שערי תשובה
GATES OF
REPENTANCE

שַׁעֲרֵי תְשׁוּבָה לְעוֹלָם פְּתוּחִין.

The gates of repentance are always open.

—DEUTERONOMY RABBAH 2.12

"בַּחוּץ לֹא־יָלִין גֵּר." שֶׁאֵין הַקָּדוֹשׁ בָּרוּךְ הוּא פּוֹסֵל לִבְרִיָּה
אֶלָּא לַכֹּל הוּא מְקַבֵּל. הַשְּׁעָרִים נִפְתָּחִין בְּכָל־שָׁעָה, וְכָל־מִי
שֶׁהוּא מְבַקֵּשׁ לְכָנֵס יִכָּנֵס.

"No stranger need lodge in the street (Job 31.32)." The Holy
One does not reject a single creature. Rather, all are acceptable
to God. The gates are open at all times, and all who wish may
enter.

—EXODUS RABBAH 19.4

שַׁעֲרֵי תְּשׁוּבָה

GATES OF
REPENTANCE

The New Union Prayerbook
for the
Days of Awe

CENTRAL CONFERENCE OF AMERICAN RABBIS

5738   New York   1978

Library of Congress Cataloging in Publication Data

Jews.   Liturgy and ritual.
   [High Holy Day prayers (Reform, Central Conference of American Rabbis)]
          שערי תשובה = Gates of repentance.

   English and/or Hebrew.
      I.   Stern, Chaim.   II.   Central Conference of American Rabbis.   III.   Jews. Liturgy
   and ritual. Reform rite, Central Conference of American Rabbis.   IV.   Title.   V.   Title:
   Gates of repentance.   VI.   The new Union prayerbook for the Days of Awe. Title roman-
   ized: Sha'are teshuvah.
   BM675.H5Z667   1978   296.4'3   78-3667

Contents

Page

Index to Psalms

This index cites Psalms appearing in whole or in substantial part

Introduction

With the publication of *Shaarei Teshuvah, Gates of Repentance: The New Union Prayerbook for the Days of Awe,* the Central Conference of American Rabbis offers the Reform Synagogue and the wider Jewish community a liturgy for Rosh Hashanah and Yom Kippur. Grateful for the kind reception accorded our earlier publications, *Gates of Prayer* (1975) and *Gates of the House* (1977), we hope that this volume will satisfy the deepest needs of our people when on the Days of Awe they enter into prayerful dialogue with their God and with themselves.

At this season we turn from our ordinary ways to contemplate extraordinary issues, to ponder large—and largely unanswerable—questions: What are we? Whence do we come? Whither are we going? What is the divine, and what our relation to the One whose name conceals more than it reveals? Measuring ourselves against our ideals during this season, we are moved to express regret for past errors and to reaffirm our aspirations for the future. This our tradition calls *cheshbon hanefesh,* 'the examined life.' This is the season of self-judgment, of struggle, of inward turning, the season when a whole people labors heroically to remake itself. Though year after year that effort meets with little success, still we believe that it must ultimately succeed. To the extent that our effort is honest and undeceived, constant and undespairing, we gain strength, though it comes in small, undramatic, perhaps unnoticed accretions. And this is a season equally for the individual and the folk. Universal in its message, reaching out to all humanity, it derives much of its power from its particularity: it is *our* searching, *our* aspiration, *our* effort, *our* unique path to self-transcendence and self-renewal. Hence its timeless hold upon the imagination of the Jew. One confronts this season, its stern demands, its awesome potentialities, with trepidation.

In the introduction to *Gates of Prayer* we set forth the principles which govern the creation of a liturgy for Reform Judaism.

These principles have been applied as well to the present volume. In sum, they are our sense of continuity with Jewish tradition, our desire to combine the old with the new, our appreciation of the diversity of thought and feeling within the Jewish people in general and the Reform movement in particular, and our need to confront the circumstances in which we find ourselves. We have once again responded to the Holocaust and the rebirth of Israel, the modern crisis of faith and the longing for a tradition in which we can feel at home, the new consciousness of women and the need for straightforward and elegant expression.

Gates of Repentance replaces *The Union Prayerbook, Part II,* which was last revised in 1945. It owes much to that volume, more to *Gate of Repentance* (London, 1973), and most to the traditional *Machzor,* the pattern upon which all modern liturgies for the Days of Awe are fashioned. We have, in addition, drawn liberally from *Gates of Prayer,* because the Holyday services have always been built upon the weekday and Shabbat liturgy. Finally, we have included many new prayers and meditations, because faith and aspiration live on in the House of Israel.

We call this prayerbook *Shaarei Teshuvah, Gates of Repentance,* though *teshuvah* might have been translated, perhaps more felicitously, 'turning.' To the Jew, to repent is to turn back to the Source of goodness and truth. May this prayerbook help us turn to one another, and find the Eternal You, the Friend amid all that is, the Nameless One whose 'name' is Hope.

אתה הבדלת אנוש מראש, ותכירהו לעמוד לפניך . . .
ותקבלנו בתשובה שלמה לפניך.

ערב שבת קדש יוארא' תשל"ח

28 Tevet 5738

Chaim Stern
CHAPPAQUA, NEW YORK

X

A Note on Usage

As in *Gates of Prayer,* the typeface suggests how the service might be conducted. In place of the conventional rubrics 'Reader,' 'All Reading,' 'Singing,' and the like, we use Roman type for 'Reader,' *italics* for 'All Reading,' and sans-serif (in the English) for Hebrew passages that are generally sung. In congregations where a Cantor shares the service, some of the 'Reader' passages will no doubt be chanted.

This prayerbook offers two services for both the evening and the morning of Rosh Hashanah. Some congregations will alternate these services over a two year period. Congregations which hold successive services on the evening or the morning of Rosh Hashanah may use both liturgies. Those congregations which observe Rosh Hashanah for two days will, we trust, find the two services helpful. Some congregations may choose to combine sections from both services. However, it should be noted that in *Gates of Repentance* each service is complete in itself. There need be no announcements of pages once the service has begun, unless some part of the liturgy is to be omitted.

It should also be pointed out that, for both the evening and morning of Rosh Hashanah, Service II is somewhat shorter than Service I.

One or more of the Meditations that precede the Evening Service for Rosh Hashanah and Yom Kippur may be read as a prelude to worship or may be inserted into the service. Likewise, the section entitled 'Additional Prayers,' which follows the Yom Kippur Morning Service, may be read at that time, either in whole or in part, or selections from it may be incorporated into other services. The 'Additional Prayers' are arranged by theme, such as 'On Human Nature,' 'On Responsibility,' and 'On Turning.'

This prayerbook affords each congregation latitude in establishing its own patterns of worship. Local custom or necessity will prescribe what part of the service will be read and what part sung, what in Hebrew and what in English, what will be set for silent meditation and what will be spoken. While Hebrew and English are generally joined on the same page, it is not contemplated that all Hebrew and English passages will be read in the course of a single service.

It should be remarked that where an English passage is introduced by the symbol (°), it is offered as a free interpretation of the Hebrew text, rather than as a translation of it. The English is intended to convey not the literal meaning of the classic prayer, but the timeless truth we discern in it.

Acknowledgments

The Central Conference of American Rabbis wishes to express its gratitude to all who helped shape the contents of this volume. Many suggestions, comments, and criticisms were received during the course of its preparation. All were carefully considered. They came from individuals and from congregations in North America and Europe. We thank them all.

The Conference takes this opportunity to record its special indebtedness to a number of individuals.

As he did for *Gates of Prayer* and *Gates of the House,* Rabbi Chaim Stern, creative liturgist and gifted poet, served as Editor of *Gates of Repentance.* In that capacity he planned the book, and in consultation with the Liturgy Committee, he prepared three drafts, compiling, shaping, and revising the material in them, translating the Hebrew, writing many new prayers and meditations, searching out and adapting many others. After the final text had been accepted by vote of the members of the Conference, Rabbi Stern prepared the manuscript for the printer, a task which included page design and correction of proofs.

The Conference wishes to record its profound gratitude and sense of indebtedness to Rabbi A. Stanley Dreyfus, who served as Chairman of the Liturgy Committee throughout the years during which this prayerbook was created. Rabbi Dreyfus gave hours beyond reckoning to this project, making many fruitful suggestions, helping to rework texts and translations, sharing the labor of design and correction. His contribution was invaluable.

Dr. Edward Graham read the entire manuscript. His expert knowledge of English literature and prose style, and his sensitive understanding of liturgy, resulted in many improvements. Rabbis Herbert Bronstein and Lawrence A. Hoffman devoted much time and effort and made substantial contributions to the book. Their meetings with Rabbi Stern and Dreyfus in the final months of revision were especially helpful. Susan Stern studied the entire manuscript, and her contribution is gratefully recorded. Rabbi Julius Rosenthal assisted the Editor and Rabbi Dreyfus with the proofreading. His assistance went beyond the correction of errors. We thank Ismar David, whose calligraphy enhances the title page. We are grateful to Bernard Scharfstein of Ktav Publishing House, and his associates, for their expert and courteous service in setting the type. Rabbi Elliot L. Stevens was unfailingly helpful in overseeing the technical details of production and publication. And we thank Rabbi Joseph B. Glaser, Executive Vice-President of the Conference, whose dedication to the accomplishment of this task was boundless. His work on its behalf both initiated and helped speed it to a conclusion.

Rabbis Jay R. Brickman, Herbert Bronstein, Harvey J. Fields, Norman D. Hirsh, Gunter Hirschberg, Lawrence A. Hoffman, and Fredric A. Pomerantz served as members of the Liturgy Committee, of which Rabbi Dreyfus was Chairman. In addition to the Editor, Rabbis Joseph B. Glaser, W. Gunther Plaut, Malcolm H. Stern, and Elliot L. Stevens, and Cantor George Weinflash served *ex-officio,* the latter as delegate from the American Conference of Cantors. Their individual and collective contributions are here noted with gratitude.

The Conference records its thanks to the following people, all of whom offered detailed suggestions: Rabbis Michael L. Abraham, Arthur J. Abrams, Joseph Asher, Albert S. Axelrad, Henry Bamberger, Terry R. Bard, Morton A. Bauman, Robert M. Benjamin, H. Philip Berkowitz, Bernard H. Bloom, William G. Braude, Stanley R. Brav, Sidney H. Brooks, Jonathan M. Brown, Gustav Buchdahl, Eli L. Cooper, Jerome P. David, Stanley M. Davids, Jason Z. Edelstein, Michael Farhi, Stephen J. Einstein, Jonathan H. Gerard, Roland B. Gittelsohn, Joseph Goldman, Albert A. Gordon, Theodore H. Gordon, Paul Gorin, Alan S. Green, Frederick E. Greenspan, Stanley Greenstein, Henry Guttmann, David Hachen, Sheldon J. Harr, Meyer Heller, Bennett M. Hermann, Eric H. Hoffman, Samuel Horowitz, Walter Jacob, Samuel Z. Jaffe, Wolli Kaelter, Robert I. Kahn, Daniel L. Kaplan, Earl Kaplan, Robert L. Katz, Bernard P. King, Ralph P. Kingsley, Abraham J.

xiv

Klausner, Peter Knobel, Neil Kominsky, Charles A. Kroloff, Ronald Kronish, William J. Leffler, Arthur J. Lelyveld, Charles B. Lesser, Eugene J. Lipman, Ernst M. Lorge, Allen S. Maller, Robert D. Marx, Ralph D. Mecklenburger, Kurt L. Metzger, James R. Michaels, Arnold H. Miller, Judea B. Miller, Meyer Miller, Joseph R. Narot, Norman R. Patz, Jordan Pearlson, Jakob J. Petuchowski, Ely E. Pilchik, W. Gunther Plaut, David Polish, Albert Plotkin, Sally J. Priesand, Seymour Prystowsky, Gerald Raiskin, Lawrence W. Raphael, Daniel A. Roberts, Andrew J. Robins, Michael A. Robinson, Sanford E. Rosen, Roy A. Rosenberg, Elliot D. Rosenstock, Richard Rosenthal, Harry A. Roth, Byron T. Rubenstein, Alvan D. Rubin, William N. Sajowitz, Jay J. Sangerman, Elbert L. Sapinsley, Scott B. Saulson, Harold I. Saperstein, Herman E. Schaalman, Bernard Schachtel, Amos Schauss, Robert J. Schur, Sylvan D. Schwartzman, Robert A. Seigel, Max Selinger, Howard Shapiro, Max A. Shapiro, Alan R. Sherman, Albert M. Shulman, Martin I. Silverman, Marcus S. Simmons, Mordecai I. Soloff, Rav A. Soloff, Fred Solomon, Ned J. Soltz, Edwin N. Soslow, H. D. U. Smith, George M. Stern, Michael S. Stroh, Frank M. Sundheim, Michael M. Szenes, Roy D. Tanenbaum, Peter E. Tarlow, Leo Trepp, Leo E. Turitz, Harold B. Waintrup, Gerry H. Walter, Gerald Weider, Stephen E. Weisberg, Steven R. Westman, Herbert Wilner, Leonard Winograd, Michael R. Zedek, Henry A. Zoob; Cantors Jason N. Bauch, Henry H. Danziger, Marshall M. Glatzer, and Jacob Seully. We thank as well Professor Werner Weinberg, Hebrew Union College-Jewish Institute of Religion. In addition, Annette Daum, Cecile Fallon, and Edith Miller made helpful suggestions.

We cannot mention the many others who contributed valuable criticisms and advice, but their assistance is here gratefully noted. They include rabbinic and cantorial students of the Hebrew Union College-Jewish Institute of Religion, and the members of congregations where the various drafts of the text of this volume were used, wholly or in part, and useful experience gained as a result.

The late Harriet Sanders of Temple Israel, Dayton, Ohio, provided a substantial bequest for the support of this project. Her memory is a blessing for ever.

◆ ◆

Every effort has been made to ascertain the owners of copyrights for selections used in this volume, and to obtain permission to reprint copyrighted passages. For the use of the passages indicated, the Central Conference of American Rabbis expresses its gratitude to those whose names appear below. The Conference will be pleased, in subsequent editions, to correct any inadvertent errors or omissions that may be pointed out.

A. S. BARNES AND COMPANY, INC.: Two poems from *The Golden Peacock: A Worldwide Treasury of Yiddish Poetry,* compiled, translated and edited by Dr. Joseph Leftwich; and a passage from *A Treasury of Jewish Quotations,* edited by Joseph L. Baron. Reprinted by permission.
ALFRED A. KNOPF, INC.: From *Selected Poems of Robert Nathan.* Copyright © 1935 and renewed © 1953 by Robert Nathan. Reprinted by permission of Alfred A. Knopf, Inc.
ARBOR HOUSE, INC.: From *Star Eternal,* by Ka-tzetnik 135633 (Yechiel De-Nur). English translation copyright © 1971 by Nina De-Nur.
ATHENEUM PUBLISHING COMPANY, INC.: From a poem in *The Hard Hours,* by Anthony Hecht. Copyright © 1967 by Anthony Hecht. Reprinted by permission.
BANTAM BOOKS, INC.: From *The Dybbuk and other Great Yiddish Plays,* edited and translated by Joseph C. Landis. Copyright © 1966 by Bantam Books, Ic.
BEACON PRESS: From *Hymns for the Celebration of Life,* by the Unitarian Universalist Hymnbook Commission. Copyright © 1964 by the Unitarian Universalist Association.
BLOCH PUBLISHING COMPANY, INC.: From *A Hasidic Anthology,* edited by Louis I. Newman and H. Spitz. Copyright © 1944. Reprinted by permission.
BRIN, RUTH S.: "Atonement," a poem from *Interpretations for the Weekly Torah Reading.* Copyright © 1965. Reprinted by permission.

ACKNOWLEDGMENTS

CAMBRIDGE UNIVERSITY PRESS: From *Science and the Modern World,* by Alfred North Whitehead. Reprinted by permission.

CHARLES SCRIBNER'S SONS, INC.: From *Man's Quest for God,* by Abraham Joshua Heschel. Copyright © 1954 by Charles Scribner's Sons, Inc. Reprinted by permission.

CURTIS BROWN LTD.: From *Belief and Action,* by Viscount Herbert Samuel. Reprinted by permission.

DORRANCE AND CO., INC.: "Erev Yom Kippur," by Mollie R. Golomb, in *How Fair My Faith and Other Poems,* 1968.

DOUBLEDAY AND COMPANY, INC.: "The Road," from *This Blind Rose,* by Humbert Wolfe. Copyright © 1929. Reprinted by permission.

FABER AND FABER LTD.: From *Collected Poems* by Stephen Spender. Reprinted by permission.

FARRAR STRAUS & GIROUX, INC.: From *The Wisdom of Heschel: Writing of A. J. Heschel,* by Ruth Marcus Goodhill. Copyright © 1970, 1972, 1975 by Sylvia Heschel, Executrix of the Estate of Abraham Joshua Heschel.

FINE, ALVIN I.: "Birth is a Beginning." Used by permission.

GASTER, THEODOR: From *Festivals of the Jewish Year,* by Theodor Gaster. William Sloane Associates, N.Y. Copyright © 1952, 1953 by Theodor Gaster.

GEORGE ALLEN & UNWIN LTD.: From *The Art of Loving,* by Erich Fromm and from *The Thought of the Prophets,* by Israel I. Mattuck, copyright © 1953. Both reprinted by permission.

HARCOURT BRACE JOVANOVICH, INC; From *Basic Judaism,* by Milton Steinberg. Copyright © 1947 by Milton Steinberg. Used by permission.

HARPER & ROW, INC.: From *The Art of Loving,* by Erich Fromm. Copyright © 1974.

HEBREW UNION COLLEGE-JEWISH INSTITUTE OF RELIGION: From "Prayer," in *Essays,* by Henry Slonimsky. Copyright © 1967. Reprinted by permission.

HOLT, RINEHART & WINSTON, INC.: From *Leo Baeck, Teacher of Theresienstadt,* by Albert H. Friedlander. Copyright © 1968 by Albert H. Friedlander; and from *A Treasury of Yiddish Poetry,* edited by Irving Howe and Eliezer Greenberg. Copyright © 1969 by the editors.

THE JEWISH PUBLICATION SOCIETY OF AMERICA: From *The Torah, Isaiah, Jeremiah,* and *Jonah,* for occasional use of the translations. Used by permission.

JEWISH RECONSTRUCTIONIST FOUNDATION, INC.: Some passages in pp.

412–17 are adapted from the *High Holy Day Prayer Book, Volume II,* pp. 366–75. Copyright © 1948. Reprinted by permission.

KETER PUBLISHING HOUSE JERUSALEM, LTD.: "The Moon's Brightness," by Haim Lensky, from *Anthology of Modern Hebrew Poetry, Vol. 2,* edited by S. Y. Penueli and A. Ukhmani, and translated © 1966 by Robert Friend. Reprinted by permission.

KOREN PUBLISHERS JERUSALEM, LTD.: For permission to use photo-offset reprints of the Torah and Haftarah Readings for Rosh Hashanah and Yom Kippur, from the *Koren Bible.*

MEDIA JUDAICA PRESS, INC.: For "We cannot Pray to You," and "Now is the Time for Turning," by Jack Riemer, in *New Prayers for the High Holy Days.* Copyright © 1970, 1971.

MACMILLAN ADMINISTRATION (BASINGSTOKE) LTD.: From *Outlines of Liberal Judaism* (1912) and from *Liberal Judaism* (1903) by Claude G. Montefiore. Reprinted by permission of Macmillan, London and Basingstoke.

MACMILLAN PUBLISHING CO., INC.: From *Science and the Modern World,* by Alfred North Whitehead, copyright © 1925 by Macmillan Publishing Co., Inc., copyright renewed © 1953 by Evelyn Whitehead. Reprinted by permission.

MINDLIN, HILARY: "God of our Fathers," by Hilary Mindlin. Used by permission.

OXFORD UNIVERSITY PRESS: From *The New English Bible.* Copyright © by The Delegates of the Oxford University Press and The Syndics of the Cambridge University Press 1961, 1970. Reprinted by permission.

PHILOSOPHICAL LIBRARY PUBLISHING CO., INC.: From *Survival for What?* by Zvi Kolitz. Reprinted by permission.

THE RABBINICAL ASSEMBLY: From *Mahzor for Rosh Hashanah and Yom Kippur,* copyright © 1972, and for two poems by Joanne Greenberg, in *Yearnings II,* copyright © 1974. Both volumes edited by Rabbi Jules Harlow. Reprinted by permission.

RANDOM HOUSE, INC.: "I Think Continually Of Those Who Were Truly Great, copyright © 1934 and renewed © 1962 by Stephen Spender. Reprinted from *Selected Poems,* by Stephen Spender. And for "Travelogue for Exiles," copyright © 1942 and renewed © 1970 by Karl Shapiro. Both of the above are copyrighted by Random House, Inc., and reprinted by permission of Random House, Inc.

RUDIN, JACOB P.: For a passage beginning: "When we are dead. . . . "

SCHOCKEN BOOKS, INC.: From *Tales of the Hasidim: The Early Masters,* by Martin Buber. Copyright © 1947; copyright renewed ©

1975; from *The Way of Response: Martin Buber,* edited by Nahum N. Glatzer. Copyright © 1946, 1961; copyright renewed © 1974; from *Days of Awe,* edited by S. Y. Agnon. Copyright © 1948, 1965; copyright renewed © 1975; from *The Essence of Judaism,* by Leo Baeck. Copyright © 1948; copyright renewed © 1975. All of the above are copyrighted by Schocken Books, Inc., and reprinted by permission of Schocken Books, Inc.

SPERBER, SHMUEL: For a brief extract from a Shiur held in Jerusalem.

STEPHENSON HARWOOD & TATHAM (Executors of Siegfried Sassoon, deceased): From *Collected Poems* by Siegfried Sassoon. Copyright © 1920 by E. P. Dutton & Company. Reprinted by permission.

UNIVERSITY OF CALIFORNIA PRESS: "Solemn Hour" and "Evening," from *Fifty Selected Poems,* by Rainer Maria Rilke, translated by C. F. MacIntyre. Copyright © 1968. Reprinted by permission of the University of California Press.

UNION OF AMERICAN HEBREW CONGREGATIONS: From *The Jew in the Medieval World,* edited by Jacob R. Marcus, copyright© 1938; and from *Out of the Whirlwind,* edited by Albert H. Friedlander, copyright © 1968.

VICTOR GOLLANCZ, LTD.: From *A Year of Grace,* copyright © 1950, and *From Darkness to Light,* copyright © 1956, both edited by Victor Gollancz. Reprinted by permissitn

VIKING PENGUIN, INC.: From *Collected Poems* by Siegfried Sassoon. Copyright © 1920 by E. P. Dutton & Company. Reprinted by permission of The Viking Press.

GATES OF REPENTANCE

Meditations ה

1

Just as the hand, held before the eye, can hide the tallest mountain, so the routine of everyday life can keep us from seeing the vast radiance and the secret wonders that fill the world.

Chasidic, 18th Century

2

Rabbi Elazar would always give a coin to a poor person before praying. In explanation, he would quote: "As for me, I shall behold Your face *betzedek,* in righteousness (Psalm 17.15)." (*Tzedek* and *tzedakah* were always synonyms for righteousness and later *tzedakah* acquired the meaning of charity.)

Talmud

3

Our Rabbis taught: Do not stand up to pray in a morose spirit, nor in a mood of ribaldry, frivolity, levity, or idle chatter, but only in the joy of the Mitzvah.

Talmud

4

Rabbi Chiyah and Rabbi Shimon bar Abba were engaged in study. One said: When we pray we must direct our eyes downward, for it is written: "My eyes and My heart will be there (on earth) for all time (I Kings 9.3)." The other said: Our eyes must be directed upward, for it is written: "Let us lift up our hearts and hands to God in heaven (Lamentations 3.41)." Meanwhile, Rabbi Yishmael ben Rabbi Yosei happened along. He said: What are you discussing? They told him. Then he said: This was the view of Abba: When we pray we must direct our eyes downward and our hearts upward, thus fulfilling both verses.

Talmud

5

The Baal Shem Tov said: The first time an event occurs in nature it is called a miracle; later it comes to seem natural and is taken for granted. Let your worship and your service be your miracle each day. Only such worship, performed from the heart with the enthusiasm of fresh wonder, is acceptable.

Chasidic, 18th Century

6

In the beginning God created the heavens and the earth . . . . And God said: 'Let there be light!'; and there was light . . . . And God saw that it was good.

Genesis

7

"And God said: 'Let there be light!' " This first light God made before making the sun and stars. God showed it to David, who burst into song. This was the light Moses saw on Sinai! At the creation, the universe from end to end radiated light — but it was withdrawn . . . and now it is stored away for the righteous, until all the worlds will be in harmony again and all will be united and whole. But until this future world is established, this light, coming out of darkness and formed by the Most Secret, is hidden: "Light is sown for the righteous (Psalm 97.11)."

Zohar

8

Rabbi Akiva said: How greatly God must have loved us to create us in the image of God; yet even greater love did God show us in making us conscious that we are created in the divine image.

Mishnah

9

Rabbi Berechya said: The Holy One, just before the creation of Adam, saw that both saints and sinners would be numbered among his descendants. The Holy One considered: If I create Adam, I create sinners as well; but if I do not create Adam, how will the righteous come into existence? Therefore the Holy One ignored the sinners who were destined to be born, took hold of mercy, and created Adam!

Midrash

10

Why did creation begin with a single human being? For the sake of the righteous and the wicked, that none might ascribe their differing characters to hereditary differences. And lest families boast of their high lineage. This they do nonetheless—how much worse it would be if all were not descended from a single source!

Talmud

11

Therefore was a single human being created: to teach you that to destroy a single human soul is equivalent to destroying an entire world; and that to sustain a single human soul is equivalent to sustaining an entire world. And a single human being was created to keep peace among human beings, that no one might say to another: My lineage is greater than yours!

Mishnah

12

We experience our belonging to an infinity.
    It presses upon us,
    whether we go into ourselves
    or go beyond ourselves.
We live in space without end
    and are a part of it,
    in time without stop as a segment of it.
Space and time are fundamentally one here,
    they come from the one, omnipresent, eternal God.
World and eternity are here one word (עולם),
    both signify the same unendingness.
We live in this unendingness and from it.
Our domain is the opposite of mere location,
    of that which has its boundary and written description.

5

Our day is the opposite of finality, of fate.
Our domain is a going outward that points to the faraway,
    our day is the direction that leads into the distance.
All that has come into existence and has been given
    becomes a path to the beyond,
    and to that which is in the process of becoming,
    to the world beyond and to the coming day.
All creation wants to be revelation,
    all of the past becomes the future.

Leo Baeck

13

An ancient Jewish word says:
God creates, in order to continue to create . . . .
All creation has its force, its constant birth.
Creation and revelation,
becoming and designation belong together;
they determine one another.
The world is not mere fate . . . .
It is the world of God:
a world; and nevertheless, God's domain.
Space; and nevertheless, unendingness;
Time; and nevertheless, eternity.
Just so an ancient Jewish word again says:
God is the space of the world,
but the world is not the space of God . . . .
It is the creation and revelation of God
and therefore a world filled with tension.
It is an interweaving of opposites,
an immanence of the transcendent,
a being at one with the other,
the covenanting of the finite and temporal
with the infinite eternal.
Both become one within religious feeling,
the current moves between the poles . . . .

Leo Baeck

14

Free will is given to every human being. If we wish to incline ourselves toward goodness and righteousness, we are free to do so; and if we wish to incline ourselves toward evil, we are also free to do that. From Scripture (Genesis 3.22) we learn that the human species, with its knowledge of good and evil, is unique among all earth's creatures. Of our own accord, by our own faculty of intelligence and understanding, we can distinguish between good and evil, doing as we choose. Nothing holds us back from making this choice between good and evil—the power is in our hands.

Maimonides, 12th Century

15

All is foreseen—and free will is given.
Everything is in the hands of God except reverence for God.

Talmud

16

If you choose to pollute yourself with sin, you will find all the gates open before you; and if you desire to attain the highest purity, you will find all the forces of goodness ready to help you.

Talmud

17

Do not imagine that character is determined at birth. We have been given free will. Any person can become as righteous as Moses or as wicked as Jereboam. We ourselves decide whether to make ourselves learned or ignorant, compassionate or cruel, generous or miserly. No one forces us, no one decides for us, no one drags us along one path or the other; we ourselves, by our own volition, choose our own way.

Maimonides, 12th Century

18

In connection with the Mitzvah of following the right path, it has been taught: As God is called gracious, so must you be gracious; as God is compassionate, so must you be; as God is holy, so must you follow the path of holiness. Therefore the prophets described God as possessing these attributes: endlessly patient and loving, just and upright, whole-hearted, and the like. Their intention was to teach us that these are the good and praiseworthy paths for us to follow as we attempt, according to our capacities, to imitate God.

Maimonides, 12th Century

19

With regard to all human traits, the middle of the road is the right path. For example: Do not be hot-tempered, easily angered. Nor, on the other hand, should you be unfeeling like a corpse. Rather, take the middle of the road: keep an even disposition, reserving your anger for occasions when it is truly warranted. Similarly, do not cultivate a desire for luxuries; keep your eye fixed only on genuine necessities. In giving to others, do not hold back what you can afford, but do not give so lavishly that you yourself will be impoverished. Avoid both hysterical gaiety and somber dejection, and instead be calmly joyful always, showing a cheerful countenance. Act similarly with regard to all the dispositions. This is the path followed by the wise.

Maimonides, 12th Century

20

How do we fix these traits into our character? By repeatedly doing them, returning to them until they become second nature. And because these attributes are divine, this path, the one that avoids extremes, is called the 'path of God,' and Abraham taught his descendants to follow it. Whoever follows it gains goodness and blessing, as it is said: "For I have known him, that he might command his children and those who follow him to keep the Lord's path, doing justice and right, that the Lord may fulfill for Abraham the divine purpose (Genesis 18.19)."

Maimonides, 12th Century

21

Smooth speech and deception are forbidden us. Our words must not differ from our thoughts; the inner and outer person must be the same;

what is in the heart should be on the lips. We are forbidden to deceive anyone, Jew or Gentile, even in seemingly small matters. For example, one must not urge food on another, knowing that the other cannot eat it; one must not offer gifts that cannot be accepted; a storekeeper opening a bottle in order to sell its contents must not pretend to be opening it in honor of a particular person, and the like. Honest speech, integrity, and a pure heart—that is what is required of us.

Maimonides, 12th Century

22

If you see a friend sinning or pursuing an unworthy life, it is a Mitzvah to try to restore that person to the right path. Let your friend know that wrong actions are self-inflicted hurts, but speak softly and gently, making it clear that you speak only because of your concern for your friend's well-being.

Maimonides, 12th Century

23

Our sages taught: One who shames another in public has no share in the world-to-come. Therefore one must take great care not to shame another in public, whether young or old, either by shameful name-calling or by tale-bearing.

Maimonides, 12th Century

24

This fragile life between birth and death can nevertheless be a fulfillment—if it is a dialogue. In our life and experience we are addressed; by thought and speech and action, by producing and by influencing we are able to answer. For the most part we do not listen to the address, or we break into it with chatter. But if the word comes to us and the answer proceeds from us, then human life exists, though brokenly, in the world. The kindling of the response in that 'spark' of the soul, the blazing up of the response, which occurs time and again, to the unexpectedly approaching speech, we term responsibility . . . .

Martin Buber

25

Ethical life has entered into religious life, and cannot be extracted from it. There is no responsibility unless there is One to whom one is responsible, for there is no response where there is no address . . . .

Martin Buber

26

We shall accomplish nothing at all if we divide our world and our life into two domains: one in which God's command is paramount, the other governed by the laws of economics, politics, and the 'simple self-assertion' of the group . . . . Stopping one's ears so as not to hear the voice from above is breaking the connection between existence and the meaning of existence.

Martin Buber

27

It was the favorite saying of the sages of Yavneh: I am a creature of God and you are a creature of God. My work may be in the city, yours is perhaps in the field. As you rise early to your work, so I rise early to my work. As you do not claim that your work is superior to mine, so I do not claim that mine is superior to yours. And should one say, I do more important work and the other less important work, we have already learned: more or less, it does not matter, so long as the heart is turned toward heaven.

Talmud

28

"The Lord loves the righteous (Psalm 146.8)." The Holy One loves the righteous because their righteousness is not a matter of birth. The priests and Levites are members of ancestral houses; one cannot choose to join them. But anyone, Jew or Gentile, can choose to be righteous. Of their own accord the righteous give themselves to God in love. Therefore, the Holy One loves them.

Midrash

29

"And an angel of the Lord called to him from heaven and said: Abraham, Abraham! (Genesis 22.11)" Rabbi Eliezer ben Jacob said: The repetition of 'Abraham' signifies that he was calling not only to Abraham, but to all subsequent generations. For there is no generation without its Abraham, none without its counterpart of Jacob, its Moses, and its Samuel.

Midrash

30

Every human being has merits and faults. The righteous person has more merits than faults, the wicked one more faults than merits. The average person is (more or less) evenly balanced between the two. A community, too, is judged in this manner: if the merits of its citizens outweigh their faults, it is called righteous; if their faults outweigh their merits, it is called wicked.

Maimonides, 12th Century

31

Rabbi Shimon ben Elazar said: The will-to-evil is like iron in a forge: While it is there, one can shape it, make utensils of it, anything you like. So with the will-to-evil: There is only one way to shape it aright, through the words of the Torah, which is like fire.

Midrash

32

Rabbi Bunam said to his followers: Our great transgression is not that we commit sins—temptation is strong and our strength is slight! No, our transgression is that at every instant we can turn to God—and we do not turn!

Chasidic, 18th-19th Century

33

Though the Torah warns the wicked of punishment, God is merciful. "Therefore God instructs sinners in the way (Psalm 25.8)"—this is the

way of repentance. When we ask: What is the fate of sinners? the
Books of Wisdom reply: "Misfortune pursues sinners (Proverbs
13.21)." The Books of Prophecy reply: "The soul that sins shall die
(Ezekiel 18.4)." The Books of the Torah reply: "Let them bring an offering and be forgiven (Leviticus 1.4; 5.6, 16)." But the Holy One
replies: Let them repent and be forgiven. As it is written: "God instructs sinners in the way"—the way of repentance.

Palestinian Talmud

34

Who is truly repentant? The one who, when the temptation to sin is
repeated, refrains from sinning.

Talmud

35

Do not think you are obliged to repent only for transgressions invol-
ving acts, such as stealing, robbing, and sexual immorality. Just as we
must repent such acts, so must we examine our evil feelings and repent
our anger, our jealousy, our mocking thoughts, our excessive ambition
and greed. We must repent all these. Therefore it is written: "Let the
wicked forsake their ways, the unrighteous their thoughts (Isaiah
55.7)."

Maimonides, 12th Century

36

There are many reasons for the sounding of the Shofar. Among them
are these: Rosh Hashanah marks the beginning of Creation, and we,
on Rosh Hashanah, accept the Creator as our Sovereign, as it is said:
"With trumpets and the sound of the Shofar acclaim the Sovereign
Lord (Psalm 98.6)." Secondly, since Rosh Hashanah is the first of the
Ten Days of Repentance, the Shofar is sounded to herald their beginning, as though to say: Let all who desire to repent, turn now. Thirdly,
the Shofar reminds us of our stand at Sinai, as it is said: "The blast of
the Shofar grew louder and louder (Exodus 19.19)," in order that we
may take upon ourselves what our ancestors took upon themselves
when they said: "We will do and we will hear (Exodus 24.7)."
Fourthly, it reminds us of the Binding of Isaac, who offered himself to

Heaven and was replaced by the ram caught by its horns in a thicket. So ought we to be ready at all times to offer our lives for the sanctification of God's name. Finally, it reminds us of redemption, that we may long passionately for it, as it is said: "It shall come to pass on that day, that a great Shofar will be sounded; and all the lost shall return (Isaiah 27.13)."

Saadia Gaon, 10th Century

37

From year to year the need becomes more urgent for a religion that teaches reverence for life as its highest principle. Judaism is such a religion. The God it worships does not desire the death of sinners, but that they may turn and live. That God's word is 'Seek Me and live,' and 'Choose life.' It is a religion which teaches that to destroy a single life is to destroy an entire world, and to sustain a single life is to sustain an entire world. It is a religion that yearns, above all things, for the day when swords will be beaten into plowshares and spears into pruninghooks; whose aim, in the words of a modern Jewish writer, is 'the creation of a human being unable to shed blood;' whose toast is *Lechayim,* 'To life!' It is the religion of the Akedah, which is a symbol of life, not death, *because Abraham is forbidden to sacrifice his son.* It is a religion whose New Year is a celebration of life and a plea for its continuance: 'Remember us unto life, O King who delights in life, and inscribe us in the Book of Life, for Your sake, O God of life.'

John D. Rayner

38

Glory to those who hope!
For the future is theirs;
Those who stand unflinching against the mountain
Shall gain its summit.
 So hopes the river, running to the sea,
 To fulfill its dreams in the crash of waters.
 So longs the tree, branching skyward
 At last to touch the palm of sun.
Therefore we love dawn as a promise of day,
The nightingale's love-song as a longing for birth,

The flowing of streams as the beat of dreams made real,
Streams cutting channels for rivers of the future
And never growing weary.
And all who join hands, trusting creation—
These are the companions of hope.
Forge, then, the vision of days to come:
As the waves shape the rocky shore,
As the smith moulds white-hot steel at will,
Form dreams of faithfulness.
Desolation will not leave the desert,
Until it leaves the heart.

David Rokeach

39

There is a grace that every dawn renews,
A loveliness making every morning fresh.
We will endure, we will prevail—
We, the children of Hope,
Children of the One
Who crowds the heavens with stars,
Endows the earth with glory,
And fills the mind with wonder!

Chaim Stern

תפלת ערבית לראש השנה

ROSH HASHANAH EVENING
SERVICE

Readings and meditations begin on page 3

15

*For congregations where the blessing over the lights
is recited in the synagogue*

הדלקת הנרות

Creator of beginnings, as You created the world on this
day, uniting fragments into a universe, so help unite our
hearts and the hearts of all Jews to serve You. Illumine
our lives with the light of Your Torah, for by Your light
do we see light. Grant us this year a glimpse of the light of
redemption, the light of healing and of peace. Amen.

• •

בָּרוּךְ אַתָּה, יְיָ אֱלֹהֵינוּ, מֶלֶךְ הָעוֹלָם, אֲשֶׁר קִדְּשָׁנוּ
בְּמִצְוֹתָיו וְצִוָּנוּ לְהַדְלִיק נֵר שֶׁל (שַׁבָּת וְשֶׁל) יוֹם טוֹב.

Blessed is the Lord our God, Ruler of the universe, who
hallows us with mitzvot, and commands us to kindle the
lights of (Shabbat and) Yom Tov.

בָּרוּךְ אַתָּה, יְיָ אֱלֹהֵינוּ, מֶלֶךְ הָעוֹלָם, שֶׁהֶחֱיָנוּ וְקִיְּמָנוּ
וְהִגִּיעָנוּ לַזְּמַן הַזֶּה.

Blessed is the Lord our God, Ruler of the universe, for
giving us life, for sustaining us, and for enabling us to
reach this season.

הנני

הִנְנִי הֶעָנִי מִמַּעַשׂ, נִרְעָשׁ וְנִפְחָד מִפַּחַד יוֹשֵׁב תְּהִלּוֹת יִשְׂרָאֵל. בָּאתִי לַעֲמֹד וּלְחַנֵּן לְפָנֶיךָ עַל עַמְּךָ יִשְׂרָאֵל אֲשֶׁר שְׁלָחוּנִי, אַף עַל פִּי שֶׁאֵינִי כְדַי וְהָגוּן לְכָךְ. עַל כֵּן אֲבַקֶּשְׁךָ, אֱלֹהֵי אַבְרָהָם, אֱלֹהֵי יִצְחָק וֵאלֹהֵי יַעֲקֹב, יְיָ, יְיָ, אֵל רַחוּם וְחַנּוּן, אֱלֹהֵי יִשְׂרָאֵל, שַׁדַּי אָיֹם וְנוֹרָא: הֱיֵה נָא מַצְלִיחַ דַּרְכִּי אֲשֶׁר אָנֹכִי הוֹלֵךְ, לַעֲמֹד לְבַקֵּשׁ רַחֲמִים עָלַי וְעַל שׁוֹלְחָי. וְנָא אַל תַּפְשִׁיעֵם בְּחַטֹּאתַי וְאַל תְּחַיְּבֵם בַּעֲוֹנוֹתַי, כִּי חוֹטֵא וּפוֹשֵׁעַ אָנִי. וְאַל יִכָּלְמוּ בִּפְשָׁעַי וְאַל יֵבֹשׁוּ בָהֶם. וְקַבֵּל תְּפִלָּתִי כִּתְפִלַּת זָקֵן וְרָגִיל וּפִרְקוֹ נָאֶה וּזְקָנוֹ נָעִים, וּמְעֹרָב בְּדַעַת עִם הַבְּרִיּוֹת. וְיִהִי נָא דִגְלֵנוּ עָלֶיךָ אַהֲבָה, וְעַל כָּל־פְּשָׁעִים תְּכַסֶּה בְּאַהֲבָה. וְכָל־צָרוֹת וְרָעוֹת הֲפָךְ־לָנוּ וּלְכָל־יִשְׂרָאֵל לְשָׂשׂוֹן וּלְשִׂמְחָה לְחַיִּים וּלְשָׁלוֹם. הָאֱמֶת וְהַשָּׁלוֹם אֱהָבוּ, וְלֹא יְהִי שׁוּם מִכְשׁוֹל בִּתְפִלָּתִי.

וִיהִי רָצוֹן לְפָנֶיךָ, יְיָ אֱלֹהֵי אַבְרָהָם, אֱלֹהֵי יִצְחָק וֵאלֹהֵי יַעֲקֹב, הָאֵל הַגָּדוֹל, הַגִּבּוֹר וְהַנּוֹרָא, אֵל עֶלְיוֹן, אֶהְיֶה אֲשֶׁר אֶהְיֶה, שֶׁתָּבוֹא תְּפִלָּתִי לִפְנֵי כִסֵּא כְבוֹדֶךָ, בַּעֲבוּר כָּל־הַצַּדִּיקִים וְהַחֲסִידִים, הַתְּמִימִים וְהַיְשָׁרִים, וּבַעֲבוּר כְּבוֹד שִׁמְךָ הַגָּדוֹל וְהַנּוֹרָא. כִּי אַתָּה שׁוֹמֵעַ תְּפִלַּת עַמְּךָ יִשְׂרָאֵל בְּרַחֲמִים. בָּרוּךְ אַתָּה, שׁוֹמֵעַ תְּפִלָּה.

HINENI

Behold me, of little merit, trembling and afraid, as I stand before You to plead for Your people. O gracious God, the One enthroned by Israel's praises, Lord of compassion and love, accept my petition and that of my people. Let them not be put to shame because of me, nor I because of them. Sinners though we are, let our prayers come before You innocent and sweet and pleasing, as though from hearts more worthy than ours. Let love be the banner we raise in Your sight, and let that love conceal all our sins and make them as though they had not been. Change our afflictions to joy and gladness, our misdeeds to acts of life. May our love of truth and peace remove all that hinders us from sincere and fruitful prayer.

O God supreme, God of every age, God eternal, let my prayer find favor, for the sake of the righteous, the loyal, the honest and upright, and for the sake of Your own glorious purpose on earth. For You are the One who in mercy hears our prayer. Blessed are You, who hearkens to prayer.

HOPE FOR A NEW DAY

Hear Me, Jacob,
Israel, whom I have called:
I am the One,
the Beginning and the End.
My own hand founded the earth
and spread out the skies.
Thus says the Eternal One,
who created the heavens and stretched them out,
who made the earth and all that grows in it,
who gives breath to its people
and spirit to those who walk on it.

I, the Eternal, have called you to righteousness,
and taken you by the hand, and kept you;
I have made you a covenant people,
a light to the nations:
to open blind eyes,
to bring the captives out of prison,
and those who sit in darkness from their dungeons.

Thus says the Eternal One,
Creator of heavens,
the One Who Is:

I am; I will be; there is none else.
Justice is My speech,
right, My declaration.
The troubled past is forgotten,
hidden from My sight.

For behold,
I create a new heaven and a new earth,
the past forgotten, never called to mind.
Be glad, then,
and rejoice for ever in My creation.

Before us lies a new day,
and in the distance a new world,
ours to create,
by the strength of our faith.

◆ ◆

Psalm 121

אֶשָּׂא עֵינַי אֶל־הֶהָרִים, מֵאַיִן יָבוֹא עֶזְרִי? עֶזְרִי מֵעִם
יְיָ, עֹשֵׂה שָׁמַיִם וָאָרֶץ. אַל־יִתֵּן לַמּוֹט רַגְלֶךָ, אַל־יָנוּם
שֹׁמְרֶךָ. הִנֵּה לֹא־יָנוּם וְלֹא יִישָׁן, שׁוֹמֵר יִשְׂרָאֵל. יְיָ
שֹׁמְרֶךָ, יְיָ צִלְּךָ עַל־יַד יְמִינֶךָ. יוֹמָם הַשֶּׁמֶשׁ לֹא־
יַכֶּכָּה, וְיָרֵחַ בַּלָּיְלָה. יְיָ יִשְׁמָרְךָ מִכָּל־רָע, יִשְׁמֹר אֶת־
נַפְשֶׁךָ. יְיָ יִשְׁמָר־צֵאתְךָ וּבוֹאֶךָ, מֵעַתָּה וְעַד־עוֹלָם.

I lift up my eyes to the mountains; what is the source of my
help? My help will come from the Lord, Maker of heaven and
earth. God will not allow your foot to slip; your Guardian will not
slumber. Behold, the Guardian of Israel neither slumbers nor
sleeps. The Eternal is your Keeper, the Lord is your shade at
your right hand. The sun shall not harm you by day, nor the
moon by night. The Lord will guard you from all evil, and
protect your being. The Lord will guard you, coming and going,
from this time forth, and for ever.

◆ ◆

WE WILL NOT FORGET YOU

God of our people, hear our prayer:
We who speak are Jews.
⠀⠀⠀⠀Remember
The bush You kindled once in the desert air,
Years ago, on Horeb's lonely sand,
That fire You lit to set the centuries aflame
And say to us Your endless, perfect Name,

21

'I am what I will be'—
It burns eternally now, that light
Upon our altars now, against the night.
And there are deserts still. We are the Jews;
We do not forget.

Remember
The words You spoke in stone
And thunder.
The mountain smoked
And the dismayed multitude
Stood off, hearing the first time
The words they could not refuse,
Fearing the burden and the God that set
Them into history.
And there are mountains still. We are the Jews.
We cannot forget.

We come here then. But something far more deep
Compels: the ancient desert dream we keep,
A people touched by God, a certain grace
That tells of You. We are
Locked with You in old identity,
Remembering the lightning of that place;
Something in us of Your awesome will,
Something of that mountain's thunder, still.

Love us, as much as we will let You.
We are Your Jews,
We will not forget You.

SACRED ASSEMBLY   בחדש השביעי

In the seventh month,   בַּחֹדֶשׁ הַשְּׁבִיעִי,
on the first day of the month,   בְּאֶחָד לַחֹדֶשׁ,
there shall be a sacred assembly,
a cessation from work,   יִהְיֶה לָכֶם שַׁבָּתוֹן,
a day of commemoration   זִכְרוֹן תְּרוּעָה,
proclaimed by the sound
of the Shofar.   מִקְרָא־קֹדֶשׁ.
                                       כָּל־מְלֶאכֶת עֲבוֹדָה
                                       לֹא תַעֲשׂוּ.

◆

All rise

תִּקְעוּ בַחֹדֶשׁ שׁוֹפָר, בַּכֶּסֶה לְיוֹם חַגֵּנוּ.
כִּי חֹק לְיִשְׂרָאֵל הוּא, מִשְׁפָּט לֵאלֹהֵי יַעֲקֹב.

Sound the Shofar when the new moon appears,
at the turning of the year,
at the returning of our solemn celebration.
For this is a statute binding on Israel,
an ordinance of the God of Jacob.

The Ark is opened

THE YEAR   יהי רצון

יְהִי רָצוֹן מִלְּפָנֶיךָ, יְיָ אֱלֹהֵינוּ וֵאלֹהֵי אֲבוֹתֵינוּ,
שֶׁתְּחַדֵּשׁ עָלֵינוּ וְעַל־כָּל־בֵּית יִשְׂרָאֵל אֶת־הַשָּׁנָה
הַזֹּאת, שְׁנַת חֲמֵשֶׁת אֲלָפִים וּשְׁבַע מֵאוֹת וּ. . . . ,,
לְחַיִּים וּלְשָׁלוֹם, לְשָׂשׂוֹן וּלְשִׂמְחָה, לִישׁוּעָה
וּלְנֶחָמָה, וְנֹאמַר: אָמֵן.

23

May it be Your will, Eternal our God, God of all generations, that the year five thousand seven hundred and . . .
bring to us and the whole House of Israel life and peace,
joy and exaltation, redemption and comfort; and let us
say: Amen.

◆ ◆

שמע וברכותיה

בָּרְכוּ אֶת־יְיָ הַמְבֹרָךְ!

Praise the Lord, to whom our praise is due!

בָּרוּךְ יְיָ הַמְבֹרָךְ לְעוֹלָם וָעֶד!

*Praised be the Lord, to whom our praise is due,
now and for ever!*

◆ ◆

*The Ark is closed
Remain standing*

THE WILL THAT ORDERS THE STARS   מעריב ערבים

בָּרוּךְ אַתָּה, יְיָ אֱלֹהֵינוּ, מֶלֶךְ הָעוֹלָם, אֲשֶׁר בִּדְבָרוֹ
מַעֲרִיב עֲרָבִים. בְּחָכְמָה פּוֹתֵחַ שְׁעָרִים, וּבִתְבוּנָה
מְשַׁנֶּה עִתִּים, וּמַחֲלִיף אֶת־הַזְּמַנִּים, וּמְסַדֵּר אֶת־
הַכּוֹכָבִים בְּמִשְׁמְרוֹתֵיהֶם בָּרָקִיעַ כִּרְצוֹנוֹ. בּוֹרֵא יוֹם
וָלַיְלָה, גּוֹלֵל אוֹר מִפְּנֵי חֹשֶׁךְ וְחֹשֶׁךְ מִפְּנֵי אוֹר,
וּמַעֲבִיר יוֹם וּמֵבִיא לַיְלָה, וּמַבְדִּיל בֵּין יוֹם וּבֵין
לַיְלָה, יְיָ צְבָאוֹת שְׁמוֹ. אֵל חַי וְקַיָּם, תָּמִיד יִמְלוֹךְ
עָלֵינוּ, לְעוֹלָם וָעֶד. בָּרוּךְ אַתָּה, יְיָ, הַמַּעֲרִיב עֲרָבִים.

24

There was silence; there was chaos; there was a voice. A mind went forth to form worlds: now order reigns where chaos once held sway.

The law makes evening fall; the law brings on the dawn.

The moon follows accustomed paths, constellations their patterned ways.

Sovereign is the will that orders the stars in their courses in the endless skies: Sovereign is that will!

◆ ◆

HEART STILL TURNED TO LOVE　　　　　　　　אהבת עולם

אַהֲבַת עוֹלָם בֵּית יִשְׂרָאֵל עַמְּךָ אָהָבְתָּ: תּוֹרָה
וּמִצְוֹת, חֻקִּים וּמִשְׁפָּטִים אוֹתָנוּ לִמַּדְתָּ.
עַל־כֵּן, יְיָ אֱלֹהֵינוּ, בְּשָׁכְבֵּנוּ וּבְקוּמֵנוּ נָשִׂיחַ בְּחֻקֶּיךָ,
וְנִשְׂמַח בְּדִבְרֵי תוֹרָתֶךָ וּבְמִצְוֹתֶיךָ לְעוֹלָם וָעֶד.
כִּי הֵם חַיֵּינוּ וְאֹרֶךְ יָמֵינוּ, וּבָהֶם נֶהְגֶּה יוֹמָם וָלָיְלָה.
וְאַהֲבָתְךָ אַל־תָּסִיר מִמֶּנּוּ לְעוֹלָמִים! בָּרוּךְ אַתָּה, יְיָ,
אוֹהֵב עַמּוֹ יִשְׂרָאֵל.

°And how unyielding is the will of our people Israel! After the long nights, after the days and years when our ashes blackened the sky, Israel endures, heart still turned to love, soul turning still to life.

So day and night, early and late, we will rejoice in the study of Torah, we will walk by the light of Mitzvot: they are our

---

°This symbol indicates that the English is a variation suggested by the theme of the Hebrew.

25

life and the length of our days. Praised be the Source of life
and love, and Israel our people!

◆ ◆

שְׁמַע יִשְׂרָאֵל: יְיָ אֱלֹהֵינוּ, יְיָ אֶחָד!

Hear, O Israel: the Lord is our God, the Lord is One!

בָּרוּךְ שֵׁם כְּבוֹד מַלְכוּתוֹ לְעוֹלָם וָעֶד!

Blessed is His glorious kingdom for ever and ever!

All are seated

וְאָהַבְתָּ אֵת יְיָ אֱלֹהֶיךָ בְּכָל־לְבָבְךָ וּבְכָל־נַפְשְׁךָ
וּבְכָל־מְאֹדֶךָ. וְהָיוּ הַדְּבָרִים הָאֵלֶּה, אֲשֶׁר אָנֹכִי מְצַוְּךָ
הַיּוֹם, עַל־לְבָבֶךָ. וְשִׁנַּנְתָּם לְבָנֶיךָ, וְדִבַּרְתָּ בָּם
בְּשִׁבְתְּךָ בְּבֵיתֶךָ, וּבְלֶכְתְּךָ בַדֶּרֶךְ, וּבְשָׁכְבְּךָ וּבְקוּמֶךָ.
וּקְשַׁרְתָּם לְאוֹת עַל־יָדֶךָ, וְהָיוּ לְטֹטָפֹת בֵּין עֵינֶיךָ,
וּכְתַבְתָּם עַל־מְזֻזוֹת בֵּיתֶךָ, וּבִשְׁעָרֶיךָ.

You shall love the Lord your God with all your mind, with all
your strength, with all your being. Set these words, which I
command you this day, upon your heart. Teach them
faithfully to your children; speak of them in your home and
on your way, when you lie down and when you rise up. Bind
them as a sign upon your hand; let them be a symbol before
your eyes; inscribe them on the doorposts of your house, and
on your gates.

לְמַעַן תִּזְכְּרוּ וַעֲשִׂיתֶם אֶת־כָּל־מִצְוֹתָי, וִהְיִיתֶם
קְדֹשִׁים לֵאלֹהֵיכֶם. אֲנִי יְיָ אֱלֹהֵיכֶם, אֲשֶׁר הוֹצֵאתִי
אֶתְכֶם מֵאֶרֶץ מִצְרַיִם לִהְיוֹת לָכֶם לֵאלֹהִים. אֲנִי יְיָ
אֱלֹהֵיכֶם.

26

Be mindful of all My Mitzvot, and do them: so shall you consecrate yourselves to your God. I, the Lord, am your God who led you out of Egypt to be your God; I, the Lord, am your God.

◆ ◆

OUR FAITH IN TOMORROW   גאולה

What does it mean to be a Jew? "You shall be holy."

In the face of the many, to stand for the one; in the presence of fragments, to make them whole.

What does it mean to be a Jew? "You shall be a holy people."

To hold fast to our vision of truth, to retain our faith in tomorrow.

Holy in our past is the memory of redemption from Egyptian bondage.

Holy in our day is the hope of a redemption we still await.

Twice holy in our past are those who gave their lives to hallow this world.

Holy is the Jew, today and tomorrow, who bears witness to the goodness of life.

And holy are those whose lives are songs in freedom's cause:

·

27

מִי־כָמְכָה בָּאֵלִם, יְיָ?

Who is like You, Eternal One, among
the gods that are worshipped?

מִי כָּמְכָה, נֶאְדָּר בַּקֹּדֶשׁ,
נוֹרָא תְהִלֹּת, עְֹשֵׂה פֶלֶא?

Who is like You, majestic in holiness,
awesome in splendor, doing wonders?

מַלְכוּתְךָ רָאוּ בָנֶיךָ, בּוֹקֵעַ יָם לִפְנֵי מֹשֶׁה; "זֶה אֵלִי!"
עָנוּ וְאָמְרוּ: "יְיָ יִמְלֹךְ לְעֹלָם וָעֶד!"

In their escape from the sea, Your children saw Your sovereign
might displayed. "This is my God!" they cried. "The Eternal will
reign for ever and ever!"

וְנֶאֱמַר: "כִּי־פָדָה יְיָ אֶת־יַעֲקֹב, וּגְאָלוֹ מִיַּד חָזָק
מִמֶּנּוּ." בָּרוּךְ אַתָּה, יְיָ, גָּאַל יִשְׂרָאֵל.

°Now let all come to say: The Eternal has redeemed Israel and
all the oppressed. Blessed is the Eternal God.

• •

RISE UP TO LIFE RENEWED   הַשְׁכִּיבֵנוּ

הַשְׁכִּיבֵנוּ, יְיָ אֱלֹהֵינוּ, לְשָׁלוֹם, וְהַעֲמִידֵנוּ, מַלְכֵּנוּ,
לְחַיִּים. וּפְרוֹשׂ עָלֵינוּ סֻכַּת שְׁלוֹמֶךָ, וְתַקְּנֵנוּ בְּעֵצָה
טוֹבָה מִלְּפָנֶיךָ, וְהוֹשִׁיעֵנוּ לְמַעַן שְׁמֶךָ, וְהָגֵן בַּעֲדֵנוּ.
וְהָסֵר מֵעָלֵינוּ אוֹיֵב, דֶּבֶר וְחֶרֶב וְרָעָב וְיָגוֹן; וְהָסֵר
שָׂטָן מִלְּפָנֵינוּ וּמֵאַחֲרֵינוּ; וּבְצֵל כְּנָפֶיךָ תַּסְתִּירֵנוּ, כִּי
אֵל שׁוֹמְרֵנוּ וּמַצִּילֵנוּ אָתָּה, כִּי אֵל מֶלֶךְ חַנּוּן וְרַחוּם
אָתָּה. וּשְׁמֹר צֵאתֵנוּ וּבוֹאֵנוּ לְחַיִּים וּלְשָׁלוֹם, מֵעַתָּה
וְעַד עוֹלָם, וּפְרוֹשׂ עָלֵינוּ סֻכַּת שְׁלוֹמֶךָ. בָּרוּךְ אַתָּה,

יְיָ, הַפּוֹרֵשׂ סֻכַּת שָׁלוֹם עָלֵינוּ, וְעַל־כָּל־עַמּוֹ יִשְׂרָאֵל
וְעַל יְרוּשָׁלָֽיִם.

°May we lie down this night in peace, and rise up to life renewed. May night spread over us a shelter of peace, of quiet and calm, the blessing of rest.

There will come a time when morning will bring no word of war or famine or anguish; there will come a day of happiness, of contentment and peace.

Praised be the source of joy within us, for the night and its rest, for the promise of peace.

• •

ON SHABBAT

THE COVENANT OF SHABBAT   ושמרו

וְשָׁמְרוּ בְנֵי־יִשְׂרָאֵל אֶת־הַשַּׁבָּת, לַעֲשׂוֹת אֶת־הַשַּׁבָּת
לְדֹרֹתָם בְּרִית עוֹלָם. בֵּינִי וּבֵין בְּנֵי יִשְׂרָאֵל אוֹת הִיא
לְעֹלָם, כִּי שֵֽׁשֶׁת יָמִים עָשָׂה יְיָ אֶת־הַשָּׁמַֽיִם וְאֶת־
הָאָֽרֶץ, וּבַיּוֹם הַשְּׁבִיעִי שָׁבַת וַיִּנָּפַשׁ.

• •

READER'S KADDISH   חצי קדיש

יִתְגַּדַּל וְיִתְקַדַּשׁ שְׁמֵהּ רַבָּא בְּעָלְמָא דִּי־בְרָא כִרְעוּתֵהּ, וְיַמְלִיךְ
מַלְכוּתֵהּ בְּחַיֵּיכוֹן וּבְיוֹמֵיכוֹן וּבְחַיֵּי דְכָל־בֵּית יִשְׂרָאֵל, בַּעֲגָלָא
וּבִזְמַן קָרִיב, וְאִמְרוּ: אָמֵן. יְהֵא שְׁמֵהּ רַבָּא מְבָרַךְ לְעָלַם
וּלְעָלְמֵי עָלְמַיָּא. יִתְבָּרַךְ וְיִשְׁתַּבַּח, וְיִתְפָּאַר וְיִתְרוֹמַם
וְיִתְנַשֵּׂא, וְיִתְהַדָּר וְיִתְעַלֶּה וְיִתְהַלָּל שְׁמֵהּ דְּקוּדְשָׁא, בְּרִיךְ
הוּא, לְעֵֽלָּא מִן כָּל־בִּרְכָתָא וְשִׁירָתָא, תֻּשְׁבְּחָתָא וְנֶחֱמָתָא
דַּאֲמִירָן בְּעָלְמָא, וְאִמְרוּ: אָמֵן.

29

All rise

תפלה

אֲדֹנָי, שְׂפָתַי תִּפְתָּח, וּפִי יַגִּיד תְּהִלָּתֶךָ.

Eternal God, open my lips, that my mouth may declare Your glory.

GOD OF ALL GENERATIONS   **אבות**

בָּרוּךְ אַתָּה, יְיָ אֱלֹהֵינוּ וֵאלֹהֵי אֲבוֹתֵינוּ, אֱלֹהֵי
אַבְרָהָם, אֱלֹהֵי יִצְחָק, וֵאלֹהֵי יַעֲקֹב: הָאֵל הַגָּדוֹל,
הַגִּבּוֹר וְהַנּוֹרָא, אֵל עֶלְיוֹן. גּוֹמֵל חֲסָדִים טוֹבִים,
וְקוֹנֵה הַכֹּל, וְזוֹכֵר חַסְדֵי אָבוֹת, וּמֵבִיא גְאֻלָּה לִבְנֵי
בְנֵיהֶם, לְמַעַן שְׁמוֹ, בְּאַהֲבָה.

We praise You, Lord our God and God of all generations;
God of Abraham, God of Isaac, God of Jacob; great,
mighty, and awesome God, God supreme.

*Master of all the living, Your ways are ways of love. You
remember the faithfulness of our ancestors, and in love bring
redemption to their children's children, for the sake of Your
name.*

Remember us unto life, O King who delights in life, and
inscribe us in the Book of Life, for Your sake, O God of
life.

זָכְרֵנוּ לְחַיִּים, מֶלֶךְ חָפֵץ בַּחַיִּים, וְכָתְבֵנוּ בְּסֵפֶר
הַחַיִּים, לְמַעַנְךָ אֱלֹהִים חַיִּים. מֶלֶךְ עוֹזֵר וּמוֹשִׁיעַ
וּמָגֵן. בָּרוּךְ אַתָּה, יְיָ, מָגֵן אַבְרָהָם.

You are our King and our Help, our Savior and our
Shield. Blessed is the Lord, the Shield of Abraham.

30

אַתָּה גִּבּוֹר לְעוֹלָם, אֲדֹנָי, מְחַיֵּה הַכֹּל אַתָּה, רַב
לְהוֹשִׁיעַ.

מְכַלְכֵּל חַיִּים בְּחֶסֶד, מְחַיֵּה הַכֹּל בְּרַחֲמִים רַבִּים.
סוֹמֵךְ נוֹפְלִים, וְרוֹפֵא חוֹלִים, וּמַתִּיר אֲסוּרִים,
וּמְקַיֵּם אֱמוּנָתוֹ לִישֵׁנֵי עָפָר.

*Great is Your might, O Lord, in this world; great is Your
power in the worlds beyond.*

*Your love sustains the living, Your great compassion is the
source of life. Your power is in the help that comes to the
falling, in the healing that comes to the sick, in the freedom
You bring to the captive, in the faith You keep with those
who sleep in the dust.*

מִי כָמוֹךָ, בַּעַל גְּבוּרוֹת, וּמִי דּוֹמֶה לָּךְ, מֶלֶךְ מֵמִית
וּמְחַיֵּה וּמַצְמִיחַ יְשׁוּעָה? מִי כָמוֹךָ אַב הָרַחֲמִים,
זוֹכֵר יְצוּרָיו לְחַיִּים בְּרַחֲמִים? וְנֶאֱמָן אַתָּה לְהַחֲיוֹת
הַכֹּל. בָּרוּךְ אַתָּה, יְיָ, מְחַיֵּה הַכֹּל.

Who is like You, Master of Might? Who is Your equal, O
Lord of life and death, Source of salvation?

*Who is like You, Source of mercy? In compassion You sus-
tain the life of your children.*

*We trust in You to restore our life. Blessed is the Lord,
Source of all life.*

◆ ◆

31

GOD'S HOLINESS   קדושת השם

אַתָּה קָדוֹשׁ וְשִׁמְךָ קָדוֹשׁ, וּקְדוֹשִׁים בְּכָל־יוֹם
יְהַלְלוּךָ סֶּלָה.

You are holy, Your name is holy, and those who strive to
be holy declare Your glory day by day.

All are seated

♦

וּבְכֵן תֵּן פַּחְדְּךָ, יְיָ אֱלֹהֵינוּ, עַל כָּל־מַעֲשֶׂיךָ, וְאֵימָתְךָ
עַל כָּל־מַה־שֶּׁבָּרָאתָ. וְיִירָאוּךָ כָּל־הַמַּעֲשִׂים, וְיִשְׁתַּחֲווּ
לְפָנֶיךָ כָּל־הַבְּרוּאִים, וְיֵעָשׂוּ כֻלָּם אֲגֻדָּה אַחַת
לַעֲשׂוֹת רְצוֹנְךָ בְּלֵבָב שָׁלֵם, כְּמוֹ שֶׁיָּדַעְנוּ, יְיָ אֱלֹהֵינוּ,
שֶׁהַשִּׁלְטוֹן לְפָנֶיךָ, עֹז בְּיָדְךָ וּגְבוּרָה בִּימִינֶךָ, וְשִׁמְךָ
נוֹרָא עַל כָּל־מַה־שֶּׁבָּרָאתָ.

Lord our God, cause all Your works to stand in awe
before You, and all that You have made to tremble at
Your presence. Let all that lives revere You, and all creation turn to You in worship. Let them all become a single
family, doing Your will with a perfect heart. For well we
know, O Lord our God, that Yours is the majesty, Yours
the might; and awesome is Your name in all creation.

וּבְכֵן תֵּן כָּבוֹד, יְיָ, לְעַמֶּךָ, תְּהִלָּה לִירֵאֶיךָ וְתִקְוָה
לְדוֹרְשֶׁיךָ, וּפִתְחוֹן פֶּה לַמְיַחֲלִים לָךְ, שִׂמְחָה לְאַרְצֶךָ
וְשָׂשׂוֹן לְעִירֶךָ, וּצְמִיחַת קֶרֶן לְכָל־יוֹשְׁבֵי תֵבֵל.

*Grant honor, Lord, to Your people, glory to those who
revere You, hope to those who seek You, and courage to
those who trust You; bless Your land with gladness and
Your city with joy, and cause the light of redemption to
dawn for all who dwell on earth.*

וּבְכֵן צַדִּיקִים יִרְאוּ וְיִשְׂמָחוּ וִישָׁרִים יַעֲלֹזוּ וַחֲסִידִים
בְּרִנָּה יָגִילוּ, וְעוֹלָתָה תִּקְפָּץ־פִּיהָ וְכָל־הָרִשְׁעָה כֻּלָּהּ
כְּעָשָׁן תִּכְלֶה. כִּי תַעֲבִיר מֶמְשֶׁלֶת זָדוֹן מִן הָאָרֶץ.
וְתִמְלֹךְ אַתָּה, יְיָ, לְבַדֶּךָ עַל כָּל־מַעֲשֶׂיךָ, כַּכָּתוּב
בְּדִבְרֵי קָדְשֶׁךָ:

יִמְלֹךְ יְיָ לְעוֹלָם, אֱלֹהַיִךְ צִיּוֹן, לְדֹר וָדֹר. הַלְלוּיָהּ!

Then the just shall see and exult, the upright be glad, and
the faithful sing for joy. Violence shall rage no more, and
evil shall vanish like smoke; the rule of tyranny shall pass
away from the earth, and You alone, O Lord, shall have
dominion over all Your works, as it is written:

*The Lord shall reign for ever; your God, O Zion, from
generation to generation. Halleluyah!*

קָדוֹשׁ אַתָּה וְנוֹרָא שְׁמֶךָ, וְאֵין אֱלוֹהַּ מִבַּלְעָדֶיךָ,
כַּכָּתוּב:

וַיִּגְבַּהּ יְיָ צְבָאוֹת בַּמִּשְׁפָּט, וְהָאֵל הַקָּדוֹשׁ נִקְדַּשׁ
בִּצְדָקָה.

You are holy; awesome is Your name; there is no God but
You, as it is written:

*The Lord of Hosts is exalted by justice; the holy God is
sanctified by righteousness.*

בָּרוּךְ אַתָּה, יְיָ, הַמֶּלֶךְ הַקָּדוֹשׁ.

Blessed is the Lord, the holy King.

◆ ◆

33

THE HOLINESS OF THIS DAY   קדושת היום

אַתָּה בְחַרְתָּנוּ מִכָּל־הָעַמִּים, אָהַבְתָּ אוֹתָנוּ וְרָצִיתָ
בָּנוּ, וְרוֹמַמְתָּנוּ מִכָּל־הַלְשׁוֹנוֹת וְקִדַּשְׁתָּנוּ בְּמִצְוֹתֶיךָ,
וְקֵרַבְתָּנוּ מַלְכֵּנוּ לַעֲבוֹדָתֶךָ, וְשִׁמְךָ הַגָּדוֹל וְהַקָּדוֹשׁ
עָלֵינוּ קָרָאתָ.

וַתִּתֶּן־לָנוּ, יְיָ אֱלֹהֵינוּ, בְּאַהֲבָה אֶת־יוֹם (הַשַּׁבָּת הַזֶּה
וְאֶת־יוֹם) הַזִּכָּרוֹן הַזֶּה, יוֹם תְּרוּעָה, מִקְרָא קֹדֶשׁ,
זֵכֶר לִיצִיאַת מִצְרָיִם.

In love and favor, O God, You have chosen us from all
the peoples, hallowing us with Your Mitzvot. Our
Sovereign, You have summoned us to Your service, that
through us Your great and holy name may become known
in all the earth.

In Your love, O God, You have given us this (Shabbat
and this) Day of Remembrance, to hear the sound of the
Shofar, to unite in worship, and to recall the Exodus from
Egypt.

אֱלֹהֵינוּ וֵאלֹהֵי אֲבוֹתֵינוּ, יַעֲלֶה וְיָבֹא וְיֵרָאֶה וְיִזָּכֵר זִכְרוֹנֵנוּ
וְזִכְרוֹן כָּל־עַמְּךָ בֵּית יִשְׂרָאֵל לְפָנֶיךָ, לְטוֹבָה לְחֵן
לְחֶסֶד וּלְרַחֲמִים, לְחַיִּים וּלְשָׁלוֹם בְּיוֹם הַזִּכָּרוֹן הַזֶּה.
זָכְרֵנוּ, יְיָ אֱלֹהֵינוּ, בּוֹ לְטוֹבָה.   אָמֵן.
וּפָקְדֵנוּ בוֹ לִבְרָכָה.   אָמֵן.
וְהוֹשִׁיעֵנוּ בוֹ לְחַיִּים.   אָמֵן.

Our God and God of all ages, be mindful of Your people
Israel on this Day of Remembrance, and renew in us love
and compassion, goodness, life, and peace.
This day remember us for well-being.   Amen.
This day bless us with Your nearness.   Amen.
This day help us to live.   Amen.

34

אֱלֹהֵינוּ וֵאלֹהֵי אֲבוֹתֵינוּ, מְלוֹךְ עַל כָּל־הָעוֹלָם כֻּלּוֹ
בִּכְבוֹדֶךָ וְהִנָּשֵׂא עַל כָּל־הָאָרֶץ בִּיקָרֶךָ, וְהוֹפַע בַּהֲדַר
גְּאוֹן עֻזֶּךָ עַל כָּל־יוֹשְׁבֵי תֵבֵל אַרְצֶךָ. וְיֵדַע כָּל־פָּעוּל
כִּי אַתָּה פְעַלְתּוֹ, וְיָבִין כָּל־יָצוּר כִּי אַתָּה יְצַרְתּוֹ,
וְיֹאמַר כֹּל אֲשֶׁר נְשָׁמָה בְאַפּוֹ: יְיָ אֱלֹהֵי יִשְׂרָאֵל מֶלֶךְ,
וּמַלְכוּתוֹ בַּכֹּל מָשָׁלָה.

Our God and God of our ancestors, may You rule in glory
over all the earth, and let Your grandeur be acclaimed
throughout the world. Reveal the splendor of Your majesty to all who dwell on earth, that all Your works may
know You as their Maker, and all the living acknowledge
You as their Creator. Then all who breathe shall say: 'The
Lord God of Israel is the King whose dominion extends to
all creation.'

אֱלֹהֵינוּ וֵאלֹהֵי אֲבוֹתֵינוּ, (רְצֵה בִמְנוּחָתֵנוּ,) קַדְּשֵׁנוּ
בְּמִצְוֹתֶיךָ וְתֵן חֶלְקֵנוּ בְּתוֹרָתֶךָ. שַׂבְּעֵנוּ מִטּוּבֶךָ,
וְשַׂמְּחֵנוּ בִּישׁוּעָתֶךָ, (וְהַנְחִילֵנוּ, יְיָ אֱלֹהֵינוּ, בְּאַהֲבָה
וּבְרָצוֹן שַׁבַּת קָדְשֶׁךָ, וְיָנוּחוּ בָהּ יִשְׂרָאֵל מְקַדְּשֵׁי
שְׁמֶךָ,) וְטַהֵר לִבֵּנוּ לְעָבְדְּךָ בֶּאֱמֶת, כִּי אַתָּה אֱלֹהִים
אֱמֶת, וּדְבָרְךָ אֱמֶת וְקַיָּם לָעַד. בָּרוּךְ אַתָּה, יְיָ, מֶלֶךְ
עַל כָּל־הָאָרֶץ, מְקַדֵּשׁ (הַשַּׁבָּת וְ) יִשְׂרָאֵל וְיוֹם
הַזִּכָּרוֹן.

*Our God and God of our ancestors, sanctify us with Your
Mitzvot, and let Your Torah be our way of life. (May our
rest on this day be pleasing in Your sight.) Satisfy us with
Your goodness, gladden us with Your salvation, and purify
our hearts to serve You in truth; for You, O God, are Truth,
and Your word is true for ever. (In Your gracious love, O
Lord our God, let Your holy Sabbath remain our heritage,
that all Israel, hallowing Your name, may find rest and*

35

peace.) **Blessed is the Lord, who hallows (the Sabbath,) the
House of Israel and the Day of Remembrance.**

❖ ❖

WORSHIP   עבודה

רְצֵה, יְיָ אֱלֹהֵינוּ, בְּעַמְּךָ יִשְׂרָאֵל, וּתְפִלָּתָם בְּאַהֲבָה
תְקַבֵּל, וּתְהִי לְרָצוֹן תָּמִיד עֲבוֹדַת יִשְׂרָאֵל עַמֶּךָ. אֵל
קָרוֹב לְכָל־קֹרְאָיו, פְּנֵה אֶל עֲבָדֶיךָ וְחָנֵּנוּ; שְׁפוֹךְ
רוּחֲךָ עָלֵינוּ, וְתֶחֱזֶינָה עֵינֵינוּ בְּשׁוּבְךָ לְצִיּוֹן בְּרַחֲמִים.

Be gracious, O Lord our God, to Your people Israel, and
receive our prayers with love. O may our worship always
be acceptable to You.
Fill us with the knowledge that You are near to all who
seek You in truth. Pour out Your spirit upon us; let our
eyes behold Your presence in our midst and in the midst
of our people in Zion.

*Blessed is the Lord, whose presence gives life to Zion and all
Israel.*

בָּרוּךְ אַתָּה, יְיָ, הַמַּחֲזִיר שְׁכִינָתוֹ לְצִיּוֹן.

❖ ❖

THANKSGIVING   הודאה

מוֹדִים אֲנַחְנוּ לָךְ, שָׁאַתָּה הוּא יְיָ אֱלֹהֵינוּ וֵאלֹהֵי
אֲבוֹתֵינוּ לְעוֹלָם וָעֶד. צוּר חַיֵּינוּ, מָגֵן יִשְׁעֵנוּ, אַתָּה
הוּא לְדוֹר וָדוֹר. נוֹדֶה לְךָ וּנְסַפֵּר תְּהִלָּתֶךָ, עַל־חַיֵּינוּ
הַמְּסוּרִים בְּיָדֶךָ, וְעַל־נִשְׁמוֹתֵינוּ הַפְּקוּדוֹת לָךְ, וְעַל־
נִסֶּיךָ שֶׁבְּכָל־יוֹם עִמָּנוּ, וְעַל־נִפְלְאוֹתֶיךָ וְטוֹבוֹתֶיךָ
שֶׁבְּכָל־עֵת, עֶרֶב וָבֹקֶר וְצָהֳרָיִם. הַטּוֹב: כִּי לֹא־כָלוּ

36

רַחֲמֶיךָ, וְהַמְרַחֵם: כִּי־לֹא תַמּוּ חֲסָדֶיךָ, מֵעוֹלָם קִוְּינוּ
לָךְ.

We gratefully acknowledge that You are the Lord our God
and God of our people, the God of all generations. You are
the Rock of our life, the Power that shields us in every age.
We thank You and sing Your praises: for our lives, which
are in Your hand; for our souls, which are in Your keeping;
for the miracles which are daily with us; and for Your
wondrous gifts at all times, morning, noon, and night. You
are Goodness: Your mercies never end; You are Compas-
sion: Your love never fails. You have always been our hope.

וְעַל כֻּלָּם יִתְבָּרַךְ וְיִתְרוֹמַם שִׁמְךָ, מַלְכֵּנוּ, תָּמִיד
לְעוֹלָם וָעֶד.

וּכְתוֹב לְחַיִּים טוֹבִים כָּל־בְּנֵי בְרִיתֶךָ.

וְכֹל הַחַיִּים יוֹדוּךָ סֶּלָה, וִיהַלְלוּ אֶת שִׁמְךָ בֶּאֱמֶת,
הָאֵל יְשׁוּעָתֵנוּ וְעֶזְרָתֵנוּ סֶלָה. בָּרוּךְ אַתָּה, יְיָ, הַטּוֹב
שִׁמְךָ וּלְךָ נָאֶה לְהוֹדוֹת.

For all these things, O Sovereign God, let Your name be
for ever exalted and blessed, and let life abundant be the
heritage of all the children of Your covenant. O God our
Redeemer and Helper, let all who live affirm You and
praise Your name in truth. Lord, whose nature is
Goodness, we give You thanks and praise.

◆ ◆

PEACE   ברכת שלום

שָׁלוֹם רָב עַל־יִשְׂרָאֵל עַמְּךָ תָּשִׂים לְעוֹלָם, כִּי אַתָּה
הוּא מֶלֶךְ אָדוֹן לְכָל הַשָּׁלוֹם. וְטוֹב בְּעֵינֶיךָ לְבָרֵךְ
אֶת־עַמְּךָ יִשְׂרָאֵל בְּכָל־עֵת וּבְכָל־שָׁעָה בִּשְׁלוֹמֶךָ.
בְּסֵפֶר חַיִּים, בְּרָכָה וְשָׁלוֹם וּפַרְנָסָה טוֹבָה נִזָּכֵר

וְנִכָּתֵב לְפָנֶיךָ, אֲנַחְנוּ וְכָל־עַמְּךָ בֵּית יִשְׂרָאֵל, לְחַיִּים
טוֹבִים וּלְשָׁלוֹם. בָּרוּךְ אַתָּה, יְיָ, עוֹשֶׂה הַשָּׁלוֹם.

°*Grant us peace, Your most precious gift, O Eternal Source
of peace, and give us the will to proclaim its message to all
the peoples of the earth. Bless our country, that it may
always be a stronghold of peace, and its advocate among the
nations. May contentment reign within its borders, health
and happiness within its homes. Strengthen the bonds of
friendship among the inhabitants of all lands, and may the
love of Your name hallow every home and every heart. Teach
us, O God, to labor for righteousness, and inscribe us in the
Book of life, blessing, and peace. Blessed is the Eternal God,
the Source of peace.*

◆ ◆

SILENT PRAYER

אֱלֹהַי, נְצֹר לְשׁוֹנִי מֵרָע, וּשְׂפָתַי מִדַּבֵּר מִרְמָה,
וְלִמְקַלְלַי נַפְשִׁי תִדּוֹם, וְנַפְשִׁי כֶּעָפָר לַכֹּל תִּהְיֶה.
פְּתַח לִבִּי בְּתוֹרָתֶךָ, וּבְמִצְוֹתֶיךָ תִּרְדּוֹף נַפְשִׁי, וְכֹל
הַחוֹשְׁבִים עָלַי רָעָה, מְהֵרָה הָפֵר עֲצָתָם וְקַלְקֵל
מַחֲשַׁבְתָּם. עֲשֵׂה לְמַעַן שְׁמֶךָ, עֲשֵׂה לְמַעַן יְמִינֶךָ,
עֲשֵׂה לְמַעַן קְדֻשָּׁתֶךָ, עֲשֵׂה לְמַעַן תוֹרָתֶךָ. לְמַעַן
יֵחָלְצוּן יְדִידֶיךָ, הוֹשִׁיעָה יְמִינְךָ וַעֲנֵנִי.

O God, keep my tongue from evil and my lips from deceit.
Help me to be silent in the face of derision, humble in the
presence of all. Open my heart to Your Torah, that I may
hasten to do Your Mitzvot. Save me with Your power; in
time of trouble be my answer, that those who love You
may be delivered.

◆ ◆

38

יִהְיוּ לְרָצוֹן אִמְרֵי־פִי וְהֶגְיוֹן לִבִּי לְפָנֶיךָ, יְיָ, צוּרִי
וְגוֹאֲלִי.

May the words of my mouth, and the meditations of my heart,
be acceptable to You, O Lord, my Rock and my Redeemer.

or

עֹשֶׂה שָׁלוֹם בִּמְרוֹמָיו, הוּא יַעֲשֶׂה שָׁלוֹם עָלֵינוּ וְעַל
כָּל־יִשְׂרָאֵל, וְאִמְרוּ אָמֵן.

May the One who causes peace to reign in the high heavens let
peace descend on us, on all Israel, and all the world.

39

All rise
The Ark is opened

אבינו מלכנו

אָבִינוּ מַלְכֵּנוּ, שְׁמַע קוֹלֵנוּ.

Our Father, our King, hear our voice.

אָבִינוּ מַלְכֵּנוּ, חָטָאנוּ לְפָנֶיךָ.

Our Father, our King, we have sinned against You.

אָבִינוּ מַלְכֵּנוּ, חֲמוֹל עָלֵינוּ וְעַל עוֹלָלֵינוּ וְטַפֵּנוּ.

Our Father, our King, have compassion on us and on our children.

אָבִינוּ מַלְכֵּנוּ, כַּלֵּה דֶּבֶר וְחֶרֶב וְרָעָב מֵעָלֵינוּ.

Our Father, our King, make an end to sickness, war, and famine.

אָבִינוּ מַלְכֵּנוּ, כַּלֵּה כָּל־צַר וּמַשְׂטִין מֵעָלֵינוּ.

Our Father, our King, make an end to all oppression.

אָבִינוּ מַלְכֵּנוּ, כָּתְבֵנוּ בְּסֵפֶר חַיִּים טוֹבִים.

Our Father, our King, inscribe us for blessing in the Book of Life.

אָבִינוּ מַלְכֵּנוּ, חַדֵּשׁ עָלֵינוּ שָׁנָה טוֹבָה.

Our Father, our King, let the new year be a good year for us.

אָבִינוּ מַלְכֵּנוּ, הָרֵם קֶרֶן יִשְׂרָאֵל עַמֶּךָ.

Our Father, our King, give strength to Your people Israel.

אָבִינוּ מַלְכֵּנוּ, חָנֵּנוּ וַעֲנֵנוּ, כִּי אֵין בָּנוּ מַעֲשִׂים, עֲשֵׂה
עִמָּנוּ צְדָקָה וָחֶסֶד וְהוֹשִׁיעֵנוּ.

Our Father, our King, be gracious and answer us, for we have little merit. Treat us generously and with kindness, and be our help.

The Ark is closed

קדוש

בָּרוּךְ אַתָּה, יְיָ אֱלֹהֵינוּ, מֶלֶךְ הָעוֹלָם, בּוֹרֵא פְּרִי הַגָּפֶן.

בָּרוּךְ אַתָּה, יְיָ אֱלֹהֵינוּ, מֶלֶךְ הָעוֹלָם, אֲשֶׁר בָּחַר בָּנוּ מִכָּל־עָם, וְרוֹמְמָנוּ מִכָּל־לָשׁוֹן, וְקִדְּשָׁנוּ בְּמִצְוֹתָיו. וַתִּתֶּן־לָנוּ, יְיָ אֱלֹהֵינוּ, בְּאַהֲבָה אֶת־יוֹם (הַשַּׁבָּת הַזֶּה וְאֶת־יוֹם) הַזִּכָּרוֹן הַזֶּה, יוֹם תְּרוּעָה, מִקְרָא קֹדֶשׁ, זֵכֶר לִיצִיאַת מִצְרָיִם. כִּי בָנוּ בָחַרְתָּ, וְאוֹתָנוּ קִדַּשְׁתָּ מִכָּל־הָעַמִּים, וּדְבָרְךָ אֱמֶת וְקַיָּם לָעַד. בָּרוּךְ אַתָּה, יְיָ, מֶלֶךְ עַל כָּל־הָאָרֶץ, מְקַדֵּשׁ (הַשַּׁבָּת וְ)יִשְׂרָאֵל וְיוֹם הַזִּכָּרוֹן.

בָּרוּךְ אַתָּה, יְיָ אֱלֹהֵינוּ, מֶלֶךְ הָעוֹלָם, שֶׁהֶחֱיָנוּ וְקִיְּמָנוּ וְהִגִּיעָנוּ לַזְּמַן הַזֶּה.

Blessed is the Lord our God, Ruler of the universe, Creator of the fruit of the vine.

Blessed is the Lord our God, Ruler of the universe, who has chosen us from all the peoples, hallowing us with the Mitzvot. In Your love, O Lord our God, You have given us this (Shabbat and this) Day of Remembrance, to hear the sound of the Shofar, to unite in worship, and to recall the Exodus from Egypt. For You have chosen us from all peoples, consecrating us to Your service, and Your word is truth eternal.

Blessed is the Sovereign God, Ruler of all the world, who hallows (the Sabbath,) the House of Israel and the Day of Remembrance.

Blessed is the Lord our God, Ruler of the universe, for giving us life, for sustaining us, and for enabling us to reach this season.

עָלֵינוּ

All rise

עָלֵינוּ לְשַׁבֵּחַ לַאֲדוֹן הַכֹּל, לָתֵת גְּדֻלָּה לְיוֹצֵר
בְּרֵאשִׁית, שֶׁלֹּא עָשָׂנוּ כְּגוֹיֵי הָאֲרָצוֹת, וְלֹא שָׂמָנוּ
כְּמִשְׁפְּחוֹת הָאֲדָמָה; שֶׁלֹּא שָׂם חֶלְקֵנוּ כָּהֶם, וְגֹרָלֵנוּ
כְּכָל־הֲמוֹנָם.

We must praise the Lord of all, the Maker of heaven and earth,
who has set us apart from the other families of earth, giving us a
destiny unique among the nations.

וַאֲנַחְנוּ כּוֹרְעִים וּמִשְׁתַּחֲוִים וּמוֹדִים לִפְנֵי מֶלֶךְ מַלְכֵי
הַמְּלָכִים, הַקָּדוֹשׁ בָּרוּךְ הוּא,

We therefore bow in awe and thanksgiving before the One who
is Sovereign over all, the Holy One, blessed be He.

All are seated

שֶׁהוּא נוֹטֶה שָׁמַיִם וְיוֹסֵד אָרֶץ, וּמוֹשַׁב יְקָרוֹ בַּשָּׁמַיִם
מִמַּעַל, וּשְׁכִינַת עֻזּוֹ בְּגָבְהֵי מְרוֹמִים. הוּא אֱלֹהֵינוּ,
אֵין עוֹד; אֱמֶת מַלְכֵּנוּ, אֶפֶס זוּלָתוֹ, כַּכָּתוּב בְּתוֹרָתוֹ:
"וְיָדַעְתָּ הַיּוֹם וַהֲשֵׁבֹתָ אֶל־לְבָבֶךָ, כִּי יְיָ הוּא הָאֱלֹהִים
בַּשָּׁמַיִם מִמַּעַל וְעַל־הָאָרֶץ מִתָּחַת, אֵין עוֹד."

He spread out the heavens and established the earth; He is
our God; there is none else. In truth He alone is our King,
as it is written: "Know then this day and take it to heart:
the Lord is God in the heavens above and on the earth
below; there is none else."

עַל־כֵּן נְקַוֶּה לְךָ, יְיָ אֱלֹהֵינוּ, לִרְאוֹת מְהֵרָה בְּתִפְאֶרֶת
עֻזֶּךָ, לְהַעֲבִיר גִּלּוּלִים מִן־הָאָרֶץ, וְהָאֱלִילִים כָּרוֹת

43

יְבָרְתוּן, לְתַקֵּן עוֹלָם בְּמַלְכוּת שַׁדַּי. וְכָל־בְּנֵי בָשָׂר
יִקְרְאוּ בִשְׁמֶךָ, לְהַפְנוֹת אֵלֶיךָ כָּל־רִשְׁעֵי אָרֶץ.
יַכִּירוּ וְיֵדְעוּ כָּל־יוֹשְׁבֵי תֵבֵל כִּי לְךָ תִּכְרַע כָּל־בֶּרֶךְ,
תִּשָּׁבַע כָּל־לָשׁוֹן. לְפָנֶיךָ, יְיָ אֱלֹהֵינוּ, יִכְרְעוּ וְיִפֹּלוּ,
וְלִכְבוֹד שִׁמְךָ יְקָר יִתֵּנוּ, וִיקַבְּלוּ כֻלָּם אֶת־עֹל
מַלְכוּתֶךָ, וְתִמְלוֹךְ עֲלֵיהֶם מְהֵרָה לְעוֹלָם וָעֶד.

*We therefore hope, O Lord our God, soon to behold the
glory of Your might. Then will false gods vanish from our
hearts, and the world will be perfected under Your unchal-
lenged rule. And then will all acclaim You as their God, and,
forsaking evil, turn to You alone.*

*Let all who dwell on earth acknowledge that unto You every
knee must bend and every tongue swear loyalty. Before You,
O Lord our God, let them humble themselves. To Your
glorious name let them give honor. Let all accept the yoke of
Your kingdom, that You may rule over them soon and for
ever.*

כִּי הַמַּלְכוּת שֶׁלְךָ הִיא, וּלְעוֹלְמֵי עַד תִּמְלוֹךְ בְּכָבוֹד,
כַּכָּתוּב בְּתוֹרָתֶךָ: "יְיָ יִמְלֹךְ לְעֹלָם וָעֶד."

*For the kingdom is Yours, and to all eternity You will reign
in glory, as it is written: "The Lord will reign for ever and
ever."*

וְנֶאֱמַר: "וְהָיָה יְיָ לְמֶלֶךְ עַל־כָּל־הָאָרֶץ; בַּיּוֹם הַהוּא
יִהְיֶה יְיָ אֶחָד וּשְׁמוֹ אֶחָד."

And it has been said: "The Lord shall reign over all the earth; on
that day the Lord shall be One and His name shall be One."

◆ ◆

44

At this sacred moment we turn our thoughts to those who have gone from life. We recall the joy of their companionship. We feel a pang, the echo of that intenser grief when first their death lay before our stricken eyes. Now we know that they will never vanish, so long as heart and thought remain within us. By love are they remembered, and in memory they live.

O God, grant that their memory may bring strength and blessing. May the nobility in their lives and the high ideals they cherished endure in our thoughts and live on in our deeds. May we, carrying on their work, help to redeem Your promise that life shall yet prevail.

MOURNER'S KADDISH   קדיש יתום

יִתְגַּדַּל וְיִתְקַדַּשׁ שְׁמֵהּ רַבָּא בְּעָלְמָא דִּי־בְרָא
כִרְעוּתֵהּ, וְיַמְלִיךְ מַלְכוּתֵהּ בְּחַיֵּיכוֹן וּבְיוֹמֵיכוֹן וּבְחַיֵּי
דְכָל־בֵּית יִשְׂרָאֵל, בַּעֲגָלָא וּבִזְמַן קָרִיב, וְאִמְרוּ: אָמֵן.

Yit·ga·dal ve·yit·ka·dash she·mei ra·ba be·al·ma di·ve·ra
chi·re·u·tei, ve·yam·lich mal·chu·tei be·cha·yei·chon
u·ve·yo·mei·chon u·ve·cha·yei de·chol beit Yis·ra·eil, ba·a·ga·la
u·vi·ze·man ka·riv, ve·i·me·ru: a·mein.

יְהֵא שְׁמֵהּ רַבָּא מְבָרַךְ לְעָלַם וּלְעָלְמֵי עָלְמַיָּא.

Ye·hei she·mei ra·ba me·va·rach le·a·lam u·le·al·mei al·ma·ya.

יִתְבָּרַךְ וְיִשְׁתַּבַּח, וְיִתְפָּאַר וְיִתְרוֹמַם וְיִתְנַשֵּׂא,
וְיִתְהַדָּר וְיִתְעַלֶּה וְיִתְהַלָּל שְׁמֵהּ דְּקוּדְשָׁא, בְּרִיךְ
הוּא, לְעֵלָּא מִן־כָּל־בִּרְכָתָא וְשִׁירָתָא, תֻּשְׁבְּחָתָא
וְנֶחֱמָתָא דַּאֲמִירָן בְּעָלְמָא, וְאִמְרוּ: אָמֵן.

Yit·ba·rach ve·yish·ta·bach, ve·yit·pa·ar ve·yit·ro·mam
ve·yit·na·sei, ve·yit·ha·dar ve·yit·a·leh ve·yit·ha·lal she·mei
de·ku·de·sha, be·rich hu, le·ei·la min kol bi·re·cha·ta

ve·shi·ra·ta, tush·be·cha·ta ve·ne·che·ma·ta, da·a·mi·ran
be·al·ma, ve·i·me·ru: a·mein.

יְהֵא שְׁלָמָא רַבָּא מִן־שְׁמַיָּא וְחַיִּים עָלֵינוּ וְעַל־כָּל־
יִשְׂרָאֵל, וְאִמְרוּ: אָמֵן.

Ye·hei she·la·ma ra·ba min she·ma·ya ve·cha·yim a·lei·nu ve·al
kol Yis·ra·eil, ve·i·me·ru: a·mein.

עֹשֶׂה שָׁלוֹם בִּמְרוֹמָיו, הוּא יַעֲשֶׂה שָׁלוֹם עָלֵינוּ וְעַל־
כָּל־יִשְׂרָאֵל, וְאִמְרוּ: אָמֵן.

O·seh sha·lom bi·me·ro·mav, hu ya·a·seh sha·lom a·lei·nu ve·al
kol Yis·ra·eil, ve·i·me·ru: a·mein.

Let the glory of God be extolled, let His great name be hallowed
in the world whose creation He willed. May His kingdom soon
prevail, in our own day, our own lives, and the life of all Israel,
and let us say: Amen.
Let His great name be blessed for ever and ever.
Let the name of the Holy One, blessed is He, be glorified, exalted, and honored, though He is beyond all the praises, songs,
and adorations that we can utter, and let us say: Amen.
For us and for all Israel, may the blessing of peace and the
promise of life come true, and let us say: Amen.
May the One who causes peace to reign in the high heavens, let
peace descend on us, on all Israel, and all the world, and let us
say: Amen.

◆ ◆

May the Source of peace send peace to all who mourn,
and comfort to all who are bereaved. Amen.

46

ADON OLAM   אדון עולם

A·don o·lam, a·sher ma·lach   אֲדוֹן עוֹלָם, אֲשֶׁר מָלַךְ

be·te·rem kol ye·tsir niv·ra,   בְּטֶרֶם כָּל־יְצִיר נִבְרָא,

le·eit na·a·sa ve·chef·tso kol,   לְעֵת נַעֲשָׂה בְחֶפְצוֹ כֹּל,

a·zai me·lech she·mo nik·ra.   אֲזַי מֶלֶךְ שְׁמוֹ נִקְרָא.

Ve·a·cha·rei ki·che·lot ha·kol,   וְאַחֲרֵי כִּכְלוֹת הַכֹּל,

le·va·do yim·loch no·ra,   לְבַדּוֹ יִמְלֹךְ נוֹרָא,

ve·hu ha·ya, ve·hu ho·veh,   וְהוּא הָיָה, וְהוּא הֹוֶה,

ve·hu yi·he·yeh be·tif·a·ra.   וְהוּא יִהְיֶה בְּתִפְאָרָה.

Ve·hu e·chad, ve·ein shei·ni   וְהוּא אֶחָד, וְאֵין שֵׁנִי

le·ham·shil lo, le·hach·bi·ra,   לְהַמְשִׁיל לוֹ, לְהַחְבִּירָה,

be·li rei·shit, be·li tach·lit,   בְּלִי רֵאשִׁית, בְּלִי תַכְלִית,

ve·lo ha·oz ve·ha·mis·ra.   וְלוֹ הָעֹז וְהַמִּשְׂרָה.

Ve·hu Ei·li, ve·chai go·a·li,   וְהוּא אֵלִי, וְחַי גּוֹאֲלִי,

ve·tsur chev·li be·eit tsa·ra,   וְצוּר חֶבְלִי בְּעֵת צָרָה,

ve·hu ni·si u·ma·nos li,   וְהוּא נִסִּי וּמָנוֹס לִי,

me·nat ko·si be·yom ek·ra.   מְנָת כּוֹסִי בְּיוֹם אֶקְרָא.

Be·ya·do af·kid ru·chi   בְּיָדוֹ אַפְקִיד רוּחִי

be·eit i·shan ve·a·i·ra,   בְּעֵת אִישַׁן וְאָעִירָה,

ve·im ru·chi ge·vi·ya·ti: וְעִם־רוּחִי גְוִיָּתִי:

A·do·nai li, ve·lo i·ra.   יְיָ לִי, וְלֹא אִירָא.

He is the eternal Lord, who reigned before any being had yet
been created; when all was done according to His will, already
then His name was King.

And after all has ceased to be, still will He reign in solitary majesty; He was, He is, and He shall be in glory.

And He is one; none other can compare to Him, or consort with
Him; He is without beginning, without end; to Him belong
power and dominion.

47

And He is *my* God, my living Redeemer, my Rock in time of trouble and distress; He is my banner and my refuge, my benefactor when I call on Him.

Into His hands I entrust my spirit, when I sleep and when I wake; and with my spirit, my body also: the Lord is with me, I will not fear.

THE LORD OF ALL

The Lord of all, who reigned supreme,
Ere first creation's form was framed;
When all was finished by His will,
His name Almighty was proclaimed.

When this, our world, shall be no more.
In majesty He still shall reign,
Who was, who is, who will remain,
His endless glory we proclaim.

Alone is He, beyond compare,
Without division or ally,
Without initial date or end,
Omnipotent He rules on high.

He is my God, my Savior He,
To whom I turn in sorrow's hour—
My banner proud, my refuge sure,
Who hears and answers with His pow'r.

Then in His hand myself I lay,
And trusting sleep, and wake with cheer;
My soul and body are His care;
The Lord does guard, I have no fear.

48

Evening Service II

תפלת ערבית ב

הדלקת הנרות

With the setting of this evening's sun, united with Jews of every place and time, we proclaim a new year of hope. May the light of the divine shine forth to lead us, to show us the good we must do, the harmony we must create. Let the fire we kindle be for us a warming flame, whose brightness shows us the path of life.

◆ ◆

בָּרוּךְ אַתָּה, יְיָ אֱלֹהֵינוּ, מֶלֶךְ הָעוֹלָם, אֲשֶׁר קִדְּשָׁנוּ בְּמִצְוֹתָיו וְצִוָּנוּ לְהַדְלִיק נֵר שֶׁל (שַׁבָּת וְשֶׁל) יוֹם טוֹב.

°Blessed is the eternal Power that inspires us to kindle the light of (Shabbat and) Yom Tov. Blessed is the Source of life and light.

בָּרוּךְ אַתָּה, יְיָ אֱלֹהֵינוּ, מֶלֶךְ הָעוֹלָם, שֶׁהֶחֱיָנוּ וְקִיְּמָנוּ וְהִגִּיעָנוּ לַזְּמַן הַזֶּה.

°Blessed is the eternal Power of the universe, for giving us life, for sustaining us, and for enabling us to reach this season.

°This symbol indicates that the English is a variation suggested by the theme of the Hebrew.

MEDITATION

From Psalms 3 and 5

Lord, I cry out to You,
and from Your holy mountain's summit
Your answer comes.
I lie down and sleep,
and then I am awake,
safe in Your hand,
and unafraid . . .
Lord, rise up;
help me, O my God,
for You, Lord, are the One
from whom help comes,
and Your blessing rests upon Your people.

As for me, in Your abundant lovingkindness
let me enter Your house,
reverently to worship in Your holy temple.

For all who trust in You
there is joy and everlasting song;
You will give them shelter;
and all who love Your name
shall exult in You.
For You give your benediction to the just;
Lord, You throw Your favor about them like a shield.

❖ ❖

Psalm 121

אֶשָּׂא עֵינַי אֶל־הֶהָרִים, מֵאַיִן יָבוֹא עֶזְרִי? עֶזְרִי מֵעִם
יְיָ, עֹשֵׂה שָׁמַיִם וָאָרֶץ. אַל־יִתֵּן לַמּוֹט רַגְלֶךָ, אַל־יָנוּם
שֹׁמְרֶךָ. הִנֵּה לֹא־יָנוּם וְלֹא יִישָׁן, שׁוֹמֵר יִשְׂרָאֵל. יְיָ
שֹׁמְרֶךָ, יְיָ צִלְּךָ עַל־יַד יְמִינֶךָ. יוֹמָם הַשֶּׁמֶשׁ לֹא־
יַכֶּכָּה, וְיָרֵחַ בַּלָּיְלָה. יְיָ יִשְׁמָרְךָ מִכָּל־רָע, יִשְׁמֹר אֶת־
נַפְשֶׁךָ. יְיָ יִשְׁמָר־צֵאתְךָ וּבוֹאֶךָ, מֵעַתָּה וְעַד־עוֹלָם.

I lift up my eyes to the mountains; what is the source of my
help? My help will come from the Lord, Maker of heaven and
earth. God will not allow your foot to slip; your Guardian will not
slumber. Behold, the Guardian of Israel neither slumbers nor
sleeps. The Eternal is your Keeper, the Lord is your shade at
your right hand. The sun shall not harm you by day, nor the
moon by night. The Lord will guard you from all evil, and
protect your being. The Lord will guard you, coming and going,
from this time forth, and for ever.

◆ ◆

IN THE TWILIGHT

In the twilight of the vanishing year, we lift up our hearts
in thanksgiving.

*Our souls are stirred by the memory of joy, as the new year
begins.*

We were sustained by love and kindness; comforted in
times of sorrow; found happiness in our homes, and
gladness with our friends. We lift up our hearts in
thanksgiving, as the new year begins.

As the new year begins, our spirits rise in grateful song.

But there were dreams that came to naught . . . and times when we refused to dream. These, with much regret, we now remember, as the new year begins.

As the new year begins, contrition fills our thoughts.

Some of our days were dark with grief. Many a tear furrowed our cheeks: alas for the tender ties that were broken! We look back with sorrow, as the new year begins.

As the new year begins, tears well up within us.

Yet we look ahead with hope, giving thanks for the daily miracle of renewal, for the promise of good to come. May this Rosh Hashanah, birthday of the world, be our day of rebirth into life and peace, serenity and safety, as the new year begins.

As the new year begins, so is hope reborn with us!

◆ ◆

SACRED ASSEMBLY

בחדש השביעי

In the seventh month,
on the first day of the month,
there shall be a sacred assembly,
a cessation from work,
a day of commemoration
proclaimed by the sound
of the Shofar.

בַּחְׂדֶשׁ הַשְּׁבִיעִי,
בְּאֶחָד לַחְׂדֶשׁ,
יִהְיֶה לָכֶם שַׁבָּתוֹן,
זִכְרוֹן תְּרוּעָה,
מִקְרָא־קְׂדֶשׁ.
כָּל־מְלֶאכֶת עֲבוֹדָה
לֹא תַעֲשׂוּ.

◆

52

All rise

תִּקְעוּ בַחֹדֶשׁ שׁוֹפָר, בַּכֶּסֶה לְיוֹם חַגֵּנוּ.
כִּי חֹק לְיִשְׂרָאֵל הוּא, מִשְׁפָּט לֵאלֹהֵי יַעֲקֹב.

Sound the Shofar when the new moon appears,
at the turning of the year,
at the returning of our solemn celebration.
For this is a statute binding on Israel,
an ordinance of the God of Jacob.

The Ark is opened

THE YEAR   יהי רצון

יְהִי רָצוֹן מִלְפָנֶיךָ, יְיָ אֱלֹהֵינוּ וֵאלֹהֵי אֲבוֹתֵינוּ,
שֶׁתְּחַדֵּשׁ עָלֵינוּ וְעַל־כָּל־בֵּית יִשְׂרָאֵל אֶת־הַשָּׁנָה
הַזֹּאת, שְׁנַת חֲמֵשֶׁת אֲלָפִים וּשְׁבַע מֵאוֹת וְ . . . . ,,
לְחַיִּים וּלְשָׁלוֹם, לְשָׂשׂוֹן וּלְשִׂמְחָה, לִישׁוּעָה
וּלְנֶחָמָה, וְנֹאמַר: אָמֵן.

°May this new year, called five thousand seven hundred
and . . ., bring to us and the whole House of Israel life and
peace, joy and exaltation, redemption and comfort.

*May this new year bring us life and peace, joy and exalta-
tion, redemption and comfort. Amen.*

◆ ◆

53

שמע וברכותיה

בָּרְכוּ אֶת־יְיָ הַמְבֹרָךְ!

Praise the Lord, to whom our praise is due!

בָּרוּךְ יְיָ הַמְבֹרָךְ לְעוֹלָם וָעֶד!

Praised be the Lord, to whom our praise is due,
now and for ever!

The Ark is closed
Remain standing

◆ ◆

CREATION   מעריב ערבים

בָּרוּךְ אַתָּה, יְיָ אֱלֹהֵינוּ, מֶלֶךְ הָעוֹלָם, אֲשֶׁר בִּדְבָרוֹ
מַעֲרִיב עֲרָבִים. בְּחָכְמָה פּוֹתֵחַ שְׁעָרִים, וּבִתְבוּנָה
מְשַׁנֶּה עִתִּים, וּמַחֲלִיף אֶת־הַזְּמַנִּים, וּמְסַדֵּר אֶת־
הַכּוֹכָבִים בְּמִשְׁמְרוֹתֵיהֶם בָּרָקִיעַ כִּרְצוֹנוֹ. בּוֹרֵא יוֹם
וָלַיְלָה, גּוֹלֵל אוֹר מִפְּנֵי חֹשֶׁךְ וְחֹשֶׁךְ מִפְּנֵי אוֹר,
וּמַעֲבִיר יוֹם וּמֵבִיא לָיְלָה, וּמַבְדִּיל בֵּין יוֹם וּבֵין
לָיְלָה, יְיָ צְבָאוֹת שְׁמוֹ. אֵל חַי וְקַיָּם, תָּמִיד יִמְלוֹךְ
עָלֵינוּ, לְעוֹלָם וָעֶד.

Praised be the Lord our God, Ruler of the universe, whose
word brings on the evening.

With wisdom You open heaven's gates; with understanding
You make the ages pass and the seasons alternate.

Your will controls the stars as they travel through the sky.

Creator of day and night, You roll light away from darkness

54

*and darkness from light; You cause day to pass and bring on
the night; the Lord of Hosts is Your name. O living and eternal God, rule us always, to the end of time! Blessed is the
Lord, whose word makes evening fall.*

בָּרוּךְ אַתָּה, יְיָ, הַמַּעֲרִיב עֲרָבִים.

◆ ◆

REVELATION   אהבת עולם

אַהֲבַת עוֹלָם בֵּית יִשְׂרָאֵל עַמְּךָ אָהַבְתָּ: תּוֹרָה
וּמִצְוֹת, חֻקִּים וּמִשְׁפָּטִים אוֹתָנוּ לִמַּדְתָּ. עַל־כֵּן, יְיָ
אֱלֹהֵינוּ, בְּשָׁכְבֵּנוּ וּבְקוּמֵנוּ נָשִׂיחַ בְּחֻקֶּיךָ, וְנִשְׂמַח
בְּדִבְרֵי תוֹרָתְךָ וּבְמִצְוֹתֶיךָ לְעוֹלָם וָעֶד. כִּי הֵם חַיֵּינוּ
וְאֹרֶךְ יָמֵינוּ, וּבָהֶם נֶהְגֶּה יוֹמָם וָלָיְלָה. וְאַהֲבָתְךָ אַל־
תָּסִיר מִמֶּנּוּ לְעוֹלָמִים!

Unending is Your love for Your people, the House of
Israel: Torah and Mitzvot, laws and precepts have You
taught us. Therefore, O Lord our God, when we lie down
and when we rise up, we will meditate on Your laws and
rejoice in Your Torah and Mitzvot for ever.

*Day and night we will reflect on them, for they are our life
and the length of our days. O may Your love never depart
from our hearts! Blessed are You, O Lord: You love Your
people Israel.*

בָּרוּךְ אַתָּה, יְיָ, אוֹהֵב עַמּוֹ יִשְׂרָאֵל.

◆ ◆

55

שְׁמַע יִשְׂרָאֵל: יְיָ אֱלֹהֵינוּ, יְיָ אֶחָד!

Hear, O Israel: the Lord is our God, the Lord is One!

בָּרוּךְ שֵׁם כְּבוֹד מַלְכוּתוֹ לְעוֹלָם וָעֶד!

Blessed is His glorious kingdom for ever and ever!

All are seated

וְאָהַבְתָּ אֵת יְיָ אֱלֹהֶיךָ בְּכָל־לְבָבְךָ וּבְכָל־נַפְשְׁךָ
וּבְכָל־מְאֹדֶךָ. וְהָיוּ הַדְּבָרִים הָאֵלֶּה, אֲשֶׁר אָנֹכִי מְצַוְּךָ
הַיּוֹם, עַל־לְבָבֶךָ. וְשִׁנַּנְתָּם לְבָנֶיךָ, וְדִבַּרְתָּ בָּם
בְּשִׁבְתְּךָ בְּבֵיתֶךָ, וּבְלֶכְתְּךָ בַדֶּרֶךְ, וּבְשָׁכְבְּךָ וּבְקוּמֶךָ.
וּקְשַׁרְתָּם לְאוֹת עַל־יָדֶךָ, וְהָיוּ לְטֹטָפֹת בֵּין עֵינֶיךָ,
וּכְתַבְתָּם עַל־מְזֻזוֹת בֵּיתֶךָ, וּבִשְׁעָרֶיךָ.

*You shall love the Lord your God with all your mind, with all
your strength, with all your being. Set these words, which I
command you this day, upon your heart. Teach them
faithfully to your children; speak of them in your home and
on your way, when you lie down and when you rise up. Bind
them as a sign upon your hand; let them be a symbol before
your eyes; inscribe them on the doorposts of your house, and
on your gates.*

לְמַעַן תִּזְכְּרוּ וַעֲשִׂיתֶם אֶת־כָּל־מִצְוֹתָי, וִהְיִיתֶם
קְדֹשִׁים לֵאלֹהֵיכֶם. אֲנִי יְיָ אֱלֹהֵיכֶם, אֲשֶׁר הוֹצֵאתִי
אֶתְכֶם מֵאֶרֶץ מִצְרַיִם לִהְיוֹת לָכֶם לֵאלֹהִים. אֲנִי יְיָ
אֱלֹהֵיכֶם.

*Be mindful of all My Mitzvot, and do them: so shall you
consecrate yourselves to your God. I, the Lord, am your God
who led you out of Egypt to be your God; I, the Lord, am
your God.*

◆ ◆

56

גְּאוּלָה

אֱמֶת וֶאֱמוּנָה כָּל־זֹאת, וְקַיָּם עָלֵינוּ כִּי הוּא יְיָ
אֱלֹהֵינוּ וְאֵין זוּלָתוֹ, וַאֲנַחְנוּ יִשְׂרָאֵל עַמּוֹ. הַפּוֹדֵנוּ
מִיַּד מְלָכִים, מַלְכֵּנוּ הַגּוֹאֲלֵנוּ מִכַּף כָּל־הֶעָרִיצִים.
הָעֹשֶׂה גְדֹלוֹת עַד אֵין חֵקֶר, וְנִפְלָאוֹת עַד־אֵין
מִסְפָּר. הַשָּׂם נַפְשֵׁנוּ בַּחַיִּים, וְלֹא־נָתַן לַמּוֹט רַגְלֵנוּ.

All this we hold to be true and sure: You alone are our
God; there is none else, and we are Israel Your people.

You are our King, delivering us from the hand of oppressors,
saving us from the fist of tyrants, doing wonders without
number, marvels that pass our understanding. You give us
our life; with Your help our people has survived all our op-
pressors.

הָעֹשֶׂה לָּנוּ נִסִּים בְּפַרְעֹה, אוֹתוֹת וּמוֹפְתִים בְּאַדְמַת
בְּנֵי חָם. וַיּוֹצֵא אֶת־עַמּוֹ יִשְׂרָאֵל מִתּוֹכָם לְחֵרוּת
עוֹלָם.

You did wonders for us in the land of Egypt, miracles and
marvels in the land of Pharaoh.

You led Your people Israel out, for ever to serve You in
freedom.

וְרָאוּ בָנָיו גְּבוּרָתוֹ; שִׁבְּחוּ וְהוֹדוּ לִשְׁמוֹ. וּמַלְכוּתוֹ
בְּרָצוֹן קִבְּלוּ עֲלֵיהֶם. מֹשֶׁה וּבְנֵי יִשְׂרָאֵל לְךָ עָנוּ
שִׁירָה בְּשִׂמְחָה רַבָּה, וְאָמְרוּ כֻלָּם:

When Your children witnessed Your power, they extolled
You and gave You thanks; freely they acclaimed You
King; and, full of joy, Moses and all Israel sang this song:

מִי־כָמְֽכָה בָּאֵלִם, יְיָ?

Who is like You, Eternal One, among
the gods that are worshipped?

מִי כָּמֹֽכָה, נֶאְדָּר בַּקֹֽדֶשׁ,
נוֹרָא תְהִלֹּת, עֹֽשֵׂה פֶֽלֶא?

Who is like You, majestic in holiness,
awesome in splendor, doing wonders?

מַלְכוּתְךָ רָאוּ בָנֶֽיךָ, בּוֹקֵֽעַ יָם לִפְנֵי מֹשֶׁה; "זֶה אֵלִי!"
עָנוּ וְאָמְרוּ: "יְיָ יִמְלֹךְ לְעֹלָם וָעֶד!"

In their escape from the sea, Your children saw Your sovereign
might displayed. "This is my God!" they cried. "The Eternal will
reign for ever and ever!"

וְנֶאֱמַר: "כִּי־פָדָה יְיָ אֶת־יַעֲקֹב, וּגְאָלוֹ מִיַּד חָזָק
מִמֶּֽנּוּ." בָּרוּךְ אַתָּה, יְיָ, גָּאַל יִשְׂרָאֵל.

°Now let all come to say: The Eternal has redeemed Israel and
all the oppressed. Blessed is the Eternal God .

◆ ◆

RISE UP TO LIFE RENEWED   הַשְׁכִּיבֵֽנוּ

הַשְׁכִּיבֵֽנוּ, יְיָ אֱלֹהֵֽינוּ, לְשָׁלוֹם, וְהַעֲמִידֵֽנוּ, מַלְכֵּֽנוּ,
לְחַיִּים. וּפְרוֹשׂ עָלֵֽינוּ סֻכַּת שְׁלוֹמֶֽךָ, וְתַקְּנֵֽנוּ בְּעֵצָה
טוֹבָה מִלְּפָנֶֽיךָ, וְהוֹשִׁיעֵֽנוּ לְמַֽעַן שְׁמֶֽךָ, וְהָגֵן בַּעֲדֵֽנוּ.
וְהָסֵר מֵעָלֵֽינוּ אוֹיֵב, דֶּֽבֶר וְחֶֽרֶב וְרָעָב וְיָגוֹן; וְהָסֵר
שָׂטָן מִלְּפָנֵֽינוּ וּמֵאַחֲרֵינוּ; וּבְצֵל כְּנָפֶֽיךָ תַּסְתִּירֵֽנוּ, כִּי
אֵל שׁוֹמְרֵֽנוּ וּמַצִּילֵֽנוּ אָֽתָּה, כִּי אֵל מֶֽלֶךְ חַנּוּן וְרַחוּם
אָֽתָּה. וּשְׁמוֹר צֵאתֵֽנוּ וּבוֹאֵֽנוּ לְחַיִּים וּלְשָׁלוֹם, מֵעַתָּה
וְעַד עוֹלָם, וּפְרוֹשׂ עָלֵֽינוּ סֻכַּת שְׁלוֹמֶֽךָ. בָּרוּךְ אַתָּה,

58

יְיָ, הַפּוֹרֵשׂ סֻכַּת שָׁלוֹם עָלֵינוּ, וְעַל־כָּל־עַמּוֹ יִשְׂרָאֵל
וְעַל יְרוּשָׁלָיִם.

Cause us, O Eternal God, to lie down in peace, and raise
us up, O Sovereign, to life renewed. Spread over us the
shelter of Your peace; guide us with Your good counsel;
and for Your name's sake, be our Help.

*Shield us from hatred and plague; keep us from war and
famine and anguish; subdue our inclination to evil. O God,
our Guardian and Helper, our gracious and merciful Ruler,
give us refuge in the shadow of Your wings. Guard our coming and our going, that now and always we have life and
peace.*

Blessed are You, O Lord, whose shelter of peace is spread
over us, over all Israel, and over Jerusalem.

◆ ◆

ON SHABBAT

THE COVENANT OF SHABBAT   ושמרו

וְשָׁמְרוּ בְנֵי־יִשְׂרָאֵל אֶת־הַשַּׁבָּת, לַעֲשׂוֹת אֶת־הַשַּׁבָּת
לְדֹרֹתָם בְּרִית עוֹלָם. בֵּינִי וּבֵין בְּנֵי יִשְׂרָאֵל אוֹת הִיא
לְעֹלָם, כִּי שֵׁשֶׁת יָמִים עָשָׂה יְיָ אֶת־הַשָּׁמַיִם וְאֶת־
הָאָרֶץ, וּבַיּוֹם הַשְּׁבִיעִי שָׁבַת וַיִּנָּפַשׁ.

The people of Israel shall keep the Sabbath, observing the Sabbath in every generation as a covenant for all time. It is a sign for
ever between Me and the people of Israel, for in six days the
Eternal God made heaven and earth, and on the seventh day
He rested from His labors.

◆ ◆

59

חצי קדיש

יִתְגַּדַּל וְיִתְקַדַּשׁ שְׁמֵהּ רַבָּא בְּעָלְמָא דִּי־בְרָא כִרְעוּתֵהּ, וְיַמְלִיךְ
מַלְכוּתֵהּ בְּחַיֵּיכוֹן וּבְיוֹמֵיכוֹן וּבְחַיֵּי דְכָל־בֵּית יִשְׂרָאֵל, בַּעֲגָלָא
וּבִזְמַן קָרִיב, וְאִמְרוּ: אָמֵן. יְהֵא שְׁמֵהּ רַבָּא מְבָרַךְ לְעָלַם
וּלְעָלְמֵי עָלְמַיָּא. יִתְבָּרַךְ וְיִשְׁתַּבַּח, וְיִתְפָּאַר וְיִתְרוֹמַם
וְיִתְנַשֵּׂא, וְיִתְהַדָּר וְיִתְעַלֶּה וְיִתְהַלַּל שְׁמֵהּ דְּקוּדְשָׁא, בְּרִיךְ
הוּא, לְעֵלָּא מִן כָּל־בִּרְכָתָא וְשִׁירָתָא, תֻּשְׁבְּחָתָא וְנֶחֱמָתָא
דַּאֲמִירָן בְּעָלְמָא, וְאִמְרוּ: אָמֵן.

Let the glory of God be extolled, let His great name be hallowed
in the world whose creation He willed. May His kingdom soon
prevail, in our own day, our own lives, and the life of all Israel,
and let us say: Amen.

Let His great name be blessed for ever and ever.

Let the name of the Holy One, blessed is He, be glorified, exalted and honored, though He is beyond all the praises, songs,
and adorations that we can utter, and let us say: Amen.

◆ ◆

All rise

תפלה

WE ARE THEIR FUTURE **אבות**

בָּרוּךְ אַתָּה, יְיָ אֱלֹהֵינוּ וֵאלֹהֵי אֲבוֹתֵינוּ, אֱלֹהֵי
אַבְרָהָם, אֱלֹהֵי יִצְחָק, וֵאלֹהֵי יַעֲקֹב: הָאֵל הַגָּדוֹל,
הַגִּבּוֹר וְהַנּוֹרָא, אֵל עֶלְיוֹן. גּוֹמֵל חֲסָדִים טוֹבִים,
וְקוֹנֵה הַכֹּל, וְזוֹכֵר חַסְדֵי אָבוֹת, וּמֵבִיא גְאֻלָּה לִבְנֵי
בְנֵיהֶם, לְמַעַן שְׁמוֹ, בְּאַהֲבָה.

°Lord, You are our God, even as You were the God of
Abraham and Sarah, the God of our fathers and mothers,
the God of all the ages of Israel.

They are our past as we are their future.

We recall their vision and pray for the strength to keep it
alive: Help us, O God and Shield, to keep their faith.

O God, Shield of Abraham, Sarah's Help, in all generations
be our Help, our Shield, our God!

זָכְרֵנוּ לְחַיִּים, מֶלֶךְ חָפֵץ בַּחַיִּים, וְכָתְבֵנוּ בְּסֵפֶר
הַחַיִּים, לְמַעַנְךָ אֱלֹהִים חַיִּים. מֶלֶךְ עוֹזֵר וּמוֹשִׁיעַ
וּמָגֵן. בָּרוּךְ אַתָּה, יְיָ, מָגֵן אַבְרָהָם.

Remember us unto life, O Sovereign who delights in life,
and inscribe us in the Book of Life, O God of life.

▪ ◆

IMMORTAL YEARNINGS, UNDYING HOPES   גבורות

אַתָּה גִבּוֹר לְעוֹלָם, אֲדֹנָי, מְחַיֵּה הַכֹּל אַתָּה, רַב
לְהוֹשִׁיעַ. מְכַלְכֵּל חַיִּים בְּחֶסֶד, מְחַיֵּה הַכֹּל בְּרַחֲמִים
רַבִּים. סוֹמֵךְ נוֹפְלִים, וְרוֹפֵא חוֹלִים, וּמַתִּיר
אֲסוּרִים, וּמְקַיֵּם אֱמוּנָתוֹ לִישֵׁנֵי עָפָר.
מִי כָמוֹךָ, בַּעַל גְּבוּרוֹת, וּמִי דוֹמֶה לָּךְ, מֶלֶךְ מֵמִית
וּמְחַיֵּה וּמַצְמִיחַ יְשׁוּעָה? מִי כָמוֹךָ אַב הָרַחֲמִים,
זוֹכֵר יְצוּרָיו לְחַיִּים בְּרַחֲמִים? וְנֶאֱמָן אַתָּה לְהַחֲיוֹת
הַכֹּל. בָּרוּךְ אַתָּה, יְיָ, מְחַיֵּה הַכֹּל.

For two readers or more, or responsively

°Love is the thread that binds our lives in a lasting fabric
which time shall fray,

Which time shall fray, but only to be rewoven by each generation.

Each generation will lift the fallen to their feet and hold them as they learn to walk.

And as they learn to walk, the sickness of our time will be healed by those who drink deep from ancient wells of truth.

From ancient wells of truth they will draw strength to keep faith with those who sleep in the dust.

We praise the Source of life and power, who has implanted within us immortal yearning, undying hopes.

◆ ◆

IN PRAISE OF THE HOLY   קְדוּשַׁת הַשֵּׁם

אַתָּה קָדוֹשׁ וְשִׁמְךָ קָדוֹשׁ, וּקְדוֹשִׁים בְּכָל־יוֹם יְהַלְלוּךָ סֶּלָה.

All are seated

◆

וּבְכֵן תֵּן פַּחְדְּךָ, יְיָ אֱלֹהֵינוּ, עַל כָּל־מַעֲשֶׂיךָ, וְאֵימָתְךָ עַל כָּל־מַה־שֶּׁבָּרָאתָ. וְיִירָאוּךָ כָּל־הַמַּעֲשִׂים, וְיִשְׁתַּחֲווּ לְפָנֶיךָ כָּל־הַבְּרוּאִים, וְיֵעָשׂוּ כֻלָּם אֲגֻדָּה אַחַת לַעֲשׂוֹת רְצוֹנְךָ בְּלֵבָב שָׁלֵם, כְּמוֹ שֶׁיָּדַעְנוּ, יְיָ אֱלֹהֵינוּ, שֶׁהַשִּׁלְטוֹן לְפָנֶיךָ, עֹז בְּיָדְךָ וּגְבוּרָה בִּימִינֶךָ, וְשִׁמְךָ נוֹרָא עַל כָּל־מַה־שֶּׁבָּרָאתָ.

°Now in awe we behold the wonder of being: an awesome pageant of shapes and forms—yet all akin, one family of life!

וּבְכֵן תֵּן כָּבוֹד, יְיָ, לְעַמֶּךָ, תְּהִלָּה לִירֵאֶיךָ וְתִקְנָה לְדוֹרְשֶׁיךָ, וּפִתְחוֹן פֶּה לַמְיַחֲלִים לָךְ, שִׂמְחָה לְאַרְצֶךָ וְשָׂשׂוֹן לְעִירֶךָ, וּצְמִיחַת קֶרֶן לְכָל-יוֹשְׁבֵי תֵבֵל.

°We pray for wisdom to treasure all creation; we ask for insight to see its glory; we hope for courage to trust its goodness; we yearn for grace to fill the world with gladness; we seek the strength to help redeem it.

וּבְכֵן צַדִּיקִים יִרְאוּ וְיִשְׂמָחוּ וִישָׁרִים יַעֲלֹזוּ וַחֲסִידִים בְּרִנָּה יָגִילוּ, וְעוֹלָתָה תִּקְפָּץ־פִּיהָ וְכָל־הָרִשְׁעָה כֻּלָּה כְּעָשָׁן תִּכְלֶה. כִּי תַעֲבִיר מֶמְשֶׁלֶת זָדוֹן מִן הָאָרֶץ. וְתִמְלֹךְ אַתָּה, יְיָ, לְבַדֶּךָ עַל כָּל־מַעֲשֶׂיךָ, כַּכָּתוּב בְּדִבְרֵי קָדְשֶׁךָ:

°A world released from sorrow to joy! The bowed head shall be raised, the bent back made straight. Those who dragged their chains shall dance and sing. O may violence give way to goodness, the land be cleansed of tyrants, and the prophet's word redeemed: Peace shall rule the earth!

יִמְלֹךְ יְיָ לְעוֹלָם, אֱלֹהַיִךְ צִיּוֹן, לְדֹר וָדֹר. הַלְלוּיָהּ!

The Lord shall reign for ever; your God, O Zion, from generation to generation. Halleluyah!

קָדוֹשׁ אַתָּה וְנוֹרָא שְׁמֶךָ, וְאֵין אֱלוֹהַּ מִבַּלְעָדֶיךָ, כַּכָּתוּב:

°Holy is life, awesome its Source. One Mind unites all being; one Law rules all creation. As it is written:

וַיִּגְבַּה יְיָ צְבָאוֹת בַּמִּשְׁפָּט, וְהָאֵל הַקָּדוֹשׁ נִקְדַּשׁ בִּצְדָקָה.

63

The Lord of Hosts is exalted by justice; the holy God is sanctified by righteousness.

בָּרוּךְ אַתָּה, יְיָ, הַמֶּלֶךְ הַקָּדוֹשׁ.

°*Blessed is creation, and blessed the love that sustains it.*

◆ ◆

THE HOLINESS OF THIS DAY   קדושת היום

אַתָּה בְחַרְתָּנוּ מִכָּל־הָעַמִּים, אָהַבְתָּ אוֹתָנוּ וְרָצִיתָ
בָּנוּ, וְרוֹמַמְתָּנוּ מִכָּל־הַלְּשׁוֹנוֹת וְקִדַּשְׁתָּנוּ בְּמִצְוֹתֶיךָ,
וְקֵרַבְתָּנוּ מַלְכֵּנוּ לַעֲבוֹדָתֶךָ, וְשִׁמְךָ הַגָּדוֹל וְהַקָּדוֹשׁ
עָלֵינוּ קָרָאתָ. וַתִּתֶּן־לָנוּ, יְיָ אֱלֹהֵינוּ, בְּאַהֲבָה אֶת־יוֹם
(הַשַּׁבָּת הַזֶּה וְאֶת־יוֹם) הַזִּכָּרוֹן הַזֶּה, יוֹם תְּרוּעָה,
מִקְרָא קֹדֶשׁ, זֵכֶר לִיצִיאַת מִצְרָיִם.

°The House of Israel is called to holiness, to a covenant with the Eternal for all time.

We are called to serve the Most High; may we rejoice in this heritage for ever.

May this day add meaning to our lives. Let the Shofar's sound awaken the voice of conscience, our common worship unite us in love, our memories of bondage impel us to help the oppressed.

אֱלֹהֵינוּ וֵאלֹהֵי אֲבוֹתֵינוּ, יַעֲלֶה וְיָבֹא וְיֵרָאֶה וְיִזָּכֵר זִכְרוֹנֵנוּ
וְזִכְרוֹן כָּל־עַמְּךָ בֵּית יִשְׂרָאֵל לְפָנֶיךָ, לְטוֹבָה לְחֵן
לְחֶסֶד וּלְרַחֲמִים, לְחַיִּים וּלְשָׁלוֹם בְּיוֹם הַזִּכָּרוֹן הַזֶּה.
זָכְרֵנוּ, יְיָ אֱלֹהֵינוּ, בּוֹ לְטוֹבָה.   אָמֵן.
וּפָקְדֵנוּ בוֹ לִבְרָכָה.   אָמֵן.
וְהוֹשִׁיעֵנוּ בוֹ לְחַיִּים.   אָמֵן.

64

°*On this Day of Remembrance we pray for awareness. Let love and compassion grow among us, and goodness be our daily care. This day may we find well being. This day may we discover the eternal strength that abides among us. This day may we be helped to a life that is whole. Amen.*

אֱלֹהֵינוּ וֵאלֹהֵי אֲבוֹתֵינוּ, מְלוֹךְ עַל כָּל־הָעוֹלָם כֻּלּוֹ בִּכְבוֹדֶךָ וְהִנָּשֵׂא עַל כָּל־הָאָרֶץ בִּיקָרֶךָ, וְהוֹפַע בַּהֲדַר גְּאוֹן עֻזֶּךָ עַל כָּל־יוֹשְׁבֵי תֵבֵל אַרְצֶךָ. וְיֵדַע כָּל־פָּעוּל כִּי אַתָּה פְּעַלְתּוֹ. וְיָבִין כָּל־יָצוּר כִּי אַתָּה יְצַרְתּוֹ, וְיֹאמַר כֹּל אֲשֶׁר נְשָׁמָה בְאַפּוֹ: יְיָ אֱלֹהֵי יִשְׂרָאֵל מֶלֶךְ, וּמַלְכוּתוֹ בַּכֹּל מָשָׁלָה.

°You transcend our deepest thought and elude the keenest eye, yet all who dwell on earth may find You. Every creature's form proclaims Your glory, for all that breathes is one creation, children of a single kingdom. Thus was it written of old: "The Eternal God of Israel is the King whose dominion extends to all creation."

אֱלֹהֵינוּ וֵאלֹהֵי אֲבוֹתֵינוּ, (רְצֵה בִמְנוּחָתֵנוּ,) קַדְּשֵׁנוּ בְּמִצְוֹתֶיךָ וְתֵן חֶלְקֵנוּ בְּתוֹרָתֶךָ. שַׂבְּעֵנוּ מִטּוּבֶךָ, וְשַׂמְּחֵנוּ בִּישׁוּעָתֶךָ, (וְהַנְחִילֵנוּ, יְיָ אֱלֹהֵינוּ, בְּאַהֲבָה וּבְרָצוֹן שַׁבַּת קָדְשֶׁךָ, וְיָנוּחוּ בָהּ יִשְׂרָאֵל מְקַדְּשֵׁי שְׁמֶךָ,) וְטַהֵר לִבֵּנוּ לְעָבְדְּךָ בֶּאֱמֶת, כִּי אַתָּה אֱלֹהִים אֱמֶת, וּדְבָרְךָ אֱמֶת וְקַיָּם לָעַד. בָּרוּךְ אַתָּה, יְיָ, מֶלֶךְ עַל כָּל־הָאָרֶץ, מְקַדֵּשׁ (הַשַּׁבָּת וְ) יִשְׂרָאֵל וְיוֹם הַזִּכָּרוֹן.

°*The kingdom of law is the domain of freedom. Blessed is the law that sets us free to find gladness and joy. (May this day's rest renew all who observe it; and let the holiness of*

65

Shabbat remain our heritage, that all Israel, hallowing its life, may find rest and peace.) Praised be the Power that makes for freedom, that blesses (the Sabbath,) the House of Israel and the Day of Remembrance.

◆ ◆

SILENT PRAYER

THE SPIRIT THAT SINGS WITHIN US   עבודה

רְצֵה, יְיָ אֱלֹהֵינוּ, בְּעַמְּךָ יִשְׂרָאֵל, וּתְפִלָּתָם בְּאַהֲבָה
תְקַבֵּל, וּתְהִי לְרָצוֹן תָּמִיד עֲבוֹדַת יִשְׂרָאֵל עַמֶּךָ.
בָּרוּךְ אַתָּה, יְיָ, שֶׁאוֹתְךָ לְבַדְּךָ בְּיִרְאָה נַעֲבוֹד.

°Let our thoughts be gentle, gracious our deeds, and kindness rule our lips and hearts! Blessed is the spirit, a hymn of love within us, that calls us to prayer.

◆ ◆

SING OF WONDERS   הודאה

מוֹדִים אֲנַחְנוּ לָךְ, שָׁאַתָּה הוּא יְיָ אֱלֹהֵינוּ וֵאלֹהֵי
אֲבוֹתֵינוּ, אֱלֹהֵי כָל־בָּשָׂר, יוֹצְרֵנוּ יוֹצֵר בְּרֵאשִׁית.
בְּרָכוֹת וְהוֹדָאוֹת לְשִׁמְךָ הַגָּדוֹל וְהַקָּדוֹשׁ עַל־
שֶׁהֶחֱיִיתָנוּ וְקִיַּמְתָּנוּ.

°O world, where miracles spring up to meet us along the way, we hold you close and give thanks for morning light, for evening calm.

Sun and moon, sea and sky, snow and mist, city streets and country lanes: what joy to know you, how excellent to touch you!

66

כֵּן תְּחַיֵּנוּ וּתְקַיְּמֵנוּ, יְיָ אֱלֹהֵינוּ, וּתְאַמְּצֵנוּ לִשְׁמֹר
חֻקֶּיךָ, לַעֲשׂוֹת רְצוֹנֶךָ, וּלְעָבְדְּךָ בְּלֵבָב שָׁלֵם. וּכְתוֹב
לְחַיִּים טוֹבִים כָּל־בְּנֵי בְרִיתֶךָ. בָּרוּךְ אֵל הַהוֹדָאוֹת.

To live, and nothing more, would be enough to make us
glad. Yet morning, noon, and night, a task awaits us:

*The lost and hungry to be found and fed, the sick and sad to
be healed and cheered, a peaceful world to be built and kept.*

Blessed is the gift of life, blessed the Source of life and its
tasks!

◆ ◆

For two readers or more, or responsively

SEEK PEACE AND PURSUE IT   ברכת שלום

Words there are and prayers, but justice there is not, nor
yet peace.

The prophet said: In the end of days the Lord shall
judge between the nations; they shall beat their
swords into plowshares and their spears into
pruninghooks.

Although we must wait for judgment, we may not wait for
peace to fall like rain upon us.

The teacher said: Those who have made peace in their
house, it is as though they have brought peace to all
Israel, indeed, to all the world.

Peace will remain a distant vision until we do the work of
peace ourselves. If peace is to be brought into the world,
we must bring it first to our families and communities.

The psalmist said: Seek peace and pursue it.

Be not content to make peace only in your own household; go forth and work for peace wherever men and women are struggling in its cause.

◆ ◆

MEDITATION

Rabbi Eliezer said: Repent one day before your death. His disciples asked: How can one know which day that will be? He replied: Precisely! Repent today, therefore, in case you should die tomorrow. Thus will you spend all your days wisely.

◆ ◆

יִהְיוּ לְרָצוֹן אִמְרֵי־פִי וְהֶגְיוֹן לִבִּי לְפָנֶיךָ, יְיָ, צוּרִי וְגוֹאֲלִי.

or

עֹשֶׂה שָׁלוֹם בִּמְרוֹמָיו, הוּא יַעֲשֶׂה שָׁלוֹם עָלֵינוּ וְעַל כָּל־יִשְׂרָאֵל, וְאִמְרוּ אָמֵן.

68

All rise
The Ark is opened

אבינו מלכנו

אָבִינוּ מַלְכֵּנוּ, שְׁמַע קוֹלֵנוּ.

Our Father, our King, hear our voice.

אָבִינוּ מַלְכֵּנוּ, חָטָאנוּ לְפָנֶיךָ.

Our Father, our King, we have sinned against You.

אָבִינוּ מַלְכֵּנוּ, חֲמוֹל עָלֵינוּ וְעַל עוֹלָלֵינוּ וְטַפֵּנוּ.

Our Father, our King, have compassion on us and on our
children.

אָבִינוּ מַלְכֵּנוּ, כַּלֵּה דֶּבֶר וְחֶרֶב וְרָעָב מֵעָלֵינוּ.

Our Father, our King, make an end to sickness, war, and
famine.

אָבִינוּ מַלְכֵּנוּ, כַּלֵּה כָּל־צַר וּמַשְׂטִין מֵעָלֵינוּ.

Our Father, our King, make an end to all oppression.

אָבִינוּ מַלְכֵּנוּ, כָּתְבֵנוּ בְּסֵפֶר חַיִּים טוֹבִים.

Our Father, our King, inscribe us for blessing in the Book of
Life.

אָבִינוּ מַלְכֵּנוּ, חַדֵּשׁ עָלֵינוּ שָׁנָה טוֹבָה.

Our Father, our King, let the new year be a good year for us.

אָבִינוּ מַלְכֵּנוּ, הָרֵם קֶרֶן יִשְׂרָאֵל עַמֶּךָ.

Our Father, our King, give strength to Your people Israel.

אָבִינוּ מַלְכֵּנוּ, חָנֵּנוּ וַעֲנֵנוּ, כִּי אֵין בָּנוּ מַעֲשִׂים,
עֲשֵׂה עִמָּנוּ צְדָקָה וָחֶסֶד וְהוֹשִׁיעֵנוּ.

Our Father, our King, be gracious and answer us, for we have little merit. Treat us generously and with kindness, and be our help.

The Ark is closed

קדוש

בָּרוּךְ אַתָּה, יְיָ אֱלֹהֵינוּ, מֶלֶךְ הָעוֹלָם, בּוֹרֵא פְּרִי הַגָּפֶן.

בָּרוּךְ אַתָּה, יְיָ אֱלֹהֵינוּ, מֶלֶךְ הָעוֹלָם, אֲשֶׁר בָּחַר בָּנוּ מִכָּל־עָם, וְרוֹמְמָנוּ מִכָּל־לָשׁוֹן, וְקִדְּשָׁנוּ בְּמִצְוֹתָיו. וַתִּתֶּן־לָנוּ, יְיָ אֱלֹהֵינוּ, בְּאַהֲבָה אֶת־יוֹם (הַשַּׁבָּת הַזֶּה וְאֶת־יוֹם) הַזִּכָּרוֹן הַזֶּה, יוֹם תְּרוּעָה, מִקְרָא קֹדֶשׁ, זֵכֶר לִיצִיאַת מִצְרָיִם. כִּי בָנוּ בָחַרְתָּ, וְאוֹתָנוּ קִדַּשְׁתָּ מִכָּל־הָעַמִּים, וּדְבָרְךָ אֱמֶת וְקַיָּם לָעַד. בָּרוּךְ אַתָּה, יְיָ, מֶלֶךְ עַל כָּל־הָאָרֶץ, מְקַדֵּשׁ (הַשַּׁבָּת וְ)יִשְׂרָאֵל וְיוֹם הַזִּכָּרוֹן.

בָּרוּךְ אַתָּה, יְיָ אֱלֹהֵינוּ, מֶלֶךְ הָעוֹלָם, שֶׁהֶחֱיָנוּ וְקִיְּמָנוּ וְהִגִּיעָנוּ לַזְּמַן הַזֶּה.

Blessed is the Lord our God, Ruler of the universe, Creator of the fruit of the vine.

Blessed is the Lord our God, Ruler of the universe, who has chosen us from all the peoples, hallowing us with the Mitzvot. In Your love, O Lord our God, You have given us this (Shabbat and this) Day of Remembrance, to hear the sound of the Shofar, to unite in worship, and to recall the Exodus from Egypt. For You have chosen us from all peoples, consecrating us to Your service, and Your word is truth eternal.

Blessed is the Sovereign God, Ruler of all the world, who hallows (the Sabbath,) the House of Israel and the Day of Remembrance.

Blessed is the Lord our God, Ruler of the universe, for giving us life, for sustaining us, and for enabling us to reach this season.

71

עָלֵינוּ

All rise

Let us adore	עָלֵינוּ לְשַׁבֵּחַ לַאֲדוֹן הַכֹּל,
the ever-living God,	לָתֵת גְּדֻלָּה לְיוֹצֵר בְּרֵאשִׁית,
and render praise	
unto Him	שֶׁהוּא נוֹטֶה שָׁמַיִם וְיוֹסֵד אֶרֶץ,
who spread out the heavens	וּמוֹשַׁב יְקָרוֹ בַּשָּׁמַיִם מִמַּעַל,
and established the earth,	
whose glory	וּשְׁכִינַת עֻזּוֹ בְּגָבְהֵי מְרוֹמִים.
is revealed in the heavens above,	הוּא אֱלֹהֵינוּ, אֵין עוֹד.
and whose greatness	
is manifest throughout the world.	
He is our God;	
there is none else.	

וַאֲנַחְנוּ כּוֹרְעִים וּמִשְׁתַּחֲוִים וּמוֹדִים לִפְנֵי מֶלֶךְ מַלְכֵי
הַמְּלָכִים, הַקָּדוֹשׁ בָּרוּךְ הוּא.

We therefore bow in awe and thanksgiving before the One who
is Sovereign over all, the Holy and Blessed One.

All are seated

May the time not be distant, O God, when Your name
shall be worshipped in all the earth, when unbelief shall
disappear and error be no more. Fervently we pray that
the day may come when all shall turn to You in love, when
corruption and evil shall give way to integrity and
goodness, when superstition shall no longer enslave the
mind, nor idolatry blind the eye, when all who dwell on
earth shall know that You alone are God. O may all,
created in Your image, become one in spirit and one in
friendship, for ever united in Your service. Then shall
Your kingdom be established on earth, and the word of
Your prophet fulfilled: "The Lord will reign for ever and
ever."

72

בַּיּוֹם הַהוּא יִהְיֶה יְיָ אֶחָד וּשְׁמוֹ אֶחָד.

*On that day the Lord shall be One and His name shall be
One.*

◆ ◆

The light of life is a finite flame. Like a candle, life is
kindled: it burns, it glows, it is radiant with warmth and
beauty. But soon it fades; its substance is consumed, and it
is no more.

In light we see; in light we are seen. The flames dance and
our lives are full. But as night follows day, the candle of
our life burns down and gutters. There is an end to the
flames. We see no more and are no more seen. Yet we do
not despair, for we are more than a memory slowly fading
into the darkness. With our lives we give life. Something
of us can never die: we move in the eternal cycle of
darkness and death, of light and life.

MOURNER'S KADDISH   קדיש יתום

יִתְגַּדַּל וְיִתְקַדַּשׁ שְׁמֵהּ רַבָּא בְּעָלְמָא דִּי־בְרָא
כִרְעוּתֵהּ, וְיַמְלִיךְ מַלְכוּתֵהּ בְּחַיֵּיכוֹן וּבְיוֹמֵיכוֹן וּבְחַיֵּי
דְכָל־בֵּית יִשְׂרָאֵל, בַּעֲגָלָא וּבִזְמַן קָרִיב, וְאִמְרוּ: אָמֵן.

Yit·ga·dal ve·yit·ka·dash she·mei ra·ba be·al·ma di·ve·ra
chi·re·u·tei, ve·yam·lich mal·chu·tei be·cha·yei·chon
u·ve·yo·mei·chon u·ve·cha·yei de·chol beit Yis·ra·eil, ba·a·ga·la
u·vi·ze·man ka·riv, ve·i·me·ru: a·mein.

יְהֵא שְׁמֵהּ רַבָּא מְבָרַךְ לְעָלַם וּלְעָלְמֵי עָלְמַיָּא.

Ye·hei she·mei ra·ba me·va·rach le·a·lam u·le·al·mei al·ma·ya.

יִתְבָּרַךְ וְיִשְׁתַּבַּח, וְיִתְפָּאַר וְיִתְרוֹמַם וְיִתְנַשֵּׂא,
וְיִתְהַדָּר וְיִתְעַלֶּה וְיִתְהַלָּל שְׁמֵהּ דְּקוּדְשָׁא, בְּרִיךְ

73

הוּא, לְעֵלָּא מִן־כָּל־בִּרְכָתָא וְשִׁירָתָא, תֻּשְׁבְּחָתָא
וְנֶחֱמָתָא דַּאֲמִירָן בְּעָלְמָא, וְאִמְרוּ: אָמֵן.

Yit·ba·rach ve·yish·ta·bach, ve·yit·pa·ar ve·yit·ro·mam
ve·yit·na·sei, ve·yit·ha·dar ve·yit·a·leh ve·yit·ha·lal she·mei
de·ku·de·sha, be·rich hu, le·ei·la min kol bi·re·cha·ta
ve·shi·ra·ta, tush·be·cha·ta ve·ne·che·ma·ta, da·a·mi·ran
be·al·ma, ve·i·me·ru: a·mein.

יְהֵא שְׁלָמָא רַבָּא מִן־שְׁמַיָּא וְחַיִּים עָלֵינוּ וְעַל־כָּל־
יִשְׂרָאֵל, וְאִמְרוּ: אָמֵן.

Ye·hei she·la·ma ra·ba min she·ma·ya ve·cha·yim a·lei·nu ve·al
kol Yis·ra·eil, ve·i·me·ru: a·mein.

עֹשֶׂה שָׁלוֹם בִּמְרוֹמָיו, הוּא יַעֲשֶׂה שָׁלוֹם עָלֵינוּ וְעַל־
כָּל־יִשְׂרָאֵל, וְאִמְרוּ: אָמֵן.

O·seh sha·lom bi·me·ro·mav, hu ya·a·seh sha·lom a·lei·nu ve·al
kol Yis·ra·eil, ve·i·me·ru: a·mein.

Let the glory of God be extolled, let His great name be hallowed
in the world whose creation He willed. May His kingdom soon
prevail, in our own day, our own lives, and the life of all Israel,
and let us say: Amen.
Let His great name be blessed for ever and ever.
Let the name of the Holy One, blessed is He, be glorified, exalted, and honored, though He is beyond all the praises, songs,
and adorations that we can utter, and let us say: Amen.
For us and for all Israel, may the blessing of peace and the
promise of life come true, and let us say: Amen.
May the One who causes peace to reign in the high heavens, let
peace descend on us, on all Israel, and all the world, and let us
say: Amen.

◆ ◆

May the Source of peace send peace to all who mourn,
and comfort to all who are bereaved. Amen.

ADON OLAM

אֲדוֹן עוֹלָם

A·don o·lam, a·sher ma·lach	אֲדוֹן עוֹלָם, אֲשֶׁר מָלַךְ
be·te·rem kol ye·tsir niv·ra,	בְּטֶרֶם כָּל־יְצִיר נִבְרָא,
le·eit na·a·sa ve·chef·tso kol,	לְעֵת נַעֲשָׂה בְחֶפְצוֹ כֹּל,
a·zai me·lech she·mo nik·ra.	אֲזַי מֶלֶךְ שְׁמוֹ נִקְרָא.
Ve·a·cha·rei ki·che·lot ha·kol,	וְאַחֲרֵי כִּכְלוֹת הַכֹּל,
le·va·do yim·loch no·ra,	לְבַדּוֹ יִמְלֹךְ נוֹרָא,
ve·hu ha·ya, ve·hu ho·veh,	וְהוּא הָיָה, וְהוּא הֹוֶה,
ve·hu yi·he·yeh be·tif·a·ra.	וְהוּא יִהְיֶה בְּתִפְאָרָה.
Ve·hu e·chad, ve·ein shei·ni	וְהוּא אֶחָד, וְאֵין שֵׁנִי
le·ham·shil lo, le·hach·bi·ra,	לְהַמְשִׁיל לוֹ, לְהַחְבִּירָה,
be·li rei·shit, be·li tach·lit,	בְּלִי רֵאשִׁית, בְּלִי תַכְלִית,
ve·lo ha·oz ve·ha·mis·ra.	וְלוֹ הָעֹז וְהַמִּשְׂרָה.
Ve·hu Ei·li, ve·chai go·a·li,	וְהוּא אֵלִי, וְחַי גּוֹאֲלִי,
ve·tsur chev·li be·eit tsa·ra,	וְצוּר חֶבְלִי בְּעֵת צָרָה,
ve·hu ni·si u·ma·nos li,	וְהוּא נִסִּי וּמָנוֹס לִי,
me·nat ko·si be·yom ek·ra.	מְנָת כּוֹסִי בְּיוֹם אֶקְרָא.
Be·ya·do af·kid ru·chi	בְּיָדוֹ אַפְקִיד רוּחִי
be·eit i·shan ve·a·i·ra,	בְּעֵת אִישַׁן וְאָעִירָה,
ve·im ru·chi ge·vi·ya·ti:	וְעִם־רוּחִי גְוִיָּתִי:
A·do·nai li, ve·lo i·ra.	יְיָ לִי, וְלֹא אִירָא.

The translation of Adon Olam
is on page 47

75

תפלת שחרית לראש השנה

ROSH HASHANAH MORNING
SERVICE

Reading and meditations begin on page 3

For those who wear the Tallit

Praise the Lord, O my soul!
O Lord my God, You are very great!
Arrayed in glory and majesty,
You wrap Yourself in light as with a garment,
You stretch out the heavens like a curtain.

בָּרְכִי נַפְשִׁי אֶת יְיָ!

יְיָ אֱלֹהַי, גָּדַלְתָּ מְּאֹד!

הוֹד וְהָדָר לָבָשְׁתָּ,

עֹטֶה אוֹר כַּשַּׂלְמָה,

נוֹטֶה שָׁמַיִם כַּיְרִיעָה.

בָּרוּךְ אַתָּה, יְיָ אֱלֹהֵינוּ, מֶלֶךְ הָעוֹלָם,

אֲשֶׁר קִדְּשָׁנוּ בְּמִצְוֹתָיו וְצִוָּנוּ לְהִתְעַטֵּף בַּצִּיצִת.

Blessed is the Lord our God, Ruler of the universe, who hallows
us with Mitzvot, and teaches us to wrap ourselves in the fringed
Tallit.

Morning Blessings

Some or all the Morning Blessings may be used for private prayer. In public worship, any or all may be read or sung. Poems of Praise begin on page 91. Barechu is on page 99.

FOR THE BLESSING OF WORSHIP

How lovely are Your tents, O Jacob, your dwelling-places, O Israel!

In Your abundant lovingkindness, O God, let me enter Your house, reverently to worship in Your holy temple.

Lord, I love Your house, the place where Your glory dwells. So I would worship with humility; I would seek blessing in the presence of God, my Maker.

May my prayer now, O Lord, find favor before You.
In Your great love, O God, answer me with Your saving truth.

◆ ◆

Psalm 100

Shout joyfully to the Lord, all the earth!
Serve the Lord with gladness!
Come into His presence with singing!
Acknowledge that the Lord is God.
He made us and we are His,
His people, His beloved flock.
Enter His gates with thanksgiving,
His courts with praise.
Give thanks to Him, bless His name!
For the Lord is good,
His love is everlasting,
His faithfulness for all generations.

◆ ◆

בִּרְכוֹת הַשַּׁחַר

מַה טֹּבוּ

מַה־טֹּבוּ אֹהָלֶיךָ, יַעֲקֹב, מִשְׁכְּנֹתֶיךָ, יִשְׂרָאֵל!

וַאֲנִי, בְּרֹב חַסְדְּךָ אָבֹא בֵיתֶךָ,
אֶשְׁתַּחֲוֶה אֶל־הֵיכַל קָדְשְׁךָ בְּיִרְאָתֶךָ.

יְיָ, אָהַבְתִּי מְעוֹן בֵּיתֶךָ, וּמְקוֹם מִשְׁכַּן כְּבוֹדֶךָ.
וַאֲנִי אֶשְׁתַּחֲוֶה וְאֶכְרָעָה, אֶבְרְכָה לִפְנֵי־יְיָ עֹשִׂי.

וַאֲנִי תְפִלָּתִי לְךָ, יְיָ, עֵת רָצוֹן.
אֱלֹהִים, בְּרָב־חַסְדֶּךָ, עֲנֵנִי בֶּאֱמֶת יִשְׁעֶךָ.

∵

הָרִיעוּ לַיְיָ כָּל־הָאָרֶץ!
עִבְדוּ אֶת־יְיָ בְּשִׂמְחָה!
בֹּאוּ לְפָנָיו בִּרְנָנָה!
דְּעוּ כִּי־יְיָ הוּא אֱלֹהִים.
הוּא עָשָׂנוּ וְלוֹ אֲנַחְנוּ,
עַמּוֹ וְצֹאן מַרְעִיתוֹ.
בֹּאוּ שְׁעָרָיו בְּתוֹדָה,
חֲצֵרֹתָיו בִּתְהִלָּה.
הוֹדוּ לוֹ, בָּרְכוּ שְׁמוֹ!
כִּי־טוֹב יְיָ,
לְעוֹלָם חַסְדּוֹ,
וְעַד־דֹּר וָדֹר אֱמוּנָתוֹ.

Psalm 15

יְיָ, מִי־יָגוּר בְּאָהֳלֶךָ, מִי־יִשְׁכֹּן בְּהַר קָדְשֶׁךָ?
הוֹלֵךְ תָּמִים וּפֹעֵל צֶדֶק וְדֹבֵר אֱמֶת בִּלְבָבוֹ.

Lord, who may abide in Your house? Who may dwell in
Your holy mountain?

*Those who are upright; who do justly; who speak the truth
within their hearts.*

לֹא־רָגַל עַל־לְשֹׁנוֹ, לֹא־עָשָׂה לְרֵעֵהוּ רָעָה,
וְחֶרְפָּה לֹא נָשָׂא עַל־קְרֹבוֹ.
נִבְזֶה בְּעֵינָיו נִמְאָס, וְאֶת־יִרְאֵי יְיָ יְכַבֵּד.

Who do not slander others, or wrong them, or bring
shame upon them.

Who scorn the base, but honor those who revere the Lord.

נִשְׁבַּע לְהָרַע וְלֹא יָמִיר.
כַּסְפּוֹ לֹא־נָתַן בְּנֶשֶׁךְ וְשֹׁחַד עַל־נָקִי לֹא לָקָח.

Who give their word, and, come what may, do not retract.

Who do not exploit others, who never take bribes.

עֹשֵׂה אֵלֶּה לֹא יִמּוֹט לְעוֹלָם.

Those who live in this way shall never be shaken.

◆ ◆

YOUR ENDLESS BLESSING   אב גדול

אָב גָּדוֹל וְקָדוֹשׁ, אֲבִי כָּל־בָּאֵי עוֹלָם:

Great and holy Maker of all the living,

אַתָּה בוֹרֵא אֶת־עוֹלָמְךָ בִּנְךָ, בְּכָל־מְעוּף עָיִן.

You create the world, Your child, anew at every moment.

אִם כְּהֶרֶף עַיִן תָּסִיר אֶת־חֶסֶד יְצִירָתְךָ וְהָיָה הַכֹּל
אַיִן וָאָפֶס.

*An instant's pause in Your creative love, and all things would
turn to naught.*

אֲבָל אַתָּה מֵרִיק עַל יְצִירֶיךָ־פָּנֶיךָ צִנּוֹרֵי בְרָכָה בְּכָל־
רֶגַע וָרֶגַע.

But Your blessing glows in every spark of time.

וְעוֹד הַפַּעַם יוֹפִיעוּ כּוֹכְבֵי שַׁחַר וְשָׁרוּ שִׁירַת אַהֲבָה
לְפָנֶיךָ

Again and again the morning stars unite to hymn Your love.

וְעוֹד הַפַּעַם יֵצֵא שֶׁמֶשׁ בִּגְבוּרָתוֹ וְשָׁר שִׁירַת אוֹר
לְפָנֶיךָ

Again the sun comes forth to sing Your light.

וְעוֹד הַפַּעַם יָשִׁירוּ מַלְאָכִים שִׁירַת קֹדֶשׁ לְפָנֶיךָ

Again the angels sing their sacred chant to You.

וְעוֹד הַפַּעַם תָּשֵׁרְנָה נְשָׁמוֹת שִׁירַת צִמָּאוֹן לְפָנֶיךָ

Again souls intone their need for You.

וְעוֹד הַפַּעַם יָשִׁירוּ עִשְׂבֵי שָׂדֶה שִׁירַת גַּעֲגוּעִים
לְפָנֶיךָ

Again the grasses sing their thirst for You.

וְעוֹד הַפַּעַם תָּשֵׁרְנָה צִפֳּרִים שִׁירַת גִּיל לְפָנֶיךָ

Again the birds chirp their joy before You.

83

וְעוֹד הַפַּעַם יָשִׁירוּ אֶפְרוֹחִים עֲזוּבִים שִׁירַת יְתוֹמִים
לְפָנֶיךָ

Again abandoned chicks voice their orphan-song to You.

וְעוֹד הַפַּעַם יְלְחַשׁ מַעְיָן אֶת־תְּפִלָּתוֹ.

Again springs softly bubble their prayer to You.

וְעוֹד הַפַּעַם יַעֲטֹף עָנִי וְשָׁפַךְ אֶת־שִׂיחוֹ לְפָנֶיךָ

And still the afflicted pour out their complaint to You.

וְעוֹד הַפַּעַם נִשְׁמָתוֹ־תְּפִלָּתוֹ בּוֹקַעַת רְקִיעֶךָ־שְׁחָקֶיךָ
בַּעֲלוֹתָהּ לְפָנֶיךָ

And still their souls' prayer splits Your heavens.

וְעוֹד הַפַּעַם פָּרוֹר יִתְפּוֹרֵר גֵּוּ מֵאֵימַת כְּבוֹדֶךָ

And still they tremble in awe of Your glory.

וְעוֹד הַפַּעַם עֵינוֹ נְשׂוּאָה אֵלֶיךָ.

And still in hope they lift up their eyes to You.

רַק קַו אֶחָד מֵאוֹרְךָ וְהָיִיתִי חֲדוּר אוֹרָה.

One ray of Your light, and we are bathed in light!

רַק דָּבָר אֶחָד מִדְּבָרֶיךָ וְקַמְתִּי לִתְחִיָּה.

One word from You, and we are reborn!

רַק תְּנוּעָה אַחַת מֵחַיֵּי נִצְחֲךָ וְהָיִיתִי רָווּי טַל
יַלְדוּת.

*One hint of Your eternal presence, and we are refreshed with
the dew of youth!*

הֲלֹא אַתָּה בּוֹרֵא הַכֹּל מְחָדָשׁ, בְּרָא נָא אָבִי אוֹתִי,
יַלְדְּךָ, מְחָדָשׁ.

*Author of life, as You renew all things, take us, Your
children, and make us new.*

נְשֹׁם בִּי מִנִּשְׁמַת אַפְּךָ וְחָיִיתִי חַיִּים חֲדָשִׁים, חַיֵּי
יַלְדוּת חֲדָשָׁה.

*Breathe Your spirit into us, that we may start life afresh,
with childhood's unbounded promise.*

◆ ◆

THE MIRACLES OF DAILY LIFE   נסים בכל יום

בָּרוּךְ אַתָּה, יְיָ אֱלֹהֵינוּ, מֶלֶךְ הָעוֹלָם, אֲשֶׁר נָתַן
לַשֶּׂכְוִי בִינָה לְהַבְחִין בֵּין יוֹם וּבֵין לָיְלָה.

*Blessed is the Eternal our God, Ruler of the universe, who
has implanted mind and instinct within every living being.*

בָּרוּךְ אַתָּה, יְיָ אֱלֹהֵינוּ, מֶלֶךְ הָעוֹלָם, הַמַּעֲבִיר שֵׁנָה
מֵעֵינַי וּתְנוּמָה מֵעַפְעַפָּי.

*Blessed is the Eternal our God, who removes sleep from the
eyes, slumber from the eyelids.*

בָּרוּךְ אַתָּה, יְיָ אֱלֹהֵינוּ, מֶלֶךְ הָעוֹלָם, פּוֹקֵחַ עִוְרִים.

*Blessed is the Eternal our God, who opens the eyes of the
blind.*

בָּרוּךְ אַתָּה, יְיָ אֱלֹהֵינוּ, מֶלֶךְ הָעוֹלָם, זוֹקֵף כְּפוּפִים.

*Blessed is the Eternal our God, whose power lifts up the fal-
len.*

בָּרוּךְ אַתָּה, יְיָ אֱלֹהֵינוּ, מֶלֶךְ הָעוֹלָם, הַנּוֹתֵן לַיָּעֵף
כְּחַ.

*Blessed is the Eternal our God, who gives strength to the
weary.*

בָּרוּךְ אַתָּה, יְיָ אֱלֹהֵינוּ, מֶלֶךְ הָעוֹלָם, הַמֵּכִין מִצְעֲדֵי־גָבֶר.

Blessed is the Eternal our God, who makes firm each person's steps.

בָּרוּךְ אַתָּה, יְיָ אֱלֹהֵינוּ, מֶלֶךְ הָעוֹלָם, מַלְבִּישׁ עֲרֻמִּים.

Blessed is the Eternal our God, who provides clothes for the naked.

בָּרוּךְ אַתָּה, יְיָ אֱלֹהֵינוּ, מֶלֶךְ הָעוֹלָם, שֶׁעָשַׂנִי בֶּן חוֹרִין.

Blessed is the Eternal our God, who has made me to be free.

בָּרוּךְ אַתָּה, יְיָ אֱלֹהֵינוּ, מֶלֶךְ הָעוֹלָם, מַתִּיר אֲסוּרִים.

Blessed is the Eternal our God, who brings freedom to the captive.

בָּרוּךְ אַתָּה, יְיָ אֱלֹהֵינוּ, מֶלֶךְ הָעוֹלָם, שֶׁעָשַׂנִי יִשְׂרָאֵל.

Blessed is the Eternal our God, who has made me a Jew.

בָּרוּךְ אַתָּה, יְיָ אֱלֹהֵינוּ, מֶלֶךְ הָעוֹלָם, אוֹזֵר יִשְׂרָאֵל בִּגְבוּרָה.

Blessed is the Eternal our God, who girds our people Israel with strength.

בָּרוּךְ אַתָּה, יְיָ אֱלֹהֵינוּ, מֶלֶךְ הָעוֹלָם, עוֹטֵר יִשְׂרָאֵל בְּתִפְאָרָה.

Blessed is the Eternal our God, who crowns Israel with glory.

✦ ✦

FOR THE BODY אשר יצר

בָּרוּךְ אַתָּה, יְיָ אֱלֹהֵינוּ, מֶלֶךְ הָעוֹלָם, אֲשֶׁר יָצַר אֶת־
הָאָדָם בְּחָכְמָה, וּבָרָא בוֹ נְקָבִים נְקָבִים, חֲלוּלִים
חֲלוּלִים. גָּלוּי וְיָדוּעַ לִפְנֵי כִסֵּא כְבוֹדֶךָ, שֶׁאִם יִפָּתֵחַ
אֶחָד מֵהֶם, אוֹ יִסָּתֵם אֶחָד מֵהֶם, אִי אֶפְשַׁר לְהִתְקַיֵּם
וְלַעֲמוֹד לְפָנֶיךָ. בָּרוּךְ אַתָּה, יְיָ, רוֹפֵא כָל־בָּשָׂר
וּמַפְלִיא לַעֲשׂוֹת.

Blessed is our Eternal God, Creator of the universe, who
has made our bodies with wisdom, combining veins,
arteries, and vital organs in a finely balanced system.
Wondrous Fashioner and Sustainer of life, Source of our
health and our strength, we give You thanks and praise.

◆ ◆

FOR THE SOUL אלהי נשמה

אֱלֹהַי, נְשָׁמָה שֶׁנָּתַתָּ בִּי טְהוֹרָה הִיא! אַתָּה בְרָאתָהּ,
אַתָּה יְצַרְתָּהּ, אַתָּה נְפַחְתָּהּ בִּי, וְאַתָּה מְשַׁמְּרָהּ
בְּקִרְבִּי. כָּל־זְמַן שֶׁהַנְּשָׁמָה בְקִרְבִּי, מוֹדֶה אֲנִי לְפָנֶיךָ,
יְיָ אֱלֹהַי וֵאלֹהֵי אֲבוֹתַי, רִבּוֹן כָּל־הַמַּעֲשִׂים, אֲדוֹן
כָּל־הַנְּשָׁמוֹת. בָּרוּךְ אַתָּה, יְיָ, אֲשֶׁר בְּיָדוֹ נֶפֶשׁ כָּל־חָי,
וְרוּחַ כָּל־בְּשַׂר־אִישׁ.

The soul that You have given me, O God, is pure! You
have created it. You have formed it. You have breathed it
into me, and within me You sustain it. So long as I have
breath, therefore, I will give thanks to You, O Lord my
God and God of all ages, Master of all creation, Lord of
every human spirit.

Blessed is the Lord, in whose hands are the souls of all the
living and the spirits of all flesh.

87

OUR SMALLNESS AND OUR GREATNESS מה אנחנו

רִבּוֹן כָּל־הָעוֹלָמִים, לֹא עַל־צִדְקוֹתֵינוּ אֲנַחְנוּ
מַפִּילִים תַּחֲנוּנֵינוּ לְפָנֶיךָ, כִּי עַל רַחֲמֶיךָ הָרַבִּים.

מָה אֲנַחְנוּ, מֶה חַיֵּינוּ, מֶה חַסְדֵּנוּ, מַה־צִּדְקֵנוּ, מַה־
יְשׁוּעָתֵנוּ, מַה־כֹּחֵנוּ, מַה־גְּבוּרָתֵנוּ? מַה־נֹּאמַר
לְפָנֶיךָ, יְיָ אֱלֹהֵינוּ וֵאלֹהֵי אֲבוֹתֵינוּ?

Master of all the worlds, not in reliance upon the
righteousness of our deeds do we place our longings
before You; we look instead to Your abundant mercy.

*For what are we? What is our life, and what our faithful-
ness? What is our goodness, and what our vaunted strength?
What can we say in Your presence, O Lord our God and
God of all ages?*

הֲלֹא כָל־הַגִּבּוֹרִים כְּאַיִן לְפָנֶיךָ, וְאַנְשֵׁי הַשֵּׁם כְּלֹא
הָיוּ, וַחֲכָמִים כִּבְלִי מַדָּע, וּנְבוֹנִים כִּבְלִי הַשְׂכֵּל, כִּי
רֹב מַעֲשֵׂיהֶם תֹּהוּ, וִימֵי חַיֵּיהֶם הֶבֶל לְפָנֶיךָ; וּמוֹתַר
הָאָדָם מִן הַבְּהֵמָה אָיִן, כִּי הַכֹּל הָבֶל.

אֲבָל אֲנַחְנוּ עַמְּךָ בְּנֵי בְרִיתֶךָ, וְאוֹתָנוּ קָרָאתָ
לַעֲבוֹדָתֶךָ. לְפִיכָךְ אֲנַחְנוּ חַיָּבִים לְהוֹדוֹת לְךָ
וּלְשַׁבֵּחַךָ, וּלְבָרֵךְ וּלְקַדֵּשׁ אֶת־שְׁמֶךָ.

Are not all the conquerors as nothing before You, and
those of renown as though they had not been, the learned
as if they had no knowledge, and the wise as if without understanding? Many of our works are vain, and our days
pass away like a shadow. Our life would be altogether
vanity, were it not for the soul which, fashioned in Your
own image, gives us assurance of our higher destiny and
imparts to our fleeting days an abiding value.

Despite all our frailty, we are Your people, bound to Your covenant, and called to Your service. We therefore thank You and bless You, and proclaim the holiness of Your name.

◆ ◆

How greatly we are blessed!	אַשְׁרֵינוּ!
How good is our portion!	מַה־טוֹב חֶלְקֵנוּ,
How pleasant our lot!	וּמַה־נָּעִים גּוֹרָלֵנוּ,
How beautiful our heritage!	וּמַה־יָּפָה יְרֻשָּׁתֵנוּ!

◆ ◆

FOR TORAH   לעסוק בדברי תורה

גֶּפֶן מִמִּצְרַיִם הֶעֱלָה אֱלֹהֵינוּ,
וַיְגָרֶשׁ גּוֹיִם וַיִּטָּעָה.
מַיִם מִסִּינַי הִשְׁקָה אוֹתָהּ,
וְנוֹזְלִים מֵחוֹרֵב.

You raised up a vine out of Egypt, O God,
You scattered our foes and planted us.

You gave us water from Sinai's well,
You nourished us from Horeb's spring.

◆

בָּרוּךְ אַתָּה, יְיָ אֱלֹהֵינוּ, מֶלֶךְ הָעוֹלָם, אֲשֶׁר קִדְּשָׁנוּ
בְּמִצְוֹתָיו וְצִוָּנוּ לַעֲסוֹק בְּדִבְרֵי תוֹרָה.

Blessed is the Eternal our God, Ruler of the universe, who hallows us with Mitzvot, and who commands us to engage in the study of Torah.

◆

אֵלּוּ דְבָרִים שֶׁאֵין לָהֶם שִׁעוּר, שֶׁאָדָם אוֹכֵל
פֵּרוֹתֵיהֶם בָּעוֹלָם הַזֶּה וְהַקֶּרֶן קַיֶּמֶת לוֹ לָעוֹלָם הַבָּא,
וְאֵלּוּ הֵן:

These are obligations without measure; their fruit we eat now, their essence remains for us in the life to come:

To honor father and mother;	כִּבּוּד אָב וָאֵם,
to perform acts of love and kindness;	וּגְמִילוּת חֲסָדִים,
to attend the house of study daily;	וְהַשְׁכָּמַת בֵּית הַמִּדְרָשׁ שַׁחֲרִית וְעַרְבִית,
to welcome the stranger;	וְהַכְנָסַת אוֹרְחִים,
to visit the sick;	וּבִקּוּר חוֹלִים,
to rejoice with bride and groom;	וְהַכְנָסַת כַּלָּה,
to console the bereaved;	וּלְוָיַת הַמֵּת,
to pray with sincerity;	וְעִיּוּן תְּפִלָּה,
to make peace when there is strife.	וַהֲבָאַת שָׁלוֹם בֵּין אָדָם לַחֲבֵרוֹ;
	וְתַלְמוּד תּוֹרָה כְּנֶגֶד כֻּלָּם.

But the study of Torah is equal to them all.

◆

וְהַעֲרֶב־נָא, יְיָ אֱלֹהֵינוּ, אֶת־דִּבְרֵי תוֹרָתְךָ בְּפִינוּ,
וּבְפִי עַמְּךָ בֵּית יִשְׂרָאֵל, וְנִהְיֶה אֲנַחְנוּ וְצֶאֱצָאֵינוּ,
וְצֶאֱצָאֵי עַמְּךָ בֵּית יִשְׂרָאֵל, כֻּלָּנוּ יוֹדְעֵי שְׁמֶךָ וְלוֹמְדֵי

תּוֹרָתֶךָ לִשְׁמָהּ. בָּרוּךְ אַתָּה, יְיָ, הַמְלַמֵּד תּוֹרָה לְעַמּוֹ
יִשְׂרָאֵל.

Eternal our God, make the words of Your Torah sweet to
us, and to the House of Israel, Your people, that we and
our children may be lovers of Your name and students of
Your Torah for its own sake.

*Blessed are You, the Eternal One, Teacher of Torah to
Israel.*

• •

Poems of Praise פסוקי דזמרה

One or more of the following passages may be read or chanted.
Then continue with Barechu, page 99.

FOR LIFE ברוך שאמר

בָּרוּךְ שֶׁאָמַר וְהָיָה הָעוֹלָם, בָּרוּךְ הוּא.
בָּרוּךְ עוֹשֶׂה בְרֵאשִׁית, בָּרוּךְ אוֹמֵר וְעוֹשֶׂה.
בָּרוּךְ גּוֹזֵר וּמְקַיֵּם, בָּרוּךְ מְרַחֵם עַל הָאָרֶץ.
בָּרוּךְ מְרַחֵם עַל הַבְּרִיּוֹת, בָּרוּךְ מְשַׁלֵּם שָׂכָר טוֹב
לִירֵאָיו. בָּרוּךְ חַי לָעַד וְקַיָּם לָנֶצַח, בָּרוּךְ פּוֹדֶה
וּמַצִּיל, בָּרוּךְ שְׁמוֹ. בִּשְׁבָחוֹת וּבִזְמִירוֹת נְגַדֶּלְךָ
וּנְשַׁבֵּחֲךָ וּנְפָאֶרְךָ, וְנַזְכִּיר שִׁמְךָ וְנַמְלִיכְךָ, מַלְכֵּנוּ,
אֱלֹהֵינוּ. יָחִיד, חֵי הָעוֹלָמִים, מֶלֶךְ, מְשֻׁבָּח וּמְפֹאָר
עֲדֵי־עַד שְׁמוֹ הַגָּדוֹל. בָּרוּךְ אַתָּה, יְיָ, מֶלֶךְ מְהֻלָּל
בַּתִּשְׁבָּחוֹת.

Praised be the One who spoke, and the world came to be.
Praised be the Source of creation.

91

Praised be the One whose word is deed, whose thought is fact.

Praised be the One whose compassion covers the earth and all its creatures.

Praised be the living and eternal God, Ruler of the universe, Source of our deliverance and help.

With songs of praise we extol You and proclaim Your sovereignty, our God and King, for You are the Author of life in the universe.

Blessed is the Eternal King, to whom our praise is due.

◆ ◆

From Psalm 19

הַשָּׁמַיִם מְסַפְּרִים כְּבוֹד־אֵל, וּמַעֲשֵׂה יָדָיו מַגִּיד
הָרָקִיעַ.

The heavens declare the glory of God; the arch of sky reveals His handiwork.

יוֹם לְיוֹם יַבִּיעַ אֹמֶר, וְלַיְלָה לְלַיְלָה יְחַוֶּה־דָּעַת.

Day after day the word pours out; night after night knowledge goes forth.

אֵין־אֹמֶר וְאֵין דְּבָרִים, בְּלִי נִשְׁמָע קוֹלָם—

There is no speech, there are no words, no voice is heard—

בְּכָל־הָאָרֶץ יָצָא קַוָּם, וּבִקְצֵה תֵבֵל מִלֵּיהֶם!

Yet their call goes through all the earth, and their words to the edge of the universe!

◆ ◆

92

From Psalm 33

רַנְּנוּ צַדִּיקִים בַּיְיָ;
לַיְשָׁרִים נָאוָה תְהִלָּה.

הוֹדוּ לַיְיָ בְּכִנּוֹר; בְּנֵבֶל עָשׂוֹר זַמְּרוּ־לוֹ.
שִׁירוּ לוֹ שִׁיר חָדָשׁ; הֵיטִיבוּ נַגֵּן בִּתְרוּעָה.

כִּי־יָשָׁר דְּבַר־יְיָ, וְכָל־מַעֲשֵׂהוּ בֶּאֱמוּנָה.
אֹהֵב צְדָקָה וּמִשְׁפָּט; חֶסֶד יְיָ מָלְאָה הָאָרֶץ.

בִּדְבַר יְיָ שָׁמַיִם נַעֲשׂוּ, וּבְרוּחַ פִּיו כָּל־צְבָאָם.
כִּי הוּא אָמַר וַיֶּהִי; הוּא־צִוָּה וַיַּעֲמֹד.

עֲצַת יְיָ לְעוֹלָם תַּעֲמֹד;
מַחְשְׁבוֹת לִבּוֹ לְדֹר וָדֹר.

הַיֹּצֵר יַחַד לִבָּם;
הַמֵּבִין אֶל־כָּל־מַעֲשֵׂיהֶם.

נַפְשֵׁנוּ חִכְּתָה לַיְיָ; עֶזְרֵנוּ וּמָגִנֵּנוּ הוּא.
כִּי־בוֹ יִשְׂמַח לִבֵּנוּ; כִּי בְשֵׁם קָדְשׁוֹ בָטָחְנוּ.
יְהִי־חַסְדְּךָ, יְיָ, עָלֵינוּ; כַּאֲשֶׁר יִחַלְנוּ לָךְ.

Let all who are righteous sing God's song;
the upright do well to acclaim Him.

Thank the Lord with the harp; accompany your chant
with strings.
Sing to Him a new song; grace your song with skillful play.

For the word of the Lord holds good; His work commands our trust.
He loves justice and right; His steadfast love fills the earth.

The heavens were made by the word of the Lord; their starry host by the power of His thought.
For He spoke and it was; He commanded and it stood firm.

The Lord's plan will stand for ever;
His thought will endure for all time.

He fashioned the hearts of us all;
He understands the meaning of our lives.

Therefore we trust in the Lord; He is our Help and our Shield. In Him will we rejoice; in His holy being will we trust.
Let Your steadfast love rest upon us, O Lord, as we put our trust in You.

◆ ◆

Psalm 150

Halleluyah!	הַלְלוּיָהּ!
Praise God in His sanctuary;	הַלְלוּ־אֵל בְּקָדְשׁוֹ,
Praise Him whose power the	הַלְלוּהוּ בִּרְקִיעַ עֻזּוֹ.
heavens proclaim.	הַלְלוּהוּ בִגְבוּרֹתָיו,
Praise Him for His mighty acts;	הַלְלוּהוּ כְּרֹב גֻּדְלוֹ.
Praise Him for His surpassing greatness.	
Praise Him with shofar blast;	הַלְלוּהוּ בְּתֵקַע שׁוֹפָר,
Praise Him with harp and lute.	הַלְלוּהוּ בְּנֵבֶל וְכִנּוֹר.
Praise Him with drum and dance;	הַלְלוּהוּ בְתֹף וּמָחוֹל,
Praise Him with strings and pipe.	הַלְלוּהוּ בְּמִנִּים וְעֻגָב.
Praise Him with cymbals sounding;	הַלְלוּהוּ בְּצִלְצְלֵי־שָׁמַע,

94

Praise Him with cymbals resounding.
Let every soul praise the Lord.
Halleluyah!

הַלְלוּהוּ בְּצִלְצְלֵי תְרוּעָה.
כֹּל הַנְּשָׁמָה תְּהַלֵּל יָהּ.
הַלְלוּיָהּ!

◆ ◆

OUR IMMEASURABLE DEBT TO GOD נשמת כל־חי

נִשְׁמַת כָּל־חַי תְּבָרֵךְ אֶת־שִׁמְךָ, יְיָ אֱלֹהֵינוּ, וְרוּחַ כָּל־
בָּשָׂר תְּפָאֵר וּתְרוֹמֵם זִכְרְךָ, מַלְכֵּנוּ, תָּמִיד. מִן־
הָעוֹלָם וְעַד־הָעוֹלָם אַתָּה אֵל; אֵין לָנוּ מֶלֶךְ אֶלָּא
אָתָּה.

Let every living soul bless Your name, O Lord our God,
and let every human being acclaim Your majesty, for ever
and ever. Through all eternity You are God; we have no
King but You.

אֱלֹהֵי הָרִאשׁוֹנִים וְהָאַחֲרוֹנִים, אֱלוֹהַּ כָּל־בְּרִיּוֹת,
אֲדוֹן כָּל־תּוֹלָדוֹת, הַמְהֻלָּל בְּרֹב הַתִּשְׁבָּחוֹת, הַמְנַהֵג
עוֹלָמוֹ בְּחֶסֶד וּבְרִיּוֹתָיו בְּרַחֲמִים. וַיְיָ לֹא יָנוּם וְלֹא
יִישָׁן; הַמְעוֹרֵר יְשֵׁנִים וְהַמֵּקִיץ נִרְדָּמִים וְהַמֵּשִׂיחַ
אִלְּמִים, וְהַמַּתִּיר אֲסוּרִים וְהַסּוֹמֵךְ נוֹפְלִים וְהַזּוֹקֵף
כְּפוּפִים. לְךָ לְבַדְּךָ אֲנַחְנוּ מוֹדִים.

God of all ages, Ruler of all creatures, Lord of all generations: all praise to You. You guide the world with steadfast love, Your creatures with tender mercy. You neither
slumber nor sleep; You awaken the sleeping and arouse
the dormant. You give speech to the silent, freedom to the
enslaved, and justice to the oppressed. To You alone we
give thanks.

אִלּוּ פִינוּ מָלֵא שִׁירָה כַּיָּם, וּלְשׁוֹנֵנוּ רִנָּה כַּהֲמוֹן גַּלָּיו,
וְשִׂפְתוֹתֵינוּ שֶׁבַח כְּמֶרְחֲבֵי רָקִיעַ, וְעֵינֵינוּ מְאִירוֹת
כַּשֶּׁמֶשׁ וְכַיָּרֵחַ, וְיָדֵינוּ פְרוּשׂוֹת כְּנִשְׁרֵי שָׁמָיִם,
וְרַגְלֵינוּ קַלּוֹת כָּאַיָּלוֹת—אֵין אֲנַחְנוּ מַסְפִּיקִים
לְהוֹדוֹת לְךָ, יְיָ אֱלֹהֵינוּ וֵאלֹהֵי אֲבוֹתֵינוּ, וּלְבָרֵךְ אֶת־
שְׁמֶךָ עַל־אַחַת מֵאֶלֶף, אֶלֶף אַלְפֵי אֲלָפִים וְרִבֵּי
רְבָבוֹת פְּעָמִים הַטּוֹבוֹת שֶׁעָשִׂיתָ עִם־אֲבוֹתֵינוּ וְעִמָּנוּ.

*Though our mouths should overflow with song as the sea,
our tongues with melody as the roaring waves, our lips with
praise as the heavens' wide expanse; and though our eyes
were to shine as the sun and the moon, our arms extend like
eagles' wings, our feet speed swiftly as deer—still we could
not fully thank You, Lord our God and God of all ages, or
bless Your name enough, for even one of Your infinite
kindnesses to our ancestors and to us.*

עַל כֵּן אֵבָרִים שֶׁפִּלַּגְתָּ בָּנוּ, וְרוּחַ וּנְשָׁמָה שֶׁנָּפַחְתָּ
בְּאַפֵּינוּ, וְלָשׁוֹן אֲשֶׁר שַׂמְתָּ בְּפִינוּ, הֵן הֵם יוֹדוּ
וִיבָרְכוּ וִישַׁבְּחוּ וִיפָאֲרוּ אֶת־שְׁמְךָ, מַלְכֵּנוּ. כִּי כָל־פֶּה
לְךָ יוֹדֶה, וְכָל־לָשׁוֹן לְךָ תִשָּׁבַע, וְכָל־בֶּרֶךְ לְךָ תִכְרַע,
וְכָל־קוֹמָה לְפָנֶיךָ תִשְׁתַּחֲוֶה, וְכָל־לְבָבוֹת יִירָאוּךָ,
וְכָל־קֶרֶב וּכְלָיוֹת יְזַמְּרוּ לִשְׁמֶךָ. כַּדָּבָר שֶׁכָּתוּב: כָּל־
עַצְמוֹתַי תֹּאמַרְנָה: "יְיָ, מִי כָמוֹךָ?" כָּאָמוּר, "לְדָוִד,
בָּרְכִי, נַפְשִׁי, אֶת־יְיָ, וְכָל־קְרָבַי אֶת־שֵׁם קָדְשׁוֹ!"

Therefore, O God, limbs and tongue and heart and mind
shall join to praise Your name; every tongue will yet affirm You, and every soul give You allegiance. As it is
written: All my limbs shall say: "Lord, who is like You?"

96

And David sang: "Bless the Lord, O my soul, and let all
that is within me bless His holy name!"

◆ ◆

הָאֵל בְּתַעֲצֻמוֹת עֻזֶּךָ, הַגָּדוֹל בִּכְבוֹד שְׁמֶךָ, הַגִּבּוֹר
לָנֶצַח וְהַנּוֹרָא בְּנוֹרְאוֹתֶיךָ.

You are tremendous in power, O God, glorious in being,
mighty for ever and awesome in Your works.

הַמֶּלֶךְ הַיּוֹשֵׁב עַל כִּסֵּא רָם וְנִשָּׂא.

O KING supreme and exalted,

שׁוֹכֵן עַד, מָרוֹם וְקָדוֹשׁ שְׁמוֹ. וְכָתוּב: רַנְּנוּ צַדִּיקִים
בַּיְיָ; לַיְשָׁרִים נָאוָה תְהִלָּה.

You abide for ever, the High and Holy One. Therefore let
all who are righteous sing Your song; the upright do well
to acclaim You.

בְּפִי יְשָׁרִים תִּתְהַלָּל; וּבְדִבְרֵי צַדִּיקִים תִּתְבָּרַךְ;
וּבִלְשׁוֹן חֲסִידִים תִּתְרוֹמָם; וּבְקֶרֶב קְדוֹשִׁים
תִּתְקַדָּשׁ.

*The mouths of the upright acclaim You; the words of the
righteous bless You; the tongues of the faithful exalt You;
the hearts of all who seek holiness sanctify You.*

וּבְמַקְהֲלוֹת רִבְבוֹת עַמְּךָ, בֵּית יִשְׂרָאֵל, בְּרִנָּה יִתְפָּאַר
שִׁמְךָ, מַלְכֵּנוּ, בְּכָל־דּוֹר וָדוֹר. יִשְׁתַּבַּח שִׁמְךָ לָעַד,
מַלְכֵּנוּ, הָאֵל הַמֶּלֶךְ הַגָּדוֹל וְהַקָּדוֹשׁ בַּשָּׁמַיִם וּבָאָרֶץ.

O King, the assembled hosts of Your people, the house of
Israel, in every generation glorify Your name in song. O

Sovereign God, great and holy King, let Your name be
praised for ever in heaven and on earth.

בָּרוּךְ אַתָּה, יְיָ, אֵל מֶלֶךְ, גָּדוֹל בַּתִּשְׁבָּחוֹת, אֵל
הַהוֹדָאוֹת, אֲדוֹן הַנִּפְלָאוֹת, הַבּוֹחֵר בְּשִׁירֵי זִמְרָה,
מֶלֶךְ אֵל חֵי הָעוֹלָמִים.

*Blessed is the Lord, the Sovereign God, the Lord of wonders
who delights in song, the Only One, the Life of the universe.*

✦ ✦

READER'S KADDISH   חצי קדיש

יִתְגַּדַּל וְיִתְקַדַּשׁ שְׁמֵהּ רַבָּא בְּעָלְמָא דִּי־בְרָא כִרְעוּתֵהּ, וְיַמְלִיךְ
מַלְכוּתֵהּ בְּחַיֵּיכוֹן וּבְיוֹמֵיכוֹן וּבְחַיֵּי דְכָל־בֵּית יִשְׂרָאֵל, בַּעֲגָלָא
וּבִזְמַן קָרִיב, וְאִמְרוּ: אָמֵן.
יְהֵא שְׁמֵהּ רַבָּא מְבָרַךְ לְעָלַם וּלְעָלְמֵי עָלְמַיָּא.
יִתְבָּרַךְ וְיִשְׁתַּבַּח, וְיִתְפָּאַר וְיִתְרוֹמַם וְיִתְנַשֵּׂא, וְיִתְהַדָּר
וְיִתְעַלֶּה וְיִתְהַלַּל שְׁמֵהּ דְּקוּדְשָׁא, בְּרִיךְ הוּא, לְעֵלָּא מִן כָּל־
בִּרְכָתָא וְשִׁירָתָא, תֻּשְׁבְּחָתָא וְנֶחֱמָתָא דַּאֲמִירָן בְּעָלְמָא,
וְאִמְרוּ: אָמֵן.

Let the glory of God be extolled, let His great name be hallowed
in the world whose creation He willed. May His kingdom soon
prevail, in our own day, our own lives, and the life of all Israel,
and let us say: Amen.
Let His great name be blessed for ever and ever.
Let the name of the Holy One, blessed is He, be glorified, exalted and honored, though He is beyond all the praises, songs,
and adorations that we can utter, and let us say: Amen.

✦ ✦

All rise

שמע וברכותיה

בָּרְכוּ אֶת־יְיָ הַמְבֹרָךְ!

Praise the Lord, to whom our praise is due!

בָּרוּךְ יְיָ הַמְבֹרָךְ לְעוֹלָם וָעֶד!

Praised be the Lord, to whom our praise is due,
now and for ever!

◦ ◦

THAT CROWNS THE SKY WITH STARS   **יוצר**

בָּרוּךְ אַתָּה, יְיָ אֱלֹהֵינוּ, מֶלֶךְ הָעוֹלָם, יוֹצֵר אוֹר
וּבוֹרֵא חְשֶׁךְ, עֹשֶׂה שָׁלוֹם וּבוֹרֵא אֶת־הַכֹּל.
הַמֵּאִיר לָאָרֶץ וְלַדָּרִים עָלֶיהָ בְּרַחֲמִים, וּבְטוּבוֹ
מְחַדֵּשׁ בְּכָל־יוֹם תָּמִיד מַעֲשֵׂה בְרֵאשִׁית.
מָה רַבּוּ מַעֲשֶׂיךָ, יְיָ! כֻּלָּם בְּחָכְמָה עָשִׂיתָ, מָלְאָה
הָאָרֶץ קִנְיָנֶךָ.
תִּתְבָּרַךְ, יְיָ אֱלֹהֵינוּ, עַל־שֶׁבַח מַעֲשֵׂה יָדֶיךָ, וְעַל־
מְאוֹרֵי־אוֹר שֶׁעָשִׂיתָ: יְפָאֲרוּךָ. סֶלָה. בָּרוּךְ אַתָּה, יְיָ,
יוֹצֵר הַמְּאוֹרוֹת.

◦Blessed is the grace that crowns the sky with stars, and
keeps the planets on their ways; the law that turns our
night to day, and fills the eye with light; the love that
keeps us whole, and day by day sustains us.

◦*This symbol indicates that the English is a variation suggested by the theme of*
the Hebrew.

*Praised be the Power that brings renewal to the soul, the
vital song that makes creation dance.*

Blessed is the murmuring dark, blessed is light to the eyes!

The fall of dusk, the flow of dawn, the turn of noon—

O give thanks for life's renewal, the radiant return of the
sun!

Blessed is the power of creation, praised be the light!

✦ ✦

A FLAME THAT NEVER FAILS   אהבה רבה

אַהֲבָה רַבָּה אֲהַבְתָּנוּ, יְיָ אֱלֹהֵינוּ, חֶמְלָה גְדוֹלָה
וִיתֵרָה חָמַלְתָּ עָלֵינוּ. אָבִינוּ מַלְכֵּנוּ, בַּעֲבוּר אֲבוֹתֵינוּ
שֶׁבָּטְחוּ בְךָ וַתְּלַמְּדֵם חֻקֵּי חַיִּים, כֵּן תְּחָנֵּנוּ וּתְלַמְּדֵנוּ.
אָבִינוּ, הָאָב הָרַחֲמָן, הַמְרַחֵם, רַחֵם עָלֵינוּ וְתֵן בְּלִבֵּנוּ
לְהָבִין וּלְהַשְׂכִּיל, לִשְׁמֹעַ לִלְמֹד וּלְלַמֵּד, לִשְׁמֹר
וְלַעֲשׂוֹת וּלְקַיֵּם אֶת־כָּל־דִּבְרֵי תַלְמוּד תּוֹרָתֶךָ
בְּאַהֲבָה.

°The Law has been our garden of delight; the Law has
been our life. In deepest darkness, we have held it fast; in
the valley of tears, it has upheld us. Therefore shall we
learn this Law and reveal it to our children: our truth, our
way, our joy. It makes us one, a single heart.

וְהָאֵר עֵינֵינוּ בְּתוֹרָתֶךָ, וְדַבֵּק לִבֵּנוּ בְּמִצְוֹתֶיךָ, וְיַחֵד
לְבָבֵנוּ לְאַהֲבָה וּלְיִרְאָה אֶת־שְׁמֶךָ. וְלֹא־נֵבוֹשׁ
לְעוֹלָם וָעֶד, כִּי בְשֵׁם קָדְשְׁךָ הַגָּדוֹל וְהַנּוֹרָא בָּטָחְנוּ.
נָגִילָה וְנִשְׂמְחָה בִּישׁוּעָתֶךָ, כִּי אֵל פּוֹעֵל יְשׁוּעוֹת
אָתָּה, וּבָנוּ בָחַרְתָּ וְקֵרַבְתָּנוּ לְשִׁמְךָ הַגָּדוֹל סֶלָה

בֶּאֱמֶת, לְהוֹדוֹת לְךָ וּלְיַחֶדְךָ בְּאַהֲבָה. בָּרוּךְ אַתָּה, יְיָ,
הַבּוֹחֵר בְּעַמּוֹ יִשְׂרָאֵל בְּאַהֲבָה.

*United in love, we shall walk unafraid. Blessed is the law of
love that gives us strength to live, and blessed the Torah that
makes all Israel one.*

‧ ‧

שְׁמַע יִשְׂרָאֵל: יְיָ אֱלֹהֵינוּ, יְיָ אֶחָד!

Hear, O Israel: the Lord is our God, the Lord is One!

בָּרוּךְ שֵׁם כְּבוֹד מַלְכוּתוֹ לְעוֹלָם וָעֶד!

Blessed is His glorious kingdom for ever and ever!

All are seated

וְאָהַבְתָּ אֵת יְיָ אֱלֹהֶיךָ בְּכָל־לְבָבְךָ וּבְכָל־נַפְשְׁךָ
וּבְכָל־מְאֹדֶךָ. וְהָיוּ הַדְּבָרִים הָאֵלֶּה, אֲשֶׁר אָנֹכִי מְצַוְּךָ
הַיּוֹם, עַל־לְבָבֶךָ. וְשִׁנַּנְתָּם לְבָנֶיךָ, וְדִבַּרְתָּ בָּם
בְּשִׁבְתְּךָ בְּבֵיתֶךָ, וּבְלֶכְתְּךָ בַדֶּרֶךְ, וּבְשָׁכְבְּךָ וּבְקוּמֶךָ.
וּקְשַׁרְתָּם לְאוֹת עַל־יָדֶךָ, וְהָיוּ לְטֹטָפֹת בֵּין עֵינֶיךָ,
וּכְתַבְתָּם עַל־מְזֻזוֹת בֵּיתֶךָ, וּבִשְׁעָרֶיךָ.

*You shall love the Lord your God with all your mind, with all
your strength, with all your being. Set these words, which I
command you this day, upon your heart. Teach them
faithfully to your children; speak of them in your home and
on your way, when you lie down and when you rise up. Bind
them as a sign upon your hand; let them be a symbol before
your eyes; inscribe them on the doorposts of your house, and
on your gates.*

לְמַעַן תִּזְכְּרוּ וַעֲשִׂיתֶם אֶת־כָּל־מִצְוֹתָי, וִהְיִיתֶם
קְדֹשִׁים לֵאלֹהֵיכֶם. אֲנִי יְיָ אֱלֹהֵיכֶם, אֲשֶׁר הוֹצֵאתִי

אֶתְכֶם מֵאֶרֶץ מִצְרַיִם לִהְיוֹת לָכֶם לֵאלֹהִים. אֲנִי יְיָ
אֱלֹהֵיכֶם.

*Be mindful of all My Mitzvot, and do them: so shall you
consecrate yourselves to your God. I, the Lord, am your God
who led you out of Egypt to be your God; I, the Lord, am
your God.*

◆ ◆

THE POWER THAT MAKES FOR FREEDOM   גאולה

°We worship the power that unites all the universe into
one great harmony. That oneness, however, is not yet. We
see imperfection, disorder, and evil all about us. But
before our eyes is a vision of perfection, order, and
goodness: these too we have known in some measure.
There is evil enough to break the heart, enough good to
exalt the soul. Our people has experienced untold suffering and wondrous redemptions; we await a redemption
more lasting and more splendid than any of the past.

•

אֱמֶת וְיַצִּיב, וְאָהוּב וְחָבִיב, וְנוֹרָא וְאַדִּיר, וְטוֹב וְיָפֶה
הַדָּבָר הַזֶּה עָלֵינוּ לְעוֹלָם וָעֶד. אֱמֶת, אֱלֹהֵי עוֹלָם
מַלְכֵּנוּ, צוּר יַעֲקֹב מָגֵן יִשְׁעֵנוּ.
לְדֹר וָדֹר הוּא קַיָּם, וּשְׁמוֹ קַיָּם, וְכִסְאוֹ נָכוֹן,
וּמַלְכוּתוֹ וֶאֱמוּנָתוֹ לָעַד קַיָּמֶת. וּדְבָרָיו חָיִים וְקַיָּמִים,
נֶאֱמָנִים וְנֶחֱמָדִים, לָעַד וּלְעוֹלְמֵי עוֹלָמִים.
מִמִּצְרַיִם גְּאַלְתָּנוּ, יְיָ אֱלֹהֵינוּ, וּמִבֵּית עֲבָדִים פְּדִיתָנוּ.
עַל־זֹאת שִׁבְּחוּ אֲהוּבִים וְרוֹמְמוּ אֵל, וְנָתְנוּ יְדִידִים

102

זְמִירוֹת, שִירוֹת וְתִשְׁבָּחוֹת, בְּרָכוֹת וְהוֹדָאוֹת
לַמֶּלֶךְ, אֵל חַי וְקַיָּם.

°When will redemption come?

When we master the violence that fills our world.

When we look upon others as we would have them look
upon us.

When we grant to every person the rights we claim for
ourselves.

רָם וְנִשָּׂא, גָּדוֹל וְנוֹרָא, מַשְׁפִּיל גֵּאִים וּמַגְבִּיהַּ
שְׁפָלִים, מוֹצִיא אֲסִירִים וּפוֹדֶה עֲנָוִים, וְעוֹזֵר דַּלִּים,
וְעוֹנֶה לְעַמּוֹ בְּעֵת שַׁוְּעָם אֵלָיו.

תְּהִלּוֹת לְאֵל עֶלְיוֹן, בָּרוּךְ הוּא וּמְבֹרָךְ. מֹשֶׁה וּבְנֵי
יִשְׂרָאֵל לְךָ עָנוּ שִׁירָה בְּשִׂמְחָה רַבָּה, וְאָמְרוּ כֻלָּם:

Once we were in bondage, then we were free. In that first
liberation our people saw revealed the power of the Most
High. They perceived that His presence redeems time and
event from the hands of tyrants. We, too, affirm the power
that makes for freedom. We sing the song that celebrates
our deliverance from Egypt and all bondage.

מִי־כָמְכָה בָּאֵלִם, יְיָ ?

Who is like You, Eternal One, among
the gods that are worshipped?

מִי כָּמְכָה, נֶאְדָּר בַּקֹּדֶשׁ,
נוֹרָא תְהִלֹּת, עֹשֵׂה פֶלֶא?

Who is like You, majestic in holiness,
awesome in splendor, doing wonders?

שִׁירָה חֲדָשָׁה שִׁבְּחוּ גְאוּלִים לְשִׁמְךָ עַל־שְׂפַת הַיָּם;

יַחַד כֻּלָּם הוֹדוּ וְהִמְלִיכוּ וְאָמְרוּ: "יְיָ יִמְלֹךְ לְעוֹלָם וָעֶד!"

With great joy the redeemed shall accept You as their King, and all will say with one accord: "The Eternal will reign for ever and ever!"

צוּר יִשְׂרָאֵל, קוּמָה בְּעֶזְרַת יִשְׂרָאֵל, וּפְדֵה כִנְאֻמֶךָ יְהוּדָה וְיִשְׂרָאֵל. גְּאָלֵנוּ יְיָ צְבָאוֹת שְׁמוֹ, קְדוֹשׁ יִשְׂרָאֵל. בָּרוּךְ אַתָּה, יְיָ, גָּאַל יִשְׂרָאֵל.

O Rock of Israel, come to Israel's help. Fulfill Your promise of redemption for Judah and Israel. Our Redeemer is the Lord of Hosts, the Holy One of Israel. Blessed is the Lord, the Redeemer of Israel.

◆ ◆

All rise

תפלה

אֲדֹנָי, שְׂפָתַי תִּפְתָּח, וּפִי יַגִּיד תְּהִלָּתֶךָ.

Eternal God, open my lips, that my mouth may declare Your glory.

GOD OF ALL GENERATIONS   אבות

בָּרוּךְ אַתָּה, יְיָ אֱלֹהֵינוּ וֵאלֹהֵי אֲבוֹתֵינוּ, אֱלֹהֵי אַבְרָהָם, אֱלֹהֵי יִצְחָק, וֵאלֹהֵי יַעֲקֹב: הָאֵל הַגָּדוֹל, הַגִּבּוֹר וְהַנּוֹרָא, אֵל עֶלְיוֹן, גּוֹמֵל חֲסָדִים טוֹבִים, וְקוֹנֵה הַכֹּל, וְזוֹכֵר חַסְדֵי אָבוֹת, וּמֵבִיא גְאֻלָּה לִבְנֵי בְנֵיהֶם, לְמַעַן שְׁמוֹ, בְּאַהֲבָה.

We praise You, Lord our God and God of all generations;

God of Abraham, God of Isaac, God of Jacob; great, mighty, and awesome God, God supreme.

Master of all the living, Your ways are ways of love. You remember the faithfulness of our ancestors, and in love bring redemption to their children's children, for the sake of Your name.

Remember us unto life, O King who delights in life, and inscribe us in the Book of Life, for Your sake, O God of life.

זָכְרֵנוּ לְחַיִּים, מֶלֶךְ חָפֵץ בַּחַיִּים, וְכָתְבֵנוּ בְּסֵפֶר הַחַיִּים, לְמַעַנְךָ אֱלֹהִים חַיִּים. מֶלֶךְ עוֹזֵר וּמוֹשִׁיעַ וּמָגֵן. בָּרוּךְ אַתָּה, יְיָ, מָגֵן אַבְרָהָם.

You are our King and our Help, our Savior and our Shield. Blessed is the Lord, the Shield of Abraham.

◆ ◆

GOD'S POWER   גבורות

אַתָּה גִּבּוֹר לְעוֹלָם, אֲדֹנָי, מְחַיֵּה הַכֹּל אַתָּה, רַב לְהוֹשִׁיעַ.
מְכַלְכֵּל חַיִּים בְּחֶסֶד, מְחַיֵּה הַכֹּל בְּרַחֲמִים רַבִּים. סוֹמֵךְ נוֹפְלִים, וְרוֹפֵא חוֹלִים, וּמַתִּיר אֲסוּרִים, וּמְקַיֵּם אֱמוּנָתוֹ לִישֵׁנֵי עָפָר.

Great is Your might, O Lord, in this world; great is Your power in the worlds beyond.

Your love sustains the living, Your great compassion is the source of life. Your power is in the help that comes to the falling, in the healing that comes to the sick, in the freedom You bring to the captive, in the faith You keep with those who sleep in the dust.

מִי כָמוֹךָ, בַּעַל גְּבוּרוֹת, וּמִי דּוֹמֶה לָּךְ, מֶלֶךְ מֵמִית
וּמְחַיֶּה וּמַצְמִיחַ יְשׁוּעָה? מִי כָמוֹךָ אַב הָרַחֲמִים,
זוֹכֵר יְצוּרָיו לְחַיִּים בְּרַחֲמִים? וְנֶאֱמָן אַתָּה לְהַחֲיוֹת
הַכֹּל. בָּרוּךְ אַתָּה, יְיָ, מְחַיֵּה הַכֹּל.

Who is like You, Master of Might? Who is Your equal, O
Lord of life and death, Source of Salvation?

*Who is like You, Source of mercy? In compassion You sus-
tain the life of Your children.*

*We trust in You to restore our life. Blessed is the Lord,
Source of all life.*

All are seated

◆ ◆

ונתנה תקף

MEDITATION

It is said that the words we are about to utter were born of the
martyrdom of Rabbi Amnon of Mayence. He chose to die that
his faith might live. He said: *Unetaneh tokef kedushat hayom,*
Let us proclaim the sacred power of this day; it is awesome and
full of dread. Now the divine Judge looks upon our deeds, and
determines our destiny.

A legend . . . and yet, surely our deeds do not pass away un-
recorded. Every word, every act inscribes itself in the Book of
Life. Freely we choose, and what we have chosen to become
stands in judgment over what we may yet hope to be. In our
choices we are not always free. But if only we make the effort to
turn, every force of goodness, within and without, will help us,
while we live, to escape that death of the heart which leads to
sin.

106

וּנְתַנֶּה תְּקֶף קְדֻשַׁת הַיּוֹם כִּי הוּא נוֹרָא וְאָים. וּבוֹ
תִּנָּשֵׂא מַלְכוּתֶךָ וְיִכּוֹן בְּחֶסֶד כִּסְאֶךָ וְתֵשֵׁב עָלָיו
בֶּאֱמֶת. אֱמֶת כִּי אַתָּה הוּא דַיָּן וּמוֹכִיחַ וְיוֹדֵעַ וָעֵד,
וְכוֹתֵב וְחוֹתֵם וְסוֹפֵר וּמוֹנֶה, וְתִזְכֹּר כָּל־הַנִּשְׁכָּחוֹת,
וְתִפְתַּח אֶת־סֵפֶר הַזִּכְרוֹנוֹת, וּמֵאֵלָיו יִקָּרֵא וְחוֹתָם
יַד כָּל־אָדָם בּוֹ.

Let us proclaim the sacred power of this day;
it is awesome and full of dread.
For on this day Your dominion is exalted,
Your throne established in steadfast love;
there in truth You reign.
In truth You are
Judge and Arbiter, Counsel and Witness.
You write and You seal, You record and recount.
You remember deeds long forgotten.
You open the book of our days,
and what is written there proclaims itself,
for it bears the signature
of every human being.

וּבְשׁוֹפָר גָּדוֹל יִתָּקַע, וְקוֹל דְּמָמָה דַקָּה יִשָּׁמַע,
וּמַלְאָכִים יֵחָפֵזוּן וְחִיל וּרְעָדָה יֹאחֵזוּן וְיֹאמְרוּ: הִנֵּה
יוֹם הַדִּין. לִפְקֹד עַל צְבָא מָרוֹם בַּדִּין, כִּי לֹא יִזְכּוּ
בְעֵינֶיךָ בַּדִּין. וְכָל־בָּאֵי עוֹלָם יַעַבְרוּן לְפָנֶיךָ כִּבְנֵי
מָרוֹן. כְּבַקָּרַת רוֹעֶה עֶדְרוֹ, מַעֲבִיר צֹאנוֹ תַּחַת
שִׁבְטוֹ, כֵּן תַּעֲבִיר וְתִסְפֹּר וְתִמְנֶה וְתִפְקֹד נֶפֶשׁ כָּל־
חָי, וְתַחְתֹּךְ קִצְבָה לְכָל־בְּרִיָּה וְתִכְתֹּב אֶת־גְּזַר דִּינָם.

The great Shofar is sounded,
the still, small voice is heard;
the angels,
gripped by fear and trembling,
declare in awe:

This is the Day of Judgment!
For even the hosts of heaven are judged,
as all who dwell on earth
stand arrayed before You.

As the shepherd seeks out his flock,
and makes the sheep pass under his staff,
so do You muster and number and consider
every soul,
setting the bounds of every creature's life,
and decreeing its destiny.

בְּרֹאשׁ הַשָּׁנָה יִכָּתֵבוּן וּבְיוֹם צוֹם כִּפּוּר יֵחָתֵמוּן.
כַּמָּה יַעַבְרוּן וְכַמָּה יִבָּרֵאוּן, מִי יִחְיֶה וּמִי יָמוּת, מִי
בְקִצּוֹ וּמִי לֹא בְקִצּוֹ, מִי בָאֵשׁ וּמִי בַמַּיִם, מִי בַחֶרֶב
וּמִי בַחַיָּה, מִי בָרָעָב וּמִי בַצָּמָא, מִי בָרַעַשׁ וּמִי
בַמַּגֵּפָה, מִי בַחֲנִיקָה וּמִי בַסְּקִילָה. מִי יָנוּחַ וּמִי יָנוּעַ,
מִי יַשְׁקִיט וּמִי יְטֹרַף, מִי יִשָּׁלֵו וּמִי יִתְיַסָּר, מִי יֵעָנִי
וּמִי יֵעָשִׁיר, מִי יִשָּׁפֵל וּמִי יָרוּם.

On Rosh Hashanah it is written,
on Yom Kippur it is sealed:
How many shall pass on, how many shall come to be;
who shall live and who shall die;
who shall see ripe age and who shall not;
who shall perish by fire and who by water;
who by sword and who by beast;
who by hunger and who by thirst;
who by earthquake and who by plague;
who by strangling and who by stoning;
who shall be secure and who shall be driven;
who shall be tranquil and who shall be troubled;
who shall be poor and who shall be rich;
who shall be humbled and who exalted.

וּתְשׁוּבָה וּתְפִלָּה וּצְדָקָה
מַעֲבִירִין אֶת־רֹעַ הַגְּזֵרָה.

*But REPENTANCE, PRAYER and CHARITY
temper judgment's severe decree.*

כִּי כְּשִׁמְךָ כֵּן תְּהִלָּתֶךָ, קָשֶׁה לִכְעֹס וְנוֹחַ לִרְצוֹת. כִּי
לֹא תַחְפֹּץ בְּמוֹת הַמֵּת כִּי אִם בְּשׁוּבוֹ מִדַּרְכּוֹ וְחָיָה.
וְעַד יוֹם מוֹתוֹ תְּחַכֶּה־לּוֹ, אִם יָשׁוּב מִיַּד תְּקַבְּלוֹ.
אֱמֶת כִּי אַתָּה הוּא יוֹצְרָם וְיוֹדֵעַ יִצְרָם כִּי הֵם בָּשָׂר
וָדָם.

This is Your glory: You are
slow to anger, ready to forgive.
Lord, it is not the death of sinners You seek,
but that they should turn from their ways
and live.
Until the last day You wait for them,
welcoming them
as soon as they turn to You.

*You have created us and know what we are;
we are but flesh and blood.*

אָדָם יְסוֹדוֹ מֵעָפָר וְסוֹפוֹ לֶעָפָר. בְּנַפְשׁוֹ יָבִיא לַחְמוֹ.
מָשׁוּל כַּחֶרֶס הַנִּשְׁבָּר, כְּחָצִיר יָבֵשׁ וּכְצִיץ נוֹבֵל, כְּצֵל
עוֹבֵר וּכְעָנָן כָּלָה, וּכְרוּחַ נוֹשָׁבֶת, וּכְאָבָק פּוֹרֵחַ,
וְכַחֲלוֹם יָעוּף.

וְאַתָּה הוּא מֶלֶךְ אֵל חַי וְקַיָּם!

Man's origin is dust,
and dust is his end.
Each of us is a shattered urn,
grass that must wither,

109

a flower that will fade,
a shadow moving on,
a cloud passing by,
a particle of dust floating on the wind,
a dream soon forgotten.

But You are the King,
the everlasting God!

All rise

SANCTIFICATION   קדושה

נְקַדֵּשׁ אֶת־שִׁמְךָ בָּעוֹלָם כְּשֵׁם שֶׁמַּקְדִּישִׁים אוֹתוֹ
בִּשְׁמֵי מָרוֹם, כַּכָּתוּב עַל יַד נְבִיאֶךָ, וְקָרָא זֶה אֶל־זֶה
וְאָמַר:

We sanctify Your name on earth, even as all things, to the
ends of time and space, proclaim Your holiness; and in the
words of the prophet we say:

קָדוֹשׁ, קָדוֹשׁ, קָדוֹשׁ יְיָ צְבָאוֹת, מְלֹא כָל־הָאָרֶץ
כְּבוֹדוֹ.

Holy, Holy, Holy is the Lord of Hosts; the fullness of the
whole earth is His glory!

אַדִּיר אַדִּירֵנוּ, יְיָ אֲדוֹנֵינוּ, מָה אַדִּיר שִׁמְךָ בְּכָל־
הָאָרֶץ!

Source of our strength, sovereign Lord, how majestic is
Your presence in all the earth!

בָּרוּךְ כְּבוֹד־יְיָ מִמְּקוֹמוֹ.

Blessed is the glory of God in heaven and earth.

אֶחָד הוּא אֱלֹהֵינוּ, הוּא אָבִינוּ, הוּא מַלְכֵּנוּ, הוּא
מוֹשִׁיעֵנוּ, וְהוּא יַשְׁמִיעֵנוּ בְּרַחֲמָיו לְעֵינֵי כָּל־חָי.

He alone is our God and our Creator; He is our Ruler and
our Helper; and in His mercy He reveals Himself in the
sight of all the living:

I AM ADONAI YOUR GOD!   "אֲנִי יְיָ אֱלֹהֵיכֶם!"

יִמְלֹךְ יְיָ לְעוֹלָם, אֱלֹהַיִךְ צִיּוֹן, לְדֹר וָדֹר. הַלְלוּיָהּ!

*The Lord shall reign for ever; your God, O Zion, from
generation to generation. Halleluyah!*

All are seated

לְדוֹר וָדוֹר נַגִּיד גָּדְלֶךָ, וּלְנֵצַח נְצָחִים קְדֻשָּׁתְךָ
נַקְדִּישׁ. וְשִׁבְחֲךָ, אֱלֹהֵינוּ, מִפִּינוּ לֹא יָמוּשׁ לְעוֹלָם
וָעֶד.

To all generations we will make known Your greatness,
and to all eternity proclaim Your holiness. Your praise, O
God, shall never depart from our lips.

וּבְכֵן תֵּן פַּחְדְּךָ, יְיָ אֱלֹהֵינוּ, עַל כָּל־מַעֲשֶׂיךָ, וְאֵימָתְךָ
עַל כָּל־מַה־שֶּׁבָּרָאתָ. וְיִירָאוּךָ כָּל־הַמַּעֲשִׂים,
וְיִשְׁתַּחֲווּ לְפָנֶיךָ כָּל־הַבְּרוּאִים, וְיֵעָשׂוּ כֻלָּם אֲגֻדָּה
אַחַת לַעֲשׂוֹת רְצוֹנְךָ בְּלֵבָב שָׁלֵם, כְּמוֹ שֶׁיָּדַעְנוּ, יְיָ
אֱלֹהֵינוּ, שֶׁהַשִּׁלְטוֹן לְפָנֶיךָ, עֹז בְּיָדְךָ וּגְבוּרָה בִּימִינֶךָ,
וְשִׁמְךָ נוֹרָא עַל כָּל־מַה־שֶּׁבָּרָאתָ.

*Lord our God, cause all Your works to stand in awe before
You, and all that You have made to tremble at Your
presence. Let all that lives revere You, and all creation turn
to You in worship. Let them all become a single family, doing Your will with a perfect heart. For well we know, O Lord
our God, that Yours is the majesty, Yours the might; and
awesome is Your name in all creation.*

וּבְכֵן תֵּן כָּבוֹד, יְיָ, לְעַמֶּךְ, תְּהִלָּה לִירֵאֶיךָ וְתִקְוָה
לְדוֹרְשֶׁיךָ, וּפִתְחוֹן פֶּה לַמְיַחֲלִים לָךְ, שִׂמְחָה לְאַרְצֶךְ
וְשָׂשׂוֹן לְעִירֶךָ, וּצְמִיחַת קֶרֶן לְכָל־יוֹשְׁבֵי תֵבֵל.

Grant honor, Lord, to Your people, glory to those who
revere You, hope to those who seek You, and courage to
those who trust You; bless Your land with gladness and
Your city with joy, and cause the light of redemption to
dawn for all who dwell on earth.

וּבְכֵן צַדִּיקִים יִרְאוּ וְיִשְׂמָחוּ וִישָׁרִים יַעֲלֹזוּ וַחֲסִידִים
בְּרִנָּה יָגִילוּ, וְעוֹלָתָה תִּקְפָּץ־פִּיהָ וְכָל־הָרִשְׁעָה כֻּלָּהּ
כְּעָשָׁן תִּכְלֶה, כִּי תַעֲבִיר מֶמְשֶׁלֶת זָדוֹן מִן הָאָרֶץ.
וְתִמְלֹךְ אַתָּה, יְיָ, לְבַדֶּךָ עַל כָּל־מַעֲשֶׂיךָ, כַּכָּתוּב
בְּדִבְרֵי קָדְשֶׁךָ:

Then the just shall see and exult, the upright be glad, and the
faithful sing for joy. Violence shall rage no more, and evil
shall vanish like smoke; the rule of tyranny shall pass away
from the earth, and You alone, O Lord, shall have dominion
over all Your works, as it is written:

יִמְלֹךְ יְיָ לְעוֹלָם, אֱלֹהַיִךְ צִיּוֹן, לְדֹר וָדֹר. הַלְלוּיָהּ!

The Lord shall reign for ever; your God, O Zion, from
generation to generation. Halleluyah!

קָדוֹשׁ אַתָּה וְנוֹרָא שְׁמֶךָ, וְאֵין אֱלוֹהַּ מִבַּלְעָדֶיךָ,
כַּכָּתוּב:

You are holy; awesome is Your name; there is no God but
You.

וַיִּגְבַּה יְיָ צְבָאוֹת בַּמִּשְׁפָּט, וְהָאֵל הַקָּדוֹשׁ נִקְדַּשׁ
בִּצְדָקָה.

The Lord of Hosts is exalted by justice; the holy God is
sanctified by righteousness.

בָּרוּךְ אַתָּה, יְיָ, הַמֶּלֶךְ הַקָּדוֹשׁ.

Blessed is the Lord, the holy King.

✦ ✦

THE HOLINESS OF THIS DAY   **קְדוּשַׁת הַיּוֹם**

אַתָּה בְחַרְתָּנוּ מִכָּל־הָעַמִּים, אָהַבְתָּ אוֹתָנוּ וְרָצִיתָ
בָּנוּ, וְרוֹמַמְתָּנוּ מִכָּל־הַלְּשׁוֹנוֹת וְקִדַּשְׁתָּנוּ בְּמִצְוֹתֶיךָ,
וְקֵרַבְתָּנוּ מַלְכֵּנוּ לַעֲבוֹדָתֶךָ, וְשִׁמְךָ הַגָּדוֹל וְהַקָּדוֹשׁ
עָלֵינוּ קָרָאתָ. וַתִּתֶּן־לָנוּ, יְיָ אֱלֹהֵינוּ, בְּאַהֲבָה אֶת־יוֹם
(הַשַּׁבָּת הַזֶּה וְאֶת־יוֹם) הַזִּכָּרוֹן הַזֶּה, יוֹם תְּרוּעָה,
מִקְרָא קֹדֶשׁ, זֵכֶר לִיצִיאַת מִצְרָיִם.

In love and favor, O God, You have chosen us from all
the peoples, hallowing us with Your Mitzvot. Our
Sovereign, You have summoned us to Your service, that
through us Your great and holy name may become known
in all the earth.

In Your love, O God, You have given us this (Sabbath
and this) Day of Remembrance, to hear the sound of the
Shofar, to unite in worship, and to recall the Exodus from
Egypt.

✦

ON SHABBAT

יִשְׂמְחוּ בְמַלְכוּתְךָ שׁוֹמְרֵי שַׁבָּת וְקוֹרְאֵי עֹנֶג. עַם
מְקַדְּשֵׁי שְׁבִיעִי כֻּלָּם יִשְׂבְּעוּ וְיִתְעַנְּגוּ מִטּוּבֶךָ.
וְהַשְּׁבִיעִי רָצִיתָ בּוֹ וְקִדַּשְׁתּוֹ. חֶמְדַּת יָמִים אוֹתוֹ
קָרָאתָ, זֵכֶר לְמַעֲשֵׂה בְרֵאשִׁית.

"Those who keep the Sabbath and call it a delight shall rejoice in Your kingdom. All who hallow the seventh day shall be gladdened by Your goodness. This day is Israel's festival of the spirit, sanctified and blessed by You, the most precious of days, a symbol of the joy of creation.

•

אֱלֹהֵֽינוּ וֵאלֹהֵי אֲבוֹתֵֽינוּ, יַעֲלֶה וְיָבֹא וְיִזָּכֵר זִכְרוֹנֵֽנוּ
וְזִכְרוֹן כָּל־עַמְּךָ בֵּית יִשְׂרָאֵל לְפָנֶֽיךָ, לְטוֹבָה לְחֵן
לְחֶֽסֶד וּלְרַחֲמִים, לְחַיִּים וּלְשָׁלוֹם בְּיוֹם הַזִּכָּרוֹן הַזֶּה.
זָכְרֵֽנוּ, יְיָ אֱלֹהֵֽינוּ, בּוֹ לְטוֹבָה. אָמֵן.
וּפָקְדֵֽנוּ בוֹ לִבְרָכָה. אָמֵן.
וְהוֹשִׁיעֵֽנוּ בוֹ לְחַיִּים. אָמֵן.

Our God and God of all ages, be mindful of Your people Israel on this Day of Remembrance, and renew in us love and compassion, goodness, life, and peace.
This day remember us for well-being. *Amen.*
This day bless us with Your nearness. *Amen.*
This day help us to live. *Amen.*

•

אֱלֹהֵֽינוּ וֵאלֹהֵי אֲבוֹתֵֽינוּ, (רְצֵה בִמְנוּחָתֵֽנוּ,) קַדְּשֵֽׁנוּ
בְּמִצְוֹתֶֽיךָ וְתֵן חֶלְקֵֽנוּ בְּתוֹרָתֶֽךָ. שַׂבְּעֵֽנוּ מִטּוּבֶֽךָ,
וְשַׂמְּחֵֽנוּ בִּישׁוּעָתֶֽךָ, (וְהַנְחִילֵֽנוּ, יְיָ אֱלֹהֵֽינוּ, בְּאַהֲבָה
וּבְרָצוֹן שַׁבַּת קָדְשֶֽׁךָ, וְיָנֽוּחוּ בָהּ יִשְׂרָאֵל, מְקַדְּשֵׁי
שְׁמֶֽךָ,) וְטַהֵר לִבֵּֽנוּ לְעָבְדְּךָ בֶּאֱמֶת, כִּי אַתָּה אֱלֹהִים
אֱמֶת, וּדְבָרְךָ אֱמֶת וְקַיָּם לָעַד. בָּרוּךְ אַתָּה, יְיָ, מֶֽלֶךְ
עַל כָּל־הָאָֽרֶץ, מְקַדֵּשׁ (הַשַּׁבָּת וְ) יִשְׂרָאֵל וְיוֹם
הַזִּכָּרוֹן.

114

Our God and God of our ancestors, sanctify us with Your Mitzvot, and let Your Torah be our way of life. (May our rest on this day be pleasing in Your sight.) Satisfy us with Your goodness, gladden us with Your salvation, and purify our hearts to serve You in truth; for You, O God, are truth, and Your word is true for ever. (In Your gracious love, O Lord our God, let Your holy Sabbath remain our heritage, that all Israel, hallowing Your name, may find rest and peace.) Blessed is the Lord, who hallows (the Sabbath,) the House of Israel and the Day of Remembrance.

◆ ◆

WHOM ALONE WE SERVE IN REVERENCE   עבודה

רְצֵה, יְיָ אֱלֹהֵינוּ, בְּעַמְּךָ יִשְׂרָאֵל, וּתְפִלָּתָם בְּאַהֲבָה
תְקַבֵּל, וּתְהִי לְרָצוֹן תָּמִיד עֲבוֹדַת יִשְׂרָאֵל עַמֶּךָ.
בָּרוּךְ אַתָּה, יְיָ, שֶׁאוֹתְךָ לְבַדְּךָ בְּיִרְאָה נַעֲבוֹד.

Look with favor, O Lord, upon us, and may our service be acceptable to You.

Blessed is the Eternal God, whom alone we serve in reverence.

◆ ◆

TO WHOM OUR THANKS ARE DUE   הודאה

מוֹדִים אֲנַחְנוּ לָךְ, שָׁאַתָּה הוּא יְיָ אֱלֹהֵינוּ וֵאלֹהֵי
אֲבוֹתֵינוּ לְעוֹלָם וָעֶד. צוּר חַיֵּינוּ, מָגֵן יִשְׁעֵנוּ, אַתָּה
הוּא לְדוֹר וָדוֹר.

We gratefully acknowledge, O Lord our God, that You are our Creator and Preserver, the Rock of our life and our protecting Shield.

נוֹדֶה לְךָ וּנְסַפֵּר תְּהִלָּתֶךָ, עַל־חַיֵּינוּ הַמְּסוּרִים בְּיָדֶךָ,
וְעַל־נִשְׁמוֹתֵינוּ הַפְּקוּדוֹת לָךְ, וְעַל־נִסֶּיךָ שֶׁבְּכָל־יוֹם
עִמָּנוּ, וְעַל־נִפְלְאוֹתֶיךָ וְטוֹבוֹתֶיךָ שֶׁבְּכָל־עֵת, עֶרֶב
וָבְקֶר וְצָהֳרָיִם. הַטּוֹב: כִּי לֹא־כָלוּ רַחֲמֶיךָ, וְהַמְרַחֵם:
כִּי־לֹא תַמּוּ חֲסָדֶיךָ, מֵעוֹלָם קִוִּינוּ לָךְ.
וּכְתֹב לְחַיִּים טוֹבִים כָּל־בְּנֵי בְרִיתֶךָ. בָּרוּךְ אַתָּה, יְיָ,
הַטּוֹב שִׁמְךָ, וּלְךָ נָאֶה לְהוֹדוֹת.

*We give thanks to You for our lives which are in Your hand,
for our souls which are ever in Your keeping, for Your
wondrous providence and Your continuous goodness, which
You bestow upon us day by day. Truly, Your mercies never
fail, and Your love and kindness never cease. Therefore do
we forever put our trust in You.*

✦ ✦

ברכת שלום

אֱלֹהֵינוּ וֵאלֹהֵי אֲבוֹתֵינוּ, בָּרְכֵנוּ בַּבְּרָכָה הַמְשֻׁלֶּשֶׁת
הַכְּתוּבָה בַּתּוֹרָה:

Our God and God of all generations, bless us with the
threefold benediction of the Torah:

יְבָרֶכְךָ יְיָ וְיִשְׁמְרֶךָ.

May the Lord bless you and keep you.

כֵּן יְהִי רָצוֹן!

Be this God's will!

יָאֵר יְיָ פָּנָיו אֵלֶיךָ וִיחֻנֶּךָּ.

May the light of the Lord's presence shine upon you and
be gracious to you.

כֵּן יְהִי רָצוֹן!

Be this God's will!

116

יִשָּׂא יְיָ פָּנָיו אֵלֶיךָ וְיָשֵׂם לְךָ שָׁלוֹם.

May the Lord bestow favor upon you and give you peace.

כֵּן יְהִי רָצוֹן!

Be this God's will!

שִׂים שָׁלוֹם, טוֹבָה וּבְרָכָה, חֵן וָחֶסֶד וְרַחֲמִים, עָלֵינוּ
וְעַל כָּל־יִשְׂרָאֵל עַמֶּךָ. בָּרְכֵנוּ אָבִינוּ, כֻּלָּנוּ כְּאֶחָד,
בְּאוֹר פָּנֶיךָ, כִּי בְאוֹר פָּנֶיךָ נָתַתָּ לָּנוּ, יְיָ אֱלֹהֵינוּ,
תּוֹרַת חַיִּים, וְאַהֲבַת חֶסֶד, וּצְדָקָה וּבְרָכָה וְרַחֲמִים,
וְחַיִּים וְשָׁלוֹם. וְטוֹב בְּעֵינֶיךָ לְבָרֵךְ אֶת־עַמְּךָ יִשְׂרָאֵל
בְּכָל־עֵת וּבְכָל־שָׁעָה בִּשְׁלוֹמֶךָ. בְּסֵפֶר חַיִּים בְּרָכָה
וְשָׁלוֹם וּפַרְנָסָה טוֹבָה נִזָּכֵר וְנִכָּתֵב לְפָנֶיךָ, אֲנַחְנוּ
וְכָל־עַמְּךָ בֵּית יִשְׂרָאֵל, לְחַיִּים טוֹבִים וּלְשָׁלוֹם. בָּרוּךְ
אַתָּה, יְיָ, עוֹשֵׂה הַשָּׁלוֹם.

°*Grant peace and happiness, blessing and mercy, to all Israel
and all the world. Bless us, our God, all of us together, with
the light of Your presence, for in the light of Your presence
we have found a teaching of life, the love of mercy, the law of
justice, and the way of peace: for it is ever Your will that
Your people Israel be blessed with peace.*

*Teach us, O God, to labor for righteousness, and inscribe us
in the Book of life, blessing, and peace.*

Blessed is the Lord, the Source of peace.

✦ ✦

117

MEDITATION

We pause in reverence before the gift of self:
The vessel shatters, the divine spark shines through,
And our solitary self becomes a link
    in Israel's golden chain.
For what we are, we are by sharing. And as we share
We move toward the light.

We pause in reverence before the mystery of a presence:
The near and far reality of God.
Not union, but communion is our aim.
And we approach the mystery
With deeds. Words lead us to the edge of action.
But it is deeds that bring us closer to the God of light.

We pause in terror before the human deed:
The cloud of annihilation, the concentrations for death,
The cruelly casual way of each to each.
But in the stillness of this hour
We find our way from darkness into light.

May we find our life so precious
That we cannot but share it with the other,
That light may shine brighter than a thousand suns,
With the presence among us of the God of light.

◆ ◆

יִהְיוּ לְרָצוֹן אִמְרֵי־פִי וְהֶגְיוֹן לִבִּי לְפָנֶיךָ, יְיָ, צוּרִי
וְגוֹאֲלִי.

May the words of my mouth, and the meditations of my heart,
be acceptable to You, O Lord, my Rock and my Redeemer.

or

עֹשֶׂה שָׁלוֹם בִּמְרוֹמָיו, הוּא יַעֲשֶׂה שָׁלוֹם עָלֵינוּ וְעַל כָּל־יִשְׂרָאֵל, וְאִמְרוּ אָמֵן.

May the One who causes peace to reign in the high heavens let peace descend on us, on all Israel, and all the world.

❖ ❖

סדר קריאת התורה

For the Reading of the Torah

אֵין כָּמְוֹךָ בָאֱלֹהִים, יְיָ, וְאֵין כְּמַעֲשֶׂיךָ. מַלְכוּתְךָ
מַלְכוּת כָּל־עוֹלָמִים וּמֶמְשַׁלְתְּךָ בְּכָל־דּוֹר וָדֹר.

There is none like You, O Lord, among the gods that are
worshipped, and there are no deeds like Yours. Your
kingdom is an everlasting kingdom, and Your dominion
endures through all generations.

יְיָ מֶלֶךְ, יְיָ מָלָךְ, יְיָ יִמְלֹךְ לְעוֹלָם וָעֶד. יְיָ עֹז לְעַמּוֹ
יִתֵּן, יְיָ יְבָרֵךְ אֶת־עַמּוֹ בַשָּׁלוֹם.

*The Lord rules; the Lord will reign for ever and ever. Lord,
give strength to Your people; Lord, bless Your people with
peace.*

◆ ◆

*All rise
The Ark is opened*

Avinu, Malkeinu: A hundred generations have stood as we
do now before the open Ark. That they found in
themselves little merit, testifies to their humility. They
repented and amended their ways. They fell, only to rise
again, as they climbed toward the Light. Strong was the
faith of those who stood here before us, while we are of a
generation that has sought to dethrone You.

Many have said to the works of their hands: you are our
gods. Strange, then, to see the emptiness in those who cast
You out! Strange to see the agonies of our time grow more
numerous and more intense, the more our worship centers
on ourselves. Strange that men and women grow smaller
without You, smaller without the faith that You are with

them. We pray, therefore, that this day which yet restores Your people, may help us come close to You, the living God, the God of life. For You are with us whenever we seek Your presence, You are absent only when we shut You out, only when, full of ourselves, we leave no room for You within our hearts.

We call you *Avinu.* As a loving parent, forgive our sins and failings, and reach for us as we reach for You. We call You *Malkeinu.* As a wise ruler, teach us to add our strength to Your love, that we may redeem this world and build Your Kingdom.

To this vision, to this possibility, to this task, we offer ourselves anew.

◆

אבינו מלכנו

אָבִינוּ מַלְכֵּנוּ, שְׁמַע קוֹלֵנוּ.

Our Father, our King, hear our voice.

אָבִינוּ מַלְכֵּנוּ, חָטָאנוּ לְפָנֶיךָ.

Our Father, our King, we have sinned against You.

אָבִינוּ מַלְכֵּנוּ, חֲמוֹל עָלֵינוּ וְעַל עוֹלָלֵינוּ וְטַפֵּנוּ.

Our Father, our King, have compassion on us and on our children.

אָבִינוּ מַלְכֵּנוּ, כַּלֵּה דֶּבֶר וְחֶרֶב וְרָעָב מֵעָלֵינוּ.

Our Father, our King, make an end to sickness, war, and famine.

אָבִינוּ מַלְכֵּנוּ, כַּלֵּה כָּל־צַר וּמַשְׂטִין מֵעָלֵינוּ.

Our Father, our King, make an end to all oppression.

121

אָבִֽינוּ מַלְכֵּֽנוּ, כָּתְבֵֽנוּ בְּסֵֽפֶר חַיִּים טוֹבִים.

Our Father, our King, inscribe us for blessing in the Book of Life.

אָבִֽינוּ מַלְכֵּֽנוּ, חַדֵּשׁ עָלֵֽינוּ שָׁנָה טוֹבָה.

Our Father, our King, let the new year be a good year for us.

אָבִֽינוּ מַלְכֵּֽנוּ, מַלֵּא יָדֵֽינוּ מִבִּרְכוֹתֶֽיךָ.

Our Father, our King, fill our hands with blessing.

אָבִֽינוּ מַלְכֵּֽנוּ, חָנֵּֽנוּ וַעֲנֵֽנוּ, כִּי אֵין בָּֽנוּ מַעֲשִׂים,
עֲשֵׂה עִמָּֽנוּ צְדָקָה וָחֶֽסֶד וְהוֹשִׁיעֵֽנוּ.

Our Father, our King, be gracious and answer us, for we have little merit. Treat us generously and with kindness, and be our help.

◆ ◆

יְיָ, יְיָ אֵל רַחוּם וְחַנּוּן, אֶֽרֶךְ אַפַּֽיִם וְרַב־חֶֽסֶד וֶאֱמֶת,
נוֹצֵר חֶֽסֶד לָאֲלָפִים, נֹשֵׂא עָוֹן וָפֶֽשַׁע וְחַטָּאָה וְנַקֵּה.

The Lord, the Lord God is merciful and gracious, endlessly patient, loving, and true, showing mercy to thousands,
forgiving iniquity, transgression, and sin, and granting
pardon.

◆ ◆

The Torah is taken from the Ark

בֵּית יַעֲקֹב: לְכוּ, וְנֵלְכָה בְּאוֹר יְיָ.

O House of Jacob: come, let us walk by the light of the
Lord.

◆ ◆

בָּרוּךְ שֶׁנָּתַן תּוֹרָה לְעַמּוֹ יִשְׂרָאֵל בִּקְדֻשָּׁתוֹ.

Praised be the One who in His holiness has given the Torah to
His people Israel.

◆ ◆

שְׁמַע יִשְׂרָאֵל: יְיָ אֱלֹהֵינוּ, יְיָ אֶחָד!

Hear, O Israel; the Lord is our God, the Lord is One!

אֶחָד אֱלֹהֵינוּ, גָּדוֹל אֲדוֹנֵינוּ, קָדוֹשׁ וְנוֹרָא שְׁמוֹ.

Our God is One; our Lord is great; holy and awesome is His
name.

◆ ◆

לְךָ, יְיָ, הַגְּדֻלָּה וְהַגְּבוּרָה וְהַתִּפְאֶרֶת וְהַנֵּצַח וְהַהוֹד,
כִּי כֹל בַּשָּׁמַיִם וּבָאָרֶץ, לְךָ יְיָ הַמַּמְלָכָה וְהַמִּתְנַשֵּׂא
לְכֹל לְרֹאשׁ.

Yours, Lord, is the greatness, the power, the glory, the victory,
and the majesty: for all that is in heaven and earth is Yours.
Yours is the kingdom, O Lord: You are supreme over all.

All are seated

◆ ◆

123

Reading of the Torah

Before the Reading

בָּרְכוּ אֶת־יְיָ הַמְבֹרָךְ!
בָּרוּךְ יְיָ הַמְבֹרָךְ לְעוֹלָם וָעֶד!
בָּרוּךְ אַתָּה, יְיָ אֱלֹהֵינוּ, מֶלֶךְ הָעוֹלָם, אֲשֶׁר בָּחַר־בָּנוּ
מִכָּל־הָעַמִּים וְנָתַן־לָנוּ אֶת־תּוֹרָתוֹ. בָּרוּךְ אַתָּה, יְיָ,
נוֹתֵן הַתּוֹרָה.

• •

Another reading from the Torah is on page 192.

Genesis 22.1—19

וַיְהִי אַחַר הַדְּבָרִים הָאֵלֶּה וְהָאֱלֹהִים נִסָּה אֶת־אַבְרָהָם וַיֹּאמֶר
אֵלָיו אַבְרָהָם וַיֹּאמֶר הִנֵּנִי: וַיֹּאמֶר קַח־נָא אֶת־בִּנְךָ אֶת־
יְחִידְךָ אֲשֶׁר־אָהַבְתָּ אֶת־יִצְחָק וְלֶךְ־לְךָ אֶל־אֶרֶץ הַמֹּרִיָּה
וְהַעֲלֵהוּ שָׁם לְעֹלָה עַל אַחַד הֶהָרִים אֲשֶׁר אֹמַר אֵלֶיךָ: וַיַּשְׁכֵּם
אַבְרָהָם בַּבֹּקֶר וַיַּחֲבֹשׁ אֶת־חֲמֹרוֹ וַיִּקַּח אֶת־שְׁנֵי נְעָרָיו אִתּוֹ
וְאֵת יִצְחָק בְּנוֹ וַיְבַקַּע עֲצֵי עֹלָה וַיָּקָם וַיֵּלֶךְ אֶל־הַמָּקוֹם אֲשֶׁר־
אָמַר־לוֹ הָאֱלֹהִים: בַּיּוֹם הַשְּׁלִישִׁי וַיִּשָּׂא אַבְרָהָם אֶת־עֵינָיו
וַיַּרְא אֶת־הַמָּקוֹם מֵרָחֹק: וַיֹּאמֶר אַבְרָהָם אֶל־נְעָרָיו שְׁבוּ־לָכֶם
פֹּה עִם־הַחֲמוֹר וַאֲנִי וְהַנַּעַר נֵלְכָה עַד־כֹּה וְנִשְׁתַּחֲוֶה וְנָשׁוּבָה
אֲלֵיכֶם: וַיִּקַּח אַבְרָהָם אֶת־עֲצֵי הָעֹלָה וַיָּשֶׂם עַל־יִצְחָק בְּנוֹ
וַיִּקַּח בְּיָדוֹ אֶת־הָאֵשׁ וְאֶת־הַמַּאֲכֶלֶת וַיֵּלְכוּ שְׁנֵיהֶם יַחְדָּו:
וַיֹּאמֶר יִצְחָק אֶל־אַבְרָהָם אָבִיו וַיֹּאמֶר אָבִי וַיֹּאמֶר הִנֶּנִּי בְנִי
וַיֹּאמֶר הִנֵּה הָאֵשׁ וְהָעֵצִים וְאַיֵּה הַשֶּׂה לְעֹלָה: וַיֹּאמֶר אַבְרָהָם

Reading of the Torah

Before the Reading

Praise the Lord, to whom our praise is due!
Praised be the Lord, to whom our praise is due,
now and for ever!

Praised be the Lord our God, Ruler of the universe, who
has chosen us from all peoples by giving us His Torah.
Blessed is the Lord, Giver of the Torah.

◆ ◆

Another reading from the Torah is on page 193.

Genesis 22.1—19

There came a time when God put Abraham to the
test.'Abraham!', God said to him, and he answered: 'Here
I am.' Then God said: 'Take your son, your precious one,
Isaac, whom you love, and go to the land of Moriah; there
you shall offer him up as a burnt offering on one of the
hills that I will point out to you.' Early next morning,
Abraham, having first split wood for the burnt offering,
saddled his donkey, took with him two of his servants and
his son Isaac, and set out for the place of which God had
told him. On the third day, as he looked up, Abraham saw
the place from afar. He said to his lads: 'Stay here with the
donkey while I and the boy go up to worship; then we will
return to you.' Abraham took the wood for the sacrifice,
and laid it on Isaac, his son. He himself carried the
firestone and the knife; and the two walked on together.

Then Isaac broke the silence and said to his father
Abraham: 'Father!' And he said: 'Here I am, my son.'
And he said: 'I see the firestone and the wood; but where

אֱלֹהִים יִרְאֶה־לּוֹ הַשֶּׂה לְעֹלָה בְּנִי וַיֵּלְכוּ שְׁנֵיהֶם יַחְדָּו: וַיָּבֹאוּ
אֶל־הַמָּקוֹם אֲשֶׁר אָמַר־לוֹ הָאֱלֹהִים וַיִּבֶן שָׁם אַבְרָהָם אֶת־
הַמִּזְבֵּחַ וַיַּעֲרֹךְ אֶת־הָעֵצִים וַיַּעֲקֹד אֶת־יִצְחָק בְּנוֹ וַיָּשֶׂם אֹתוֹ
עַל־הַמִּזְבֵּחַ מִמַּעַל לָעֵצִים: וַיִּשְׁלַח אַבְרָהָם אֶת־יָדוֹ וַיִּקַּח
אֶת־הַמַּאֲכֶלֶת לִשְׁחֹט אֶת־בְּנוֹ: וַיִּקְרָא אֵלָיו מַלְאַךְ יהוה
מִן־הַשָּׁמַיִם וַיֹּאמֶר אַבְרָהָם ׀ אַבְרָהָם וַיֹּאמֶר הִנֵּנִי: וַיֹּאמֶר אַל־
תִּשְׁלַח יָדְךָ אֶל־הַנַּעַר וְאַל־תַּעַשׂ לוֹ מְאוּמָה כִּי ׀ עַתָּה יָדַעְתִּי
כִּי־יְרֵא אֱלֹהִים אַתָּה וְלֹא חָשַׂכְתָּ אֶת־בִּנְךָ אֶת־יְחִידְךָ מִמֶּנִּי:
וַיִּשָּׂא אַבְרָהָם אֶת־עֵינָיו וַיַּרְא וְהִנֵּה־אַיִל אַחַר נֶאֱחַז בַּסְּבַךְ
בְּקַרְנָיו וַיֵּלֶךְ אַבְרָהָם וַיִּקַּח אֶת־הָאַיִל וַיַּעֲלֵהוּ לְעֹלָה תַּחַת
בְּנוֹ: וַיִּקְרָא אַבְרָהָם שֵׁם־הַמָּקוֹם הַהוּא יהוה ׀ יִרְאֶה אֲשֶׁר
יֵאָמֵר הַיּוֹם בְּהַר יהוה יֵרָאֶה: וַיִּקְרָא מַלְאַךְ יהוה אֶל־אַבְרָהָם
שֵׁנִית מִן־הַשָּׁמַיִם: וַיֹּאמֶר בִּי נִשְׁבַּעְתִּי נְאֻם־יהוה כִּי יַעַן אֲשֶׁר
עָשִׂיתָ אֶת־הַדָּבָר הַזֶּה וְלֹא חָשַׂכְתָּ אֶת־בִּנְךָ אֶת־יְחִידֶךָ: כִּי־
בָרֵךְ אֲבָרֶכְךָ וְהַרְבָּה אַרְבֶּה אֶת־זַרְעֲךָ כְּכוֹכְבֵי הַשָּׁמַיִם וְכַחוֹל
אֲשֶׁר עַל־שְׂפַת הַיָּם וְיִרַשׁ זַרְעֲךָ אֵת שַׁעַר אֹיְבָיו: וְהִתְבָּרֲכוּ
בְזַרְעֲךָ כֹּל גּוֹיֵי הָאָרֶץ עֵקֶב אֲשֶׁר שָׁמַעְתָּ בְּקֹלִי: וַיָּשָׁב אַבְרָהָם
אֶל־נְעָרָיו וַיָּקֻמוּ וַיֵּלְכוּ יַחְדָּו אֶל־בְּאֵר שָׁבַע וַיֵּשֶׁב אַבְרָהָם
בִּבְאֵר שָׁבַע:

∴

is the lamb for the burnt offering?' Abraham replied: 'God will see to the lamb for the burnt offering, my son.' And the two walked on together.

They came to the place of which God had told him. Abraham built an altar there. He laid on the wood. He tied up his son Isaac. He laid him on the altar on top of the wood. He reached for the knife to slay his son. But an angel of the Lord called to him from heaven: 'Abraham, Abraham!' 'Here I am,' he answered. And the angel said: 'Do not raise your hand against the boy, nor do the least thing to him; for now I know you stand in awe of God, since you did not withhold from Me your own son, your precious one.'

As Abraham looked up, his eye fell upon a ram caught in the thicket by its horns. So he went and took the ram and offered it as a burnt offering in place of his son. And Abraham named that place 'The Lord Sees;' as it is said to this day: 'On the mountain of the Lord there is vision.'

The angel of the Lord called to Abraham out of heaven a second time and said: 'By Myself do I swear, says the Lord, that because you have done this, and did not withhold your son, your precious one, from Me, I will bless you greatly, and make your descendants as numerous as the stars of heaven and the sands of the seashore; and your descendants shall come to possess the gates of your enemies. All the nations of the earth shall be blessed through your descendants, because you obeyed My command.'

Abraham then returned to his servants, and they left together for Beer-sheba. And Abraham stayed in Beer-sheba.

◆ ◆

After the Reading

בָּרוּךְ אַתָּה, יְיָ אֱלֹהֵינוּ, מֶלֶךְ הָעוֹלָם, אֲשֶׁר נָתַן לָנוּ
תּוֹרַת אֱמֶת וְחַיֵּי עוֹלָם נָטַע בְּתוֹכֵנוּ. בָּרוּךְ אַתָּה, יְיָ,
נוֹתֵן הַתּוֹרָה.

As the reading is completed, the Torah might be held high
while this is said or sung:

וְזֹאת הַתּוֹרָה אֲשֶׁר־שָׂם מֹשֶׁה לִפְנֵי בְּנֵי יִשְׂרָאֵל, עַל־
פִּי יְיָ בְּיַד־מֹשֶׁה.

◆◆

Reading of the Haftarah

Before the Reading

בָּרוּךְ אַתָּה, יְיָ אֱלֹהֵינוּ, מֶלֶךְ הָעוֹלָם, אֲשֶׁר בָּחַר
בִּנְבִיאִים טוֹבִים וְרָצָה בְדִבְרֵיהֶם הַנֶּאֱמָרִים בֶּאֱמֶת.
בָּרוּךְ אַתָּה, יְיָ, הַבּוֹחֵר בַּתּוֹרָה וּבְמֹשֶׁה עַבְדּוֹ
וּבְיִשְׂרָאֵל עַמּוֹ וּבִנְבִיאֵי הָאֱמֶת וָצֶדֶק.

An alternative Haftarah is on page 132.

From First Samuel 1

וַיְהִי אִישׁ אֶחָד מִן־הָרָמָתַיִם צוֹפִים מֵהַר אֶפְרָיִם וּשְׁמוֹ אֶלְקָנָה
בֶּן־יְרֹחָם בֶּן־אֱלִיהוּא בֶּן־תֹּחוּ בֶן־צוּף אֶפְרָתִי: וְלוֹ שְׁתֵּי נָשִׁים
שֵׁם אַחַת חַנָּה וְשֵׁם הַשֵּׁנִית פְּנִנָּה וַיְהִי לִפְנִנָּה יְלָדִים וּלְחַנָּה
אֵין יְלָדִים: וְעָלָה הָאִישׁ הַהוּא מֵעִירוֹ מִיָּמִים וְיָמִימָה
לְהִשְׁתַּחֲוֹת וְלִזְבֹּחַ לַיהוָה צְבָאוֹת בְּשִׁלֹה וְשָׁם שְׁנֵי בְנֵי־עֵלִי
חָפְנִי וּפִנְחָס כֹּהֲנִים לַיהוָה: וַיְהִי הַיּוֹם וַיִּזְבַּח אֶלְקָנָה וְנָתַן

After the Reading

Praised be the Lord our God, Ruler of the universe, who has given us a Torah of truth, implanting within us eternal life. Blessed is the Lord, Giver of the Torah.

◆ ◆

As the reading is completed, the Torah might be held high while this is said or sung:

This is the Torah that Moses placed before the people of Israel to fulfill the word of God.

◆ ◆

Reading of the Haftarah

Before the Reading

Praised be the Lord our God, Ruler of the universe, who has chosen faithful prophets to speak words of truth. Blessed is the Lord, for the revelation of Torah, for Moses His servant and Israel His people, and for the prophets of truth and righteousness.

An alternative Haftarah is on page 133.

From First Samuel 1

There was a man from Ramatayim, a Zuphite from the highlands of Ephraim, whose name was Elkanah son of Yerucham. He had two wives, one named Hannah and the other Peninah. Peninah had children, but Hannah had none. This man used to go up from his town annually to worship and to offer sacrifice to the Lord of Hosts in Shiloh. There, Eli's two sons, Chofni and Pinchas, were priests of the Lord. When Elkanah offered a sacrifice, he

לִפְנִנָּה אִשְׁתּוֹ וּלְכָל־בָּנֶיהָ וּבְנוֹתֶיהָ מָנוֹת: וּלְחַנָּה יִתֵּן מָנָה
אַחַת אַפָּיִם כִּי אֶת־חַנָּה אָהֵב וַיהוָה סָגַר רַחְמָהּ:
וַתָּקָם חַנָּה אַחֲרֵי אָכְלָה בְשִׁלֹה וְאַחֲרֵי
שָׁתֹה וְעֵלִי הַכֹּהֵן יֹשֵׁב עַל־הַכִּסֵּא עַל־מְזוּזַת הֵיכַל יְהוָה: וְהִיא
מָרַת נָפֶשׁ וַתִּתְפַּלֵּל עַל־יְהוָה וּבָכֹה תִבְכֶּה: וַתִּדֹּר נֶדֶר וַתֹּאמַר
יְהוָה צְבָאוֹת אִם־רָאֹה תִרְאֶה ׀ בָּעֳנִי אֲמָתֶךָ וּזְכַרְתַּנִי וְלֹא־
תִשְׁכַּח אֶת־אֲמָתֶךָ וְנָתַתָּה לַאֲמָתְךָ זֶרַע אֲנָשִׁים וּנְתַתִּיו
לַיהוָה כָּל־יְמֵי חַיָּיו וּמוֹרָה לֹא־יַעֲלֶה עַל־רֹאשׁוֹ: וְהָיָה כִּי
הִרְבְּתָה לְהִתְפַּלֵּל לִפְנֵי יְהוָה וְעֵלִי שֹׁמֵר אֶת־פִּיהָ: וְחַנָּה הִיא
מְדַבֶּרֶת עַל־לִבָּהּ רַק שְׂפָתֶיהָ נָּעוֹת וְקוֹלָהּ לֹא יִשָּׁמֵעַ וַיַּחְשְׁבֶהָ
עֵלִי לְשִׁכֹּרָה: וַיֹּאמֶר אֵלֶיהָ עֵלִי עַד־מָתַי תִּשְׁתַּכָּרִין הָסִירִי
אֶת־יֵינֵךְ מֵעָלָיִךְ: וַתַּעַן חַנָּה וַתֹּאמֶר לֹא אֲדֹנִי אִשָּׁה קְשַׁת־
רוּחַ אָנֹכִי וְיַיִן וְשֵׁכָר לֹא שָׁתִיתִי וָאֶשְׁפֹּךְ אֶת־נַפְשִׁי לִפְנֵי יְהוָה:
אַל־תִּתֵּן אֶת־אֲמָתְךָ לִפְנֵי בַּת־בְּלִיָּעַל כִּי־מֵרֹב שִׂיחִי וְכַעְסִי
דִּבַּרְתִּי עַד־הֵנָּה: וַיַּעַן עֵלִי וַיֹּאמֶר לְכִי לְשָׁלוֹם וֵאלֹהֵי יִשְׂרָאֵל
יִתֵּן אֶת־שֵׁלָתֵךְ אֲשֶׁר שָׁאַלְתְּ מֵעִמּוֹ: וַתֹּאמֶר תִּמְצָא שִׁפְחָתְךָ
חֵן בְּעֵינֶיךָ וַתֵּלֶךְ הָאִשָּׁה לְדַרְכָּהּ וַתֹּאכַל וּפָנֶיהָ לֹא־הָיוּ־לָהּ
עוֹד: וַיַּשְׁכִּמוּ בַבֹּקֶר וַיִּשְׁתַּחֲווּ לִפְנֵי יְהוָה וַיָּשֻׁבוּ וַיָּבֹאוּ אֶל־
בֵּיתָם הָרָמָתָה וַיֵּדַע אֶלְקָנָה אֶת־חַנָּה אִשְׁתּוֹ וַיִּזְכְּרֶהָ יְהוָה:
וַיְהִי לִתְקֻפוֹת הַיָּמִים וַתַּהַר חַנָּה וַתֵּלֶד בֵּן וַתִּקְרָא אֶת־שְׁמוֹ
שְׁמוּאֵל כִּי מֵיהוָה שְׁאִלְתִּיו: וַיַּעַל הָאִישׁ אֶלְקָנָה וְכָל־בֵּיתוֹ
לִזְבֹּחַ לַיהוָה אֶת־זֶבַח הַיָּמִים וְאֶת־נִדְרוֹ: וְחַנָּה לֹא עָלָתָה כִּי־
אָמְרָה לְאִישָׁהּ עַד יִגָּמֵל הַנַּעַר וַהֲבִאֹתִיו וְנִרְאָה אֶת־פְּנֵי יְהוָה
וְיָשַׁב שָׁם עַד־עוֹלָם: וַיֹּאמֶר לָהּ אֶלְקָנָה אִישָׁהּ עֲשִׂי הַטּוֹב
בְּעֵינַיִךְ שְׁבִי עַד־גָּמְלֵךְ אֹתוֹ אַךְ יָקֵם יְהוָה אֶת־דְּבָרוֹ וַתֵּשֶׁב

would give portions to Peninah his wife and to each of her sons and daughters; but, although he loved her, he would give to Hannah only one portion, since the Lord had made her barren. Her rival would torment her about her misfortune, that the Lord had made her barren. This went on year by year; when they went up to the house of the Lord, her rival would so torment her that she would weep and not eat. Elkanah would say to her: 'Hannah, why do you weep? Why don't you eat? Why are you so unhappy? Am I not dearer to you than ten sons?'

Once Hannah rose after they had eaten in Shiloh and went to the temple of the Lord, at whose entrance was sitting Eli the priest. In bitter grief she prayed to the Lord, weeping copious tears. She took a vow, saying: 'Lord of Hosts, if You take notice of Your servant's affliction, if You keep me in mind and do not forget Your servant, giving Your servant a son, I will dedicate him to the Lord for life . . . .'

As she continued to pray before the Lord, Eli's attention was drawn to her lips. Hannah was praying silently; though her lips were moving, she made no sound, so that Eli took her for a drunkard. Eli said to her: 'How long do you propose to carry on drunk like this! Get rid of your wine!' 'You mistake me, my lord,' Hannah replied. 'I am a sober woman; I have had neither wine nor liquor, but have been pouring out my heart before the Lord. Do not think your servant so debased. All this time I have been speaking out of my great sorrow and grief.' Then Eli replied: 'Go in peace; and may the God of Israel grant your request.' 'May your humble servant always find favor with you,' she said. So the woman went on her way. She ate, and was downcast no longer.

Early in the morning they arose, worshipped before the Lord, and returned to their home in Ramah. Then the Lord was mindful of her. In due time, Hannah conceived

הָאִשָּׁה וַתֵּינֶק אֶת־בְּנָהּ עַד־גָּמְלָהּ אֹתוֹ: וַתַּעֲלֵהוּ עִמָּהּ כַּאֲשֶׁר
גְּמָלַתּוּ בְּפָרִים שְׁלֹשָׁה וְאֵיפָה אַחַת קֶמַח וְנֵבֶל יַיִן וַתְּבִאֵהוּ
בֵית־יְהוָה שִׁלוֹ וְהַנַּעַר נָעַר: וַיִּשְׁחֲטוּ אֶת־הַפָּר וַיָּבִיאוּ אֶת־
הַנַּעַר אֶל־עֵלִי: וַתֹּאמֶר בִּי אֲדֹנִי חֵי נַפְשְׁךָ אֲדֹנִי אֲנִי הָאִשָּׁה
הַנִּצֶּבֶת עִמְּכָה בָּזֶה לְהִתְפַּלֵּל אֶל־יְהוָה: אֶל־הַנַּעַר הַזֶּה
הִתְפַּלָּלְתִּי וַיִּתֵּן יְהוָה לִי אֶת־שְׁאֵלָתִי אֲשֶׁר שָׁאַלְתִּי מֵעִמּוֹ:
וְגַם אָנֹכִי הִשְׁאִלְתִּהוּ לַיהוָה כָּל־הַיָּמִים אֲשֶׁר הָיָה הוּא שָׁאוּל
לַיהוָה וַיִּשְׁתַּחוּ שָׁם לַיהוָה:

The benediction after the Haftarah is on page 134.

An alternative Haftarah

From Nehemiah 8

וַיַּגַּע הַחֹדֶשׁ הַשְּׁבִיעִי וּבְנֵי יִשְׂרָאֵל בְּעָרֵיהֶם:
וַיֵּאָסְפוּ כָל־הָעָם כְּאִישׁ אֶחָד אֶל־הָרְחוֹב אֲשֶׁר לִפְנֵי שַׁעַר־
הַמָּיִם וַיֹּאמְרוּ לְעֶזְרָא הַסֹּפֵר לְהָבִיא אֶת־סֵפֶר תּוֹרַת מֹשֶׁה
אֲשֶׁר־צִוָּה יְהוָה אֶת־יִשְׂרָאֵל: וַיָּבִיא עֶזְרָא הַכֹּהֵן אֶת־הַתּוֹרָה
לִפְנֵי הַקָּהָל מֵאִישׁ וְעַד־אִשָּׁה וְכֹל מֵבִין לִשְׁמֹעַ בְּיוֹם אֶחָד
לַחֹדֶשׁ הַשְּׁבִיעִי: וַיִּקְרָא־בוֹ לִפְנֵי הָרְחוֹב אֲשֶׁר לִפְנֵי שַׁעַר־
הַמַּיִם מִן־הָאוֹר עַד־מַחֲצִית הַיּוֹם נֶגֶד הָאֲנָשִׁים וְהַנָּשִׁים
וְהַמְּבִינִים וְאָזְנֵי כָל־הָעָם אֶל־סֵפֶר הַתּוֹרָה:
וַיֹּאמֶר נְחֶמְיָה הוּא
הַתִּרְשָׁתָא וְעֶזְרָא הַכֹּהֵן הַסֹּפֵר וְהַלְוִיִּם הַמְּבִינִים אֶת־הָעָם
לְכָל־הָעָם הַיּוֹם קָדֹשׁ־הוּא לַיהוָה אֱלֹהֵיכֶם אַל־תִּתְאַבְּלוּ
וְאַל־תִּבְכּוּ כִּי בוֹכִים כָּל־הָעָם כְּשָׁמְעָם אֶת־דִּבְרֵי הַתּוֹרָה:
וַיֹּאמֶר לָהֶם לְכוּ אִכְלוּ מַשְׁמַנִּים וּשְׁתוּ מַמְתַּקִּים וְשִׁלְחוּ

and gave birth to a son, whom she named Samuel, saying: 'I asked him of the Lord (and was heard).'

When she had weaned him, she brought him up to the house of the Lord at Shiloh, together with a three-year-old bull, an ephah of meal, and a skin of wine, though he was still but a child. They slaughtered the bull, and brought the lad to Eli. Then she said: 'O my lord, I am the woman who stood near you right here, praying to the Lord. It was for this lad that I prayed, and the Lord has granted my request. I therefore dedicate him to the Lord. So long as he lives he is dedicated to the Lord.' And they worshipped the Lord there.

The benediction after the Haftarah is on page 135.

An alternative Haftarah

From Nehemiah 8

At the coming of the seventh month, when the people of Israel were in their towns, all the people gathered as one body in the square in front of the Water Gate. They asked Ezra the scribe to bring the book of the Law of Moses which the Lord had enjoined upon Israel. On the first day of the seventh month, Ezra the priest brought the Law before the assembly, both men and women, and all who could understand; and he read from it, facing the square in front of the Water Gate, from early morning till noon. . . . Then Nehemiah the governor, and Ezra the priestly scribe, and the Levites who taught the people, said to them: 'This day is holy to the Lord your God; do not mourn or weep.' For all the people had been weeping when they heard the words of the Law. Then he said to them: 'Go now, eat of the best, drink sweet wine, and send portions to those for whom nothing is prepared; for this

מָנוֹת לְאֵין נָכוֹן לוֹ כִּי־קָדוֹשׁ הַיּוֹם לַאֲדֹנֵינוּ וְאַל־תֵּעָצֵבוּ כִּי־חֶדְוַת יהוה הִיא מָעֻזְּכֶם:

: :

After the Reading

An alternative version of this Benediction follows below

בָּרוּךְ אַתָּה, יְיָ אֱלֹהֵינוּ, מֶלֶךְ הָעוֹלָם, צוּר כָּל־הָעוֹלָמִים, צַדִּיק בְּכָל־הַדּוֹרוֹת, הָאֵל הַנֶּאֱמָן, הָאוֹמֵר וְעוֹשֶׂה, הַמְדַבֵּר וּמְקַיֵּם, שֶׁכָּל־דְּבָרָיו אֱמֶת וָצֶדֶק.

עַל הַתּוֹרָה וְעַל הָעֲבוֹדָה וְעַל הַנְּבִיאִים (וְעַל יוֹם הַשַּׁבָּת הַזֶּה) וְעַל יוֹם הַזִּכָּרוֹן הַזֶּה, שֶׁנָּתַתָּ לָנוּ, יְיָ אֱלֹהֵינוּ, (לִקְדֻשָּׁה וְלִמְנוּחָה) לְכָבוֹד וּלְתִפְאָרֶת, עַל הַכֹּל, יְיָ אֱלֹהֵינוּ, אֲנַחְנוּ מוֹדִים לָךְ, וּמְבָרְכִים אוֹתָךְ. יִתְבָּרַךְ שִׁמְךָ בְּפִי כָּל־חַי תָּמִיד לְעוֹלָם וָעֶד. וּדְבָרְךָ אֱמֶת וְקַיָּם לָעַד. בָּרוּךְ אַתָּה, יְיָ, מֶלֶךְ עַל כָּל־הָאָרֶץ, מְקַדֵּשׁ (הַשַּׁבָּת וְ) יִשְׂרָאֵל וְיוֹם הַזִּכָּרוֹן.

Continue on page 138.

Alternative Version

בָּרוּךְ אַתָּה, יְיָ אֱלֹהֵינוּ, מֶלֶךְ הָעוֹלָם, צוּר כָּל־הָעוֹלָמִים, צַדִּיק בְּכָל־הַדּוֹרוֹת, הָאֵל הַנֶּאֱמָן, הָאוֹמֵר וְעוֹשֶׂה, הַמְדַבֵּר וּמְקַיֵּם, שֶׁכָּל־דְּבָרָיו אֱמֶת וָצֶדֶק.

day is holy to our Lord. Do not be sad, for the joy of the Lord is your strength.'

♦ ♦

After the Reading

An alternative version of this Benediction follows below

Praised be the Lord our God, Ruler of the universe, Rock of all creation, righteous in all generations, the faithful God whose word is deed, whose every command is just and true.

For the Torah, for the privilege of worship, for the prophets, and for this (Shabbat and this) Day of Remembrance that You, O Lord our God, have given us (for holiness and rest,) for honor and glory, we thank and bless You. May Your name be blessed for ever by every living being, for Your word is true for ever. Blessed is the Lord, King of all the earth, for the holiness of (the Sabbath,) the House of Israel and the Day of Remembrance.

Continue on page 138.

Alternative Version

Praised be the Lord our God, Ruler of the universe, Rock of all creation, righteous in all generations, the faithful God whose word is deed, whose every command is just and true.

נֶאֱמָן אַתָּה הוּא יְיָ אֱלֹהֵינוּ, וְנֶאֱמָנִים דְּבָרֶיךָ, וְדָבָר אֶחָד מִדְּבָרֶיךָ אָחוֹר לֹא־יָשׁוּב רֵיקָם, כִּי אֵל מֶלֶךְ נֶאֱמָן וְרַחֲמָן אָתָּה. בָּרוּךְ אַתָּה, יְיָ, הָאֵל הַנֶּאֱמָן בְּכָל־דְּבָרָיו.

רַחֵם עַל־צִיּוֹן כִּי הִיא בֵּית חַיֵּינוּ, וְלַעֲלוּבַת נֶפֶשׁ תּוֹשִׁיעַ בִּמְהֵרָה בְיָמֵינוּ. בָּרוּךְ אַתָּה, יְיָ, מְשַׂמֵּחַ צִיּוֹן בְּבָנֶיהָ.

שַׂמְּחֵנוּ, יְיָ אֱלֹהֵינוּ, בְּאֵלִיָּהוּ הַנָּבִיא עַבְדֶּךָ, וּבְמַלְכוּת בֵּית דָּוִד מְשִׁיחֶךָ, בִּמְהֵרָה יָבֹא וְיָגֵל לִבֵּנוּ. עַל־כִּסְאוֹ לֹא־יֵשֵׁב זָר וְלֹא־יִנְחֲלוּ עוֹד אֲחֵרִים אֶת־כְּבוֹדוֹ. כִּי בְשֵׁם קָדְשְׁךָ נִשְׁבַּעְתָּ לּוֹ שֶׁלֹּא־יִכְבֶּה נֵרוֹ לְעוֹלָם וָעֶד. בָּרוּךְ אַתָּה, יְיָ, מָגֵן דָּוִד.

עַל הַתּוֹרָה וְעַל הָעֲבוֹדָה וְעַל הַנְּבִיאִים (וְעַל יוֹם הַשַּׁבָּת הַזֶּה) וְעַל יוֹם הַזִּכָּרוֹן הַזֶּה שֶׁנָּתַתָּ לָּנוּ, יְיָ אֱלֹהֵינוּ, (לִקְדֻשָּׁה וְלִמְנוּחָה) לְכָבוֹד וּלְתִפְאָרֶת, עַל הַכֹּל, יְיָ אֱלֹהֵינוּ, אֲנַחְנוּ מוֹדִים לָךְ, וּמְבָרְכִים אוֹתָךְ. יִתְבָּרַךְ שִׁמְךָ בְּפִי כָּל־חַי תָּמִיד לְעוֹלָם וָעֶד. וּדְבָרְךָ אֱמֶת וְקַיָּם לָעַד. בָּרוּךְ אַתָּה, יְיָ, מֶלֶךְ עַל כָּל־הָאָרֶץ, מְקַדֵּשׁ (הַשַּׁבָּת וְ) יִשְׂרָאֵל וְיוֹם הַזִּכָּרוֹן.

You are the Faithful One, O Lord our God, and faithful is Your word. Not one word of Yours goes forth without accomplishing its task, O faithful and compassionate God and King. Blessed is the Lord, the faithful God.

Show compassion for Zion, our House of Life, and speedily, in our own day, deliver those who despair. Blessed is the Lord, who brings joy to Zion's children.

Lord our God, bring us the joy of Your kingdom: let our dream of Elijah and David bear fruit. Speedily let redemption come to gladden our hearts. Let Your solemn promise be fulfilled: David's light shall not for ever be extinguished! Blessed is the Lord, the Shield of David.

For the Torah, for the privilege of worship, for the prophets, and for this (Shabbat and this) Day of Remembrance that You, O Lord our God, have given us (for holiness and rest,) for honor and glory, we thank and bless You. May Your name be blessed for ever by every living being, for Your word is true for ever. Blessed is the Lord, King of all the earth, for the holiness of (the Sabbath,) the House of Israel and the Day of Remembrance.

סדר תקיעת שופר

The Sounding of the Shofar

Note: In ancient Israel the sound of the ram's horn announced the beginning of a new month, the Jubilee year, the coronation of a king, and all the solemn moments of the year. But when the new moon of the seventh month came to be observed as the New Year, new and deeper meanings gathered around the sounding of the Shofar. These meanings, deepening still, awaken within us each time we hear the Shofar call.

In the seventh month,
on the first day of the month,
there shall be a sacred assembly,
a cessation from work,
a day of commemoration
proclaimed by the sound
of the Shofar.

וּבַחֹדֶשׁ הַשְּׁבִיעִי,
בְּאֶחָד לַחֹדֶשׁ,
מִקְרָא־קֹדֶשׁ יִהְיֶה לָכֶם;
כָּל־מְלֶאכֶת עֲבוֹדָה לֹא תַעֲשׂוּ;
יוֹם תְּרוּעָה יִהְיֶה לָכֶם.

◆

Hear now the Shofar; acclaim the world's creation!

And now recall Isaac's awesome trial!

Hear now the Shofar, you who stand at Sinai!

And now proclaim the rule of Israel's God!

Hear now the call, and turn in true repentance!

And now affirm the triumph of good!

We are made in the divine image!

*We are the House of Israel,
a kingdom of priests, a holy people!*

Know then the sound; discover its meaning:

◆

עוּרוּ, יְשֵׁנִים, מִשְּׁנַתְכֶם, וְנִרְדָּמִים, הָקִיצוּ
מִתַּרְדֵּמַתְכֶם! וְחַפְּשׂוּ בְּמַעֲשֵׂיכֶם, וְחִזְרוּ בִּתְשׁוּבָה,
וְזִכְרוּ בּוֹרַאֲכֶם, אֵלּוּ הַשּׁוֹכְחִים אֶת־הָאֱמֶת בְּהַבְלֵי
הַזְּמַן, וְשׁוֹגִים כָּל־שְׁנָתָם בְּהֶבֶל וָרִיק אֲשֶׁר לֹא יוֹעִיל
וְלֹא יַצִּיל. הַבִּיטוּ לְנַפְשׁוֹתֵיכֶם וְהֵיטִיבוּ דַרְכֵיכֶם
וּמַעַלְלֵיכֶם, וְיַעֲזֹב כָּל־אֶחָד מִכֶּם דַּרְכּוֹ הָרָעָה,
וּמַחֲשַׁבְתּוֹ אֲשֶׁר לֹא טוֹבָה.

Awake, you sleepers, from your sleep! Rouse yourselves,
you slumberers, out of your slumber! Examine your
deeds, and turn to God in repentance. Remember your
Creator, you who are caught up in the daily round, losing
sight of eternal truth; you who are wasting your years in
vain pursuits that neither profit nor save. Look closely at
yourselves; improve your ways and your deeds. Abandon
your evil ways, your unworthy schemes, every one of you!

◆ ◆

MALCHUYOT   מלכויות

SOVEREIGNTY

All rise

עָלֵינוּ לְשַׁבֵּחַ לַאֲדוֹן הַכֹּל, לָתֵת גְּדֻלָּה לְיוֹצֵר
בְּרֵאשִׁית, שֶׁלֹּא עָשָׂנוּ כְּגוֹיֵי הָאֲרָצוֹת, וְלֹא שָׂמָנוּ
כְּמִשְׁפְּחוֹת הָאֲדָמָה; שֶׁלֹּא שָׂם חֶלְקֵנוּ כָּהֶם, וְגֹרָלֵנוּ
כְּכָל־הֲמוֹנָם.

וַאֲנַחְנוּ כּוֹרְעִים וּמִשְׁתַּחֲוִים וּמוֹדִים לִפְנֵי מֶלֶךְ מַלְכֵי הַמְּלָכִים, הַקָּדוֹשׁ בָּרוּךְ הוּא.

We must praise the Lord of all, the Maker of heaven and earth, who has set us apart from the other families of earth, giving us a destiny unique among the nations.

We therefore bow in awe and thanksgiving before the One who is Sovereign over all, the Holy and Blessed One.

All are seated

יַכִּירוּ וְיֵדְעוּ כָּל־יוֹשְׁבֵי תֵבֵל כִּי לְךָ תִּכְרַע כָּל־בֶּרֶךְ, תִּשָּׁבַע כָּל־לָשׁוֹן. לְפָנֶיךָ, יְיָ אֱלֹהֵינוּ, יִכְרְעוּ וְיִפֹּלוּ, וְלִכְבוֹד שִׁמְךָ יְקָר יִתֵּנוּ, וִיקַבְּלוּ כֻלָּם אֶת־עֹל מַלְכוּתֶךָ, וְתִמְלוֹךְ עֲלֵיהֶם מְהֵרָה לְעוֹלָם וָעֶד. כִּי הַמַּלְכוּת שֶׁלְּךָ הִיא וּלְעוֹלְמֵי עַד תִּמְלוֹךְ בְּכָבוֹד.

Let all who dwell on earth acknowledge that unto You every knee must bend and every tongue swear loyalty. Before You, O Lord our God, let them humble themselves. To Your glorious name let them give honor. Let all accept the yoke of Your kingdom, that You may rule over them soon and for ever.

For the kingdom is Yours, and to all eternity You will reign in glory.

∙ ∙

כַּכָּתוּב בְּתוֹרָתֶךָ: "יְיָ אֱלֹהָיו עִמּוֹ וּתְרוּעַת מֶלֶךְ בּוֹ."

וּבְדִבְרֵי קָדְשְׁךָ כָּתוּב לֵאמֹר: "שְׂאוּ שְׁעָרִים רָאשֵׁיכֶם, וְהִנָּשְׂאוּ פִּתְחֵי עוֹלָם, וְיָבוֹא מֶלֶךְ הַכָּבוֹד!

140

מִי הוּא זֶה מֶלֶךְ הַכָּבוֹד? יְיָ צְבָאוֹת—הוּא מֶלֶךְ
הַכָּבוֹד! סֶלָה."

וְעַל יְדֵי עֲבָדֶיךָ הַנְּבִיאִים כָּתוּב לֵאמֹר: "כֹּה אָמַר יְיָ,
מֶלֶךְ יִשְׂרָאֵל וְגֹאֲלוֹ, יְיָ צְבָאוֹת, אֲנִי רִאשׁוֹן וַאֲנִי
אַחֲרוֹן, וּמִבַּלְעָדַי אֵין אֱלֹהִים."

וּבְתוֹרָתְךָ כָּתוּב לֵאמֹר: "שְׁמַע יִשְׂרָאֵל: יְיָ אֱלֹהֵינוּ,
יְיָ אֶחָד!"

The Torah proclaims: The Lord your God is with you;
shout acclaim to your King!

*The psalmist affirms: Lift up your heads, O gates! Lift
yourselves up, O ancient doors! Let the King of Glory enter.
Who is this King of Glory? The Lord of Hosts — He is the
King of Glory!*

The prophet declares: I am the First and I am the Last; I
am the Only One.

*As it is written in the Torah: Hear, O Israel: the Lord is our
God, the Lord is One!*

· ·

אֱלֹהֵינוּ וֵאלֹהֵי אֲבוֹתֵינוּ, מְלוֹךְ עַל כָּל־הָעוֹלָם כֻּלּוֹ
בִּכְבוֹדֶךָ וְהִנָּשֵׂא עַל כָּל־הָאָרֶץ בִּיקָרֶךָ, וְהוֹפַע בַּהֲדַר
גְּאוֹן עֻזֶּךָ עַל כָּל־יוֹשְׁבֵי תֵבֵל אַרְצֶךָ. וְיֵדַע כָּל־פָּעוּל
כִּי אַתָּה פְעַלְתּוֹ, וְיָבִין כָּל־יָצוּר כִּי אַתָּה יְצַרְתּוֹ,
וְיֹאמַר כֹּל אֲשֶׁר נְשָׁמָה בְאַפּוֹ: יְיָ אֱלֹהֵי יִשְׂרָאֵל מֶלֶךְ,
וּמַלְכוּתוֹ בַּכֹּל מָשָׁלָה. בָּרוּךְ אַתָּה, יְיָ, מֶלֶךְ עַל כָּל־
הָאָרֶץ, מְקַדֵּשׁ (הַשַּׁבָּת וְ) יִשְׂרָאֵל וְיוֹם הַזִּכָּרוֹן.

141

Our God and God of our ancestors, may You rule in glory over all the earth, and let Your grandeur be acclaimed throughout the world. Reveal the splendor of Your majesty to all who dwell on earth, that all Your works may know You as their Maker, and all the living acknowledge You as their Creator. Then all who breathe shall say: 'The Lord God of Israel is the King whose dominion extends to all creation.' Blessed is the Lord, King of all the earth, who hallows (the Sabbath,) the House of Israel and the Day of Remembrance.

◆ ◆

All rise

בָּרוּךְ אַתָּה, יְיָ אֱלֹהֵינוּ, מֶלֶךְ הָעוֹלָם, אֲשֶׁר קִדְּשָׁנוּ
בְּמִצְוֹתָיו וְצִוָּנוּ לִשְׁמֹעַ קוֹל שׁוֹפָר.
בָּרוּךְ אַתָּה, יְיָ אֱלֹהֵינוּ, מֶלֶךְ הָעוֹלָם, שֶׁהֶחֱיָנוּ וְקִיְּמָנוּ
וְהִגִּיעָנוּ לַזְּמַן הַזֶּה.

Blessed is the Lord our God, Ruler of the universe, who hallows us with Mitzvot, and calls us to hear the sound of the Shofar.

Blessed is the Lord our God, Ruler of the universe, for giving us life, for sustaining us, and for enabling us to reach this season.

The Shofar is sounded

TEKIAH SHEVARIM-TERUAH	תקיעה שברים־תרועה
TEKIAH	תקיעה
TEKIAH SHEVARIM TEKIAH	תקיעה שברים תקיעה
TEKIAH TERUAH TEKIAH	תקיעה תרועה תקיעה

All are seated

◆ ◆

הַיּוֹם הֲרַת עוֹלָם. הַיּוֹם יַעֲמִיד בַּמִּשְׁפָּט כָּל־יְצוּרֵי
עוֹלָמִים אִם כְּבָנִים אִם כַּעֲבָדִים. אִם כְּבָנִים, רַחֲמֵנוּ
כְּרַחֵם אָב עַל בָּנִים. וְאִם כַּעֲבָדִים, עֵינֵינוּ לְךָ תְלוּיוֹת
עַד שֶׁתְּחָנֵּנוּ וְתוֹצִיא כָאוֹר מִשְׁפָּטֵנוּ, אָיֹם קָדוֹשׁ.

This is the day of the world's birth. This day all creatures stand
before You, whether as children or as slaves. As we are Your
children, show us a parent's compassion; as we are slaves, we
look to You for mercy: shed the light of Your judgment upon us,
O holy and awesome God.

◆ ◆

אֲרֶשֶׁת שְׂפָתֵינוּ יֶעֱרַב לְפָנֶיךָ, אֵל רָם וְנִשָּׂא, מֵבִין
וּמַאֲזִין מַבִּיט וּמַקְשִׁיב לְקוֹל תְּקִיעָתֵנוּ, וּתְקַבֵּל
בְּרַחֲמִים וּבְרָצוֹן סֵדֶר מַלְכִיּוֹתֵינוּ.

O God Supreme, accept the offering of our lips, the sound
of the Shofar. In love and favor hear us, as we acclaim
Your SOVEREIGNTY.

◆ ◆

ZICHRONOT   זכרונות

REMEMBRANCE

אַתָּה זוֹכֵר מַעֲשֵׂה עוֹלָם וּפוֹקֵד כָּל־יְצוּרֵי קֶדֶם.
לְפָנֶיךָ נִגְלוּ כָּל־תַּעֲלוּמוֹת וַהֲמוֹן נִסְתָּרוֹת
שֶׁמִּבְּרֵאשִׁית. כִּי אֵין שִׁכְחָה לִפְנֵי כִסֵּא כְבוֹדֶךָ וְאֵין
נִסְתָּר מִנֶּגֶד עֵינֶיךָ. אַתָּה זוֹכֵר אֶת־כָּל־הַמִּפְעָל וְגַם
כָּל־הַיְצוּר לֹא נִכְחָד מִמֶּךָּ. הַכֹּל גָּלוּי וְיָדוּעַ לְפָנֶיךָ, יְיָ
אֱלֹהֵינוּ, צוֹפֶה וּמַבִּיט עַד סוֹף כָּל־הַדּוֹרוֹת, כִּי תָבִיא

חֹק זִכָּרוֹן לְהִפָּקֵד כָּל־רוּחַ וָנָפֶשׁ, לְהִזָּכֵר מַעֲשִׂים
רַבִּים וַהֲמוֹן בְּרִיּוֹת לְאֵין תַּכְלִית. מֵרֵאשִׁית כָּזֹאת
הוֹדַעְתָּ וּמִלְּפָנִים אוֹתָהּ גִּלִּיתָ.

You remember the work of creation, You are mindful of
all that You have made. You unravel every mystery; all
secret things are known to You. For there is no forgetfulness in Your presence, nothing hidden from Your sight.
You remember every deed; You know every doer. All
things past and present are known to You, Eternal God,
and every person's acts are remembered and judged. This
You made known from the beginning; this You revealed
from of old.

זֶה הַיּוֹם תְּחִלַּת מַעֲשֶׂיךָ, זִכָּרוֹן לְיוֹם רִאשׁוֹן. כִּי חֹק
לְיִשְׂרָאֵל הוּא, מִשְׁפָּט לֵאלֹהֵי יַעֲקֹב. וְעַל הַמְּדִינוֹת
בּוֹ יֵאָמֵר: אֵיזוֹ לַחֶרֶב וְאֵיזוֹ לַשָּׁלוֹם, אֵיזוֹ לָרָעָב
וְאֵיזוֹ לַשֹּׂבַע. וּבְרִיּוֹת בּוֹ יִפָּקֵדוּ לְהַזְכִּירָם לַחַיִּים
וְלַמָּוֶת. מִי לֹא נִפְקָד כְּהַיּוֹם הַזֶּה, כִּי זֵכֶר כָּל־הַיְצוּר
לְפָנֶיךָ בָּא, מַעֲשֵׂה אִישׁ וּפְקֻדָּתוֹ וַעֲלִילוֹת מִצְעֲדֵי־
גָבֶר, מַחְשְׁבוֹת אָדָם וְתַחְבּוּלוֹתָיו וְיִצְרֵי מַעַלְלֵי־
אִישׁ.

This is the day of the world's beginning; now we recall
creation's first day. On this day the fate of nations is in the
balance—for war or peace, for famine or plenty. So too
with every single creature: life and death are in the
balance. Every mortal's record is set before You, our acts
and our schemes, our thoughts and desires.

אַשְׁרֵי אִישׁ שֶׁלֹּא יִשְׁכָּחֶךָ וּבֶן־אָדָם יִתְאַמֶּץ־בָּךְ. כִּי
דוֹרְשֶׁיךָ לְעוֹלָם לֹא יִכָּשֵׁלוּ, וְלֹא יִכָּלְמוּ לָנֶצַח כָּל־
הַחוֹסִים בָּךְ. כִּי זֵכֶר כָּל־הַמַּעֲשִׂים לְפָנֶיךָ בָּא.

*Blessed is the one who does not forget You, who looks to
You and finds courage. Those who seek You shall not stumble; those who trust You shall not be ashamed.*

• •

כַּכָּתוּב בְּתוֹרָתֶךָ: "וַיִּשְׁמַע אֱלֹהִים אֶת־נַאֲקָתָם,
וַיִּזְכֹּר אֱלֹהִים אֶת־בְּרִיתוֹ אֶת־אַבְרָהָם אֶת־יִצְחָק
וְאֶת־יַעֲקֹב."

וּבְדִבְרֵי קָדְשְׁךָ כָּתוּב לֵאמֹר: "וַיִּזְכֹּר לָהֶם בְּרִיתוֹ,
וַיִּנָּחֶם כְּרֹב חֲסָדָיו."

וְעַל יְדֵי עֲבָדֶיךָ הַנְּבִיאִים כָּתוּב לֵאמֹר: "וְזָכַרְתִּי אֲנִי
אֶת־בְּרִיתִי אוֹתָךְ בִּימֵי נְעוּרָיִךְ, וַהֲקִימוֹתִי לָךְ בְּרִית
עוֹלָם."

וּבְתוֹרָתְךָ כָּתוּב לֵאמֹר: "וְזָכַרְתִּי לָהֶם בְּרִית
רִאשֹׁנִים, אֲשֶׁר הוֹצֵאתִי אֹתָם מֵאֶרֶץ מִצְרַיִם לְעֵינֵי
הַגּוֹיִם, לִהְיוֹת לָהֶם לֵאלֹהִים, אֲנִי יְיָ."

The Torah proclaims: God heard the enslaved people's
groaning, and remembered the covenant with Abraham,
Isaac, and Jacob.

*The psalmist affirms: You remembered Your covenant with
us; in Your great love, You comforted us.*

The prophet declares: I will remember the covenant I

made with you in the days of your youth, and I will establish with you an everlasting covenant.

As it is written in the Torah: I will remember the covenant with their ancestors whom I led out of Egypt in the sight of the nations, to be their God. I am the Lord.

◆ ◆

אֱלֹהֵינוּ וֵאלֹהֵי אֲבוֹתֵינוּ, זָכְרֵנוּ בְּזִכָּרוֹן טוֹב לְפָנֶיךָ
וּפָקְדֵנוּ בִּפְקֻדַּת יְשׁוּעָה וְרַחֲמִים מִשְּׁמֵי שְׁמֵי קֶדֶם.
וּזְכָר־לָנוּ, יְיָ אֱלֹהֵינוּ, אֶת־הַבְּרִית וְאֶת־הַחֶסֶד וְאֶת־
הַשְּׁבוּעָה אֲשֶׁר נִשְׁבַּעְתָּ לְאַבְרָהָם אָבִינוּ בְּהַר
הַמּוֹרִיָּה. וְתֵרָאֶה לְפָנֶיךָ עֲקֵדָה שֶׁעָקַד אַבְרָהָם
אָבִינוּ אֶת־יִצְחָק בְּנוֹ עַל גַּב הַמִּזְבֵּחַ וְכָבַשׁ רַחֲמָיו
לַעֲשׂוֹת רְצוֹנְךָ בְּלֵבָב שָׁלֵם. כֵּן יִכְבְּשׁוּ רַחֲמֶיךָ אֶת־
כַּעַסְךָ מֵעָלֵינוּ, וּבְטוּבְךָ הַגָּדוֹל יָשׁוּב חֲרוֹן אַפְּךָ
מֵעַמְּךָ וּמֵעִירְךָ וּמִנַּחֲלָתֶךָ. כִּי זוֹכֵר כָּל־הַנִּשְׁכָּחוֹת
אַתָּה הוּא מֵעוֹלָם, וְאֵין שִׁכְחָה לִפְנֵי כִסֵּא כְבוֹדֶךָ.
בָּרוּךְ אַתָּה, יְיָ, זוֹכֵר הַבְּרִית.

Our God and God of all generations, remember us with favor and grant us Your compassionate deliverance. Remember Your love for us, the covenant You made with Abraham on Mount Moriah. Remember his boundless love for You, his willingness to offer You all that was his. Show us Your compassion, then, and in Your goodness look with favor upon Your people and Your loved ones.

For You are the One who remembers all that has been forgotten; there is no forgetfulness in Your presence. Blessed is the Lord, who remembers the covenant.

All rise
The Shofar is sounded:

TEKIAH SHEVARIM-TERUAH	תקיעה שברים־תרועה
TEKIAH	תקיעה
TEKIAH SHEVARIM TEKIAH	תקיעה שברים תקיעה
TEKIAH TERUAH TEKIAH	תקיעה תרועה תקיעה

All are seated

❖ ❖

הַיּוֹם הֲרַת עוֹלָם. הַיּוֹם יַעֲמִיד בַּמִּשְׁפָּט כָּל־יְצוּרֵי
עוֹלָמִים אִם כְּבָנִים אִם כַּעֲבָדִים. אִם כְּבָנִים, רַחֲמֵנוּ
כְּרַחֵם אָב עַל בָּנִים. וְאִם כַּעֲבָדִים, עֵינֵינוּ לְךָ תְלוּיוֹת
עַד שֶׁתְּחָנֵּנוּ וְתוֹצִיא כָאוֹר מִשְׁפָּטֵנוּ, אָיֹם קָדוֹשׁ.

This is the day of the world's birth. This day all creatures stand
before You, whether as children or as slaves. As we are Your
children, show us a parent's compassion; as we are slaves, we
look to You for mercy: shed the light of Your judgment upon us,
O holy and awesome God.

❖ ❖

אֲרֶשֶׁת שְׂפָתֵינוּ יֶעֱרַב לְפָנֶיךָ, אֵל רָם וְנִשָּׂא, מֵבִין
וּמַאֲזִין מַבִּיט וּמַקְשִׁיב לְקוֹל תְּקִיעָתֵנוּ, וּתְקַבֵּל
בְּרַחֲמִים וּבְרָצוֹן סֵדֶר זִכְרוֹנוֹתֵינוּ.

O God Supreme, accept the offering of our lips, the sound
of the Shofar. In love and favor hear us, as we invoke
Your REMEMBRANCE.

❖ ❖

SHOFAROT שופרות

REVELATION

אַתָּה נִגְלֵיתָ בַּעֲנַן כְּבוֹדֶךָ, עַל עַם קָדְשְׁךָ לְדַבֵּר עִמָּם. מִן הַשָּׁמַיִם הִשְׁמַעְתָּם קוֹלֶךָ, וְנִגְלֵיתָ עֲלֵיהֶם בְּעַרְפְּלֵי טְהַר. גַּם כָּל־הָעוֹלָם כֻּלּוֹ חָל מִפָּנֶיךָ וּבְרִיּוֹת בְּרֵאשִׁית חָרְדוּ מִמֶּךָ. בְּהִגָּלוֹתְךָ מַלְכֵּנוּ עַל הַר סִינַי לְלַמֵּד לְעַמְּךָ תּוֹרָה וּמִצְוֹת, וַתַּשְׁמִיעֵם אֶת־הוֹד קוֹלֶךָ, וְדִבְּרוֹת קָדְשְׁךָ מִלַּהֲבוֹת אֵשׁ. בְּקוֹלוֹת וּבְרָקִים עֲלֵיהֶם נִגְלֵיתָ וּבְקוֹל שׁוֹפָר עֲלֵיהֶם הוֹפָעְתָּ.

In a cloud of glory You spoke in holy address to Your people. We felt Your presence, a luminous mist, Your voice resounding from the very heavens. As all creation trembled, You revealed Your Torah to us at Sinai.

We heard the majesty of Your voice; Your sacred word came forth amid flashes of fire. There was thunder and lightning; and, with the sound of a Shofar, You were manifest to us.

◆ ◆

כַּכָּתוּב בְּתוֹרָתֶךָ: "וַיְהִי בַיּוֹם הַשְּׁלִישִׁי, בִּהְיֹת הַבֹּקֶר, וַיְהִי קֹלֹת וּבְרָקִים וְעָנָן כָּבֵד עַל הָהָר, וְקֹל שֹׁפָר חָזָק מְאֹד, וַיֶּחֱרַד כָּל־הָעָם אֲשֶׁר בַּמַּחֲנֶה."

וּבְדִבְרֵי קָדְשְׁךָ כָּתוּב לֵאמֹר: "עָלָה אֱלֹהִים בִּתְרוּעָה, יְיָ בְּקוֹל שׁוֹפָר."

וְעַל יְדֵי עֲבָדֶיךָ הַנְּבִיאִים כָּתוּב לֵאמֹר: "כָּל־יֹשְׁבֵי

תֵּבֵל וְשֹׁכְנֵי אָרֶץ, כִּנְשֹׂא נֵס הָרִים תִּרְאוּ, וְכִתְקֹעַ
שׁוֹפָר תִּשְׁמָעוּ."

וְנֶאֱמַר: "וַיְיָ עֲלֵיהֶם יֵרָאֶה וְיָצָא כַבָּרָק חִצּוֹ, וַאדֹנָי
אֱלֹהִים בַּשּׁוֹפָר יִתְקָע וְהָלַךְ בְּסַעֲרוֹת תֵּימָן. יְיָ
צְבָאוֹת יָגֵן עֲלֵיהֶם." כֵּן תָּגֵן עַל עַמְּךָ יִשְׂרָאֵל
בִּשְׁלוֹמֶךָ.

The Torah proclaims: As the third day dawned at Sinai,
there was thunder and lightning, a dense cloud over the
mountain, and a loud blast of the Shofar; the people
trembled.

The psalmist affirms: God stands revealed amid acclama-
tion; the Lord, amid the sound of the Shofar.

The prophet declares: All you who dwell on earth, who in-
habit the world, when a banner is raised, take note; and
when the Shofar is sounded, take heed!

As it is written: 'The Eternal will appear; God's arrow will
flash like lightning. The Eternal God will cause the Shofar
to be sounded, and stride forth with the storm-winds of the
South.' Thus, O God, will You shield Your people with
peace.

••

אֱלֹהֵינוּ וֵאלֹהֵי אֲבוֹתֵינוּ, תְּקַע בְּשׁוֹפָר גָּדוֹל
לְחֵרוּתֵנוּ, וְשָׂא נֵס לְקַבֵּץ גָּלֻיּוֹתֵינוּ וְלִפְדוּת
עֲשׁוּקֵינוּ. וְקוֹל דְּרוֹר יִשָּׁמַע בְּאַרְבַּע כַּנְפוֹת הָאָרֶץ,
וְתֵן שִׂמְחַת עוֹלָם לְצִיּוֹן עִירֶךָ וְלִירוּשָׁלַיִם בֵּית
מִקְדָּשֶׁךָ. כִּי אַתָּה שׁוֹמֵעַ קוֹל שׁוֹפָר וּמַאֲזִין תְּרוּעָה,

149

וְאֵין דּוֹמֶה לָּךְ. בָּרוּךְ אַתָּה, יְיָ, שׁוֹמֵעַ קוֹל תְּרוּעַת
עַמּוֹ יִשְׂרָאֵל בְּרַחֲמִים.

Our God and God of all generations: Sound the great
Shofar to proclaim our freedom; raise the banner for the
redemption of the oppressed; signal liberty for all who are
in exile; bring lasting joy to Zion and to Jerusalem, Your
holy city.

*We praise You, the merciful God who hearkens to the sound
of the Shofar.*

◆ ◆

All rise
The Shofar is sounded:

TEKIAH SHEVARIM-TERUAH	תקיעה שברים־תרועה
TEKIAH	תקיעה
TEKIAH SHEVARIM TEKIAH	תקיעה שברים תקיעה
TEKIAH TERUAH TEKIAH GEDOLAH	תקיעה תרועה תקיעה גדולה

All are seated

◆ ◆

הַיּוֹם הֲרַת עוֹלָם. הַיּוֹם יַעֲמִיד בַּמִּשְׁפָּט כָּל־יְצוּרֵי
עוֹלָמִים אִם כְּבָנִים אִם כַּעֲבָדִים. אִם כְּבָנִים, רַחֲמֵנוּ
כְּרַחֵם אָב עַל בָּנִים. וְאִם כַּעֲבָדִים, עֵינֵינוּ לְךָ תְלוּיוֹת
עַד שֶׁתְּחָנֵּנוּ וְתוֹצִיא כָאוֹר מִשְׁפָּטֵנוּ, אָיֹם קָדוֹשׁ.

This is the day of the world's birth. This day all creatures stand
before You, whether as children or as slaves. As we are Your
children, show us a parent's compassion; as we are slaves, we

look to You for mercy: shed the light of Your judgment upon us,
O awesome and holy God.

• •

אֲרֶשֶׁת שְׂפָתֵינוּ יֶעֱרַב לְפָנֶיךָ, אֵל רָם וְנִשָּׂא, מֵבִין
וּמַאֲזִין מַבִּיט וּמַקְשִׁיב לְקוֹל תְּקִיעָתֵנוּ, וּתְקַבֵּל
בְּרַחֲמִים וּבְרָצוֹן סֵדֶר שׁוֹפְרוֹתֵינוּ.

O God Supreme, accept the offering of our lips, the sound
of the Shofar. In love and favor hear us, as we call to You
with THE SOUND OF THE SHOFAR.

• •

All rise

FOR OUR CONGREGATION AND OUR PEOPLE

Lord, we pray to You for the whole House of Israel, scattered over the earth, yet bound together by a common history and united by a common heritage of faith and hope.

Be with our brothers and sisters whose lives are made hard because they are Jews. Give them strength to endure, and lead them soon from bondage to freedom, from darkness to light.

Bless this holy congregation and all who serve it, together with all other holy congregations, in all lands near and far. Uphold us, shield us, and bestow upon us abundant life and health and peace and happiness. Bring to fulfillment the blessing of Moses: The Lord your God make you a thousand times as many as you are, and bless you as He has promised you. Amen.

O God, send Your healing to the sick, Your comfort to all who are in pain or anxiety, Your tender love to the sorrowing hearts among us. Be their refuge through their time of trial, as they pass from weakness to strength, from suffering to consolation, from lonely fear to the courage of faith. Amen.

FOR OUR NATION AND ITS RULERS

We pray for all who hold positions of leadership and responsibility in our national life. Let Your blessing rest upon them, and make them responsive to Your will, so that our nation may be to the world an example of justice and compassion.

Deepen our love for our country and our desire to serve it. Strengthen our power of self-sacrifice for our nation's welfare. Teach us to uphold its good name by our own right conduct.

Cause us to see clearly that the well-being of our nation is in the hands of all its citizens; imbue us with zeal for the cause of liberty in our own land and in all lands; and help us always to keep our homes safe from affliction, strife, and war. Amen.

FOR THE STATE OF ISRAEL

We pray for the land of Israel and its people. May its borders know peace, its inhabitants tranquility. And may the bonds of faith and fate which unite the Jews of all lands be a source of strength to Israel and to us all. God of all lands and ages, answer our constant prayer with a Zion once more aglow with light for us and for all the world, and let us say: Amen.

Returning the Torah to the Ark

יְהַלְלוּ אֶת־שֵׁם יְיָ, כִּי־נִשְׂגָּב שְׁמוֹ לְבַדּוֹ.

Let us praise the name of the Lord, whose name alone is exalted.

הוֹדוֹ עַל אֶרֶץ וְשָׁמָיִם, וַיָּרֶם קֶרֶן לְעַמּוֹ, תְּהִלָּה לְכָל־
חֲסִידָיו, לִבְנֵי יִשְׂרָאֵל עַם קְרוֹבוֹ. הַלְלוּיָהּ.

God's splendor covers heaven and earth; He is the strength of His people, making glorious His faithful ones, Israel, a people close to Him. Halleluyah!

◆ ◆

תּוֹרַת יְיָ תְּמִימָה, מְשִׁיבַת נָפֶשׁ;
עֵדוּת יְיָ נֶאֱמָנָה, מַחְכִּימַת פֶּתִי;

The law of the Lord is perfect, restoring the soul;

The teaching of the Lord is sure, making wise the simple;

פִּקּוּדֵי יְיָ יְשָׁרִים, מְשַׂמְּחֵי־לֵב;
מִצְוַת יְיָ בָּרָה, מְאִירַת עֵינָיִם;

The precepts of the Lord are right, rejoicing the heart;

The Mitzvah of the Lord is clear, giving light to the eyes;

יִרְאַת יְיָ טְהוֹרָה, עֹמֶדֶת לָעַד;
מִשְׁפְּטֵי יְיָ אֱמֶת, צָדְקוּ יַחְדָּו.

The word of the Lord is pure, enduring for ever;

The judgments of the Lord are true, and altogether just.

◆ ◆

כִּי לֶקַח טוֹב נָתַתִּי לָכֶם, תּוֹרָתִי אַל־תַּעֲזֹבוּ.
עֵץ־חַיִּים הִיא לַמַּחֲזִיקִים בָּה, וְתֹמְכֶיהָ מְאֻשָּׁר.
דְּרָכֶיהָ דַרְכֵי־נֹעַם, וְכָל־נְתִיבוֹתֶיהָ שָׁלוֹם.

Behold, a good doctrine has been given you, do not forsake it. It is a tree of life to those who hold it fast, and all
who cling to it find happiness. Its ways are ways of
pleasantness, and all its paths are peace.

הֲשִׁיבֵנוּ יְיָ אֵלֶיךָ, וְנָשׁוּבָה. חַדֵּשׁ יָמֵינוּ כְּקֶדֶם.

Help us to return to You, O Lord; then truly shall we return.
Renew our days as in the past.

The Ark is closed
All are seated

עָלֵינוּ

All rise

עָלֵינוּ לְשַׁבֵּחַ לַאֲדוֹן הַכֹּל, לָתֵת גְּדֻלָּה לְיוֹצֵר בְּרֵאשִׁית, שֶׁלֹּא עָשָׂנוּ כְּגוֹיֵי הָאֲרָצוֹת, וְלֹא שָׂמָנוּ כְּמִשְׁפְּחוֹת הָאֲדָמָה; שֶׁלֹּא שָׂם חֶלְקֵנוּ כָּהֶם, וְגֹרָלֵנוּ כְּכָל־הֲמוֹנָם.

We must praise the Lord of all, the Maker of heaven and earth, who has set us apart from the other families of earth, giving us a destiny unique among the nations.

וַאֲנַחְנוּ כּוֹרְעִים וּמִשְׁתַּחֲוִים וּמוֹדִים לִפְנֵי מֶלֶךְ מַלְכֵי הַמְּלָכִים, הַקָּדוֹשׁ בָּרוּךְ הוּא,

We therefore bow in awe and thanksgiving before the One who is Sovereign over all, the Holy and Blessed One.

All are seated

שֶׁהוּא נוֹטֶה שָׁמַיִם וְיוֹסֵד אָרֶץ, וּמוֹשַׁב יְקָרוֹ בַּשָּׁמַיִם מִמַּעַל, וּשְׁכִינַת עֻזּוֹ בְּגָבְהֵי מְרוֹמִים. הוּא אֱלֹהֵינוּ, אֵין עוֹד; אֱמֶת מַלְכֵּנוּ, אֶפֶס זוּלָתוֹ, כַּכָּתוּב בְּתוֹרָתוֹ: "וְיָדַעְתָּ הַיּוֹם וַהֲשֵׁבֹתָ אֶל־לְבָבֶךָ, כִּי יְיָ הוּא הָאֱלֹהִים בַּשָּׁמַיִם מִמַּעַל וְעַל־הָאָרֶץ מִתָּחַת, אֵין עוֹד."

He spread out the heavens and established the earth; He is our God; there is none else. In truth He alone is our King, as it is written: "Know then this day and take it to heart: the Lord is God in the heavens above and on the earth below; there is none else."

עַל־כֵּן נְקַוֶּה לְךָ, יְיָ אֱלֹהֵינוּ, לִרְאוֹת מְהֵרָה בְּתִפְאֶרֶת עֻזֶּךָ, לְהַעֲבִיר גִּלּוּלִים מִן־הָאָרֶץ, וְהָאֱלִילִים כָּרוֹת

יְבָרֵתוּן, לְתַקֵּן עוֹלָם בְּמַלְכוּת שַׁדַּי. וְכָל־בְּנֵי בָשָׂר
יִקְרְאוּ בִשְׁמֶךָ, לְהַפְנוֹת אֵלֶיךָ כָּל־רִשְׁעֵי אָרֶץ. יַכִּירוּ
וְיֵדְעוּ כָּל־יוֹשְׁבֵי תֵבֵל כִּי לְךָ תִּכְרַע כָּל־בֶּרֶךְ, תִּשָּׁבַע
כָּל־לָשׁוֹן. לְפָנֶיךָ, יְיָ אֱלֹהֵינוּ, יִכְרְעוּ וְיִפֹּלוּ, וְלִכְבוֹד
שִׁמְךָ יְקָר יִתֵּנוּ, וִיקַבְּלוּ כֻלָּם אֶת־עֹל מַלְכוּתֶךָ,
וְתִמְלֹךְ עֲלֵיהֶם מְהֵרָה לְעוֹלָם וָעֶד.

*We therefore hope, O Lord our God, soon to behold the
glory of Your might. Then will false gods vanish from our
hearts, and the world will be perfected under Your unchal-
lenged rule. And then will all acclaim You as their God, and,
forsaking evil, turn to You alone.*

*Let all who dwell on earth acknowledge that unto You every
knee must bend and every tongue swear loyalty. Before You,
O Lord our God, let them humble themselves. To Your
glorious name let them give honor. Let all accept the yoke of
Your kingdom, that You may rule over them soon and for
ever.*

כִּי הַמַּלְכוּת שֶׁלְּךָ הִיא, וּלְעוֹלְמֵי עַד תִּמְלוֹךְ בְּכָבוֹד,
כַּכָּתוּב בְּתוֹרָתֶךָ: "יְיָ יִמְלֹךְ לְעוֹלָם וָעֶד."

*For the kingdom is Yours, and to all eternity You will reign
in glory, as it is written: "The Lord will reign for ever and
ever."*

וְנֶאֱמַר: "וְהָיָה יְיָ לְמֶלֶךְ עַל־כָּל־הָאָרֶץ; בַּיּוֹם הַהוּא
יִהְיֶה יְיָ אֶחָד וּשְׁמוֹ אֶחָד."

And it has been said: "The Lord shall reign over all the earth; on
that day the Lord shall be One and His name shall be One."

• •

Lord, You give us dear ones and make them the strength of our life, the light of our eyes. They depart from us and leave us bereaved; but You are the living Source of our healing. To You the stricken look for comfort and the sorrow-laden for consolation. On this solemn day of the New Year, we see life as through windows that open on eternity. We see that love abides, the soul abides, as You, O God, abide for ever. We see that our years are more than grass that withers, more than flowers that fade. They weave a pattern of life that is timeless and unite us with a world that is from end to end the abode of Your love and the vesture of Your glory. In life and in death we cannot go where You are not, and where You are, all is well. Sustained by this assurance, we praise Your name, O God of life:

MOURNER'S KADDISH   קדיש יתום

יִתְגַּדַּל וְיִתְקַדַּשׁ שְׁמֵהּ רַבָּא בְּעָלְמָא דִי־בְרָא
כִרְעוּתֵהּ, וְיַמְלִיךְ מַלְכוּתֵהּ בְּחַיֵּיכוֹן וּבְיוֹמֵיכוֹן וּבְחַיֵּי
דְכָל־בֵּית יִשְׂרָאֵל, בַּעֲגָלָא וּבִזְמַן קָרִיב, וְאִמְרוּ: אָמֵן.

Yit·ga·dal ve·yit·ka·dash she·mei ra·ba be·al·ma di·ve·ra
chi·re·u·tei, ve·yam·lich mal·chu·tei be·cha·yei·chon
u·ve·yo·mei·chon u·ve·cha·yei de·chol beit Yis·ra·eil, ba·a·ga·la
u·vi·ze·man ka·riv, ve·i·me·ru: a·mein.

יְהֵא שְׁמֵהּ רַבָּא מְבָרַךְ לְעָלַם וּלְעָלְמֵי עָלְמַיָּא.

Ye·hei she·mei ra·ba me·va·rach le·a·lam u·le·al·mei al·ma·ya.

יִתְבָּרַךְ וְיִשְׁתַּבַּח, וְיִתְפָּאַר וְיִתְרוֹמַם וְיִתְנַשֵּׂא,
וְיִתְהַדַּר וְיִתְעַלֶּה וְיִתְהַלָּל שְׁמֵהּ דְּקוּדְשָׁא, בְּרִיךְ
הוּא, לְעֵלָּא מִן־כָּל־בִּרְכָתָא וְשִׁירָתָא, תֻּשְׁבְּחָתָא
וְנֶחֱמָתָא דַּאֲמִירָן בְּעָלְמָא, וְאִמְרוּ: אָמֵן.

Yit·ba·racn ve·yish·ta·bach, ve·yit·pa·ar ve·yit·ro·mam
ve·yit·na·sei, ve·yit·ha·dar ve·yit·a·leh ve·yit·ha·lal she·mei

158

de·ku·de·sha, be·rich hu, le·ei·la min kol bi·re·cha·ta
ve·shi·ra·ta, tush·be·cha·ta ve·ne·che·ma·ta, da·a·mi·ran
be·al·ma, ve·i·me·ru: a·mein.

יְהֵא שְׁלָמָא רַבָּא מִן־שְׁמַיָּא וְחַיִּים עָלֵינוּ וְעַל־כָּל־
יִשְׂרָאֵל, וְאִמְרוּ: אָמֵן.

Ye·hei she·la·ma ra·ba min she·ma·ya ve·cha·yim a·lei·nu ve·al
kol Yis·ra·eil, ve·i·me·ru: a·mein.

עֹשֶׂה שָׁלוֹם בִּמְרוֹמָיו, הוּא יַעֲשֶׂה שָׁלוֹם עָלֵינוּ וְעַל־
כָּל־יִשְׂרָאֵל, וְאִמְרוּ: אָמֵן.

O·seh sha·lom bi·me·ro·mav, hu ya·a·seh sha·lom a·lei·nu ve·al
kol Yis·ra·eil, ve·i·me·ru: a·mein.

Let the glory of God be extolled, let His great name be hallowed
in the world whose creation He willed. May His kingdom soon
prevail, in our own day, our own lives, and the life of all Israel,
and let us say: Amen.
Let His great name be blessed for ever and ever.
Let the name of the Holy One, blessed is He, be glorified, exalted, and honored, though He is beyond all the praises, songs,
and adorations that we can utter, and let us say: Amen.
For us and for all Israel, may the blessing of peace and the
promise of life come true, and let us say: Amen.
May the One who causes peace to reign in the high heavens, let
peace descend on us, on all Israel, and all the world, and let us
say: Amen.

◆ ◆

May the Source of peace send peace to all who mourn,
and comfort to all who are bereaved. Amen.

ALL THE WORLD   וְיֶאֱתָיוּ

וְיֶאֱתָיוּ כֹל לְעָבְדֶךָ, וִיבָרְכוּ שֵׁם כְּבוֹדֶךָ, וְיַגִּידוּ בָאִיִּים
צִדְקֶךָ. וְיִדְרְשׁוּךָ עַמִּים לֹא יְדָעוּךָ, וִיהַלְלוּךָ כָּל־
אַפְסֵי אָרֶץ, וְיֹאמְרוּ תָמִיד: יִגְדַּל יְיָ.

וְיִזְבְּחוּ לְךָ אֶת־זִבְחֵיהֶם, וְיִזְנְחוּ אֶת־עֲצַבֵּיהֶם,
וְיַחְפְּרוּ עִם פְּסִילֵיהֶם, וְיַטּוּ שְׁכֶם אֶחָד לְעָבְדֶךָ.
וְיִרָאוּךָ עִם שֶׁמֶשׁ מְבַקְשֵׁי פָנֶיךָ, וְיַכִּירוּ כֹּחַ
מַלְכוּתֶךָ, וִילַמְּדוּ תוֹעִים בִּינָה.

וְיִפְצְחוּ הָרִים רִנָּה, וְיִצְהֲלוּ אִיִּים בְּמָלְכֶךָ, וִיקַבְּלוּ עֹל
מַלְכוּתֶךָ. וִירוֹמְמוּךָ בִּקְהַל עָם, וְיִשְׁמְעוּ רְחוֹקִים
וְיָבוֹאוּ, וְיִתְּנוּ לְךָ כֶּתֶר מְלוּכָה.

Ve·ye·e·ta·yu kol le·ov·de·cha, vi·va·re·chu sheim ke·vo·de·cha,
ve·ya·gi·du va·i·yim tsid·ke·cha. Ve·yid·re·shu·cha a·mim lo
ye·da·u·cha, vi·ha·le·lu·cha kol a·fe·sei a·rets, ve·yo·me·ru
ta·mid: yig·dal A·do·nai.

Ve·yiz·be·chu le·cha et zi·ve·chei·hem, ve·yiz·ne·chu et a·
tsa·bei·hem, ve·yach·pe·ru im pe·si·lei·hem, ve·ya·tu she·chem
e·chad le·ov·de·cha. Ve·yi·ra·u·cha im she·mesh me·va·ke·shei
fa·ne·cha, ve·ya·ki·ru ko·ach mal·chu·te·cha, ve·yil·me·du to·im
bi·na.

Ve·yif·tse·chu ha·rim ri·na, ve·yits·ha·lu i·yim be·mo·le·che·cha,
vi·ka·be·lu ol mal·chu·te·cha. Vi·ro·me·mu·cha bi·ke·hal am,
ve·yish·me·u re·cho·kim ve·ya·vo·u, ve·yi·te·nu le·cha ke·ter
me·lu·cha.

All the world shall come to serve You,
  And bless Your glorious name,
And Your righteousness triumphant
  The islands shall proclaim.

And the peoples shall go seeking
    Who knew You not before.
And the ends of earth shall praise You,
    And tell Your greatness o'er.

They shall build for You their altars,
    Their idols overthrown,
And their graven gods shall shame them,
    As they turn to You alone.
They shall worship You at sunrise,
    And feel Your kingdom's might,
And impart their understanding
    To those astray in night.

With the coming of Your kingdom
    The hills shall shout with song,
And the islands laugh exultant
    That they to God belong.
And through all Your congregations
    So loud Your praise shall ring,
That the utmost peoples, hearing,
    Shall hail You crowned King.

Benediction

And now, at the beginning of a new year,
we pray for blessing:

The spirit of wisdom and understanding. *Amen.*

The spirit of insight and courage. *Amen.*

The spirit of knowledge and reverence. *Amen.*

May we overcome trouble, pain, and sorrow. *Amen.*

May our days and years increase. *Amen.*

יְהִי רָצוֹן מִלְּפָנֶיךָ, יְיָ אֱלֹהֵינוּ וֵאלֹהֵי אֲבוֹתֵינוּ,
שֶׁתְּחַדֵּשׁ עָלֵינוּ שָׁנָה טוֹבָה וּמְתוּקָה.

Eternal our God and God of our people,
renew us for a good year.

Amen and Amen.

Morning Service II

תפלת שחרית ב

עדת ישראל,
Congregation Israel,
Israel My witness,
Congregation as witness to the One!
Our rabbis taught:
'I am God, and you are My witnesses.'
I can be God only when you are My witnesses.

The word of God is of no avail
unless the congregation bears witness.

Congregation, witness,
Congregation when you become one
in the service of the Highest
you can comprehend.

What do we serve here?
To what end is our effort?
Why do we assemble?
To whose voice do we hearken?

Here we are,
our presence a question,
yet every word a hope.
Challenged by this time,
let each begin response,

Maker, Parent, Teacher, Shaper,
bless us, bless us,
and Your Presence be a light.
Resting here and dwelling here,
Your Name, Torah, and Teaching
be a light, a lamp, a warming flame.
In us renew the love
with which our life begins,

sacred, joyful, fresh and free,
bright with fables and with song;
in us renew the life
in which our love begins.

עדת ישראל,
Congregation Israel!
Israel is your name.
Israel, 'God will rule,' is your name.
The search for the Highest is your name.

'The toppling of idols,
quest for a beyond,'
that is our name:
beyond the lower, beyond the lesser,
beyond the slavish and debased.

Israel!
You have become a name
for purpose and life.
Still you are called
to the service of One
who dwells within
our hymn of praise.

◆ ◆

If desired, the Morning Blessings and Poems of Praise, pages 79-98,
may be read here, in whole or in part. Then continue on page 165.

Sweet hymns and songs will I recite
To sing of You, by day and night.
Of You, who are my soul's delight.

How does my soul within me yearn
Beneath Your shadow to return,
Your secret mysteries to learn.

And e'en while yet Your glory fires
My words, and hymns of praise inspires,
Your love it is my heart desires.

My meditation day and night,
May it be pleasant in Your sight,
For You are all my soul's delight.

אַנְעִים זְמִירוֹת וְשִׁירִים
אֶאֱרוֹג,
כִּי אֵלֶיךָ נַפְשִׁי תַעֲרוֹג.
נַפְשִׁי חִמְדָה בְּצֵל יָדֶךָ,
לָדַעַת כָּל־רָז סוֹדֶךָ.
מִדֵּי דַבְּרִי בִּכְבוֹדֶךָ,
הוֹמֶה לִבִּי אֶל־דּוֹדֶיךָ.
יֶעֱרַב־נָא שִׂיחִי עָלֶיךָ,
כִּי נַפְשִׁי תַעֲרוֹג אֵלֶיךָ.

◆ ◆

MEDITATION

This Rosh Hashanah, each of us enters this sanctuary
with a different need.

Some hearts are full of gratitude and joy:
They are overflowing with the happiness of love
and the joy of life;
they are eager to confront the day, to make the world more fair;
they are recovering from illness or have escaped misfortune.
And we rejoice with them.

Some hearts ache with sorrow:
Disappointments weigh heavily upon them, and they have
tasted despair; families have been broken;
loved ones lie on a bed of pain;
death has taken those whom they cherished.
May our presence and sympathy bring them comfort.

Some hearts are embittered:
They have sought answers in vain;

have had their ideals mocked and betrayed:
life has lost its meaning and value.
May the knowledge that we too are searching,
restore their hope that there is something to find.

Some spirits hunger:
They long for friendship; they crave understanding;
they yearn for warmth.
May we in our common need gain strength from one another:
sharing our joys, lightening each other's burdens, and praying
for the welfare of our community.

◆ ◆

O Source of light and truth, Creator of the eternal law of
goodness, and of the impulse within us for justice and
mercy, we pray that this hour of worship may be one of vision and inspiration. Help us to find knowledge by which
to live; lead us to take the words we shall speak into our
hearts and our lives.

*Bless all who enter this sanctuary in search and in need, all
who bring to this place the offering of their hearts. May our
worship here lead us to fulfill our words and our hopes with
acts of kindness, peace, and love. Amen.*

◆ ◆

READER'S KADDISH   חצי קדיש

יִתְגַּדַּל וְיִתְקַדַּשׁ שְׁמֵהּ רַבָּא בְּעָלְמָא דִּי־בְרָא כִרְעוּתֵהּ, וְיַמְלִיךְ
מַלְכוּתֵהּ בְּחַיֵּיכוֹן וּבְיוֹמֵיכוֹן וּבְחַיֵּי דְכָל־בֵּית יִשְׂרָאֵל, בַּעֲגָלָא
וּבִזְמַן קָרִיב, וְאִמְרוּ: אָמֵן.
יְהֵא שְׁמֵהּ רַבָּא מְבָרַךְ לְעָלַם וּלְעָלְמֵי עָלְמַיָּא.
יִתְבָּרַךְ וְיִשְׁתַּבַּח, וְיִתְפָּאַר וְיִתְרוֹמַם וְיִתְנַשֵּׂא, וְיִתְהַדָּר

166

וְיִתְעַלֶּה וְיִתְהַלָּל שְׁמֵהּ דְּקוּדְשָׁא, בְּרִיךְ הוּא, לְעֵלָּא מִן כָּל־
בִּרְכָתָא וְשִׁירָתָא, תֻּשְׁבְּחָתָא וְנֶחֱמָתָא דַּאֲמִירָן בְּעָלְמָא,
וְאִמְרוּ: אָמֵן.

Let the glory of God be extolled, let His great name be hallowed
in the world whose creation He willed. May His kingdom soon
prevail, in our own day, our own lives, and the life of all Israel,
and let us say: Amen.
Let His great name be blessed for ever and ever.
Let the name of the Holy One, blessed is He, be glorified, exalted, and honored, though He is beyond all the praises, songs,
and adorations that we can utter, and let us say: Amen.

* *

All rise

שמע וברכותיה

בָּרְכוּ אֶת־יְיָ הַמְבֹרָךְ!

Praise the Lord, to whom our praise is due!

בָּרוּךְ יְיָ הַמְבֹרָךְ לְעוֹלָם וָעֶד!

*Praised be the Lord, to whom our praise is due,
now and for ever!*

* *

CREATION   יוצר

בָּרוּךְ אַתָּה, יְיָ אֱלֹהֵינוּ, מֶלֶךְ הָעוֹלָם, יוֹצֵר אוֹר
וּבוֹרֵא חְשֶׁךְ, עֹשֶׂה שָׁלוֹם וּבוֹרֵא אֶת־הַכֹּל.

כָּל כּוֹכְבֵי בְקֶר לְךָ יָשִׁירוּ, כִּי זָהֳרֵיהֶם מִמְּךָ יַזְהִירוּ.
וּבְנֵי אֱלֹהִים עֹמְדִים עַל מִשְׁמָרוֹת לַיְל וְיוֹם, שָׁם

167

נֶאְדָּר יַאְדִירוּ, וּקְהַל קְדוֹשִׁים קִבְּלוּ מֵהֶם וְכָל־
שַׁחַר לְשַׁחַר בֵּיתְךָ יָעִירוּ.

Praised be the Lord our God, Ruler of the universe, who
makes light and creates darkness, who ordains peace and
fashions all things.

To You the stars of morning sing,
From You their bright radiance must spring.

And steadfast in their vigils, day and night,
The sons of God, flooded with fervor, ring
Your praise; they teach the holy ones to bring
Into Your house the breath of early light.

הַמֵּאִיר לָאָרֶץ וְלַדָּרִים עָלֶיהָ בְּרַחֲמִים, וּבְטוּבוֹ
מְחַדֵּשׁ בְּכָל־יוֹם תָּמִיד מַעֲשֵׂה בְרֵאשִׁית.

מָה רַבּוּ מַעֲשֶׂיךָ, יְיָ! כֻּלָּם בְּחָכְמָה עָשִׂיתָ, מָלְאָה
הָאָרֶץ קִנְיָנֶךָ.

תִּתְבָּרַךְ, יְיָ אֱלֹהֵינוּ, עַל־שֶׁבַח מַעֲשֵׂה יָדֶיךָ, וְעַל־
מְאוֹרֵי־אוֹר שֶׁעָשִׂיתָ: יְפָאֲרוּךָ. סֶּלָה. בָּרוּךְ אַתָּה, יְיָ,
יוֹצֵר הַמְּאוֹרוֹת.

With compassion You give light to the earth and all who
dwell there; with goodness You renew the work of creation
continually, day by day.

How manifold are Your works, O Lord; in wisdom You
have made them all; the earth in its fullness is Yours.

Beyond our praise is the work of Your hands; beyond ex-
pression, the wonder of Your light.

Blessed is the Lord, the Maker of light.

◆ ◆

168

אַהֲבָה רַבָּה אֲהַבְתָּנוּ, יְיָ אֱלֹהֵינוּ, חֶמְלָה גְדוֹלָה
וִיתֵרָה חָמַלְתָּ עָלֵינוּ. אָבִינוּ מַלְכֵּנוּ, בַּעֲבוּר אֲבוֹתֵינוּ
שֶׁבָּטְחוּ בְךָ וַתְּלַמְּדֵם חֻקֵּי חַיִּים, כֵּן תְּחָנֵּנוּ וּתְלַמְּדֵנוּ.
אָבִינוּ, הָאָב הָרַחֲמָן, הַמְרַחֵם, רַחֵם עָלֵינוּ וְתֵן בְּלִבֵּנוּ
לְהָבִין וּלְהַשְׂכִּיל, לִשְׁמֹעַ לִלְמֹד וּלְלַמֵּד, לִשְׁמֹר
וְלַעֲשׂוֹת וּלְקַיֵּם אֶת־כָּל־דִּבְרֵי תַלְמוּד תּוֹרָתֶךָ
בְּאַהֲבָה.

Great is Your love for us, O Lord our God, and deep
Your compassion. Our Maker and King, our ancestors
trusted in You, and You taught them the laws of life: be
gracious now to us, and teach us.

Have compassion upon us, O Source of mercy, and guide
us to know and understand, to learn and teach, to observe
and uphold with love all the teachings of Your Torah.

וְהָאֵר עֵינֵינוּ בְּתוֹרָתֶךָ, וְדַבֵּק לִבֵּנוּ בְּמִצְוֹתֶיךָ, וְיַחֵד
לְבָבֵנוּ לְאַהֲבָה וּלְיִרְאָה אֶת־שְׁמֶךָ. וְלֹא־נֵבוֹשׁ
לְעוֹלָם וָעֶד, כִּי בְשֵׁם קָדְשְׁךָ הַגָּדוֹל וְהַנּוֹרָא בָּטָחְנוּ.
נָגִילָה וְנִשְׂמְחָה בִּישׁוּעָתֶךָ, כִּי אֵל פּוֹעֵל יְשׁוּעוֹת
אָתָּה, וּבָנוּ בָחַרְתָּ וְקֵרַבְתָּנוּ לְשִׁמְךָ הַגָּדוֹל סֶלָה
בֶּאֱמֶת, לְהוֹדוֹת לְךָ וּלְיַחֶדְךָ בְּאַהֲבָה. בָּרוּךְ אַתָּה, יְיָ,
הַבּוֹחֵר בְּעַמּוֹ יִשְׂרָאֵל בְּאַהֲבָה.

Enlighten us with Your Teaching, help us to hold fast to
Your Mitzvot, and unite our hearts to love and revere
Your name.

Then shall we never be shamed, for we shall put our trust in
You, the great, holy, and awesome One. We shall rejoice

*and be glad in Your salvation, for You, O God, are the
Author of many deliverances. In love You have chosen us and
drawn us near to serve You in faithfulness and to proclaim
Your unity.*

Blessed are You, O Lord: You have chosen Your people
Israel in love.

◆ ◆

שְׁמַע יִשְׂרָאֵל: יְיָ אֱלֹהֵינוּ, יְיָ אֶחָד!

Hear, O Israel: The Lord is our God, the Lord is One!

בָּרוּךְ שֵׁם כְּבוֹד מַלְכוּתוֹ לְעוֹלָם וָעֶד!

Blessed is His glorious kingdom for ever and ever!

All are seated

וְאָהַבְתָּ אֵת יְיָ אֱלֹהֶיךָ בְּכָל־לְבָבְךָ וּבְכָל־נַפְשְׁךָ
וּבְכָל־מְאֹדֶךָ. וְהָיוּ הַדְּבָרִים הָאֵלֶּה, אֲשֶׁר אָנֹכִי מְצַוְּךָ
הַיּוֹם, עַל־לְבָבֶךָ. וְשִׁנַּנְתָּם לְבָנֶיךָ, וְדִבַּרְתָּ בָּם
בְּשִׁבְתְּךָ בְּבֵיתֶךָ, וּבְלֶכְתְּךָ בַדֶּרֶךְ, וּבְשָׁכְבְּךָ וּבְקוּמֶךָ.
וּקְשַׁרְתָּם לְאוֹת עַל־יָדֶךָ, וְהָיוּ לְטֹטָפֹת בֵּין עֵינֶיךָ,
וּכְתַבְתָּם עַל־מְזֻזוֹת בֵּיתֶךָ, וּבִשְׁעָרֶיךָ.

*You shall love the Lord your God with all your mind, with all
your strength, with all your being. Set these words, which I
command you this day, upon your heart. Teach them
faithfully to your children; speak of them in your home and
on your way, when you lie down and when you rise up. Bind
them as a sign upon your hand; let them be a symbol before
your eyes; inscribe them on the doorposts of your house, and
on your gates.*

לְמַעַן תִּזְכְּרוּ וַעֲשִׂיתֶם אֶת־כָּל־מִצְוֹתָי, וִהְיִיתֶם
קְדֹשִׁים לֵאלֹהֵיכֶם. אֲנִי יְיָ אֱלֹהֵיכֶם, אֲשֶׁר הוֹצֵאתִי
אֶתְכֶם מֵאֶרֶץ מִצְרַיִם לִהְיוֹת לָכֶם לֵאלֹהִים. אֲנִי יְיָ
אֱלֹהֵיכֶם.

*Be mindful of all My Mitzvot, and do them: so shall you
consecrate yourselves to your God. I, the Lord, am your God
who led you out of Egypt to be your God; I, the Lord, am
your God.*

✦ ✦

גאולה

אֱמֶת וְיַצִּיב, וְאָהוּב וְחָבִיב, וְנוֹרָא וְאַדִּיר, וְטוֹב וְיָפֶה
הַדָּבָר הַזֶּה עָלֵינוּ לְעוֹלָם וָעֶד. אֱמֶת, אֱלֹהֵי עוֹלָם
מַלְכֵּנוּ, צוּר יַעֲקֹב מָגֵן יִשְׁעֵנוּ.

True and enduring, beloved and precious, awesome, good,
and beautiful is this eternal teaching.
*This truth we hold to be for ever certain: the Eternal God is
our King; the Rock of Jacob is our protecting Shield.*

לְדֹר וָדֹר הוּא קַיָּם, וּשְׁמוֹ קַיָּם, וְכִסְאוֹ נָכוֹן,
וּמַלְכוּתוֹ וֶאֱמוּנָתוֹ לָעַד קַיֶּמֶת. וּדְבָרָיו חָיִים וְקַיָּמִים,
נֶאֱמָנִים וְנֶחֱמָדִים, לָעַד וּלְעוֹלְמֵי עוֹלָמִים.

You abide through all generations; Your name is Eternal.
Your throne stands firm; Your sovereignty and
faithfulness are everlasting.
Your words live and endure, true and precious to all eternity.

מִמִּצְרַיִם גְּאַלְתָּנוּ, יְיָ אֱלֹהֵינוּ, וּמִבֵּית עֲבָדִים פְּדִיתָנוּ.

Lord our God, You redeemed us from Egypt;
You set us free from the house of bondage.

עַל־זֹאת שִׁבְּחוּ אֲהוּבִים וְרוֹמְמוּ אֵל, וְנָתְנוּ יְדִידִים
זְמִירוֹת, שִׁירוֹת וְתִשְׁבָּחוֹת, בְּרָכוֹת וְהוֹדָאוֹת
לַמֶּלֶךְ, אֵל חַי וְקַיָּם.

For this the people who felt Your love sang songs of
praise to You:
The living God, high and exalted, mighty and awesome,

רָם וְנִשָּׂא, גָּדוֹל וְנוֹרָא, מַשְׁפִּיל גֵּאִים וּמַגְבִּיהַּ
שְׁפָלִים, מוֹצִיא אֲסִירִים וּפוֹדֶה עֲנָוִים, וְעוֹזֵר דַּלִּים,
וְעוֹנֶה לְעַמּוֹ בְּעֵת שַׁוְּעָם אֵלָיו.

Who humbles the proud and raises the lowly,
who frees the captive and redeems the oppressed.
You are the Answer to all who cry out to You.

תְּהִלּוֹת לְאֵל עֶלְיוֹן, בָּרוּךְ הוּא וּמְבֹרָךְ. מֹשֶׁה וּבְנֵי
יִשְׂרָאֵל לְךָ עָנוּ שִׁירָה בְּשִׂמְחָה רַבָּה, וְאָמְרוּ כֻלָּם:

All praise to God Most High, the Source of blessing! Like
Moses and Israel, we sing to You this song of rejoicing:

מִי־כָמְכָה בָּאֵלִם, יְיָ?

Who is like You, Eternal One, among
the gods that are worshipped?

מִי כָּמְכָה, נֶאְדָּר בַּקֹּדֶשׁ,
נוֹרָא תְהִלֹּת, עֹשֵׂה פֶלֶא?

Who is like You, majestic in holiness,
awesome in splendor, doing wonders?

שִׁירָה חֲדָשָׁה שִׁבְּחוּ גְאוּלִים לְשִׁמְךָ עַל־שְׂפַת הַיָּם;

172

יַחַד כֻּלָּם הוֹדוּ וְהִמְלִיכוּ וְאָמְרוּ: "יְיָ יִמְלֹךְ לְעוֹלָם
וָעֶד!"

A new song the redeemed sang to Your name. At the shore of
the Sea, saved from destruction, we proclaimed Your sovereign
power: "The Eternal will reign for ever and ever!"

צוּר יִשְׂרָאֵל, קוּמָה בְּעֶזְרַת יִשְׂרָאֵל, וּפְדֵה כִנְאֻמֶךָ
יְהוּדָה וְיִשְׂרָאֵל. גֹּאֲלֵנוּ יְיָ צְבָאוֹת שְׁמוֹ, קְדוֹשׁ
יִשְׂרָאֵל. בָּרוּךְ אַתָּה, יְיָ, גָּאַל יִשְׂרָאֵל.

O Rock of Israel, come to Israel's help. Fulfill Your promise of
redemption for Judah and Israel. Our Redeemer is the Lord of
Hosts, the Holy One of Israel. Blessed is the Lord, the
Redeemer of Israel.

• •

All rise

תפלה

אֲדֹנָי, שְׂפָתַי תִּפְתָּח, וּפִי יַגִּיד תְּהִלָּתֶךָ.

Eternal God, open my lips, that my mouth may declare Your
glory.

MERIT OF OUR ANCESTORS   אבות

בָּרוּךְ אַתָּה, יְיָ אֱלֹהֵינוּ וֵאלֹהֵי אֲבוֹתֵינוּ, אֱלֹהֵי
אַבְרָהָם, אֱלֹהֵי יִצְחָק, וֵאלֹהֵי יַעֲקֹב: הָאֵל הַגָּדוֹל,
הַגִּבּוֹר וְהַנּוֹרָא, אֵל עֶלְיוֹן. גּוֹמֵל חֲסָדִים טוֹבִים,
וְקוֹנֵה הַכֹּל, וְזוֹכֵר חַסְדֵי אָבוֹת, וּמֵבִיא גְאֻלָּה לִבְנֵי
בְנֵיהֶם, לְמַעַן שְׁמוֹ, בְּאַהֲבָה.

173

°Each generation has its path; each a vision of its own.

Yet each is linked to all; their origin and goal are one.

Our mothers and fathers kindled light:

To lead us to the day of shining hope,
with mercy our companion along the way.

A life unmarred by hate and war;

A time of steadfast love, our journey's end!

Homage to the faithful who came before us;

And blessed the light that is ours to kindle!

Honor to the generations of Israel, our people!

All honor to those who illumine our paths!

זָכְרֵנוּ לְחַיִּים, מֶלֶךְ חָפֵץ בַּחַיִּים, וְכָתְבֵנוּ בְּסֵפֶר
הַחַיִּים, לְמַעַנְךָ אֱלֹהִים חַיִּים. מֶלֶךְ עוֹזֵר וּמוֹשִׁיעַ
וּמָגֵן. בָּרוּךְ אַתָּה, יְיָ, מָגֵן אַבְרָהָם.

Remember us unto life, O Sovereign who delights in life,
and inscribe us in the Book of Life, O God of life.

◆ ◆

THE POWER TO LIVE AND ACT   גבורות

אַתָּה גִבּוֹר לְעוֹלָם, אֲדֹנָי, מְחַיֵּה הַכֹּל אַתָּה, רַב
לְהוֹשִׁיעַ. מְכַלְכֵּל חַיִּים בְּחֶסֶד, מְחַיֵּה הַכֹּל בְּרַחֲמִים

°This symbol indicates that the English is a variation suggested by the theme
of the Hebrew.

רַבִּים. סוֹמֵךְ נוֹפְלִים, וְרוֹפֵא חוֹלִים, וּמַתִּיר
אֲסוּרִים, וּמְקַיֵּם אֱמוּנָתוֹ לִישֵׁנֵי עָפָר. מִי כָמְוֹךָ, בַּעַל
גְּבוּרוֹת, וּמִי דּוֹמֶה לָּךְ, מֶלֶךְ מֵמִית וּמְחַיֶּה וּמַצְמִיחַ
יְשׁוּעָה? מִי כָמְוֹךָ אַב הָרַחֲמִים, זוֹכֵר יְצוּרָיו לְחַיִּים
בְּרַחֲמִים? וְנֶאֱמָן אַתָּה לְהַחֲיוֹת הַכֹּל. בָּרוּךְ אַתָּה, יְיָ,
מְחַיֵּה הַכֹּל.

°Great is the eternal power at the heart of life; mighty the
love that is stronger than death.

*Faithful love gives life to all, and acts of grace restore our
strength.*

Life's harsh winds uproot the weak; its hard rains beat
down upon our kin. Let those who stand support the falling, keep faith with those who lie in the dust.

*To the sick, we must bring healing; and to those who are
bound, release.*

How good to redeem the ancient pledge, for joy to blossom in arid soil!

*We give thanks for the power to live and to act, and for the
blessing of love that is stronger than death.*

All are seated

• •

ונתנה תקף

MEDITATION

It is said that the words we are about to utter were born of the
martyrdom of Rabbi Amnon of Mayence. He chose to die that

his faith might live. He said: *Unetaneh tokef kedushat hayom,*
Let us proclaim the sacred power of this day; it is awesome and
full of dread. Now the divine Judge looks upon our deeds, and
determines our destiny.

A legend . . . and yet, surely our deeds do not pass away un-
recorded. Every word, every act inscribes itself in the Book of
Life. Freely we choose, and what we have chosen to become
stands in judgment over what we may yet hope to be. In our
choices we are not always free. But if only we make the effort to
turn, every force of goodness, within and without, will help us,
while we live, to escape that death of the heart which leads to
sin.

◆◆

וּנְתַנֶּה תְּקֶף קְדֻשַּׁת הַיּוֹם כִּי הוּא נוֹרָא וְאָיֹם. וּבוֹ
תִנָּשֵׂא מַלְכוּתֶךָ וְיִכּוֹן בְּחֶסֶד כִּסְאֶךָ וְתֵשֵׁב עָלָיו
בֶּאֱמֶת. אֱמֶת כִּי אַתָּה הוּא דַיָּן וּמוֹכִיחַ וְיוֹדֵעַ וָעֵד,
וְכוֹתֵב וְחוֹתֵם וְסוֹפֵר וּמוֹנֶה, וְתִזְכֹּר כָּל־הַנִּשְׁכָּחוֹת,
וְתִפְתַּח אֶת־סֵפֶר הַזִּכְרוֹנוֹת, וּמֵאֵלָיו יִקָּרֵא וְחוֹתַם
יַד כָּל־אָדָם בּוֹ.

Let us proclaim the sacred power of this day;
it is awesome and full of dread.
For on this day Your dominion is exalted,
Your throne established in steadfast love;
there in truth You reign.
In truth You are
Judge and Arbiter, Counsel and Witness.
You write and You seal, You record and recount.
You remember deeds long forgotten.
You open the book of our days,
and what is written there proclaims itself,
for it bears the signature
of every human being.

וּבְשׁוֹפָר גָּדוֹל יִתָּקַע וְקוֹל דְּמָמָה דַקָּה יִשָּׁמַע.
וּמַלְאָכִים יֵחָפֵזוּן וְחִיל וּרְעָדָה יֹאחֵזוּן וְיֹאמְרוּ: הִנֵּה
יוֹם הַדִּין. לִפְקֹד עַל צְבָא מָרוֹם בַּדִּין, כִּי לֹא יִזְכּוּ
בְעֵינֶיךָ בַּדִּין. וְכָל־בָּאֵי עוֹלָם יַעַבְרוּן לְפָנֶיךָ כִּבְנֵי
מָרוֹן. כְּבַקָּרַת רוֹעֶה עֶדְרוֹ, מַעֲבִיר צֹאנוֹ תַּחַת
שִׁבְטוֹ, כֵּן תַּעֲבִיר וְתִסְפֹּר וְתִמְנֶה וְתִפְקֹד נֶפֶשׁ כָּל־
חָי, וְתַחְתֹּךְ קִצְבָה לְכָל־בְּרִיָּה וְתִכְתֹּב אֶת־גְּזַר דִּינָם.

The great Shofar is sounded,
the still, small voice is heard;
the angels,
gripped by fear and trembling,
declare in awe:
This is the Day of Judgment!
For even the hosts of heaven are judged,
as all who dwell on earth
stand arrayed before You.

As the shepherd seeks out his flock,
and makes the sheep pass under his staff,
so do You muster and number and consider
every soul,
setting the bounds of every creature's life,
and decreeing its destiny.

בְּרֹאשׁ הַשָּׁנָה יִכָּתֵבוּן וּבְיוֹם צוֹם כִּפּוּר יֵחָתֵמוּן.
כַּמָּה יַעַבְרוּן וְכַמָּה יִבָּרֵאוּן, מִי יִחְיֶה וּמִי יָמוּת, מִי
בְקִצּוֹ וּמִי לֹא בְקִצּוֹ, מִי בָאֵשׁ וּמִי בַמַּיִם, מִי בַחֶרֶב
וּמִי בַחַיָּה, מִי בָרָעָב וּמִי בַצָּמָא וּמִי בָרַעַשׁ וּמִי
בַמַּגֵּפָה, מִי בַחֲנִיקָה וּמִי בַסְּקִילָה. מִי יָנוּחַ וּמִי יָנוּעַ,
מִי יַשְׁקִיט וּמִי יְטֹרַף, מִי יִשָּׁלֵו וּמִי יִתְיַסַּר, מִי יֵעָנִי
וּמִי יַעֲשִׁיר, מִי יִשָּׁפֵל וּמִי יָרוּם.

On Rosh Hashanah it is written,
on Yom Kippur it is sealed:

How many shall pass on, how many shall come to be;
who shall live and who shall die;
who shall see ripe age and who shall not;
who shall perish by fire and who by water;
who by sword and who by beast;
who by hunger and who by thirst;
who by earthquake and who by plague;
who by strangling and who by stoning;
who shall be secure and who shall be driven;
who shall be tranquil and who shall be troubled;
who shall be poor and who shall be rich;
who shall be humbled and who exalted.

וּתְשׁוּבָה וּתְפִלָּה וּצְדָקָה
מַעֲבִירִין אֶת־רֹעַ הַגְּזֵרָה.

But REPENTANCE, PRAYER, and CHARITY
temper judgment's severe decree.

כִּי כְשִׁמְךָ כֵּן תְּהִלָּתֶךָ, קָשֶׁה לִכְעֹס וְנְוֹחַ לִרְצוֹת. כִּי
לֹא תַחְפֹּץ בְּמוֹת הַמֵּת כִּי אִם בְּשׁוּבוֹ מִדַּרְכּוֹ וְחָיָה.
וְעַד יוֹם מוֹתוֹ תְּחַכֶּה־לּוֹ, אִם יָשׁוּב מִיַּד תְּקַבְּלוֹ.
אֱמֶת כִּי אַתָּה הוּא יוֹצְרָם וְיוֹדֵעַ יִצְרָם כִּי הֵם בָּשָׂר
וָדָם.

This is Your glory: You are
slow to anger, ready to forgive.
Lord, it is not the death of sinners You seek,
but that they should turn from their ways
and live.
Until the last day You wait for them,
welcoming them
as soon as they turn to You.

You have created us and know what we are;
we are but flesh and blood.

אָדָם יְסוֹדוֹ מֵעָפָר וְסוֹפוֹ לֶעָפָר. בְּנַפְשׁוֹ יָבִיא לַחְמוֹ.
מָשׁוּל כַּחֶרֶס הַנִּשְׁבָּר, כְּחָצִיר יָבֵשׁ וּכְצִיץ נוֹבֵל, כְּצֵל
עוֹבֵר וּכְעָנָן כָּלֶה, וּכְרוּחַ נוֹשֶׁבֶת, וּכְאָבָק פּוֹרֵחַ,
וְכַחֲלוֹם יָעוּף.

וְאַתָּה הוּא מֶלֶךְ אֵל חַי וְקַיָּם!

Man's origin is dust,
and dust is his end.
Each of us is a shattered urn,
grass that must wither,
a flower that will fade,
a shadow moving on,
a cloud passing by,
a particle of dust floating on the wind,
a dream soon forgotten.

But You are the King,
the everlasting God!

All rise

HOLY, HOLY, HOLY   קְדוּשָׁה

נְקַדֵּשׁ אֶת־שִׁמְךָ בָּעוֹלָם כְּשֵׁם שֶׁמַּקְדִּישִׁים אוֹתוֹ
בִּשְׁמֵי מָרוֹם, כַּכָּתוּב עַל יַד נְבִיאֶךָ, וְקָרָא זֶה אֶל־זֶה
וְאָמַר:
קָדוֹשׁ, קָדוֹשׁ, קָדוֹשׁ יְיָ צְבָאוֹת, מְלֹא כָל־הָאָרֶץ
כְּבוֹדוֹ.
אַדִּיר אַדִּירֵנוּ, יְיָ אֲדוֹנֵינוּ, מָה אַדִּיר שִׁמְךָ בְּכָל־
הָאָרֶץ!
בָּרוּךְ כְּבוֹד־יְיָ מִמְּקוֹמוֹ.
אֶחָד הוּא אֱלֹהֵינוּ, הוּא אָבִינוּ, הוּא מַלְכֵּנוּ, הוּא

מוֹשִׁיעֵנוּ; וְהוּא יַשְׁמִיעֵנוּ בְּרַחֲמָיו לְעֵינֵי כָּל־חָי.
"אֲנִי יְיָ אֱלֹהֵיכֶם!"
יִמְלֹךְ יְיָ לְעוֹלָם, אֱלֹהַיִךְ צִיּוֹן, לְדֹר וָדֹר. הַלְלוּיָהּ!
לְדוֹר וָדוֹר נַגִּיד גָּדְלֶךָ, וּלְנֵצַח נְצָחִים קְדֻשָּׁתְךָ
נַקְדִּישׁ. וְשִׁבְחֲךָ, אֱלֹהֵינוּ, מִפִּינוּ לֹא יָמוּשׁ לְעוֹלָם
וָעֶד.

°Holy is the dignity that is human; sacred the mystery we
call divine.

*Holy is the sacrifice made for those we love; precious the
pains they take for us.*

Sublime the glory of the heavens above us; sacred the
beauty that glows within us.

*Noble is the mind in search of meaning. The heart is happy
that finds its way.*

Awesome is the power that rules our being;

Holy the kinship that makes us one.

All are seated

MEDITATION

Why be concerned with meaning? why not be content with
satisfaction of desires and needs? The vital drives of food, sex,
and power, as well as the mental functions aimed at satisfying
them, are as characteristic of animals as they are of us. Being
human is a characteristic of a being who faces the question:
After satisfaction, what?

◆

It is not enough for me to be able to say: "I am;" I want to know *who I am,* and in relation to whom I live. It is not enough for me to ask questions; I want to know how to answer the one question that seems to encompass everything I face: What am I here for?

·

What is the meaning of my being? My quest is not for theoretical knowledge about myself. What I look for is not how to gain a firm hold on myself and on life, but primarily how to live a life that would deserve and evoke an eternal Amen.

♦ ♦

וּבְכֵן תֵּן פַּחְדְּךָ, יְיָ אֱלֹהֵינוּ, עַל כָּל־מַעֲשֶׂיךָ, וְאֵימָתְךָ עַל כָּל־מַה־שֶּׁבָּרֶאתָ. וְיִירָאוּךָ כָּל־הַמַּעֲשִׂים, וְיִשְׁתַּחֲווּ לְפָנֶיךָ כָּל־הַבְּרוּאִים, וְיֵעָשׂוּ כֻלָּם אֲגֻדָּה אַחַת לַעֲשׂוֹת רְצוֹנְךָ בְּלֵבָב שָׁלֵם, כְּמוֹ שֶׁיָּדַעְנוּ, יְיָ אֱלֹהֵינוּ, שֶׁהַשִּׁלְטוֹן לְפָנֶיךָ, עֹז בְּיָדְךָ וּגְבוּרָה בִּימִינֶךָ, וְשִׁמְךָ נוֹרָא עַל כָּל־מַה־שֶּׁבָּרֶאתָ.

WE STAND IN AWE OF CREATION

°We stand in awe of all created things,
the power within them that gives them form,
the ancient law that rules them all:
fish of the sea, birds of the air,
the quiet stone and the beating wave,
all woven from a single loom.

We stand in awe of all created things.

וּבְכֵן תֵּן כָּבוֹד, יְיָ, לְעַמֶּךָ, תְּהִלָּה לִירֵאֶיךָ, וְתִקְוָה לְדוֹרְשֶׁיךָ, וּפִתְחוֹן פֶּה לַמְיַחֲלִים לָךְ, שִׂמְחָה לְאַרְצֶךָ וְשָׂשׂוֹן לְעִירֶךָ, וּצְמִיחַת קֶרֶן לְכָל־יוֹשְׁבֵי תֵבֵל.

181

°We stand in awe of courage:

Honor to those who endure:
the seeker, the giver, the one who loves;
all who sing and all who weep;
the one who makes his loss a gain;
the one who gives his heart to life.

וּבְכֵן צַדִּיקִים יִרְאוּ וְיִשְׂמָחוּ, וִישָׁרִים יַעֲלֹזוּ, וַחֲסִידִים
בְּרִנָּה יָגִילוּ, וְעוֹלָתָה תִּקְפָּץ־פִּיהָ, וְכָל־הָרִשְׁעָה כֻּלָּהּ
כְּעָשָׁן תִּכְלֶה, כִּי תַעֲבִיר מֶמְשֶׁלֶת זָדוֹן מִן הָאָרֶץ.

°Honor to those who endure!

And honor to all who are just:

To be just, upright, and faithful:
let this and this alone give joy.
To reach as high as one may dare,
and do no hurt, and kill no hope:
let this and this alone give joy.
O when will arrogance end
and wickedness cease,
and when will tyrants be no more?
On that day, rejoice!
The faithful will rejoice,
and all who breathe be glad.

וְתִמְלֹךְ אַתָּה, יְיָ, לְבַדְּךָ עַל כָּל־מַעֲשֶׂיךָ, כַּכָּתוּב
בְּדִבְרֵי קָדְשֶׁךָ:
יִמְלֹךְ יְיָ לְעוֹלָם, אֱלֹהַיִךְ צִיּוֹן, לְדֹר וָדֹר. הַלְלוּיָהּ!

°*For goodness shall reign for ever,*
justice shall be exalted,
righteousness hold sway.

As it is written:

182

וַיִּגְבַּה יְיָ צְבָאוֹת בַּמִּשְׁפָּט, וְהָאֵל הַקָּדוֹשׁ נִקְדַּשׁ
בִּצְדָקָה.

The Lord of Hosts is exalted by justice;
the holy God is sanctified by righteousness.

קָדוֹשׁ אַתָּה וְנוֹרָא שְׁמֶךָ, וְאֵין אֱלוֹהַ מִבַּלְעָדֶיךָ.

°We stand in awe of all created things, of all that is holy, of
all we cannot name.

בָּרוּךְ אַתָּה, יְיָ, הַמֶּלֶךְ הַקָּדוֹשׁ.

°*Blessed is the power of holiness that leads the world to the*
rule of goodness.

• •

אַתָּה בְחַרְתָּנוּ מִכָּל־הָעַמִּים, אָהַבְתָּ אוֹתָנוּ וְרָצִיתָ
בָּנוּ, וְרוֹמַמְתָּנוּ מִכָּל־הַלְּשׁוֹנוֹת וְקִדַּשְׁתָּנוּ בְּמִצְוֹתֶיךָ,
וְקֵרַבְתָּנוּ מַלְכֵּנוּ לַעֲבוֹדָתֶךָ, וְשִׁמְךָ הַגָּדוֹל וְהַקָּדוֹשׁ
עָלֵינוּ קָרָאתָ. וַתִּתֶּן־לָנוּ, יְיָ אֱלֹהֵינוּ, בְּאַהֲבָה אֶת־יוֹם
(הַשַּׁבָּת הַזֶּה וְאֶת־יוֹם) הַזִּכָּרוֹן הַזֶּה, יוֹם תְּרוּעָה,
מִקְרָא קֹדֶשׁ, זֵכֶר לִיצִיאַת מִצְרָיִם.

°Out of the mystery of time and event has come the call to
serve the Highest, to hallow this life, this time and place.

°*Now we remember the call. Again it comes on this (Shabbat*
and this) Day of Remembrance, as we hear the sound of the
Shofar, unite in worship, and recall the beginning of all our
liberations, when our people walked upright from the land of
bondage and turned to the Land of Promise.

•

ON SHABBAT

יִשְׂמְחוּ בְמַלְכוּתְךָ שׁוֹמְרֵי שַׁבָּת וְקוֹרְאֵי עֹנֶג. עַם
מְקַדְּשֵׁי שְׁבִיעִי כֻּלָּם יִשְׂבְּעוּ וְיִתְעַנְּגוּ מִטּוּבֶךָ.
וְהַשְּׁבִיעִי רָצִיתָ בּוֹ וְקִדַּשְׁתּוֹ. חֶמְדַּת יָמִים אוֹתוֹ
קָרָאתָ, זֵכֶר לְמַעֲשֵׂה בְרֵאשִׁית.

°Those who keep the Sabbath and call it a delight shall rejoice
in Your kingdom. All who hallow the seventh day shall be gladdened by Your goodness. This day is Israel's festival of the
spirit, sanctified and blessed by You, the most precious of
days, a symbol of the joy of creation.

⋅

אֱלֹהֵינוּ וֵאלֹהֵי אֲבוֹתֵינוּ, יַעֲלֶה וְיָבֹא וְיֵרָאֶה וְיִזָּכֵר זִכְרוֹנֵנוּ
וְזִכְרוֹן כָּל־עַמְּךָ בֵּית יִשְׂרָאֵל לְפָנֶיךָ, לְטוֹבָה, לְחֵן
לְחֶסֶד וּלְרַחֲמִים, לְחַיִּים וּלְשָׁלוֹם בְּיוֹם הַזִּכָּרוֹן הַזֶּה.
זָכְרֵנוּ, יְיָ אֱלֹהֵינוּ, בּוֹ לְטוֹבָה.   אָמֵן.
וּפָקְדֵנוּ בוֹ לִבְרָכָה.   אָמֵן.
וְהוֹשִׁיעֵנוּ בוֹ לְחַיִּים.   אָמֵן.

°As in the heart of matter a flame flares unseen to bring us
warmth, so in the human heart a spark of goodness glows,
a portent of renewal, of life and of peace. This day may we
grow in self-knowledge. This day may we reach out for a
full life. Amen.

⋅

אֱלֹהֵינוּ וֵאלֹהֵי אֲבוֹתֵינוּ, (רְצֵה בִמְנוּחָתֵנוּ,) קַדְּשֵׁנוּ
בְּמִצְוֹתֶיךָ וְתֵן חֶלְקֵנוּ בְּתוֹרָתֶךָ. שַׂבְּעֵנוּ מִטּוּבֶךָ,
וְשַׂמְּחֵנוּ בִּישׁוּעָתֶךָ, (וְהַנְחִילֵנוּ, יְיָ אֱלֹהֵינוּ, בְּאַהֲבָה
וּבְרָצוֹן שַׁבַּת קָדְשֶׁךָ, וְיָנוּחוּ בָהּ יִשְׂרָאֵל, מְקַדְּשֵׁי
שְׁמֶךָ,) וְטַהֵר לִבֵּנוּ לְעָבְדְּךָ בֶּאֱמֶת, כִּי אַתָּה אֱלֹהִים

184

אֱמֶת, וּדְבָרְךָ אֱמֶת וְקַיָּם לָעַד. בָּרוּךְ אַתָּה, יְיָ, מֶלֶךְ
עַל כָּל־הָאָרֶץ, מְקַדֵּשׁ (הַשַּׁבָּת וְ) יִשְׂרָאֵל וְיוֹם
הַזִּכָּרוֹן.

°*We give thanks for the Mitzvot which hallow our days, and
pray for wisdom to guide our lives by Torah. May our
redemptive labors make us glad, our struggle for purity not
fail, our striving for good bring us joy. Blessed is the vision
of holiness that exalts (the Sabbath,) the House of Israel
and the Day of Remembrance.*

• •

THE MIRACLE OF PRAYER   עבודה

רְצֵה, יְיָ אֱלֹהֵינוּ, בְּעַמְּךָ יִשְׂרָאֵל, וּתְפִלָּתָם בְּאַהֲבָה
תְקַבֵּל, וּתְהִי לְרָצוֹן תָּמִיד עֲבוֹדַת יִשְׂרָאֵל עַמֶּךְ.
בָּרוּךְ אַתָּה, יְיָ, שֶׁאוֹתְךָ לְבַדְּךָ בְּיִרְאָה נַעֲבוֹד.

°O fill our minds with knowledge and our hearts with
wisdom;
Praised be the Mind that unifies all creation.

Remind us of the best that is in us:
Praised be the Will that gives us power to choose our way.

Help us to feel the anguish of the afflicted and oppressed;
*Praised be the Heart that inspires in us a vision of justice
and love.*

Make us bring knowledge and skill to help the infirm;
Praised be the Power that brings healing to the sick.

Teach us to stand in awe before the mystery of being.
Praised be the One who is present in the miracle of prayer.

• •

185

ALL OUR BLESSINGS · הודאה

מוֹדִים אֲנַחְנוּ לָךְ, שָׁאַתָּה הוּא יְיָ אֱלֹהֵינוּ וֵאלֹהֵי
אֲבוֹתֵינוּ, אֱלֹהֵי כָל־בָּשָׂר, יוֹצְרֵנוּ יוֹצֵר בְּרֵאשִׁית.
בְּרָכוֹת וְהוֹדָאוֹת לְשִׁמְךָ הַגָּדוֹל וְהַקָּדוֹשׁ עַל־
שֶׁהֶחֱיִיתָנוּ וְקִיַּמְתָּנוּ. כֵּן תְּחַיֵּנוּ וּתְקַיְּמֵנוּ, יְיָ אֱלֹהֵינוּ,
וְתֶאֱסֹף גָּלֻיּוֹתֵינוּ לְחַצְרוֹת קָדְשֶׁךָ, לַעֲשׂוֹת רְצוֹנֶךָ, וּלְעָבְדְּךָ
בְּלֵבָב שָׁלֵם. בָּרוּךְ אֵל הַהוֹדָאוֹת.

°*Many are our blessings on this Day of Remembrance. We
give thanks for life itself, for all that sustains body and mind,
for love and friendship, for the delights of the senses, and for
the excellence of the Torah, which deepens our life and
enriches our days. O let abundant life be the heritage of all
earth's children!*

∙∙

PEACE AND BLESSING · ברכת שלום

אֱלֹהֵינוּ וֵאלֹהֵי אֲבוֹתֵינוּ, בָּרְכֵנוּ בַּבְּרָכָה הַמְשֻׁלֶּשֶׁת
בַּתּוֹרָה:
יְבָרֶכְךָ יְיָ וְיִשְׁמְרֶךָ.
יָאֵר יְיָ פָּנָיו אֵלֶיךָ וִיחֻנֶּךָּ.
יִשָּׂא יְיָ פָּנָיו אֵלֶיךָ וְיָשֵׂם לְךָ שָׁלוֹם.

שִׂים שָׁלוֹם, טוֹבָה וּבְרָכָה, חֵן וָחֶסֶד וְרַחֲמִים, עָלֵינוּ
וְעַל כָּל־יִשְׂרָאֵל עַמֶּךָ. בָּרְכֵנוּ אָבִינוּ, כֻּלָּנוּ כְּאֶחָד,
בְּאוֹר פָּנֶיךָ, כִּי בְאוֹר פָּנֶיךָ נָתַתָּ לָנוּ, יְיָ אֱלֹהֵינוּ,
תּוֹרַת חַיִּים, וְאַהֲבַת חֶסֶד, וּצְדָקָה וּבְרָכָה וְרַחֲמִים,
וְחַיִּים וְשָׁלוֹם. וְטוֹב בְּעֵינֶיךָ לְבָרֵךְ אֶת־עַמְּךָ יִשְׂרָאֵל
בְּכָל־עֵת וּבְכָל־שָׁעָה בִּשְׁלוֹמֶךָ. בְּסֵפֶר חַיִּים בְּרָכָה

וְשָׁלוֹם וּפַרְנָסָה טוֹבָה נִזָּכֵר וְנִכָּתֵב לְפָנֶיךָ, אֲנַחְנוּ
וְכָל־עַמְּךָ בֵּית יִשְׂרָאֵל, לְחַיִּים טוֹבִים וּלְשָׁלוֹם. בָּרוּךְ
אַתָּה, יְיָ, עוֹשֵׂה הַשָּׁלוֹם.

°Peace, happiness, and blessing; grace and love and mercy:
may these descend on us, on all Israel, and all the world.

*May all who breathe affirm the law of life: to love kindness
and mercy, to seek blessing, life, and peace.*

A divine light will shine upon us, one and all, as we struggle to bless the world with righteousness and peace.

*Blessed is the Power that makes for peace, and praised be
those who labor to bring it into the world.*

◆ ◆

MEDITATION

Be among those who cherish truth above ease, and whose
prayers are shafts of light in the darkness that, otherwise, would
envelop us. Be the same within and without. Aspire to be loving,
compassionate, humane, and hopeful. Become the prayer for
goodness your lips have uttered. Become Israel, exemplar of the
Highest, and serve all that is great within you.

◆ ◆

יִהְיוּ לְרָצוֹן אִמְרֵי־פִי וְהֶגְיוֹן לִבִּי לְפָנֶיךָ, יְיָ, צוּרִי
וְגוֹאֲלִי.

or

עֹשֶׂה שָׁלוֹם בִּמְרוֹמָיו, הוּא יַעֲשֶׂה שָׁלוֹם עָלֵינוּ וְעַל
כָּל־יִשְׂרָאֵל, וְאִמְרוּ אָמֵן.

◆ ◆

187

סדר קריאת התורה

For the Reading of the Torah

From Psalm 24

לַייָ הָאָרֶץ וּמְלוֹאָהּ, תֵּבֵל וְיֹשְׁבֵי בָהּ. כִּי־הוּא עַל־
יַמִּים יְסָדָהּ, וְעַל־נְהָרוֹת יְכוֹנְנֶהָ. מִי־יַעֲלֶה בְהַר־יְיָ,
וּמִי־יָקוּם בִּמְקוֹם קָדְשׁוֹ?

The earth is the Lord's and all its fullness, the world and
all who dwell there. For He has laid its foundations in the
sea, and established it upon the currents. Who may ascend
the mountain of the Lord? Who may stand in His holy
place?

נְקִי כַפַּיִם וּבַר־לֵבָב, אֲשֶׁר לֹא־נָשָׂא לַשָּׁוְא נַפְשׁוֹ וְלֹא
נִשְׁבַּע לְמִרְמָה. יִשָּׂא בְרָכָה מֵאֵת יְיָ וּצְדָקָה מֵאֱלֹהֵי
יִשְׁעוֹ. זֶה דּוֹר דֹּרְשָׁו, מְבַקְשֵׁי פָנֶיךָ, יַעֲקֹב. סֶלָה.

*Those with clean hands and pure hearts, who never speak
with malice, who never swear deceitfully. They shall receive
blessings from the Lord, justice from God, their Helper.*

Such are the people who turn to Him, who seek Your
presence, O God of Jacob.

◆ ◆

Lift up your heads, O gates!	שְׂאוּ שְׁעָרִים רָאשֵׁיכֶם,
Lift yourselves up, O ancient doors!	וְהִנָּשְׂאוּ פִּתְחֵי עוֹלָם,
Let the King of Glory enter.	וְיָבוֹא מֶלֶךְ הַכָּבוֹד!
Who is this King of Glory?	מִי הוּא זֶה מֶלֶךְ הַכָּבוֹד?
The Lord of Hosts—	יְיָ צְבָאוֹת—
He is the King of Glory!	הוּא מֶלֶךְ הַכָּבוֹד! סֶלָה.

All rise
The Ark is opened

Avinu, Malkeinu: A hundred generations have stood as we do now before the open Ark. That they found in themselves little merit, testifies to their humility. They repented and amended their ways. They fell, only to rise again, as they climbed toward the Light. Strong was the faith of those who stood here before us, while we are of a generation that has sought to dethrone You.

Many have said to the works of their hands: you are our gods. Strange, then, to see the emptiness in those who cast You out! Strange to see the agonies of our time grow more numerous and more intense, the more our worship centers on ourselves. Strange that men and women grow smaller without You, smaller without the faith that You are with them. We pray, therefore, that this day which yet restores Your people, may help us come close to You, the living God, the God of life. For You are with us whenever we seek Your presence. You are absent only when we shut You out, only when, full of ourselves, we leave no room for You within our hearts.

We call You *Avinu*. As a loving parent, forgive our sins and failings, and reach for us as we reach for You. We call you *Malkeinu*. As a wise ruler, teach us to add our strength to Your love, that we may redeem this world and build Your Kingdom.

To this vision, to this possibility, to this task, we offer ourselves anew.

◆

אבינו מלכנו

אָבִינוּ מַלְכֵּנוּ, שְׁמַע קוֹלֵנוּ.

Our Father, our King, hear our voice.

אָבִֽינוּ מַלְכֵּֽנוּ, חָטָֽאנוּ לְפָנֶֽיךָ.

Our Father, our King, we have sinned against You.

אָבִֽינוּ מַלְכֵּֽנוּ, חֲמוֹל עָלֵֽינוּ וְעַל עוֹלָלֵֽינוּ וְטַפֵּֽנוּ.

Our Father, our King, have compassion on us and on our children.

אָבִֽינוּ מַלְכֵּֽנוּ, כַּלֵּה דֶּֽבֶר וְחֶֽרֶב וְרָעָב מֵעָלֵֽינוּ.

Our Father, our King, make an end to sickness, war, and famine.

אָבִֽינוּ מַלְכֵּֽנוּ, כַּלֵּה כָּל־צַר וּמַשְׂטִין מֵעָלֵֽינוּ.

Our Father, our King, make an end to all oppression.

אָבִֽינוּ מַלְכֵּֽנוּ, כָּתְבֵֽנוּ בְּסֵֽפֶר חַיִּים טוֹבִים.

Our Father, our King, inscribe us for blessing in the Book of Life.

אָבִֽינוּ מַלְכֵּֽנוּ, חַדֵּשׁ עָלֵֽינוּ שָׁנָה טוֹבָה.

Our Father, our King, let the new year be a good year for us.

אָבִֽינוּ מַלְכֵּֽנוּ, מַלֵּא יָדֵֽינוּ מִבִּרְכוֹתֶֽיךָ.

Our Father, our King, fill our hands with blessing.

אָבִֽינוּ מַלְכֵּֽנוּ, חָנֵּֽנוּ וַעֲנֵֽנוּ, כִּי אֵין בָּֽנוּ מַעֲשִׂים,
עֲשֵׂה עִמָּֽנוּ צְדָקָה וָחֶֽסֶד וְהוֹשִׁיעֵֽנוּ.

Our Father, our King, be gracious and answer us, for we have little merit. Treat us generously and with kindness, and be our help.

◆◆

יְיָ, יְיָ אֵל רַחוּם וְחַנּוּן, אֶֽרֶךְ אַפַּֽיִם וְרַב חֶֽסֶד וֶאֱמֶת,
נוֹצֵר חֶֽסֶד לָאֲלָפִים, נֹשֵׂא עָוֹן וָפֶֽשַׁע וְחַטָּאָה וְנַקֵּה.

The Lord, the Lord God is merciful and gracious, endlessly patient, loving, and true, showing mercy to thousands,
forgiving iniquity, transgression, and sin, and granting
pardon.

◆ ◆

The Torah is taken from the Ark

בֵּית יַעֲקֹב: לְכוּ, וְנֵלְכָה בְּאוֹר יְיָ.

O House of Jacob: come, let us walk by the light of the
Lord.

◆ ◆

בָּרוּךְ שֶׁנָּתַן תּוֹרָה לְעַמּוֹ יִשְׂרָאֵל בִּקְדֻשָּׁתוֹ.

Praised be the One who in His holiness has given the Torah to
His people Israel.

◆ ◆

שְׁמַע יִשְׂרָאֵל: יְיָ אֱלֹהֵינוּ, יְיָ אֶחָד!

Hear, O Israel: The Lord is our God, the Lord is One!

אֶחָד אֱלֹהֵינוּ, גָּדוֹל אֲדוֹנֵינוּ, קָדוֹשׁ וְנוֹרָא שְׁמוֹ.

Our God is One; our Lord is great; holy and awesome is His
name.

◆ ◆

לְךָ, יְיָ, הַגְּדֻלָּה וְהַגְּבוּרָה וְהַתִּפְאֶרֶת וְהַנֵּצַח וְהַהוֹד,
כִּי כֹל בַּשָּׁמַיִם וּבָאָרֶץ, לְךָ יְיָ הַמַּמְלָכָה וְהַמִּתְנַשֵּׂא
לְכֹל לְרֹאשׁ.

Yours, Lord, is the greatness, the power, the glory, the victory,
and the majesty; for all that is in heaven and earth is Yours.
Yours is the kingdom, O Lord; You are supreme over all.

All are seated

191

Reading of the Torah.

Before the Reading

בָּרְכוּ אֶת־יְיָ הַמְבֹרָךְ!

בָּרוּךְ יְיָ הַמְבֹרָךְ לְעוֹלָם וָעֶד!

בָּרוּךְ אַתָּה, יְיָ אֱלֹהֵינוּ, מֶלֶךְ הָעוֹלָם, אֲשֶׁר בָּחַר־בָּנוּ

מִכָּל־הָעַמִּים וְנָתַן־לָנוּ אֶת־תּוֹרָתוֹ. בָּרוּךְ אַתָּה, יְיָ,

נוֹתֵן הַתּוֹרָה.

❖ ❖

Another reading from the Torah is on page 124.

Genesis 1.1-2.3

בְּרֵאשִׁית בָּרָא אֱלֹהִים אֵת הַשָּׁמַיִם וְאֵת הָאָרֶץ: וְהָאָרֶץ
הָיְתָה תֹהוּ וָבֹהוּ וְחֹשֶׁךְ עַל־פְּנֵי תְהוֹם וְרוּחַ אֱלֹהִים מְרַחֶפֶת
עַל־פְּנֵי הַמָּיִם: וַיֹּאמֶר אֱלֹהִים יְהִי־אוֹר וַיְהִי־אוֹר: וַיַּרְא אֱלֹהִים
אֶת־הָאוֹר כִּי־טוֹב וַיַּבְדֵּל אֱלֹהִים בֵּין הָאוֹר וּבֵין הַחֹשֶׁךְ: וַיִּקְרָא
אֱלֹהִים ׀ לָאוֹר יוֹם וְלַחֹשֶׁךְ קָרָא לָיְלָה וַיְהִי־עֶרֶב וַיְהִי־בֹקֶר יוֹם
אֶחָד:
וַיֹּאמֶר אֱלֹהִים יְהִי רָקִיעַ בְּתוֹךְ הַמָּיִם וִיהִי מַבְדִּיל בֵּין מַיִם
לָמָיִם: וַיַּעַשׂ אֱלֹהִים אֶת־הָרָקִיעַ וַיַּבְדֵּל בֵּין הַמַּיִם אֲשֶׁר
מִתַּחַת לָרָקִיעַ וּבֵין הַמַּיִם אֲשֶׁר מֵעַל לָרָקִיעַ וַיְהִי־כֵן: וַיִּקְרָא
אֱלֹהִים לָרָקִיעַ שָׁמָיִם וַיְהִי־עֶרֶב וַיְהִי־בֹקֶר יוֹם שֵׁנִי:
וַיֹּאמֶר אֱלֹהִים יִקָּווּ הַמַּיִם מִתַּחַת הַשָּׁמַיִם אֶל־מָקוֹם אֶחָד
וְתֵרָאֶה הַיַּבָּשָׁה וַיְהִי־כֵן: וַיִּקְרָא אֱלֹהִים ׀ לַיַּבָּשָׁה אֶרֶץ וּלְמִקְוֵה
הַמַּיִם קָרָא יַמִּים וַיַּרְא אֱלֹהִים כִּי־טוֹב: וַיֹּאמֶר אֱלֹהִים תַּדְשֵׁא

Reading of the Torah.

Before the Reading

Praise the Lord, to whom our praise is due!
Praised be the Lord, to whom our praise is due,
now and for ever!

Praised be the Lord our God, Ruler of the universe, who
has chosen us from all peoples by giving us His Torah.
Blessed is the Lord, Giver of the Torah.

◆ ◆

Another reading from the Torah is on page 125.

Genesis 1.1-2.3

In the beginning God created the heavens and the earth.
And the earth was without form and void, and there was
darkness upon the face of the deep, and the spirit of God
moved over the surface of the waters. Then God said: Let
there be light! and there was light. God saw that the light
was good, and God separated the light from the darkness.
God called the light Day, and the darkness Night. And
there was evening and there was morning, one day.

God said: Let there be an expanse in the midst of the
water, that it may separate water from water. God made
the expanse, and it separated the water which was below
the expanse from the water which was above the expanse.
And it was so. God called the expanse Sky. And there was
evening and there was morning, a second day.

God said: Let the water below the sky be gathered into
one area, that the dry land may appear. And it was so.
God called the dry land Earth, and the gathering of

הָאָרֶץ דֶּשֶׁא עֵשֶׂב מַזְרִיעַ זֶרַע עֵץ פְּרִי עֹשֶׂה פְּרִי לְמִינוֹ אֲשֶׁר
זַרְעוֹ־בוֹ עַל־הָאָרֶץ וַיְהִי־כֵן: וַתּוֹצֵא הָאָרֶץ דֶּשֶׁא עֵשֶׂב מַזְרִיעַ
זֶרַע לְמִינֵהוּ וְעֵץ עֹשֶׂה־פְּרִי אֲשֶׁר זַרְעוֹ־בוֹ לְמִינֵהוּ וַיַּרְא אֱלֹהִים
כִּי־טוֹב: וַיְהִי־עֶרֶב וַיְהִי־בֹקֶר יוֹם שְׁלִישִׁי:
וַיֹּאמֶר אֱלֹהִים יְהִי מְאֹרֹת בִּרְקִיעַ הַשָּׁמַיִם לְהַבְדִּיל בֵּין הַיּוֹם
וּבֵין הַלָּיְלָה וְהָיוּ לְאֹתֹת וּלְמוֹעֲדִים וּלְיָמִים וְשָׁנִים: וְהָיוּ
לִמְאוֹרֹת בִּרְקִיעַ הַשָּׁמַיִם לְהָאִיר עַל־הָאָרֶץ וַיְהִי־כֵן: וַיַּעַשׂ
אֱלֹהִים אֶת־שְׁנֵי הַמְּאֹרֹת הַגְּדֹלִים אֶת־הַמָּאוֹר הַגָּדֹל לְמֶמְשֶׁלֶת
הַיּוֹם וְאֶת־הַמָּאוֹר הַקָּטֹן לְמֶמְשֶׁלֶת הַלַּיְלָה וְאֵת הַכּוֹכָבִים:
וַיִּתֵּן אֹתָם אֱלֹהִים בִּרְקִיעַ הַשָּׁמַיִם לְהָאִיר עַל־הָאָרֶץ: וְלִמְשֹׁל
בַּיּוֹם וּבַלַּיְלָה וּלְהַבְדִּיל בֵּין הָאוֹר וּבֵין הַחֹשֶׁךְ וַיַּרְא אֱלֹהִים
כִּי־טוֹב: וַיְהִי־עֶרֶב וַיְהִי־בֹקֶר יוֹם רְבִיעִי:
וַיֹּאמֶר אֱלֹהִים יִשְׁרְצוּ הַמַּיִם שֶׁרֶץ נֶפֶשׁ חַיָּה וְעוֹף יְעוֹפֵף עַל־
הָאָרֶץ עַל־פְּנֵי רְקִיעַ הַשָּׁמָיִם: וַיִּבְרָא אֱלֹהִים אֶת־הַתַּנִּינִם
הַגְּדֹלִים וְאֵת כָּל־נֶפֶשׁ הַחַיָּה। הָרֹמֶשֶׂת אֲשֶׁר שָׁרְצוּ הַמַּיִם
לְמִינֵהֶם וְאֵת כָּל־עוֹף כָּנָף לְמִינֵהוּ וַיַּרְא אֱלֹהִים כִּי־טוֹב:
וַיְבָרֶךְ אֹתָם אֱלֹהִים לֵאמֹר פְּרוּ וּרְבוּ וּמִלְאוּ אֶת־הַמַּיִם בַּיַּמִּים
וְהָעוֹף יִרֶב בָּאָרֶץ: וַיְהִי־עֶרֶב וַיְהִי־בֹקֶר יוֹם חֲמִישִׁי:
וַיֹּאמֶר אֱלֹהִים תּוֹצֵא הָאָרֶץ נֶפֶשׁ חַיָּה לְמִינָהּ בְּהֵמָה וָרֶמֶשׂ
וְחַיְתוֹ־אֶרֶץ לְמִינָהּ וַיְהִי־כֵן: וַיַּעַשׂ אֱלֹהִים אֶת־חַיַּת הָאָרֶץ לְמִינָהּ
וְאֶת־הַבְּהֵמָה לְמִינָהּ וְאֵת כָּל־רֶמֶשׂ הָאֲדָמָה לְמִינֵהוּ וַיַּרְא
אֱלֹהִים כִּי־טוֹב: וַיֹּאמֶר אֱלֹהִים נַעֲשֶׂה אָדָם בְּצַלְמֵנוּ כִּדְמוּתֵנוּ
וְיִרְדּוּ בִדְגַת הַיָּם וּבְעוֹף הַשָּׁמַיִם וּבַבְּהֵמָה וּבְכָל־הָאָרֶץ וּבְכָל־
הָרֶמֶשׂ הָרֹמֵשׂ עַל־הָאָרֶץ: וַיִּבְרָא אֱלֹהִים। אֶת־הָאָדָם בְּצַלְמוֹ
בְּצֶלֶם אֱלֹהִים בָּרָא אֹתוֹ זָכָר וּנְקֵבָה בָּרָא אֹתָם: וַיְבָרֶךְ

waters, Seas. And God saw that it was good. And God said: Let the earth sprout vegetation: seed-bearing plants, fruit trees of every kind on earth that bear fruit with the seed in it. And it was so. The earth brought forth vegetation: seed-bearing plants of every kind, and trees of every kind with the seed in it. And God saw that it was good. And there was evening and there was morning, a third day.

God said: Let there be lights in the expanse of the sky to separate day from night; they shall serve as signs for the set times—the days and the years; and they shall serve as lights in the expanse of the sky to shine upon the earth. And it was so. God made the two great lights, the greater light to dominate the day and the lesser light to dominate the night, and the stars. And God set them in the expanse of the sky to shine upon the earth, to dominate the day and the night, and to separate light from darkness. And God saw that it was good. And there was evening and there was morning, a fourth day.

God said: Let the waters teem with swarms of living creatures, and let birds fly above the earth across the vault of heaven. God made the great sea monsters, and all the living creatures of every kind that creep, which the waters brought forth in swarms; and all the winged birds of every kind. And God saw that it was good. God blessed them, saying: Be fruitful and multiply, fill the waters in the seas, and let the birds multiply on the earth. And there was evening and there was morning, a fifth day.

God said: Let the earth bring forth living creatures, according to their kinds: cattle, reptiles, and land animals, according to their kinds. And it was so. God made wild beasts of every kind and cattle of every kind, and every kind of reptile. And God saw that it was good. And God said: Let us make a being in our image, after our likeness,

אֹתָם אֱלֹהִים וַיֹּאמֶר לָהֶם אֱלֹהִים פְּרוּ וּרְבוּ וּמִלְאוּ אֶת־הָאָרֶץ
וְכִבְשֻׁהָ וּרְדוּ בִּדְגַת הַיָּם וּבְעוֹף הַשָּׁמַיִם וּבְכָל־חַיָּה הָרֹמֶשֶׂת
עַל־הָאָרֶץ: וַיֹּאמֶר אֱלֹהִים הִנֵּה נָתַתִּי לָכֶם אֶת־כָּל־עֵשֶׂב ׀ זֹרֵעַ
זֶרַע אֲשֶׁר עַל־פְּנֵי כָל־הָאָרֶץ וְאֶת־כָּל־הָעֵץ אֲשֶׁר־בּוֹ פְרִי־עֵץ
זֹרֵעַ זָרַע לָכֶם יִהְיֶה לְאָכְלָה: וּלְכָל־חַיַּת הָאָרֶץ וּלְכָל־עוֹף
הַשָּׁמַיִם וּלְכֹל ׀ רוֹמֵשׂ עַל־הָאָרֶץ אֲשֶׁר־בּוֹ נֶפֶשׁ חַיָּה אֶת־כָּל־
יֶרֶק עֵשֶׂב לְאָכְלָה וַיְהִי־כֵן: וַיַּרְא אֱלֹהִים אֶת־כָּל־אֲשֶׁר עָשָׂה
וְהִנֵּה־טוֹב מְאֹד וַיְהִי־עֶרֶב וַיְהִי־בֹקֶר יוֹם הַשִּׁשִּׁי:
וַיְכֻלּוּ הַשָּׁמַיִם וְהָאָרֶץ וְכָל־צְבָאָם: וַיְכַל אֱלֹהִים בַּיּוֹם הַשְּׁבִיעִי
מְלַאכְתּוֹ אֲשֶׁר עָשָׂה וַיִּשְׁבֹּת בַּיּוֹם הַשְּׁבִיעִי מִכָּל־מְלַאכְתּוֹ
אֲשֶׁר עָשָׂה: וַיְבָרֶךְ אֱלֹהִים אֶת־יוֹם הַשְּׁבִיעִי וַיְקַדֵּשׁ אֹתוֹ כִּי
בוֹ שָׁבַת מִכָּל־מְלַאכְתּוֹ אֲשֶׁר־בָּרָא אֱלֹהִים לַעֲשׂוֹת:

⁖

After the Reading

בָּרוּךְ אַתָּה, יְיָ אֱלֹהֵינוּ, מֶלֶךְ הָעוֹלָם, אֲשֶׁר נָתַן לָנוּ
תּוֹרַת אֱמֶת וְחַיֵּי עוֹלָם נָטַע בְּתוֹכֵנוּ. בָּרוּךְ אַתָּה, יְיָ,
נוֹתֵן הַתּוֹרָה.

⁖

and let it have dominion over the fish of the sea and the birds of the air, and over the cattle; over all the earth and over every creature that crawls upon it. Thus God created us in the divine image, creating us in the image of God, creating us male and female. And God blessed us, and said to us: Be fruitful and multiply; fill the earth and subdue it; and have dominion over the fish of the sea and the birds of the air, and over every living thing that moves upon the earth.

God said: See, I have given you every seed-bearing plant that is upon all the earth, and every tree that has seed-bearing fruit; they shall be yours for food. And to all the animals on land, to all the birds of the air, and to everything that creeps on earth, in which there is the breath of life, I give all the green plants for food. And it was so. And God saw all creation, and found it very good. And there was evening and there was morning, the sixth day.

Now the whole universe— earth, sky, and all their array— was completed. With the seventh day God ended the work of creation, resting on the seventh day, with all the work completed. Then God blessed the seventh day and called it holy, for with it God had completed the work of creation.

✦ ✦

After the Reading

Praised be the Lord our God, Ruler of the universe, who has given us a Torah of truth, implanting within us eternal life. Blessed is the Lord, Giver of the Torah.

✦ ✦

*As the reading is completed, the Torah might be held high
while this is said or sung:*

וְזֹאת הַתּוֹרָה אֲשֶׁר־שָׂם מֹשֶׁה לִפְנֵי בְּנֵי יִשְׂרָאֵל, עַל־
פִּי יְיָ בְּיַד־מֹשֶׁה.

◆ ◆

Reading of the Haftarah

Before the Reading

בָּרוּךְ אַתָּה, יְיָ אֱלֹהֵינוּ, מֶלֶךְ הָעוֹלָם, אֲשֶׁר בָּחַר
בִּנְבִיאִים טוֹבִים וְרָצָה בְדִבְרֵיהֶם הַנֶּאֱמָרִים בֶּאֱמֶת.
בָּרוּךְ אַתָּה, יְיָ, הַבּוֹחֵר בַּתּוֹרָה וּבְמֹשֶׁה עַבְדּוֹ
וּבְיִשְׂרָאֵל עַמּוֹ וּבִנְבִיאֵי הָאֱמֶת וָצֶדֶק.

An alternative Haftarah is on page 200.

Isaiah 55.6–13

דִּרְשׁוּ יְהֹוָה בְּהִמָּצְאוֹ קְרָאֻהוּ
בִּהְיוֹתוֹ קָרוֹב: יַעֲזֹב רָשָׁע דַּרְכּוֹ וְאִישׁ אָוֶן מַחְשְׁבֹתָיו וְיָשֹׁב
אֶל־יְהֹוָה וִירַחֲמֵהוּ וְאֶל־אֱלֹהֵינוּ כִּי־יַרְבֶּה לִסְלוֹחַ: כִּי לֹא
מַחְשְׁבוֹתַי מַחְשְׁבוֹתֵיכֶם וְלֹא דַרְכֵיכֶם דְּרָכָי נְאֻם יְהֹוָה: כִּי־
גָבְהוּ שָׁמַיִם מֵאָרֶץ כֵּן גָּבְהוּ דְרָכַי מִדַּרְכֵיכֶם וּמַחְשְׁבֹתַי
מִמַּחְשְׁבֹתֵיכֶם: כִּי כַּאֲשֶׁר יֵרֵד הַגֶּשֶׁם וְהַשֶּׁלֶג מִן־הַשָּׁמַיִם
וְשָׁמָּה לֹא יָשׁוּב כִּי אִם־הִרְוָה אֶת־הָאָרֶץ וְהוֹלִידָהּ וְהִצְמִיחָהּ
וְנָתַן זֶרַע לַזֹּרֵעַ וְלֶחֶם לָאֹכֵל: כֵּן יִהְיֶה דְבָרִי אֲשֶׁר יֵצֵא מִפִּי
לֹא־יָשׁוּב אֵלַי רֵיקָם כִּי אִם־עָשָׂה אֶת־אֲשֶׁר חָפַצְתִּי וְהִצְלִיחַ
אֲשֶׁר שְׁלַחְתִּיו: כִּי־בְשִׂמְחָה תֵצֵאוּ וּבְשָׁלוֹם תּוּבָלוּן הֶהָרִים

As the reading is completed, the Torah might be held high while this is said or sung:

This is the Torah that Moses placed before the people of Israel to fulfill the word of God.

◆ ◆

Reading of the Haftarah

Before the Reading

Praised be the Lord our God, Ruler of the universe, who has chosen faithful prophets to speak words of truth. Blessed is the Lord, for the revelation of Torah, for Moses His servant and Israel His people, and for the prophets of truth and righteousness.

An alternative Haftarah is on page 201.

Isaiah 55.6–13

Seek the Lord while there is yet time; cry out while God is near. Let the wicked forsake their ways, those bent on evil, their thoughts. Let them return to the Lord, who will show them mercy; to our God, who will graciously pardon.

For My thoughts are not your thoughts, nor are My ways your ways, says the Lord. But as the heavens are high above the earth, so are My ways high above your ways, and My thoughts above yours. For as rain and snow come down from heaven and do not return until they have watered the earth, making it blossom and bear fruit, giving you seed to sow and bread to eat, so shall the word that comes from My mouth prevail: it shall not return to

וְהַגְּבָעוֹת יִפְצְחוּ לִפְנֵיכֶם רִנָּה וְכָל־עֲצֵי הַשָּׂדֶה יִמְחֲאוּ־כָף:
תַּחַת הַנַּעֲצוּץ יַעֲלֶה בְרוֹשׁ תַּחַת הַסִּרְפַּד יַעֲלֶה הֲדַס וְהָיָה
לַיהוה לְשֵׁם לְאוֹת עוֹלָם לֹא יִכָּרֵת:

•   •

The benediction after the reading is on page 204.

•   •

An alternative Haftarah

Jeremiah 31.1–19

כֹּה אָמַר יהוה מָצָא חֵן בַּמִּדְבָּר עַם
שְׂרִידֵי חָרֶב הָלוֹךְ לְהַרְגִּיעוֹ יִשְׂרָאֵל: מֵרָחוֹק יהוה נִרְאָה לִי
וְאַהֲבַת עוֹלָם אֲהַבְתִּיךְ עַל־כֵּן מְשַׁכְתִּיךְ חָסֶד: עוֹד אֶבְנֵךְ
וְנִבְנֵית בְּתוּלַת יִשְׂרָאֵל עוֹד תַּעְדִּי תֻפַּיִךְ וְיָצָאת בִּמְחוֹל
מְשַׂחֲקִים: עוֹד תִּטְּעִי כְרָמִים בְּהָרֵי שֹׁמְרוֹן נָטְעוּ נֹטְעִים
וְחִלֵּלוּ: כִּי יֶשׁ־יוֹם קָרְאוּ נֹצְרִים בְּהַר אֶפְרָיִם קוּמוּ וְנַעֲלֶה צִיּוֹן
אֶל־יהוה אֱלֹהֵינוּ: כִּי־כֹה ׀ אָמַר יהוה רָנּוּ
לְיַעֲקֹב שִׂמְחָה וְצַהֲלוּ בְּרֹאשׁ הַגּוֹיִם הַשְׁמִיעוּ הַלְלוּ וְאִמְרוּ
הוֹשַׁע יהוה אֶת־עַמְּךָ אֵת שְׁאֵרִית יִשְׂרָאֵל: הִנְנִי מֵבִיא אוֹתָם
מֵאֶרֶץ צָפוֹן וְקִבַּצְתִּים מִיַּרְכְּתֵי־אָרֶץ בָּם עִוֵּר וּפִסֵּחַ הָרָה
וְיֹלֶדֶת יַחְדָּו קָהָל גָּדוֹל יָשׁוּבוּ הֵנָּה: בִּבְכִי יָבֹאוּ וּבְתַחֲנוּנִים

Me empty, without having accomplished its purpose or having succeeded in its mission.

You shall then go out with joy, and be led forth in peace. The mountains and hills shall burst into song before you, and all the trees of the field shall clap their hands. Fir trees shall grow instead of thorns, myrtles instead of briars. These shall stand as a testimony to the Lord, as a sign for ever that shall not perish.

✦ ✦

The benediction after the reading is on page 205.

✦ ✦

An alternative Haftarah

Jeremiah 31.1–19

The people escaped from the sword found favor in the wilderness; when Israel was marching homeward, the Lord appeared to them. Thus says the Lord: Eternal love I conceived for you then; therefore I continue My grace to you. I will build you up again, O innocent daughter of Israel, I will build you up! Again you shall take up your timbrels, and go forth to the rhythm of the dancers. Again you shall plant vineyards on the hills of Samaria; you shall plant and live to enjoy them. For the day is coming when watchers shall proclaim on the heights of Ephraim: Come, let us go up to Zion, to the Lord our God!

For thus says the Lord: Cry out in joy for Jacob, lead the nations, crying loud and clear! Sing aloud in praise, and say: The Lord has saved His people, the remnant of Israel. I will bring them in from the north, gather them from the ends of the earth, the blind and the lame among them, those with child and those in labor, a vast throng. They

אוֹבִילֵם אֶל־נַחֲלֵי מַיִם בְּדֶרֶךְ יָשָׁר לֹא יִכָּשְׁלוּ בָּהּ כִּי־
הָיִיתִי לְיִשְׂרָאֵל לְאָב וְאֶפְרַיִם בְּכֹרִי הוּא: שִׁמְעוּ
דְבַר־יְהוָה גּוֹיִם וְהַגִּידוּ בָאִיִּים מִמֶּרְחָק וְאִמְרוּ מְזָרֵה יִשְׂרָאֵל
יְקַבְּצֶנּוּ וּשְׁמָרוֹ כְּרֹעֶה עֶדְרוֹ: כִּי־פָדָה יְהוָה אֶת־יַעֲקֹב וּגְאָלוֹ
מִיַּד חָזָק מִמֶּנּוּ: וּבָאוּ וְרִנְּנוּ בִמְרוֹם־צִיּוֹן וְנָהֲרוּ אֶל־טוּב יְהוָה
עַל־דָּגָן וְעַל־תִּירֹשׁ וְעַל־יִצְהָר וְעַל־בְּנֵי־צֹאן וּבָקָר וְהָיְתָה
נַפְשָׁם כְּגַן רָוֶה וְלֹא־יוֹסִיפוּ לְדַאֲבָה עוֹד: אָז תִּשְׂמַח בְּתוּלָה
בְּמָחוֹל וּבַחֻרִים וּזְקֵנִים יַחְדָּו וְהָפַכְתִּי אֶבְלָם לְשָׂשׂוֹן וְנִחַמְתִּים
וְשִׂמַּחְתִּים מִיגוֹנָם: וְרִוֵּיתִי נֶפֶשׁ הַכֹּהֲנִים דָּשֶׁן וְעַמִּי אֶת־טוּבִי
יִשְׂבָּעוּ נְאֻם־יְהוָה: כֹּה ׀ אָמַר יְהוָה קוֹל בְּרָמָה
נִשְׁמָע נְהִי בְּכִי תַמְרוּרִים רָחֵל מְבַכָּה עַל־בָּנֶיהָ מֵאֲנָה לְהִנָּחֵם
עַל־בָּנֶיהָ כִּי אֵינֶנּוּ:   כֹּה ׀ אָמַר יְהוָה מִנְעִי קוֹלֵךְ
מִבֶּכִי וְעֵינַיִךְ מִדִּמְעָה כִּי יֵשׁ שָׂכָר לִפְעֻלָּתֵךְ נְאֻם־יְהוָה וְשָׁבוּ
מֵאֶרֶץ אוֹיֵב: וְיֵשׁ־תִּקְוָה לְאַחֲרִיתֵךְ נְאֻם־יְהוָה וְשָׁבוּ בָנִים
לִגְבוּלָם: שָׁמוֹעַ שָׁמַעְתִּי אֶפְרַיִם מִתְנוֹדֵד יִסַּרְתַּנִי וָאִוָּסֵר כְּעֵגֶל
לֹא לֻמָּד הֲשִׁבֵנִי וְאָשׁוּבָה כִּי אַתָּה יְהוָה אֱלֹהָי: כִּי־אַחֲרֵי שׁוּבִי
נִחַמְתִּי וְאַחֲרֵי הִוָּדְעִי סָפַקְתִּי עַל־יָרֵךְ בֹּשְׁתִּי וְגַם־נִכְלַמְתִּי כִּי
נָשָׂאתִי חֶרְפַּת נְעוּרָי: הֲבֵן יַקִּיר לִי אֶפְרַיִם אִם יֶלֶד שַׁעֲשׁוּעִים
כִּי־מִדֵּי דַבְּרִי בּוֹ זָכֹר אֶזְכְּרֶנּוּ עוֹד עַל־כֵּן הָמוּ מֵעַי לוֹ רַחֵם
אֲרַחֲמֶנּוּ נְאֻם־יְהוָה:

∴

shall come with weeping, and as I lead them, I will comfort them. I will lead them to flowing streams, by a level road where they shall not stumble. For I am ever the Lover of Israel, and Ephraim is My firstborn.

Hear the word of the Lord, O nations, and tell it to the isles far-off: the One who scattered Israel will gather them in, and watch over them as a shepherd the flock. For the Lord has delivered Jacob, and redeemed them from the hand of the mighty. Radiant over the bounty of the Lord, the grain, the wine, the oil, the sheep and cattle, they shall come with shouts of joy to Zion's heights. They shall become like a watered garden, never again to languish. Then girls shall dance with joy, young and old shall exult. I will turn their mourning into gladness, I will comfort and hearten them in their grief.

Thus says the Lord: A voice is heard in Ramah; lamentation and bitter weeping! Rachel is weeping for her children, refusing to be comforted for her children, for they are gone. Thus says the Lord: Restrain your voice from weeping and your eyes from tears! For your labor shall have its reward. They shall return from the enemy's land. There is hope for your future: your children shall return to their own land.

I can hear Ephraim lamenting: 'You have chastised me, I am chastised like a calf that has not been broken. Receive me back, let me return, for You, O Lord, are my God. Now that I have turned back, I am filled with remorse; now that I am made aware, I beat my breast in shame and contrition, for I bear the disgrace of my youth.' O Ephraim, are you not My precious child, My own beloved offspring? Even when I reproach you, I think of you with tenderness. My heart yearns for you, I will receive you back in love, says the Lord.

✦ ✦

After the Reading

An alternative version of this Benediction follows below

בָּרוּךְ אַתָּה, יְיָ אֱלֹהֵינוּ, מֶלֶךְ הָעוֹלָם, צוּר כָּל־
הָעוֹלָמִים, צַדִּיק בְּכָל־הַדּוֹרוֹת, הָאֵל הַנֶּאֱמָן,
הָאוֹמֵר וְעוֹשֶׂה, הַמְדַבֵּר וּמְקַיֵּם, שֶׁכָּל־דְּבָרָיו אֱמֶת
וָצֶדֶק.

עַל הַתּוֹרָה וְעַל הָעֲבוֹדָה וְעַל הַנְּבִיאִים (וְעַל יוֹם
הַשַּׁבָּת הַזֶּה) וְעַל יוֹם הַזִּכָּרוֹן הַזֶּה, שֶׁנָּתַתָּ לָּנוּ, יְיָ
אֱלֹהֵינוּ, (לִקְדֻשָּׁה וְלִמְנוּחָה) לְכָבוֹד וּלְתִפְאָרֶת, עַל
הַכֹּל, יְיָ אֱלֹהֵינוּ, אֲנַחְנוּ מוֹדִים לָךְ, וּמְבָרְכִים אוֹתָךְ.
יִתְבָּרַךְ שִׁמְךָ בְּפִי כָּל־חַי תָּמִיד לְעוֹלָם וָעֶד. וּדְבָרְךָ
אֱמֶת וְקַיָּם לָעַד. בָּרוּךְ אַתָּה, יְיָ, מֶלֶךְ עַל כָּל־הָאָרֶץ,
מְקַדֵּשׁ (הַשַּׁבָּת וְ) יִשְׂרָאֵל וְיוֹם הַזִּכָּרוֹן.

Continue on page 208.

Alternative Version

בָּרוּךְ אַתָּה, יְיָ אֱלֹהֵינוּ, מֶלֶךְ הָעוֹלָם, צוּר כָּל־
הָעוֹלָמִים, צַדִּיק בְּכָל־הַדּוֹרוֹת, הָאֵל הַנֶּאֱמָן,
הָאוֹמֵר וְעוֹשֶׂה, הַמְדַבֵּר וּמְקַיֵּם, שֶׁכָּל־דְּבָרָיו אֱמֶת
וָצֶדֶק.

נֶאֱמָן אַתָּה הוּא יְיָ אֱלֹהֵינוּ, וְנֶאֱמָנִים דְּבָרֶיךָ, וְדָבָר
אֶחָד מִדְּבָרֶיךָ אָחוֹר לֹא־יָשׁוּב רֵיקָם, כִּי אֵל מֶלֶךְ
נֶאֱמָן וְרַחֲמָן אָתָּה. בָּרוּךְ אַתָּה, יְיָ, הָאֵל הַנֶּאֱמָן
בְּכָל־דְּבָרָיו.

After the Reading

An alternative version of this Benediction follows below

Praised be the Lord our God, Ruler of the universe, Rock of all creation, righteous in all generations, the faithful God whose word is deed, whose every command is just and true.

For the Torah, for the privilege of worship, for the prophets, and for this (Shabbat and this) Day of Remembrance that You, O Lord our God, have given us (for holiness and rest,) for honor and glory, we thank and bless You. May Your name be blessed for ever by every living being, for Your word is true for ever. Blessed is the Lord, King of all the earth, for the holiness of (the Sabbath,) the House of Israel and the Day of Remembrance.

Continue on page 208.

Alternative Version

Praised be the Lord our God, Ruler of the universe, Rock of all creation, righteous in all generations, the faithful God whose word is deed, whose every command is just and true.

You are the Faithful One, O Lord our God, and faithful is Your word. Not one word of Yours goes forth without accomplishing its task, O faithful and compassionate God and King. Blessed is the Lord, the faithful God.

205

רַחֵם עַל־צִיּוֹן כִּי הִיא בֵּית חַיֵּינוּ, וְלַעֲלוּבַת נֶפֶשׁ
תּוֹשִׁיעַ בִּמְהֵרָה בְיָמֵינוּ. בָּרוּךְ אַתָּה, יְיָ, מְשַׂמֵּחַ צִיּוֹן
בְּבָנֶיהָ.

שַׂמְּחֵנוּ, יְיָ אֱלֹהֵינוּ, בְּאֵלִיָּהוּ הַנָּבִיא עַבְדֶּךָ, וּבְמַלְכוּת
בֵּית דָּוִד מְשִׁיחֶךָ, בִּמְהֵרָה יָבֹא וְיָגֵל לִבֵּנוּ. עַל־כִּסְאוֹ
לֹא־יֵשֶׁב זָר וְלֹא־יִנְחֲלוּ עוֹד אֲחֵרִים אֶת־כְּבוֹדוֹ. כִּי
בְשֵׁם קָדְשְׁךָ נִשְׁבַּעְתָּ לּוֹ שֶׁלֹּא־יִכְבֶּה נֵרוֹ לְעוֹלָם וָעֶד.
בָּרוּךְ אַתָּה, יְיָ, מָגֵן דָּוִד.

עַל הַתּוֹרָה וְעַל הָעֲבוֹדָה וְעַל הַנְּבִיאִים (וְעַל יוֹם
הַשַּׁבָּת הַזֶּה) וְעַל יוֹם הַזִּכָּרוֹן הַזֶּה שֶׁנָּתַתָּ לָּנוּ, יְיָ
אֱלֹהֵינוּ, (לִקְדֻשָּׁה וְלִמְנוּחָה) לְכָבוֹד וּלְתִפְאָרֶת, עַל
הַכֹּל, יְיָ אֱלֹהֵינוּ, אֲנַחְנוּ מוֹדִים לָךְ, וּמְבָרְכִים אוֹתָךְ.
יִתְבָּרַךְ שִׁמְךָ בְּפִי כָל־חַי תָּמִיד לְעוֹלָם וָעֶד. וּדְבָרְךָ
אֱמֶת וְקַיָּם לָעַד. בָּרוּךְ אַתָּה, יְיָ, מֶלֶךְ עַל כָּל־הָאָרֶץ,
מְקַדֵּשׁ (הַשַּׁבָּת וְ) יִשְׂרָאֵל וְיוֹם הַזִּכָּרוֹן.

• •

Show compassion for Zion, our House of Life, and speedily, in our own day, deliver those who despair. Blessed is the Lord, who brings joy to Zion's children.

Lord our God, bring us the joy of Your kingdom: let our dream of Elijah and David bear fruit. Speedily let redemption come to gladden our hearts. Let Your solemn promise be fulfilled: David's light shall not for ever be extinguished! Blessed is the Lord, the Shield of David.

For the Torah, for the privilege of worship, for the prophets, and for this (Shabbat and this) Day of Remembrance that You, O Lord our God, have given us (for holiness and rest,) for honor and glory, we thank and bless you. May Your name be blessed for ever by every living being, for Your word is true for ever. Blessed is the Lord, King of all the earth, for the holiness of (the Sabbath,) the House of Israel and the Day of Remembrance.

◆ ◆

סדר תקיעת שופר

The Sounding of the Shofar

Note: In ancient Israel the sound of the ram's horn announced the beginning of a new month, the Jubilee year, the coronation of a king, and all the solemn moments of the year. But when the new moon of the seventh month came to be observed as the New Year, new and deeper meanings gathered around the sounding of the Shofar. These meanings, deepening still, awaken within us each time we hear the Shofar call.

In the seventh month,
on the first day of the month,
there shall be a sacred assembly,
a cessation from work,
a day of commemoration
proclaimed by the sound
of the Shofar.

וּבַחֹדֶשׁ הַשְּׁבִיעִי,
בְּאֶחָד לַחֹדֶשׁ,
מִקְרָא־קֹדֶשׁ יִהְיֶה לָכֶם;
כָּל־מְלֶאכֶת עֲבוֹדָה לֹא תַעֲשׂוּ;
יוֹם תְּרוּעָה יִהְיֶה לָכֶם.

•

Hear now the Shofar; acclaim the world's creation!

And now recall Isaac's awesome trial!

Hear now the Shofar, you who stand at Sinai!

And now proclaim the rule of Israel's God!

Hear now the call, and turn in true repentance!

And now affirm the triumph of good!

We are made in the divine image!

We are the House of Israel,
a kingdom of priests, a holy people!

Know then the sound; discover its meaning:

•

עוּרוּ, יְשֵׁנִים, מִשְּׁנַתְכֶם, וְנִרְדָּמִים, הָקִיצוּ
מִתַּרְדֵּמַתְכֶם! וְחַפְּשׂוּ בְּמַעֲשֵׂיכֶם, וְחִזְרוּ בִּתְשׁוּבָה,
וְזִכְרוּ בּוֹרַאֲכֶם, אֵלּוּ הַשּׁוֹכְחִים אֶת־הָאֱמֶת בְּהַבְלֵי
הַזְּמַן, וְשׁוֹגִים כָּל־שְׁנָתָם בְּהֶבֶל וָרֵיק אֲשֶׁר לֹא יוֹעִיל
וְלֹא יַצִּיל. הַבִּיטוּ לְנַפְשׁוֹתֵיכֶם וְהֵיטִיבוּ דַרְכֵיכֶם
וּמַעַלְלֵיכֶם, וְיַעֲזֹב כָּל־אֶחָד מִכֶּם דַּרְכּוֹ הָרָעָה,
וּמַחֲשַׁבְתּוֹ אֲשֶׁר לֹא טוֹבָה.

Awake, you sleepers, from your sleep! Rouse yourselves,
you slumberers, out of your slumber! Examine your
deeds, and turn to God in repentance. Remember your
Creator, you who are caught up in the daily round, losing
sight of eternal truth; you who are wasting your years in
vain pursuits that neither profit nor save. Look closely at
yourselves; improve your ways and your deeds. Abandon
your evil ways, your unworthy schemes, every one of you!

◆ ◆

מלכויות   MALCHUYOT

CREATION

All rise

עָלֵינוּ לְשַׁבֵּחַ לַאֲדוֹן הַכֹּל, לָתֵת גְּדֻלָּה לְיוֹצֵר
בְּרֵאשִׁית, שֶׁהוּא נוֹטֶה שָׁמַיִם וְיוֹסֵד אָרֶץ, וּמוֹשַׁב
יְקָרוֹ בַּשָּׁמַיִם מִמַּעַל, וּשְׁכִינַת עֻזּוֹ בְּגָבְהֵי מְרוֹמִים.
הוּא אֱלֹהֵינוּ, אֵין עוֹד.
וַאֲנַחְנוּ כּוֹרְעִים וּמִשְׁתַּחֲוִים וּמוֹדִים לִפְנֵי מֶלֶךְ מַלְכֵי
הַמְּלָכִים, הַקָּדוֹשׁ בָּרוּךְ הוּא.

All are seated

209

God of space and time, Yours is the word that laid the foundations of the world. By Your command it went forth to the seas: thus far shall you come, but no further, and here shall your proud waves be stayed. When the morning stars sang together, and the hosts of heaven shouted for joy, then Your creative word made the light to break through the darkness, and life to issue forth from the marriage of heaven and earth.

And as You shaped all things from the beginning, so do You rule and sustain them day by day. You are Infinite Spirit, giving all things their form. Amid the ebb and flow of the ages, only You abide unchanged. Yours is the kingdom, and Your dominion will endure for ever.

◆ ◆

In the beginning God created the heavens and the earth.

The heavens were made by the word of the Lord; their starry host by the power of God's thought.

The heavens declare the glory of God, the skies proclaim God's creative work.

Yet these are a mere glimpse of Your ways, and how faint a whisper we hear of You!

For You, the Eternal, are a great God, a Ruler high above the idols of every age.

'I am the First, and I am the Last; besides Me there is no God.'

Dominion is Yours, Lord, and You rule the nations.

Declare to the nations: 'God reigns; now the world is secure and firmly based.'

God reigns; let the earth rejoice, the many nations be glad.

The Lord will reign for ever and ever.

❖ ❖

בָּרוּךְ אַתָּה, יְיָ, מֶלֶךְ עַל כָּל־הָאָרֶץ, מְקַדֵּשׁ (הַשַׁבָּת וְ)
יִשְׂרָאֵל וְיוֹם הַזִּכָּרוֹן.

Blessed is the Eternal God, Ruler of all the world, for the
holiness of (the Sabbath,) the House of Israel and the Day
of Remembrance.

❖ ❖

All rise

בָּרוּךְ אַתָּה, יְיָ אֱלֹהֵינוּ, מֶלֶךְ הָעוֹלָם, אֲשֶׁר קִדְּשָׁנוּ
בְּמִצְוֹתָיו וְצִוָּנוּ לִשְׁמוֹעַ קוֹל שׁוֹפָר.
בָּרוּךְ אַתָּה, יְיָ אֱלֹהֵינוּ, מֶלֶךְ הָעוֹלָם, שֶׁהֶחֱיָנוּ וְקִיְּמָנוּ
וְהִגִּיעָנוּ לַזְּמַן הַזֶּה.

*Blessed is the Lord our God, Ruler of the universe, who hal-
lows us with Mitzvot, and calls us to hear the sound of the
Shofar.*

*Blessed is the Lord our God, Ruler of the universe, for giving
us life, for sustaining us, and for enabling us to reach this
season.*

The Shofar is sounded:

TEKIAH SHEVARIM-TERUAH   תקיעה שברים־תרועה
TEKIAH   תקיעה

TEKIAH SHEVARIM TEKIAH   תקיעה שברים תקיעה

TEKIAH TERUAH TEKIAH   תקיעה תרועה תקיעה

All are seated

◆ ◆

יְיָ מָלָךְ, גֵּאוּת לָבֵשׁ; לָבֵשׁ יְיָ, עֹז הִתְאַזָּר; אַף־תִּכּוֹן
תֵּבֵל, בַּל־תִּמּוֹט. נָכוֹן כִּסְאֲךָ מֵאָז, מֵעוֹלָם אָתָּה.

The Lord reigns; God is robed in majesty.
The Lord is robed and girded with strength;
the world is established, it cannot be moved.
Your throne is established from of old;
You are from everlasting.

◆ ◆

ZICHRONOT   זכרונות

MEANING IN TIME

God of all lands and ages, the ground under our feet is
holy; the light that shines for us is Yours; the world glows
with Your presence. You are just beyond the horizon of
the mind, a vision new to us yet seen before, like a
memory of the future, a promise already kept.

We remember Abraham and Isaac walking together
toward their mountain; Jacob dreaming of a ladder to link
heaven and earth; Moses turning aside to look at the common bush burning with a divine flame; David dancing
before the Ark of Your covenant; a shepherd prophet
roaring Your word like a lion; the days and years of our
own lives—a search for light in a dark and dusty time.
And we remember a rainbow.

We remember the prophets, whose vision will not grow dim;
we remember the sages, for whom goodness was daily bread.
As we remember, we affirm the heritage that gives our life
its worth.

We remember what You mean to us—
as signs appear
when paths diverge.
We remember what You mean to us—
when empty days
are now fulfilled.

We remember what You mean to us—
now, together,
we have endured hope's touch
in the dark wood
through which we walk.

◆ ◆

Lord, Your love is everlasting to those who revere You;
Your righteousness continues to children's children, to
those who keep Your covenant, who remember Your
commandments and do them.

Never will I forget Your precepts, for by them You have
given me life.

I remember Your kindnesses, Lord, Your great goodness
to the House of Israel.

You remember Your covenant, the pledge You gave for a
thousand generations.

The Lord your God is a God of compassion who will not
forget the sworn covenant with your fathers and mothers.

I remember Your ordinances from of old, O Lord, and I am comforted.

I will meditate on Your precepts, and keep Your ways before my eyes.

I will find joy in Your statutes; I will not forget Your word.

Justice, justice shall you follow, that you may live.

Let justice roll down like waters, and righteousness as a mighty stream.

◆ ◆

בָּרוּךְ אַתָּה, יְיָ, זוֹכֵר הַבְּרִית.

Blessed is the Eternal God, who remembers the covenant.

◆ ◆

All rise
The Shofar is sounded:

TEKIAH SHEVARIM-TERUAH	תקיעה שברים־תרועה
TEKIAH	תקיעה
TEKIAH SHEVARIM TEKIAH	תקיעה שברים תקיעה
TEKIAH TERUAH TEKIAH	תקיעה תרועה תקיעה

All are seated

◆ ◆

For the mountains may depart,
and the hills be removed,
but My kindness shall not depart
from you,

כִּי הֶהָרִים יָמוּשׁוּ,
וְהַגְּבָעוֹת תְּמוּטֶינָה,
וְחַסְדִּי מֵאִתֵּךְ לֹא־יָמוּשׁ,

214

neither shall My covenant of peace be removed,
says the Lord, who has compassion upon you.

וּבְרִית שְׁלוֹמִי לֹא־תָמוּט,
אָמַר מְרַחֲמֵךְ יְיָ.

◆ ◆

SHOFAROT שופרות

REVELATION AND REDEMPTION

Now we call to mind the great moment when Israel stood at Sinai, and heard the voice of the Shofar. There our people entered into Your covenant, to be Your witness to the world. From there they went forth to proclaim the laws by which the free may live and the enslaved find hope. That covenant we renew when we hear the sound of the Shofar.

From that day to this have we, a people acquainted with miracle and disaster, encountered You again and again on the path of our life. And You are present, O Eternal One, not on peaks of vision alone; at any moment we may turn, and find You. The whisper of a thought, the most humble touch of being, may lead us to You. So, endlessly revealed amid Your concealments, You stand awaiting our search, to lead us, with many a fall, upward to heights we tremble to climb.

All this we hear, when the voice of the Shofar, stranger among sounds, is heard.

And that Shofar-sound heralds yet another day, whose promise is our hope. Then shall begin the time of peace of which we dream; a world of truth shall be revealed to us; and together we shall rejoice in the kingdom of God.

Distant the goal; at times it fades from sight. For we are free: free to love, free to build the kingdom; free to hate, free to tear it down. And yet the dream is not forgotten, the vision does not fail—it is the meaning of our lives. Come what may, we shall hold fast to it. And even when the hope seems lost, we shall say: "The kingdom of heaven could begin today, if we would but hearken to God's voice."

The great trumpet will sound and summon us to serve under Your banner of truth, of purity, and of peace.

On that day the great Shofar shall be sounded.

You shall cause the Shofar to be sounded, and proclaim liberty throughout the earth to all its inhabitants.

Happy is the people that knows the joyful sound.

They shall walk, O Lord, in the light of Your presence.

And it shall be said on that day: 'This is our God for whom we wait, whose deliverance we await in hope.'

'This is the Lord for whom we have waited, in whose deliverance we shall rejoice and be glad.'

Every valley shall be exalted, every mountain and hill made low; the uneven ground shall be made level, and the rough places a plain.

The glory of the Lord shall be revealed, and, united, all shall see it, for the mouth of the Lord has spoken.

Shout joyfully to the Lord, all the earth! Break forth, sing aloud, shout praise!

With trumpet-sound and Shofar-blast acclaim the Sovereign God!

בָּרוּךְ אַתָּה, יְיָ, שׁוֹמֵעַ קוֹל תְּרוּעַת עַמּוֹ יִשְׂרָאֵל
בְּרַחֲמִים.

*We praise You, the merciful God who hearkens to the sound
of the Shofar.*

◆ ◆

All rise
The Shofar is sounded:

TEKIAH SHEVARIM-TERUAH	תקיעה שברים־תרועה
TEKIAH	תקיעה
TEKIAH SHEVARIM TEKIAH	תקיעה שברים תקיעה
TEKIAH TERUAH TEKIAH GEDOLAH	תקיעה תרועה תקיעה
	גדולה

All you dwellers on earth, when the Shofar is sounded, hearken;
and when the great trumpet is blown, come all and worship the
Lord at the holy mountain. The Lord of Hosts shall be a shield
unto you.

◆ ◆

FOR OUR CONGREGATION AND OUR PEOPLE

Lord, we pray to You for the whole House of Israel, scattered over the earth, yet bound together by a common history, and united by a common heritage of faith and hope.

Be with our brothers and sisters whose lives are made hard because they are Jews. Give them strength to endure, and lead them soon from bondage to freedom, from darkness to light.

Bless this holy congregation and all who serve it, together with all other holy congregations, in all lands near and far. Uphold us, shield us, and bestow upon us abundant life and health and peace and happiness. Bring to fulfillment the blessing of Moses: The Lord your God make you a thousand times as many as you are, and bless you as He has promised you. Amen.

O God, send Your healing to the sick, Your comfort to all who are in pain or anxiety, Your tender love to the sorrowing hearts among us. Be their refuge through their time of trial, as they pass from weakness to strength, from suffering to consolation, from lonely fear to the courage of faith. Amen.

FOR OUR NATION AND ITS RULERS

We pray for all who hold positions of leadership and responsibility in our national life. Let Your blessing rest upon them, and make them responsive to Your will, so that our nation may be to the world an example of justice and compassion.

Deepen our love for our country and our desire to serve it. Strengthen our power of self-sacrifice for our nation's welfare. Teach us to uphold its good name by our own right conduct.

Cause us to see clearly that the well being of our nation is in the hands of all its citizens; imbue us with zeal for the cause of liberty in our own land and in all lands; and help us always to keep our homes safe from affliction, strife, and war. Amen.

FOR THE STATE OF ISRAEL

We pray for the land of Israel and its people. May its borders know peace, its inhabitants tranquility. And may the bonds of faith and fate which unite the Jews of all lands be a source of strength to Israel and to us all. God of all lands and ages, answer our constant prayer with a Zion once more aglow with light for us and for all the world, and let us say: Amen.

Returning the Torah to the Ark

יְהַלְלוּ אֶת־שֵׁם יְיָ, כִּי־נִשְׂגָּב שְׁמוֹ לְבַדּוֹ.

Let us praise the name of the Lord, whose name alone is exalted.

הוֹדוֹ עַל אֶרֶץ וְשָׁמָיִם, וַיָּרֶם קֶרֶן לְעַמּוֹ, תְּהִלָּה לְכָל־
חֲסִידָיו, לִבְנֵי יִשְׂרָאֵל עַם קְרוֹבוֹ. הַלְלוּיָהּ.

God's splendor covers heaven and earth; He is the strength of His people, making glorious His faithful ones, Israel, a people close to Him. Halleluyah!

◆ ◆

תּוֹרַת יְיָ תְּמִימָה, מְשִׁיבַת נָפֶשׁ;
עֵדוּת יְיָ נֶאֱמָנָה, מַחְכִּימַת פֶּתִי;

The law of the Lord is perfect, restoring the soul;

The teaching of the Lord is sure, making wise the simple;

פִּקּוּדֵי יְיָ יְשָׁרִים, מְשַׂמְּחֵי־לֵב;
מִצְוַת יְיָ בָּרָה, מְאִירַת עֵינָיִם;

The precepts of the Lord are right, rejoicing the heart;

The Mitzvah of the Lord is clear, giving light to the eyes;

יִרְאַת יְיָ טְהוֹרָה, עוֹמֶדֶת לָעַד;
מִשְׁפְּטֵי יְיָ אֱמֶת, צָדְקוּ יַחְדָּו.

The word of the Lord is pure, enduring for ever;

The judgments of the Lord are true, and altogether just.

◆ ◆

כִּי לֶקַח טוֹב נָתַתִּי לָכֶם, תּוֹרָתִי אַל־תַּעֲזֹבוּ.
עֵץ־חַיִּים הִיא לַמַּחֲזִיקִים בָּהּ, וְתֹמְכֶיהָ מְאֻשָּׁר.
דְּרָכֶיהָ דַרְכֵי־נֹעַם, וְכָל־נְתִיבוֹתֶיהָ שָׁלוֹם.

Behold, a good doctrine has been given you, do not forsake it. It is a tree of life to those who hold it fast, and all
who cling to it find happiness. Its ways are ways of
pleasantness, and all its paths are peace.

הֲשִׁיבֵנוּ יְיָ אֵלֶיךָ, וְנָשׁוּבָה. חַדֵּשׁ יָמֵינוּ כְּקֶדֶם.

Help us to return to You, O Lord; then truly shall we return.
Renew our days as in the past.

The Ark is closed

All are seated

עָלֵינוּ

All rise

Let us adore
the ever-living God,
and render praise
unto Him
who spread out the heavens
and established the earth,
whose glory
is revealed in the heavens above,
and whose greatness
is manifest throughout the world.
He is our God; there is none else.

עָלֵינוּ לְשַׁבֵּחַ לַאֲדוֹן הַכֹּל,
לָתֵת גְּדֻלָּה לְיוֹצֵר בְּרֵאשִׁית,
שֶׁהוּא נוֹטֶה שָׁמַיִם
וְיוֹסֵד אָרֶץ,
וּמוֹשַׁב יְקָרוֹ בַּשָּׁמַיִם מִמַּעַל,
וּשְׁכִינַת עֻזּוֹ בְּגָבְהֵי מְרוֹמִים.
הוּא אֱלֹהֵינוּ, אֵין עוֹד.

וַאֲנַחְנוּ כּוֹרְעִים וּמִשְׁתַּחֲוִים וּמוֹדִים לִפְנֵי מֶלֶךְ מַלְכֵי
הַמְּלָכִים, הַקָּדוֹשׁ בָּרוּךְ הוּא.

We therefore bow in awe and thanksgiving before the One who
is Sovereign over all, the Holy and Blessed One.

All are seated

May the time not be distant, O God, when Your name
shall be worshipped in all the earth, when unbelief shall
disappear and error be no more. Fervently we pray that
the day may come when all shall turn to You in love, when
corruption and evil shall give way to integrity and
goodness, when superstition shall no longer enslave the
mind, nor idolatry blind the eye, when all who dwell on
earth shall know that You alone are God. O may all,
created in Your image, become one in spirit and one in
friendship, for ever united in Your service. Then shall
Your kingdom be established on earth, and the word of
Your prophet fulfilled: "The Lord will reign for ever and
ever."

בַּיּוֹם הַהוּא יִהְיֶה יְיָ אֶחָד וּשְׁמוֹ אֶחָד.

On that day the Lord shall be One and His name shall be One.

◆ ◆

Life and death alike are mysteries. We journey through a country dimly seen by the uncertain light of thought and feeling, and death is undiscovered territory, a land without report. Yet as we now remember our loved ones who have died, we look ahead with faith and hope. They have faded from our sight, but they live on in God's presence, where nothing good can perish. In the Eternal, all beauty shines for ever.

As we turn from thoughts of death to tasks of life, may we, like those who came before us, be builders of God's kingdom, a world of justice and joy.

MOURNER'S KADDISH   קדיש יתום

יִתְגַּדַּל וְיִתְקַדַּשׁ שְׁמֵהּ רַבָּא בְּעָלְמָא דִּי־בְרָא
כִרְעוּתֵהּ, וְיַמְלִיךְ מַלְכוּתֵהּ בְּחַיֵּיכוֹן וּבְיוֹמֵיכוֹן וּבְחַיֵּי
דְכָל־בֵּית יִשְׂרָאֵל, בַּעֲגָלָא וּבִזְמַן קָרִיב, וְאִמְרוּ: אָמֵן.

Yit·ga·dal ve·yit·ka·dash she·mei ra·ba be·al·ma di·ve·ra
chi·re·u·tei, ve·yam·lich mal·chu·tei be·cha·yei·chon
u·ve·yo·mei·chon u·ve·cha·yei de·chol beit Yis·ra·eil, ba·a·ga·la
u·vi·ze·man ka·riv, ve·i·me·ru: a·mein.

יְהֵא שְׁמֵהּ רַבָּא מְבָרַךְ לְעָלַם וּלְעָלְמֵי עָלְמַיָּא.

Ye·hei she·mei ra·ba me·va·rach le·a·lam u·le·al·mei al·ma·ya.

יִתְבָּרַךְ וְיִשְׁתַּבַּח, וְיִתְפָּאַר וְיִתְרוֹמַם וְיִתְנַשֵּׂא,
וְיִתְהַדָּר וְיִתְעַלֶּה וְיִתְהַלָּל שְׁמֵהּ דְּקוּדְשָׁא, בְּרִיךְ

223

הוּא, לְעֵלָּא מִן־כָּל־בִּרְכָתָא וְשִׁירָתָא, תֻּשְׁבְּחָתָא
וְנֶחֱמָתָא דַּאֲמִירָן בְּעָלְמָא, וְאִמְרוּ: אָמֵן.

Yit·ba·rach ve·yish·ta·bach, ve·yit·pa·ar ve·yit·ro·mam
ve·yit·na·sei, ve·yit·ha·dar ve·yit·a·leh ve·yit·ha·lal she·mei
de·ku·de·sha, be·rich hu, le·ei·la min kol bi·re·cha·ta
ve·shi·ra·ta, tush·be·cha·ta ve·ne·che·ma·ta, da·a·mi·ran
be·al·ma, ve·i·me·ru: a·mein.

יְהֵא שְׁלָמָא רַבָּא מִן־שְׁמַיָּא וְחַיִּים עָלֵינוּ וְעַל־כָּל־
יִשְׂרָאֵל, וְאִמְרוּ: אָמֵן.

Ye·hei she·la·ma ra·ba min she·ma·ya ve·cha·yim a·lei·nu ve·al
kol Yis·ra·eil, ve·i·me·ru: a·mein.

עֹשֶׂה שָׁלוֹם בִּמְרוֹמָיו, הוּא יַעֲשֶׂה שָׁלוֹם עָלֵינוּ
וְעַל־כָּל־יִשְׂרָאֵל, וְאִמְרוּ: אָמֵן.

O·seh sha·lom bi·me·ro·mav, hu ya·a·seh sha·lom a·lei·nu ve·al
kol Yis·ra·eil, ve·i·me·ru: a·mein.

Let the glory of God be extolled, let His great name be hallowed
in the world whose creation He willed. May His kingdom soon
prevail, in our own day, our own lives, and the life of all Israel,
and let us say: Amen.
Let His great name be blessed for ever and ever.
Let the name of the Holy One, blessed is He, be glorified, exalted, and honored, though He is beyond all the praises, songs,
and adorations that we can utter, and let us say: Amen.
For us and for all Israel, may the blessing of peace and the
promise of life come true, and let us say: Amen.
May the One who causes peace to reign in the high heavens, let
peace descend on us, on all Israel, and all the world, and let us
say: Amen.

◆ ◆

May the Source of peace send peace to all who mourn,
and comfort to all who are bereaved. Amen.

EIN KEILOHEINU   אין כאלהינו

אֵין כֵּאלֹהֵינוּ, אֵין כַּאדוֹנֵינוּ,
אֵין כְּמַלְכֵּנוּ, אֵין כְּמוֹשִׁיעֵנוּ.

Ein kei·lo·hei·nu, ein ka·do·nei·nu,
ein ke·mal·kei·nu, ein ke·mo·shi·ei·nu.

מִי כֵאלֹהֵינוּ? מִי כַאדוֹנֵינוּ?
מִי כְמַלְכֵּנוּ? מִי כְמוֹשִׁיעֵנוּ?

Mi chei·lo·hei·nu? Mi cha·do·nei·nu?
Mi che·mal·kei·nu? Mi che·mo·shi·ei·nu?

נוֹדֶה לֵאלֹהֵינוּ, נוֹדֶה לַאדוֹנֵינוּ,
נוֹדֶה לְמַלְכֵּנוּ, נוֹדֶה לְמוֹשִׁיעֵנוּ.

No·deh lei·lo·hei·nu, no·deh la·do·nei·nu,
no·deh le·mal·kei·nu, no·deh le·mo·shi·ei·nu.

בָּרוּךְ אֱלֹהֵינוּ, בָּרוּךְ אֲדוֹנֵינוּ,
בָּרוּךְ מַלְכֵּנוּ, בָּרוּךְ מוֹשִׁיעֵנוּ.

Ba·ruch E·lo·hei·nu, ba·ruch A·do·nei·nu,
ba·ruch Mal·kei·nu, ba·ruch Mo·shi·ei·nu.

אַתָּה הוּא אֱלֹהֵינוּ, אַתָּה הוּא אֲדוֹנֵינוּ,
אַתָּה הוּא מַלְכֵּנוּ, אַתָּה הוּא מוֹשִׁיעֵנוּ.

A·ta hu E·lo·hei·nu, a·ta hu A·do·nei·nu,
a·ta hu Mal·kei·nu, a·ta hu Mo·shi·ei·nu.

There is none like our God; there is none like our Lord; there is none
like our King; there is none like our Savior.

Who is like our God? Who is like our Lord? Who is like our King?
Who is like our Savior?

We will give thanks to our God; we will give thanks to our Lord; we
will give thanks to our King; we will give thanks to our Savior.

Blessed is our God; blessed is our Lord; blessed is our King; blessed is
our Savior.

You are our God; You are our Lord: You are our King; You are our
Savior.

Benediction

And now, at the beginning of a new year,
we pray for blessing:

The spirit of wisdom and understanding.   *Amen.*

The spirit of insight and knowledge.   *Amen.*

The spirit of knowledge and reverence.   *Amen.*

May we overcome trouble, pain, and sorrow.   *Amen.*

May our days and years increase.   *Amen.*

יְהִי רָצוֹן מִלְפָנֶיךָ, יְיָ אֱלֹהֵינוּ וֵאלֹהֵי אֲבוֹתֵינוּ,
שֶׁתְּחַדֵּשׁ עָלֵינוּ שָׁנָה טוֹבָה וּמְתוּקָה.

Eternal our God and God of our people,
renew us for a good year.

Amen and Amen.

תפלת ערבית ליום כפור

YOM KIPPUR EVENING
SERVICE

Meditations   הגיונות

I

"And this shall be to you a law for all time: In the seventh month, on the tenth day of the month, you shall practice self-denial (Leviticus 16.29; cf. Leviticus 23.27, Numbers 29.7)."

Three times the Torah links Yom Kippur with the practice of 'self-denial.' By tradition we fulfill this command in part by fasting. The three-fold utterance may suggest three reasons for fasting.

Judaism calls for self-discipline. When we control our appetites on Yom Kippur, we remember that on other days, too, we can be masters, not slaves, of our desires.

Judaism calls for empathy. When we consciously experience hunger, we are more likely to consider the millions who need no Yom Kippur in order to suffer hunger. For some, most days are days without food enough for themselves and their children.

Judaism calls for penitence. The confession we make with our lips is a beginning. The penance we inflict upon our bodies through fasting, leads us along further still toward the acknowledgment that we have sinned against ourselves and others.

Only that fast is good which helps us move toward that transformation of self and society whose achievement is the ultimate end of our worship on Yom Kippur.

Chaim Stern

2

"Let all that breathes praise the Lord (Psalm 150.6)." Let us praise our Maker with and for every single breath we take.

Midrash

3

"O God who hears prayer, to You shall all flesh come (Psalm 65.3)." When the poor speak, we pay little attention; when the rich open their mouths, we are all attention. Before God, however, all are equal—

female and male, master and servant, rich and poor. Two verses of Scripture make this clear. In regard to Moses, greatest of the prophets, it is written: "A prayer of Moses, the man of God (Psalm 90.1);" while in regard to the poor it is written: "A prayer of the poor, when they are faint and pouring out their grievances before the Lord (Psalm 102.1)." The identical word, *tefillah,* 'a prayer,' is used in both cases—from which we learn that great and small are equal before God.

Midrash

4

To seek God is to strive for the good; to find God is to do good.

Leo Baeck

5

Rabbi Baruch's grandson, Yechiel, was playing hide-and-seek with another boy. He hid himself well and waited for his playmate to find him. After waiting a long time, he came from his hiding place, but the other was nowhere in sight. Now he realized that the boy had not looked for him. Weeping, he came to his grandfather to complain of his faithless friend. Rabbi Baruch's eyes, too, brimmed with tears, and he said: God says the same thing: I hide, but no one wants to seek Me!

Chasidic, 18th Century

6

Rabbi Baruch once said: Elijah's great work was not that he performed miracles, but that, when, in his conflict with the priests of Baal on Mt. Carmel, fire fell from Heaven, the people did not speak of miracles, but cried: "The Lord is God (I Kings 18.39)!"

Chasidic, 18th Century

7

Rabbi Shneur Zalman of Liadi asked a disciple: Mosheh, what do we mean when we say 'God'? The disciple, taken aback, was silent. He asked a second and a third time. Finally, he said: Why are you silent? Because, came the reply, I do not know. Shneur Zalman rejoined: Do you think I know? And yet I must say it, I must say it. I must say: God is . . . .

Chasidic, 18th Century

8

Once the Baal Shem became so depressed that he thought: I have no share in the world-to-come. And then he said to himself: If I love God, what need have I of paradise?

Chasidic, 18th Century

9

His disciples went to visit Rabban Yochanan ben Zakkai as he lay ill. They said: Master, give us your blessing. He replied: May you fear God as much as you fear human beings. They said: No more than that? He replied: That is more than enough, believe me! Do you not know that when we are about to commit a transgression we dismiss God from our minds and hope that no human eye may notice us!

Talmud

10

A disciple asked the Baal Shem: Why does one who ordinarily feels close to God, sometimes experience a sense of remoteness from the divine presence? He replied: When a parent begins to teach a baby to walk, the parent steadies the child with both hands, and the guiding presence is always felt. Then, bit by bit, the parent moves away, establishing 'growing' distances which the child learns to traverse on its own. God may seem to move away from us sometimes, but perhaps He wants us to grow by taking hesitant steps toward Him.

Chasidic, 18th Century

11

But the child must grow. It must emerge from mother's womb, from mother's breast; it must eventually become a completely separate human being. The very essence of motherly love is to care for the child's growth, and that means to want the child's separation from herself. Here lies the basic difference to erotic love. In erotic love, two people who were separate become one. In motherly love, two people who were one become separate. The mother must not only tolerate, she must wish and support the child's separation. It is only at this stage that motherly love becomes such a difficult task, that it requires unselfishness, the ability to give everything and to want nothing but the happiness of the loved one.

Erich Fromm

12

Religion offers answers without obliterating the questions. They become blunted and will not attack you with the same ferocity. But without them the answer would dry up and wither away. The question is a great religious act; it helps you live great religious truth.

Shmuel Sperber

13

Keep two truths in your pocket, and take them out according to the need of the moment. Let one be: 'For my sake was the world created.' And the other: 'I am dust and ashes.'

Chasidic, 18th Century

14

The Great Maggid of Mezritch had a room adjoining the bedchamber of his disciples. Sometimes he would enter with a light in his hand, and look into their sleeping faces. Once he bent down to the low bench on which young Shneur Zalman of Liadi lay under a threadbare, three-cornered cover. He looked a long time and then thought: Miracle of miracles, that so great a God lives in so frail a dwelling!

Chasidic, 18th Century

15

Israel is committed by the Covenant to serve as the special steward of the Torah, the agent and exemplar of the divine dispensation in the world of humanity. Wholeness and holiness are conditions of that commitment: "You shall be holy unto Me; for I, the Lord, am holy, and have set you apart from the peoples, to make you Mine (Leviticus

20.26)." Any diminution of them—any tarnishing of the divine by the corruption of the human—is therefore not only an individual offense, a blot on individual character, but also a breach of the Covenant, a positive impediment to the discharge of its obligations. Conversely, any individual enhancement of them is at the same time a contribution to the collective endeavor.

For this reason, Yom Kippur is a public institution as well as a private experience. The confessions which are recited on this day are couched, significantly enough, in the first person plural; and what is envisaged is a purification not only of individual souls but also of the whole House of Israel.

Theodor Gaster

16

Whoever spreads malicious gossip is like one who denies God. One is also forbidden to listen to malicious gossip. Our sages taught that four types of people cannot receive the Divine Presence: scoffers, liars, flatterers, and those who spread malicious gossip.

All are obliged to be merciful, as it is written: "Do not harden your heart or shut your hand against the poor, your kin (Deuteronomy 15.7)." We must avoid arrogance, as it is written: "The arrogant are repellent to the Lord (Proverbs 16.5)."

Free yourself of hatred, as it is written: "You shall not hate another in your heart (Leviticus 19.18a)," and "Love your neighbor as yourself; I am the Lord (Leviticus 19.18b)." Our sages declared this to be the essence of the Torah. For through love of one's neighbor, and through peace-making, the people of Israel translate the Torah's teachings into reality.

Jonah ben Abraham Gerondi, 13th Century

17

Days are scrolls: write on them only what you want remembered.

Bachya ibn Pakuda, 11th Century

18

Rabbi Rafael said: Measured behavior is a dreadful evil. We do a great wrong when we trim our actions to suit others. It is as if we were always manipulating weights and measures.

Chasidic, 18th Century

19

What do you call 'profaning God's name?' Rav said: In my case, since I am reputed to live strictly under the discipline of Torah, it would be failing to pay the butcher promptly.

Talmud

20

There are birds of passage which fly to warm countries in the autumn. In one of those lands the people once saw a glorious multicolored bird amidst a flock journeying through the sky. Never had eyes seen a bird so beautiful. He alighted at the top of a very tall tree and nested in the leaves. Now when the king heard of it, he wanted it for himself. Some men were ordered to make a human ladder, each to stand on the other's shoulders until they reached the nest. It took a long time to build this living ladder. When reaching fingertips had almost grasped the bird, those who stood nearest the ground grew restive, shook themselves free—and everything collapsed.

Chasidic, 18th Century

21

A rich man once came to the Maggid of Koznitz for blessing. 'What are you in the habit of eating?' asked the Maggid. The man replied: 'I am modest in my demands. Bread and salt, a drink of water, I need no more.' 'What are you thinking of! You must eat roast meat and drink mead, like all the rich.' And the rabbi did not let him go until he had promised to change his ways. Later, to his puzzled chasidim, the Maggid explained: 'Not until he eats meat will he realize that the poor need bread. As long as he himself eats only bread, he will think the poor can live on stones.'

Chasidic, 18th Century

22

The law fuses the individual and the community into a moral unity. The dichotomy, individual and society, is dissolved under the dominion of the law of God. It commands respect for the life, dignity, and rights of human beings; it imposes social duties on individuals. Under the moral law, individual righteousness and social justice work together to give individuals their rights and society its righteousness. Conflicts between the rights of individuals and the needs of society could not arise in the thought of the Prophets because the law of God covered them both. The rights of individuals were guaranteed by the obligations laid on society, and the needs of society were met by the duties commanded to individuals.

Israel I. Mattuck

23

Rabbi Levi Yitzchak turned to the people standing around him and said: Do you know the difference between our Father Abraham, peace be with him, and his nephew Lot? Why does such a spirit of satisfaction pervade the story of how Abraham set before the angels curd and milk and tender calf? Did not Lot also bake for them and give them food? In Lot's case it is written that angels came to Sodom. But concerning Abraham, Scripture says: ". . . and he looked up and saw three men standing opposite him (Genesis 18.2)." Lot saw angelic shapes; Abraham saw poor, dusty wayfarers in need of food and rest.

Chasidic, 18th Century

24

See how great is the peacemaker's reward! It is written: "You shall build the altar of the Lord with unhewn stones (Deuteronomy 27.6)." Though they cannot hear, see, smell, or speak, these stones are spared the touch of the sword, as it is commanded: "You shall lift no iron tool upon them (Deuteronomy 27.5)." Why? Because the sacrifices offered upon them helped people make peace with one another. As for human beings, who *can* hear, see, smell, and speak—how much greater is their reward when they make peace among themselves!

Midrash

25

Our masters taught: His disciples came to visit Rabbi Eliezer as he lay ill. They said: Master, teach us the paths by which we may attain eternal life. He replied: Show concern for the honor of your friends; set your children at the feet of the wise, who will keep them from idle thoughts; and, when you pray, know before Whom you stand. Thus will you win eternal life.

Talmud

26

Wherever you stand to lift up your eyes to heaven, that place is a Holy of Holies. Every human being created by God in God's own image and likeness is a High Priest. Each day of your life is the Day of Atonement; and every word spoken from the heart is the name of the Lord. Therefore the sin of any of us, whether of commission or omission, brings the ruin of a whole world in its train.

S. Ansky, The Dibbuk

27

There was that law of life, so cruel and so just, which demanded that one must grow or else pay more for remaining the same.

Norman Mailer

Increase your knowledge, or you will decrease it!

Mishnah

28

Rabbi Michal gave this command to his sons: Pray for your enemies that all may be well with them. And rest assured that, far from opposing God's will, these prayers of yours, more than any others, will be in God's service.

Chasidic, 18th Century

29

The Holy One said to Israel: My children, I have created the evil inclination, and I have created the Torah as its antidote. Occupy yourselves with the Torah, and the evil inclination will not control you.

Talmud

30

The disciples of Rabbi Pinchas were talking with animation when their master entered the House of Study. Upon his arrival, they fell silent. He asked them: What were you talking about? They replied: We were discussing our fear that the evil inclination will pursue us. He replied: You need not worry. You have not yet reached so high a plane. For the time being, *you* are still pursuing *it*.

Chasidic, 18th Century

31

Self-deceit is a strong fort;
It will last a lifetime.

Self-truth is a lightning bolt lost as I grasp it.
And the fires that it strikes can raze my house.

You ask me to yearn after truth, Lord,
But who would choose to be whipped with fire?—

—Unless in the burning there can be great light,
Unless the lightning that strikes terror
Lights enough to show the boundaries
Where terror ends,
And at the limits, still enduring and alive,
Shows me myself
And a hope no longer blind.

Joanne Greenberg

32

When Akabya ben Mahalalel was dying, his son said to him: Father, commend me to your colleagues. He replied: I will not commend you.

His son said: Have you found in me some cause for complaint? Akabya answered: No, but your own deeds will commend you to them, or your own deeds will estrange you from them.

Mishnah

33

Rabbi Michal once said to his sons: My life was blessed, because I never needed anything until I had it.

Chasidic, 18th Century

34

At first sin is like a spider's web; in the end it becomes as thick as a ship's cable. At first it is a visitor; in the end it becomes the master of the house.

Midrash

35

One good deed leads to another, and one transgression to another.

Mishnah

36

Happy are you, O Israel! Before whom are you made clean, and before whom do you cleanse yourselves? Your Maker in heaven, as it is said: "I will sprinkle clean water upon you, and you shall be clean (Ezekiel 36.25)."

Mishnah

37

Some louts in Rabbi Meir's neighborhood were giving him a great deal of trouble, and in exasperation he prayed for their deaths. His wife Beruriah said to him: How can you think that such prayer is permitted? Pray for an end to sin; then, sin having ceased, there will be no more sinners. Pray that they may turn from their ways. Then Rabbi Meir prayed on their behalf.

Talmud

38

For us there is but one atonement—the atonement wrought by human repentance and the divine forgiveness; by God's grace and help on the one hand, by human remorse and effort on the other. The process is doubtless subtle, but put into words it is simple, and in practice it is efficacious and works. That is the Jewish atonement: we know no other.

Claude G. Montefiore

39

"Open to Me (Song of Songs 5.2)." Make for Me an opening (of repentance), an opening as narrow as the point of a needle, and I will make the opening so wide (for pardon) that camps full of soldiers and siege engines could enter it.

Midrash

40

One who says: I will sin and repent, then I will sin again and repent again, is not really repentant. And one who says: I will sin, and the Day of Atonement will atone for me, will find that that day will not avail for atonement.

Mishnah

41

For transgressions against God, the Day of Atonement atones; but for transgressions of one human being against another, the Day of Atonement does not atone until they have made peace with one another.

Mishnah

42

If we are guilty of sin and confess it and yet do not change our ways, we may be compared to those who hold a defiling object even while they are immersed in purifying waters! Will all the world's waters help them? So long as we cling to defilement, the uncleanness remains.

Talmud

43

We do not ask that our past sins may be forgiven in the sense that their effects may be cancelled, for that is impossible. All we can ask and do ask for is better insight, purer faith, fuller strength. We want to grow in holiness of life and in the love of God. For this we ask God's help, for this we try by earnest prayer to realise better the true vileness of sin, how it separates us from God, and weakens and defiles us; for this only we make repentance and seek atonement.

Claude G. Montefiore

44

When you talk about and reflect upon an evil deed you have done, you become the captive of your thoughts—all your soul is utterly caught up in the evil, for you are what you think. And then you are prevented from turning, for your spirit will coarsen, your heart grow infirm, and, in addition, melancholy may disable you. After all, if you stir filth this way or that, it is still filth. What is the use of weighing and measuring our sins? In the time I am brooding on this, I could be stringing pearls for the joy of heaven. That is why it is written: "Depart from evil, and do good (Psalm 34.15)" —turn wholly from evil, do not brood about it, and do good. You have done wrong? Then balance it by doing right.

Chasidic, 19th Century

45

After the flood, Noah opened the ark and looked out. He saw the earth desolate, forests and gardens uprooted, corpses visible everywhere. There was no grass, no vegetation; the world was a wasteland. In pain and dismay, he cried out to his Master: Sovereign of all creation, in six days You made the earth and all that grows in it: it was like a garden, like a table prepared for a feast; now You Yourself have brought the work of Your hands to nought, uprooting all that You planted, tearing down all that You built. Why did You not show compassion for Your creatures? God then replied: O faithless shepherd! Now, after the destruction, You come to Me and complain. But when I said to you: Make an ark for yourself, for I am going to flood the earth to destroy all flesh, you did not plead for your neighbors! How differently Abraham will act; he will pray on behalf of the people of Sodom and Gomorrah. And Moses, when his people anger Me with their calf of gold, will offer his life for them. But you—when you saw that judgment was about to strike the world—you thought only of yourself and your household, while all else perished by fire and water!

Then Noah understood that he had sinned.

Midrash

46

"Return, O Israel, to the Lord your God (Hosea 14.2)." Rabbi Judah bar Simon said: Return, even if you have denied the Source of all existence. Rabbi Elazar said: When one person insults another in public, the injured party usually demands a public apology before there can be a reconciliation. But even if one blasphemes by publicly denying God, the Holy One declares: Repent even in private and I shall welcome you. As it is written: "I will heal their apostasy; I will love them freely (Hosea 14.5)."

Midrash

47

God says: My hands reach out to the penitent; I reject none who give Me their hearts. Therefore we read: "Peace, peace, to all, far and near (Isaiah 57.19)." God says: Though you be far from Me, I will draw near and heal you—if you come toward Me!

Midrash

48

Friends, what does it say about the people of Nineveh? Not, "God saw their sackcloth and their fasting," but, "God saw their deeds—that they had turned back from their evil way (Jonah 3.10)." And in his admonition, the prophet says: "Rend your hearts, and not your garments (Joel 2.13)."

Mishnah

49

Atonement with God means redemption from sinfulness. It does not redeem us from an earthly fate. We are not transported into the other world as a consolation for suffering. We are redeemed from the illusion that our share in evil is unavoidable . . . . God in mercy can grant atonement only to those who strive for the good, who recognize sin and wish to avoid it. Without our moral work in repentance, God would be unable to redeem us.

Hermann Cohen

50

Our Rabbis have taught: Those who are persecuted and do not persecute in turn, those who listen to contemptuous insults and do not reply, those who act out of love and are glad of sufferings, concerning them the Torah says: "They that love God are like the sun going forth in his strength (Judges 5.31)."

Talmud

51

To act out of love and to be willing to bear the suffering which the good and true man must inevitably bear in a world like ours, in a world which is only partly divine and which must be won for God through the efforts of man—that is the deepest utterance of the rabbis and the culminating idea of Jewish religiosity and of Jewish prayer.

Henry Slonimsky

52

One can always find warm hearts who in a glow of emotion would like to make the whole world happy but who have never attempted the sober experiment of bringing a real blessing to a single human being. It is easy to revel enthusiastically in one's love of man, but it is more difficult to do good to someone solely because he is a human being. When we are approached by a human being demanding his right, we cannot replace definite ethical action by mere vague goodwill.

Leo Baeck

53

One wears his mind out in study, and yet has more mind with which to study. One gives away his heart in love and yet has more heart to give away. One perishes out of pity for a suffering world, and is the stronger therefor. So, too, it is possible at one and the same time to hold on to life and let it go.

Milton Steinberg

54

When we are dead, and people weep for us and grieve, let it be because we touched their lives with beauty and simplicity. Let it not be said that life was good to us, but, rather, that we were good to life.

Jacob P. Rudin

55

There was a villager who, on the Days of Awe, would pray in the Baal Shem Tov's Synagogue. His son was a dull lad who had not learned to read his letters, much less the prayer book. So his father never took him with him. But when the boy reached the age of Bar Mitzvah, his father took him to the synagogue on Yom Kippur, to keep an eye on him, lest, out of sheer ignorance, he eat on the holy fast day. This boy had a little flute which he would play while in the field tending his flock. Though his father did not know it, he had taken it with him to the synagogue. All day long the boy sat in silence in the House of Prayer. During the Additional Prayer, the boy had whispered to his father: Father, I want to play my flute. Terrified, his father had spoken to him sharply, and the boy had subsided. This happened again during the afternoon service, and at its conclusion. Each time his father restrained the boy. Finally, however, during the concluding service, the boy forced the flute out of his pocket and blew a blast so loud that all were taken aback. When the Baal Shem Tov (who was the Reader) heard the sound, he shortened his prayer.

At the end, the Baal Shem Tov said: This child's flute lifted up all our prayers. Through the strength of his yearning he played his heart's note perfectly. This was very dear to God, and all our prayers were accepted for his sake.

Chasidic, 18th Century

56

Rabbi Joshua came upon the prophet Elijah as he stood at the entrance of Rabbi Shimon bar Yochai's cave. He asked the prophet: When will the Messiah come? Elijah answered: You will find him before the gates of Rome, sitting among the poor. His body, like theirs, is covered with running sores. The others first remove all their dressings and then apply fresh bandages. But he never changes more than one dressing at a time, for he thinks: when I hear the call, I must be able to come without delay!

Rabbi Joshua went and found him. He said: Peace be with you, my master and teacher! The reply was: Peace be with you, son of Levi! Then Joshua asked: When are you coming, master? And he answered: Today! But when the day had come to an end, the Messiah had not arrived, and Rabbi Joshua turned to Elijah, and said: He lied to me, oh, he lied to me! Today! he said, and he did not come. He lied . . . But Elijah said: You must understand what he meant, for it is written: "Today—if you will but hearken to God's voice (Psalm 95.7)!"

Talmud

57

Rav Beroka of Bei Hozae was often in the market of Bei Lapat. There he would meet Elijah. Once he said to Elijah: Is there anyone in this market who has earned eternal life? Elijah said to him: No. They were standing there when two men came along. Elijah said to him: These men have earned eternal life. Rav Beroka went to them and said: What do you do? They replied: We are jesters, and make the sad to laugh. When we see two people quarreling, we strain ourselves to make peace between them.

Talmud

58

Darkness is not the road to light, dictatorship and paternalism are not the paths to freedom and independence, terror is no express train to the golden age.

Chaim Greenberg

59

Everyone suddenly burst out singing;
And I was filled with such delight
As prisoned birds must find in freedom,
Winging wildly across the white
Orchards and dark-green fields;
    on—on—and out of sight.
Everyone's voice was suddenly lifted;
And beauty came like the setting sun;
My heart was shaken with tears; and horror
Drifted away . . . Oh, but everyone
Was a bird; and the song was wordless—
    the singing will never be done.

Siegfried Sassoon

Evening Service

All rise

Before the open Ark

רִבּוֹנוֹ שֶׁל עוֹלָם, הִנְנִי עוֹמֵד לְפָנֶיךָ בְּיִרְאָה וּבְשִׁפְלוּת
לְהִתְפַּלֵּל עִם עַמְּךָ בְּנֵי יִשְׂרָאֵל וּבַעֲדָם. יוֹדֵעַ אֲנִי שֶׁאֵינִי כְדַאי
וְהָגוּן לְכָךְ, כִּי טְמֵא־שְׂפָתַיִם אָנֹכִי, וּבְתוֹךְ עַם־טְמֵא שְׂפָתַיִם
אָנֹכִי יוֹשֵׁב. מִי יָקוּם בִּמְקוֹם קָדְשֶׁךָ? וְאִם עֲוֹנוֹת תִּשְׁמָר, מִי
יַעֲמֹד? וְאַתָּה יוֹשֵׁב תְּהִלּוֹת יִשְׂרָאֵל, וּמַתִּיר לְהִתְפַּלֵּל עִם
הָעֲבַרְיָנִים. עַל־כֵּן, בְּרַחֲמֶיךָ הָרַבִּים, רַחֵם עָלַי וְעַל שׁוֹלְחָי.
אַל יִכָּלְמוּ בִי, וְאַל אֶכָּלֵם בָּהֶם. הֱיֵה עִם פִּיפִיּוֹת שְׁלוּחֵי עַמֶּךָ.
חַזֵּק אֱמוּנָתֵנוּ, וְטַהֵר מַחְשְׁבוֹתֵינוּ, וּפְשָׁעֵינוּ תְּכַסֶּה בְּאַהֲבָה,
וְתָבֹא תְפִלָּתֵנוּ הַיּוֹם לִפְנֵי כִסֵּא כְבוֹדֶךָ.

Lord of the universe, in awe and humility I have come to
stand before You to pray with Your people Israel and on
their behalf. Who is fit for such a task? Yet You are present to us whenever our voices rise in praise. In Your great
mercy, have compassion on me and on us all. Let my congregation not falter on my account, nor I on theirs. Guide
the lips of those who lead Your people in worship.
Strengthen our faith and purify our thoughts, and let
Your love draw a veil over all our failings. So may our
prayers ascend this day to the throne of Your glory.

The Ark is closed

All are seated

••

*For congregations where the blessing over the lights
is recited in the synagogue*

הדלקת הנרות

בָּרוּךְ אַתָּה, יְיָ אֱלֹהֵינוּ, מֶלֶךְ הָעוֹלָם, אֲשֶׁר קִדְּשָׁנוּ בְּמִצְוֹתָיו וְצִוָּנוּ לְהַדְלִיק נֵר שֶׁל (שַׁבָּת וְשֶׁל) יוֹם הַכִּפּוּרִים.

Blessed is the Lord our God, Ruler of the universe, who
hallows us with Mitzvot, and commands us to kindle the
lights of (Shabbat and) the Day of Atonement.

בָּרוּךְ אַתָּה,יְיָ אֱלֹהֵינוּ, מֶלֶךְ הָעוֹלָם, שֶׁהֶחֱיָנוּ וְקִיְּמָנוּ וְהִגִּיעָנוּ לַזְּמַן הַזֶּה.

Blessed is the Lord our God, Ruler of the universe, for
giving us life, for sustaining us, and for enabling us to
reach this season.

◆ ◆

248

MEDITATION

In the beginning God created heaven and earth,
and the earth brought forth life,
and life gave birth to man and woman.
And they became conscious:
Aware that they were free
to create or destroy,
to live or to die.
Conscious also that they were not alone.
Slowly they became aware of a Presence
greater than themselves,
whose will must be done
if we are to endure
and become what we can be.
This vision was seen by the founders of our people.
At the Mountain they pledged themselves
and us, their children,
to live by its light,
to share it with others.
Here we stand, heirs of the past
and makers of the future—
priestly, privileged,
but heavily burdened
with blindness, folly, unfaithfulness.
Can we re-open our eyes to wisdom,
to be, or hope to be, at one with the One?
This day, if any day, can make us whole.
Trembling, we pray to gain
a new heart, a new spirit.

◆ ◆

Once more Atonement Day has come.
All pretense gone,
naked heart revealed to the hiding self,
we stand on holy ground,
between the day that was
and the one that must be.

We tremble.
At what did we aim?
How did we stumble?
What did we take? What did we give?
To what were we blind?
Last year's confession came easily to the lips.
Will this year's come from deeper than the skin?
Say then:
Why are our paths strewn with promises like
fallen leaves?
Say then:
When shall our lust be for wisdom?
Say now:
Love and truth shall meet;
justice and peace shall embrace.

O Hope of Israel:
In our weakness, give us strength.
In our blindness, be our guide.
When we falter, hold our hand.

Make consistent our impulse for good;
let us know the joy of walking in Your ways.

◆ ◆

MEDITATION

Kol Nidrei is the prayer of people not free to make their own decisions, people forced to say what they do not mean. In repeating this prayer, we identify with the agony of our forebears who had to say 'yes' when they meant 'no.' Kol Nidrei is also a confession: we are all transgressors, all exiled from the Highest we know, all in need of the healing of forgiveness and reconciliation. For what we have done, for what we may yet do, we ask pardon; for rash words, broken pledges, insincere assurances, and foolish promises, may we find forgiveness.

◆ ◆

עֲבֵרוֹת שֶׁבֵּין אָדָם לַמָּקוֹם, יוֹם הַכִּפּוּרִים מְכַפֵּר. עֲבֵרוֹת שֶׁבֵּין אָדָם לַחֲבֵרוֹ, אֵין יוֹם הַכִּפּוּרִים מְכַפֵּר עַד שֶׁיְרַצֶּה אֶת־חֲבֵרוֹ.

For transgressions against God, the Day of Atonement atones; but for transgressions of one human being against another, the Day of Atonement does not atone until they have made peace with one another.

◆ ◆

All rise

The Ark is opened

אוֹר זָרֻעַ לַצַּדִּיק, וּלְיִשְׁרֵי־לֵב שִׂמְחָה.

Light is sown for the righteous,
and gladness for the upright in heart.

◆ ◆

The Scrolls are taken from the Ark

בִּישִׁיבָה שֶׁל מַעְלָה וּבִישִׁיבָה שֶׁל מַטָּה,
עַל דַּעַת הַמָּקוֹם וְעַל דַּעַת הַקָּהָל,
אָנוּ מַתִּירִין לְהִתְפַּלֵּל עִם הָעֲבַרְיָנִים.

In the sight of God and of the congregation, no matter how far some of us may have transgressed by departing from our people and our heritage, we pray as one on this Night of Repentance.

Kol Nidrei: a whisper of wings, as promises are remembered. Saint and sinner alike communes with the Most High. We are at one.

Heart of all life, from this Day of Atonement to the next—

*may we reach it in peace—all Israel makes these vows: to turn
from sin and wrongdoing, and to walk in the way of Your Law, the
path of justice and right. Yet we know our weakness—how prone
we are to fail: help us to keep these vows made with contrite
hearts. We have come to seek pardon and forgiveness.*

ALL VOWS   כל נדרי

כָּל־נִדְרֵי וֶאֱסָרֵי וַחֲרָמֵי וְקוֹנָמֵי וְכִנּוּיֵי וְקִנּוּסֵי
וּשְׁבוּעוֹת, דִּנְדַרְנָא וּדְאִשְׁתְּבַּעְנָא וּדְאַחֲרִימְנָא
וְדַאֲסָרְנָא עַל נַפְשָׁתָנָא, מִיּוֹם כִּפּוּרִים זֶה עַד יוֹם
כִּפּוּרִים הַבָּא עָלֵינוּ לְטוֹבָה, כֻּלְּהוֹן אִחֲרַטְנָא בְהוֹן,
כֻּלְּהוֹן יְהוֹן שָׁרָן, שְׁבִיקִין שְׁבִיתִין, בְּטֵלִין וּמְבֻטָּלִין,
לָא שְׁרִירִין וְלָא קַיָּמִין. נִדְרָנָא לָא נִדְרֵי, וֶאֱסָרָנָא לָא
אֱסָרֵי, וּשְׁבוּעָתָנָא לָא שְׁבוּעוֹת.

Let all our vows and oaths, all the promises we make and the
obligations we incur to You, O God, between this Yom Kippur
and the next, be null and void should we, after honest effort,
find ourselves unable to fulfill them. Then may we be absolved
of them.

◆ ◆

וְנִסְלַח לְכָל־עֲדַת בְּנֵי יִשְׂרָאֵל וְלַגֵּר הַגָּר בְּתוֹכָם, כִּי
לְכָל־הָעָם בִּשְׁגָגָה.

Knowingly or not, the whole community of Israel and all
who live among them have sinned; let them be forgiven.

סְלַח נָא לַעֲוֹן הָעָם הַזֶּה כְּגֹדֶל חַסְדֶּךָ, וְכַאֲשֶׁר נָשָׂאתָ
לָעָם הַזֶּה מִמִּצְרַיִם וְעַד הֵנָּה.

*As, in Your love, You have been patient with this people
from the time You led us out of Egypt to the present day, so,
in Your great love, may You forgive Your people now.*

252

וַיֹּאמֶר יְיָ: "סָלַחְתִּי כִּדְבָרֶךָ."

And the Lord said: I have pardoned in response to your
plea.

• •

בָּרוּךְ אַתָּה, יְיָ אֱלֹהֵינוּ, מֶלֶךְ הָעוֹלָם, שֶׁהֶחֱיָנוּ וְקִיְּמָנוּ
וְהִגִּיעָנוּ לַזְּמַן הַזֶּה.

*Blessed is the Lord our God, Ruler of the universe, for giving
us life, for sustaining us, and for enabling us to reach this
season.*

• •

The Scrolls are returned to the Ark
Remain standing

שמע וברכותיה

בָּרְכוּ אֶת־יְיָ הַמְבֹרָךְ!

Praise the Lord, to whom our praise is due!

בָּרוּךְ יְיָ הַמְבֹרָךְ לְעוֹלָם וָעֶד!

Praised be the Lord, to whom our praise is due,
now and for ever!

• •

AS CLOSE TO US AS BREATHING   מעריב ערבים

בָּרוּךְ אַתָּה, יְיָ אֱלֹהֵינוּ, מֶלֶךְ הָעוֹלָם, אֲשֶׁר בִּדְבָרוֹ
מַעֲרִיב עֲרָבִים. בְּחָכְמָה פּוֹתֵחַ שְׁעָרִים, וּבִתְבוּנָה
מְשַׁנֶּה עִתִּים, וּמַחֲלִיף אֶת־הַזְּמַנִּים, וּמְסַדֵּר אֶת־

253

הַכּוֹכָבִים בְּמִשְׁמְרוֹתֵיהֶם בָּרָקִיעַ כִּרְצוֹנוֹ. בּוֹרֵא יוֹם
וָלַיְלָה, גּוֹלֵל אוֹר מִפְּנֵי חֹשֶׁךְ וְחֹשֶׁךְ מִפְּנֵי אוֹר,
וּמַעֲבִיר יוֹם וּמֵבִיא לַיְלָה, וּמַבְדִּיל בֵּין יוֹם וּבֵין
לַיְלָה, יְיָ צְבָאוֹת שְׁמוֹ. אֵל חַי וְקַיָּם, תָּמִיד יִמְלוֹךְ
עָלֵינוּ, לְעוֹלָם וָעֶד. בָּרוּךְ אַתָּה, יְיָ, הַמַּעֲרִיב עֲרָבִים.

°O God, how can we know You? Where can we find You?
You are as close to us as breathing, yet You are farther
than the farthermost star.

You are as mysterious as the vast solitudes of night, yet as
familiar to us as the light of the sun. To Moses You said:
"You cannot see My face, but I will make all My
goodness pass before you."

Even so does Your goodness pass before us: in the realm
of nature, and in the varied experiences of our lives.

◆ ◆

YOUR GOODNESS ENTERS OUR LIVES   אהבת עולם

אַהֲבַת עוֹלָם בֵּית יִשְׂרָאֵל עַמְּךָ אָהָבְתָּ: תּוֹרָה
וּמִצְוֹת, חֻקִּים וּמִשְׁפָּטִים אוֹתָנוּ לִמַּדְתָּ.
עַל־כֵּן, יְיָ אֱלֹהֵינוּ, בְּשָׁכְבֵּנוּ וּבְקוּמֵנוּ נָשִׂיחַ בְּחֻקֶּיךָ,
וְנִשְׂמַח בְּדִבְרֵי תוֹרָתֶךָ וּבְמִצְוֹתֶיךָ לְעוֹלָם וָעֶד.
כִּי הֵם חַיֵּינוּ וְאֹרֶךְ יָמֵינוּ, וּבָהֶם נֶהְגֶּה יוֹמָם וָלָיְלָה.
וְאַהֲבָתְךָ אַל־תָּסִיר מִמֶּנּוּ לְעוֹלָמִים! בָּרוּךְ אַתָּה, יְיָ,
אוֹהֵב עַמּוֹ יִשְׂרָאֵל.

°When justice burns within us like a flaming fire, when love
evokes willing sacrifice from us, when, to the last full

°This symbol indicates that the English is a variation suggested by the theme
of the Hebrew.

*measure of selfless devotion, we demonstrate our belief in
the ultimate triumph of truth and righteousness, then Your
goodness enters our lives; then You live within our hearts,
and we through righteousness behold Your presence.*

✦ ✦

שְׁמַע יִשְׂרָאֵל: יְיָ אֱלֹהֵינוּ, יְיָ אֶחָד!

Hear, O Israel: the Lord is our God, the Lord is One!

בָּרוּךְ שֵׁם כְּבוֹד מַלְכוּתוֹ לְעוֹלָם וָעֶד!

Blessed is His glorious kingdom for ever and ever!

All are seated

וְאָהַבְתָּ אֵת יְיָ אֱלֹהֶיךָ בְּכָל־לְבָבְךָ וּבְכָל־נַפְשְׁךָ
וּבְכָל־מְאֹדֶךָ. וְהָיוּ הַדְּבָרִים הָאֵלֶּה, אֲשֶׁר אָנֹכִי מְצַוְּךָ
הַיּוֹם, עַל־לְבָבֶךָ. וְשִׁנַּנְתָּם לְבָנֶיךָ, וְדִבַּרְתָּ בָּם
בְּשִׁבְתְּךָ בְּבֵיתֶךָ, וּבְלֶכְתְּךָ בַדֶּרֶךְ, וּבְשָׁכְבְּךָ וּבְקוּמֶךָ.
וּקְשַׁרְתָּם לְאוֹת עַל־יָדֶךָ, וְהָיוּ לְטֹטָפֹת בֵּין עֵינֶיךָ,
וּכְתַבְתָּם עַל־מְזֻזוֹת בֵּיתֶךָ, וּבִשְׁעָרֶיךָ.

*You shall love the Lord your God with all your mind, with all
your strength, with all your being. Set these words, which I
command you this day, upon your heart. Teach them
faithfully to your children; speak of them in your home and
on your way, when you lie down and when you rise up. Bind
them as a sign upon your hand; let them be a symbol before
your eyes; inscribe them on the doorposts of your house and
on your gates.*

לְמַעַן תִּזְכְּרוּ וַעֲשִׂיתֶם אֶת־כָּל־מִצְוֹתָי, וִהְיִיתֶם
קְדֹשִׁים לֵאלֹהֵיכֶם. אֲנִי יְיָ אֱלֹהֵיכֶם, אֲשֶׁר הוֹצֵאתִי
אֶתְכֶם מֵאֶרֶץ מִצְרַיִם לִהְיוֹת לָכֶם לֵאלֹהִים. אֲנִי יְיָ
אֱלֹהֵיכֶם.

255

Be mindful of all My mitzvot, and do them; so shall you consecrate yourselves to your God. I, the Lord, am your God who led you out of Egypt to be your God; I, the Lord, am your God.

◆ ◆

THE HELP OF OUR PEOPLE   גְּאוּלָה

אֱמֶת וֶאֱמוּנָה כָּל־זֹאת, וְקַיָּם עָלֵינוּ כִּי הוּא יְיָ
אֱלֹהֵינוּ וְאֵין זוּלָתוֹ, וַאֲנַחְנוּ יִשְׂרָאֵל עַמּוֹ. הַפּוֹדֵנוּ
מִיַּד מְלָכִים, מַלְכֵּנוּ הַגּוֹאֲלֵנוּ מִכַּף כָּל־הֶעָרִיצִים.
הָעֹשֶׂה גְדֹלוֹת עַד אֵין חֵקֶר, וְנִפְלָאוֹת עַד־אֵין
מִסְפָּר. הַשָּׂם נַפְשֵׁנוּ בַּחַיִּים, וְלֹא־נָתַן לַמּוֹט רַגְלֵנוּ.
הָעֹשֶׂה לָּנוּ נִסִּים בְּפַרְעֹה, אוֹתוֹת וּמוֹפְתִים בְּאַדְמַת
בְּנֵי חָם. וַיּוֹצֵא אֶת־עַמּוֹ יִשְׂרָאֵל מִתּוֹכָם לְחֵרוּת
עוֹלָם. וְרָאוּ בָנָיו גְּבוּרָתוֹ; שִׁבְּחוּ וְהוֹדוּ לִשְׁמוֹ.
וּמַלְכוּתוֹ בְּרָצוֹן קִבְּלוּ עֲלֵיהֶם. מֹשֶׁה וּבְנֵי יִשְׂרָאֵל לְךָ
עָנוּ שִׁירָה בְּשִׂמְחָה רַבָּה, וְאָמְרוּ כֻלָּם:

°True and enduring are the words spoken by our prophets.

You are the living God; Your word brings life and light to the soul.

You are the First and the Last:

besides You there is no redeemer or savior.

You are the strength of our life, the Power that saves us.

Your kingdom and Your truth abide for ever.

You have been the help of our people in time of trouble;

You are our refuge in all generations.

Your power was manifest when we went free out of Egypt;

in every liberation from bondage we see it.

May Your law of freedom rule the hearts of all Your children,

and Your law of justice unite them in friendship.

May the righteous of all nations rejoice in Your love and triumph by Your power.

O God, our refuge and our hope, we glorify Your name now as did our people in ancient days:

מִי־כָמֹכָה בָּאֵלִם, יְיָ?

Who is like You, Eternal One, among
the gods that are worshipped?

מִי כָּמֹכָה, נֶאְדָּר בַּקֹּדֶשׁ,
נוֹרָא תְהִלֹּת, עֹשֵׂה פֶלֶא?

Who is like You, majestic in holiness,
awesome in splendor, doing wonders?

מַלְכוּתְךָ רָאוּ בָנֶיךָ, בּוֹקֵעַ יָם לִפְנֵי מֹשֶׁה; "זֶה אֵלִי!"
עָנוּ וְאָמְרוּ: "יְיָ יִמְלֹךְ לְעֹלָם וָעֶד!"

In their escape from the sea, Your children saw your sovereign
might displayed. "This is my God!" they cried. "The Eternal will
reign for ever and ever!"

וְנֶאֱמַר: "כִּי־פָדָה יְיָ אֶת־יַעֲקֹב, וּגְאָלוֹ מִיַּד חָזָק
מִמֶּנּוּ." בָּרוּךְ אַתָּה, יְיָ, גָּאַל יִשְׂרָאֵל.

°Now let all come to say: The Eternal has redeemed Israel and
all the oppressed. Blessed is the Eternal God.

◆ ◆

257

THE SUDDEN LIGHT THAT LIFTS THE HEART   השכיבנו

הַשְׁכִּיבֵנוּ, יְיָ אֱלֹהֵינוּ, לְשָׁלוֹם, וְהַעֲמִידֵנוּ, מַלְכֵּנוּ,
לְחַיִּים. וּפְרוֹשׂ עָלֵינוּ סֻכַּת שְׁלוֹמֶךָ, וְתַקְּנֵנוּ בְּעֵצָה
טוֹבָה מִלְּפָנֶיךָ, וְהוֹשִׁיעֵנוּ לְמַעַן שְׁמֶךָ, וְהָגֵן בַּעֲדֵנוּ.
וְהָסֵר מֵעָלֵינוּ אוֹיֵב, דֶּבֶר וְחֶרֶב וְרָעָב וְיָגוֹן; וְהָסֵר
שָׂטָן מִלְּפָנֵינוּ וּמֵאַחֲרֵינוּ; וּבְצֵל כְּנָפֶיךָ תַּסְתִּירֵנוּ, כִּי
אֵל שׁוֹמְרֵנוּ וּמַצִּילֵנוּ אָתָּה, כִּי אֵל מֶלֶךְ חַנּוּן וְרַחוּם
אָתָּה. וּשְׁמוֹר צֵאתֵנוּ וּבוֹאֵנוּ לְחַיִּים וּלְשָׁלוֹם, מֵעַתָּה
וְעַד עוֹלָם, וּפְרוֹשׂ עָלֵינוּ סֻכַּת שְׁלוֹמֶךָ. בָּרוּךְ אַתָּה,
יְיָ, הַפּוֹרֵשׂ סֻכַּת שָׁלוֹם עָלֵינוּ, וְעַל־כָּל־עַמּוֹ יִשְׂרָאֵל,
וְעַל־יְרוּשָׁלָיִם.

°The shadows fall, but end of day fills the eye with brightness; the infinite heavens glow, and all creation sings its hymn of glory. With hope, therefore, we pray for light within: O God, reveal Yourself; hide no more; let Your face shine on all who seek You.

Eternal and infinite God, banish our darkness! Be present to us as the sudden light that lifts the heart and brings us joy.

Then shall we be at peace, O God, whose peaceful shelter we seek through all the days and nights of our lives.

• •

ON SHABBAT

THE COVENANT OF SHABBAT   ושמרו

וְשָׁמְרוּ בְנֵי־יִשְׂרָאֵל אֶת־הַשַּׁבָּת, לַעֲשׂוֹת אֶת־הַשַּׁבָּת
לְדֹרֹתָם בְּרִית עוֹלָם. בֵּינִי וּבֵין בְּנֵי יִשְׂרָאֵל אוֹת הִיא

לְעֹלָם, כִּי שֵׁשֶׁת יָמִים עָשָׂה יְיָ אֶת־הַשָּׁמַיִם וְאֶת־הָאָרֶץ, וּבַיּוֹם הַשְּׁבִיעִי שָׁבַת וַיִּנָּפַשׁ.

The people of Israel shall keep the Sabbath, observing the Sabbath in every generation as a covenant for all time. It is a sign for ever between Me and the people of Israel, for in six days the Eternal God made heaven and earth, and on the seventh day He rested from His labors.

∴

ON THIS DAY   כי ביום הזה

כִּי בַיּוֹם הַזֶּה יְכַפֵּר עֲלֵיכֶם, לְטַהֵר אֶתְכֶם; מִכֹּל חַטֹּאתֵיכֶם לִפְנֵי יְיָ תִּטְהָרוּ.

For on this day atonement shall be made for you, to purify you; you shall be cleansed from all your sins before the Lord.

∴

READER'S KADDISH   חצי קדיש

יִתְגַּדַּל וְיִתְקַדַּשׁ שְׁמֵהּ רַבָּא בְּעָלְמָא דִּי־בְרָא כִרְעוּתֵהּ, וְיַמְלִיךְ מַלְכוּתֵהּ בְּחַיֵּיכוֹן וּבְיוֹמֵיכוֹן וּבְחַיֵּי דְכָל־בֵּית יִשְׂרָאֵל, בַּעֲגָלָא וּבִזְמַן קָרִיב, וְאִמְרוּ: אָמֵן.
יְהֵא שְׁמֵהּ רַבָּא מְבָרַךְ לְעָלַם וּלְעָלְמֵי עָלְמַיָּא.
יִתְבָּרַךְ וְיִשְׁתַּבַּח, וְיִתְפָּאַר וְיִתְרוֹמַם וְיִתְנַשֵּׂא, וְיִתְהַדָּר וְיִתְעַלֶּה וְיִתְהַלָּל שְׁמֵהּ דְּקוּדְשָׁא, בְּרִיךְ הוּא, לְעֵלָּא מִן כָּל־בִּרְכָתָא וְשִׁירָתָא, תֻּשְׁבְּחָתָא וְנֶחֱמָתָא דַּאֲמִירָן בְּעָלְמָא, וְאִמְרוּ: אָמֵן.

Let the glory of God be extolled, let His great name be hallowed in the world whose creation He willed. May His kingdom soon prevail, in our own day, our own lives, and the life of all Israel, and let us say: Amen.

Let His great name be blessed for ever and ever.
Let the name of the Holy One, blessed is He, be glorified, exalted and honored, though He is beyond all the praises, songs,
and adorations that we can utter, and let us say: Amen.

◆ ◆

All rise

תפלה

אֲדֹנָי, שְׂפָתַי תִּפְתָּח, וּפִי יַגִּיד תְּהִלָּתֶךָ.

°May our lips and our lives be one in serving eternal truth.

THE DISTANT SHORES OF BLESSING   אבות

בָּרוּךְ אַתָּה, יְיָ אֱלֹהֵינוּ וֵאלֹהֵי אֲבוֹתֵינוּ, אֱלֹהֵי
אַבְרָהָם, אֱלֹהֵי יִצְחָק, וֵאלֹהֵי יַעֲקֹב: הָאֵל הַגָּדוֹל,
הַגִּבּוֹר וְהַנּוֹרָא, אֵל עֶלְיוֹן. גּוֹמֵל חֲסָדִים טוֹבִים,
וְקוֹנֵה הַכֹּל, וְזוֹכֵר חַסְדֵי אָבוֹת, וּמֵבִיא גְאֻלָּה לִבְנֵי
בְנֵיהֶם, לְמַעַן שְׁמוֹ, בְּאַהֲבָה.

°Praised be the Lord our God and God of all generations,
God of our mothers and fathers, of Abraham, Isaac, and
Jacob, Sarah, Rebekah, Rachel, and Leah, great, mighty
and exalted.

*You bestow love and kindness on all Your children. You
remember the devotion of our ancestors. In Your love, You
bring redemption to their descendants for the sake of Your
name.*

Remember us unto life, O King, who delights in life, and inscribe us in the Book of Life, for Your sake, O God of life.

זָכְרֵנוּ לְחַיִּים, מֶלֶךְ חָפֵץ בַּחַיִּים, וְכָתְבֵנוּ בְּסֵפֶר הַחַיִּים, לְמַעַנְךָ אֱלֹהִים חַיִּים. מֶלֶךְ עוֹזֵר וּמוֹשִׁיעַ וּמָגֵן. בָּרוּךְ אַתָּה, יְיָ, מָגֵן אַבְרָהָם.

°*You are our Ruler and our Helper, our Savior and Protector. Blessed is our Eternal God, Shield of our people in every age.*

•••

THE POWER TO LIVE AND ACT   גבורות

אַתָּה גִבּוֹר לְעוֹלָם, אֲדֹנָי, מְחַיֶּה הַכֹּל אַתָּה, רַב לְהוֹשִׁיעַ.

מְכַלְכֵּל חַיִּים בְּחֶסֶד, מְחַיֶּה הַכֹּל בְּרַחֲמִים רַבִּים. סוֹמֵךְ נוֹפְלִים, וְרוֹפֵא חוֹלִים, וּמַתִּיר אֲסוּרִים, וּמְקַיֵּם אֱמוּנָתוֹ לִישֵׁנֵי עָפָר.

מִי כָמוֹךָ, בַּעַל גְבוּרוֹת, וּמִי דּוֹמֶה לָךְ, מֶלֶךְ מֵמִית וּמְחַיֶּה וּמַצְמִיחַ יְשׁוּעָה? מִי כָמוֹךָ אַב הָרַחֲמִים, זוֹכֵר יְצוּרָיו לְחַיִּים בְּרַחֲמִים? וְנֶאֱמָן אַתָּה לְהַחֲיוֹת הַכֹּל. בָּרוּךְ אַתָּה, יְיָ, מְחַיֶּה הַכֹּל.

°Great is the eternal power at the heart of life; mighty the love that is stronger than death.

Faithful love gives life to all, and acts of grace restore our strength.

Life's harsh winds uproot the weak; its hard rains beat down upon our kin. Let those who stand support the falling, keep faith with those who lie in the dust.

To the sick, we must bring healing; and to those who are bound, release.

How good to redeem the ancient pledge, for joy to blossom in arid soil.

We give thanks for the power to live and act, for the blessing of love that is stronger than death.

All are seated

• •

GOD'S HOLINESS   **קְדוּשַׁת הַשֵּׁם**

אַתָּה קָדוֹשׁ וְשִׁמְךָ קָדוֹשׁ, וּקְדוֹשִׁים בְּכָל־יוֹם יְהַלְלוּךָ סֶּלָה.

וּבְכֵן תֵּן פַּחְדְּךָ, יְיָ אֱלֹהֵינוּ, עַל כָּל־מַעֲשֶׂיךָ, וְאֵימָתְךָ עַל כָּל־מַה־שֶּׁבָּרָאתָ. וְיִירָאוּךָ כָּל־הַמַּעֲשִׂים, וְיִשְׁתַּחֲווּ לְפָנֶיךָ כָּל־הַבְּרוּאִים, וְיֵעָשׂוּ כֻלָּם אֲגֻדָּה אַחַת לַעֲשׂוֹת רְצוֹנְךָ בְּלֵבָב שָׁלֵם, כְּמוֹ שֶׁיָּדַעְנוּ, יְיָ אֱלֹהֵינוּ, שֶׁהַשִּׁלְטוֹן לְפָנֶיךָ, עֹז בְּיָדְךָ וּגְבוּרָה בִימִינֶךָ, וְשִׁמְךָ נוֹרָא עַל כָּל־מַה־שֶּׁבָּרָאתָ.

°Lord our God, let Your presence be manifest to us in all Your works, that reverence may fill the hearts of all Your creatures. Make all Your children mindful of Your glory, that we may unite to do Your will with perfect heart. For Yours are dominion and power, and the impress of Your hand is upon all that You have made.

וּבְכֵן תֵּן כָּבוֹד, יְיָ, לְעַמֶּךָ, תְּהִלָּה לִירֵאֶיךָ וְתִקְוָה לְדוֹרְשֶׁיךָ, וּפִתְחוֹן פֶּה לַמְיַחֲלִים לָךְ, שִׂמְחָה לְאַרְצֶךָ וְשָׂשׂוֹן לְעִירֶךָ, וּצְמִיחַת קֶרֶן לְכָל־יוֹשְׁבֵי תֵבֵל.

°Grant honor to those who revere You, inspire with courage those who wait for You, and fulfill the hope of all who trust in Your name.

262

וּבְכֵן צַדִּיקִים יִרְאוּ וְיִשְׂמֶחוּ וִישָׁרִים יַעֲלֹזוּ וַחֲסִידִים
בְּרִנָּה יָגִילוּ, וְעוֹלָתָה תִּקְפָּץ־פִּיהָ וְכָל־הָרִשְׁעָה כֻּלָּה
כֶּעָשָׁן תִּכְלֶה. כִּי תַעֲבִיר מֶמְשֶׁלֶת זָדוֹן מִן הָאָרֶץ.

°Hasten the day that will bring gladness to all who dwell
on earth and victory of the spirit to those who bear
witness to Your truth.

*Then the just shall see and exult, the upright be glad, and
Your servants sing for joy. Then shall iniquity be made
dumb, and wickedness vanish like smoke; for the dominion
of arrogance shall have passed away from the earth.*

וְתִמְלֹךְ אַתָּה, יְיָ, לְבַדֶּךָ עַל כָּל־מַעֲשֶׂיךָ, כַּכָּתוּב
בְּדִבְרֵי קָדְשֶׁךָ:

You alone, O Lord, shall reign over all Your works, as it
is written:

יִמְלֹךְ יְיָ לְעוֹלָם, אֱלֹהַיִךְ צִיּוֹן, לְדֹר וָדֹר. הַלְלוּיָהּ!

*The Lord shall reign for ever; your God, O Zion, from
generation to generation. Halleluyah!*

קָדוֹשׁ אַתָּה וְנוֹרָא שְׁמֶךָ, וְאֵין אֱלוֹהַּ מִבַּלְעָדֶיךָ,
כַּכָּתוּב:

You are holy; awesome is Your name; there is no God but
You.

וַיִּגְבַּהּ יְיָ צְבָאוֹת בַּמִּשְׁפָּט, וְהָאֵל הַקָּדוֹשׁ נִקְדַּשׁ
בִּצְדָקָה.

*The Lord of Hosts is exalted by justice; the holy God is
sanctified by righteousness.*

263

בָּרוּךְ אַתָּה, יְיָ, הַמֶּלֶךְ הַקָּדוֹשׁ.

Blessed is the Lord, the holy King.

◆ ◆

קדושת היום

THE HOLINESS OF THIS DAY

אַתָּה בְחַרְתָּנוּ מִכָּל־הָעַמִּים, אָהַבְתָּ אוֹתָנוּ וְרָצִיתָ
בָּנוּ, וְרוֹמַמְתָּנוּ מִכָּל־הַלְּשׁוֹנוֹת וְקִדַּשְׁתָּנוּ בְּמִצְוֹתֶיךָ,
וְקֵרַבְתָּנוּ מַלְכֵּנוּ לַעֲבוֹדָתֶךָ, וְשִׁמְךָ הַגָּדוֹל וְהַקָּדוֹשׁ
עָלֵינוּ קָרָאתָ.

°We render thanks to You that You have called us to
Your service, to bring the knowledge of Your word to the
four corners of the earth.

*You have called us Your servant, to give faithful witness even
in suffering and deprivation.*

וַתִּתֶּן־לָנוּ, יְיָ אֱלֹהֵינוּ, בְּאַהֲבָה אֶת־יוֹם (הַשַּׁבָּת הַזֶּה
לִקְדֻשָּׁה וְלִמְנוּחָה וְאֶת־יוֹם) הַכִּפּוּרִים הַזֶּה לִמְחִילָה
וְלִסְלִיחָה וְלְכַפָּרָה וְלִמְחָל־בּוֹ אֶת־כָּל־עֲוֹנוֹתֵינוּ,
מִקְרָא קֹדֶשׁ, זֵכֶר לִיצִיאַת מִצְרָיִם.

°In this solemn hour, O God, we would draw near to You;
may the observance of this Day of Atonement help us to
remember Israel's sacred heritage. Teach us to build our
lives on the abiding foundations of Your law; open our
eyes to the goodness of life and its sacred opportunities for
service.

אֱלֹהֵינוּ וֵאלֹהֵי אֲבוֹתֵינוּ, מְחַל לַעֲוֹנוֹתֵינוּ בְּיוֹם
(הַשַּׁבָּת הַזֶּה וּבְיוֹם) הַכִּפּוּרִים הַזֶּה; מְחֵה וְהַעֲבֵר
פְּשָׁעֵינוּ וְחַטֹּאתֵינוּ מִנֶּגֶד עֵינֶיךָ, כָּאָמוּר: "אָנֹכִי, אָנֹכִי
הוּא מֹחֶה פְשָׁעֶיךָ לְמַעֲנִי, וְחַטֹּאתֶיךָ לֹא אֶזְכֹּר."

264

וְנֶאֱמַר: "מָחִיתִי כָעָב פְּשָׁעֶיךָ, וְכֶעָנָן חַטֹּאתֶיךָ,
שׁוּבָה אֵלַי, כִּי גְאַלְתִּיךָ." וְנֶאֱמַר: "כִּי בַיּוֹם הַזֶּה
יְכַפֵּר עֲלֵיכֶם לְטַהֵר אֶתְכֶם; מִכֹּל חַטֹּאתֵיכֶם לִפְנֵי יְיָ
תִּטְהָרוּ."

°O Source of mercy, give us the grace to show forbearance to
those who offend against us. When the wrongs and injustices
of others wound us, may our hearts not despair of human
good. May no trial, however severe, embitter our souls and
destroy our trust. When beset by trouble and sorrow, our
mothers and fathers put on the armor of faith and fortitude.
May we too find strength to meet adversity with quiet
courage and unshaken will. Help us to understand that injustice and hate will not for ever afflict the human race; that
righteousness and mercy will triumph in the end.

אֱלֹהֵינוּ וֵאלֹהֵי אֲבוֹתֵינוּ, (רְצֵה בִמְנוּחָתֵנוּ,) קַדְּשֵׁנוּ
בְּמִצְוֹתֶיךָ וְתֵן חֶלְקֵנוּ בְּתוֹרָתֶךָ. שַׂבְּעֵנוּ מִטּוּבֶךָ,
וְשַׂמְּחֵנוּ בִּישׁוּעָתֶךָ, (וְהַנְחִילֵנוּ, יְיָ אֱלֹהֵינוּ, בְּאַהֲבָה
וּבְרָצוֹן שַׁבַּת קָדְשֶׁךָ, וְיָנוּחוּ בָהּ יִשְׂרָאֵל מְקַדְּשֵׁי
שְׁמֶךָ,) וְטַהֵר לִבֵּנוּ לְעָבְדְּךָ בֶּאֱמֶת. כִּי אַתָּה סָלְחָן
לְיִשְׂרָאֵל וּמָחֳלָן לְשִׁבְטֵי יְשֻׁרוּן בְּכָל־דּוֹר וָדוֹר,
וּמִבַּלְעָדֶיךָ אֵין לָנוּ מֶלֶךְ מוֹחֵל וְסוֹלֵחַ אֶלָּא אָתָּה.
בָּרוּךְ אַתָּה, יְיָ, מֶלֶךְ מוֹחֵל וְסוֹלֵחַ לַעֲוֹנוֹתֵינוּ
וְלַעֲוֹנוֹת עַמּוֹ בֵּית יִשְׂרָאֵל, וּמַעֲבִיר אַשְׁמוֹתֵינוּ בְּכָל־
שָׁנָה וְשָׁנָה, מֶלֶךְ עַל כָּל־הָאָרֶץ, מְקַדֵּשׁ (הַשַּׁבָּת וְ)
יִשְׂרָאֵל וְיוֹם הַכִּפּוּרִים.

Sanctify us with Your Mitzvot and bring us near to Your
service, that we may be worthy to proclaim Your truth to
all the world.

Satisfy us with Your goodness, and gladden us with Your

265

salvation. Purify our hearts that we may serve You in truth.
For You, O God, are Truth, and Your word endures for ever.
Blessed is the Lord, who sanctifies (the Sabbath,) Israel and
the Day of Atonement.

◆ ◆

WORSHIP עבודה

רְצֵה, יְיָ אֱלֹהֵינוּ, בְּעַמְּךָ יִשְׂרָאֵל, וּתְפִלָּתָם בְּאַהֲבָה
תְקַבֵּל, וּתְהִי לְרָצוֹן תָּמִיד עֲבוֹדַת יִשְׂרָאֵל עַמֶּךָ. אֵל
קָרוֹב לְכָל־קֹרְאָיו, פְּנֵה אֶל עֲבָדֶיךָ וְחָנֵּנוּ; שְׁפוֹךְ
רוּחֲךָ עָלֵינוּ, וְתֶחֱזֶינָה עֵינֵינוּ בְּשׁוּבְךָ לְצִיּוֹן בְּרַחֲמִים.

Be gracious, O Lord our God, to Your people Israel, and
receive our prayers with love. O may our worship always
be acceptable to You. Fill us with the knowledge that You
are near to all who seek You in truth. Pour out Your spirit
upon us; let our eyes behold Your presence in our midst
and in the midst of our people in Zion.

Blessed is the Lord, whose presence gives life to Zion and all
Israel.

בָּרוּךְ אַתָּה, יְיָ, הַמַּחֲזִיר שְׁכִינָתוֹ לְצִיּוֹן.

◆ ◆

TO WHOM OUR THANKS ARE DUE הודאה

מוֹדִים אֲנַחְנוּ לָךְ, שָׁאַתָּה הוּא יְיָ אֱלֹהֵינוּ וֵאלֹהֵי
אֲבוֹתֵינוּ לְעוֹלָם וָעֶד. צוּר חַיֵּינוּ, מָגֵן יִשְׁעֵנוּ, אַתָּה
הוּא לְדוֹר וָדוֹר. נוֹדֶה לְךָ וּנְסַפֵּר תְּהִלָּתֶךָ, עַל־חַיֵּינוּ
הַמְּסוּרִים בְּיָדֶךָ, וְעַל־נִשְׁמוֹתֵינוּ הַפְּקוּדוֹת לָךְ, וְעַל־
נִסֶּיךָ שֶׁבְּכָל־יוֹם עִמָּנוּ, וְעַל־נִפְלְאוֹתֶיךָ וְטוֹבוֹתֶיךָ

שֶׁבְּכָל־עֵת, עֶרֶב וָבְקֶר וְצָהֳרָיִם. הַטּוֹב: כִּי לֹא־כָלוּ
רַחֲמֶיךָ, וְהַמְרַחֵם: כִּי־לֹא תַמּוּ חֲסָדֶיךָ, מֵעוֹלָם קִוִּינוּ
לָךְ.

*We gratefully acknowledge, O Lord our God, that You are
our Creator and Preserver, the Rock of our life and our
protecting Shield. We give thanks to You for our lives which
are in Your hand, for our souls which are ever in Your keeping, for Your wondrous providence and Your continuous
goodness, which You bestow upon us day by day. Truly,
Your mercies never fail, and Your lovingkindness never
ceases. Therefore do we for ever put our trust in You. O
God, let life abundant be the heritage of all the children of
Your covenant! Blessed is the Eternal God, to whom our
thanks are due.*

PEACE   ברכת שלום

שָׁלוֹם רָב עַל יִשְׂרָאֵל עַמְּךָ וְעַל כָּל־הָעַמִּים תָּשִׂים
לְעוֹלָם, כִּי אַתָּה הוּא מֶלֶךְ אָדוֹן לְכָל־הַשָּׁלוֹם. וְטוֹב
בְּעֵינֶיךָ לְבָרֵךְ אֶת־עַמְּךָ יִשְׂרָאֵל בְּכָל־עֵת וּבְכָל־שָׁעָה
בִּשְׁלוֹמֶךָ. בְּסֵפֶר חַיִּים בְּרָכָה וְשָׁלוֹם וּפַרְנָסָה טוֹבָה
נִזָּכֵר וְנִכָּתֵב לְפָנֶיךָ, אֲנַחְנוּ וְכָל־עַמְּךָ בֵּית יִשְׂרָאֵל,
לְחַיִּים טוֹבִים וּלְשָׁלוֹם. בָּרוּךְ אַתָּה, יְיָ, עוֹשֵׂה
הַשָּׁלוֹם.

°Grant us peace, Your most precious gift, O Eternal
Source of peace, and give us the will to proclaim its message to all the peoples of the earth. Bless our country, that
it may always be a stronghold of peace, and its advocate
among the nations. May contentment reign within its
borders, health and happiness within its homes.
Strengthen the bonds of friendship among the inhabitants
of all lands; and may the love of Your name hallow every
home and every heart. Teach us, O God, to labor for

righteousness, and inscribe us in the Book of life, blessing, and peace. Blessed is the Eternal God, the Source of peace.

◆ ◆

MEDITATION

Do not say after you have sinned, 'There is no restoration for me,' but trust in the Lord and repent, and God will receive you. And do not say, 'If I confess, I shall be disgraced,' but hold position in contempt, humble yourself, and return in repentance.

◆

What is genuine repentance? When an opportunity for transgression occurs and we resist it, not out of fear or weakness, but because we have repented.

◆ ◆

יִהְיוּ לְרָצוֹן אִמְרֵי־פִי וְהֶגְיוֹן לִבִּי לְפָנֶיךָ, יְיָ, צוּרִי וְגוֹאֲלִי.

May the words of my mouth, and the meditations of my heart, be acceptable to You, O Lord, my Rock and my Redeemer.

or

עֹשֶׂה שָׁלוֹם בִּמְרוֹמָיו, הוּא יַעֲשֶׂה שָׁלוֹם עָלֵינוּ וְעַל כָּל־יִשְׂרָאֵל, וְאִמְרוּ אָמֵן.

May the One who causes peace to reign in the high heavens let peace descend on us, on all Israel, and all the world.

◆ ◆

CONFESSION OF SIN   וִדּוּי

All rise

אֱלֹהֵינוּ וֵאלֹהֵי אֲבוֹתֵינוּ, תָּבוֹא לְפָנֶיךָ תְּפִלָּתֵנוּ וְאַל
תִּתְעַלַּם מִתְּחִנָּתֵנוּ, שֶׁאֵין אֲנַחְנוּ עַזֵּי פָנִים וּקְשֵׁי עֹרֶף
לוֹמַר לְפָנֶיךָ, יְיָ אֱלֹהֵינוּ וֵאלֹהֵי אֲבוֹתֵינוּ, צַדִּיקִים
אֲנַחְנוּ וְלֹא חָטָאנוּ, אֲבָל אֲנַחְנוּ חָטָאנוּ. חָטָאנוּ,
עָוִינוּ, פָּשָׁעְנוּ.

Our God, God of our mothers and fathers, grant that our prayers may reach You. Do not be deaf to our pleas, for we are not so arrogant and stiff-necked as to say before You, Lord our God and God of all ages, we are perfect and have not sinned; rather do we confess: we have gone astray, we have sinned, we have transgressed.

All are seated

◆

אָשַׁמְנוּ, בָּגַדְנוּ, גָּזַלְנוּ, דִּבַּרְנוּ דְפִי. הֶעֱוִינוּ, וְהִרְשַׁעְנוּ,
זַדְנוּ, חָמַסְנוּ, טָפַלְנוּ שֶׁקֶר. יָעַצְנוּ רָע, כִּזַּבְנוּ, לַצְנוּ,
מָרַדְנוּ, נִאַצְנוּ. סָרַרְנוּ, עָוִינוּ, פָּשַׁעְנוּ, צָרַרְנוּ, קִשִּׁינוּ
עֹרֶף. רָשַׁעְנוּ, שִׁחַתְנוּ, תִּעַבְנוּ, תָּעִינוּ, תִּעְתָּעְנוּ.

°We all have committed offenses; together we confess these human sins:

The sins of arrogance, bigotry, and cynicism; of deceit and egotism, flattery and greed, injustice and jealousy.

Some of us kept grudges, were lustful, malicious, or narrow-minded.

269

Others were obstinate or possessive, quarrelsome, rancorous, or selfish.

There was violence, weakness of will, xenophobia.

We yielded to temptation, and showed zeal for bad causes.

•

סָרְנוּ מִמִּצְוֹתֶיךָ וּמִמִּשְׁפָּטֶיךָ הַטּוֹבִים וְלֹא שָׁוָה לָנוּ.
וְאַתָּה צַדִּיק עַל כָּל־הַבָּא עָלֵינוּ, כִּי אֱמֶת עָשִׂיתָ
וַאֲנַחְנוּ הִרְשָׁעְנוּ.

We have turned aside from Your commandments and from Your precepts, and it has not availed us; You are just, whatever befalls us; You call us to righteousness, but we bring evil upon ourselves.

מַה־נֹּאמַר לְפָנֶיךָ יוֹשֵׁב מָרוֹם, וּמַה־נְּסַפֵּר לְפָנֶיךָ
שׁוֹכֵן שְׁחָקִים? הֲלֹא כָּל־הַנִּסְתָּרוֹת וְהַנִּגְלוֹת אַתָּה
יוֹדֵעַ? אַתָּה יוֹדֵעַ רָזֵי עוֹלָם וְתַעֲלוּמוֹת סִתְרֵי כָל־חָי.
אַתָּה חוֹפֵשׂ כָּל־חַדְרֵי־בָטֶן וּבוֹחֵן כְּלָיוֹת וָלֵב. אֵין
דָּבָר נֶעְלָם מִמֶּךָ וְאֵין נִסְתָּר מִנֶּגֶד עֵינֶיךָ.

What can we say before You, who dwell on high? What shall we plead before You, enthroned beyond the stars? Are not all things known to You, both the mysteries of eternity and the dark secrets of all that live? You search the inmost chambers of the heart, and probe the deep recesses of the soul. Nothing is concealed from Your sight.

וּבְכֵן יְהִי רָצוֹן מִלְּפָנֶיךָ, יְיָ אֱלֹהֵינוּ וֵאלֹהֵי אֲבוֹתֵינוּ,
שֶׁתִּסְלַח לָנוּ עַל כָּל־חַטֹּאתֵינוּ וְתִמְחַל לָנוּ עַל כָּל־
עֲונוֹתֵינוּ וּתְכַפֶּר־לָנוּ עַל כָּל־פְּשָׁעֵינוּ.

Now may it be Your will, O Lord God of all generations, to forgive all our sins, to pardon all our wrongdoings, and to blot out all our transgressions:

על חטא

עַל חֵטְא שֶׁחָטָאנוּ לְפָנֶיךָ בְּאֹנֶס וּבְרָצוֹן,

The sin we have committed against You under duress or by choice,

עַל חֵטְא שֶׁחָטָאנוּ לְפָנֶיךָ בְּזָדוֹן וּבִשְׁגָגָה,

the sin we have committed against You consciously or un-consciously,

וְעַל חֵטְא שֶׁחָטָאנוּ לְפָנֶיךָ בַּגָּלוּי וּבַסָּתֶר.

and the sin we have committed against You openly or secret-ly.

עַל חֵטְא שֶׁחָטָאנוּ לְפָנֶיךָ בְּהַרְהוֹר הַלֵּב,

The sin we have committed against You in our thoughts,

עַל חֵטְא שֶׁחָטָאנוּ לְפָנֶיךָ בְּדִבּוּר פֶּה,

the sin we have committed against You with our words,

וְעַל חֵטְא שֶׁחָטָאנוּ לְפָנֶיךָ בְּחֹזֶק יָד.

and the sin we have committed against You by the abuse of power.

וְעַל כֻּלָּם, אֱלוֹהַ סְלִיחוֹת, סְלַח־לָנוּ, מְחַל־לָנוּ, כַּפֶּר־לָנוּ!

For all these, O God of mercy, forgive us, pardon us, grant us atonement!

עַל חֵטְא שֶׁחָטָאנוּ לְפָנֶיךָ בְּאִמּוּץ הַלֵּב,

The sin we have committed against You by hardening our hearts,

271

עַל חֵטְא שֶׁחָטָאנוּ לְפָנֶיךָ בְּחִלּוּל הַשֵׁם,

the sin we have committed against You by profaning Your name,

וְעַל חֵטְא שֶׁחָטָאנוּ לְפָנֶיךָ בְּזִלְזוּל הוֹרִים וּמוֹרִים.

and the sin we have committed against You by disrespect for parents and teachers.

עַל חֵטְא שֶׁחָטָאנוּ לְפָנֶיךָ בִּלְשׁוֹן הָרָע,

The sin we have committed against You by speaking slander,

עַל חֵטְא שֶׁחָטָאנוּ לְפָנֶיךָ בְּמַשָׂא וּבְמַתָּן,

the sin we have committed against You by dishonesty in our work,

וְעַל חֵטְא שֶׁחָטָאנוּ לְפָנֶיךָ בְּהוֹנָאַת רֵעַ.

and the sin we have committed against You by hurting others in any way.

וְעַל כֻּלָּם, אֱלוֹהַּ סְלִיחוֹת, סְלַח לָנוּ, מְחַל לָנוּ, כַּפֶּר־לָנוּ!

For all these, O God of mercy, forgive us, pardon us, grant us atonement!

◆ ◆

SILENT PRAYER

From Psalm 51

In Your love, O God, be gracious to me; in Your great mercy, wipe out my transgressions. Wash away my guilt, and free me from my sin; for I know my transgressions, and my sin is always before me.

Against You, You alone, have I sinned, and done what is evil in

Your sight, so that You accuse me rightly, and condemn me justly. You love truth in the inner being; therefore teach me wisdom in my heart. Purify me, that I may become clean; wash me, till I am whiter than snow.

Let me hear the sound of joy and gladness, so that my oppressed being may exult. Turn Your face from my sins, and wipe out all my iniquities. Create in me a clean heart, O God, and renew a willing spirit within me. Do not cast me away from Your presence, do not remove Your holy spirit from me. Let me know again the joy of Your help, and keep alive in me a generous spirit. Then will I teach transgressors Your way, and cause sinners to return to You. Save me from bloodshed, O God, redeeming God! Then I will sing the praises of Your goodness. Eternal God, open my lips, and my mouth shall declare Your glory!

◆ ◆

PRAYERS FOR FORGIVENESS   סליחות

Psalm 130

שִׁיר הַמַּעֲלוֹת. מִמַּעֲמַקִּים קְרָאתִיךָ, יְיָ.
אֲדֹנָי, שִׁמְעָה בְקוֹלִי; תִּהְיֶינָה אָזְנֶיךָ קַשֻּׁבוֹת לְקוֹל
תַּחֲנוּנָי.
אִם עֲוֹנוֹת תִּשְׁמָר־יָהּ, אֲדֹנָי, מִי יַעֲמֹד?

Out of the depths I call to You, O Lord. Lord, listen to my cry; let Your ear be attentive to my plea for mercy.

If You kept account of sins, O Lord, who could stand erect?

כִּי עִמְּךָ הַסְּלִיחָה, לְמַעַן תִּוָּרֵא.
קִוִּיתִי יְיָ, קִוְּתָה נַפְשִׁי, וְלִדְבָרוֹ הוֹחָלְתִּי.

273

But Yours is the power to forgive, and therefore You are
held in awe.

Truly I wait, I wait for the Lord, whose promise is my hope.

נַפְשִׁי לַאדֹנָי מִשֹּׁמְרִים לַבֹּקֶר, שֹׁמְרִים לַבֹּקֶר.

יַחֵל יִשְׂרָאֵל אֶל יְיָ, כִּי עִם יְיָ הַחֶסֶד וְהַרְבֵּה עִמּוֹ
פְדוּת.

וְהוּא יִפְדֶּה אֶת־יִשְׂרָאֵל מִכֹּל עֲוֹנֹתָיו.

I am more eager for the Lord than watchers for the morning, as they keep vigil for the dawn. O Israel, hope in the
Lord; for with the Lord is steadfast love, and great power
to set us free.

You, O God, will set us free from all our faults!

⋄ ⋄

יַעֲלֶה תַחֲנוּנֵינוּ מֵעֶרֶב, וְיָבֹא שַׁוְעָתֵנוּ מִבֹּקֶר,
וְיֵרָאֶה רַנּוּנֵנוּ עַד עָרֶב:
יַעֲלֶה קוֹלֵנוּ מֵעֶרֶב, וְיָבֹא צִדְקָתֵנוּ מִבֹּקֶר,
וְיֵרָאֶה פִּדְיוֹנֵנוּ עַד עָרֶב.
יַעֲלֶה עֲתִירָתֵנוּ מֵעֶרֶב, וְיָבֹא סְלִיחָתֵנוּ מִבֹּקֶר,
וְיֵרָאֶה נַאֲקָתֵנוּ עַד עָרֶב.
יַעֲלֶה מְנוּסֵנוּ מֵעֶרֶב, וְיָבֹא לְמַעֲנוֹ מִבֹּקֶר,
וְיֵרָאֶה כִּפּוּרֵנוּ עַד עָרֶב.

יַעֲלֶה יִשְׁעֵנוּ מֵעֶרֶב, וְיָבֹא טָהֳרֵנוּ מִבֹּקֶר,
וְיֵרָאֶה חִנּוּנֵנוּ עַד עָרֶב.
יַעֲלֶה זִכְרוֹנֵנוּ מֵעֶרֶב, וְיָבֹא וְעוּדֵנוּ מִבֹּקֶר,
וְיֵרָאֶה הַדְרָתֵנוּ עַד עָרֶב.

יַעֲלֶה דָפְקֵנוּ מֵעֶרֶב, וְיָבֹא גִילֵנוּ מִבְּקֶר,
וְיֵרָאֶה בַּקָּשָׁתֵנוּ עַד עָרֶב.
יַעֲלֶה אֶנְקָתֵנוּ מֵעֶרֶב, וְיָבֹא אֵלֶיךָ מִבְּקֶר,
וְיֵרָאֶה אֵלֵינוּ עַד עָרֶב.

Unto You with contrite spirits,
Do we come this eventide;
And throughout the morrow's passing
We will in Your presence bide.
O that ere the great Day closes
We be cleansed and purified!

How this solemn evening's advent
Bids us search and look within,
And until the morrow's twilight,
To confront our secret sin!
O that ere the great Day closes
Our true penitence begin!

We of guilt, alas, are conscious
As we usher in this night;
And we would make full confession
Through the lengthened morrow's flight.
O that ere the great Day closes
To our souls will come the light!

Our petitions and our prayers
Yearning rise to You this eve,
And until the morrow's twilight
Will our chastened spirits grieve.
O that ere the great Day closes
Your forgiveness we receive!

◆ ◆

Eternal God, keep before us the vision of Your kingdom.

Eternal God, draw us near to Your service.

Eternal God, remove from us the deafness that keeps us from hearing You.

Eternal God, remove from us the blindness that obscures Your glory.

Eternal God, remove from us the stubbornness that leads us to resist Your will.

Eternal God, remove from us the selfishness that makes us small.

Eternal God, teach us Your law of righteousness.

Lord, help us to rise above what we have been. Imbue us with love for all life and reverence for all being; teach us to respond to Your greatness with awe. Strengthen us with Your love, and guide us in the paths of righteousness. On this Sabbath of Sabbaths, kindle within us a light that shall illumine all other days.

✦ ✦

Who among us is righteous
enough to say: 'I have not sinned?'
Born of love to love,
we grow weary,
heavy with regret,
sorry for ourselves,
and afraid to know
what might have been.

*We have sinned against You, O God,
and against each other.*

Look now to the cities:
see the broken streets,
poor and decayed,

and all afraid.
See them and ask:
What have we done?

Help us to turn, O God;
help us to find forgiveness.

Behold water and air and soil, and see:
Still we beat plowshares into swords,
and make spears out of pruning-hooks.

Disfigured lies the human form divine,
estranged from its center!
"Your iniquities have separated you from your God."
Vision fades as the Presence recedes;
the voice grows still;
the search for God is over and gone.
We are alone, all alone,
our meaning unremembered.

Help us to turn, O God;
help us to find ourselves;
help us to learn where to seek You.

Here, now, on Atonement Day
we need not be alone
with our failings.
Let us recall, together,
blessed moments when clouds parted
and the sun appeared. We looked. We saw.
There was healing and the hope of joy;
we were at peace and knew the joy of hope.
O God, turn us to the heights
where human goodness finds its dwelling;
lead us to Your holy mountain,
Your hand stretched forth in welcome
to help us on the way.

Help us on our way, O God;
lead us on our path.

∴

אֱלֹהֵינוּ וֵאלֹהֵי אֲבוֹתֵינוּ, אַל תַּעַזְבֵנוּ וְאַל תִּטְּשֵׁנוּ
וְאַל תַּכְלִימֵנוּ, וְאַל תָּפֵר בְּרִיתְךָ אִתָּנוּ. קָרְבֵנוּ
לְתוֹרָתֶךָ, לַמְּדֵנוּ מִצְוֹתֶיךָ, הוֹרֵנוּ דְרָכֶיךָ, הַט לִבֵּנוּ
לְיִרְאָה אֶת־שְׁמֶךָ, וּמוֹל אֶת־לְבָבֵנוּ לְאַהֲבָתֶךָ, וְנָשׁוּב
אֵלֶיךָ בֶּאֱמֶת וּבְלֵב שָׁלֵם.

°Our God, God of all generations, may the sense of Your
presence never leave us; may it keep us ever faithful to
Your covenant. Make us responsive to Your Teaching,
that we may walk in Your ways. Fill our souls with awe,
and our hearts with love, that we may return to You in
truth, and with all our being.

Lord our God, let the strength of our longing for You help us
to grow in the wise use of our powers, that through us Your
power may be magnified in human life. So we may hallow
this world and labor to redeem it.

∴

שְׁמַע קוֹלֵנוּ, יְיָ אֱלֹהֵינוּ, חוּס וְרַחֵם עָלֵינוּ, וְקַבֵּל
בְּרַחֲמִים וּבְרָצוֹן אֶת־תְּפִלָּתֵנוּ. הֲשִׁיבֵנוּ יְיָ אֵלֶיךָ
וְנָשׁוּבָה, חַדֵּשׁ יָמֵינוּ כְּקֶדֶם.
אֲמָרֵינוּ הַאֲזִינָה, יְיָ; בִּינָה הֲגִיגֵנוּ.
אַל תַּשְׁלִיכֵנוּ מִלְּפָנֶיךָ, וְרוּחַ קָדְשְׁךָ אַל תִּקַּח מִמֶּנּוּ.
אַל תַּשְׁלִיכֵנוּ לְעֵת זִקְנָה, כִּכְלוֹת כֹּחֵנוּ אַל תַּעַזְבֵנוּ.
אַל תַּעַזְבֵנוּ, יְיָ אֱלֹהֵינוּ, אַל תִּרְחַק מִמֶּנּוּ.
כִּי לְךָ, יְיָ, הוֹחָלְנוּ; אַתָּה תַעֲנֶה, אֲדֹנָי אֱלֹהֵינוּ.

278

Hear our voice, Lord our God; have compassion upon us, and with that compassion accept our prayer.

Help us to return to You, O Lord; then truly shall we return. Renew our days as in the past.

Consider our words, Lord: look into our inmost thoughts.

Do not cast us away from Your presence, do not remove Your holy spirit.

Do not cast us away when we are old; as our strength diminishes, do not abandon us.

Do not abandon us, Lord our God; do not be far from us.

For You, Lord, do we wait; and You, our God, will answer.

＊ ＊

We are Your people
You are our King.
We are Your children
You are our Father.
We are Your possession
You are our Portion.
We are Your flock
You are our Shepherd.
We are Your vineyard
You are our Keeper.
We are Your beloved
You are our Friend.

כִּי אָנוּ עַמֶּךָ, וְאַתָּה מַלְכֵּנוּ.

אָנוּ בָנֶיךָ, וְאַתָּה אָבִינוּ.

אָנוּ נַחֲלָתֶךָ, וְאַתָּה גוֹרָלֵנוּ.

אָנוּ צֹאנֶךָ, וְאַתָּה רוֹעֵנוּ.

אָנוּ כַרְמֶךָ, וְאַתָּה נוֹטְרֵנוּ.

אָנוּ רַעְיָתֶךָ, וְאַתָּה דוֹדֵנוּ.

＊ ＊

279

All rise

The Ark is opened

אבינו מלכנו

אָבִינוּ מַלְכֵּנוּ, שְׁמַע קוֹלֵנוּ.

Our Father, our King, hear our prayer.

אָבִינוּ מַלְכֵּנוּ, פְּתַח שַׁעֲרֵי שָׁמַיִם לִתְפִלָּתֵנוּ.

Our Father, our King, let the gates of heaven be open to our plea.

אָבִינוּ מַלְכֵּנוּ, תְּהֵא הַשָּׁעָה הַזֹּאת שְׁעַת רַחֲמִים וְעֵת רָצוֹן מִלְּפָנֶיךָ.

Our Father, our King, let this be an hour of compassion and favor.

אָבִינוּ מַלְכֵּנוּ, הָרֵם קֶרֶן יִשְׂרָאֵל עַמֶּךָ.

Our Father, our King, give strength to Your people Israel.

אָבִינוּ מַלְכֵּנוּ, עֲשֵׂה לְמַעַן הֲרוּגִים עַל שֵׁם קָדְשֶׁךָ.

Our Father, our King, remember those slain for their love of Your name.

אָבִינוּ מַלְכֵּנוּ, עֲשֵׂה לְמַעַן בָּאֵי בָאֵשׁ וּבַמַּיִם עַל קִדּוּשׁ שְׁמֶךָ.

Our Father, our King, remember those who went through fire and water for Your sake.

אָבִינוּ מַלְכֵּנוּ, עֲשֵׂה לְמַעַנְךָ וְהוֹשִׁיעֵנוּ.

Our Father, our King, be mindful of us, and help us.

אָבִינוּ מַלְכֵּנוּ, כָּתְבֵנוּ בְּסֵפֶר סְלִיחָה וּמְחִילָה.

Our Father our King, inscribe us in the Book of Forgiveness.

אָבִינוּ מַלְכֵּנוּ, כָּתְבֵנוּ בְּסֵפֶר חַיִּים טוֹבִים.

Our Father, our King, inscribe us for blessing in the Book of Life.

אָבִינוּ מַלְכֵּנוּ, כָּתְבֵנוּ בְּסֵפֶר גְּאֻלָּה וִישׁוּעָה.

Our Father, our King, inscribe us in the Book of deliverance and redemption.

אָבִינוּ מַלְכֵּנוּ, חָנֵּנוּ וַעֲנֵנוּ, כִּי אֵין בָּנוּ מַעֲשִׂים, עֲשֵׂה עִמָּנוּ צְדָקָה וָחֶסֶד וְהוֹשִׁיעֵנוּ.

Our Father, our King, be gracious and answer us, for we have little merit. Treat us generously and with kindness, and be our help.

All are seated

The Ark is closed

All rise

עָלֵינוּ

Let us revere the God of life, and sing the praise of Nature's Lord, who spread out the heavens and established the earth, whose glory is proclaimed by the starry skies, and whose wonders are revealed in the human heart. He is our God; there is none else. With love and awe we acclaim the Eternal God, the Holy One, blessed be He.

עָלֵינוּ לְשַׁבֵּחַ לַאֲדוֹן הַכֹּל,
לָתֵת גְּדֻלָּה לְיוֹצֵר בְּרֵאשִׁית,
שֶׁהוּא נוֹטֶה שָׁמַיִם
וְיוֹסֵד אָרֶץ,
וּמוֹשַׁב יְקָרוֹ בַּשָּׁמַיִם מִמַּעַל,
וּשְׁכִינַת עֻזּוֹ בְּגָבְהֵי מְרוֹמִים.
הוּא אֱלֹהֵינוּ, אֵין עוֹד.

וַאֲנַחְנוּ כּוֹרְעִים וּמִשְׁתַּחֲוִים וּמוֹדִים לִפְנֵי מֶלֶךְ מַלְכֵי
הַמְּלָכִים, הַקָּדוֹשׁ בָּרוּךְ הוּא.

All are seated

The day will come when all shall turn with trust to God, hearkening to His voice, bearing witness to His truth.

We pray with all our hearts: let violence be gone; let the day come soon when evil shall give way to goodness, when war shall be forgotten, hunger be no more, and all at last shall live in freedom.

O Source of life: may we, created in Your image, embrace one another in friendship and in joy. Then shall we be one family, and then shall Your kingdom be established on earth, and the word of Your prophet fulfilled: "The Lord will reign for ever and ever."

וְנֶאֱמַר: "וְהָיָה יְיָ לְמֶלֶךְ עַל־כָּל־הָאָרֶץ; בַּיּוֹם הַהוּא
יִהְיֶה יְיָ אֶחָד וּשְׁמוֹ אֶחָד."

And it has been said: "The Lord shall reign over all the earth; on that day the Lord shall be One and His name shall be One."

יְהִי שֵׁם יְיָ מְבֹרָךְ מֵעַתָּה וְעַד־עוֹלָם, וְיִמָּלֵא כְבוֹדוֹ
אֶת־כָּל־הָאָרֶץ. אָמֵן וְאָמֵן.

Blessed be the name of the Lord for ever; and let the whole world be filled with His glory. Amen and Amen.

• •

Birth is a beginning
And death a destination.
And life is a journey:
From childhood to maturity
And youth to age;
From innocence to awareness
And ignorance to knowing;
From foolishness to discretion
    And then, perhaps, to wisdom;
From weakness to strength
Or strength to weakness—
    And, often, back again;
From health to sickness
    And back, we pray, to health again;
From offense to forgiveness,
From loneliness to love,
From joy to gratitude,
From pain to compassion,
And grief to understanding—
    From fear to faith;
From defeat to defeat to defeat—
Until, looking backward or ahead,
We see that victory lies
Not at some high place along the way,
But in having made the journey, stage by stage,
    A sacred pilgrimage.
Birth is a beginning

And death a destination.
And life is a journey,
A sacred pilgrimage—
    To life everlasting.

MOURNER'S KADDISH   קדיש יתום

יִתְגַּדַּל וְיִתְקַדַּשׁ שְׁמֵהּ רַבָּא בְּעָלְמָא דִּי־בְרָא
כִרְעוּתֵהּ, וְיַמְלִיךְ מַלְכוּתֵהּ בְּחַיֵּיכוֹן וּבְיוֹמֵיכוֹן וּבְחַיֵּי
דְכָל־בֵּית יִשְׂרָאֵל, בַּעֲגָלָא וּבִזְמַן קָרִיב, וְאִמְרוּ: אָמֵן.

Yit·ga·dal ve·yit·ka·dash she·mei ra·ba be·al·ma di·ve·ra
chi·re·u·tei, ve·yam·lich mal·chu·tei be·cha·yei·chon
u·ve·yo·mei·chon u·ve·cha·yei de·chol beit Yis·ra·eil, ba·a·ga·la
u·vi·ze·man ka·riv, ve·i·me·ru: a·mein.

יְהֵא שְׁמֵהּ רַבָּא מְבָרַךְ לְעָלַם וּלְעָלְמֵי עָלְמַיָּא.

Ye·hei she·mei ra·ba me·va·rach le·a·lam u·le·al·mei al·ma·ya.

יִתְבָּרַךְ וְיִשְׁתַּבַּח, וְיִתְפָּאַר וְיִתְרוֹמַם וְיִתְנַשֵּׂא,
וְיִתְהַדָּר וְיִתְעַלֶּה וְיִתְהַלָּל שְׁמֵהּ דְּקוּדְשָׁא, בְּרִיךְ
הוּא, לְעֵלָּא מִן־כָּל־בִּרְכָתָא וְשִׁירָתָא, תֻּשְׁבְּחָתָא
וְנֶחֱמָתָא דַּאֲמִירָן בְּעָלְמָא, וְאִמְרוּ: אָמֵן.

Yit·ba·rach ve·yish·ta·bach, ve·yit·pa·ar ve·yit·ro·mam
ve·yit·na·sei, ve·yit·ha·dar ve·yit·a·leh ve·yit·ha·lal she·mei
de·ku·de·sha, be·rich hu, le·ei·la min kol bi·re·cha·ta
ve·shi·ra·ta, tush·be·cha·ta ve·ne·che·ma·ta, da·a·mi·ran
be·al·ma, ve·i·me·ru: a·mein.

יְהֵא שְׁלָמָא רַבָּא מִן־שְׁמַיָּא וְחַיִּים עָלֵינוּ וְעַל־כָּל־
יִשְׂרָאֵל, וְאִמְרוּ: אָמֵן.

Ye·hei she·la·ma ra·ba min she·ma·ya ve·cha·yim a·lei·nu ve·al
kol Yis·ra·eil, ve·i·me·ru: a·mein.

עֹשֶׂה שָׁלוֹם בִּמְרוֹמָיו, הוּא יַעֲשֶׂה שָׁלוֹם עָלֵינוּ וְעַל
כָּל־יִשְׂרָאֵל, וְאִמְרוּ: אָמֵן.

O·seh sha·lom bi·me·ro·mav, hu ya·a·seh sha·lom a·lei·nu ve·al
kol Yis·ra·eil, ve·i·me·ru: a·mein.

Let the glory of God be extolled, let His great name be hallowed
in the world whose creation He willed. May His kingdom soon
prevail, in our own day, our own lives, and the life of all Israel,
and let us say: Amen.

Let His great name be blessed for ever and ever.

Let the name of the Holy One, blessed is He, be glorified, exalted, and honored, though He is beyond all the praises, songs,
and adorations that we can utter, and let us say: Amen.

For us and for all Israel, may the blessing of peace and the
promise of life come true, and let us say: Amen.

May the One who causes peace to reign in the high heavens, let
peace descend on us, on all Israel, and all the world, and let us
say: Amen.

◆ ◆

May the Source of peace send peace to all who mourn,
and comfort to all who are bereaved. Amen.

YIGDAL

יִגְדַּל

יִגְדַּל אֱלֹהִים חַי וְיִשְׁתַּבַּח,
נִמְצָא וְאֵין עֵת אֶל־מְצִיאוּתוֹ.
אֶחָד וְאֵין יָחִיד כְּיִחוּדוֹ,
נֶעְלָם וְגַם אֵין סוֹף לְאַחְדוּתוֹ.
אֵין לוֹ דְמוּת הַגּוּף וְאֵינוֹ גוּף,
לֹא נַעֲרוֹךְ אֵלָיו קְדֻשָּׁתוֹ.
קַדְמוֹן לְכָל־דָּבָר אֲשֶׁר נִבְרָא,
רִאשׁוֹן וְאֵין רֵאשִׁית לְרֵאשִׁיתוֹ.
הִנּוֹ אֲדוֹן עוֹלָם, לְכָל־נוֹצָר
יוֹרֶה גְדֻלָּתוֹ וּמַלְכוּתוֹ.
שֶׁפַע נְבוּאָתוֹ נְתָנוֹ,
אֶל־אַנְשֵׁי סְגֻלָּתוֹ וְתִפְאַרְתּוֹ.
לֹא קָם בְּיִשְׂרָאֵל כְּמֹשֶׁה עוֹד
נָבִיא וּמַבִּיט אֶת־תְּמוּנָתוֹ.
תּוֹרַת אֱמֶת נָתַן לְעַמּוֹ אֵל,
עַל יַד נְבִיאוֹ נֶאֱמַן בֵּיתוֹ.
לֹא יַחֲלִיף הָאֵל, וְלֹא יָמִיר
דָּתוֹ, לְעוֹלָמִים לְזוּלָתוֹ.
צוֹפֶה וְיוֹדֵעַ סְתָרֵינוּ,
מַבִּיט לְסוֹף דָּבָר בְּקַדְמָתוֹ.
גּוֹמֵל לְאִישׁ חֶסֶד כְּמִפְעָלוֹ,
נוֹתֵן לְרָשָׁע רַע כְּרִשְׁעָתוֹ.
יִשְׁלַח לְקֵץ יָמִין פְּדוּת עוֹלָם,
כָּל־חַי וְיֵשׁ יַכִּיר יְשׁוּעָתוֹ.
חַיֵּי עוֹלָם נָטַע בְּתוֹכֵנוּ,
בָּרוּךְ עֲדֵי עַד שֵׁם תְּהִלָּתוֹ.

Yig·dal E·lo·him chai ve·yish·ta·bach,
nim·tsa ve·ein eit el me·tsi·u·to.
E·chad ve·ein ya·chid ke·yi·chu·do,
ne·lam ve·gam ein sof le·ach·du·to.

Ein lo de·mut ha·guf ve·ei·no guf,
lo na·a·roch ei·lav ke·du·sha·to.
Kad·mon le·chol da·var a·sher niv·ra,
ri·shon ve·ein rei·shit le·rei·shi·to.

Hi·no a·don o·lam, le·chol no·tsar
yo·reh ge·du·la·to u·mal·chu·to.
She·fa ne·vu·a·to ne·ta·no,
el a·ne·shei se·gu·la·to ve·tif·ar·to.

Lo kam be·yis·ra·eil ke·mo·sheh od
na·vi u·ma·bit et te·mu·na·to.
To·rat e·met na·tan le·a·mo Eil,
al yad ne·vi·o ne·e·man bei·to.

Lo ya·cha·lif ha·eil, ve·lo ya·mir
da·to, le·o·la·mim le·zu·la·to.
Tso·feh ve·yo·dei·a se·ta·rei·nu,
ma·bit le·sof da·var be·kad·ma·to.

Go·meil le·ish che·sed ke·mif·a·lo,
no·tein le·ra·sha ra ke·rish·a·to.
Yish·lach le·keits ya·min pe·dut o·lam,
kol chai ve·yeish ya·kir ye·shu·a·to.

Cha·yei o·lam na·ta be·to·chei·nu,
ba·ruch a·dei ad sheim te·hi·la·to.

YIGDAL

We praise the living God,
For ever praise His name,
Who was and is and is to be
For e'er the same;
The One eternal God
Before our world appears,
And there can be no end of time
Beyond His years.

Without a form is He,
Nor can we comprehend
The measure of His love for us—
Without an end.
For He is Lord of all,
Creation speaks His praise.
The human race and all that grows
His will obeys.

He knows our every thought,
Our birth and death ordains;
He understands our fervent dreams,
Our hopes and our pains.
Eternal life has He
Implanted in our soul.
We dedicate our life to Him—
His way, our goal!

תפלת שחרית ליום כפור

YOM KIPPUR MORNING
SERVICE

Readings and Meditations begin on page 229

Morning Service

תפלת שחרית

For those who wear the Tallit

Praise the Lord, O my soul!   בָּרְכִי נַפְשִׁי אֶת יְיָ!

O Lord my God, You are very great!   יְיָ אֱלֹהַי, גָּדַלְתָּ מְּאֹד!

Arrayed in glory and majesty,   הוֹד וְהָדָר לָבָשְׁתָּ,

You wrap Yourself in light as with a garment,   עֹטֶה אוֹר כַּשַּׂלְמָה,

You stretch out the heavens like a curtain.   נוֹטֶה שָׁמַיִם כַּיְרִיעָה.

בָּרוּךְ אַתָּה, יְיָ אֱלֹהֵינוּ, מֶלֶךְ הָעוֹלָם,
אֲשֶׁר קִדְּשָׁנוּ בְּמִצְוֹתָיו וְצִוָּנוּ לְהִתְעַטֵּף בַּצִּיצִת.

Blessed is the Lord our God, Ruler of the universe, who hallows
us with Mitzvot, and teaches us to wrap ourselves in the fringed
Tallit.

*If desired, the Morning Blessings, pages 80–91,
may be read here. Then continue on page 292.*

Opening Prayers and Songs of Praise

Hear the word of the Lord:
When you come to appear before Me,
bring Me no more vain offerings;
incense is an abomination to Me.
New moon and Sabbath
and the calling of assemblies—
iniquity with solemn assembly—
I cannot endure.
Therefore I will hide My eyes from you;
though you make many prayers,
I will not listen,
so long as your hands are full of blood.
Wash yourselves; make yourselves clean;
remove the evil of your doings
from before My eyes;
cease to do evil; learn to do good;
seek justice; correct oppression;
defend the orphan; plead for the widow.
Seek good and not evil, that you may live.
And so the Lord, the God of Hosts,
will be with you.

Let justice well up as waters,
and righteousness as a mighty stream.

• •

שחר אבקשך

שַׁחַר אֲבַקֶּשְׁךָ, צוּרִי וּמִשְׂגַּבִּי,
אֶעֱרוֹךְ לְפָנֶיךָ שַׁחְרִי וְגַם עַרְבִּי.
לִפְנֵי גְדֻלָּתָךְ אֶעֱמֹד וְאֶבָּהֵל,
כִּי עֵינְךָ תִרְאֶה כָּל מַחְשְׁבוֹת לִבִּי.
מַה־זֶּה אֲשֶׁר יוּכַל הַלֵּב וְהַלָּשׁוֹן

292

לַעֲשׂוֹת, וּמַה כֹּחַ רוּחִי בְּתוֹךְ קִרְבִּי?
הִנֵּה לְךָ תִּיטַב זִמְרַת אֱנוֹשׁ; עַל כֵּן
אוֹדְךָ בְּעוֹד תִּהְיֶה נִשְׁמַת אֱלוֹהַּ בִּי.

Early will I seek You,
God my refuge strong;
Late prepare to meet You
With my evening song.

Though unto Your greatness
I with trembling soar,
Yet my inmost thinking
Lies Your eyes before.

What this frail heart's dreaming,
And my tongue's poor speech,
Can they even distant
To Your greatness reach?

Being great in mercy,
You will not despise
Praises which till death's hour
From my soul will rise.

◆ ◆

THE DAY OF DECISION

This is the day of God. On this day we are called to the
sanctuary by a summons as exalting and enduring as the
everlasting hills: Prepare to meet your God, O Israel.

This is the day of awe. What are we, as we stand in Your
presence, O God? A leaf in the storm, a fleeting moment
in the flow of time, a whisper lost among the stars.

This is the day of decision. Today we invoke You as the
Molder of our destiny. Help us to mend the evil of our
ways, to right the heart's old wrongs. On this Sabbath of
the soul, inscribe us for blessing in the Book of Life.

This is the day of our atonement. We would return to You as penitent children long to return to a loving parent. We confess our sins on this day, knowing that the gates of repentance are always open. Receive us with compassion, and bless us with Your forgiving love.

♦ ♦

MEANING TO OUR FLEETING DAYS

We are tenants in the house of life; our days on earth are but a span.

Time, like a river, rolls on, flowing year after year into the sea of eternity.

Its passing leaves bitter memories of hours misspent.

Now they come back to accuse us, and we tremble to think of them.

But Your purpose gives meaning to our fleeting days, Your teaching guides us, and Your love sustains us.

To You we pray for the knowledge and strength to live responsibly.

Deliver us from bondage to the past; release us from the stranglehold of evil habits; make us free to start afresh.

Let this be for us the beginning of a new season of life and health.

Liberate us from the fear of death, and from the scornful laughter that mocks our labors.

Though our lives be short, let them be full; hold our mortal days in Your hands as eternal moments.

We, dust and ashes, are endowed with divinity; compounded of clay , we live in dimensions clay cannot enter, regions where the air vibrates with Your presence.

Judge us less harshly than we can judge ourselves; judge us with mercy, O Fountain of life, in whose light we see light!

◆ ◆

FOR ALL YOUR CHILDREN

Not for ourselves alone do we pray,
not for ourselves alone,
but for all Your children.

Knowing our failings,
let us be patient with those of others.
Knowing our will to goodness,
may we see in others a dignity that is human,
a beauty inviolate for ever.
Every soul, Lord, is precious in Your sight,
and every life is Your gift to us.
Yet one stands poised to strike the next;
armies uproot vines and fig-trees,
as war and war's alarms make all afraid.

Not for ourselves alone, therefore,
not for ourselves alone,
but for all Your children
do we invoke Your love.

◆

COME WITH THE DAY

God of pity and love, return to this earth.
Go not so far away, leaving us to evil.
Return, O Lord, return. Come with the day.

Come with the light, that we may see once more
Across this earth's uncomfortable floor
The kindly path, the old and loving way.
Let us not die of evil in the night.
Let there be God again. Let there be light.

◆ ◆

From Psalm 139

Lord, You see through me; You know me. You know my
coming and my going; You understand my every thought.
You measure my going about and my lying down; You
are acquainted with all my ways.

*Whither can I go from Your spirit? Whither can I flee from
Your presence? If I ascend to the heavens, You are there! If I
make my home in the lower depths, behold, You are there! If
I take up the wings of the morning, and dwell on the ocean's
farthest shore, even there Your hand will lead me, Your right
hand will hold me. If I say, 'Surely darkness will conceal me,
night will hide me from view,' even the darkness is not too
dark for You, the night is clear as the day.*

O God, what mysteries I find in You, how inexhaustible
are their themes! I try to count them—they outnumber the
grains of sand; I wake from my reverie—and still am lost
in You.

*Search me, O God; look into my heart. Try me; enter my
thoughts. Keep me from walking the path of grief, and guide
me in the way everlasting.*

◆ ◆

O Lord, where shall I find You?
Hid is Your lofty place;
And where shall I not find You,
Whose glory fills all space?
You formed the world, abiding
Within the soul alway;
Refuge to those who seek You,
Ransom for those who stray.

O, how shall mortals praise You,
When angels strive in vain,
Or build for You a dwelling,
Whom worlds cannot contain?
Longing to draw near You
With all my heart I pray,
Then going forth to seek You,
You meet me on the way.

I find You in the marvels
Of Your creative might,
In visions in Your temple,
In dreams that bless the night.
Who say they have not seen You?
Your heavens refute their word;
Their hosts declare Your glory,
Though never voice be heard.

• •

אשרי

אַשְׁרֵי יוֹשְׁבֵי בֵיתֶךָ; עוֹד יְהַלְלוּךָ סֶּלָה.
אַשְׁרֵי הָעָם שֶׁכָּכָה לּוֹ; אַשְׁרֵי הָעָם שֶׁיְיָ אֱלֹהָיו.

Happy are those who dwell in Your house;
they will sing Your praise for ever.

Happy the people to whom such blessing falls;
happy the people whose God is the Lord.

Psalm 145

תְּהִלָּה לְדָוִד.
אֲרוֹמִמְךָ, אֱלוֹהַי הַמֶּלֶךְ, וַאֲבָרְכָה שִׁמְךָ לְעוֹלָם וָעֶד.
בְּכָל־יוֹם אֲבָרְכֶךָּ, וַאֲהַלְלָה שִׁמְךָ לְעוֹלָם וָעֶד.

I will exalt You, my Sovereign God;
I will bless Your name for ever.

Every day will I bless You;
I will extol Your name for ever.

גָּדוֹל יְיָ וּמְהֻלָּל מְאֹד, וְלִגְדֻלָּתוֹ אֵין חֵקֶר.
דּוֹר לְדוֹר יְשַׁבַּח מַעֲשֶׂיךָ, וּגְבוּרֹתֶיךָ יַגִּידוּ.

Great is the Lord and worthy of praise;
His greatness is infinite.

One generation shall acclaim Your work to the next;
they shall tell of Your mighty acts.

הֲדַר כְּבוֹד הוֹדֶךָ,
וְדִבְרֵי נִפְלְאֹתֶיךָ אָשִׂיחָה.

They shall consider Your radiant glory;

they shall reflect on Your wondrous works.

וֶעֱזוּז נוֹרְאֹתֶיךָ יֹאמֵרוּ, וּגְדֻלָּתְךָ אֲסַפְּרֶנָּה.
זֵכֶר רַב־טוּבְךָ יַבִּיעוּ, וְצִדְקָתְךָ יְרַנֵּנוּ.

They shall speak of Your awesome might,
and make known Your greatness.

They shall tell the world of Your great goodness,
and sing of Your righteousness.

חַנּוּן וְרַחוּם יְיָ, אֶרֶךְ אַפַּיִם וּגְדָל־חָסֶד.
טוֹב־יְיָ לַכֹּל, וְרַחֲמָיו עַל־כָּל־מַעֲשָׂיו.

298

"The Lord is gracious and compassionate,
endlessly patient, overflowing with love."

*"The Lord is good to all; His compassion
shelters all His creatures."*

יוֹדְוּךָ יְיָ כָּל־מַעֲשֶׂיךָ,
וַחֲסִידֶיךָ יְבָרְכְוּכָה.

All Your works, O Lord, shall thank You;

Your faithful shall bless You.

כְּבוֹד מַלְכוּתְךָ יֹאמֵרוּ, וּגְבוּרָתְךָ יְדַבֵּרוּ,
לְהוֹדִיעַ לִבְנֵי הָאָדָם גְּבוּרֹתָיו, וּכְבוֹד הֲדַר מַלְכוּתוֹ.

They shall speak of the glory of Your kingdom,
and tell of Your strength:

*to reveal Your power to the world, and
the glorious splendor of Your kingdom.*

מַלְכוּתְךָ מַלְכוּת כָּל־עֹלָמִים,
וּמֶמְשַׁלְתְּךָ בְּכָל־דּוֹר וָדֹר.

Your kingdom is an everlasting kingdom;

Your dominion endures through all generations.

סוֹמֵךְ יְיָ לְכָל־הַנֹּפְלִים, וְזוֹקֵף לְכָל־הַכְּפוּפִים.
עֵינֵי כֹל אֵלֶיךָ יְשַׂבֵּרוּ, וְאַתָּה נוֹתֵן־לָהֶם אֶת־אָכְלָם
בְּעִתּוֹ.

Lord, You support the falling;
You raise up all who are bowed down.

*The eyes of all are turned to You;
You sustain them in time of need.*

פּוֹתֵחַ אֶת־יָדֶךָ, וּמַשְׂבִּיעַ לְכָל־חַי רָצוֹן.
צַדִּיק יְיָ בְּכָל־דְּרָכָיו, וְחָסִיד בְּכָל־מַעֲשָׂיו.

299

You open Your hand to fulfill the needs of all the living.

Lord, You are just in all Your ways, loving in all Your deeds.

קָרוֹב יְיָ לְכָל־קֹרְאָיו, לְכֹל אֲשֶׁר יִקְרָאֻהוּ בֶאֱמֶת.
רְצוֹן־יְרֵאָיו יַעֲשֶׂה, וְאֶת־שַׁוְעָתָם יִשְׁמַע וְיוֹשִׁיעֵם.

The Lord is near to all who call upon Him,
to all who call upon Him in truth.

He will fulfill the hope of all who revere Him;
He will hear their cry and help them.

שׁוֹמֵר יְיָ אֶת־כָּל־אֹהֲבָיו,
וְאֵת כָּל־הָרְשָׁעִים יַשְׁמִיד.

The Lord preserves those who love Him,

but the lawless He brings to grief.

תְּהִלַּת יְיָ יְדַבֶּר־פִּי
וִיבָרֵךְ כָּל־בָּשָׂר שֵׁם קָדְשׁוֹ לְעוֹלָם וָעֶד.
וַאֲנַחְנוּ נְבָרֵךְ יָהּ מֵעַתָּה וְעַד־עוֹלָם. הַלְלוּיָהּ.

My lips shall declare the glory of the Lord;
let all flesh bless His holy name for ever and ever.

We will bless the Lord now and always. Halleluyah!

∙∙

OUR IMMEASURABLE DEBT TO GOD נִשְׁמַת כָּל־חַי

נִשְׁמַת כָּל־חַי תְּבָרֵךְ אֶת־שִׁמְךָ, יְיָ אֱלֹהֵינוּ, וְרוּחַ כָּל־
בָּשָׂר תְּפָאֵר וּתְרוֹמֵם זִכְרְךָ, מַלְכֵּנוּ, תָּמִיד. מִן־
הָעוֹלָם וְעַד־הָעוֹלָם אַתָּה אֵל; אֵין לָנוּ מֶלֶךְ אֶלָּא
אָתָּה.

Let every living soul bless Your name, O Lord our God,
and let every human being acclaim Your majesty, for ever

and ever. Through all eternity You are God; we have no King but You.

אֱלֹהֵי הָרִאשׁוֹנִים וְהָאַחֲרוֹנִים, אֱלֽוֹהַ כָּל־בְּרִיּוֹת,
אֲדוֹן כָּל־תּוֹלָדוֹת, הַמְהֻלָּל בְּרֹב הַתִּשְׁבָּחוֹת, הַמְנַהֵג
עוֹלָמוֹ בְּחֶסֶד וּבְרִיּוֹתָיו בְּרַחֲמִים. וַיְיָ לֹא יָנוּם וְלֹא
יִישָׁן; הַמְעוֹרֵר יְשֵׁנִים וְהַמֵּקִיץ נִרְדָּמִים וְהַמֵּשִׂיחַ
אִלְּמִים, וְהַמַּתִּיר אֲסוּרִים וְהַסּוֹמֵךְ נוֹפְלִים וְהַזּוֹקֵף
כְּפוּפִים. לְךָ לְבַדְּךָ אֲנַחְנוּ מוֹדִים.

God of all ages, Ruler of all creatures, Lord of all generations: all praise to You. You guide the world with steadfast love, Your creatures with tender mercy. You neither
slumber nor sleep; You awaken the sleeping and arouse
the dormant. You give speech to the silent, freedom to the
enslaved, and justice to the oppressed. To You alone we
give thanks.

אִלּוּ פִינוּ מָלֵא שִׁירָה כַיָּם, וּלְשׁוֹנֵנוּ רִנָּה כַּהֲמוֹן גַּלָּיו,
וְשִׂפְתוֹתֵינוּ שֶׁבַח כְּמֶרְחֲבֵי רָקִיעַ, וְעֵינֵינוּ מְאִירוֹת
כַּשֶּׁמֶשׁ וְכַיָּרֵחַ, וְיָדֵינוּ פְרוּשׂוֹת כְּנִשְׁרֵי שָׁמָיִם,
וְרַגְלֵינוּ קַלּוֹת כָּאַיָּלוֹת—אֵין אֲנַחְנוּ מַסְפִּיקִים
לְהוֹדוֹת לְךָ, יְיָ אֱלֹהֵינוּ וֵאלֹהֵי אֲבוֹתֵינוּ, וּלְבָרֵךְ אֶת־
שְׁמֶךָ עַל־אַחַת מֵאֶלֶף, אֶלֶף אַלְפֵי אֲלָפִים וְרִבֵּי
רְבָבוֹת פְּעָמִים הַטּוֹבוֹת שֶׁעָשִׂיתָ עִם־אֲבוֹתֵינוּ וְעִמָּנוּ.

Though our mouths should overflow with song as the sea, our
tongues with melody as the roaring waves, our lips with
praise as the heavens' wide expanse; and though our eyes
were to shine as the sun and the moon, our arms extend like
eagles' wings, our feet speed swiftly as deer—still we could
not fully thank You, Lord our God and God of all ages, or
bless Your name enough, for even one of Your infinite
kindnesses to our ancestors and to us.

301

עַל כֵּן אֵבָרִים שֶׁפִּלַּגְתָּ בָּנוּ, וְרוּחַ וּנְשָׁמָה שֶׁנָּפַחְתָּ
בְּאַפֵּינוּ, וְלָשׁוֹן אֲשֶׁר שַׂמְתָּ בְּפִינוּ, הֵן הֵם יוֹדוּ
וִיבָרְכוּ וִישַׁבְּחוּ וִיפָאֲרוּ אֶת־שְׁמְךָ, מַלְכֵּנוּ. כִּי כָל־פֶּה
לְךָ יוֹדֶה, וְכָל־לָשׁוֹן לְךָ תִשָּׁבַע, וְכָל־בֶּרֶךְ לְךָ תִכְרַע,
וְכָל־קוֹמָה לְפָנֶיךָ תִשְׁתַּחֲוֶה, וְכָל־לְבָבוֹת יִירָאוּךָ,
וְכָל־קֶרֶב וּכְלָיוֹת יְזַמְּרוּ לִשְׁמֶךָ. כַּדָּבָר שֶׁכָּתוּב: כָּל־
עַצְמוֹתַי תֹּאמַרְנָה: "יְיָ, מִי כָמוֹךָ?" כָּאָמוּר, "לְדָוִד,
בָּרְכִי, נַפְשִׁי, אֶת־יְיָ, וְכָל־קְרָבַי אֶת־שֵׁם קָדְשׁוֹ!"

Therefore, O God, limbs and tongue and heart and mind
shall join to praise Your name; every tongue will yet affirm You, and every soul give You allegiance. As it is written: All my limbs shall say: "Lord, who is like You?" And
David sang: "Bless the Lord, O my soul, and let all that is
within me bless His holy name!"

.．

הָאֵל בְּתַעֲצֻמוֹת עֻזֶּךָ, הַגָּדוֹל בִּכְבוֹד שְׁמֶךָ, הַגִּבּוֹר
לָנֶצַח וְהַנּוֹרָא בְּנוֹרְאוֹתֶיךָ.

You are tremendous in power, O God, glorious in being,
mighty for ever and awesome in Your works.

הַמֶּלֶךְ הַיּוֹשֵׁב עַל כִּסֵּא רָם וְנִשָּׂא.

O KING supreme and exalted,

שׁוֹכֵן עַד, מָרוֹם וְקָדוֹשׁ שְׁמוֹ. וְכָתוּב: רַנְּנוּ צַדִּיקִים
בַּיְיָ; לַיְשָׁרִים נָאוָה תְהִלָּה.

You abide for ever, the High and Holy One. Therefore let

all who are righteous sing Your song; the upright do well
to acclaim You.

בְּפִי יְשָׁרִים תִּתְהַלָּל; וּבְדִבְרֵי צַדִּיקִים תִּתְבָּרַךְ;
וּבִלְשׁוֹן חֲסִידִים תִּתְרוֹמָם; וּבְקֶרֶב קְדוֹשִׁים
תִּתְקַדָּשׁ.

*The mouths of the upright acclaim You; the words of the
righteous bless You; the tongues of the faithful exalt You;
the hearts of all who seek holiness sanctify You.*

וּבְמַקְהֲלוֹת רִבְבוֹת עַמְּךָ, בֵּית יִשְׂרָאֵל, בְּרִנָּה יִתְפָּאֵר
שִׁמְךָ, מַלְכֵּנוּ, בְּכָל־דּוֹר וָדוֹר. יִשְׁתַּבַּח שִׁמְךָ לָעַד
מַלְכֵּנוּ, הָאֵל הַמֶּלֶךְ הַגָּדוֹל וְהַקָּדוֹשׁ בַּשָּׁמַיִם וּבָאָרֶץ.

O King, the assembled hosts of Your people, the house of
Israel, in every generation glorify Your name in song. O
Sovereign God, great and holy King, let Your name be
praised for ever in heaven and on earth.

בָּרוּךְ אַתָּה, יְיָ, אֵל מֶלֶךְ, גָּדוֹל בַּתִּשְׁבָּחוֹת, אֵל
הַהוֹדָאוֹת, אֲדוֹן הַנִּפְלָאוֹת, הַבּוֹחֵר בְּשִׁירֵי זִמְרָה,
מֶלֶךְ אֵל חֵי הָעוֹלָמִים.

*Blessed is the Lord, the Sovereign God, the Lord of wonders
who delights in song, the Only One, the Life of the universe.*

❖ ❖

READER'S KADDISH חצי קדיש

יִתְגַּדַּל וְיִתְקַדַּשׁ שְׁמֵהּ רַבָּא בְּעָלְמָא דִּי־בְרָא כִרְעוּתֵהּ, וְיַמְלִיךְ
מַלְכוּתֵהּ בְּחַיֵּיכוֹן וּבְיוֹמֵיכוֹן וּבְחַיֵּי דְכָל־בֵּית יִשְׂרָאֵל, בַּעֲגָלָא
וּבִזְמַן קָרִיב, וְאִמְרוּ: אָמֵן.
יְהֵא שְׁמֵהּ רַבָּא מְבָרַךְ לְעָלַם וּלְעָלְמֵי עָלְמַיָּא.
יִתְבָּרַךְ וְיִשְׁתַּבַּח, וְיִתְפָּאַר וְיִתְרוֹמַם וְיִתְנַשֵּׂא, וְיִתְהַדָּר

וְיִתְעַלֶּה וְיִתְהַלַּל שְׁמֵהּ דְּקוּדְשָׁא, בְּרִיךְ הוּא, לְעֵלָּא מִן כָּל־
בִּרְכָתָא וְשִׁירָתָא, תֻּשְׁבְּחָתָא וְנֶחֱמָתָא דַּאֲמִירָן בְּעָלְמָא,
וְאִמְרוּ: אָמֵן.

Let the glory of God be extolled, let His great name be hallowed
in the world whose creation He willed. May His kingdom soon
prevail, in our own day, our own lives, and the life of all Israel,
and let us say: Amen.

Let His great name be blessed for ever and ever.

Let the name of the Holy One, blessed is He, be glorified, exalted and honored, though He is beyond all the praises, songs,
and adorations that we can utter, and let us say: Amen.

◆ ◆

All rise

שמע וברכותיה

בָּרְכוּ אֶת־יְיָ הַמְבֹרָךְ!

Praise the Lord, to whom our praise is due!

בָּרוּךְ יְיָ הַמְבֹרָךְ לְעוֹלָם וָעֶד!

Praised be the Lord, to whom our praise is due,
now and for ever!

◆ ◆

BE WITH US   יוצר

בָּרוּךְ אַתָּה, יְיָ אֱלֹהֵינוּ, מֶלֶךְ הָעוֹלָם, יוֹצֵר אוֹר
וּבוֹרֵא חְשֶׁךְ, עֹשֶׂה שָׁלוֹם וּבוֹרֵא אֶת־הַכֹּל.

הַמֵּאִיר לָאָרֶץ וְלַדָּרִים עָלֶיהָ בְּרַחֲמִים, וּבְטוּבוֹ
מְחַדֵּשׁ בְּכָל־יוֹם תָּמִיד מַעֲשֵׂה בְרֵאשִׁית.

מָה רַבּוּ מַעֲשֶׂיךָ, יְיָ! כֻּלָּם בְּחָכְמָה עָשִׂיתָ, מָלְאָה
הָאָרֶץ קִנְיָנֶךָ.

304

תִּתְבָּרַךְ, יְיָ אֱלֹהֵינוּ, עַל־שֶׁבַח מַעֲשֵׂה יָדֶיךָ, וְעַל־
מְאוֹרֵי־אוֹר שֶׁעָשִׂיתָ: יְפָאֲרוּךְ. סֶלָה. בָּרוּךְ אַתָּה, יְיָ,
יוֹצֵר הַמְּאוֹרוֹת.

°Lord of darkness and dawn,
the God who opens the gates of mercy,
who gives light to all who await forgiveness,
be with us on this Atonement Day.

God of times and seasons, be with us this day.

Lord God of hope and joy, be with us this day.

God of the loving heart, be with us this day.

Be with us as we look for strength to be free, freedom to
struggle against those who worship power, and power to
resist all who would oppress us.

God of freedom and right, be with us this day.

• •

YOUR POWER AND YOUR LOVE   אהבה רבה

אַהֲבָה רַבָּה אֲהַבְתָּנוּ, יְיָ אֱלֹהֵינוּ, חֶמְלָה גְדוֹלָה
וִיתֵרָה חָמַלְתָּ עָלֵינוּ. אָבִינוּ מַלְכֵּנוּ, בַּעֲבוּר אֲבוֹתֵינוּ
שֶׁבָּטְחוּ בְךָ וַתְּלַמְּדֵם חֻקֵּי חַיִּים, כֵּן תְּחָנֵּנוּ וּתְלַמְּדֵנוּ.
אָבִינוּ, הָאָב הָרַחֲמָן, הַמְרַחֵם, רַחֵם עָלֵינוּ וְתֵן בְּלִבֵּנוּ
לְהָבִין וּלְהַשְׂכִּיל, לִשְׁמֹעַ לִלְמֹד וּלְלַמֵּד, לִשְׁמֹר
וְלַעֲשׂוֹת וּלְקַיֵּם אֶת־כָּל־דִּבְרֵי תַלְמוּד תּוֹרָתֶךָ
בְּאַהֲבָה.

°This symbol indicates that the English is a variation suggested by the theme
of the Hebrew.

305

וְהָאֵר עֵינֵינוּ בְּתוֹרָתֶךָ, וְדַבֵּק לִבֵּנוּ בְּמִצְוֹתֶיךָ, וְיַחֵד
לְבָבֵנוּ לְאַהֲבָה וּלְיִרְאָה אֶת־שְׁמֶךָ. וְלֹא־נֵבוֹשׁ
לְעוֹלָם וָעֶד, כִּי בְשֵׁם קָדְשְׁךָ הַגָּדוֹל וְהַנּוֹרָא בָּטָחְנוּ.
נָגִילָה וְנִשְׂמְחָה בִּישׁוּעָתֶךָ, כִּי אֵל פּוֹעֵל יְשׁוּעוֹת
אָתָּה, וּבָנוּ בָחַרְתָּ וְקֵרַבְתָּנוּ לְשִׁמְךָ הַגָּדוֹל סֶלָה
בֶּאֱמֶת, לְהוֹדוֹת לְךָ וּלְיַחֶדְךָ בְּאַהֲבָה. בָּרוּךְ אַתָּה, יְיָ,
הַבּוֹחֵר בְּעַמּוֹ יִשְׂרָאֵל בְּאַהֲבָה.

°O One and Only God, You have made each of us unique,
and formed us to be united in one family of life. Be with
us, Eternal One, as we seek to unite our lives with Your
power and Your love.

*We proclaim now Your Oneness and our own hope for unity;
we acclaim Your creative power in the universe and in
ourselves, the Law that binds world to world and heart to
heart:*

• •

שְׁמַע יִשְׂרָאֵל: יְיָ אֱלֹהֵינוּ, יְיָ אֶחָד!

Hear, O Israel: the Lord is our God, the Lord is One!

בָּרוּךְ שֵׁם כְּבוֹד מַלְכוּתוֹ לְעוֹלָם וָעֶד!

Blessed is His glorious kingdom for ever and ever!

All are seated

וְאָהַבְתָּ אֵת יְיָ אֱלֹהֶיךָ בְּכָל־לְבָבְךָ וּבְכָל־נַפְשְׁךָ
וּבְכָל־מְאֹדֶךָ. וְהָיוּ הַדְּבָרִים הָאֵלֶּה, אֲשֶׁר אָנֹכִי מְצַוְּךָ
הַיּוֹם, עַל־לְבָבֶךָ. וְשִׁנַּנְתָּם לְבָנֶיךָ, וְדִבַּרְתָּ בָּם
בְּשִׁבְתְּךָ בְּבֵיתֶךָ, וּבְלֶכְתְּךָ בַדֶּרֶךְ, וּבְשָׁכְבְּךָ

306

וּבְקוּמֶךָ. וּקְשַׁרְתָּם לְאוֹת עַל־יָדֶךָ, וְהָיוּ לְטֹטָפֹת בֵּין
עֵינֶיךָ, וּכְתַבְתָּם עַל־מְזֻזוֹת בֵּיתֶךָ, וּבִשְׁעָרֶיךָ.

*You shall love the Lord your God with all your mind, with
all your strength, with all your being. Set these words, which
I command you this day, upon your heart. Teach them
faithfully to your children; speak of them in your home and
on your way, when you lie down and when you rise up. Bind
them as a sign upon your hand; let them be a symbol before
your eyes; inscribe them on the doorposts of your house, and
on your gates.*

לְמַעַן תִּזְכְּרוּ וַעֲשִׂיתֶם אֶת־כָּל־מִצְוֹתָי, וִהְיִיתֶם
קְדֹשִׁים לֵאלֹהֵיכֶם. אֲנִי יְיָ אֱלֹהֵיכֶם, אֲשֶׁר הוֹצֵאתִי
אֶתְכֶם מֵאֶרֶץ מִצְרַיִם לִהְיוֹת לָכֶם לֵאלֹהִים. אֲנִי יְיָ
אֱלֹהֵיכֶם.

*Be mindful of all My Mitzvot and do them: so shall you con-
secrate yourselves to your God. I, the Lord, am your God
who led you out of Egypt to be your God; I, the Lord, am
your God.*

MAKE THE DAY OF FREEDOM DAWN   גאולה

In this world waiting to be redeemed, our hearts cry out:
Cannot our dearest hopes at last come true?

Many are our defeats, yet how many our deliverances!
After servitude to Pharaoh, we choose service to God;
after exile in Babylon, we rebuild God's shrine; yesterday's wounds, so nearly fatal, begin to heal; and Israel,
living still, plants new seeds of redemption.

*Let the time come when all the peoples will be joined in
bonds that cannot break. The nations will yet be at peace;
the earth will yield good fruit. Mountains and waters will*

*exult, those who sowed in tears will reap in joy, and all will
sing with one accord:*

מִי־כָמְכָה בָּאֵלִם, יְיָ?

Who is like You, Eternal One, among
the gods that are worshipped?

מִי כָּמְכָה, נֶאְדָּר בַּקֹּדֶשׁ,
נוֹרָא תְהִלֹּת, עֹשֵׂה פֶלֶא?

Who is like You, majestic in holiness,
awesome in splendor, doing wonders?

שִׁירָה חֲדָשָׁה שִׁבְּחוּ גְאוּלִים לְשִׁמְךָ עַל־שְׂפַת הַיָּם;
יַחַד כֻּלָּם הוֹדוּ וְהִמְלִיכוּ וְאָמְרוּ: "יְיָ יִמְלֹךְ לְעוֹלָם
וָעֶד!"

A new song the redeemed sang to Your name. At the shore of
the Sea, saved from destruction, they proclaimed Your
sovereign power: "The Eternal will reign for ever and ever!"

צוּר יִשְׂרָאֵל, קוּמָה בְּעֶזְרַת יִשְׂרָאֵל, וּפְדֵה כִנְאֻמֶךָ
יְהוּדָה וְיִשְׂרָאֵל. גֹּאֲלֵנוּ יְיָ צְבָאוֹת שְׁמוֹ, קְדוֹשׁ
יִשְׂרָאֵל. בָּרוּךְ אַתָּה, יְיָ, גָּאַל יִשְׂרָאֵל.

O Rock of Israel, come to Israel's help. Fulfill Your promise of
redemption for Judah and Israel. Our Redeemer is the Lord of
Hosts, the Holy One of Israel. Blessed is the Lord, the
Redeemer of Israel.

• •

All rise

תפלה

אֲדֹנָי, שְׂפָתַי תִּפְתָּח, וּפִי יַגִּיד תְּהִלָּתֶךָ.

Eternal God, open my lips, that my mouth may declare Your
glory.

A COVENANT PEOPLE, ETERNAL . . .   אבות

בָּרוּךְ אַתָּה, יְיָ אֱלֹהֵינוּ וֵאלֹהֵי אֲבוֹתֵינוּ, אֱלֹהֵי
אַבְרָהָם, אֱלֹהֵי יִצְחָק, וֵאלֹהֵי יַעֲקֹב: הָאֵל הַגָּדוֹל,
הַגִּבּוֹר וְהַנּוֹרָא, אֵל עֶלְיוֹן. גּוֹמֵל חֲסָדִים טוֹבִים,
וְקוֹנֵה הַכֹּל, וְזוֹכֵר חַסְדֵי אָבוֹת, וּמֵבִיא גְאֻלָּה לִבְנֵי
בְנֵיהֶם, לְמַעַן שְׁמוֹ, בְּאַהֲבָה.

°Lord, You are the God of all generations: the ones that
are past, and those yet unborn. You are our God.

You are the First; You are the Last: You are the Only One.

You made the earth and brought us forth to dwell in it.

*You called Abraham to righteousness, his children to bear
witness to Your glory.*

You formed us to be a covenant people, eternal as the
hosts of heaven.

*O God, You are the Shield of our people, our everlasting
light.*

זָכְרֵנוּ לְחַיִּים, מֶלֶךְ חָפֵץ בַּחַיִּים, וְכָתְבֵנוּ בְּסֵפֶר
הַחַיִּים, לְמַעַנְךָ אֱלֹהִים חַיִּים. מֶלֶךְ עוֹזֵר וּמוֹשִׁיעַ
וּמָגֵן. בָּרוּךְ אַתָּה, יְיָ, מָגֵן אַבְרָהָם.

Remember us unto life, O King who delights in life, and
inscribe us in the Book of Life, for Your sake, O God of
life.

◆ ◆

גבורות

אַתָּה גִּבּוֹר לְעוֹלָם, אֲדֹנָי, מְחַיֵּה הַכֹּל אַתָּה, רַב
לְהוֹשִׁיעַ. מְכַלְכֵּל חַיִּים בְּחֶסֶד, מְחַיֵּה הַכֹּל בְּרַחֲמִים
רַבִּים. סוֹמֵךְ נוֹפְלִים, וְרוֹפֵא חוֹלִים, וּמַתִּיר
אֲסוּרִים, וּמְקַיֵּם אֱמוּנָתוֹ לִישֵׁנֵי עָפָר. מִי כָמוֹךָ, בַּעַל
גְּבוּרוֹת, וּמִי דּוֹמֶה לָךְ, מֶלֶךְ מֵמִית וּמְחַיֶּה וּמַצְמִיחַ
יְשׁוּעָה? מִי כָמוֹךָ אַב הָרַחֲמִים, זוֹכֵר יְצוּרָיו לְחַיִּים
בְּרַחֲמִים? וְנֶאֱמָן אַתָּה לְהַחֲיוֹת הַכֹּל. בָּרוּךְ אַתָּה, יְיָ,
מְחַיֵּה הַכֹּל.

°Your might, O God, is everlasting;

Help us to use our strength for good and not for evil.

You are the Source of life and blessing;

Help us to choose life for ourselves and our children.

You are the Support of the falling;

Help us to lift up the fallen.

You are the Author of freedom;

Help us to set free the captive.

You are our Hope in death as in life;

Help us to keep faith with those who sleep in the dust.

Your might, O God, is everlasting;

Help us to use our strength for good.

All are seated

♦ ♦

ונתנה תקף

On Rosh Hashanah we reflect,
On Yom Kippur we consider:
Who shall live for the sake of others,
Who, dying, shall leave a heritage of life.

Who shall burn with the fires of greed,
Who shall drown in the waters of despair.

Whose hunger shall be for the good,
Who shall thirst for justice and right.

Whose tongue shall be a thrusting sword,
Whose words shall make for peace.

Who shall be plagued by fear of the world,
Who shall strangle for lack of friends.

Who shall rest at the end of day,
Who lie sleepless on a bed of pain.

Who shall go forth in the quest for truth,

Who shall be locked in the prison of self.

Who shall be serene in every storm,
Who shall be troubled by the passing breeze.

Who shall be poor in the midst of possessions,
Who shall be rich, content with their lot.

Repentance, prayer, and charity:
These return us to our God.

Forgiven the past, renewed for tomorrow,
May we go forth with rejoicing,
To a year of great goodness.

◆

וּנְתַנֶּה תְּקֶף קְדֻשַׁת הַיּוֹם כִּי הוּא נוֹרָא וְאָים. וּבוֹ
תִנַּשֵׂא מַלְכוּתֶךָ וְיִכּוֹן בְּחֶסֶד כִּסְאֶךָ וְתֵשֵׁב עָלָיו
בֶּאֱמֶת. אֱמֶת כִּי אַתָּה הוּא דַיָּן וּמוֹכִיחַ וְיוֹדֵעַ וָעֵד,
וְכוֹתֵב וְחוֹתֵם וְסוֹפֵר וּמוֹנֶה, וְתִזְכֹּר כָּל־הַנִּשְׁכָּחוֹת,
וְתִפְתַּח אֶת־סֵפֶר הַזִּכְרוֹנוֹת, וּמֵאֵלָיו יִקָּרֵא וְחוֹתַם
יַד כָּל־אָדָם בּוֹ.

Let us proclaim the sacred power of this day:
it is awesome and full of dread.
For on this day Your dominion is exalted,
Your throne established in steadfast love;
there in truth You reign.
In truth You are
Judge and Arbiter, Counsel and Witness.
You write and You seal, You record and recount.
You remember deeds long forgotten.
You open the book of our days,
and what is written there proclaims itself,
for it bears the signature
of every human being.

וּבְשׁוֹפָר גָּדוֹל יִתָּקַע וְקוֹל דְּמָמָה דַקָּה יִשָּׁמַע.
וּמַלְאָכִים יֵחָפֵזוּן וְחִיל וּרְעָדָה יֹאחֵזוּן וְיֹאמְרוּ: הִנֵּה
יוֹם הַדִּין. לִפְקֹד עַל צְבָא מָרוֹם בַּדִּין, כִּי לֹא יִזְכּוּ
בְעֵינֶיךָ בַּדִּין. וְכָל־בָּאֵי עוֹלָם יַעַבְרוּן לְפָנֶיךָ כִּבְנֵי
מָרוֹן. כְּבַקָּרַת רוֹעֶה עֶדְרוֹ, מַעֲבִיר צֹאנוֹ תַּחַת
שִׁבְטוֹ, כֵּן תַּעֲבִיר וְתִסְפֹּר וְתִמְנֶה וְתִפְקֹד נֶפֶשׁ כָּל־
חָי, וְתַחְתֹּךְ קִצְבָה לְכָל־בְּרִיָּה וְתִכְתֹּב אֶת־גְּזַר דִּינָם.

The great Shofar is sounded,
the still, small voice is heard;
the angels,
gripped by fear and trembling,
declare in awe:

312

This is the Day of Judgment!
For even the hosts of heaven are judged,
as all who dwell on earth
stand arrayed before You.

As the shepherd seeks out his flock,
and makes the sheep pass under his staff,
so do You muster and number and consider
every soul,
setting the bounds of every creature's life,
and decreeing its destiny.

בְּרֹאשׁ הַשָּׁנָה יִכָּתֵבוּן וּבְיוֹם צוֹם כִּפּוּר יֵחָתֵמוּן.
כַּמָּה יַעַבְרוּן וְכַמָּה יִבָּרֵאוּן, מִי יִחְיֶה וּמִי יָמוּת, מִי
בְקִצּוֹ וּמִי לֹא בְקִצּוֹ, מִי בָאֵשׁ וּמִי בַמַּיִם, מִי בַחֶרֶב
וּמִי בַחַיָּה, מִי בָרָעָב   וּמִי בַצָּמָא, מִי בָרַעַשׁ וּמִי
בַמַּגֵּפָה, מִי בַחֲנִיקָה וּמִי בַסְּקִילָה. מִי יָנוּחַ וּמִי יָנוּעַ,
מִי יַשְׁקִיט וּמִי יְטֹרֵף, מִי יִשָּׁלֵו וּמִי יִתְיַסָּר, מִי יֵעָנִי
וּמִי יֵעָשִׁיר, מִי יִשָּׁפֵל וּמִי יָרוּם.

On Rosh Hashanah it is written,
on Yom Kippur it is sealed:
How many shall pass on, how many shall come to be;
who shall live and who shall die;
who shall see ripe age and who shall not;
who shall perish by fire and who by water;
who by sword and who by beast;
who by hunger and who by thirst;
who by earthquake and who by plague;
who by strangling and who by stoning;
who shall be secure and who shall be driven;
who shall be tranquil and who shall be troubled;
who shall be poor and who shall be rich;
who shall be humbled and who exalted.

וּתְשׁוּבָה וּתְפִלָּה וּצְדָקָה
מַעֲבִירִין אֶת־רֹעַ הַגְּזֵרָה.

But REPENTANCE, PRAYER, and CHARITY
temper judgment's severe decree.

כִּי כְשִׁמְךָ כֵּן תְּהִלָּתֶךָ, קָשֶׁה לִכְעֹס וְנוֹחַ לִרְצוֹת. כִּי
לֹא תַחְפֹּץ בְּמוֹת הַמֵּת כִּי אִם בְּשׁוּבוֹ מִדַּרְכּוֹ וְחָיָה.
וְעַד יוֹם מוֹתוֹ תְּחַכֶּה־לּוֹ, אִם יָשׁוּב מִיַּד תְּקַבְּלוֹ.
אֱמֶת כִּי אַתָּה הוּא יוֹצְרָם וְיוֹדֵעַ יִצְרָם כִּי הֵם בָּשָׂר
וָדָם.

This is Your glory: You are
slow to anger, ready to forgive.
Lord, it is not the death of sinners You seek,
but that they should turn from their ways
and live.
Until the last day You wait for them,
welcoming them
as soon as they turn to You.

You have created us and know what we are;
we are but flesh and blood.

אָדָם יְסוֹדוֹ מֵעָפָר וְסוֹפוֹ לֶעָפָר. בְּנַפְשׁוֹ יָבִיא לַחְמוֹ.
מָשׁוּל כַּחֶרֶס הַנִּשְׁבָּר, כְּחָצִיר יָבֵשׁ וּכְצִיץ נוֹבֵל, כְּצֵל
עוֹבֵר וּכְעָנָן כָּלָה, וּכְרוּחַ נוֹשָׁבֶת, וּכְאָבָק פּוֹרֵחַ,
וְכַחֲלוֹם יָעוּף.

וְאַתָּה הוּא מֶלֶךְ אֵל חַי וְקַיָּם!

Man's origin is dust,
and dust is his end.
Each of us is a shattered urn,
grass that must wither,

a flower that will fade,
a shadow moving on,
a cloud passing by,
a particle of dust floating on the wind,
a dream soon forgotten.

But You are the King,
the everlasting God!

All rise

SANCTIFICATION   קדושה

נְקַדֵּשׁ אֶת־שִׁמְךָ בָּעוֹלָם כְּשֵׁם שֶׁמַּקְדִּישִׁים אוֹתוֹ
בִּשְׁמֵי מָרוֹם, כַּכָּתוּב עַל יַד נְבִיאֶךָ, וְקָרָא זֶה אֶל־זֶה
וְאָמַר:

We sanctify Your name on earth, even as all things, to the
ends of time and space, proclaim Your holiness; and in the
words of the prophet we say:

קָדוֹשׁ, קָדוֹשׁ, קָדוֹשׁ יְיָ צְבָאוֹת, מְלֹא כָל־הָאָרֶץ
כְּבוֹדוֹ.

Holy, Holy, Holy is the Lord of Hosts; the fullness of the
whole earth is His glory!

אַדִּיר אַדִּירֵנוּ, יְיָ אֲדוֹנֵינוּ, מָה אַדִּיר שִׁמְךָ בְּכָל־
הָאָרֶץ!

Source of our strength, Sovereign Lord, how majestic is
Your presence in all the earth!

בָּרוּךְ כְּבוֹד־יְיָ מִמְּקוֹמוֹ.

Blessed is the glory of God in heaven and earth.

אֶחָד הוּא אֱלֹהֵינוּ, הוּא אָבִינוּ, הוּא מַלְכֵּנוּ, הוּא
מוֹשִׁיעֵנוּ, וְהוּא יַשְׁמִיעֵנוּ בְּרַחֲמָיו לְעֵינֵי כָּל־חָי.

315

He alone is our God and our Creator; He is our Ruler and our Helper; and in His mercy He reveals Himself in the sight of all the living:

I AM ADONAI YOUR GOD!   "אֲנִי יְיָ אֱלֹהֵיכֶם!"

יִמְלֹךְ יְיָ לְעוֹלָם, אֱלֹהַיִךְ צִיּוֹן, לְדֹר וָדֹר. הַלְלוּיָהּ!

The Lord shall reign for ever; your God, O Zion, from generation to generation. Halleluyah!

All are seated

לְדוֹר וָדוֹר נַגִּיד גָּדְלֶךָ, וּלְנֵצַח נְצָחִים קְדֻשָּׁתְךָ נַקְדִּישׁ. וְשִׁבְחֲךָ, אֱלֹהֵינוּ, מִפִּינוּ לֹא יָמוּשׁ לְעוֹלָם וָעֶד.

To all generations we will make known Your greatness, and to all eternity proclaim Your holiness. Your praise, O God, shall never depart from our lips.

וּבְכֵן תֵּן פַּחְדְּךָ, יְיָ אֱלֹהֵינוּ, עַל כָּל־מַעֲשֶׂיךָ, וְאֵימָתְךָ עַל כָּל־מַה־שֶּׁבָּרָאתָ. וְיִירָאוּךָ כָּל־הַמַּעֲשִׂים, וְיִשְׁתַּחֲווּ לְפָנֶיךָ כָּל־הַבְּרוּאִים, וְיֵעָשׂוּ כֻלָּם אֲגֻדָּה אַחַת לַעֲשׂוֹת רְצוֹנְךָ בְּלֵבָב שָׁלֵם, כְּמוֹ שֶׁיָּדַעְנוּ, יְיָ אֱלֹהֵינוּ, שֶׁהַשִּׁלְטוֹן לְפָנֶיךָ, עֹז בְּיָדְךָ וּגְבוּרָה בִּימִינֶךָ, וְשִׁמְךָ נוֹרָא עַל כָּל־מַה־שֶּׁבָּרָאתָ.

Lord our God, cause all Your works to stand in awe before You, and all that You have made to tremble at Your presence. Let all that lives revere You, and all creation turn to You in worship. Let them all become a single family, doing Your will with a perfect heart. For well we know, O Lord our God, that Yours is the majesty, Yours the might; and awesome is Your name in all creation.

316

וּבְכֵן תֵּן כָּבוֹד, יְיָ, לְעַמֶּךָ, תְּהִלָּה לִירֵאֶיךָ וְתִקְנָה
לְדוֹרְשֶׁיךָ, וּפִתְחוֹן פֶּה לַמְיַחֲלִים לָךְ, שִׂמְחָה לְאַרְצֶךָ
וְשָׂשׂוֹן לְעִירֶךָ, וּצְמִיחַת קֶרֶן לְכָל־יוֹשְׁבֵי תֵבֵל.

Grant honor, Lord, to Your people, glory to those who
revere You, hope to those who seek You, and courage to
those who trust You; bless Your land with gladness and
Your city with joy, and cause the light of redemption to
dawn for all who dwell on earth.

וּבְכֵן צַדִּיקִים יִרְאוּ וְיִשְׂמָחוּ וִישָׁרִים יַעֲלֹזוּ וַחֲסִידִים
בְּרִנָּה יָגִילוּ, וְעוֹלָתָה תִּקְפָּץ־פִּיהָ וְכָל־הָרִשְׁעָה כֻּלָּהּ
כְּעָשָׁן תִּכְלֶה, כִּי תַעֲבִיר מֶמְשֶׁלֶת זָדוֹן מִן הָאָרֶץ.
וְתִמְלֹךְ אַתָּה, יְיָ, לְבַדֶּךָ עַל כָּל־מַעֲשֶׂיךָ, כַּכָּתוּב
בְּדִבְרֵי קָדְשֶׁךָ:

Then the just shall see and exult, the upright be glad, and the
faithful sing for joy. Violence shall rage no more, and evil
shall vanish like smoke; the rule of tyranny shall pass away
from the earth, and You alone, O Lord, shall have dominion
over all Your works, as it is written:

יִמְלֹךְ יְיָ לְעוֹלָם, אֱלֹהַיִךְ צִיּוֹן, לְדֹר וָדֹר. הַלְלוּיָהּ!

The Lord shall reign for ever; your God, O Zion, from
generation to generation. Halleluyah!

קָדוֹשׁ אַתָּה וְנוֹרָא שְׁמֶךָ, וְאֵין אֱלֹוהַּ מִבַּלְעָדֶיךָ,
כַּכָּתוּב:

You are holy; awesome is Your name; there is no God but
You.

וַיִּגְבַּהּ יְיָ צְבָאוֹת בַּמִּשְׁפָּט, וְהָאֵל הַקָּדוֹשׁ נִקְדַּשׁ
בִּצְדָקָה.

The Lord of Hosts is exalted by justice; the holy God is
sanctified by righteousness.

317

בָּרוּךְ אַתָּה, יְיָ, הַמֶּלֶךְ הַקָּדוֹשׁ.

°*Blessed is the Lord, who rules in holiness.*

◆ ◆

THE HOLINESS OF THIS DAY   קְדוּשַׁת הַיּוֹם

אַתָּה בְחַרְתָּנוּ מִכָּל־הָעַמִּים, אָהַבְתָּ אוֹתָנוּ וְרָצִיתָ
בָּנוּ, וְרוֹמַמְתָּנוּ מִכָּל־הַלְּשׁוֹנוֹת וְקִדַּשְׁתָּנוּ בְּמִצְוֹתֶיךָ,
וְקֵרַבְתָּנוּ מַלְכֵּנוּ לַעֲבוֹדָתֶךָ, וְשִׁמְךָ הַגָּדוֹל וְהַקָּדוֹשׁ
עָלֵינוּ קָרָאתָ. וַתִּתֶּן־לָנוּ, יְיָ אֱלֹהֵינוּ, בְּאַהֲבָה אֶת־יוֹם
(הַשַּׁבָּת הַזֶּה לִקְדֻשָּׁה וְלִמְנוּחָה וְאֶת־יוֹם) הַכִּפּוּרִים
הַזֶּה לִמְחִילָה וְלִסְלִיחָה וְלִכַפָּרָה וְלִמְחָל־בּוֹ אֶת־
כָּל־עֲוֹנוֹתֵינוּ, מִקְרָא קֹדֶשׁ, זֵכֶר לִיצִיאַת מִצְרָיִם.

°The House of Israel is called to holiness, to a covenant
with the Eternal for all time.

*We are called to serve the Most High; may we rejoice in this
heritage for ever.*

May this day add meaning to our lives. Let contrition
awaken our conscience, our common worship unite us in
love, our memories of bondage impel us to help the oppressed.

אֱלֹהֵינוּ וֵאלֹהֵי אֲבוֹתֵינוּ, יַעֲלֶה וְיָבֹא וְיִזָּכֵר זִכְרוֹנֵנוּ
וְזִכְרוֹן כָּל־עַמְּךָ בֵּית יִשְׂרָאֵל לְפָנֶיךָ, לְטוֹבָה לְחֵן
לְחֶסֶד וּלְרַחֲמִים, לְחַיִּים וּלְשָׁלוֹם בְּיוֹם הַכִּפּוּרִים
הַזֶּה.

זָכְרֵנוּ, יְיָ אֱלֹהֵינוּ, בּוֹ לְטוֹבָה. אָמֵן.

318

וּפָקְדֵנוּ בוֹ לִבְרָכָה. אָמֵן.
וְהוֹשִׁיעֵנוּ בוֹ לְחַיִּים. אָמֵן.

°*On this Day of Atonement we pray for awareness. Let love
and compassion grow among us, and goodness be our daily
care.*

This day may we find well-being. *Amen.*

This day may we discover the eternal strength that abides
among us. *Amen.*

This day may we be helped to a life that is whole. *Amen.*

אֱלֹהֵינוּ וֵאלֹהֵי אֲבוֹתֵינוּ, מְחַל לַעֲוֹנוֹתֵינוּ בְּיוֹם
(הַשַּׁבָּת הַזֶּה וּבְיוֹם) הַכִּפּוּרִים הַזֶּה, מְחֵה וְהַעֲבֵר
פְּשָׁעֵינוּ וְחַטֹּאתֵינוּ מִנֶּגֶד עֵינֶיךָ, כָּאָמוּר: "אָנֹכִי, אָנֹכִי
הוּא מֹחֶה פְשָׁעֶיךָ לְמַעֲנִי, וְחַטֹּאתֶיךָ לֹא אֶזְכֹּר."
וְנֶאֱמַר: "מָחִיתִי כָעָב פְּשָׁעֶיךָ, וְכֶעָנָן חַטֹּאתֶיךָ,
שׁוּבָה אֵלַי, כִּי גְאַלְתִּיךָ." וְנֶאֱמַר: "כִּי בַיּוֹם הַזֶּה יְכַפֵּר
עֲלֵיכֶם לְטַהֵר אֶתְכֶם; מִכֹּל חַטֹּאתֵיכֶם לִפְנֵי יְיָ
תִּטְהָרוּ."

°*We give thanks for the Mitzvot which hallow our days, and
pray for wisdom to guide our lives by Torah. May our
redemptive labors make us glad, our struggle for purity not
fail, and our striving for good bring us joy. Blessed is the vision of holiness that exalts (the Sabbath,) the House of
Israel and the Day of Atonement.*

• •

NEW STRENGTH FOR YOUR SERVICE   עבודה

רְצֵה, יְיָ אֱלֹהֵינוּ, בְּעַמְּךָ יִשְׂרָאֵל, וּתְפִלָּתָם בְּאַהֲבָה

תְּקַבֵּל, וּתְהִי לְרָצוֹן תָּמִיד עֲבוֹדַת יִשְׂרָאֵל עַמֶּךָ.
בָּרוּךְ אַתָּה, יְיָ, שֶׁאוֹתְךָ לְבַדְּךָ בְּיִרְאָה נַעֲבוֹד.

°You are with us in our prayer, in our love and our doubt,
in our longing to feel Your presence and to do Your will.
You are the still, clear voice within us. Therefore, O God,
when doubt troubles us, when anxiety makes us tremble,
and pain clouds the mind, we look inward for the answer
to our prayers. There may we find You, and there find
courage and endurance. And let our worship bring us
closer to one another, that all Israel, and all who seek
You, may find new strength for Your service.

• •

THANKSGIVING   הודאה

מוֹדִים אֲנַחְנוּ לָךְ, שָׁאַתָּה הוּא יְיָ אֱלֹהֵינוּ וֵאלֹהֵי
אֲבוֹתֵינוּ לְעוֹלָם וָעֶד. צוּר חַיֵּינוּ, מָגֵן יִשְׁעֵנוּ, אַתָּה
הוּא לְדוֹר וָדוֹר.

נוֹדֶה לְךָ וּנְסַפֵּר תְּהִלָּתֶךָ, עַל־חַיֵּינוּ הַמְּסוּרִים בְּיָדֶךָ,
וְעַל־נִשְׁמוֹתֵינוּ הַפְּקוּדוֹת לָךְ, וְעַל־נִסֶּיךָ שֶׁבְּכָל־יוֹם
עִמָּנוּ, וְעַל־נִפְלְאוֹתֶיךָ וְטוֹבוֹתֶיךָ שֶׁבְּכָל־עֵת, עֶרֶב
וָבֹקֶר וְצָהֳרָיִם. הַטּוֹב: כִּי לֹא־כָלוּ רַחֲמֶיךָ, וְהַמְרַחֵם:
כִּי־לֹא תַמּוּ חֲסָדֶיךָ, מֵעוֹלָם קִוִּינוּ לָךְ.

וּכְתֹב לְחַיִּים טוֹבִים כָּל־בְּנֵי בְרִיתֶךָ. בָּרוּךְ אַתָּה, יְיָ,
הַטּוֹב שִׁמְךָ, וּלְךָ נָאֶה לְהוֹדוֹת.

WE REJOICE

°Let us rejoice in the light of day, in the glory and warmth
of the sun, in the reawakening of life to duty and labor.

We rejoice in the light of day.

In the earth with its hills and valleys, its widespread fields of grain, its fruit and hidden treasures.

We rejoice in the beauty of earth.

In the love of fathers and mothers who have nurtured our lives, with whose blessing we have gone forth to our own work in the world.

We rejoice in the love of parents.

In the children who bless our homes, whose eager minds and hearts are the promise of tomorrow.

We rejoice in our children.

In friends who share our sorrows and joys, in the fullness of the abundant life, in the serenity of old age, and in the peace that comes at last.

We rejoice, and shall rejoice for evermore.

⋄ ⋄

PEACE · ברכת שלום

אֱלֹהֵינוּ וֵאלֹהֵי אֲבוֹתֵינוּ, בָּרְכֵנוּ בַּבְּרָכָה הַמְשֻׁלֶּשֶׁת הַכְּתוּבָה בַּתּוֹרָה:

Our God and God of all generations, bless us with the threefold benediction of the Torah:

יְבָרֶכְךָ יְיָ וְיִשְׁמְרֶךָ.

May the Lord bless you and keep you.

כֵּן יְהִי רָצוֹן!

Be this God's will!

יָאֵר יְיָ פָּנָיו אֵלֶיךָ וִיחֻנֶּךָ.

321

May the light of the Lord's presence shine upon you and
be gracious to you.

כֵּן יְהִי רָצוֹן!

Be this God's will!

יִשָּׂא יְיָ פָּנָיו אֵלֶיךָ וְיָשֵׂם לְךָ שָׁלוֹם.

May the Lord bestow favor upon you and give you peace.

כֵּן יְהִי רָצוֹן!

Be this God's will!

שִׂים שָׁלוֹם, טוֹבָה וּבְרָכָה, חֵן וָחֶסֶד וְרַחֲמִים, עָלֵינוּ
וְעַל כָּל־יִשְׂרָאֵל עַמֶּךָ. בָּרְכֵנוּ אָבִינוּ, כֻּלָּנוּ כְּאֶחָד,
בְּאוֹר פָּנֶיךָ, כִּי בְאוֹר פָּנֶיךָ נָתַתָּ לָּנוּ, יְיָ אֱלֹהֵינוּ,
תּוֹרַת חַיִּים, וְאַהֲבַת חֶסֶד, וּצְדָקָה וּבְרָכָה וְרַחֲמִים,
וְחַיִּים וְשָׁלוֹם. וְטוֹב בְּעֵינֶיךָ לְבָרֵךְ אֶת־עַמְּךָ יִשְׂרָאֵל
בְּכָל־עֵת וּבְכָל־שָׁעָה בִּשְׁלוֹמֶךָ. בְּסֵפֶר חַיִּים בְּרָכָה
וְשָׁלוֹם וּפַרְנָסָה טוֹבָה נִזָּכֵר וְנִכָּתֵב לְפָנֶיךָ, אֲנַחְנוּ
וְכָל־עַמְּךָ בֵּית יִשְׂרָאֵל, לְחַיִּים טוֹבִים וּלְשָׁלוֹם. בָּרוּךְ
אַתָּה, יְיָ, עוֹשֵׂה הַשָּׁלוֹם.

°Peace and happiness, blessing, grace, love, and mercy:
may these descend on all Israel and all the world. Bless us,
O God, one and all, with the light of Your presence; for in
the light of Your presence we find the fullness of life:
faithful love and charity, compassion, blessing, and peace.

*Help us, O God of peace, by our deeds to inscribe ourselves
in the Book of life and blessing, righteousness and peace.*

*Praised be the One who teaches Israel and all peoples to love
and pursue peace, and to bring it to all the earth.*

322

MEDITATION

Rabbi Samuel ben Nachmani said: At times the gates of prayer are open, at times the gates of prayer are barred. But the gates of repentance are never barred.

But it is reported that Rabbi Judah the Prince taught: In truth, the gates of prayer are never barred.

Rabbi Akiba taught: The gates of prayer are open, and the prayer of those who practice steadfast love is heard.

Rav Chisda taught: Though sometimes the gates of heaven seem shut to all prayers, they are open to the prayers of the wounded and the hurt.

◆ ◆

וַאֲנִי תְפִלָּתִי לְךָ, יְיָ, עֵת רָצוֹן.
אֱלֹהִים, בְּרָב־חַסְדֶּךָ, עֲנֵנִי בֶּאֱמֶת יִשְׁעֶךָ.

May my prayer now, O Lord, find favor before You. In Your great love, O God, answer me with Your saving truth.

◆ ◆

CONFESSION OF SIN   ודוי

For transgressions against God, the Day of Atonement
atones; but for transgressions of one human being against
another, the Day of Atonement does not atone until they
have made peace with one another.

*I hereby forgive all who have hurt me, all who have wronged
me, whether deliberately or inadvertently, whether by word
or by deed. May no one be punished on my account.*

*As I forgive and pardon those who have wronged me, may
those whom I have harmed forgive and pardon me, whether I
acted deliberately or inadvertently, whether by word or by
deed.*

All rise

אֱלֹהֵינוּ וֵאלֹהֵי אֲבוֹתֵינוּ, תָּבוֹא לְפָנֶיךָ תְּפִלָּתֵנוּ וְאַל
תִּתְעַלַּם מִתְּחִנָּתֵנוּ, שֶׁאֵין אֲנַחְנוּ עַזֵּי פָנִים וּקְשֵׁי עֹרֶף
לוֹמַר לְפָנֶיךָ, יְיָ אֱלֹהֵינוּ וֵאלֹהֵי אֲבוֹתֵינוּ, צַדִּיקִים
אֲנַחְנוּ וְלֹא חָטָאנוּ, אֲבָל אֲנַחְנוּ חָטָאנוּ. חָטָאנוּ,
עָוִינוּ, פָּשַׁעְנוּ.

*Our God, God of our mothers and fathers, grant that our
prayers may reach You. Do not be deaf to our pleas, for we
are not so arrogant and stiff-necked as to say before You,
Lord our God and God of all ages, we are perfect and have
not sinned; rather do we confess: we have gone astray, we
have sinned, we have transgressed.*

All are seated

⋅ ⋅

324

SILENT CONFESSION

In my individuality I turn to You, O God, and seek Your help. For You care for each of Your children. You are *my* God, and *my* Redeemer. Therefore, while around me others think their own thoughts, I think mine; and as each one of them seeks to experience Your presence, so do I.

Each person's abilities are limited by nature and by the circumstances we have had to face. Whether I have done better or worse with my capacities than others with theirs, I cannot judge.

But I do know that I have failed in many ways to live up to my potentialities and Your demands. Not that You expect the impossible. You do not ask me: 'Why have you not been great as Moses?' You do ask me: 'Why have you not been yourself? Why have you not been true to the best in *you?*'

I will not lay the blame on others, though they may have wronged me, nor on circumstances, though they may have been difficult. The fault lies mainly in myself.

I have been weak. Too often I have failed to make the required effort to do my work conscientiously, to give my full attention to those who needed me, to speak the kindly word, to do the generous deed, to express my concern for my friends. I have not loved enough, not even those closest to me.

I have also neglected my duties to my community. The Jewish people is only a remnant of what it was, a fragment of what it might have been. It needs strength to rebuild itself and to carry on the task entrusted to it by a hundred generations. Have I been a source of this strength? Have I enhanced its good name? Have I shared fully in its life? Have I even acquainted myself sufficiently with the history of my people and the teachings of my faith?

And do I not share some responsibility for the social evils which I see, hear about, and read about daily? Have I always used my opportunities as a citizen to relieve suffering, to speak out against injustice, to promote harmony in the life of my city, my country, and the nations of the world?

There is much that I failed to do. There is also much that I wish I had not done. By many words and deeds I have caused harm. It is not easy now to remember the details; out of guilt I tend to shut them out of my consciousness. But clearly or dimly, the regretted memories now come back to me. I have, in many ways, hurt my sisters and brothers; I have betrayed their trust, offended their sensibilities, damaged their self-respect. Sometimes, indeed, I have done harm from what seemed at the time good motives. Sometimes my supposed love for others was in reality only a desire to dominate them. And sometimes what I took to be righteous indignation was only uncontrolled anger or unforgiving vindictiveness.

How I wish I had learned to master myself; to control my impulses; to curb my craving for pleasure, power, and possessions; to display consistently those qualities which are most admirable in others! Have I made any progress at all in this, the greatest of all arts, the art of living? Perhaps a little; certainly not enough.

Why? Because I have not been true to myself. Because I have not nurtured sufficiently the good in me. For there *is* good in me. 'The soul that You have given me is pure!' There is that in me which condemns me when I do wrong and urges me to do right, which holds up before me the ideal, and challenges me to reach toward it. There is in me a spark of Your divinity.

How to realize the 'divine image' in me—there is the question and the answer. Surely it means to seek You more earnestly, to submit myself to Your will; to say to You: Here I am; mould me, guide me, command me, use me, let me be Your co-worker, an instrument of Your redemptive purpose.

Help me then, O God; help me always, but especially now, on this sacred Day of Atonement; help me to banish from myself whatever is mean, ugly, callous, cruel, stubborn, or otherwise unworthy of a being created in Your image. Purify me, revive me, uplift me. Forgive my past, and lead me into the future, resolved to be Your servant.

May the words of my mouth, and the meditations of my heart, be acceptable to You, O Lord, my Rock and my Redeemer. Amen.

◆ ◆

יִהְיוּ לְרָצוֹן אִמְרֵי־פִי וְהֶגְיוֹן לִבִּי לְפָנֶיךָ, יְיָ, צוּרִי
וְגוֹאֲלִי.

⋅⋅

אָשַׁמְנוּ, בָּגַדְנוּ, גָזַלְנוּ, דִּבַּרְנוּ דְפִי. הֶעֱוֵינוּ, וְהִרְשַׁעְנוּ,
זַדְנוּ, חָמַסְנוּ, טָפַלְנוּ שֶׁקֶר. יָעַצְנוּ רָע, כִּזַּבְנוּ, לַצְנוּ,
מָרַדְנוּ, נִאַצְנוּ, סָרַרְנוּ, עָוִינוּ, פָּשַׁעְנוּ, צָרַרְנוּ, קִשִּׁינוּ
עֹרֶף. רָשַׁעְנוּ, שִׁחַתְנוּ, תִּעַבְנוּ, תָּעִינוּ, תִּעְתָּעְנוּ.

°Who among us is righteous
enough to say: 'I have not sinned?'
We are arrogant, brutal, careless,
destructive, egocentric, false;
greedy, heartless, insolent,
and joyless.
Our sins are an alphabet of woe.

⋅⋅

וּבְכֵן יְהִי רָצוֹן מִלְּפָנֶיךָ, יְיָ אֱלֹהֵינוּ וֵאלֹהֵי אֲבוֹתֵינוּ,
שֶׁתִּסְלַח לָנוּ עַל כָּל־חַטֹּאתֵינוּ וְתִמְחַל לָנוּ עַל כָּל־
עֲונוֹתֵינוּ וּתְכַפֶּר־לָנוּ עַל כָּל־פְּשָׁעֵינוּ.

Now may it be Your will, O Lord God of all the generations, to pardon all our sins, to forgive all our wrongdoings, and to blot out all our transgressions:

על חטא

FAILURES OF TRUTH

We sin against You when we sin against ourselves.

For our failures of truth, O Lord, we ask forgiveness.

327

For passing judgment without knowledge of the facts,

and for distorting facts to fit our theories.

For deceiving ourselves and others with half-truths,

and for pretending to emotions we do not feel.

For using the sins of others to excuse our own,

and for denying responsibility for our own misfortunes.

For condemning in our children the faults we tolerate in ourselves,

and for condemning in our parents the faults we tolerate in ourselves.

FAILURES OF JUSTICE

We sin against You when we sin against ourselves.

For our failures of justice, O Lord, we ask forgiveness.

For keeping the poor in the chains of poverty,

and turning a deaf ear to the cry of the oppressed.

For using violence to maintain our power,

and for using violence to bring about change.

For waging aggressive war,

and for the sin of appeasing aggressors.

For obeying criminal orders,

and for the sin of silence and indifference.

For poisoning the air, and polluting land and sea,

and for all the evil means we employ to accomplish good ends.

FAILURES OF LOVE

We sin against You when we sin against ourselves.

For our failures of love, O Lord, we ask forgiveness.

For confusing love with lust,

and for pursuing fleeting pleasure at the cost of lasting hurt.

For using others as a means to gratify our desires,

and as stepping-stones to further our ambitions.

For withholding love to control those we claim to love,

and shunting aside those whose youth or age disturbs us.

For hiding from others behind an armor of mistrust,

and for the cynicism which leads us to mistrust the reality of unselfish love.

♦

Teach us to forgive ourselves for all these sins, O forgiving God, and help us to overcome them.

וְעַל כֻּלָּם, אֱלוֹהַּ סְלִיחוֹת, סְלַח־לָנוּ, מְחַל־לָנוּ, כַּפֶּר־לָנוּ!

For all these sins, O God of mercy, forgive us, pardon us, grant us atonement!

♦ ♦

עַל חֵטְא שֶׁחָטָאנוּ לְפָנֶיךָ בִּרְכִילוּת,

The sin we have committed against You by malicious gossip,

עַל חֵטְא שֶׁחָטָאנוּ לְפָנֶיךָ בְּגִלּוּי עֲרָיוֹת,

the sin we have committed against You by sexual immorality,

וְעַל חֵטְא שֶׁחָטָאנוּ לְפָנֶיךָ בְּמַאֲכָל וּבְמִשְׁתֶּה.

and the sin we have committed against You by gluttony.

עַל חֵטְא שֶׁחָטָאנוּ לְפָנֶיךָ בְּצָרוּת עָיִן,

The sin we have committed against You by narrowmindedness,

עַל חֵטְא שֶׁחָטָאנוּ לְפָנֶיךָ בְּכַחַשׁ וּבְכָזָב,

the sin we have committed against You by fraud and falsehood,

וְעַל חֵטְא שֶׁחָטָאנוּ לְפָנֶיךָ בְּשִׂנְאַת חִנָּם.

and the sin we have committed against You by hating without cause.

עַל חֵטְא שֶׁחָטָאנוּ לְפָנֶיךָ בִּנְטִיַת גָּרוֹן,

The sin we have committed against You by our arrogance,

עַל חֵטְא שֶׁחָטָאנוּ לְפָנֶיךָ בְּעַזּוּת מֶצַח,

the sin we have committed against You by our insolence,

וְעַל חֵטְא שֶׁחָטָאנוּ לְפָנֶיךָ בְּקַלּוּת רֹאשׁ.

and the sin we have committed against You by our irreverence.

עַל חֵטְא שֶׁחָטָאנוּ לְפָנֶיךָ בְּוִדּוּי פֶּה,

The sin we have committed against You by our hypocrisy,

עַל חֵטְא שֶׁחָטָאנוּ לְפָנֶיךָ בִּפְלִלוּת,

*the sin we have committed against You by passing judgment
on others,*

וְעַל חֵטְא שֶׁחָטָאנוּ לְפָנֶיךָ בְּנֶשֶׁךְ וּבְמַרְבִּית.

*and the sin we have committed against You by exploiting the
weak.*

עַל חֵטְא שֶׁחָטָאנוּ לְפָנֶיךָ בְּכַפַּת שֹׁחַד,

*The sin we have committed against You by giving and taking
bribes,*

עַל חֵטְא שֶׁחָטָאנוּ לְפָנֶיךָ בְּיֵצֶר הָרָע,

*the sin we have committed against You by giving way to our
hostile impulses,*

וְעַל חֵטְא שֶׁחָטָאנוּ לְפָנֶיךָ בְּרִיצַת רַגְלַיִם לְהָרַע.

*and the sin we have committed against You by running to do
evil.*

◆ ◆

וְעַל כֻּלָּם אֱלְוֹהַּ סְלִיחוֹת, סְלַח לָנוּ, מְחַל לָנוּ, כַּפֶּר־
לָנוּ!

*For all these sins, O God of mercy, forgive us, pardon us,
grant us atonement!*

◆ ◆

Merely to have survived is not an index of excellence.
Nor, given the way things go,
Even of low cunning.
Yet I have seen the wicked in great power,
And spreading himself like a green bay tree.
And the good as if they had never been;
Their voices are blown away on the winter wind.
And again we wander the wilderness

For our transgressions
Which are confessed in the daily papers.

Except the Lord of hosts had left unto us
A very small remnant,
We should have been as Sodom,
We should have been like unto Gomorrah.
And to what purpose, as the darkness closes about,
And the child screams in the jellied fire,
Had best be our present concern,
Here, in this wilderness of comfort
In which we dwell.

Shall we now consider
The suspicious postures of our virtue,
The deformed consequences of our love,
The painful issues of our mildest acts?
Shall we ask,
Where is there one
Mad, poor and betrayed enough to find
Forgiveness for us, saying,
"None does offend,
None, I say,
None"?
Listen, listen,
But the voices are blown away.
    And yet, this light,
    The work of thy fingers, . . .

The soul is thine, and the body is thy creation:
O have compassion on thy handiwork.
The soul is thine, and the body is thine:
O deal with us according to thy name.
We come before thee relying on thy name:
O deal with us according to thy name;
For the sake of the glory of thy name;
As the gracious and merciful God is thy name.

O Lord, for thy name's sake we plead,
Forgive us our sins, though they be very great . . . .

•

From Psalms 32 and 34

Happy are those whose transgression is forgiven, whose sin is pardoned.

Happy is the one whom the Lord holds guiltless,
and in whose spirit there is no guile.

While I kept silent, my heart groaned with anguish all day long.

For day and night Your hand was heavy upon me.

Then I confessed my sin to You, concealing my guilt no more; and You forgave me.

I sought the Lord, who answered me, delivering me from all my fears.

Taste and see that the Lord is good! Happy is the one who takes refuge in God.

Come, my children, listen to me! Let me teach you the meaning of faith.

Who among you loves life, and longs to enjoy good for many days?

Then guard your tongue from evil, and your lips from deceitful speech.

Turn away from evil, and do good; seek peace, and pursue it.

The Lord has regard for the righteous, and hearkens to their plea.

PRAYERS FOR FORGIVENESS   סליחות

On this day, Eternal God, we come to You aware of our failings. Help us to cast our sins away, and to find peace.

סְלַח לָנוּ, אָבִינוּ, כִּי בְרֹב אִוַּלְתֵּנוּ שָׁגִינוּ. מְחַל לָנוּ,
מַלְכֵּנוּ, כִּי רַבּוּ עֲוֹנֵינוּ.

Source of our life: when in our folly we go astray, forgive us.
Sovereign God, pardon our many sins.

כִּי עַל רַחֲמֶיךָ הָרַבִּים אָנוּ בְטוּחִים, וְעַל צִדְקוֹתֶיךָ
אָנוּ נִשְׁעָנִים, וְלִסְלִיחוֹתֶיךָ אָנוּ מְצַפִּים, וְלִישׁוּעָתְךָ
אָנוּ מְקַוִּים.
סְלַח לָנוּ, אָבִינוּ, כִּי חָטָאנוּ; מְחַל לָנוּ, מַלְכֵּנוּ, כִּי
פָשָׁעְנוּ; כִּי אַתָּה אֲדֹנָי טוֹב וְסַלָּח, וְרַב חֶסֶד לְכָל־
קֹרְאֶיךָ.

In Your great mercy we place our faith; Your kindness is our support. In Your forgiveness we trust; Your deliverance is our hope.

Source of our life: we have sinned; forgive us. Grant us
pardon, O Sovereign God, for we have transgressed. Lord,
You are the Good from whom forgiveness flows, and with
boundless love You respond to all who call upon You.

◆ ◆

כְּרַחֵם אָב עַל־בָּנִים, רִחַם יְיָ עַל־יְרֵאָיו. כִּי כִגְבֹהַּ
שָׁמַיִם עַל־הָאָרֶץ, גָּבַר חַסְדּוֹ עַל־יְרֵאָיו.

As parents show compassion to their children, so do You, Lord, show compassion to those who revere You. For as the heavens are high above the earth, so is Your love unending for those who serve You.

◆ ◆

334

סְלַח נָא לַעֲוֹן הָעָם הַזֶּה כְּגֹֽדֶל חַסְדֶּֽךָ, וְכַאֲשֶׁר נָשָֽׂאתָ
לָעָם הַזֶּה מִמִּצְרַֽיִם וְעַד הֵֽנָּה.

As, in Your love, You have been patient with this people
from the time You led us out of Egypt to the present day,
so, in Your great love, may You forgive Your people now.

◆

וַיֹּֽאמֶר יְיָ: "סָלַֽחְתִּי כִּדְבָרֶֽךָ."

And the Lord said: I have pardoned in response to your
plea.

◆ ◆

Who can say: I have purified my heart, and I am free from
sin?

There are none on earth so righteous that they never sin.

Cast away all the evil you have done, and get yourselves a
new heart and a new spirit.

*A new heart will I give you, a new spirit put within you. I will
remove the heart of stone from your flesh, and give you a
heart that feels.*

For thus says the Eternal God: I, I Myself will search for
My sheep, and seek them out.

*As a shepherd seeks them out when any of the flock go
astray, so will I seek out My sheep.*

I will put My spirit within you, and teach you to live by
My laws.

*For I desire love and not sacrifices, the knowledge of God
rather than burnt offerings.*

335

Wash yourselves, make yourselves clean; remove the evil of your doings from before My eyes; cease to do evil; learn to do good.

Seek justice; correct oppression; defend the orphan; plead for the widow.

Seek the Lord your God, whom you shall find if you search with all your heart and soul.

Show us Your love, O Lord, and grant us Your help.

◆ ◆

שְׁמַע קוֹלֵנוּ, יְיָ אֱלֹהֵינוּ, חוּס וְרַחֵם עָלֵינוּ, וְקַבֵּל בְּרַחֲמִים וּבְרָצוֹן אֶת־תְּפִלָּתֵנוּ. הֲשִׁיבֵנוּ יְיָ אֵלֶיךָ וְנָשׁוּבָה, חַדֵּשׁ יָמֵינוּ כְּקֶדֶם.

Hear our voice, O Lord our God; have compassion upon us, and with that compassion accept our prayer. Help us to return to You, O Lord; then truly shall we return. Renew our days as in the past.

◆ ◆

אֱלֹהֵינוּ וֵאלֹהֵי אֲבוֹתֵינוּ, אַל תַּעַזְבֵנוּ וְאַל תִּטְּשֵׁנוּ וְאַל תַּכְלִימֵנוּ, וְאַל תָּפֵר בְּרִיתְךָ אִתָּנוּ. קָרְבֵנוּ לְתוֹרָתֶךָ, לַמְּדֵנוּ מִצְוֹתֶיךָ, הוֹרֵנוּ דְרָכֶיךָ, הַט לִבֵּנוּ לְיִרְאָה אֶת־שְׁמֶךָ, וּמוֹל אֶת־לְבָבֵנוּ לְאַהֲבָתֶךָ, וְנָשׁוּב אֵלֶיךָ בֶּאֱמֶת וּבְלֵב שָׁלֵם.

°*Our God, God of all generations, may the sense of Your presence never leave us; may it keep us ever faithful to Your covenant. Make us responsive to Your teaching, that we may walk in Your ways. Fill our souls with awe, and our hearts with love, that we may return to You in truth, and with all our being.*

336

We are Your people,
You are our King.
We are Your children,
You are our Father.
We are Your possession,
You are our portion.
We are Your flock,
You are our Shepherd.
We are Your vineyard,
You are our Keeper.
We are Your beloved,
You are our Friend.

כִּי אָנוּ עַמֶּךָ, וְאַתָּה מַלְכֵּנוּ.

אָנוּ בָנֶיךָ, וְאַתָּה אָבִינוּ.

אָנוּ נַחֲלָתֶךָ, וְאַתָּה גוֹרָלֵנוּ.

אָנוּ צֹאנֶךָ, וְאַתָּה רוֹעֵנוּ.

אָנוּ כַרְמֶךָ, וְאַתָּה נוֹטְרֵנוּ.

אָנוּ רַעְיָתֶךָ, וְאַתָּה דוֹדֵנוּ.

∴

סדר קריאת התורה

For the Reading of the Torah

And Moses said: O let me behold Your glory! Then God
said: I will make all My goodness pass before you, and
will proclaim My name before you. Behold, there is a
place by Me where you shall stand upon the rock . . . .

רוֹמְמוּ יְיָ אֱלֹהֵינוּ, וְהִשְׁתַּחֲווּ לְהַר קָדְשׁוֹ, כִּי קָדוֹשׁ יְיָ
אֱלֹהֵינוּ.

Let us exalt the Lord our God, and worship at His holy mountain, for the Lord our God is holy.

◆ ◆

All rise

The Ark is opened

יְיָ, יְיָ אֵל רַחוּם וְחַנּוּן, אֶרֶךְ אַפַּיִם וְרַב־חֶסֶד וֶאֱמֶת,
נוֹצֵר חֶסֶד לָאֲלָפִים, נֹשֵׂא עָוֹן וָפֶשַׁע וְחַטָּאָה וְנַקֵּה.

The Lord, the Lord God is merciful and gracious, endlessly patient, loving, and true, showing mercy to thousands,
forgiving iniquity, transgression, and sin, and granting
pardon.

◆ ◆

338

אבינו מלכנו

אָבִֽינוּ מַלְכֵּֽנוּ, חָטָֽאנוּ לְפָנֶֽיךָ.

Our Father, our King, we have sinned before You.

אָבִֽינוּ מַלְכֵּֽנוּ, הַחֲזִירֵֽנוּ בִּתְשׁוּבָה שְׁלֵמָה לְפָנֶֽיךָ.

Our Father, our King, bring us back to You in full repentance.

אָבִֽינוּ מַלְכֵּֽנוּ, סְלַח וּמְחַל לְכָל עֲוֹנוֹתֵֽינוּ.

Our Father, our King, forgive and pardon all our misdeeds.

אָבִֽינוּ מַלְכֵּֽנוּ, חֲמוֹל עָלֵֽינוּ וְעַל עוֹלָלֵֽינוּ וְטַפֵּֽנוּ.

Our Father, our King, have compassion on us and on our children.

אָבִֽינוּ מַלְכֵּֽנוּ, כַּלֵּה דֶֽבֶר וְחֶֽרֶב וְרָעָב מֵעָלֵֽינוּ.

Our Father, our King, make an end to sickness, war, and famine.

אָבִֽינוּ מַלְכֵּֽנוּ, כָּתְבֵֽנוּ בְּסֵֽפֶר חַיִּים טוֹבִים.

Our Father, our King, inscribe us for blessing in the Book of Life.

אָבִֽינוּ מַלְכֵּֽנוּ, חַדֵּשׁ עָלֵֽינוּ שָׁנָה טוֹבָה.

Our Father, our King, let the new year be a good year for us.

אָבִֽינוּ מַלְכֵּֽנוּ, עֲשֵׂה עִמָּֽנוּ לְמַֽעַן שְׁמֶֽךָ.

Our Father, our King, help us to exalt Your name in the world.

אָבִֽינוּ מַלְכֵּֽנוּ, קַבֵּל בְּרַחֲמִים וּבְרָצוֹן אֶת־תְּפִלָּתֵֽנוּ.

Our Father, our King, in Your mercy accept our prayer.

אָבִינוּ מַלְכֵּנוּ, חָנֵּנוּ וַעֲנֵנוּ, כִּי אֵין בָּנוּ מַעֲשִׂים, עֲשֵׂה
עִמָּנוּ צְדָקָה וָחֶסֶד וְהוֹשִׁיעֵנוּ.

*Our Father, our King, be gracious and answer us, for we
have little merit. Treat us generously and with kindness, and
be our help.*

• •

The Torah is taken from the Ark

וַאֲנִי זֹאת בְּרִיתִי אוֹתָם, אָמַר יְיָ: רוּחִי אֲשֶׁר עָלֶיךָ,
וּדְבָרַי אֲשֶׁר־שַׂמְתִּי בְּפִיךָ, לֹא־יָמוּשׁוּ מִפִּיךָ וּמִפִּי
זַרְעֲךָ וּמִפִּי זֶרַע זַרְעֲךָ, אָמַר יְיָ, מֵעַתָּה וְעַד־עוֹלָם.

As for Me, this is My covenant with them, says the Lord:
Let not My spirit, and the words that I have put in your
mouth, depart from you, nor from your children or their
children, from this time forth and for ever.

• •

בָּרוּךְ שֶׁנָּתַן תּוֹרָה לְעַמּוֹ יִשְׂרָאֵל בִּקְדֻשָּׁתוֹ.

Praised be the One who in His holiness has given the Torah to
His people Israel.

• •

שְׁמַע יִשְׂרָאֵל: יְיָ אֱלֹהֵינוּ, יְיָ אֶחָד!

Hear, O Israel: the Lord is our God, the Lord is One!

אֶחָד אֱלֹהֵינוּ, גָּדוֹל אֲדוֹנֵינוּ, קָדוֹשׁ וְנוֹרָא שְׁמוֹ.

Our God is One: our Lord is great; holy and awesome is His
name.

• •

340

הָבוּ גְדֶל לֵאלֹהֵינוּ וּתְנוּ כָבוֹד לַתּוֹרָה.

Let us declare the greatness of our God and give honor to
the Torah.

◆ ◆

לְךָ, יְיָ, הַגְּדֻלָּה וְהַגְּבוּרָה וְהַתִּפְאֶרֶת וְהַנֵּצַח וְהַהוֹד,
כִּי כֹל בַּשָּׁמַיִם וּבָאָרֶץ, לְךָ יְיָ הַמַּמְלָכָה וְהַמִּתְנַשֵּׂא
לְכֹל לְרֹאשׁ.

Yours, Lord, is the greatness, the power, the glory, the victory,
and the majesty; for all that is in heaven and earth is Yours.
Yours is the kingdom, O Lord; You are supreme over all.

All are seated

◆ ◆

341

Reading of the Torah

Before the Reading

בָּרְכוּ אֶת־יְיָ הַמְבֹרָךְ!
בָּרוּךְ יְיָ הַמְבֹרָךְ לְעוֹלָם וָעֶד!
בָּרוּךְ אַתָּה, יְיָ אֱלֹהֵינוּ, מֶלֶךְ הָעוֹלָם, אֲשֶׁר בָּחַר־בָּנוּ
מִכָּל־הָעַמִּים וְנָתַן־לָנוּ אֶת־תּוֹרָתוֹ. בָּרוּךְ אַתָּה, יְיָ,
נוֹתֵן הַתּוֹרָה.

∵

Deuteronomy 29.9–14; 30.11–20

אַתֶּם נִצָּבִים הַיּוֹם כֻּלְּכֶם לִפְנֵי יהוה אֱלֹהֵיכֶם רָאשֵׁיכֶם שִׁבְטֵיכֶם
זִקְנֵיכֶם וְשֹׁטְרֵיכֶם כֹּל אִישׁ יִשְׂרָאֵל: טַפְּכֶם נְשֵׁיכֶם וְגֵרְךָ אֲשֶׁר
בְּקֶרֶב מַחֲנֶיךָ מֵחֹטֵב עֵצֶיךָ עַד שֹׁאֵב מֵימֶיךָ: לְעָבְרְךָ בִּבְרִית
יהוה אֱלֹהֶיךָ וּבְאָלָתוֹ אֲשֶׁר יהוה אֱלֹהֶיךָ כֹּרֵת עִמְּךָ הַיּוֹם:
לְמַעַן הָקִים־אֹתְךָ הַיּוֹם לוֹ לְעָם וְהוּא יִהְיֶה־לְּךָ לֵאלֹהִים כַּאֲשֶׁר
דִּבֶּר־לָךְ וְכַאֲשֶׁר נִשְׁבַּע לַאֲבֹתֶיךָ לְאַבְרָהָם לְיִצְחָק וּלְיַעֲקֹב:
וְלֹא אִתְּכֶם לְבַדְּכֶם אָנֹכִי כֹּרֵת אֶת־הַבְּרִית הַזֹּאת וְאֶת־הָאָלָה
הַזֹּאת: כִּי אֶת־אֲשֶׁר יֶשְׁנוֹ פֹּה עִמָּנוּ עֹמֵד הַיּוֹם לִפְנֵי יהוה אֱלֹהֵינוּ
וְאֵת אֲשֶׁר אֵינֶנּוּ פֹּה עִמָּנוּ הַיּוֹם:
כִּי הַמִּצְוָה הַזֹּאת אֲשֶׁר אָנֹכִי מְצַוְּךָ הַיּוֹם
לֹא־נִפְלֵאת הִוא מִמְּךָ וְלֹא־רְחֹקָה הִוא: לֹא בַשָּׁמַיִם הִוא
לֵאמֹר מִי יַעֲלֶה־לָּנוּ הַשָּׁמַיְמָה וְיִקָּחֶהָ לָּנוּ וְיַשְׁמִעֵנוּ אֹתָהּ
וְנַעֲשֶׂנָּה: וְלֹא־מֵעֵבֶר לַיָּם הִוא לֵאמֹר מִי יַעֲבָר־לָנוּ אֶל־עֵבֶר
הַיָּם וְיִקָּחֶהָ לָּנוּ וְיַשְׁמִעֵנוּ אֹתָהּ וְנַעֲשֶׂנָּה: כִּי־קָרוֹב אֵלֶיךָ הַדָּבָר
מְאֹד בְּפִיךָ וּבִלְבָבְךָ לַעֲשֹׂתוֹ: רְאֵה נָתַתִּי לְפָנֶיךָ

Reading of the Torah

Before the Reading

Praise the Lord, to whom our praise is due!
Praised be the Lord, to whom our praise is due,
now and for ever!

Praised be the Lord our God, Ruler of the universe, who
has chosen us from all peoples by giving us His Torah.
Blessed is the Lord, Giver of the Torah.

◆ ◆

Deuteronomy 29.9–14; 30.11–20

You stand this day, all of you, before the Lord your
God—the heads of your tribes, your elders and officers,
every one in Israel, men, women, and children, and the
strangers in your camp, from the one who chops your
wood to the one who draws your water—to enter into the
sworn covenant which the Lord your God makes with you
this day, in order to establish you henceforth as the people
whose only God is the Lord, as you had been promised,
and as God had sworn to your fathers, to Abraham, Isaac,
and Jacob.

And it is not with you alone that I make this sworn covenant: I make it with those who are standing here with us
today before the Lord our God, and equally with all who
are not here with us today.

For this commandment which I command you this day is
not too hard for you, nor too remote. It is not in heaven,
that you should say: 'Who will go up for us to heaven and
bring it down to us, that we may do it?' Nor is it beyond
the sea, that you should say: 'Who will cross the sea for us
and bring it over to us, that we may do it?' No, it is very

הַיּוֹם אֶת־הַחַיִּים וְאֶת־הַטּוֹב וְאֶת־הַמָּוֶת וְאֶת־הָרָע: אֲשֶׁר
אָנֹכִי מְצַוְּךָ הַיּוֹם לְאַהֲבָה אֶת־יְהוָה אֱלֹהֶיךָ לָלֶכֶת בִּדְרָכָיו
וְלִשְׁמֹר מִצְוֹתָיו וְחֻקֹּתָיו וּמִשְׁפָּטָיו וְחָיִיתָ וְרָבִיתָ וּבֵרַכְךָ יְהוָה
אֱלֹהֶיךָ בָּאָרֶץ אֲשֶׁר־אַתָּה בָא־שָׁמָּה לְרִשְׁתָּהּ: וְאִם־יִפְנֶה
לְבָבְךָ וְלֹא תִשְׁמָע וְנִדַּחְתָּ וְהִשְׁתַּחֲוִיתָ לֵאלֹהִים אֲחֵרִים
וַעֲבַדְתָּם: הִגַּדְתִּי לָכֶם הַיּוֹם כִּי אָבֹד תֹּאבֵדוּן לֹא־תַאֲרִיכֻן
יָמִים עַל־הָאֲדָמָה אֲשֶׁר אַתָּה עֹבֵר אֶת־הַיַּרְדֵּן לָבוֹא שָׁמָּה
לְרִשְׁתָּהּ: הַעִדֹתִי בָכֶם הַיּוֹם אֶת־הַשָּׁמַיִם וְאֶת־הָאָרֶץ הַחַיִּים
וְהַמָּוֶת נָתַתִּי לְפָנֶיךָ הַבְּרָכָה וְהַקְּלָלָה וּבָחַרְתָּ בַּחַיִּים לְמַעַן
תִּחְיֶה אַתָּה וְזַרְעֶךָ: לְאַהֲבָה אֶת־יְהוָה אֱלֹהֶיךָ לִשְׁמֹעַ בְּקֹלוֹ
וּלְדָבְקָה־בוֹ כִּי הוּא חַיֶּיךָ וְאֹרֶךְ יָמֶיךָ לָשֶׁבֶת עַל־הָאֲדָמָה
אֲשֶׁר נִשְׁבַּע יְהוָה לַאֲבֹתֶיךָ לְאַבְרָהָם לְיִצְחָק וּלְיַעֲקֹב לָתֵת
לָהֶם:

After the Reading

בָּרוּךְ אַתָּה, יְיָ אֱלֹהֵינוּ, מֶלֶךְ הָעוֹלָם, אֲשֶׁר נָתַן לָנוּ
תּוֹרַת אֱמֶת וְחַיֵּי עוֹלָם נָטַע בְּתוֹכֵנוּ. בָּרוּךְ אַתָּה, יְיָ,
נוֹתֵן הַתּוֹרָה.

As the reading is completed, the Torah might be held high
while this is said or sung:

וְזֹאת הַתּוֹרָה אֲשֶׁר־שָׂם מֹשֶׁה לִפְנֵי בְּנֵי יִשְׂרָאֵל, עַל־
פִּי יְיָ בְּיַד־מֹשֶׁה.

∵

near to you, in your mouth and in your heart, and you can do it.

See, I have set before you this day life and good, or death and evil. For I command you this day to love the Lord, to walk in the ways and to keep the commandments, laws, and teachings of your God, that you may live and increase, and that the Lord your God may bless you in the land that you are about to occupy. But if your heart turns away and you do not listen, but let yourself be lured away to worship other gods, and serve them, I warn you now that you will perish: you will not live long in the land which you are crossing the Jordan to enter and inherit.

I call heaven and earth to witness against you this day that I have set before you life or death, blessing or curse; choose life, therefore, that you and your descendants may live—by loving the Lord your God, listening to God's voice, and holding fast to the One who is your life and the length of your days. Then you shall endure in the land which the Lord promised to your fathers, to Abraham, Isaac, and Jacob.

After the Reading

Praised be the Lord our God, Ruler of the universe, who has given us a Torah of truth, implanting within us eternal life. Blessed is the Lord, Giver of the Torah.

◆ ◆

As the reading is completed, the Torah might be held high while this is said or sung:

This is the Torah that Moses placed before the people of Israel to fulfill the word of God.

◆ ◆

345

Reading of the Haftarah

Before the Reading

בָּרוּךְ אַתָּה, יְיָ אֱלֹהֵינוּ, מֶלֶךְ הָעוֹלָם, אֲשֶׁר בָּחַר
בִּנְבִיאִים טוֹבִים וְרָצָה בְדִבְרֵיהֶם הַנֶּאֱמָרִים בֶּאֱמֶת.
בָּרוּךְ אַתָּה, יְיָ, הַבּוֹחֵר בַּתּוֹרָה וּבְמֹשֶׁה עַבְדּוֹ
וּבְיִשְׂרָאֵל עַמּוֹ וּבִנְבִיאֵי הָאֱמֶת וָצֶדֶק.

∴

Isaiah 58.1–14

קְרָא בְגָרוֹן אַל־תַּחְשֹׂךְ כַּשּׁוֹפָר הָרֵם
קוֹלֶךָ וְהַגֵּד לְעַמִּי פִּשְׁעָם וּלְבֵית יַעֲקֹב חַטֹּאתָם: וְאוֹתִי יוֹם יוֹם
יִדְרֹשׁוּן וְדַעַת דְּרָכַי יֶחְפָּצוּן כְּגוֹי אֲשֶׁר־צְדָקָה עָשָׂה וּמִשְׁפַּט
אֱלֹהָיו לֹא עָזָב יִשְׁאָלוּנִי מִשְׁפְּטֵי־צֶדֶק קִרְבַת אֱלֹהִים יֶחְפָּצוּן:
לָמָּה צַּמְנוּ וְלֹא רָאִיתָ עִנִּינוּ נַפְשֵׁנוּ וְלֹא תֵדָע הֵן בְּיוֹם צֹמְכֶם
תִּמְצְאוּ־חֵפֶץ וְכָל־עַצְּבֵיכֶם תִּנְגֹּשׂוּ: הֵן לְרִיב וּמַצָּה תָּצוּמוּ
וּלְהַכּוֹת בְּאֶגְרֹף רֶשַׁע לֹא־תָצוּמוּ כַיּוֹם לְהַשְׁמִיעַ בַּמָּרוֹם
קוֹלְכֶם: הֲכָזֶה יִהְיֶה צוֹם אֶבְחָרֵהוּ יוֹם עַנּוֹת אָדָם נַפְשׁוֹ הֲלָכֹף
כְּאַגְמֹן רֹאשׁוֹ וְשַׂק וָאֵפֶר יַצִּיעַ הֲלָזֶה תִּקְרָא־צוֹם וְיוֹם רָצוֹן
לַיהוָה: הֲלוֹא זֶה צוֹם אֶבְחָרֵהוּ פַּתֵּחַ חַרְצֻבּוֹת רֶשַׁע הַתֵּר
אֲגֻדּוֹת מוֹטָה וְשַׁלַּח רְצוּצִים חָפְשִׁים וְכָל־מוֹטָה תְּנַתֵּקוּ: הֲלוֹא
פָרֹס לָרָעֵב לַחְמֶךָ וַעֲנִיִּים מְרוּדִים תָּבִיא בָיִת כִּי־תִרְאֶה עָרֹם
וְכִסִּיתוֹ וּמִבְּשָׂרְךָ לֹא תִתְעַלָּם: אָז יִבָּקַע כַּשַּׁחַר אוֹרֶךָ וַאֲרֻכָתְךָ
מְהֵרָה תִצְמָח וְהָלַךְ לְפָנֶיךָ צִדְקֶךָ כְּבוֹד יְהוָה יַאַסְפֶךָ: אָז
תִּקְרָא וַיהוָה יַעֲנֶה תְּשַׁוַּע וְיֹאמַר הִנֵּנִי אִם־תָּסִיר מִתּוֹכְךָ

Reading of the Haftarah

Before the Reading

Praised be the Lord our God, Ruler of the universe, who has chosen faithful prophets to speak words of truth. Blessed is the Lord, for the revelation of Torah, for Moses His servant and Israel His people, and for the prophets of truth and righteousness.

◆ ◆

Isaiah 58.1—14

God says: Cry aloud, do not hold back, let your voice resound like a Shofar: declare to My people their transgression, and to the house of Jacob their sin. Yes, they seek Me daily, as though eager to learn My ways, as if they were a nation that does what is right, and has not forsaken the teachings of its God.

They ask of Me the right way, as though eager for the nearness of God. 'When we fast,' you say, 'why do You pay no heed? Why, when we afflict ourselves, do You take no notice?'

Because on your fast day you think only of your business, and oppress all your workers! Because your fasting leads only to strife and discord, and hitting out with cruel fist! Such a way of fasting on this day will not help you to be heard on high.

Is this the fast I look for? A day of self-affliction? Bowing your head like a reed, and covering yourself with sackcloth and ashes? Is this what you call a fast, a day acceptable to the Lord? Is not *this* the fast I look for: to unlock the shackles of injustice, to undo the fetters of bondage, to let the oppressed go free, and to break every cruel

347

מוֹטָה שְׁלַח אֶצְבַּע וְדַבֶּר־אָוֶן: וְתָפֵק לָרָעֵב נַפְשֶׁךָ וְנֶפֶשׁ נַעֲנָה
תַּשְׂבִּיעַ וְזָרַח בַּחֹשֶׁךְ אוֹרֶךָ וַאֲפֵלָתְךָ כַּצָּהֳרָיִם: וְנָחֲךָ יהוה
תָּמִיד וְהִשְׂבִּיעַ בְּצַחְצָחוֹת נַפְשֶׁךָ וְעַצְמֹתֶיךָ יַחֲלִיץ וְהָיִיתָ כְּגַן
רָוֶה וּכְמוֹצָא מַיִם אֲשֶׁר לֹא־יְכַזְּבוּ מֵימָיו: וּבָנוּ מִמְּךָ חָרְבוֹת
עוֹלָם מוֹסְדֵי דוֹר־וָדוֹר תְּקוֹמֵם וְקֹרָא לְךָ גֹּדֵר פֶּרֶץ מְשׁוֹבֵב
נְתִיבוֹת לָשָׁבֶת: אִם־תָּשִׁיב מִשַּׁבָּת רַגְלֶךָ עֲשׂוֹת חֲפָצֶךָ בְּיוֹם
קָדְשִׁי וְקָרָאתָ לַשַּׁבָּת עֹנֶג לִקְדוֹשׁ יהוה מְכֻבָּד וְכִבַּדְתּוֹ
מֵעֲשׂוֹת דְּרָכֶיךָ מִמְּצוֹא חֶפְצְךָ וְדַבֵּר דָּבָר: אָז תִּתְעַנַּג עַל־
יהוה וְהִרְכַּבְתִּיךָ עַל־בָּמֳותֵי אָרֶץ וְהַאֲכַלְתִּיךָ נַחֲלַת יַעֲקֹב
אָבִיךָ כִּי פִּי יהוה דִּבֵּר:

∵

348

chain? Is it not to share your bread with the hungry, and to bring the homeless poor into your house? When you see the naked, to clothe them, and never to hide yourself from your own kin?

Then shall your light blaze forth like the dawn, and your wounds shall quickly heal; your Righteous One will walk before you, the Presence of the Lord will be your rear guard. Then, when you call, the Lord will answer; when you cry, God will say: 'Here I am.'

If you remove the chains of oppression, the menacing hand, the malicious word; if you make sacrifices for the hungry, and satisfy the needs of the afflicted; then shall your light shine in the darkness, and your night become bright as noon; the Lord will guide you always; He will slake your thirst in drought, and renew your body's strength; you shall be like a watered garden, like an unfailing spring. Your people shall rebuild the ancient ruins, and lay the foundations for ages to come. You shall be called 'Repairer of the breach, Restorer of streets to dwell in.'

If you refrain from trampling the Sabbath, from pursuing your affairs on My holy day; if you call the Sabbath a delight, and honor the Lord's holy day; if you treat it with reverence, and do not look to your business or speak of it—then you can seek the favor of the Lord. I will cause you to ride upon the high places of the earth, and I will feed you with the heritage of Jacob your father. This is the promise of the Lord.

✦ ✦

After the Reading

An alternative version of this Benediction follows below

בָּרוּךְ אַתָּה, יְיָ אֱלֹהֵינוּ, מֶלֶךְ הָעוֹלָם, צוּר כָּל־
הָעוֹלָמִים, צַדִּיק בְּכָל־הַדּוֹרוֹת, הָאֵל הַנֶּאֱמָן,
הָאוֹמֵר וְעוֹשֶׂה, הַמְדַבֵּר וּמְקַיֵּם, שֶׁכָּל־דְּבָרָיו אֱמֶת
וָצֶדֶק.

עַל הַתּוֹרָה וְעַל הָעֲבוֹדָה וְעַל הַנְּבִיאִים וְעַל (יוֹם
הַשַּׁבָּת הַזֶּה וְעַל) יוֹם הַכִּפּוּרִים הַזֶּה, שֶׁנָּתַתָּ לָּנוּ, יְיָ
אֱלֹהֵינוּ, (לִקְדֻשָּׁה וְלִמְנוּחָה) לִמְחִילָה וְלִסְלִיחָה
וּלְכַפָּרָה, לְכָבוֹד וּלְתִפְאָרֶת, עַל הַכֹּל, יְיָ אֱלֹהֵינוּ,
אֲנַחְנוּ מוֹדִים לָךְ, וּמְבָרְכִים אוֹתָךְ. יִתְבָּרַךְ שִׁמְךָ בְּפִי
כָּל־חַי תָּמִיד לְעוֹלָם וָעֶד. וּדְבָרְךָ אֱמֶת וְקַיָּם לָעַד.
בָּרוּךְ אַתָּה, יְיָ, מֶלֶךְ מוֹחֵל וְסוֹלֵחַ לַעֲוֹנוֹתֵינוּ
וְלַעֲוֹנוֹת עַמּוֹ בֵּית יִשְׂרָאֵל, וּמַעֲבִיר אַשְׁמוֹתֵינוּ בְּכָל־
שָׁנָה וְשָׁנָה, מֶלֶךְ עַל כָּל־הָאָרֶץ, מְקַדֵּשׁ (הַשַּׁבָּת וְ)
יִשְׂרָאֵל וְיוֹם הַכִּפּוּרִים.

Continue on page 354

Alternative Version

בָּרוּךְ אַתָּה, יְיָ אֱלֹהֵינוּ, מֶלֶךְ הָעוֹלָם, צוּר כָּל־
הָעוֹלָמִים, צַדִּיק בְּכָל־הַדּוֹרוֹת, הָאֵל הַנֶּאֱמָן,
הָאוֹמֵר וְעוֹשֶׂה, הַמְדַבֵּר וּמְקַיֵּם, שֶׁכָּל־דְּבָרָיו אֱמֶת
וָצֶדֶק.

נֶאֱמָן אַתָּה הוּא יְיָ אֱלֹהֵינוּ, וְנֶאֱמָנִים דְּבָרֶיךָ, וְדָבָר
אֶחָד מִדְּבָרֶיךָ אָחוֹר לֹא־יָשׁוּב רֵיקָם, כִּי אֵל מֶלֶךְ

After the Reading

An alternative version of this Benediction follows below

Praised be the Lord our God, Ruler of the universe, Rock of all creation, righteous in all generations, the faithful God whose word is deed, whose every command is just and true.

For the Torah, for the privilege of worship, for the prophets, and for this (Shabbat and this) Day of Atonement that You, O Lord our God, have given us (for holiness and rest,) for pardon, forgiveness, and atonement, for honor and for glory, we thank and bless You. May Your name be blessed for ever by every living being, for Your word is true for ever. Blessed is our Sovereign God, whose forgiving love annuls our trespasses year after year. King of all the world, You hallow (the Sabbath,) the House of Israel and the Day of Atonement.

Continue on page 354

Alternative Version

Praised be the Lord our God, Ruler of the universe, Rock of all creation, righteous in all generations, the faithful God whose word is deed, whose every command is just and true.

You are the Faithful One, O Lord our God, and faithful is Your word. Not one word of Yours goes forth without accomplishing its task, O faithful and compassionate God and King. Blessed is the Lord, the faithful God.

נֶאֱמָן וְרַחֲמָן אָתָּה. בָּרוּךְ אַתָּה, יְיָ, הָאֵל הַנֶּאֱמָן בְּכָל־דְּבָרָיו.

רַחֵם עַל־צִיּוֹן כִּי הִיא בֵּית חַיֵּינוּ, וְלַעֲלוּבַת נֶפֶשׁ תּוֹשִׁיעַ בִּמְהֵרָה בְיָמֵינוּ. בָּרוּךְ אַתָּה, יְיָ, מְשַׂמֵּחַ צִיּוֹן בְּבָנֶיהָ.

שַׂמְּחֵנוּ, יְיָ אֱלֹהֵינוּ, בְּאֵלִיָּהוּ הַנָּבִיא עַבְדֶּךָ, וּבְמַלְכוּת בֵּית דָּוִד מְשִׁיחֶךָ, בִּמְהֵרָה יָבֹא וְיָגֵל לִבֵּנוּ. עַל־כִּסְאוֹ לֹא־יֵשֵׁב זָר וְלֹא־יִנְחֲלוּ עוֹד אֲחֵרִים אֶת־כְּבוֹדוֹ. כִּי בְשֵׁם קָדְשְׁךָ נִשְׁבַּעְתָּ לּוֹ שֶׁלֹּא־יִכְבֶּה נֵרוֹ לְעוֹלָם וָעֶד. בָּרוּךְ אַתָּה, יְיָ, מָגֵן דָּוִד.

עַל הַתּוֹרָה וְעַל הָעֲבוֹדָה וְעַל הַנְּבִיאִים וְעַל (יוֹם הַשַּׁבָּת הַזֶּה וְעַל) יוֹם הַכִּפּוּרִים הַזֶּה, שֶׁנָּתַתָּ לָנוּ, יְיָ אֱלֹהֵינוּ, (לִקְדֻשָׁה וְלִמְנוּחָה) לִמְחִילָה וְלִסְלִיחָה וְלִכַפָּרָה, לְכָבוֹד וּלְתִפְאֶרֶת, עַל הַכֹּל, יְיָ אֱלֹהֵינוּ, אֲנַחְנוּ מוֹדִים לָךְ, וּמְבָרְכִים אוֹתָךְ. יִתְבָּרַךְ שִׁמְךָ בְּפִי כָּל־חַי תָּמִיד לְעוֹלָם וָעֶד. וּדְבָרְךָ אֱמֶת וְקַיָּם לָעַד. בָּרוּךְ אַתָּה, יְיָ, מֶלֶךְ מוֹחֵל וְסוֹלֵחַ לַעֲוֹנוֹתֵינוּ וְלַעֲוֹנוֹת עַמּוֹ בֵּית יִשְׂרָאֵל, וּמַעֲבִיר אַשְׁמוֹתֵינוּ בְּכָל־שָׁנָה וְשָׁנָה, מֶלֶךְ עַל כָּל־הָאָרֶץ, מְקַדֵּשׁ (הַשַּׁבָּת וְ) יִשְׂרָאֵל וְיוֹם הַכִּפּוּרִים.

Show compassion for Zion, our House of Life, and speedily, in our own day, deliver those who despair. Blessed is the Lord, who brings joy to Zion's children.

Lord our God, bring us the joy of Your kingdom: let our dream of Elijah and David bear fruit. Speedily let redemption come to gladden our hearts. Let Your solemn promise be fulfilled: David's light shall not for ever be extinguished! Blessed is the Lord, the Shield of David.

For the Torah, for the privilege of worship, for the prophets, and for this (Shabbat and this) Day of Atonement that You, O Lord our God, have given us (for holiness and rest,) for pardon, forgiveness, and atonement, for honor and for glory, we thank and bless You. May Your name be blessed for ever by every living being, for Your word is true for ever. Blessed is our Sovereign God, whose forgiving love annuls our trespasses year after year. King of all the world, You hallow (the Sabbath,) the House of Israel and the Day of Atonement.

All rise

FOR OUR CONGREGATION AND OUR PEOPLE

Lord, we pray to You for the whole House of Israel, scattered over the earth, yet bound together by a common history, and united by a common heritage of faith and hope.

Be with our brothers and sisters whose lives are made hard because they are Jews. Give them strength to endure, and lead them soon from bondage to freedom, from darkness to light.

Bless this holy congregation and all who serve it, together with all other holy congregations, in all lands near and far. Uphold us, shield us, and bestow upon us abundant life and health and peace and happiness in all our dwelling places. Bring to fulfillment the blessing of Moses: The Lord your God make you a thousand times as many as you are, and bless you as He has promised you. Amen.

O God, send Your healing to the sick, Your comfort to all who are in pain or anxiety, Your tender love to the sorrowing hearts among us. Be their refuge through their time of trial, as they pass from weakness to strength, from suffering to consolation, from lonely fear to the courage of faith. Amen.

FOR OUR NATION AND ITS LEADERS

We pray for all who hold positions of leadership and responsibility in our national life. Let Your blessing rest upon them, and make them responsive to Your will, so that our nation may be to the world an example of justice and compassion.

Deepen our love for our country and our desire to serve it. Strengthen our power of self-sacrifice for our nation's welfare. Teach us to uphold its good name by our own right conduct.

Cause us to see clearly that the well-being of our nation is in the hands of all its citizens; imbue us with zeal for the cause of liberty in our own land and in all lands; and help us always to keep our homes safe from affliction, strife, and war. Amen.

FOR THE STATE OF ISRAEL

We pray for the land of Israel and its people. May its borders know peace, its inhabitants tranquility. And may the bonds of faith and fate which unite the Jews of all lands be a source of strength to Israel and to us all. God of all lands and ages, answer our constant prayer with a Zion once more aglow with light for us and for all the world, and let us say: Amen.

Returning the Torah to the Ark

יְהַלְלוּ אֶת־שֵׁם יְיָ, כִּי נִשְׂגָּב שְׁמוֹ לְבַדּוֹ.

Let us praise the name of the Lord, whose name alone is exalted.

הוֹדוֹ עַל אֶרֶץ וְשָׁמָיִם, וַיָּרֶם קֶרֶן לְעַמּוֹ, תְּהִלָּה לְכָל־
חֲסִידָיו, לִבְנֵי יִשְׂרָאֵל עַם קְרוֹבוֹ. הַלְלוּיָה.

God's splendor covers heaven and earth; He is the strength of
His people, making glorious His faithful ones, Israel, a people
close to Him. Halleluyah!

• •

כִּי זֹאת הַבְּרִית אֲשֶׁר אֶכְרֹת אֶת־בֵּית יִשְׂרָאֵל אַחֲרֵי
הַיָּמִים הָהֵם, נְאֻם־יְיָ: נָתַתִּי אֶת־תּוֹרָתִי בְּקִרְבָּם וְעַל־
לִבָּם אֶכְתֲּבֶנָּה, וְהָיִיתִי לָהֶם לֵאלֹהִים וְהֵמָּה יִהְיוּ־לִי
לְעָם.

This is the covenant I will make with the House of Israel
in days to come: I will put My Torah within them, and
engrave it on their hearts; I will be their God, and they
shall be My people.

וְלֹא יְלַמְּדוּ עוֹד אִישׁ אֶת־רֵעֵהוּ וְאִישׁ אֶת־אָחִיו
לֵאמֹר, "דְּעוּ אֶת־יְיָ," כִּי כוּלָּם יֵדְעוּ אוֹתִי, לְמִקְּטַנָּם
וְעַד־גְּדוֹלָם, נְאֻם־יְיָ.

No longer shall anyone need to teach a neighbor to know
the Lord, for they shall all know Me, young and old!

• •

356

כִּי לֶקַח טוֹב נָתַתִּי לָכֶם, תּוֹרָתִי אַל־תַּעֲזֹבוּ.
עֵץ־חַיִּים הִיא לַמַּחֲזִיקִים בָּהּ, וְתֹמְכֶיהָ מְאֻשָּׁר.
דְּרָכֶיהָ דַרְכֵי־נֹעַם, וְכָל־נְתִיבוֹתֶיהָ שָׁלוֹם.

Behold, a good doctrine has been given you; do not forsake it. It is a tree of life to those who hold it fast, and all who cling to it find happiness. Its ways are ways of pleasantness, and all its paths are peace.

הֲשִׁיבֵנוּ יְיָ אֵלֶיךָ, וְנָשׁוּבָה. חַדֵּשׁ יָמֵינוּ כְּקֶדֶם.

Help us to return to You, O Lord: then truly shall we return. Renew our days as in the past.

The Ark is closed

All are seated

This day, strengthen us! Amen.	הַיּוֹם תְּאַמְּצֵנוּ! אָמֵן.
This day, bless us! Amen.	הַיּוֹם תְּבָרְכֵנוּ! אָמֵן.
This day, exalt us! Amen.	
This day, look with favor upon us! Amen.	הַיּוֹם תְּגַדְּלֵנוּ! אָמֵן.
	הַיּוֹם תִּדְרְשֵׁנוּ לְטוֹבָה! אָמֵן.
This day, inscribe us for a blessed life! Amen.	הַיּוֹם תִּכְתְּבֵנוּ לְחַיִּים טוֹבִים! אָמֵן.
This day, hear our plea! Amen.	הַיּוֹם תִּשְׁמַע שַׁוְעָתֵנוּ! אָמֵן.
This day, uplift us with Your righteousness! Amen.	הַיּוֹם תִּתְמְכֵנוּ בִּימִין צִדְקֶךָ! אָמֵן.

357

תפלות נוספות

ADDITIONAL PRAYERS

Readings and meditations begin on page 229

Additional Prayers

Listen to Me in silence;
let the peoples renew their strength;
let them approach;
let them speak.

Let us together draw near for judgment.

Sing to the Eternal a new song;

Sing praise from earth's end!

Let the sea roar, and all that fills it;

The coastlands, and all who dwell there.

I am the Eternal, your Holy One,
Israel's Creator, your Ruler,

who makes a way in the sea,
a path in the raging waters.

Do not look back on what has been,
forget the things of old:
it is a new thing I am doing—
see it springing forth.
I will bring streams to the wilderness,
and rivers to the desert,
to give drink to My people,

the people I formed for Myself,
to declare My praise.

I, I am the One
who blots out your transgressions;
your sins will I remember no more.
I will pour water on the thirsty land,
and streams on the dry ground.

I will pour My spirit on your descendants,

361

My blessing on your offspring.

Sing, O heavens;
shout, O depths of the earth!

Break forth into song, O mountains,
O forest—every tree!

I will make a covenant with you for ever;
for as the new heavens and the new earth
that I am making shall endure,
so shall your descendants endure,
so shall your name endure.
And from new moon to new moon,
and from Sabbath to Sabbath,
all flesh shall come to worship Me.

And it shall be said:
The people who walked in darkness
have seen a great light.

◆ ◆

This is a day of judgment; today we remember our deeds. This is a day of questioning, and we ask: What have we done with the gift of life?

"Who among you loves life and longs to enjoy good for
many days? Then guard your tongue from evil, and your lips
from deceitful speech; turn away from evil, and do good;
seek peace and pursue it."

We were made to be the crown of creation. Endowed with a portion of the divine spirit, we were commanded:

"Walk before Me, and reach for perfection."

We were called to hallow this world and bless it:

"You shall be holy, for I, the Eternal One, am holy."

A divine voice calls us to a covenant of truth and peace, a law of justice and love:

"I will betroth you to Me for ever; I will betroth you to Me in righteousness and justice, in love and compassion; I will betroth you to Me in faithfulness, and you shall know the Lord."

On this day, when memory and promise are one, the song of our lives and deeds goes forth to the God enthroned within us:

"I will sing to the Most High with my life; I will sing praises to my God with all my being."

◆ ◆

MEDITATION

There are moments when we hear the call of our higher selves, the call that links us to the divine. Then we know how blessed we are with life and love. May this be such a moment, a time of deeper attachments to the godlike in us and in our world, for which we shall give thanks and praise!

◆ ◆

קְדֹשִׁים תִּהְיוּ, כִּי קָדוֹשׁ אֲנִי יְיָ אֱלֹהֵיכֶם.

You shall be holy, for I the Lord your God am holy.

◆ ◆

ON PRAYER

We cannot pray to You, O God,
to banish war,
for You have filled the world
with paths to peace,

363

if only we would take them.

We cannot pray to You
to end starvation,
for there is food enough for all,
if only we would share it.

We cannot merely pray
for prejudice to cease,
for we might see
the good in all
that lies before our eyes,
if only we would use them.

We cannot merely pray,
'Root out despair,'
for the spark of hope
already waits within the human heart,
for us to fan it into flame.

We must not ask of You, O God,
to take the task that You have given us.
We cannot shirk,
we cannot flee away,
avoiding obligation for ever.

Therefore we pray, O God,
for wisdom and will, for courage
to do and to become,
not only to look on
with helpless yearning
as though we had no strength.

For Your sake and ours,
speedily and soon, let it be:
that our land may be safe,
that our lives may be blessed.

May our words
be pleasing in Your sight;
may our deeds
be acceptable to You, Lord,
our Rock and our Redeemer.

•

MEDITATION

'When you pray, know before whom you stand.'

To be able to pray is to know how to stand still and to dwell upon a word. This is how some worshipers of the past would act: They would repeat the same word many times, because they loved and cherished it so much that they could not part with it.

♦ ♦

ON HUMAN NATURE

וַיִּבְרָא אֱלֹהִים אֶת־הָאָדָם בְּצַלְמוֹ, בְּצֶלֶם אֱלֹהִים
בָּרָא אֹתוֹ, זָכָר וּנְקֵבָה בָּרָא אֹתָם.

We are God's own creation, made in the very image of the
divine, created as one creature with two forms, male and
female.

Our tradition says that God created us through one human being to teach us that whoever destroys a single human soul has destroyed an entire world.

And whoever sustains a single human soul has sustained an
entire world.

And a single human being was created for the sake of peace, that none might say: My lineage is greater than yours.

365

I call heaven and earth to witness: Gentile or Jew, man or woman, manservant or maidservant—all according to our deeds does the spirit of God rest upon us.

◆

MEDITATION

God of the beginning, God of the end, God of all creatures, Lord of all generations: With love You guide the world, with love You walk hand in hand with all the living.

You created us in Your image, capable of love and justice, that in creation's long unfolding we might be Your partners. You endowed people with freedom; we must not enslave them; You gave them judgment; we must not dictate their course.

You set before us many paths to tread, that we might search and find the way that is true for us. We thank You for Your gift of choice. Without it, where would our greatness lie? Where our triumphs and where our failures? Created in Your image, we are called upon to choose.

Let our reflections help us to bring into our lives the harmony we seek and the love we would share.

◆

בְּמָקוֹם שֶׁאֵין אֲנָשִׁים, הִשְׁתַּדֵּל לִהְיוֹת אִישׁ!

In a place where no one behaves like a human being, you must strive to be human!

רַבִּי עֲקִיבָא הָיָה אוֹמֵר: חָבִיב אָדָם שֶׁנִּבְרָא בְצֶלֶם;
חִבָּה יְתֵרָה נוֹדַעַת לוֹ שֶׁנִּבְרָא בְצֶלֶם.

How greatly God must have loved us to create us in His image; yet even greater love did He show us in making us conscious that we are created in His image.

366

Then Isaac asked the Eternal: King of the world, when You made the light, You said in Your Torah that it was good; when You made the expanse of heaven and earth, You said in Your Torah that they were good; and of every herb You made, and every beast, You said that they were good; but when You made us in Your image, You did not say of us in Your Torah that humanity was good. Why, Lord? And God answered him: Because you I have not yet perfected, because through the Torah you are to perfect yourselves, and to perfect the world. All other things are completed; they cannot grow. But humankind is not complete; you have yet to grow. Then I will call you good.

◆

'וְאַתֶּם עֵדַי,' נְאָם יְיָ, 'וַאֲנִי אֵל.' כְּשֶׁאַתֶּם עֵדַי, אֲנִי אֵל; וּכְשֶׁאֵין אַתֶּם עֵדַי, אֵין אֲנִי אֵל.

'You are My witnesses,' says the Lord, 'and I am God.' That is: when you are My witnesses, I am God; and when you are not My witnesses, I am, one might almost say, not God.

◆

MEDITATION

TOWERS OF HOPE

The stars of heaven, awesome in their majesty, are not more wonderful than the one who charts their courses.

The elements, arrayed in perfection, are not marvels greater than the mind that beholds them.

This miracle, matter, begets a wonder: the body thinks; insight comes from flesh; the soul is born of dust to build towers of hope, to open within us doors of lamentation and love.

For You have made us little less than divine, and crowned us with glory and honor!

Glory and honor within us: but every age has despised its endowment. And yet, O God, we look with hope beyond the near horizon. Within and beyond us, O God of life, You are there. You dwell wherever we let You in. When we flee from You, we flee from ourselves. When we seek You, we discover that we are not alone.

◆

From Psalm 139

Whither can I go from Your spirit?
Whither can I flee from Your presence?
If I ascend to the heavens,
You are there!
If I make my home in the lowest depths, behold, You are there!
If I take up the wings of the morning, and dwell on the ocean's farthest shore, even there Your hand will lead me,
Your right hand will hold me.

אָנָה אֵלֵךְ מֵרוּחֶךָ,
וְאָנָה מִפָּנֶיךָ אֶבְרָח?
אִם־אֶסַּק שָׁמַיִם,
שָׁם אָתָּה!
וְאַצִּיעָה שְּׁאוֹל, הִנֶּךָ!
אֶשָּׂא כַנְפֵי־שָׁחַר,
אֶשְׁכְּנָה בְּאַחֲרִית יָם,
גַּם־שָׁם יָדְךָ תַנְחֵנִי,
וְתֹאחֲזֵנִי יְמִינֶךָ.

◆ ◆

ON RESPONSIBILITY

Our rabbis taught: Six hundred and thirteen commandments were given to Moses. Micah reduced them to three: "Do justly, love mercy, and walk humbly with your God."

Isaiah based all the commandments upon two of them: "Keep justice and righteousness."

Amos saw one guiding principle upon which all the Mitzvot are founded: "Seek Me and live."

Habbakuk, too, expounded the Torah on the basis of a single thought: "The righteous shall live by their faith."

Akiba taught: The great principle of the Torah is expressed in the Mitzvah: "You shall love your neighbor as yourself." But Ben Azzai found a principle even more fundamental in the words: "This is the story of humanity: when God created us, He made us in His likeness."

And Hillel summed up the Torah in this maxim: What is hateful to you, do not do to others. The rest is commentary: you must go and study it.

◆

The luckless, the victims, the self-defeated: these Your children whom we often shut out of our lives: give them light and joy, and shelter from the coldness of their neighbors. And give us, O God of compassion, days when we share their failures; remove our forgetfulness and seal memory into us, that not again will we laugh at their errors or shrug at their sadness.

◆

We have learned: Say always, 'The world was created for my sake,' and never say, 'Of what concern is all this to me?' Live as if all life depended on you. Do your share to add some improvement, to supply some one thing that is missing, and to leave the world a little better for your stay in it.

369

And it has been written: "Fire shall be kept burning upon the altar continually; it shall not go out." Our heart is the altar. In every occupation let a spark of the holy fire remain within you, and fan it into a flame.

◆

MEDITATION

Raba said: At the final judgment we are asked:
Did you conduct your business honestly?
Did you set aside time for the study of Torah?
Did you cultivate your mind?
Did you try to understand the inner meaning of things?
Did you wait hopefully for redemption?
And if, in addition, reverence for the Lord was your treasure, then it is well with you.

◆ ◆

ON THE EVIL INCLINATION

The greatest victory of the evil inclination is to make us forget our royal lineage.

We were created to lift up the heavens.

When the evil inclination whispers: 'You are not worthy to fulfill the Law,' I will say: 'I am worthy.'

I am dust and ashes, and yet for my sake was the world created!

◆

In days to come the righteous will perceive their evil inclination as a mountain, while the wicked will see it as a small strand of hair. Both will weep. The righteous will say: How were we able to overcome so high a mountain!

370

The wicked will say: How could we have been unable to overcome this slender hair! And the Holy One, too, will wonder, as it is written: "Thus says the Lord of Hosts: If it be marvellous in the eyes of the remnant of this people in those days, it will also be marvellous in My eyes."

◆

Lord, we are not so arrogant as to pretend
that the trial of our lives
does not reveal our flaws.
We know ourselves,
in this moment of prayer,
to have failed
the ones we love and the stranger,
again and again.
We know how often
we did not bring to the surface of our lives
the hidden goodness within.
Where we have achieved, O Lord,
we are grateful;
where we have failed,
we ask forgiveness.
Remember how exposed we are
to the chances and terrors of life.
We were afraid.
We sometimes chose to fail.
And we ask:
Turn our thoughts from the hurt to its remedy.
Free us of the torments of guilt.

Forgiven, O Lord, we shall then forgive others;
failing, we shall learn to understand failure;
renewed and encouraged, we shall strive to be like
those who came before us: human.
Sinners sometimes, yet a blessing.

◆ ◆

ON TURNING

Now is the time for turning. The leaves are beginning to turn from green to red and orange. The birds are beginning to turn and are heading once more toward the South. The animals are beginning to turn to storing their food for the winter. For leaves, birds, and animals turning comes instinctively. But for us turning does not come so easily. It takes an act of will for us to make a turn. It means breaking with old habits. It means admitting that we have been wrong; and this is never easy. It means losing face; it means starting all over again; and this is always painful. It means saying: I am sorry. It means recognizing that we have the ability to change. These things are terribly hard to do. But unless we turn, we will be trapped for ever in yesterday's ways. Lord, help us to turn—from callousness to sensitivity, from hostility to love, from pettiness to purpose, from envy to contentment, from carelessness to discipline, from fear to faith. Turn us around, O Lord, and bring us back toward You. Revive our lives, as at the beginning. And turn us toward each other, Lord, for in isolation there is no life.

◆

MEDITATION

As for us, how can we think ourselves worthy, when the very heavens, the hosts of heaven, are not pure and faultless in Your sight? If fire can be kindled among the verdant trees, how much the sooner in the withered grass!

To You the darkness is clear as light. Your eye penetrates all creation. You dwell in mystery, and all mysteries are revealed to You.

Though we are born to trouble, we know that through our study of Torah, through our pursuit of truth, through our just and loving deeds, we can give dignity and worth to our lives. Fortunate are they whose efforts are in pursuit of truth; their end will testify to their beginning.

No one, finally, can dissemble. Our own seals bear witness to our work. No one, in the end, can play the deceiver. Our deeds bear witness against us. Only our wisdom will sustain us in old age, and only our righteous deeds will accompany us to eternity.

A good name is better than lordly titles. We are born to uncertainty, and only the hour of death can attest to the worth of our lives. Until that hour God waits for us to repent, and thus give Life to our life.

We praise You, O God, the Lord who gives life to the dead.

◆

Rabbi Chama bar Chanina said: Great is repentance, for it brings healing to the world. As it is said:

"I will heal their backsliding, I will love them freely."

Rabbi Levi said: Great is repentance, for it brings us to the Throne of Glory. As it is said:

"Return, O Israel, all the way to the Lord your God."

Rabbi Jonathan said: Great is repentance, for it brings near the time of redemption. As it is said:

"To Zion a redeemer will come, to the children of Jacob who return to God."

Resh Lakish said: Great is repentance, for on the strength of it, deliberate sins are accounted unintentional. As it is said:

"Return, O Israel, all the way to the Lord your God, for you have stumbled in your iniquity."

Rabbi Jacob used to say: Better one hour of repentance and good works in this world than all the life of the world-to-come.

And Rabbi Abahu said: Where those who have repented stand, the perfectly righteous cannot stand!

◆

MEDITATION

Repentance and the Day of Atonement suffice for forgiveness of sins against God alone, but sins against human beings, such as violence or cursing or theft, are not forgiven until restitution is made and the injured person satisfied. And restitution by itself is not enough; one must appease the injured person and ask forgiveness. By the same token, an injured person must not be cruel and unforgiving. We should be slow to anger and easily appeased. And when our forgiveness is requested, we should grant it with a whole heart and a willing spirit; we should not be vengeful or bear grudges even for a grave injury—this is the way of the upright Jew.

◆

Eternal God, what can we say in Your presence? How account for our sins? We speak of repentance, and yet are slow to change. But now we turn to You with the prayer that Your love may abide with us always, turning our hearts to Your ways, our feet to Your paths. Hope is meat and drink to us; hope sustains us. And so we pray: Do not turn us away empty-handed from Your presence. End our darkness with Your light and turn our passions to Your purpose. Help us, Lord, in this hour of turning, to make real in our lives the words of our mouths, the meditations of our hearts.

◆

MEDITATION

Your power, O God, is the worship You inspire, You are the vision that beckons to us; we are your partners in creation. May I

374

live by this knowledge day by day, fulfilling each task as though it might save the world; may I seek out opportunities for service, knowing that we depend on one another. You are the great Enabler, but I must be the doer. The sense of Your presence helps me to strive and overcome; my striving helps make the world more nearly Yours. Let me therefore draw ever nearer to You, as I endeavor to do Your work and mine: to ennoble and to bless this life, this year so full of promise.

◆

הֲשִׁיבֵנוּ יְיָ אֵלֶיךָ, וְנָשׁוּבָה. חַדֵּשׁ יָמֵינוּ כְּקֶדֶם.

Help us to return to You, O Lord; then truly shall we return.
Renew our days as in the past.

◆

Come, let us consider and examine,
Recognize our sins and vanities,
Forego weeping and sackcloth and ashes—for those
Are the privileges of other days—
And start anew our struggle to master history.

For the kingdom of God is to be our doing,
The work of women and men.

In the recesses of our souls,
Knowing full well the vast measure of the unknown,
The treachery of the human heart, even ours;
In the autumn,
The time of penitence and remembrance,
We urgently pray for the gifts of God:

For courage and love,
Order in the world,
Grace in ourselves,
And wisdom to worship the Holy One.

אֱלֹהֵינוּ וֵאלֹהֵי אֲבוֹתֵינוּ:

אָמְנָם כֵּן יֵצֶר סוֹכֵן בָּנוּ.

בָּךְ לְהַצְדֵּק, רַב צֶדֶק, וַעֲנֵנוּ: סָלַחְתִּי.

גְּעַל מְרַגֵּל וְגַם פַּגֵּל סִפְרוֹ.

דּוֹד שׁוֹאֵג בְּקוֹל יִתֵּן קוֹל דְּבָרוֹ: סָלַחְתִּי.

הַס קַטֵּגוֹר וְקַח סַנֵּגוֹר מְקוֹמוֹ.

וִיהִי יְיָ לְמִשְׁעָן לוֹ לְמַעַן נָאֲמוֹ: סָלַחְתִּי.

זְכוּת אֶזְרָח גַּם יִפְרַח לְשׁוֹשַׁנָּה.

חֵטְא הַעֲבֵר וְקוֹל הַגְּבֵר מִמְּעוֹנָה: סָלַחְתִּי.

טוֹב וְסַלָּח, מְחַל וּסְלַח אֲשֵׁמִים.

יָהּ הַקְשֵׁב וְגַם הָשֵׁב מִמְּרוֹמִים: סָלַחְתִּי.

כְּאֵב תַּחֲבוֹשׁ וּבְצוּל תִּכְבּוֹשׁ עֲוֹנִי.

לְךָ תְהִלָּה, אֱמוֹר מִלָּה לְמַעֲנִי: סָלַחְתִּי.

מְחֵה פֶּשַׁע וְגַם רֶשַׁע בְּנֵי בְרִית.

נְהַג חַסְדֶּךָ כֵּן הוֹרֶךָ לִשְׁאֵרִית: סָלַחְתִּי.

סְכוֹת רַחֲשִׁי וְגַם לַחֲשִׁי תִּרְצֶה.

עָוֹן נוֹשֵׂא, לְמַעַנְךָ עֲשֵׂה וְתִפְצֶה: סָלַחְתִּי.

פְּנֵה לְעֶלְבּוֹן מְקוֹם עֲוֹן לְהָשִׁים.

צַחַן הָסֵר וְגַם תְּבַשֵּׂר לְבָךְ חוֹסִים: סָלַחְתִּי.

קוֹלִי שְׁמַע וּרְאֵה דֶּמַע עֵינִי.

רִיב רִיבִי, שְׁעֵה נִיבִי וַהֲשִׁיבֵנִי: סָלַחְתִּי.

שֶׁמֶץ טַהֵר כְּעָב מַהֵר כְּנֶאֱמָר.

תִּמְחֶה פֶּשַׁע לְעַם נוֹשַׁע וְתֹאמַר: סָלַחְתִּי.

Yes, it is true, an evil impulse sways us;
You, abundant in grace, can clear us: O answer: I forgive.
Cast scorn on traitors, reject their accusations;
Beloved God, break out with Your mighty voice: I forgive.
Silence all accusers, let defenders take their place;

Lord, lend Your strength to our defense, and say: I forgive.
Let Abraham's merit spring up in our behalf;
Sweep sin away and loud proclaim: I forgive.
Forgiving God, cleanse and pardon all who transgress;
Give ear, Lord, and answer from the heights: I forgive.
Heal our wounds, cast away our iniquity;
Let it be Your glory to say: I forgive.
Blot out all evil from the midst of Your people;
Show us Your love and Your grandeur, and say: I forgive.
Take up our prayers, accept our plea;
Clear us of sin, act for Your sake, and declare: I forgive.
Look at our low estate, consider our sufferings;
Set sin aside, and to those who trust in You proclaim: I forgive.
Hear our voice, look upon our tears;
Plead our cause, approve our request and answer: I forgive.
Banish all wrong as the wind clears the sky of clouds;
Sweep away transgression, deliver our people, and say: I forgive.

◆ ◆

ON FORGIVENESS

From Psalm 103

Praise the Lord, O my soul, and let all that is in me praise God's holy name.

Praise the Lord, O my soul, and never forget God's blessings,

who forgives all your sins and heals all your wounds;

who redeems your life from destruction, and surrounds you with love and compassion;

who fills your life with good, renewing your youth like an eagle's.

The Lord is just, demanding justice for the oppressed.

377

You revealed Your ways to Moses, Your deeds to the people of Israel.

The Lord is merciful and gracious, endlessly patient and full of love.

As parents show compassion to their children, so do You, Lord, show compassion to all who revere You.

For You know how we are made; You remember that we are dust.

Our days are as grass; we blossom like the flower of the field.

The wind blows, and it is gone; its place knows it no more.

But Your love, Lord, rests for ever on all who revere You, and Your goodness rests on their children's children,

who keep Your covenant and remember to observe Your precepts.

The Lord is enthroned in the universe,

and all creation is God's domain.

◆

MEDITATION

"Behold, I have set before you this day life or death, blessing or curse. Choose life, therefore, that you and your children may live."

I have been created with a mind able to dwell upon good thoughts and good intentions. Unseemly thoughts have led me to unworthy deeds.

I have been created with eyes, the blessing of sight, to see the world's beauty and holiness. Often I look without seeing.

I have been created with ears to hear sacred words, to hear the sounds of wisdom, beauty, and love. Often I squander God's gift, and hear without listening. Often I debase it by listening to gossip, obscenities, and words of hatred.

I have been created with a mouth and a tongue. The gift of speech God gave to no other creature. With words I try to pray. With words I speak of love, to God and to human beings. But malice, pettiness, falsehood, and slander have sullied my speech. With words I have mocked God's gift, shaming neighbor and stranger, laughing at the pain of others, uttering false oaths, insincere pledges, and vain promises.

I have been created with hands, the ability to sense creation through touch, the capacity to transmit tenderness. Often I have clenched my fists in resentment, using my hands to injure or destroy.

I have been given legs to walk in God's path. Often I have rushed to do unworthy deeds. I have walked away from God and from my neighbor.

I have been blessed with the ability to regenerate life, and to share joy in love fulfilled. Lust and jealousy, pain and fear have sometimes corrupted this gift.

All that I am is bared. I am burdened by the choices I have made, for often I have marred the beauty of my spirit through my misdeeds. Lord, on this Day of Atonement, forgive and purify me. Give me the courage to renew my life, to change at least part of what should be changed. On this day I search for reconciliation with myself, with those whom I have offended and hurt, and with You, O Master of Mercy, the Holy and Blessed One.

◆

For all we sought and missed, or left unclaimed,
for all the dreams we had and lost, for youth,
ruffling his hair, suppled by Time, and tamed,
for love denied, or seen with too much truth,
for faith, like a sword, with long misprision rusted,
for all adventure, before the quest is ended,
abandoned or betrayed, for beauty misted
by the half-lights of vision, for pity attended
with the bitterness of those who take and give,

for heavens, that had they been accessible,
were heavens only by the side of hell,
for all of us who die, before we live,
for all the crippled feet on the long road
You made for angels, we forgive You, God.

◆

MEDITATION

Once Rabbi Yochanan ben Zakkai went forth from Jerusalem. Rabbi Joshua accompanied him. They beheld the Temple in ruins. Woe is us! cried Rabbi Joshua. The place where Israel's sins found atonement is laid waste! But Rabbi Yochanan said: Do not weep. We have a means of atonement equal to this— deeds of love. As it is said: "For it is love I desire, and not sacrifice (Hosea 6.6)."

◆

I lay my pain upon Your altar, loving God;
This is my lamb, my ram, my sacrifice,

My plea for pardon, plea for forgiveness,
For all my sins of doing and not doing.

Prayers that blossom like flowers out of pain
Above the earth-pull.

My people's pains have flamed in sacrifice
Upon Your altar through slow-moving time.

Pain for all evil, hatred, cruelty,
For the sick of body and the sick of heart,

For all the loneliness, and all the lovelessness,

The unmeasureable loss of those that know not You—

The pain of all the world, dear God, I place
Before Your shrine.

Look down in pity and forgiveness.

Cause Your countenance to shine upon us,
And give us peace.

•

כִּי הִנֵּה כַחֹמֶר בְּיַד הַיּוֹצֵר, בִּרְצוֹתוֹ מַרְחִיב וּבִרְצוֹתוֹ
מְקַצֵּר,
כֵּן אֲנַחְנוּ בְיָדְךָ, חֶסֶד נוֹצֵר,　　　 לַבְּרִית הַבֵּט
וְאַל תֵּפֶן לַיֵּצֶר.

As clay in the hand of the potter, to be thickened or thinned at will, are we in Your hand. Preserve us with Your love.

Your covenant recall, and not our imperfection.

כִּי הִנֵּה כָאֶבֶן בְּיַד הַמְסַתֵּת, בִּרְצוֹתוֹ אוֹחֵז וּבִרְצוֹתוֹ
מְכַתֵּת,
כֵּן אֲנַחְנוּ בְיָדְךָ, מְחַיֶּה וּמְמוֹתֵת,　　 לַבְּרִית הַבֵּט
וְאַל תֵּפֶן לַיֵּצֶר.

As stone in the hand of the mason, to be broken or preserved at will, are we in Your hand, Master of life and death.

Your covenant recall, and not our imperfection.

כִּי הִנֵּה כַגַּרְזֶן בְּיַד הֶחָרָשׁ, בִּרְצוֹתוֹ דִּבֵּק לָאוּר
וּבִרְצוֹתוֹ פֵּרַשׁ,
כֵּן אֲנַחְנוּ בְיָדְךָ, תּוֹמֵךְ עָנִי וָרָשׁ,　　 לַבְּרִית הַבֵּט
וְאַל תֵּפֶן לַיֵּצֶר.

As iron in the hand of the blacksmith, to be thrust into fire
or withdrawn at will, are we in Your hand. Help us to heal
our wounds with deeds of charity.

Your covenant recall, and not our imperfection.

כִּי הִנֵּה כַחֹמֶר בְּיַד הַמַּלָּח, בִּרְצוֹתוֹ אוֹחֵז וּבִרְצוֹתוֹ
שַׁלַּח,
כֵּן אֲנַחְנוּ בְיָדְךָ, אֵל טוֹב וְסַלָּח,   לַבְּרִית הַבֵּט
וְאַל תֵּפֶן לַיֵּצֶר.

As a rudder in the hands of the sailor, to be guided or
abandoned at will, are we in Your hand. Prevent our constant drifting.

Your covenant recall, and not our imperfection.

כִּי הִנֵּה כִזְכוּכִית בְּיַד הַמְזַגֵּג, בִּרְצוֹתוֹ חוֹגֵג וּבִרְצוֹתוֹ
מְמוֹגֵג,
כֵּן אֲנַחְנוּ בְיָדְךָ, מַעֲבִיר זָדוֹן וְשֶׁגֶג,   לַבְּרִית הַבֵּט
וְאַל תֵּפֶן לַיֵּצֶר.

As glass in the hand of the glazier, to be melted or shaped
at will, are we in Your hand. Maintain our fragile balance
with Your grace.

Your covenant recall, and not our imperfection.

•

From Psalm 36

Sin speaks to the wicked
deep in their hearts.
There is no fear of God
before their eyes.
They flatter themselves
that their hateful guilt

will never come to light.
Their words are cruel and false.
All wisdom and good is gone.
They lie awake plotting mischief.
The course they choose is not good;
they never tire of evil.

But Your love, O God, is high as heaven,
Your faithfulness reaches to the skies.

Your righteousness is like the mighty mountains,

Your justice is like the great deep;

Lord, You help every human, every beast.
How precious is Your faithful love, O God!

Your children take refuge in the shadow of Your wings.

We feast on the riches of Your house;
we drink from the stream of Your delights.

For with You is the fountain of life,
and by Your light do we see light.

O continue to show Your love
to those who would know You,

Your justice to the upright in heart.

◆ ◆

ON SEEKING AND FINDING

Lord, where can I find You?
Your glory fills the world.

Behold, I find You
Where the ploughman breaks the hard soil,

383

Where the quarrier explodes stone out of the hillside,
Where the miner digs metals out of the reluctant earth,
Where men and women earn their bread by the sweat of
their brow,
Among the lonely and poor, the lowly and lost.

In blazing heat and shattering storm, You are with them.

Behold, I find You
In the mind free to sail by its own star,
In words that spring from the depth of truth,
Where endeavor reaches undespairing for perfection,
Where the scientist toils to unravel the secrets of Your
world,
Where the poet makes beauty out of words,
Wherever people struggle for freedom,

Wherever noble deeds are done.

Behold, I find You
In the shouts of children merry at their play,
In the mother's lullaby, as she rocks her baby in the
cradle,
In the sleep falling on his infant eyelids,

And in the smile that dances on his sleeping lips.

Behold, I find You
When dawn comes up bearing golden gifts,
And in the fall of evening peace and rest from the Western
sea.
In the current of life flowing day and night through all
things,
Throbbing in my sinews and in the dust of the earth,

In every leaf and flower.

Behold, I find You
In the wealth of joys that quickly fade,

384

In the life that from eternity dances in my blood,
In birth, which renews the generations continually,

And in death knocking on the doors of life.

O my God,
Give me strength never to disown the poor,
Never before insolent might to bow the head.
Give me strength to raise my spirit high above daily trifles,
Lightly to bear my joys and sorrows,
And in love to surrender all my strength to Your will.

For great are Your gifts to me:
The sky and the light; this my flesh;
Life and the soul—
Treasures beyond price, treasures of life and of love.

♦

How does one find the Eternal God?

By the doing of good deeds,
by study of the Torah.

And how does the Holy One find us?

Through our love, friendship, and respect;
through companionship, truth, and peace;
through the service of scholars
and the discussion of students;
through decency and a good heart;
through a No that is truly No,
through a Yes that is really Yes.

Thus says the Holy One to Israel:
My children, what do I seek of you?
Only love one another,
honor and respect each other.
Let there be found in you

385

neither transgression nor theft,
nor aught else shameful.
As it is said:

It has been told what is good,
and what the Lord demands of you:
Do justly, love mercy,
and walk humbly with your God.

◆

How does one find the Eternal God?
In heaven and earth,
In a clap of thunder, in a whisper of the soul,
In praise on yellowed parchment in an ancient tongue,
In yearning of the heart, in a child not yet born.

Blessed is the One Who Is.

"Bless the Eternal One, O my soul."
When we see a pleasing sculpture, we say:
Blessed is the one who shaped it!

The world is pleasing:
Blessed the Presence that shaped it,
Blessed the One who fashioned it with a word!

Taste of tears and wine, sight of starry skies,
Old men's voices warping the chant, children singing,
Scientists asking, artists proclaiming:

Blessed the One Who Will Be.

Even for the sake of one righteous person,
The world would have been created.
And one good man, one good woman,
Can keep the world from perishing.

The righteous one is the foundation of the world.

All the web of creation shining in God's bright sunlight,
The dew that has gathered in darkness,
Transfixes the light of day.

Blessed the One Who Is and Will Be.

◆

"You have fashioned me after and before."
If we prove worthy, it will be said:
You preceded the angels in the order of creation!

Greater are the righteous than the ministering angels!

But if we are not worthy, it will be said:
The gnat preceded you, the worm preceded you.

Inform us in self-knowledge, Lord Creator,
One and together;
Help us understand the hunger for peace
Between people, among nations.

The world was created for the sake of choice,
For the sake of the chooser.
Each of us, for whom choice is life, shall say:
For my sake was the world created:

Let us be aware,
Labor to redeem the world,
Supply what it lacks, here and now.

Grant us another year in the Book of Life,
With its peril, injustice,
And the good daylight.

Amen and Amen.

עַל־שְׁלֹשָׁה דְבָרִים הָעוֹלָם עוֹמֵד: עַל הַתּוֹרָה וְעַל
הָעֲבוֹדָה וְעַל גְּמִילוּת חֲסָדִים.

The world is sustained by three things: by Torah, by worship, by loving deeds.

• •

ON LIFE AND DEATH

O God, You have called us into life, and set us in the midst of purposes we cannot measure or understand. Yet we thank You for the good we know, for the life we have, and for the gifts that are our daily portion:

For health and healing, for labor and repose, for the ever-renewed beauty of earth and sky, for thoughts of truth and justice which stir us to acts of goodness, and for the contemplation of Your eternal presence, which fills us with hope that what is good and lovely cannot perish.

•

For two readers or more, or responsively

We need one another when we mourn and would be comforted.

> We need one another when we are in trouble and crave help, or when we are in the deep waters of temptation and a strong hand might pull us out.

We need one another when we would accomplish some great purpose and cannot do this alone.

> We need one another in our defeats, when with encouragement we might strive again; and in the hour of success, when we look for someone to share our bliss.

And we need one another when we come to die, and

would have gentle hands prepare us for the journey.

All our lives we are in need, and others are in need of us.

We best live when we bring to one another our understanding and our solace.

◆

For two readers or more, or responsively

Who weeps now anywhere in the world,
weeps without cause,
weeps over me.

Who laughs now anywhere in the night,
laughs without cause,
laughs with me.

Who goes now anywhere in the world,
goes without cause,
goes toward me.

Who dies now anywhere in the world,
dies without cause,
rests with me.

◆

They list for me the things I may not know:

*Whence came the world? Whose hand flung out the light
Of yonder stars? How could a God of Right
Ordain for earth an ebbless tide of woe?*

Their word is right. I would not scorn their doubt
Who press their questions of the how and why.

But this I know: that from the star-strewn sky
There comes to me a peace that puts to rout
All brooding thoughts of dread, abiding death;

And, too, I know with every fragrant dawn
That Life is Lord, that, with the Winter gone,
There comes the Spring, a great reviving breath.

It is enough that Life means this to me.
What Death shall mean, some sunny morn shall see.

◆

Slowly now the evening changes his garments
held for him by a rim of ancient trees;
you gaze: and the landscape divides and leaves you,
one sinking and one rising toward the sky.

And you are left, to none belonging wholly,
not so dark as a silent house, nor quite
so surely pledged unto eternity
as that which grows to star and climbs the night.

To you is left (unspeakably confused)
your life, gigantic, ripening, full of fears,
so that it, now hemmed in, now grasping all,
is changed by you in turn to stone and stars.

◆

SILENT PRAYER

Create in me a clean heart, O God, and place a willing
spirit within me. You, who know my thoughts and understand the minds of mortals, know my longing to do
Your will.

Purify my thoughts, and free me from unworthy aims. May none of my troubles make me a stranger to You and keep me from serving You.

Lighten the weight of other burdens that keep me from bearing Yours, the commands that give me life. So, with all my heart, shall I turn to You in perfect repentance.

Body and heart may fail, but God is for ever the Rock of my heart and my life's destination.

◆

קַוֵּה אֶל יְיָ, חֲזַק וְיַאֲמֵץ לִבֶּךְ וְקַוֵּה אֶל יְיָ!

Wait for the Lord; be strong, and let your heart take courage; only wait for the Lord.

תפלת מנחה ליום כפור

YOM KIPPUR AFTERNOON
SERVICE

Readings and Meditations begin on page 229

Afternoon Service

תפלת מנחה

At this hour Israel stands before its God: in our prayers, in our hope, we are one with all Jews on earth.

This people You have formed still lives to tell Your praise.

Today we say to our children:
See this sublime design, which was revealed
at the very beginning,
and which from age to age is realized.
See this people, few in number, to the world unknown,
declaring at the beginning of its history
what will be its history;
see this people choose the mission which chooses it
in the way it has foretold. See this people.

This people You have formed still lives to tell Your praise.

To our friends we say:
See this people, exiled twice and twice surviving,
teaching in its first exile the unity of God
and, in its second, the oneness of humankind.
Know this people.

This people Israel lives to tell
God's praise, men's hopes, women's dreams.

Congregation Israel:
Can you not see an Eternal Presence abiding with your people?
Can you not see in your past
a story told for all peoples,
whose shining conclusion has yet to unfold?

This people lives when it lives God's praise.

At this hour Israel stands before its God.
In our prayers, in our hope, we are one with all Jews on earth.
We look into each other's faces, and we know who we are.

We look up to our God, and we know eternity is in us.

We look into each other's faces, and we know who we are.
We look up to our God, and we know eternity is in us.

◆ ◆

A SERVANT UNTO THEE   מי יתנני

מִי־יִתְּנֵנִי עֶבֶד אֱלוֹהַּ עֹשֵׂנִי,
וִירַחֲקֵנִי כָל־דּוֹד וְהוּא יַקְרִיבֵנִי!
יֹצְרִי וְרֹעִי, נַפְשִׁי וְגֵוִי קָנִיתָ,
בֵּנְתָּ לְרֵעִי וּמַחְשְׁבוֹתַי רָאִיתָ,
אָרְחִי וְרִבְעִי וְכָל־דְּרָכַי זֵרִיתָ.
אִם תַּעְזְרֵנִי, מִי זֶה אֲשֶׁר יַכְשִׁילֵנִי?
אוֹ תַעְצְרֵנִי, מִי בִלְתְּךָ יַתִּירֵנִי?
מִי־יִתְּנֵנִי עֶבֶד אֱלוֹהַּ עֹשֵׂנִי,
וִירַחֲקֵנִי כָל־דּוֹד וְהוּא יַקְרִיבֵנִי!

O that I might be
A servant unto Thee,
Thou God by all adored!
Then, though by friends outcast,
Thy hand would hold me fast,
And draw me near to Thee, my King and Lord.

Spirit and flesh are Thine,
O Heavenly Shepherd mine;
My hopes, my thoughts, my fears, Thou seest all,
Thou measurest my path, my steps dost know.
When Thou upholdest, who can make me fall?
When Thou restrainest, who can bid me go?

O that I might be
A servant unto Thee,
Thou God by all adored!

395

Then, though by friends outcast,
Thy hand would hold me fast,
And draw me near to Thee, my King and Lord.

• •

ALL THIS DAY   מלכי מקדם

מַלְכִּי מִקֶּדֶם פּוֹעֵל יְשׁוּעוֹת בְּקֶרֶב הֲמוֹנִי, נֹצֵר חֶסֶד
לַאֲלָפִים וְנֹשֵׂא פְּשָׁעַי וַעֲוֹנִי. כַּסֵּה חֲטָאַי וּבְרַחֲמֶיךָ
הָרַבִּים חָנֵּנִי, יְיָ.
כִּי אֵלֶיךָ אֶקְרָא כָּל־הַיּוֹם.

O Sovereign Source of salvation, You show mercy to
thousands of generations, forgiving transgression and
wrongdoing. Forgive my sins; Lord, in Your abundant
mercy, be gracious to me.

All this day, You are the One we call upon.

הַיּוֹם רַפֵּא מְשׁוּבוֹתֵינוּ, כִּי אָתָאנוּ לְךָ וְהִנֵּנוּ.
שַׁבְנוּ אֵלֶיךָ, אֱלֹהֵינוּ, וּבְחַסְדְּךָ חָנֵּנוּ. דֶּרֶךְ רֶשַׁע
עֲזַבְנוּ וְהִנֵּה אֵינֶנּוּ.
פֹּה עִמָּנוּ הַיּוֹם.

All this day we look to You: heal our wounds, forgive our
failings. We come to You in penitence; in Your steadfast
love, be gracious to us, as we strive to abandon our evil
ways.

All this day, Lord, be with us.

הַיּוֹם יִגְדַּל נָא כֹחַ יְיָ וְכַעֲוֹנוֹתֵינוּ אַל תִּגְמוֹל.
כְּרַחֵם אָב עַל־בָּנִים, רַחֵם עָלֵינוּ וַחֲמוֹל. רַחֲמֶיךָ
וַחֲסָדֶיךָ פְּנֵה אֵלֵינוּ כִּתְמוֹל שִׁלְשׁוֹם.
גַּם תְּמוֹל גַּם־הַיּוֹם.

This day let Your power grow within us, Lord; and as
parents show compassion for their children, so may You
put wrath aside, turning to us in pity and love.

All this day, Lord, be with us as in days gone by.

הַיוֹם רִשְׁעֵנוּ תָסִיר וּבְסֵפֶר הַחַיִּים אוֹתָנוּ תָחוֹק.
בְּיוֹם קָרָאנוּ אֵלֶיךָ קְרַב; אַל תַּעֲמוֹד מֵרָחוֹק.
סְלִיחָה וְכַפָּרָה שַׂמְתּוֹ לְחוֹק,
וּלְמִשְׁפָּט לְיִשְׂרָאֵל עַד־הַיּוֹם.

This day blot out our misdeeds and inscribe us in the
Book of Life. Stand not apart from us, O God, for You
are near to all who call upon You: forgiveness and pardon
are laws of Your being.

To this day, Lord, You have granted pardon to Your people
Israel.

הַיּוֹם כַּפָּיו יִפְרוֹשׁ אֵלֶיךָ וּגְבוּרוֹתֶיךָ יְמַלֵּל.
בְּצֶדֶק יֶחֱזֶה פָנֶיךָ וּבְשִׁירוֹ אוֹתְךָ יְהַלֵּל. עֲוֹנוּ מוֹדֶה
וְעוֹזֵב, יְבַקֵּשׁ מְחִילָה וְיִתְפַּלֵּל,
בַּעֲדוֹ תָמִיד כָּל־הַיּוֹם.

On this day we lift up our hearts to You, and proclaim
Your might. With song and praise we approach You. We
confess and forsake our sins, as in prayer we seek
forgiveness.

This day and all days, we find You at our side.

הַיּוֹם סְמוֹךְ עַם אֲשֶׁר דְּלָתֶיךָ דוֹפְקִים; וְתִיקַר נָא
נַפְשָׁם, כִּי עָלֶיךָ מִתְרַפְּקִים. פְּרוֹשׁ יָדְךָ לָהֶם וְקַבְּלֵם
וּבַשְּׂרֵם.

This day Your people knock at Your door; to You their
yearning souls aspire, and upon You do they lean. Stretch

forth Your hand and welcome them with Your redeeming
word.

וְאַתֶּם הַדְּבֵקִים בַּיְיָ אֱלֹהֵיכֶם, חַיִּים כֻּלְּכֶם הַיּוֹם.

You who hold fast to the Lord your God have found life, all of
you, this day.

◆ ◆

All rise

תפלה

אֲדֹנָי, שְׂפָתַי תִּפְתָּח, וּפִי יַגִּיד תְּהִלָּתֶךָ.

Eternal God, open my lips, that my mouth may declare Your glory.

THE VOICE WE HEAR   אבות

בָּרוּךְ אַתָּה, יְיָ אֱלֹהֵינוּ וֵאלֹהֵי אֲבוֹתֵינוּ, אֱלֹהֵי
אַבְרָהָם, אֱלֹהֵי יִצְחָק, וֵאלֹהֵי יַעֲקֹב: הָאֵל הַגָּדוֹל,
הַגִּבּוֹר וְהַנּוֹרָא, אֵל עֶלְיוֹן. גּוֹמֵל חֲסָדִים טוֹבִים,
וְקוֹנֵה הַכֹּל, וְזוֹכֵר חַסְדֵי אָבוֹת, וּמֵבִיא גְאֻלָּה לִבְנֵי
בְנֵיהֶם, לְמַעַן שְׁמוֹ, בְּאַהֲבָה.

°God of the past and future, God of this day, God of
Israel and all the world:

We know You, yet cannot name You. With our halting
human speech we say 'God.' God of Abraham, God of

°This symbol indicates that the English is a variation suggested by the theme of
the Hebrew.

Isaac, and God of Jacob. God of Sarah and Rebekah, God of Rachel and Leah. God of freedom and justice and mercy. God of understanding. You are the Rule by which we measure ourselves; You are the Voice we hear within us.

You are the majestic One who delights in life. Inscribe us for blessing in the Book of Life.

זָכְרֵנוּ לְחַיִּים, מֶלֶךְ חָפֵץ בַּחַיִּים, וְכָתְבֵנוּ בְּסֵפֶר הַחַיִּים, לְמַעַנְךָ אֱלֹהִים חַיִּים. מֶלֶךְ עוֹזֵר וּמוֹשִׁיעַ וּמָגֵן. בָּרוּךְ אַתָּה, יְיָ, מָגֵן אַבְרָהָם.

❖

For two readers or more, or responsively

THE POWER WHOSE GIFT IS LIFE   גבורות

אַתָּה גִבּוֹר לְעוֹלָם, אֲדֹנָי, מְחַיֵּה מֵתִים אַתָּה, רַב לְהוֹשִׁיעַ.

°We pray that we might know before whom we stand: the Power whose gift is life, who quickens those who have forgotten how to live.

מַשִּׁיב הָרוּחַ וּמוֹרִיד הַגָּשֶׁם.

We pray for winds to disperse the choking air of sadness, for cleansing rains to make parched hopes flower, and to give all of us the strength to rise up toward the sun.

מְכַלְכֵּל חַיִּים בְּחֶסֶד, מְחַיֵּה מֵתִים בְּרַחֲמִים רַבִּים.

We pray for love to encompass us for no other reason save that we are human—that we may all blossom into persons who have gained power over our own lives.

399

סוֹמֵךְ נוֹפְלִים, וְרוֹפֵא חוֹלִים, וּמַתִּיר אֲסוּרִים,
וּמְקַיֵּם אֱמוּנָתוֹ לִישֵׁנֵי עָפָר.

We pray to stand upright, we fallen; to be healed, we suf-
ferers; we pray to break the bonds that keep us from the
world of beauty; we pray for opened eyes, we who are
blind to our authentic selves.

מִי כָמוֹךָ, בַּעַל גְּבוּרוֹת, וּמִי דוֹמֶה לָךְ, מֶלֶךְ מֵמִית
וּמְחַיֶּה וּמַצְמִיחַ יְשׁוּעָה?

We pray that we may walk in the garden of a purposeful
life, our own powers in touch with the power of the world.

וְנֶאֱמָן אַתָּה לְהַחֲיוֹת מֵתִים. בָּרוּךְ אַתָּה, יְיָ, מְחַיֵּה
הַמֵּתִים.

Praised be the God whose gift is life, whose cleansing rains
let parched men and women flower toward the sun.

◆ ◆

אַתָּה קָדוֹשׁ וְשִׁמְךָ קָדוֹשׁ, וּקְדוֹשִׁים בְּכָל־יוֹם
יְהַלְלוּךָ סֶּלָה.
קָדוֹשׁ אַתָּה וְנוֹרָא שְׁמֶךָ, וְאֵין אֱלוֹהַּ מִבַּלְעָדֶיךָ,
כַּכָּתוּב:
וַיִּגְבַּה יְיָ צְבָאוֹת בַּמִּשְׁפָּט, וְהָאֵל הַקָּדוֹשׁ נִקְדַּשׁ
בִּצְדָקָה. בָּרוּךְ אַתָּה, יְיָ, הַמֶּלֶךְ הַקָּדוֹשׁ.

°God of holiness, let Your glory be with us always, as a holy
light illuminating for us the paths of righteousness. For You
are holy, Your name is holy, and those who strive to be holy

declare Your glory day by day. Blessed is the Lord, who rules in holiness.

All are seated

❖ ❖

This passage may be sung, or read silently or aloud,
after which the service continues on page 403.

וּבְכֵן לְךָ הַכֹּל יַכְתִּירוּ:
לְאֵל עוֹרֵךְ דִּין,
לְבוֹחֵן לְבָבוֹת בְּיוֹם דִּין, לְגוֹלֶה עֲמֻקוֹת בַּדִּין.
לְדוֹבֵר מֵישָׁרִים בְּיוֹם דִּין, לְהוֹגֶה דֵעוֹת בַּדִּין.
לְוָתִיק וְעוֹשֶׂה חֶסֶד בְּיוֹם דִּין, לְזוֹכֵר בְּרִיתוֹ בַּדִּין.
לְחוֹמֵל מַעֲשָׂיו בְּיוֹם דִּין, לְטַהֵר חוֹסָיו בַּדִּין.
לְיוֹדֵעַ מַחֲשָׁבוֹת בְּיוֹם דִּין, לְכוֹבֵשׁ כַּעְסוֹ בַּדִּין.
לְלוֹבֵשׁ צְדָקוֹת בְּיוֹם דִּין, לְמוֹחֵל עֲוֹנוֹת בַּדִּין.
לְנוֹרָא תְהִלּוֹת בְּיוֹם דִּין, לְסוֹלֵחַ לַעֲמוּסָיו בַּדִּין.
לְעוֹנֶה לְקוֹרְאָיו בְּיוֹם דִּין, לְפוֹעֵל רַחֲמָיו בַּדִּין.
לְצוֹפֶה נִסְתָּרוֹת בְּיוֹם דִּין, לְקוֹנֶה עֲבָדָיו בַּדִּין.
לְרַחֵם עַמּוֹ בְּיוֹם דִּין, לְשׁוֹמֵר אוֹהֲבָיו בַּדִּין.
לְתוֹמֵךְ תְּמִימָיו בְּיוֹם דִּין.

Now all acclaim You King,
the God who sits in judgment.

You search the heart on judgment day,
You uncover its depths, in judgment.

You command us to righteousness on judgment day,
You know our inmost thought, in judgment.

Your love is steadfast on judgment day,
You keep Your covenant, in judgment.

You show compassion to Your creatures on judgment day,
You purify those who trust You, in judgment.

You see through our masks on judgment day,
but You cool Your wrath, in judgment.

You are arrayed in justice on judgment day,
yet You pardon rebellion, in judgment.

Your splendor is awesome on judgment day,
You pardon the wayward, in judgment.

You answer all who call upon You on judgment day,
You act with compassion, in judgment.

You penetrate all mysteries on judgment day,
You free Your children, in judgment.

You are merciful to Your people on judgment day,
You preserve those who love You, in judgment.

You uphold all who live with integrity on judgment day.

◆ ◆

THESE CRY OUT TO US

Let now an Infinite Presence teach us a gentleness that transcends force and melts our hardness of heart. Then shall we be sensitive to the needs of our neighbors, and responsive to their pleas.

All who struggle vainly for attention;

and those who shrink from another's touch.

All whose faces we forget from one encounter to the next;

and those who never seem to find a resting-place in the family of the secure.

All whose ambition exceeds their skill;

and those whose early promise has dimmed to small achievement.

All whose minds are clouded or weak;

and those who are burdened with broken bodies.

All who wait in pain only for death;

and those who wait for news that never comes.

Those who are unloved, with none to love;

all widows and widowers, abandoned husbands and wives, neglected children.

All who are deprived by the callousness of others.

and all who have been driven from their homes by wars they never made.

To all these, O God, may we respond with open hearts!

עַל חֵטְא שֶׁחָטָאנוּ לְפָנֶיךָ . . .

We have sinned against life by failing to work for peace.

We have sinned against life by keeping silent in the face of injustice.

עַל חֵטְא שֶׁחָטָאנוּ לְפָנֶיךָ . . .

We have sinned against life by ignoring those who suffer in distant lands.

We have sinned against life by forgetting the poor in our own midst.

עַל חֵטְא שֶׁחָטָאנוּ לְפָנֶיךָ . . .

We have failed to respect those made in the image of God.

We have withheld our love from those who depend on us.

עַל חֵטְא שֶׁחָטָאנוּ לְפָנֶיךָ . . .

We have engaged in gossip and in repeated slander.

We have distorted the truth for our own advantage.

עַל חֵטְא שֶׁחָטָאנוּ לְפָנֶיךָ . . .

We have conformed to fashion and not to conscience.

We have indulged in despair and trafficked with cynics.

עַל חֵטְא שֶׁחָטָאנוּ לְפָנֶיךָ . . .

We have given meager support to our Houses of Study.

We have neglected our heritage of learning.

עַל חֵטְא שֶׁחָטָאנוּ לְפָנֶיךָ . . .

We have sinned against ourselves and paid scant heed to the life of the spirit.

We have sinned against ourselves and have not risen to fulfill the best that is in us.

וְעַל כֻּלָּם אֱלוֹהַּ סְלִיחוֹת, סְלַח לָנוּ, מְחַל לָנוּ, כַּפֶּר־
לָנוּ!

*For all these sins, O God of mercy, forgive us, pardon us,
grant us atonement!*

• •

God before whom words must be true, we acknowledge
our faults and our failings. Help us now to strengthen the
good impulse within us.

*Help us to care about wrongs from which we have been
spared; to seek forgiveness for the wrongs we shall do; to
forgive the wrongs that are done to us.*

Create in us a clean heart, and place a willing spirit within
us.

*Shed Your light upon us, O God, that we may see the
goodness in each of Your children.*

• •

THE HOLINESS OF THIS DAY   קְדוּשַׁת הַיּוֹם

אֱלֹהֵינוּ וֵאלֹהֵי אֲבוֹתֵינוּ, (רְצֵה בִמְנוּחָתֵנוּ,) קַדְּשֵׁנוּ
בְּמִצְוֹתֶיךָ וְתֵן חֶלְקֵנוּ בְּתוֹרָתֶךָ. שַׂבְּעֵנוּ מִטּוּבֶךָ,
וְשַׂמְּחֵנוּ בִּישׁוּעָתֶךָ, (וְהַנְחִילֵנוּ, יְיָ אֱלֹהֵינוּ, בְּאַהֲבָה
וּבְרָצוֹן שַׁבַּת קָדְשֶׁךָ, וְיָנוּחוּ בָהּ יִשְׂרָאֵל מְקַדְּשֵׁי
שְׁמֶךָ,) וְטַהֵר לִבֵּנוּ לְעָבְדְּךָ בֶּאֱמֶת. כִּי אַתָּה סָלְחָן
לְיִשְׂרָאֵל וּמָחֳלָן לְשִׁבְטֵי יְשֻׁרוּן בְּכָל־דּוֹר וָדוֹר,
וּמִבַּלְעָדֶיךָ אֵין לָנוּ מֶלֶךְ מוֹחֵל וְסוֹלֵחַ אֶלָּא אָתָּה.
בָּרוּךְ אַתָּה, יְיָ, מֶלֶךְ מוֹחֵל וְסוֹלֵחַ לַעֲוֹנוֹתֵינוּ
וְלַעֲוֹנוֹת עַמּוֹ בֵּית יִשְׂרָאֵל, וּמַעֲבִיר אַשְׁמוֹתֵינוּ בְּכָל־

405

שָׁנָה וְשָׁנָה, מֶלֶךְ עַל כָּל־הָאָרֶץ, מְקַדֵּשׁ (הַשַּׁבָּת וְ)
יִשְׂרָאֵל וְיוֹם הַכִּפּוּרִים.

*Our God and God of our ancestors, sanctify us with Your
Mitzvot, and let Your Torah be our way of life. (May our
rest on this day be pleasing in Your sight.) Satisfy us with
Your goodness, gladden us with Your salvation, and purify
our hearts to serve You in truth; for You alone are the One
who pardons and forgives us in every generation; we have no
God but You. Blessed is the Lord, whose forgiving love annuls our trespasses year after year. King of all the world,
You hallow (the Sabbath,) the House of Israel and the Day
of Atonement.*

• •

BECAUSE I LOVE   עבודה

רְצֵה, יְיָ אֱלֹהֵינוּ, בְּעַמְּךָ יִשְׂרָאֵל, וּתְפִלָּתָם בְּאַהֲבָה
תְקַבֵּל, וּתְהִי לְרָצוֹן תָּמִיד עֲבוֹדַת יִשְׂרָאֵל עַמֶּךָ.
בָּרוּךְ אַתָּה, יְיָ, שָׁאוֹתְךָ לְבַדְּךָ בְּיִרְאָה נַעֲבוֹד.

°Let me hear You, Lord, when I hear my spirit soaring in
prayer. May I sing because I love, not afraid to waste my
sweetness upon the void, but reflecting in my soul's flight
the universal God who sings through me.

• •

TO USE OUR LIFE FOR BLESSING   הודאה

מוֹדִים אֲנַחְנוּ לָךְ, שָׁאַתָּה הוּא יְיָ אֱלֹהֵינוּ וֵאלֹהֵי
אֲבוֹתֵינוּ, אֱלֹהֵי כָל־בָּשָׂר, יוֹצְרֵנוּ יוֹצֵר בְּרֵאשִׁית.
בְּרָכוֹת וְהוֹדָאוֹת לְשִׁמְךָ הַגָּדוֹל וְהַקָּדוֹשׁ עַל־
שֶׁהֶחֱיִיתָנוּ וְקִיַּמְתָּנוּ.

O God of Israel's past, God of this day, God of all flesh, Creator of all life: We praise You, the Most High, for the gift of life; we give thanks, O Source of good, that life endures.

כֵּן תְּחַיֵּנוּ וּתְקַיְּמֵנוּ, יְיָ אֱלֹהֵינוּ, וּתְאַמְּצֵנוּ לִשְׁמֹר חֻקֶּיךָ, לַעֲשׂוֹת רְצוֹנֶךָ, וּלְעָבְדְּךָ בְּלֵבָב שָׁלֵם. בָּרוּךְ אֵל הַהוֹדָאוֹת.

Eternal and infinite God, help us to use our life for blessing: to live by Your law, to do Your will, to walk in Your way with a whole heart. We praise You, Eternal God, for the blessing of life.

A PEACE PROFOUND AND TRUE　　　　　ברכת שלום

שִׂים שָׁלוֹם, טוֹבָה וּבְרָכָה, חֵן וָחֶסֶד וְרַחֲמִים, עָלֵינוּ וְעַל כָּל־יִשְׂרָאֵל עַמֶּךָ. בָּרְכֵנוּ אָבִינוּ, כֻּלָּנוּ כְּאֶחָד, בְּאוֹר פָּנֶיךָ, כִּי בְאוֹר פָּנֶיךָ נָתַתָּ לָּנוּ, יְיָ אֱלֹהֵינוּ, תּוֹרַת חַיִּים, וְאַהֲבַת חֶסֶד, וּצְדָקָה וּבְרָכָה וְרַחֲמִים, וְחַיִּים וְשָׁלוֹם. וְטוֹב בְּעֵינֶיךָ לְבָרֵךְ אֶת־עַמְּךָ יִשְׂרָאֵל בְּכָל־עֵת וּבְכָל־שָׁעָה בִּשְׁלוֹמֶךָ. בְּסֵפֶר חַיִּים בְּרָכָה וְשָׁלוֹם וּפַרְנָסָה טוֹבָה נִזָּכֵר וְנִכָּתֵב לְפָנֶיךָ, אֲנַחְנוּ וְכָל־עַמְּךָ בֵּית יִשְׂרָאֵל, לְחַיִּים טוֹבִים וּלְשָׁלוֹם. בָּרוּךְ אַתָּה, יְיָ, עוֹשֵׂה הַשָּׁלוֹם.

°O Source of peace, lead us to peace, a peace profound and true; lead us to a healing, to mastery of all that drives us to war within ourselves and with others.

°May our deeds inscribe us in the Book of life and blessing, righeousness and peace!

°O Source of peace, bless us with peace.

◆ ◆

SILENT PRAYER

יְהִי רָצוֹן מִלְּפָנֶיךָ, יְיָ אֱלֹהֵינוּ וֵאלֹהֵי אֲבוֹתֵינוּ, שֶׁלֹּא
תַעֲלֶה שִׂנְאָתֵנוּ עַל־לֵב אָדָם, וְלֹא שִׂנְאַת אָדָם תַּעֲלֶה
עַל לִבֵּנוּ.
וּתְיַחֵד לְבָבֵנוּ לְיִרְאָה אֶת־שְׁמֶךָ, וּתְרַחֲקֵנוּ מִכָּל־מַה
שֶּׁשָּׂנֵאתָ, וּתְקָרְבֵנוּ לְכָל־מַה שֶׁאָהַבְתָּ, וְתַעֲשֶׂה עִמָּנוּ
צְדָקָה לְמַעַן שְׁמֶךָ.

Lord our God and God of all generations, grant that none
may hate us, and let hatred for others never enter our
hearts.
Unite us in the reverence of Your name; keep us far from
the things You hate, and draw us near to the things You
love; O treat us with compassion for Your name's sake!

◆ ◆

עֹשֶׂה שָׁלוֹם בִּמְרוֹמָיו, הוּא יַעֲשֶׂה שָׁלוֹם עָלֵינוּ וְעַל
כָּל־יִשְׂרָאֵל, וְאִמְרוּ אָמֵן.

May the One who causes peace to reign in the high heavens let
peace descend on us, on all Israel, and all the world.

◆ ◆

מִי שֶׁשָּׁכֵן אֶת־שְׁמוֹ בַּבַּיִת הַזֶּה, הוּא יַשְׁכִּין בֵּינֵיכֶם
אַהֲבָה וְאַחֲוָה וְשָׁלוֹם וְרֵעוּת.

May the One whose presence dwells in this house cause
love and harmony, peace and friendship to dwell among
us, now and always.

◆ ◆

The Ark is opened
All rise

עלֵינוּ

Let us adore
the ever-living God,
and render praise
unto Him
who spread out the heavens
and established the earth,
whose glory
is revealed in the heavens above,
and whose greatness
is manifest throughout the world.
He is our God; there is none else.

עָלֵינוּ לְשַׁבֵּחַ לַאֲדוֹן הַכֹּל,
לָתֵת גְּדֻלָּה לְיוֹצֵר בְּרֵאשִׁית,
שֶׁהוּא נוֹטֶה שָׁמַיִם וְיוֹסֵד אָרֶץ,
וּמוֹשַׁב יְקָרוֹ בַּשָּׁמַיִם מִמַּעַל,
וּשְׁכִינַת עֻזּוֹ בְּגָבְהֵי מְרוֹמִים.
הוּא אֱלֹהֵינוּ, אֵין עוֹד.

וַאֲנַחְנוּ כּוֹרְעִים וּמִשְׁתַּחֲוִים וּמוֹדִים לִפְנֵי מֶלֶךְ מַלְכֵי
הַמְּלָכִים, הַקָּדוֹשׁ בָּרוּךְ הוּא.

We therefore bow in awe and reverence before the One who
is Sovereign over all, the Holy and Blessed One.

אֱמֶת מַלְכֵּנוּ אֶפֶס זוּלָתוֹ, כַּכָּתוּב בְּתוֹרָתוֹ: "וְיָדַעְתָּ
הַיּוֹם וַהֲשֵׁבֹתָ אֶל לְבָבֶךָ, כִּי יְיָ הוּא הָאֱלֹהִים בַּשָּׁמַיִם
מִמַּעַל וְעַל הָאָרֶץ מִתָּחַת, אֵין עוֹד".

In truth, God alone is our King, as it is written: "Know
then this day and take it to heart: the Lord is God in the
heavens above and on the earth below; there is none else."

The Ark is closed
All are seated

♦ ♦

From Creation to Redemption

עבודה

Two or more readers might conduct
the following section, to page 429

MEDITATION

אַתָּה כּוֹנַנְתָּ עוֹלָם מֵרֹאשׁ, יָסַדְתָּ תֵּבֵל וְהַכֹּל פָּעֲלְתָּ, וּבְרִיּוֹת
בּוֹ יָצְרְתָּ. בְּשׁוּרְךָ עוֹלָם תְּהוּ נָבְהוּ, וְחְשֶׁךְ עַל פְּנֵי תְהוֹם,
גֵּרֵשְׁתָּ אְפֶל וְהַצַּבְתָּ נְגַהּ. גְּלֶם תַּבְנִיתְךָ מִן הָאֲדָמָה יָצֵרְתָּ, וְעַל
עֵץ הַדַּעַת אוֹתוֹ פָּקַדְתָּ. דְּבָרְךָ זָנַח וְנִזְנַח מֵעֵדֶן, וְלֹא כִלִּיתוֹ
לְמַעַן אֶרֶךְ אַפֶּךָ. הִגְדַּלְתָּ פִּרְיוֹ וּבֵרַכְתָּ זַרְעוֹ, וְהִפְרִיתָם
בְּטוּבְךָ וְהוֹשַׁבְתָּם שָׁקֶט. וַיִּפְרְקוּ עֹל וַיֹּאמְרוּ לָאֵל סוּר מִמֶּנּוּ;
וַהֲסִירוֹתָ יָד, כְּרֶגַע כְּחָצִיר אָמְלָלוּ. זָכַרְתָּ בְּרִית לְתָמִים
בְּדוֹרוֹ, וּבִזְכוּתוֹ שַׂמְתָּ לָעוֹלָם שְׁאֵרִית. חֹק בְּרִית קֶשֶׁת
לְמַעֲנוּ כָּרַתָּ, וּבְאַהֲבַת נִיחֹחוֹ בָּנָיו בֵּרַכְתָּ. טָעוּ בְעָשְׂרָם וַיִּבְנוּ
מִגְדָּל, וַיֹּאמְרוּ: לְכוּ וְנַעֲלֶה, וְנִבְקִיעַ הָרָקִיעַ לְהִלָּחֶם־בּוֹ. יָחִיד,
אַב הָמוֹן, פִּתְאוֹם כְּכוֹכָב זָרַח מֵאוֹר כַּשְׂדִּים, לְהָאִיר בַּחְשֶׁךְ.

°Author of life, in the beginning You formed the universe and
established the earth.

Beholding chaos, seeing the darkness that lay upon the face of
the deep, You brought forth brightness to dispel the gloom.

Creation danced as clay took on Your image. How can dust
become the one whose thought is more than dust?

Driven by restless yearnings, we ate of the Tree of Knowledge:
Ever since, we dream of Your Garden, a vision we fled, a vision
we fly to—

For even now Your pity upholds us.

Growing in numbers, increasing our skills, we feel blessed by
Your goodness.

How then can we break our bond and say to You: Depart from us!
In an instant we wither without Your care.

Judgment follows our every deed, but You are mindful of Your
covenant; a sign of Your blessing, the rainbow, adorns the
heavens.

Knowledge grows; still we stray, and in pride assault those
heavens. Lunar cold invades us.
Many fail and fall.
Nothing abides.
O but some who shine as stars bear witness to Your love.

··

אוֹחִילָה לָאֵל, אֲחַלֶּה פָנָיו, אֶשְׁאֲלָה מִמֶּנּוּ מַעֲנֵה
לָשׁוֹן. אֲשֶׁר בִּקְהַל עָם אָשִׁירָה עֻזּוֹ, אַבִּיעָה רְנָנוֹת
בְּעַד מִפְעָלָיו. לְאָדָם מַעַרְכֵי־לֵב, וּמֵיְיָ מַעֲנֵה לָשׁוֹן.
אֲדֹנָי, שְׂפָתַי תִּפְתָּח, וּפִי יַגִּיד תְּהִלָּתֶךָ. יִהְיוּ לְרָצוֹן
אִמְרֵי־פִי וְהֶגְיוֹן לִבִּי לְפָנֶיךָ, יְיָ, צוּרִי וְגֹאֲלִי.

I wait for God, I seek God's presence, hoping for an answer to
prayer. In the midst of the people, O God, I extol Your might
and celebrate Your deeds in joyful song.

We must purify our hearts, and the Lord will answer our prayer.

Eternal God, open my lips, and my mouth shall declare Your
glory. May the words of my mouth, and the meditations of my
heart, be acceptable to You, O Lord, my Rock and my
Redeemer.

··

בְּרֵאשִׁית בָּרָא אֱלֹהִים אֵת הַשָּׁמַיִם וְאֵת הָאָרֶץ: וְהָאָרֶץ
הָיְתָה תֹהוּ וָבֹהוּ וְחֹשֶׁךְ עַל־פְּנֵי תְהוֹם וְרוּחַ אֱלֹהִים מְרַחֶפֶת
עַל־פְּנֵי הַמָּיִם: וַיֹּאמֶר אֱלֹהִים יְהִי־אוֹר וַיְהִי־אוֹר:

In the beginning God created the heavens and the earth.
And the earth was without form and void, and there was
darkness upon the face of the deep, and the spirit of God

moved over the surface of the waters. Then God said: Let
there be light! And there was light.

•

For countless ages, the sun
flooded our planet with light,
yet no eye beheld its brilliance;
the winds whispered and roared,
but no ear heard their soft murmurs
or thundering peals.

•

וַיֹּאמֶר אֱלֹהִים: "יִשְׁרְצוּ הַמַּיִם שֶׁרֶץ נֶפֶשׁ חַיָּה, וְעוֹף
יְעוֹפֵף עַל־הָאָרֶץ, עַל־פְּנֵי רְקִיעַ הַשָּׁמָיִם".
וַיֹּאמֶר אֱלֹהִים: "תּוֹצֵא הָאָרֶץ נֶפֶשׁ חַיָּה לְמִינָהּ,
בְּהֵמָה וָרֶמֶשׂ וְחַיְתוֹ־אֶרֶץ לְמִינָהּ," וַיְהִי־כֵן.

*Then God said: Let the waters teem with swarms of living
creatures, and let birds fly above the earth across the vault of
heaven.*
*And God said: Let the earth bring forth living creatures, ac-
cording to their kinds: cattle, reptiles, and land animals according to their kinds. And it was so.*

•

Creatures were born in the shallow waters,
of one substance with earth and sea and air,
but Your creative word endowed them with new powers.
They could feed and sustain themselves,
reproduce and multiply.
Some had the further gift
to perceive, explore, and apprehend their world.
And so, by Your word, the earth awoke.

A flood of light burst forth
to shape innumerable forms of life
in an endless variety of living species.

◆

From Psalm 104

Praise the Lord, O my soul! O Lord my God, You are very great.

You are arrayed in glory and majesty.

You wrap Yourself in light as with a garment.

You stretch out the heavens like a curtain.

The winds are Your messengers;

flames of fire, Your ministers.

You cause streams to spring forth in the valleys;

they run between the mountains, giving drink to all the beasts of the field.

The birds of the air nest on their banks, and sing among the leaves.

You make the moon to mark the seasons; the sun knows its time of setting.

How manifold are Your works, O Lord!

In wisdom You have made them all; the earth in its fullness is Yours.

◆

יְהִי כְבוֹד יְיָ לְעוֹלָם! יִשְׂמַח יְיָ בְּמַעֲשָׂיו!

May the glory of the Lord endure for ever! Rejoice, O Lord, in
Your works!

•

Every living creature has its native wisdom:
the fish move and multiply in the cool waters;
the birds glide through the living air;
beasts of prey go hunting without instruction;
and every creature uses an inborn cunning
to flee, to hide, and to defend itself and its young.
But to one species, more than all others,
You were lavish in Your gifts.

•

וַיֹּאמֶר אֱלֹהִים: "נַעֲשֶׂה אָדָם בְּצַלְמֵנוּ כִּדְמוּתֵנוּ,
וְיִרְדּוּ בִדְגַת הַיָּם, וּבְעוֹף הַשָּׁמַיִם, וּבַבְּהֵמָה, וּבְכָל־
הָאָרֶץ, וּבְכָל־הָרֶמֶשׂ הָרֹמֵשׂ עַל־הָאָרֶץ." וַיִּבְרָא
אֱלֹהִים אֶת־הָאָדָם בְּצַלְמוֹ, בְּצֶלֶם אֱלֹהִים בָּרָא אֹתוֹ;
זָכָר וּנְקֵבָה בָּרָא אֹתָם. וַיְבָרֶךְ אֹתָם אֱלֹהִים, וַיֹּאמֶר
לָהֶם אֱלֹהִים: "פְּרוּ וּרְבוּ, וּמִלְאוּ אֶת־הָאָרֶץ וְכִבְשֻׁהָ;
וּרְדוּ בִדְגַת הַיָּם וּבְעוֹף הַשָּׁמַיִם, וּבְכָל־חַיָּה הָרֹמֶשֶׂת
עַל־הָאָרֶץ."

Then God said: Let us make a being in our image, after
our likeness, and let it have dominion over the fish of the
sea and the birds of the air, and over the cattle; over all the
earth and over every creature that crawls upon it. Thus
God created us in the divine image, creating us in the
image of God, creating us male and female. And God
blessed us, and said to us: Be fruitful and multiply; fill the
earth and subdue it; and have dominion over the fish of

the sea and the birds of the air, and over every living thing
that moves upon the earth.

◆

We were unlike other creatures.
Not for us the tiger's claws,
the elephant's thick hide,
or the crocodile's scaly armor.
To the gazelle we were slow of foot,
to the lioness a weakling,
and the eagle thought us bound to earth.
But You gave us powers they could not comprehend:
a skillful hand,
a probing mind,
a loving heart,
a soul aspiring to know and to fulfill its destiny.

◆

From Psalm 8

Sovereign Lord, how majestic is Your presence in all the
earth!

You have stamped Your glory upon the heavens!

When I consider the heavens, the work of Your fingers;
the moon and the stars that You have established:

What are we, that You are mindful of us?

What are we mortals, that You care for us?

*Yet You have made us little less than divine, and crowned us
with glory and honor.*

◆

You gave us
the power of speech, that magic gift
by which each soul, unique and separate,
yet shares its life with others.
Though each individual,
unaided and alone, is weak and helpless,
Your gift of love brings us strength:
Not by might nor by power,
but by Your spirit—
the thirst for knowledge,
the urge to create,
the passion for justice,
the will to give love and loyalty.
Sometimes we have lived at peace with one another,
but all too often we are deaf
to the divine wisdom within us,
preferring the law of the jungle,
preferring war to peace,
preferring evil to good.

◆

וַיַּרְא יְיָ כִּי רַבָּה רָעַת הָאָדָם בָּאָרֶץ,
וְכָל־יֵצֶר מַחְשְׁבֹת לִבּוֹ רַק רַע כָּל הַיּוֹם.

And the Lord saw that our wickedness on earth was great,
and that the heart was ever bent on evil.

◆

How long shall the curse of Cain
continue to haunt the human race?
How long shall Abel's blood, the innocent blood
cruelly shed in ceaseless conflict,
plead all unheeded that we are kin,
and every one the keeper of the other?
Cannot those whose mind and will

have brought them to the moon,
do equal wonders on their native soil?

Though our deeds are stained with blood, this we know:
You have set in the inmost sanctuary of our being
Your law of justice, love, and peace.
The flame which burns upon that altar may flicker,
but it can never be quenched.
For that flame is Your eternal spirit,
burning within us.

◆

Long ago, but we remember it well,
You inspired a people, the House of Israel,
to recognize that flame and minister to it
as a kingdom of priests and a holy people.
This was to be the meaning and message
of their existence,
the calling of those who gave up home and hearth
to found a people pledged to do Your will.

◆

וַיֹּאמֶר יְיָ אֶל־אַבְרָם: ״לֶךְ־לְךָ מֵאַרְצְךָ וּמִמּוֹלַדְתְּךָ
וּמִבֵּית אָבִיךָ אֶל־הָאָרֶץ אֲשֶׁר אַרְאֶךָּ. וְאֶעֶשְׂךָ לְגוֹי
גָּדוֹל, וַאֲבָרֶכְךָ וַאֲגַדְּלָה שְׁמֶךָ, וֶהְיֵה בְּרָכָה...
וְנִבְרְכוּ בְךָ כֹּל מִשְׁפְּחֹת הָאֲדָמָה.״

Then the Lord said to Abram: 'Go forth from your
country, and your birthplace, and your ancestral home, to
the land that I will show you. And I will make of you a
great people; I will bless you, and make your name great,
and you shall be a blessing . . . . Through you shall all the
families of the earth be blessed.'

◆

Many generations later, redeemed from slavery,
Abraham's descendants stood at Mount Sinai.
The ancient promise was to be confirmed,
the ancient mandate reasserted and enlarged,
the ancient covenant renewed and sealed
to bind all future generations.

◆

When God revealed the Torah,
no bird chirped,
no fowl beat its wings,
no ox bellowed,
the angels did not sing,
the sea did not stir,
no creature uttered a sound;
the world was silent and still,
and the Divine Voice spoke:
'I, the Lord, am your God.'

◆

א אָנֹכִי יְיָ אֱלֹהֶיךָ, אֲשֶׁר הוֹצֵאתִיךָ מֵאֶרֶץ מִצְרַיִם,
מִבֵּית עֲבָדִים.

I, the Lord, am your God who led you out of the land of
Egypt, out of the house of bondage.

ב לֹא יִהְיֶה־לְךָ אֱלֹהִים אֲחֵרִים עַל־פָּנָי.

You shall have no other gods besides Me.

ג לֹא תִשָּׂא אֶת־שֵׁם־יְיָ אֱלֹהֶיךָ לַשָּׁוְא.

You shall not invoke the name of the Lord your God with
malice.

ד זָכוֹר אֶת־יוֹם הַשַּׁבָּת לְקַדְּשׁוֹ.

Remember the Sabbath day and keep it holy.

418

ה כַּבֵּד אֶת־אָבִיךָ וְאֶת־אִמֶּךָ.

Honor your father and your mother.

ו לֹא תִרְצָח.

You shall not murder.

ז לֹא תִנְאָף.

You shall not commit adultery.

ח לֹא תִגְנֹב.

You shall not steal.

ט לֹא־תַעֲנֶה בְרֵעֲךָ עֵד שָׁקֶר.

You shall not bear false witness against your neighbor.

י לֹא תַחְמֹד.

You shall not covet.

◆

Thus pledged to play a redemptive role
in the world's unfolding destiny,
Israel journeyed on from Sinai
and reached the Promised Land,
the land they loved,
and which seemed to love them in return.
On one of its mountains they built a city, Jerusalem,
and on top of the mountain, a temple,
symbol of the splendor of Israel's God.

◆

But no city is eternal; no temple stands for ever.
Centuries passed . . . . Israel stumbled and fell.
The city was stormed, the Temple burned to ashes,
the flower of the nation carried captive to the

conqueror's land.
By the waters of Babylon they sat and wept,
remembering Jerusalem.
"How shall we sing the Lord's song in a foreign land?"
But the Lord had not deserted them;
restoration was at hand.

◆

נַחֲמוּ, נַחֲמוּ עַמִּי, יֹאמַר אֱלֹהֵיכֶם. דַּבְּרוּ עַל־לֵב
יְרוּשָׁלַיִם, וְקִרְאוּ אֵלֶיהָ, כִּי מָלְאָה צְבָאָהּ, כִּי נִרְצָה
עֲוֹנָהּ; כִּי לָקְחָה מִיַּד יְיָ כִּפְלַיִם בְּכָל־חַטֹּאתֶיהָ. קוֹל
קוֹרֵא: בַּמִּדְבָּר פַּנּוּ דֶּרֶךְ יְיָ, יַשְּׁרוּ בָּעֲרָבָה מְסִלָּה
לֵאלֹהֵינוּ. כָּל־גֶּיא יִנָּשֵׂא, וְכָל־הַר וְגִבְעָה יִשְׁפָּלוּ;
וְהָיָה הֶעָקֹב לְמִישׁוֹר, וְהָרְכָסִים לְבִקְעָה. וְנִגְלָה
כְּבוֹד יְיָ, וְרָאוּ כָל־בָּשָׂר יַחְדָּו, כִּי פִי יְיָ דִּבֵּר.

Take comfort, take comfort, My people, says your God.
Speak tenderly to Jerusalem; proclaim to her that her bondage is ended, her iniquity pardoned, that she has received
from the Lord's hand ample punishment for all her sins. A
voice proclaims: Build a road for the Lord through the
wilderness, clear a highway in the desert for our God.
Every valley shall be exalted, every mountain and hill
made low; the uneven ground shall be made level, the
rough places a plain. The glory of the Lord shall be
revealed, and, united, all shall see it; for the mouth of the
Lord has spoken.

◆

How like a dream it was, but far more real:
the exiles returned to Jerusalem; they
        laughed for joy;
the Lord had done great things for them,

and with full hearts they dedicated a new temple
to the Eternal One, Creator and Sustainer of all being.
Here the ancient forms of worship were resumed,
and new ones evolved—chief among them
the Day of Atonement.

◆

The ritual begins at dawn.
Great crowds converge from far and near
upon the Temple,
until its courts are filled to overflowing
with priests and levites, men and women,
young and old.
The High Priest has prepared himself for seven days.
How can he intercede for others
if he is impure himself?
All night he has rehearsed the sacred ritual.
Robed in gold,
he burns the incense, offers the sacrifices,
dispatches a goat into the wilderness,
the goat a symbol
of the people's longing to be rid of sin.

How splendid he looks in his glittering array;
how heavy is his responsibility
as alone he enters the Holy of Holies,
that curtained chamber, mysterious yet simple,
containing nothing but a stone—
but engraved on that stone are God's Ten Words!

◆

How glorious he is,
when he comes from behind the veil of the shrine!

Three times the white-robed High Priest recites
a confession of sins:
first, for himself and for his family.

אָנָּא יְיָ, כַּפֶּר־נָא לַחֲטָאִים וְלַעֲוֹנוֹת וְלַפְּשָׁעִים
שֶׁחָטָאתִי וְשֶׁעָוְיתִי וְשֶׁפָּשַׁעְתִּי לְפָנֶיךָ, אֲנִי וּבֵיתִי,
כַּכָּתוּב: "כִּי בַיּוֹם הַזֶּה יְכַפֵּר עֲלֵיכֶם, לְטַהֵר אֶתְכֶם;
מִכֹּל חַטֹּאתֵיכֶם לִפְנֵי יְיָ תִּטְהָרוּ."

*O Lord, pardon the sins, iniquities, and transgressions that I
have committed before You, I and my household; as it has
been said: "On this day atonement shall be made for you, to
purify you; you shall be cleansed from all your sins before
the Lord."*

So, too, do we confess our own sins,
and pray on behalf of our loved ones:
Lord, let our homes be dwelling-places of Your presence,
where love and justice are taught and practiced.
May we always enter them with eager hearts,
and from them go into the world
with dedication and a firm resolve
faithfully to carry out the tasks of life.

*So may we too be priests,
ministering to the needs of others,
and making clear in the world
the beauty of holiness.*

◆

Having confessed his own sins,
the High Priest recites a similar confession
for the whole House of Aaron.

אָנָּא יְיָ, כַּפֶּר־נָא לַחֲטָאִים וְלַעֲוֹנוֹת וְלַפְּשָׁעִים
שֶׁחָטָאתִי וְשֶׁעָוְיתִי וְשֶׁפָּשַׁעְתִּי לְפָנֶיךָ, אֲנִי וּבֵיתִי וּבְנֵי

אַהֲרֹן, כַּכָּתוּב: "כִּי בַיּוֹם הַזֶּה יְכַפֵּר עֲלֵיכֶם, לְטַהֵר
אֶתְכֶם; מִכֹּל חַטֹּאתֵיכֶם לִפְנֵי יְיָ תִּטְהָרוּ."

O Lord, pardon the sins, iniquities, and transgressions that I
have committed before You, I, my household, and the sons of
Aaron; as it has been said: "On this day atonement shall be
made for you, to purify you; you shall be cleansed from all
your sins before the Lord."

Like the High Priest of old, may Israel's teachers today
bear themselves humbly and be watchful of their responsibility. May their lives in the sight of God testify to the
truths they proclaim to their people. Grant them wisdom
and strength, O God, to sing Your word with earnestness
and zeal, and thus awaken in the hearts of Your people
devotion to Your cause and confidence in their mission.

◆

Now the High Priest, having confessed for himself and his
family, and for all the priests, confesses a third time, for
the whole House of Israel.

אָנָּא יְיָ, כַּפֶּר־נָא לַחֲטָאִים וְלַעֲוֹנוֹת וְלַפְּשָׁעִים
שֶׁחָטְאוּ וְשֶׁעָווּ וְשֶׁפָּשְׁעוּ לְפָנֶיךָ עַמְּךָ בֵּית־יִשְׂרָאֵל,
כַּכָּתוּב: "כִּי בַיּוֹם הַזֶּה יְכַפֵּר עֲלֵיכֶם, לְטַהֵר אֶתְכֶם;
מִכֹּל חַטֹּאתֵיכֶם לִפְנֵי יְיָ תִּטְהָרוּ."

O Lord, pardon the sins, iniquities and transgressions that
we, Your people, the House of Israel, have committed before
You; as it has been said: "On this day atonement shall be
made for you, to purify you; you shall be cleansed from all
your sins before the Lord."

◆

423

וְהַכֹּהֲנִים וְהָעָם הָעוֹמְדִים בָּעֲזָרָה, כְּשֶׁהָיוּ שׁוֹמְעִים
אֶת־הַשֵּׁם הַנִּכְבָּד וְהַנּוֹרָא מְפוֹרָשׁ יוֹצֵא מִפִּי כֹּהֵן
גָּדוֹל בִּקְדֻשָּׁה וּבְטָהֳרָה, הָיוּ כּוֹרְעִים וּמִשְׁתַּחֲוִים
וּמוֹדִים וְנוֹפְלִים עַל פְּנֵיהֶם, וְאוֹמְרִים:

When the priests and the people who stood in the Temple
court heard the High Priest, full of reverence, utter God's
holy and awesome Name, they fell upon their faces and,
prostrate, exclaimed:

All rise

בָּרוּךְ שֵׁם כְּבוֹד מַלְכוּתוֹ לְעוֹלָם וָעֶד!

Blessed is His glorious kingdom for ever and ever!

All are seated

◆

We, too, pray not only for ourselves,
but for the Jewish people as a whole,
whose destiny is our own,
and whose hope we share.
Alas, how much there is in the life of our people
that is unworthy of its noble past
and its high calling!

◆

Some have strayed from their ancestral faith, and broken
the chain of tradition.

*Some have despised their birthright, and treated their
heritage with contempt.*

Some have dishonored the Sabbath and desecrated the
Festive Days.

424

Some are deaf to the music of Mitzvot, and they shut their eyes to the beauty of holiness.

Some have made idols of professional advancement, social status, and material reward.

Some, while pretending to love humanity, have withheld from their own people the love they deserve.

Some have forgotten that Judaism calls us to love and to serve others.

Some, by their wrong actions, or by their failure to act, have brought dishonor upon our people.

In our communal life needless conflict and groundless hatred destroy the unity of Israel.

And in the name of unity we sometimes disregard the greater virtue of integrity.

Self-seeking leaves little room for self-sacrifice,

and our high-sounding words are rarely translated into action.

◆

For all these sins we ask forgiveness, and pray that the House of Israel, purified, reconciled, and reconsecrated, may again become worthy to stand in Your presence, and to be the messenger of Your word, O Lord our God, God Most High.

◆ ◆

The Second Temple, like the First, came to an end, and all its splendid rites,

425

including those of Yom Kippur,
became a wistful memory.
But when it fell, the Synagogue,
house of the people's assembly, took its place.
No sacrifices were offered here.
Here Israel's people met
to study the word of God,
so that the law taught by Moses and the prophets
became the heritage of the congregation of Jacob;
together chanting prayer and praise
to their divine Creator,
bringing to God, instead of burnt-offerings,
the offering of their lips
and the service of their hearts;
together seeking atonement
through repentance, prayer, and charity.
Here, in the synagogues,
our people found the presence of God,
and the guidance they needed to hallow their lives.
And as they entered them, they sang:

מַה־טֹּבוּ אֹהָלֶיךָ, יַעֲקֹב, מִשְׁכְּנֹתֶיךָ, יִשְׂרָאֵל!

How lovely are Your tents, O Jacob, your dwelling-places, O
Israel!

♦ ♦

If you wish to know the fortress
to which your fathers bore their treasure,
their scrolls of Torah, their Holy of Holies;
if you would know the place of their deliverance;
if you would find the refuge
which kept your people's mighty spirit safe,
whose age—despite the years of degradation—
did not disgrace its gracious youth:

If you would know all this,

turn to the ancient, battered house of prayer.
There, to this day, your eyes may see
Jews with faces lean and lined,
Jews of the Exile, bearing its heavy weight,
forgetting their toil in a Talmud's tattered page,
their cares in chanted psalms.
How drab and strange a sight
to those who do not understand!
Your heart will tell you:
your feet touch the threshhold of our house of life,
your eyes behold the storehouse of our soul.

If God's spirit still breathes within you,
if still His solace whispers in your heart,
and if a spark of hope for better days
illumines the darkness in which you dwell,
mark well and hearken, my sister and brother:
this house is but a spark, a remnant saved
by a miracle, from that great fire
kept by our fathers always upon their altars.
Who can say? Did not the torrents of their tears
carry us safely to this shore?
Perhaps their prayers were the price of our salvation.
And was it not their deaths that bequeathed us life,
life enduring, life without end?

◆

Look back, look back on bitter suffering,
look back on noble endurance.
Behold our faith in Truth,
our heroic trust in God.
Look back and wonder:
What is this people?
What is the meaning of its life?

◆

Thus says the Lord God, who created the heavens and
stretched them out, who made the earth and all that grows
on it, who gives breath to its people and spirit to those
who walk on it:
I, the Lord, have called you to righteousness,
and taken you by the hand and kept you;
I have made you a covenant people,
a light to the nations:
to bring the captives out of prison,
and those who sit in darkness from their dungeons.

◆

You are My witnesses, says the Lord,
and My servant whom I have chosen,
that you may know Me, and trust Me,
and understand that I am the One.
Before Me no God was formed,
nor shall there be any after Me.
I, I alone am the Lord,
and besides Me there is no savior.

◆

Behold My servants, whom I uphold,
My chosen ones, in whom My soul delights;
I have put My spirit upon them,
that they may bring justice to the nations.
They shall not cry out nor shout aloud,
nor make themselves heard in the street.
Though bent like a reed,
they shall not be broken;
though their flame burns low,
they shall not be snuffed out:
faithfully shall they bring forth justice.

They shall not weaken,

they shall not be broken:
at last to establish justice in the earth,
as the most distant lands respond to their teaching.

◆

God chose us. We chose God.
There is a mystery here that reason cannot solve
nor cynicism dismiss.
We can deny that mystery, or we can humbly recognize it,
each resolving to be a part of it, and saying to God:
הנני, Here I am; send me.

אלה אזכרה

God's witnesses, God's servants! Generation after generation, in times of darkness as in times of light, we have
heard the divine word: "You shall be to Me a kingdom of
priests and a holy nation." We have felt the joy of being
God's servants. We have also felt the pain, for it has been
our destiny to be God's Suffering Servants. And so did we
appear to the nations:

From Isaiah 53

They had no outward grace to attract the eye, no beauty
to win the heart.

They were despised and rejected, a people of pains and ac-
quainted with grief.

As one from whom all turn their face, so were they
despised, and we held them of no account.

Yet it was our suffering they bore, our pains they endured.
And we supposed them punished by God, afflicted.

All the while they were wounded by our misdeeds, crushed
by our sins.

429

They were oppressed, they were afflicted, yet they never said a word.

Like lambs led to the slaughter, like sheep standing dumb before their shearers, they never uttered a cry.

By violence and injustice were they carried off.

Who cared about their fate, when they were cut off from the land of the living?

They were given graves among the wicked, a tomb among the base, though they had done no wrong, practiced no deception.

♦

The earth's crust is soaked with the tears of the innocent. The blood of every race cries out from the ground. Which is the people without its martyrs?

Now, therefore, we honor those of every race and continent: the innocent, the victims, all our companions in death and our partners in grief. Them we honor, them we mourn: may they never be forgotten; may a better world grow out of their suffering.

And especially do we remember the suffering of the House of Israel, a people of pains and acquainted with grief.

Look and remember. Look upon this land,
Far, far across the factories and the grass.
Surely, there, surely, they will let you pass.
Speak then and ask the forest and the loam.
What do you hear? What does the land command?
The earth is taken: this is not your home.

Days and years of peace: these too have been our lot.

Grandeur, greatness, quiet ages, domestic joys,
times when fear might almost be forgotten.
Yet again and again
our peace has been shattered, our land usurped, our dwell-
ings razed.
The mind grows numb, and the heart turns to stone,
to see our long travail.
Our foes were not content to give us pain;
their dream was darker still:
a world without Jews,
a world that would forget our very name!
We cannot forget this or be indifferent to its meaning.
We shall remember!

•

אֵלֶּה אֶזְכְּרָה,
וְנַפְשִׁי עָלַי אֶשְׁפְּכָה:
כִּי בְלָעוּנוּ זֵדִים
כְּעֻגָּה בְּלִי הֲפוּכָה,
כִּי בִימֵי הַשַּׂר לֹא עָלְתָה אֲרוּכָה,
לַעֲשָׂרָה הֲרוּגֵי מְלוּכָה.

*These things do I remember: through all the years, ig-
norance like a monster has devoured our martyrs as in one
long day of blood. Rulers have arisen through the endless
years, oppressive, savage in their witless power, filled with a
futile thought: to make an end of that which God has
cherished.*

•

אֵלִי צִיּוֹן וְעָרֶיהָ כְּמוֹ אִשָּׁה בְּצִירֶיהָ,
וְכִבְתוּלָה חֲגוּרַת שַׂק עַל בַּעַל נְעוּרֶיהָ.

עֲלֵי גָלוּת מְשָׁרְתֵי־אֵל, מַנְעִימֵי שִׁיר זְמָרֶיהָ,
וְעַל דָּמָם אֲשֶׁר שֻׁפַּךְ כְּמוֹ מֵימֵי יְאוֹרֶיהָ.

For Zion and her cities I mourn like a mother in her anguish, like
a woman who mourns the husband of her youth.

I mourn the exile of God's servants, makers of sweet melody,
their blood poured out like Zion's streams.

◆

I have taken an oath: to remember it all.
To remember—to forget nothing at all.
Forgetting nothing of this,
Till the tenth generation,
Till the grief disappears,
To the last, to its ending,
Till the punishing blows are ended for good.
I swear this night of terror
Shall not have passed in vain;
I swear this morning I'll not live unchanged,
As if I were no wiser even now, even now.

◆

THE TEN MARTYRS

In the time of Hadrian, emperor of Rome, the study and
practice of Torah were forbidden. Israel's leaders said:
'How survive without the Tree of Life? Why live when the
soul is dead?' And so they taught and learned and did
God's will. Israel's ten leaders were taken and doomed.

Shimon ben Gamaliel was slain. Remembering his
wisdom and witnessing his death, disciples exclaimed: 'Is
this Torah, and this its reward?' Rabbi Yishmael was next
to die. In pain and anguish, he cried out, and at his cry the
heavens trembled: 'Accept this; affirm Me; for if you fail,

the world must crumble into chaos!' Then Yishmael accepted his fate and said: 'I will trust in You even though You slay me.'

These things I remember as I pour out my heart: How the arrogant have devoured us!

Akiba had defied the decree and continued to teach. He was among those taken. He was led to his death at the time when the Shema is recited. As his flesh was flayed, he said: שמע ישראל. 'Even now?' his disciples asked. He replied: 'All my life this verse has troubled me: "Love the Lord your God with all your . . . . being . . . ."—love God, though you must die for it! I prayed always to be able to fulfill this—and now I can!' And with his final breath he said: יי אחד!—The Lord is One!, prolonging the last word until life was gone. Thus in a godless world was God affirmed.

These things I remember as I pour out my heart: How the arrogant have devoured us!

The Romans had forbidden the ordination of rabbis, decreeing death to ordainer and those ordained, and destruction for any city in which ordination would take place. Rabbi Yehudah ben Bava ordained five in the hills between two cities, Shefaram and Usha. When the enemy soldiers were upon them, Rabbi Yehudah told his disciples to flee. 'What will become of you?' they cried. He answered: 'I shall place myself before them as an immovable rock.' So he did—and the Roman lances struck him down. But the disciples escaped.

The Ten included other teachers, ten teachers among many. Dying, they did not perish. Their faith is immortal, their God eternal.

These things I remember as I pour out my heart: How the
arrogant have devoured us!

◆

In the days of the Crusades, whole communities of Jews
were massacred in the Rhineland. In one city, young and
old donned armor and stood behind their leader, Rabbi
Kalonymos ben Meshullam. The gate was smashed, their
friends had fled, and death reached out with sword and
fire. They said to one another:'Let us be strong and bear
the yoke of our holy faith, for only in this world can the
enemy kill us . . . .' In another city, as the flames mounted
high, the martyrs began to sing a song that began softly
but rose to a crescendo. Those who heard it came and
asked: 'What kind of song is this? We have never heard
such a sweet melody.' It was the Aleinu—We must praise
the Lord of all . . . .

So it was for us long ago. And only yesterday we drained
once more the cup of sorrow.

◆

קוֹל בְּרָמָה נִשְׁמָע, נְהִי בְּכִי תַמְרוּרִים! רָחֵל מְבַכָּה
עַל־בָּנֶיהָ, מֵאֲנָה לְהִנָּחֵם עַל־בָּנֶיהָ, כִּי אֵינֶנּוּ.

A voice is heard in Ramah, lamentation and bitter weeping!
Rachel is weeping for her children, refusing to be comforted
for her children, for they are gone.

◆

אַב הָרַחֲמִים, שׁוֹכֵן מְרוֹמִים, בְּרַחֲמָיו הָעֲצוּמִים,
הוּא יִפְקֹד בְּרַחֲמִים הַחֲסִידִים וְהַיְשָׁרִים וְהַתְּמִימִים,
קְהִלּוֹת הַקֹּדֶשׁ שֶׁמָּסְרוּ נַפְשָׁם עַל קְדֻשַּׁת הַשֵּׁם,
הַנֶּאֱהָבִים וְהַנְּעִימִים בְּחַיֵּיהֶם, וּבְמוֹתָם לֹא נִפְרָדוּ.

מִנְּשָׁרִים קַלּוּ, וּמֵאֲרָיוֹת גָּבֵרוּ, לַעֲשׂוֹת רְצוֹן קוֹנָם
וְחֵפֶץ צוּרָם. יִזְכְּרֵם אֱלֹהֵינוּ לְטוֹבָה עִם שְׁאָר צַדִּיקֵי
עוֹלָם, וְיִנְקֹם נִקְמַת דַּם עֲבָדָיו הַשָּׁפוּךְ, כַּכָּתוּב
בְּתוֹרַת מֹשֶׁה אִישׁ הָאֱלֹהִים: הַרְנִינוּ, גוֹיִם, עַמּוֹ, כִּי
דַם עֲבָדָיו יִקּוֹם, וְנָקָם יָשִׁיב לְצָרָיו, וְכִפֶּר אַדְמָתוֹ
עַמּוֹ . . .

Merciful God enthroned on high, in Your sublime compassion
remember the loving, the upright, and the innocent, the holy
congregations who gave their lives for the sanctification of Your
name. Loyal and honorable in their lives, in their deaths they
remained undivided. They were swifter than eagles and
stronger than lions to do the will of their Maker and the desire of
their Rock. Remember them for good with the other righteous of
the world, and bring judgment upon those who shed the blood
of Your servants. As it is written: Give praise, O nations, with His
people; for God will bring judgment upon those who shed the
blood of His servants . . . .

•

How many there are who rest in nameless graves, and how
many whose ashes were blown by the winds to every corner of the earth!

Even now the air we breathe is thick with the dust of our
martyrs. Do men and women know that they breathe it
still? And how can they not feel the earth trembling
beneath their feet as they walk upon ground under which
so many were thrust without mercy?

•

כָּל־זֹאת בָּאַתְנוּ וְלֹא שְׁכַחֲנוּךָ, וְלֹא־שִׁקַּרְנוּ בִּבְרִיתֶךָ.
כִּי־עָלֶיךָ הֹרַגְנוּ כָל־הַיּוֹם, נֶחְשַׁבְנוּ כְּצֹאן טִבְחָה.

All this has come upon us, yet we have not forgotten You, nor
been false to Your covenant.

435

For Your sake were we slain all the day long, and treated
like sheep for the slaughter.

♦

MEDITATION

We walk the world of slaughter,
stumbling and falling in wreckage,
surrounded by the fear of death,
and eyes which gaze at us in silence,
the eyes of other martyred Jews,
of hunted, harried, persecuted souls
who never had a choice,
who've huddled all together in the corner
and press each other closer still and quake.
For here it was the sharpened axes found them
and they have come to take another look
at the stark terror of their savage death.
Their staring eyes all ask the ancient question: Why?

♦ ♦

Lord our God, we have testified to Your presence in
heaven and earth. But in our day Your presence has been
an absence, Your call a silence. Long ago it was written in
Your name: "If you are My witnesses, I am the Lord, and
if you are not My witnesses, I am not the Lord." We have
struggled to live for You, and see what our fate has been!
Is not Your fate bound up with ours? How can Your
presence abide in a world where murder rules?

♦

Without Jews there is no Jewish God.
If we leave this world
The light will go out in Your tent.
Since Abraham knew You in a cloud,
You have burned in every Jewish face,

You have glowed in every Jewish eye,
And we made You in our image.

◆

Now the lifeless skulls
Add up to millions.
The stars are going out around You.
The memory of You is dimming,
The kingdom will soon be over.
Jewish seed and flower
Are embers.
The dew cries in the dead grass!
The Jewish dream and reality are ravished,
They die together.
Your witnesses are sleeping:
Infants, women,
Young men, old.
Even the Thirty-six,
Your saints, pillars of Your world,
Have fallen into a dead, an everlasting sleep.

◆

Who will dream You?
Who will remember You?
Who deny You?
Who yearn for You?
Who, on a lonely bridge,
Will leave You—in order to return?

◆

Silence.
Where in this holocaust is the word of God?
Not in the storm, nor in the shaking earth,
nor in the fire, but only within us.
The world was silent; the world was still.

YOM KIPPUR

And now, survivors stammer; their words are haunted.
Behind their words: silence.
Behind the silence,
a witness to the sin of silence.
What pains were taken to save cathedrals,
museums, monuments from destruction.
Treasures of art must be preserved—
they are the song of the human soul!
And in the camps and streets of Europe
mother and father and child lay dying,
and many looked away.
To look away from evil:
Is this not the sin of all 'good' people?

◆

MEDITATION

Perhaps some of the blame falls on me,
Because I kept silent, uttered no cry.
Fear froze my heart and confused my mind.
And I did not resist the lie.
My clear voice was choked and dumb.
And I allowed them, without protest,
To outrage and violate
What was dearest to me, holiest.
Cowardice came down and walked the earth.

We hid our true feelings from one another.
We did not hear the cry of a friend.
And our own cry we often had to smother.
Black suspicion, like the plague,
Murdered faith, and left hearts cold.
Courage was branded treason,
Betrayal was called heroic, bold.
Light hung its head in shame,
Waiting that at least one man should cry out:
'No!' but no one cried.

438

Only one thing was left—the patience to wait,
To wait that justice might prevail one day.
Perhaps that was part of my blame,
That I kept silent, did not speak,
As though I had nothing to say.

◆

מִמַּעֲמַקִּים קְרָאתִיךָ, יְיָ. אֲדֹנָי, שִׁמְעָה בְקוֹלִי.

Out of the depths I call to You, O Lord. Lord, hearken to my voice.

◆

For the sin of silence,
For the sin of indifference,
For the secret complicity of the neutral,
For the closing of borders,
For the washing of hands,
For the crime of indifference,
For the sin of silence,
For the closing of borders,
For all that was done,
For all that was not done,
Let there be no forgetfulness before the Throne of Glory;
Let there be remembrance within the human heart;
And let there at last be forgiveness
When Your children, O God,
are free and at peace.

◆

And yet even in the inferno, even there
were those we call חסידי אמות העולם,
the righteous of the nations.
Some gave their very lives to keep Jews from harm.
Who can measure such courage?
When so many were afraid to act,

439

they bore witness to the greatness
men and women can reach.
Look and take heart.
If ever such days return,
remember them and find courage.
Consider what can be done, what must be done
not to banish from our souls the image of God.

*Let the righteous who were faithful be remembered for good.
By their deeds, they have inscribed themselves in the Book of
Life!*

♦ ♦

MEDITATION

I

Is not a flower a mystery no flower can explain? Is not God the
growing, the pattern which has no end and is never quite the
same? Is not God in the heart that sees it and weeps for beauty?
Why, then, God, this mystery: that the bombs fall and the
sprays kill and the flames rise and the children go up in smoke?
Why is there still a flower to remind us of You? Why does the
sun still burn to give us life? How do we still turn to You? Why
cannot we help but turn to You, but why, why do we turn to
You so late?

II

When Leo Baeck came out of the black midnight of the con-
centration camp, he looked about at the world and at his
neighbors. Many averted their eyes. They had been silent. They
had been selfish—or they had followed the multitude to do evil.
In the darkness of the camps, Leo Baeck had not despaired. He
had fulfilled his function: he had taught and he had given comfort. And, in the darkness of the new world which had to live
with the memory of Belsen and Auschwitz, Baeck had continued to teach and to comfort his people. They say that when
Baeck lifted his hands and spoke the priestly benediction the
congregation felt very close to the Divine Presence.

'May the Lord look kindly upon you and be gracious unto you.' These words took on new meaning for the worshippers. In ancient times, the image of one Babylonian god was a clay furnace. When the fires of human sacrifice burned high, the eyes of the idol glared death upon the onlookers. To see God was to die. Biblical Israel transformed the terror into awe, and fear became love. In God's light we saw light. But in our days the world grew dark again. The pagan furnace roared, and Israel ascended into the sky as smoke. And we who are alive, wander across a darkened landscape fitfully illuminated by burning idols in which some exterminate their own human kin.

We need our teachers: those who died for the sanctification of the Divine Name, and those who lived to guide and comfort us. They tell us that the encounter with God can take place in the utmost darkness—if we are ready for it.

The blessing that shone through Leo Baeck can touch our lives. 'May God look upon us and give us peace.'

◆ ◆

זאָג ניט קיינמאָל אַז דו גייסט דעם לעצטן וועג,
וען הימלען בלײַענע פֿאַרשטעלן בלויע טעג.
וויַיל קומען וועט נאָך אונדזער אויסגעבענקטע שעה,
ס׳וועט אַ פויק טאָן אונדזער טראָט: מיר זײַנען דאָ!

פֿון גרינעם פֿאַלמען־לאַנד ביז ווײַסן לאַנד פֿון שניי,
מיר זײַנען דאָ, מיט אונדזער פּײַן, מיט אונדזער וויי.
און וווּ געפֿאַלן ס׳איז אַ שפּריץ פֿון אונדזער בלוט,
וועט אַ שפּראָץ טאָן אונדזער גבורה, אונדזער מוט.

You must not say that you now walk the final way,
Because the darkened heavens hide the blue of day.
The time we've longed for will at last draw near,
And our steps, as drums, will sound that we are here.

From land all green with palms, to lands all white with snow
We now arrive with all our pain and all our woe.
Where our blood sprayed out and came to touch the land,
There our courage and our faith will rise and stand.

◆ ◆

REBIRTH

After the suffering we rose up, refusing to die.
We rose to tend the wounded and comfort the bereaved;
to strengthen old communities and establish new ones;
to open new synagogues, to build new schools.
And we began to write a new chapter in our old book,
continuing the story of Israel, the eternal people.

Lord, teach us to do and to hear
the command that rests upon us now:
to honor the memory of the slain,
to bring our people back to life,
to bear witness before the world to Your glory
and to the goodness of life.

◆

עָזִּי וְזִמְרָת יָהּ וַיְהִי־לִי לִישׁוּעָה.
לֹא־אָמוּת כִּי־אֶחְיֶה, וַאֲסַפֵּר מַעֲשֵׂי יָהּ.

The Lord is my strength and my song, and He has become my
salvation.
I shall not die, but live, to declare the works of the Lord.

◆

In one land especially we glimpsed the rays of a new dawn:
the land of Zion, made ready for habitation by generations of pioneers. The great day came: Israel independent
at last, the millenial dream, a dream no more! Drawn by
its brightness, her children flocked to Israel from distant

lands of despair, and found hope. Though bent in mourning, they ploughed the earth deep, so that grain would grow tall. And as they restored the land to its fruitfulness, they began themselves to be restored. Israel lives: a people at home again, rooted in its soil, its way of life, its ancient faith.

◆

From Ezekiel 37

The hand of the Lord was upon me, setting me down in the midst of a valley. It was full of bones, and they were very dry. God said to me: Can these bones live? I answered: O Lord God, You alone know. Then God said to me: Prophesy to these bones, and say to them, O dry bones, hear the word of the Lord.

Behold, I will cause breath to enter you, that you may live. I will lay sinews upon you, and cause flesh to come upon you, and cover you with skin, and put breath in you, that you may live. Then you shall know that I am the Lord.

So I prophesied as God commanded me, and the breath came into them, and they lived. They stood on their feet, a very great host. Then God said to me:

These bones are the whole house of Israel. Behold, they say, our bones are dried up, our hope is lost, and we are cut off.

Therefore prophesy and say to them: Thus says the Lord God: Behold, I will open your graves, O My people, and I will bring you home to the land of Israel.

I will put My spirit within you, and you shall live. I will place you in your own land; then you shall know that I, the Lord, have spoken and acted.

◆

443

And the ransomed of the Lord shall return, and come to
Zion with singing, with everlasting joy as their crown.

*Joy and gladness shall be theirs; suffering and sorrow shall
take flight.*

In days to come, Jacob shall take root; Israel shall blossom and bud, and fill the world with fruit.

*For the Lord has comforted Zion, and shown compassion for
her afflicted.*

◆

וִיהוּדָה לְעוֹלָם תֵּשֵׁב, וִירוּשָׁלַיִם לְדוֹר וָדוֹר.

Judah shall abide for ever, Jerusalem from generation to
generation.

◆

Jerusalem is the joy of all the world!
But the whole earth is Yours, Lord,
and all who dwell there are Your children.
Wherever we seek You, we may find You.
Wherever we ponder Your teachings,
Torah makes its home.
Wherever we do justly and love mercy,
Your presence abides.
In the four corners of earth we, Your people,
are called to witness:
to the light of the Eternal,
to a teaching of compassion,
to the vision of redemption:

*It is too small a task for you to be My servant
merely to preserve the tribes of Jacob
and to restore the survivors of Israel:
I will make you a light to the nations,
that My salvation may reach to the ends of the earth.*

444

Sing, O heavens; exult, O earth!
Break out in song, you hills!

O Lord, You have comforted our people,
and shown compassion for the afflicted!

◆

The storm will end, a rain will fall,
A quiet meadow wind stir into being,

And over a dead tree trunk, a waking bluebell
With tongue of dew will carol in the morning.

◆ ◆

REDEMPTION

Today let us remember the earth's oppressed;
let us restore their human heritage
to the victims of torture,
the weak and the weary,
all who are imprisoned without cause.
Let us remember them,
bring peace to every home,
and comfort to every heart.
We know the wisdom by which You would have us
    live;
oceans of ink have been spilled to say it:
be faithful, be true, love one another as you
    love yourselves.
But the world is dark, Lord, and cold with fear
    and rage.
The hammer of Chaos beats loudly within our breasts:
How can we endure?

◆

445

This is the vision of a great and noble life:
to endure ambiguity and to make light shine through it;
to stand fast in uncertainty;
to prove capable of unlimited love and hope.

◆

Lord, today we turn to You,
uncertainly proclaiming Your glory
with scarce remembered words of a half-forgotten faith.
We have confessed our sins and promised to forsake them.
O find us as we grope for You in our darkness.
Lord, pardon us as we knock upon Your door,
for it has been said:
The gates of repentance are never barred.
And it has been taught:
We know our sin is pardoned when we no longer commit
it.

Lord, make us whole: make us one with our own hearts;
make us one with each other, at last to find ourselves at one
with You, our Friend, our Helper, and our Joy.

◆

Use us, Lord, to speed the day of reconciliation when
poverty, racial prejudice, and religious hatred no longer
threaten to destroy us;

when violence, angry conflict, and mistrust are forgotten
evils;

when our wealth is used to feed the hungry and heal the
sick;

when we cherish the world and hold it in trust for our
children's children;

446

when the weak become strong, and the strong compassionate;

and that which has been commanded shall come to pass: Let justice roll down like waters, and righteousness like a mighty stream.

• •

אֱלֹהֵֽינוּ וֵאלֹהֵי אֲבוֹתֵֽינוּ, מְלוֹךְ עַל כָּל־הָעוֹלָם כֻּלּוֹ בִּכְבוֹדֶֽךָ וְהִנָּשֵׂא עַל כָּל־הָאָֽרֶץ בִּיקָרֶֽךָ, וְהוֹפַע בַּהֲדַר גְּאוֹן עֻזֶּֽךָ עַל כָּל־יוֹשְׁבֵי תֵבֵל אַרְצֶֽךָ. וְיֵדַע כָּל־פָּעוּל כִּי אַתָּה פְעַלְתּוֹ, וְיָבִין כָּל־יָצוּר כִּי אַתָּה יְצַרְתּוֹ, וְיֹאמַר כֹּל אֲשֶׁר נְשָׁמָה בְאַפּוֹ: יְיָ אֱלֹהֵי יִשְׂרָאֵל מֶֽלֶךְ, וּמַלְכוּתוֹ בַּכֹּל מָשָֽׁלָה.

Our God and God of our ancestors, may You rule in glory over all the earth, and let Your grandeur be acclaimed throughout the world. Reveal the splendor of Your majesty to all who dwell on earth, that all Your works may know You as their Maker, and all the living acknowledge You as their Creator. Then all who breathe shall say: 'The Lord God of Israel is the King whose dominion extends to all creation.'

• •

ALL THE WORLD   וַיֶּאֱתָיוּ

וְיֶאֱתָיוּ כֹל לְעָבְדֶֽךָ, וִיבָרְכוּ שֵׁם כְּבוֹדֶֽךָ, וְיַגִּֽידוּ בָאִיִּים צִדְקֶֽךָ. וְיִדְרְשֽׁוּךָ עַמִּים לֹא יְדָעֽוּךָ, וִיהַלְלֽוּךָ כָּל־אַפְסֵי אָֽרֶץ, וְיֹאמְרוּ תָמִיד: יִגְדַּל יְיָ. וְיִזְבְּחוּ לְךָ אֶת־זִבְחֵיהֶם, וְיִזְנְחוּ אֶת־עֲצַבֵּיהֶם, וְיַחְפְּרוּ עִם פְּסִילֵיהֶם, וְיַטּוּ שְׁכֶם אֶחָד לְעָבְדֶֽךָ. וְיִירָאֽוּךָ עִם שֶֽׁמֶשׁ מְבַקְשֵׁי פָנֶֽיךָ, וְיַכִּֽירוּ כֹֽחַ

מַלְכוּתֶךָ, וִילַמְּדוּ תוֹעִים בִּינָה.
וְיִפְצְחוּ הָרִים רִנָּה, וְיִצְהֲלוּ אִיִּים בְּמָלְכֶךָ, וִיקַבְּלוּ עַל
מַלְכוּתֶךָ. וִירוֹמְמוּךָ בִּקְהַל עָם, וְיִשְׁמְעוּ רְחוֹקִים
וְיָבוֹאוּ, וְיִתְּנוּ לְךָ כֶּתֶר מְלוּכָה.

Ve·ye·e·ta·yu kol le·ov·de·cha, vi·va·re·chu sheim ke·vo·de·cha,
ve·ya·gi·du va·i·yim tsid·ke·cha. Ve·yid·re·shu·cha a·mim lo
ye·da·u·cha, vi·ha·le·lu·cha kol a·fe·sei a·rets, ve·yo·me·ru
ta·mid: yig·dal A·do·nai.

Ve·yiz·be·chu le·cha et zi·ve·chei·hem, ve·yiz·ne·chu et a·-
tsa·bei·hem, ve·yach·pe·ru im pe·si·lei·hem, ve·ya·tu she·chem
e·chad le·ov·de·cha. Ve·yi·ra·u·cha im she·mesh me·va·ke·shei
fa·ne·cha, ve·ya·ki·ru ko·ach mal·chu·te·cha, ve·yil·me·du to·im
bi·na.

Ve·yif·tse·chu ha·rim ri·na, ve·yits·ha·lu i·yim be·mo·le·che·cha,
vi·ka·be·lu ol mal·chu·te·cha. Vi·ro·me·mu·cha bi·ke·hal am,
ve·yish·me·u re·cho·kim ve·ya·vo·u, ve·yi·te·nu le·cha ke·ter
me·lu·cha.

All the world shall come to serve You,
   And bless Your glorious name,
And Your righteousness triumphant
   The islands shall proclaim.
And the peoples shall go seeking
   Who knew You not before,
And the ends of earth shall praise You,
   And tell Your greatness o'er.

They shall build for You their altars,
   Their idols overthrown,
And their graven gods shall shame them,
   As they turn to You alone.
They shall worship You at sunrise,
   And feel Your kingdom's might,
And impart their understanding
   To those astray in night.

With the coming of Your kingdom
    The hills shall shout with song,
And the islands laugh exultant
    That they to God belong.
And through all Your congregations
    So loud Your praise shall ring.,
That the utmost peoples, hearing,
    Shall hail You crowned King.

◆ ◆

סדר קריאת התורה

For the Reading of the Torah

וְהָיָה בְּאַחֲרִית הַיָּמִים, נָכוֹן יִהְיֶה הַר בֵּית־יְיָ בְּראשׁ
הֶהָרִים, וְנִשָּׂא מִגְּבָעוֹת, וְנָהֲרוּ אֵלָיו כָּל־הַגּוֹיִם.
וְהָלְכוּ עַמִּים רַבִּים וְאָמְרוּ: לְכוּ, וְנַעֲלֶה אֶל־הַר־יְיָ,
אֶל־בֵּית אֱלֹהֵי יַעֲקֹב, וְיוֹרֵנוּ מִדְּרָכָיו וְנֵלְכָה
בְּאֹרְחֹתָיו.

It shall come to pass, in the fullness of time, that the
mountain of the Lord's house shall be established as the
highest mountain, and raised above the hills; and all nations shall flow to it. Then many peoples shall say: Come,
let us go up to the mountain of the Eternal, to the house of
the God of Jacob. And they shall say:

Teach us Your ways, that we may walk in Your paths.

◆ ◆

All rise

The Ark is opened

אֵין כָּמוֹךָ בָאֱלֹהִים, יְיָ, וְאֵין כְּמַעֲשֶׂיךָ. מַלְכוּתְךָ
מַלְכוּת כָּל־עוֹלָמִים וּמֶמְשַׁלְתְּךָ בְּכָל־דּוֹר וָדֹר.
יְיָ מֶלֶךְ, יְיָ מָלָךְ, יְיָ יִמְלֹךְ לְעוֹלָם וָעֶד. יְיָ עֹז לְעַמּוֹ
יִתֵּן, יְיָ יְבָרֵךְ אֶת־עַמּוֹ בַשָּׁלוֹם.

There is none like You, O Lord, among the gods that are
worshipped, and there are no deeds like Yours. Your kingdom
is an everlasting kingdom, and Your dominion endures through
all generations.
The Lord rules; the Lord will reign for ever and ever. May the
Lord give strength to His people; may the Lord bless His people
with peace.

◆ ◆

The Torah is taken from the Ark

כִּי מִצִּיּוֹן תֵּצֵא תוֹרָה, וּדְבַר־יְיָ מִירוּשָׁלָיִם.

For out of Zion shall go forth Torah, and the word of the Lord
from Jerusalem.

בָּרוּךְ שֶׁנָּתַן תּוֹרָה לְעַמּוֹ יִשְׂרָאֵל בִּקְדֻשָּׁתוֹ.

Praised be the One who in His holiness has given the Torah to
His people Israel.

• •

בֵּית יַעֲקֹב: לְכוּ, וְנֵלְכָה בְּאוֹר יְיָ.

O house of Jacob: come, let us walk by the light of the
Lord.

• •

שְׁמַע יִשְׂרָאֵל: יְיָ אֱלֹהֵינוּ, יְיָ אֶחָד!

Hear, O Israel: the Lord is our God, the Lord is One!

אֶחָד אֱלֹהֵינוּ, גָּדוֹל אֲדוֹנֵינוּ, קָדוֹשׁ וְנוֹרָא שְׁמוֹ.

Our God is One; our Lord is great; holy and awesome is His
name.

• •

לְךָ, יְיָ, הַגְּדֻלָּה וְהַגְּבוּרָה וְהַתִּפְאֶרֶת וְהַנֵּצַח וְהַהוֹד,
כִּי כֹל בַּשָּׁמַיִם וּבָאָרֶץ, לְךָ יְיָ הַמַּמְלָכָה וְהַמִּתְנַשֵּׂא
לְכֹל לְרֹאשׁ.

Yours, Lord, is the greatness, the power, the glory, the victory,
and the majesty; for all that is in heaven and earth is Yours.
Yours is the kingdom, O Lord; You are supreme over all.

All are seated

• •

451

Reading of the Torah

Before the Reading

בָּרְכוּ אֶת־יְיָ הַמְבֹרָךְ!
בָּרוּךְ יְיָ הַמְבֹרָךְ לְעוֹלָם וָעֶד!
בָּרוּךְ אַתָּה, יְיָ אֱלֹהֵינוּ, מֶלֶךְ הָעוֹלָם, אֲשֶׁר בָּחַר־בָּנוּ
מִכָּל־הָעַמִּים וְנָתַן־לָנוּ אֶת תּוֹרָתוֹ. בָּרוּךְ אַתָּה, יְיָ,
נוֹתֵן הַתּוֹרָה.

• •

Leviticus 19.1–4, 9–18, 32–37

וַיְדַבֵּר יהוה אֶל־מֹשֶׁה לֵּאמֹר: דַּבֵּר אֶל־כָּל־עֲדַת בְּנֵי־יִשְׂרָאֵל
וְאָמַרְתָּ אֲלֵהֶם קְדֹשִׁים תִּהְיוּ כִּי קָדוֹשׁ אֲנִי יהוה אֱלֹהֵיכֶם:
אִישׁ אִמּוֹ וְאָבִיו תִּירָאוּ וְאֶת־שַׁבְּתֹתַי תִּשְׁמֹרוּ אֲנִי יהוה
אֱלֹהֵיכֶם: אַל־תִּפְנוּ אֶל־הָאֱלִילִם וֵאלֹהֵי מַסֵּכָה לֹא תַעֲשׂוּ
לָכֶם אֲנִי יהוה אֱלֹהֵיכֶם: וּבְקֻצְרְכֶם אֶת־קְצִיר
אַרְצְכֶם לֹא תְכַלֶּה פְּאַת שָׂדְךָ לִקְצֹר וְלֶקֶט קְצִירְךָ לֹא תְלַקֵּט:
וְכַרְמְךָ לֹא תְעוֹלֵל וּפֶרֶט כַּרְמְךָ לֹא תְלַקֵּט לֶעָנִי וְלַגֵּר תַּעֲזֹב
אֹתָם אֲנִי יהוה אֱלֹהֵיכֶם: לֹא תִּגְנֹבוּ וְלֹא־תְכַחֲשׁוּ וְלֹא־תְשַׁקְּרוּ
אִישׁ בַּעֲמִיתוֹ: וְלֹא־תִשָּׁבְעוּ בִשְׁמִי לַשָּׁקֶר וְחִלַּלְתָּ אֶת־שֵׁם
אֱלֹהֶיךָ אֲנִי יהוה: לֹא־תַעֲשֹׁק אֶת־רֵעֲךָ וְלֹא תִגְזֹל לֹא־תָלִין
פְּעֻלַּת שָׂכִיר אִתְּךָ עַד־בֹּקֶר: לֹא־תְקַלֵּל חֵרֵשׁ וְלִפְנֵי עִוֵּר לֹא
תִתֵּן מִכְשֹׁל וְיָרֵאתָ מֵּאֱלֹהֶיךָ אֲנִי יהוה: לֹא־תַעֲשׂוּ עָוֶל בַּמִּשְׁפָּט
לֹא־תִשָּׂא פְנֵי־דָל וְלֹא תֶהְדַּר פְּנֵי גָדוֹל בְּצֶדֶק תִּשְׁפֹּט עֲמִיתֶךָ:
לֹא־תֵלֵךְ רָכִיל בְּעַמֶּיךָ לֹא תַעֲמֹד עַל־דַּם רֵעֶךָ אֲנִי יהוה:

452

Reading of the Torah

Before the Reading

Praise the Lord, to whom our praise is due!
Praised be the Lord, to whom our praise is due,
now and for ever!
Praised be the Lord our God, Ruler of the universe, who
has chosen us from all peoples by giving us His Torah.
Blessed is the Lord, Giver of the Torah.

◆ ◆

Leviticus 19.1–4, 9–18, 32–37

The Lord spoke to Moses, saying: Speak to the whole
community of Israel, and say to them: You shall be holy,
for I, the Lord your God, am holy.

Revere your mother and your father, each one of you, and
keep My sabbaths; I, the Lord, am your God. Do not turn
to idols, nor make for yourselves molten gods; I, the Lord,
am your God.

When you reap the harvest of your land, do not reap the
corners of your field, and do not glean the fallen ears of
your crop. Nor may you strip your vineyard bare, nor
gather the overlooked grapes; you must leave them for the
poor and the stranger; I, the Lord, am your God.

You must not steal; you must not act deceitfully nor lie to
one another. And you must not swear falsely by My name,
profaning the name of your God; I am the Lord.

You must not oppress your neighbor. Do not commit rob-
bery. The wages of a laborer should not remain with you
overnight until morning. Do not curse the deaf, nor put a

לֹא־תִשְׂנָא אֶת־אָחִיךָ בִּלְבָבֶךָ הוֹכֵחַ תּוֹכִיחַ אֶת־עֲמִיתֶךָ וְלֹא־
תִשָּׂא עָלָיו חֵטְא׃ לֹא־תִקֹם וְלֹא־תִטֹּר אֶת־בְּנֵי עַמֶּךָ וְאָהַבְתָּ
לְרֵעֲךָ כָּמוֹךָ אֲנִי יהוה׃   מִפְּנֵי שֵׂיבָה תָּקוּם וְהָדַרְתָּ פְּנֵי זָקֵן
וְיָרֵאתָ מֵּאֱלֹהֶיךָ אֲנִי יהוה׃   וְכִי־יָגוּר אִתְּךָ גֵּר
בְּאַרְצְכֶם לֹא תוֹנוּ אֹתוֹ׃ כְּאֶזְרָח מִכֶּם יִהְיֶה לָכֶם הַגֵּר ׀ הַגָּר
אִתְּכֶם וְאָהַבְתָּ לוֹ כָּמוֹךָ כִּי־גֵרִים הֱיִיתֶם בְּאֶרֶץ מִצְרָיִם אֲנִי
יהוה אֱלֹהֵיכֶם׃ לֹא־תַעֲשׂוּ עָוֶל בַּמִּשְׁפָּט בַּמִּדָּה בַּמִּשְׁקָל
וּבַמְּשׂוּרָה׃ מֹאזְנֵי צֶדֶק אַבְנֵי־צֶדֶק אֵיפַת צֶדֶק וְהִין צֶדֶק יִהְיֶה
לָכֶם אֲנִי יהוה אֱלֹהֵיכֶם אֲשֶׁר־הוֹצֵאתִי אֶתְכֶם מֵאֶרֶץ מִצְרָיִם׃
וּשְׁמַרְתֶּם אֶת־כָּל־חֻקֹּתַי וְאֶת־כָּל־מִשְׁפָּטַי וַעֲשִׂיתֶם אֹתָם
אֲנִי יהוה׃

∴

After the Reading

בָּרוּךְ אַתָּה, יְיָ אֱלֹהֵינוּ, מֶלֶךְ הָעוֹלָם, אֲשֶׁר נָתַן לָנוּ
תּוֹרַת אֱמֶת וְחַיֵּי עוֹלָם נָטַע בְּתוֹכֵנוּ. בָּרוּךְ אַתָּה, יְיָ,
נוֹתֵן הַתּוֹרָה.

454

stumbling-block before the blind: show reverence for your God; I am the Lord.

Do not pervert justice, neither by favoring the poor nor by deferring to the powerful: you must judge your neighbor justly. You must not go about slandering your kin, nor may you stand by idly when your neighbor's blood is being shed; I am the Lord.

You shall not hate your brother or sister in your heart. Rather, you must reason with your kin, so that you do not incur guilt on their account. But you must not seek vengeance, nor bear a grudge against your kin; you shall love your neighbor as yourself; I am the Lord.

You shall rise in the presence of the aged and show respect for the old: you shall revere your God; I am the Lord.

When strangers live with you in your land, you must not oppress them. The strangers who live with you shall be to you like citizens, and you shall love them as yourself, for you were strangers in the land of Egypt; I, the Lord, am your God.

Do not pervert justice when you measure length, weight, or quantity. You must have honest scales, honest weights, honest dry and liquid measures; I, the Lord, am your God who led you out of the land of Egypt. You shall observe all My statutes and precepts, and do them; I am the Lord.

◆ ◆

After the Reading

Praised be the Lord our God, Ruler of the universe, who has given us a Torah of truth, implanting within us eternal life. Blessed is the Lord, Giver of the Torah.

As the reading is completed, the Torah might be held high
while this is said or sung:

וְזֹאת הַתּוֹרָה אֲשֶׁר־שָׂם מֹשֶׁה לִפְנֵי בְּנֵי יִשְׂרָאֵל, עַל־
פִּי יְיָ בְּיַד־מֹשֶׁה.

• •

רוֹמְמוּ יְיָ אֱלֹהֵינוּ, וְהִשְׁתַּחֲווּ לְהַר קָדְשׁוֹ, כִּי קָדוֹשׁ יְיָ
אֱלֹהֵינוּ.

• •

Reading of the Haftarah

Before the Reading

בָּרוּךְ אַתָּה, יְיָ אֱלֹהֵינוּ, מֶלֶךְ הָעוֹלָם, אֲשֶׁר בָּחַר
בִּנְבִיאִים טוֹבִים וְרָצָה בְדִבְרֵיהֶם הַנֶּאֱמָרִים בֶּאֱמֶת.
בָּרוּךְ אַתָּה, יְיָ, הַבּוֹחֵר בַּתּוֹרָה וּבְמֹשֶׁה עַבְדּוֹ
וּבְיִשְׂרָאֵל עַמּוֹ וּבִנְבִיאֵי הָאֱמֶת וָצֶדֶק.

• •

From the Book of Jonah

וַיְהִי דְּבַר־יהוה אֶל־יוֹנָה בֶן־אֲמִתַּי לֵאמֹר: קוּם לֵךְ אֶל־נִינְוֵה
הָעִיר הַגְּדוֹלָה וּקְרָא עָלֶיהָ כִּי־עָלְתָה רָעָתָם לְפָנָי: וַיָּקָם יוֹנָה
לִבְרֹחַ תַּרְשִׁישָׁה מִלִּפְנֵי יהוה וַיֵּרֶד יָפוֹ וַיִּמְצָא אֳנִיָּה ׀ בָּאָה
תַרְשִׁישׁ וַיִּתֵּן שְׂכָרָהּ וַיֵּרֶד בָּהּ לָבוֹא עִמָּהֶם תַּרְשִׁישָׁה מִלִּפְנֵי
יהוה: וַיהוה הֵטִיל רוּחַ־גְּדוֹלָה אֶל־הַיָּם וַיְהִי סַעַר־גָּדוֹל בַּיָּם
וְהָאֳנִיָּה חִשְּׁבָה לְהִשָּׁבֵר: וַיִּירְאוּ הַמַּלָּחִים וַיִּזְעֲקוּ אִישׁ אֶל־
אֱלֹהָיו וַיָּטִלוּ אֶת־הַכֵּלִים אֲשֶׁר בָּאֳנִיָּה אֶל־הַיָּם לְהָקֵל

456

As the reading is completed, the Torah might be held high while this is said or sung:

This is the Torah that Moses placed before the people of Israel to fulfill the word of God.

◆ ◆

Let us exalt the Lord our God, and worship at His holy mountain, for the Lord our God is holy.

◆ ◆

Reading of the Haftarah

Before the Reading

Praised be the Lord our God, Ruler of the universe, who has chosen faithful prophets to speak words of truth. Blessed is the Lord, for the revelation of Torah, for Moses His servant and Israel His people, and for the prophets of truth and righteousness.

◆ ◆

From the Book of Jonah

The word of the Eternal came to Jonah son of Amittai: Go at once to Nineveh, that great city, and proclaim judgment upon it; for their wickedness has come before Me.

Jonah started out, however, to flee to Tarshish from the service of the Eternal. He went down to Joppa and found a ship going to Tarshish. He paid the fare and went aboard to sail with the others to Tarshish, away from the service of the Eternal.

But the Eternal cast a mighty wind upon the sea, and such

מֵעֲלֵיהֶם וְיוֹנָה יָרַד אֶל־יַרְכְּתֵי הַסְּפִינָה וַיִּשְׁכַּב וַיֵּרָדַם: וַיִּקְרַב
אֵלָיו רַב הַחֹבֵל וַיֹּאמֶר לוֹ מַה־לְּךָ נִרְדָּם קוּם קְרָא אֶל־אֱלֹהֶיךָ
אוּלַי יִתְעַשֵּׁת הָאֱלֹהִים לָנוּ וְלֹא נֹאבֵד: וַיֹּאמְרוּ אִישׁ אֶל־רֵעֵהוּ
לְכוּ וְנַפִּילָה גוֹרָלוֹת וְנֵדְעָה בְּשֶׁלְּמִי הָרָעָה הַזֹּאת לָנוּ וַיַּפִּלוּ
גּוֹרָלוֹת וַיִּפֹּל הַגּוֹרָל עַל־יוֹנָה: וַיֹּאמְרוּ אֵלָיו הַגִּידָה־נָּא לָנוּ
בַּאֲשֶׁר לְמִי־הָרָעָה הַזֹּאת לָנוּ מַה־מְּלַאכְתְּךָ וּמֵאַיִן תָּבוֹא מָה
אַרְצֶךָ וְאֵי־מִזֶּה עַם אָתָּה: וַיֹּאמֶר אֲלֵיהֶם עִבְרִי אָנֹכִי וְאֶת־
יְהוָה אֱלֹהֵי הַשָּׁמַיִם אֲנִי יָרֵא אֲשֶׁר־עָשָׂה אֶת־הַיָּם וְאֶת־
הַיַּבָּשָׁה: וַיִּירְאוּ הָאֲנָשִׁים יִרְאָה גְדוֹלָה וַיֹּאמְרוּ אֵלָיו מַה־זֹּאת
עָשִׂיתָ כִּי־יָדְעוּ הָאֲנָשִׁים כִּי־מִלִּפְנֵי יְהוָה הוּא בֹרֵחַ כִּי הִגִּיד
לָהֶם: וַיֹּאמְרוּ אֵלָיו מַה־נַּעֲשֶׂה לָּךְ וְיִשְׁתֹּק הַיָּם מֵעָלֵינוּ כִּי הַיָּם
הוֹלֵךְ וְסֹעֵר: וַיֹּאמֶר אֲלֵיהֶם שָׂאוּנִי וַהֲטִילֻנִי אֶל־הַיָּם וְיִשְׁתֹּק
הַיָּם מֵעֲלֵיכֶם כִּי יוֹדֵעַ אָנִי כִּי בְשֶׁלִּי הַסַּעַר הַגָּדוֹל הַזֶּה עֲלֵיכֶם:
וַיַּחְתְּרוּ הָאֲנָשִׁים לְהָשִׁיב אֶל־הַיַּבָּשָׁה וְלֹא יָכֹלוּ כִּי הַיָּם הוֹלֵךְ
וְסֹעֵר עֲלֵיהֶם: וַיִּקְרְאוּ אֶל־יְהוָה וַיֹּאמְרוּ אָנָּה יְהוָה אַל־נָא
נֹאבְדָה בְּנֶפֶשׁ הָאִישׁ הַזֶּה וְאַל־תִּתֵּן עָלֵינוּ דָּם נָקִיא כִּי־אַתָּה
יְהוָה כַּאֲשֶׁר חָפַצְתָּ עָשִׂיתָ: וַיִּשְׂאוּ אֶת־יוֹנָה וַיְטִלֻהוּ אֶל־הַיָּם
וַיַּעֲמֹד הַיָּם מִזַּעְפּוֹ: וַיִּירְאוּ הָאֲנָשִׁים יִרְאָה גְדוֹלָה אֶת־יְהוָה
וַיִּזְבְּחוּ־זֶבַח לַיהוָה וַיִּדְּרוּ נְדָרִים: וַיְמַן יְהוָה דָּג גָּדוֹל לִבְלֹעַ אֶת־
יוֹנָה וַיְהִי יוֹנָה בִּמְעֵי הַדָּג שְׁלֹשָׁה יָמִים וּשְׁלֹשָׁה לֵילוֹת: וַיִּתְפַּלֵּל
יוֹנָה אֶל־יְהוָה אֱלֹהָיו מִמְּעֵי הַדָּגָה: וַיֹּאמֶר קָרָאתִי מִצָּרָה לִי
אֶל־יְהוָה וַיַּעֲנֵנִי מִבֶּטֶן שְׁאוֹל שִׁוַּעְתִּי שָׁמַעְתָּ קוֹלִי: וַתַּשְׁלִיכֵנִי
מְצוּלָה בִּלְבַב יַמִּים וְנָהָר יְסֹבְבֵנִי כָּל־מִשְׁבָּרֶיךָ וְגַלֶּיךָ עָלַי
עָבָרוּ: וַאֲנִי אָמַרְתִּי נִגְרַשְׁתִּי מִנֶּגֶד עֵינֶיךָ אַךְ אוֹסִיף לְהַבִּיט אֶל־

a tempest came upon the sea that the ship was in danger of breaking up. In their fright, the sailors cried out, each to his own god; and they flung the cargo overboard to make the ship lighter. Meanwhile, Jonah had gone into the hold of the vessel, where he lay down and fell asleep. The captain went over to him and cried out: 'How can you be sleeping so soundly! Up! call upon your god! Perhaps the god will be kind to us and we will not perish.'

The men said to one another: 'Let us cast lots and find out on whose account this misfortune has come upon us.' They cast lots and the lot fell on Jonah. They said to him: 'Tell us, you who have brought this misfortune upon us, what is your business? Where do you come from? What is your country, and of what people are you?' 'I am a Hebrew,' he replied. 'I worship the Eternal, the God of Heaven, who made both sea and land.' The men were greatly terrified, and they asked him: 'What have you done?' And when the men learned that he was fleeing from the service of the Eternal—for so he told them—they said to him: 'What must we do to you to make the sea calm around us?' For the sea was growing more and more stormy. He answered: 'Heave me overboard, for I know that this terrible storm came upon you on my account.' Nevertheless, the men rowed hard to regain the shore, but they could not, for the sea was growing more and more stormy around them. Before throwing him overboard, they cried out to the Eternal: 'Please do not let us perish on account of this man. Do not compel us to kill an innocent person! For You, O Eternal, by Your will, have brought this about.' And they heaved Jonah overboard, and the sea stopped raging.

The men were greatly in awe of the Eternal; they offered a sacrifice to the Eternal, and they made vows.

The Eternal provided a huge fish to swallow Jonah; and

459

הֵיכַל קָדְשֶׁךָ: אֲפָפוּנִי מַיִם עַד־נֶפֶשׁ תְּהוֹם יְסֹבְבֵנִי סוּף חָבוּשׁ
לְרֹאשִׁי: לְקִצְבֵי הָרִים יָרַדְתִּי הָאָרֶץ בְּרִחֶיהָ בַעֲדִי לְעוֹלָם
וַתַּעַל מִשַּׁחַת חַיַּי יהוה אֱלֹהָי: בְּהִתְעַטֵּף עָלַי נַפְשִׁי אֶת־יהוה
זָכָרְתִּי וַתָּבוֹא אֵלֶיךָ תְּפִלָּתִי אֶל־הֵיכַל קָדְשֶׁךָ: מְשַׁמְּרִים הַבְלֵי־
שָׁוְא חַסְדָּם יַעֲזֹבוּ: וַאֲנִי בְּקוֹל תּוֹדָה אֶזְבְּחָה־לָּךְ אֲשֶׁר נָדַרְתִּי
אֲשַׁלֵּמָה יְשׁוּעָתָה לַיהוה: וַיֹּאמֶר יהוה לַדָּג וַיָּקֵא
אֶת־יוֹנָה אֶל־הַיַּבָּשָׁה: וַיְהִי דְבַר־יהוה אֶל־יוֹנָה
שֵׁנִית לֵאמֹר: קוּם לֵךְ אֶל־נִינְוֵה הָעִיר הַגְּדוֹלָה וּקְרָא אֵלֶיהָ
אֶת־הַקְּרִיאָה אֲשֶׁר אָנֹכִי דֹּבֵר אֵלֶיךָ: וַיָּקָם יוֹנָה וַיֵּלֶךְ אֶל־נִינְוֵה
כִּדְבַר יהוה וְנִינְוֵה הָיְתָה עִיר־גְּדוֹלָה לֵאלֹהִים מַהֲלַךְ שְׁלֹשֶׁת
יָמִים: וַיָּחֶל יוֹנָה לָבוֹא בָעִיר מַהֲלַךְ יוֹם אֶחָד וַיִּקְרָא וַיֹּאמַר
עוֹד אַרְבָּעִים יוֹם וְנִינְוֵה נֶהְפָּכֶת: וַיַּאֲמִינוּ אַנְשֵׁי נִינְוֵה בֵּאלֹהִים
וַיִּקְרְאוּ־צוֹם וַיִּלְבְּשׁוּ שַׂקִּים מִגְּדוֹלָם וְעַד־קְטַנָּם: וַיִּגַּע הַדָּבָר
אֶל־מֶלֶךְ נִינְוֵה וַיָּקָם מִכִּסְאוֹ וַיַּעֲבֵר אַדַּרְתּוֹ מֵעָלָיו וַיְכַס שַׂק
וַיֵּשֶׁב עַל־הָאֵפֶר: וַיַּזְעֵק וַיֹּאמֶר בְּנִינְוֵה מִטַּעַם הַמֶּלֶךְ וּגְדֹלָיו
לֵאמֹר הָאָדָם וְהַבְּהֵמָה הַבָּקָר וְהַצֹּאן אַל־יִטְעֲמוּ מְאוּמָה אַל־
יִרְעוּ וּמַיִם אַל־יִשְׁתּוּ: וְיִתְכַּסּוּ שַׂקִּים הָאָדָם וְהַבְּהֵמָה וְיִקְרְאוּ
אֶל־אֱלֹהִים בְּחָזְקָה וְיָשֻׁבוּ אִישׁ מִדַּרְכּוֹ הָרָעָה וּמִן־הֶחָמָס אֲשֶׁר
בְּכַפֵּיהֶם: מִי־יוֹדֵעַ יָשׁוּב וְנִחַם הָאֱלֹהִים וְשָׁב מֵחֲרוֹן אַפּוֹ וְלֹא
נֹאבֵד: וַיַּרְא הָאֱלֹהִים אֶת־מַעֲשֵׂיהֶם כִּי־שָׁבוּ מִדַּרְכָּם הָרָעָה
וַיִּנָּחֶם הָאֱלֹהִים עַל־הָרָעָה אֲשֶׁר־דִּבֶּר לַעֲשׂוֹת־לָהֶם וְלֹא
עָשָׂה: וַיֵּרַע אֶל־יוֹנָה רָעָה גְדוֹלָה וַיִּחַר לוֹ: וַיִּתְפַּלֵּל אֶל־יהוה
וַיֹּאמַר אָנָּה יהוה הֲלוֹא־זֶה דְבָרִי עַד־הֱיוֹתִי עַל־אַדְמָתִי עַל־כֵּן
קִדַּמְתִּי לִבְרֹחַ תַּרְשִׁישָׁה כִּי יָדַעְתִּי כִּי אַתָּה אֵל־חַנּוּן וְרַחוּם

Jonah remained in the fish's belly three days and three nights . . . . Then the Eternal commanded the fish to spew Jonah out upon dry land.

The word of the Eternal came to Jonah a second time: 'Go at once to Nineveh, that great city, and proclaim to it what I tell you.' Jonah went at once to Nineveh in accordance with the command of the Eternal.

Nineveh was an enormously large city, a three days' walk across. Jonah started out and made his way into the city the distance of one day's walk, and proclaimed: 'Forty days more, and Nineveh shall be overthrown!'

The people of Nineveh believed God. They proclaimed a fast, and all alike put on sackcloth. When the news reached the king of Nineveh, he rose from his throne, took off his robe, put on sackcloth, and sat in ashes. And he had the word cried through Nineveh: 'By decree of the king and his nobles: Neither man nor beast shall taste anything! They shall not graze, and they shall not drink water! They shall be covered with sackcloth and shall cry mightily to God. Let all turn back from their evil ways and from the injustice of which they are guilty. Who knows but that God may turn back and relent, so that we do not perish?'

God saw what they did, how they were turning back from their evil ways. And God renounced the punishment planned for them, and did not carry it out.

This displeased Jonah greatly, and he was grieved. He prayed to the Eternal, saying: 'Eternal One! Isn't this just what I said when I was still in my own country? This is why I fled beforehand to Tarshish. For I know that You are a compassionate and gracious God, endlessly patient, abounding in love, renouncing punishment. Take my life,

אֶרֶךְ אַפַּיִם וְרַב־חֶסֶד וְנִחָם עַל־הָרָעָה: וְעַתָּה יהוה קַח־נָא
אֶת־נַפְשִׁי מִמֶּנִּי כִּי טוֹב מוֹתִי מֵחַיָּי: וַיֹּאמֶר יהוה הַהֵיטֵב חָרָה
לָךְ: וַיֵּצֵא יוֹנָה מִן־הָעִיר וַיֵּשֶׁב מִקֶּדֶם לָעִיר וַיַּעַשׂ לוֹ שָׁם סֻכָּה
וַיֵּשֶׁב תַּחְתֶּיהָ בַּצֵּל עַד אֲשֶׁר יִרְאֶה מַה־יִּהְיֶה בָּעִיר: וַיְמַן יהוה־
אֱלֹהִים קִיקָיוֹן וַיַּעַל ׀ מֵעַל לְיוֹנָה לִהְיוֹת צֵל עַל־רֹאשׁוֹ לְהַצִּיל
לוֹ מֵרָעָתוֹ וַיִּשְׂמַח יוֹנָה עַל־הַקִּיקָיוֹן שִׂמְחָה גְדוֹלָה: וַיְמַן
הָאֱלֹהִים תּוֹלַעַת בַּעֲלוֹת הַשַּׁחַר לַמָּחֳרָת וַתַּךְ אֶת־הַקִּיקָיוֹן
וַיִּיבָשׁ: וַיְהִי ׀ כִּזְרֹחַ הַשֶּׁמֶשׁ וַיְמַן אֱלֹהִים רוּחַ קָדִים חֲרִישִׁית
וַתַּךְ הַשֶּׁמֶשׁ עַל־רֹאשׁ יוֹנָה וַיִּתְעַלָּף וַיִּשְׁאַל אֶת־נַפְשׁוֹ לָמוּת
וַיֹּאמֶר טוֹב מוֹתִי מֵחַיָּי: וַיֹּאמֶר אֱלֹהִים אֶל־יוֹנָה הַהֵיטֵב חָרָה־
לְךָ עַל־הַקִּיקָיוֹן וַיֹּאמֶר הֵיטֵב חָרָה־לִי עַד־מָוֶת: וַיֹּאמֶר יהוה
אַתָּה חַסְתָּ עַל־הַקִּיקָיוֹן אֲשֶׁר לֹא־עָמַלְתָּ בּוֹ וְלֹא גִדַּלְתּוֹ
שֶׁבִּן־לַיְלָה הָיָה וּבִן־לַיְלָה אָבָד: וַאֲנִי לֹא אָחוּס עַל־נִינְוֵה
הָעִיר הַגְּדוֹלָה אֲשֶׁר יֶשׁ־בָּהּ הַרְבֵּה מִשְׁתֵּים־עֶשְׂרֵה רִבּוֹ
אָדָם אֲשֶׁר לֹא־יָדַע בֵּין־יְמִינוֹ לִשְׂמֹאלוֹ וּבְהֵמָה רַבָּה:

⋅ ⋅

After the Reading

An alternative version of this Benediction follows below

בָּרוּךְ אַתָּה, יְיָ אֱלֹהֵינוּ, מֶלֶךְ הָעוֹלָם, צוּר כָּל־
הָעוֹלָמִים, צַדִּיק בְּכָל־הַדּוֹרוֹת, הָאֵל הַנֶּאֱמָן,
הָאוֹמֵר וְעוֹשֶׂה, הַמְדַבֵּר וּמְקַיֵּם, שֶׁכָּל־דְּבָרָיו אֱמֶת
וָצֶדֶק.

עַל הַתּוֹרָה וְעַל הָעֲבוֹדָה וְעַל הַנְּבִיאִים וְעַל (יוֹם
הַשַּׁבָּת הַזֶּה וְעַל) יוֹם הַכִּפּוּרִים הַזֶּה, שֶׁנָּתַתָּ לָנוּ, יְיָ

462

then, for I would rather die than live to see this.' The Eternal One replied: 'Are you deeply grieved?'

Now Jonah had left the city and found a place east of the city. He made a booth there and sat under it in the shade, until he should see what happened to the city. The Eternal God provided a gourd, which grew up over Jonah, to provide shade for his head and save him from discomfort. Jonah was very happy about the plant. But the next day at dawn God provided a worm, which attacked the plant so that it withered. And when the sun rose, God provided a sultry east wind; the sun beat down on Jonah's head, and he became faint. He begged for death, saying: 'I would rather die than live.' Then God said to Jonah: 'Are you so deeply grieved about the plant?' 'Yes,' he replied, 'so deeply that I want to die.' Then the Eternal said: 'You care about the plant, yet you did not work on it nor cultivate it; it appeared overnight and perished overnight. And should I not care about Nineveh, that great city, in which there are more than a hundred and twenty thousand persons who do not yet know their right hand from their left, and many beasts as well!'

◆ ◆

After the Reading

An alternative version of this Benediction follows below

Praised be the Lord our God, Ruler of the universe, Rock of all creation, righteous in all generations, the faithful God whose word is deed, whose every command is just and true.

For the Torah, for the privilege of worship, for the prophets, and for this (Shabbat and this) Day of Atone-

אֱלֹהֵינוּ, (לִקְדֻשָּׁה וְלִמְנוּחָה) לִמְחִילָה וְלִסְלִיחָה
וּלְכַפָּרָה, לְכָבוֹד וּלְתִפְאָרֶת, עַל הַכֹּל, יְיָ אֱלֹהֵינוּ,
אֲנַחְנוּ מוֹדִים לָךְ, וּמְבָרְכִים אוֹתָךְ. יִתְבָּרַךְ שִׁמְךָ בְּפִי
כָּל־חַי תָּמִיד לְעוֹלָם וָעֶד. וּדְבָרְךָ אֱמֶת וְקַיָּם לָעַד.
בָּרוּךְ אַתָּה, יְיָ, מֶלֶךְ מוֹחֵל וְסוֹלֵחַ לַעֲוֹנוֹתֵינוּ
וְלַעֲוֹנוֹת עַמּוֹ בֵּית יִשְׂרָאֵל, וּמַעֲבִיר אַשְׁמוֹתֵינוּ בְּכָל־
שָׁנָה וְשָׁנָה, מֶלֶךְ עַל כָּל־הָאָרֶץ, מְקַדֵּשׁ (הַשַּׁבָּת וְ)
יִשְׂרָאֵל וְיוֹם הַכִּפּוּרִים.

Continue on page 468

Alternative Version

בָּרוּךְ אַתָּה, יְיָ אֱלֹהֵינוּ, מֶלֶךְ הָעוֹלָם, צוּר כָּל־
הָעוֹלָמִים, צַדִּיק בְּכָל־הַדּוֹרוֹת, הָאֵל הַנֶּאֱמָן,
הָאוֹמֵר וְעוֹשֶׂה, הַמְדַבֵּר וּמְקַיֵּם, שֶׁכָּל־דְּבָרָיו אֱמֶת
וָצֶדֶק.
נֶאֱמָן אַתָּה הוּא יְיָ אֱלֹהֵינוּ, וְנֶאֱמָנִים דְּבָרֶיךָ, וְדָבָר
אֶחָד מִדְּבָרֶיךָ אָחוֹר לֹא־יָשׁוּב רֵיקָם, כִּי אֵל מֶלֶךְ
נֶאֱמָן וְרַחֲמָן אָתָּה. בָּרוּךְ אַתָּה, יְיָ, הָאֵל הַנֶּאֱמָן
בְּכָל־דְּבָרָיו.

רַחֵם עַל־צִיּוֹן כִּי הִיא בֵּית חַיֵּינוּ, וְלַעֲלוּבַת נֶפֶשׁ
תּוֹשִׁיעַ בִּמְהֵרָה בְיָמֵינוּ. בָּרוּךְ אַתָּה, יְיָ, מְשַׂמֵּחַ צִיּוֹן
בְּבָנֶיהָ.

שַׂמְּחֵנוּ, יְיָ אֱלֹהֵינוּ, בְּאֵלִיָּהוּ הַנָּבִיא עַבְדֶּךָ, וּבְמַלְכוּת
בֵּית דָּוִד מְשִׁיחֶךָ, בִּמְהֵרָה יָבֹא וְיָגֵל לִבֵּנוּ. עַל־כִּסְאוֹ

ment that You, O Lord our God, have given us (for holiness and rest,) for pardon, forgiveness, and atonement, for honor and for glory, we thank and bless You. May Your name be blessed for ever by every living being, for Your word is true for ever. Blessed is our Sovereign God, whose forgiving love annuls our trespasses year after year. King of all the world, You hallow (the Sabbath,) the House of Israel and the Day of Atonement.

Continue on page 468

Alternative Version

Praised be the Lord our God, Ruler of the universe, Rock of all creation, righteous in all generations, the faithful God whose word is deed, whose every command is just and true.

You are the Faithful One, O Lord our God, and faithful is Your word. Not one word of Yours goes forth without accomplishing its task, O faithful and compassionate God and King. Blessed is the Lord, the faithful God.

Show compassion for Zion, our House of Life, and speedily, in our own day, deliver those who despair. Blessed is the Lord, who brings joy to Zion's children.

Lord our God, bring us the joy of Your kingdom: let our dream of Elijah and David bear fruit. Speedily let redemption come to gladden our hearts. Let Your solemn promise be fulfilled: David's light shall not for ever be extinguished! Blessed is the Lord, the Shield of David.

For the Torah, for the privilege of worship, for the prophets, and for this (Shabbat and this) Day of Atonement that You, O Lord our God, have given us (for holiness and rest,) for pardon, forgiveness, and atonement, for honor and for glory, we thank and bless You.

לֹא־יֵשֵׁב זָר וְלֹא־יִנְחֲלוּ עוֹד אֲחֵרִים אֶת־כְּבוֹדוֹ. כִּי
בְשֵׁם קָדְשְׁךָ נִשְׁבַּעְתָּ לּוֹ שֶׁלֹּא־יִכְבֶּה נֵרוֹ לְעוֹלָם וָעֶד.
בָּרוּךְ אַתָּה, יְיָ, מָגֵן דָּוִד.

עַל הַתּוֹרָה וְעַל הָעֲבוֹדָה וְעַל הַנְּבִיאִים וְעַל (יוֹם
הַשַּׁבָּת הַזֶּה וְעַל) יוֹם הַכִּפּוּרִים הַזֶּה, שֶׁנָּתַתָּ לָּנוּ, יְיָ
אֱלֹהֵינוּ, (לִקְדֻשָּׁה וְלִמְנוּחָה) לִמְחִילָה וְלִסְלִיחָה
וּלְכַפָּרָה, לְכָבוֹד וּלְתִפְאָרֶת, עַל הַכֹּל, יְיָ אֱלֹהֵינוּ,
אֲנַחְנוּ מוֹדִים לָךְ, וּמְבָרְכִים אוֹתָךְ. יִתְבָּרַךְ שִׁמְךָ בְּפִי
כָל־חַי תָּמִיד לְעוֹלָם וָעֶד. וּדְבָרְךָ אֱמֶת וְקַיָּם לָעַד.
בָּרוּךְ אַתָּה, יְיָ, מֶלֶךְ מוֹחֵל וְסוֹלֵחַ לַעֲוֹנוֹתֵינוּ
וְלַעֲוֹנוֹת עַמּוֹ בֵּית יִשְׂרָאֵל, וּמַעֲבִיר אַשְׁמוֹתֵינוּ בְּכָל־
שָׁנָה וְשָׁנָה, מֶלֶךְ עַל כָּל־הָאָרֶץ, מְקַדֵּשׁ (הַשַּׁבָּת וְ)
יִשְׂרָאֵל וְיוֹם הַכִּפּוּרִים.

May Your name be blessed for ever by every living being, for Your word is true for ever. Blessed is our Sovereign God, whose forgiving love annuls our trespasses year after year. King of all the world, You hallow (the Sabbath,) the House of Israel and the Day of Atonement.

Returning the Torah to the Ark

All rise

שְׁכֹן, יְיָ, בְּתוֹךְ עַמֶּךְ, וְתָנוּחַ רוּחֲךָ בְּבֵית תְּפִלָּתֶךָ.

Dwell, O Lord, among Your people; let Your spirit abide within Your house.

כִּי כָל־פֶּה וְכָל־לָשׁוֹן יִתְּנוּ הוֹד וְהָדָר לְמַלְכוּתֶךָ.

Let every human being acknowledge the splendor of Your kingdom, and its glory.

• •

הוֹדוּ עַל אֶרֶץ וְשָׁמָיִם, וַיָּרֶם קֶרֶן לְעַמּוֹ, תְּהִלָּה לְכָל־חֲסִידָיו, לִבְנֵי יִשְׂרָאֵל עַם קְרוֹבוֹ. הַלְלוּיָהּ!

God's splendor covers heaven and earth; He is the strength of His people, making glorious His faithful ones, Israel, a people close to Him. Halleluyah!

• •

אַשְׁרֵי אָדָם מָצָא חָכְמָה, וְאָדָם יָפִיק תְּבוּנָה, כִּי טוֹב סַחְרָהּ מִסְּחַר־כָּסֶף, וּמֵחָרוּץ תְּבוּאָתָהּ. יְקָרָה הִיא מִפְּנִינִים, וְכָל־חֲפָצֶיךָ לֹא יִשְׁווּ־בָהּ.

Happy is the one who finds wisdom, the one who gains understanding; For its fruits are better than silver, its yield than fine gold. It is more precious than rubies; no treasure can match it.

כִּי לֶקַח טוֹב נָתַתִּי לָכֶם, תּוֹרָתִי אַל־תַּעֲזֹבוּ. עֵץ־חַיִּים הִיא לַמַּחֲזִיקִים בָּהּ, וְתֹמְכֶיהָ מְאֻשָּׁר. דְּרָכֶיהָ דַרְכֵי־נֹעַם, וְכָל־נְתִיבֹתֶיהָ שָׁלוֹם.

468

Behold, a good doctrine has been given you, My Torah: do not forsake it. It is a tree of life to those who hold it fast, and all who cling to it find happiness. Its ways are ways of pleasantness, and all its paths are peace.

הֲשִׁיבֵנוּ יְיָ אֵלֶיךָ, וְנָשׁוּבָה. חַדֵּשׁ יָמֵינוּ כְּקֶדֶם.

Help us to return to You, O Lord; then truly shall we return. Renew our days as in the past.

The Ark is closed
All are seated

◆ ◆

JUSTICE, JUSTICE

Lord, Your earth yields enough to satisfy the needs of every living creature, but human greed thwarts Your purposes, and countless of Your children go hungry and naked. Great plenty and abject poverty, unrestrained power and utter helplessness exist side by side.

We are taught that all people are Your children, whatever their belief, whatever their shade of skin. You have ordained one law for rich and poor, one law for woman, child, and man. And we today, like those who came before us, are summoned to right the ancient wrongs in obedience to Your holy word:

Justice, justice shall you pursue, that you may live; do good and not evil, that you may live.

We often forget. Pride of possession, greed for wealth, fear of losing what we have—these blind us, and we forget: we who were strangers and slaves, we who have felt the sting of injustice, the terror of exile, the torment of inquisition, we who feel them still: how can we forget?

469

On this day of self-examination, O God, teach us to search our ways and to acknowledge that we have not been sufficiently mindful of our neighbors. We confess that in trying to keep what we have, we give too little thought to those who need us.

Inspire us, O God, to recognize and to help those men and women of vision who see the needs of others and try to assist them; may we, in our daily pursuits, help to better the world through generous sympathy and personal sacrifice.

◆ ◆

MEDITATION

As I look into the recesses of my heart on this Day of Days, I am reminded of the sacred obligations that have been placed upon me as a member of a congregation in the Household of Israel. I recall how parents and teachers and friends impressed upon me the beauty of holiness. I am pledged to discharge my duties. Now, as I aspire toward maturity of mind and heart, may I not be heedless of my faith nor neglectful of my responsibilities. Grant me a firmness of purpose and a loyal disposition that I may never shirk my task nor fail in the hour of testing. May I stand ready to assume my share of the duties of the congregation and the community of which I am a part, to uphold the hands of those who are giving of themselves to serve humanity, and increasingly to understand my own life as an opportunity for service. Grant that my daily life demonstrate the sincerity of my professions. Toward the poor and the needy, toward the bearers of burdens and the sad of heart, toward those who lead and those who follow, toward those of vision and insight, toward every Jew, toward every person, may I so act as to merit their approval and Your blessing. Amen.

◆ ◆

As we look upon our deeds in the light of Torah, we see that affliction of the body and fasting alone cannot cleanse the soul of sin and relieve the conscience of its weight of guilt. But these are the true means of atonement:

Let justice well up as waters, and righteousness as a mighty stream.

Show compassion, each one of you, to every person; do not oppress the stranger, the orphan, and the widow; do not plan evil against your neighbor. Speak the truth to your neighbor; render judgments that are true and that make for peace within your city.

Do justly, love mercy, and walk humbly with your God.

O God, grant that we may hearken to the solemn admonitions of this Sabbath of Sabbaths in true contrition and humility. Help us to fulfill our obligation to the needy and distressed. Incline our hearts to compassion, that we may aid the poor, the homeless, and the suffering; help us to be as parents to the needy, eyes to the blind, and feet to the lame. Teach us to be generous in our support of all good works. Bless all who labor unselfishly for the welfare and happiness of their brothers and sisters. On this Day of Repentance, we return to You with chastened hearts; receive us with favor, O God, our Rock and our Help. Amen.

THE LORD IS YOUR NAME   יה שמך

יָה שְׁמָךְ: אֲרוֹמִמְךָ; וְצִדְקָתְךָ לֹא אֲכַסֶּה. הֶאֱזַנְתִּי
וְהֶאֱמַנְתִּי; לֹא־אֶשְׁאַל וְלֹא־אֲנַסֶּה. וְאֵיךְ יֹאמַר כְּלִי
חֹמֶר אֱלֵי יוֹצְרוֹ: מַה־תַּעֲשֶׂה? דְּרַשְׁתִּיהוּ, פְּגַשְׁתִּיהוּ,
לְמִגְדַּל־עֹז וְצוּר מַחְסֶה. הַבָּהִיר כְּאוֹר מַזְהִיר בְּלִי
מָסָךְ וְאֵין מִכְסֶה.

יִשְׁתַּבַּח וְיִתְפָּאֵר וְיִתְרוֹמֵם וְיִתְנַשֵּׂא.

471

The Lord is Your name: I will exalt You; I will not conceal Your
righteousness.
I have heard, and will trust; I will not question or try You.
For how can a vessel of clay demand to know the potter's
mind?
I have sought You and found You:
You are a tower of strength, a sheltering rock,
A beacon shining bright whose light is not obscured.

Let God be praised and glorified, exalted and extolled.

הֲדַר כְּבוֹדְךָ וְעוֹז יָדְךָ מְסַפְּרִים הַשָּׁמַיִם, בְּעֵת
עֲלוֹתָם וְעֵת פְּנוֹתָם וְעֵת שְׁחוֹתָם אַפָּיִם. וּמַלְאָכִים
נֶהֱלָכִים בְּתוֹךְ אַבְנֵי אֵשׁ וּמַיִם, יְעִידוּךְ וְיוֹדוּךְ, בּוֹרֵא
נִיב שְׂפָתָיִם. כִּי תִסְבּוֹל וְלֹא תִבּוֹל בְּלִי זְרוֹעַ וְיָדַיִם,
תַּחְתִּיּוֹת וְעֶלְיוֹת וְהַחַיּוֹת וְהַכִּסֵּא.

יִשְׁתַּבַּח וְיִתְפָּאֵר וְיִתְרוֹמֵם וְיִתְנַשֵּׂא.

The heavens proclaim Your majesty and might at dawn and
dusk and when the dark descends.
And angels walking amid fire and water testify to You, the
Source of speech.
For You, unaging, invisibly sustain all depths and heights,
All forms of life, and Your own supernal realm.

Let God be praised and glorified, exalted and extolled.

וּמִי יְמַלֵּל כְּבוֹד מְחוֹלֵל שְׁחָקִים בַּאֲמִירָתוֹ? חֵי עוֹלָם
אֲשֶׁר נֶעְלָם בְּגָבְהֵי רוֹם מְעוֹנָתוֹ, וּבִרְצֹתוֹ בְּבֶן־בֵּיתוֹ
בְּאָהֳלוֹ שָׁת שְׁכִינָתוֹ, וְשָׁם מַרְאוֹת לַנְּבוּאוֹת לְהַבִּיט
אֶל־תְּמוּנָתוֹ, וְאֵין תַּבְנִית וְאֵין תָּכְנִית וְאֵין קֵץ
לִתְבוּנָתוֹ, רַק מַרְאָיו בְּעֵין נְבִיאָיו כְּמֶלֶךְ רָם
וּמִתְנַשֵּׂא.

יִשְׁתַּבַּח וְיִתְפָּאֵר וְיִתְרוֹמֵם וְיִתְנַשֵּׂא.

472

Who can express Your glory? You made the heavens with a
word!
Eternal, You dwell hidden in Your inaccessible domain,
Yet to Your beloved one You reveal Your presence,
Proclaiming Your nature in direct encounter.
You are the formless One, the Being of pure Mind,
Whom prophets see as a high and exalted King.

Let God be praised and glorified, exalted and extolled.

דְּבַר גְּבוּרוֹת בְּלִי סְפֹרוֹת, וּמִי יְסַפֵּר תְּהִלּוֹתָיו?
אַשְׁרֵי אִישׁ אֲשֶׁר יָחִישׁ לְהַכִּיר עֹז גְּדֻלּוֹתָיו, וְיִסָּמֵךְ
בְּאֵל תֹּמֵךְ עוֹלָם עַל־זְרוֹעוֹתָיו, וְיַעֲרִיצוּ שׁוֹב וְרָצוֹא
וְיַצְדִּיק דִּין עֲלִילוֹתָיו, וְיוֹדֶה עַל אֲשֶׁר פָּעַל, כִּי
לְמַעֲנוֹ פְּעֻלּוֹתָיו, וְכִי יֶשׁ־יוֹם לְאֵל אָיוֹם וְדִין עַל־כָּל־
הַמַּעֲשֶׂה!

יִשְׁתַּבַּח וְיִתְפָּאֵר וְיִתְרוֹמֵם וְיִתְנַשֵּׂא.

Who can recount Your praise? Your acts of power abound,
Your arms support the world!
Happy the one who runs to laud Your greatness,
Who leans on You, who clings to You, who, come what may,
accepts the rightness of Your deeds,
And who thanks the One whose purpose runs through all His
acts,
The awesome God whose Day of Judgment awaits us all!

Let God be praised and glorified, exalted and extolled.

הִשְׁתּוֹנֵן וְהִכּוֹנֵן וְהִתְבּוֹנֵן בְּסוֹדֶךָ, וְהַבַּטְתָּ: מָה אַתָּה
וּמֵאַיִן יְסוֹדֶךָ? וּמִי הֱכִינֶךָ? וְכֹחַ מִי יְנִידֶךָ? וְהַבֵּט אֶל
גְּבוּרוֹת אֵל וְהָעִירָה כְּבוֹדֶךָ. חֲקֹר פְּעָלָיו, רַק אֵלָיו
אַל־תִּשְׁלַח יָדֶךָ כִּי תִדְרֹשׁ בְּסוֹף וּבְרֹאשׁ, בַּמֻּפְלָא
וּבַמְכֻסֶּה.

יִשְׁתַּבַּח וְיִתְפָּאֵר וְיִתְרוֹמֵם וְיִתְנַשֵּׂא.

473

Reflect, consider, look within, and see:
What are you and whence have you come? Who gave you body and mind? Whose strength moves within you?
Regard God's wonders, let your sense of awe awaken.
Study God's works, search beginnings and ends, the wondrous things and the hidden, and yet you will not fathom Him. Say then:

Let God be praised and glorified, exalted and extolled.

יזכר ליום כפור

YOM KIPPUR MEMORIAL
SERVICE

Readings and Meditations begin on page 229

475

Yom Kippur Memorial Service יזכר ליום כפור

Our days are like grass.
We shoot up like flowers that fade
and die as the chill wind passes
over them, yet Your love for those
who revere You is everlasting.
Lord, Your righteousness
extends to all generations.

אֱנוֹשׁ כֶּחָצִיר יָמָיו;
כְּצִיץ הַשָּׂדֶה כֵּן יָצִיץ.
כִּי רוּחַ עָבְרָה־בּוֹ וְאֵינֶנּוּ,
וְלֹא יַכִּירֶנּוּ עוֹד מְקוֹמוֹ.
וְחֶסֶד יְיָ מֵעוֹלָם וְעַד־עוֹלָם
עַל־יְרֵאָיו, וְצִדְקָתוֹ לִבְנֵי בָנִים.

∵

Lord, I yearn only to be near You,
though at times I seem remote.
Lord, I cannot find the way unaided:
teach me the faithful service You would have me do,
show me Your ways, guide me, lead me,
release me from the prison of unknowing
while I still can make amends.
Do not despise my lowly state.
Before I grow so weak, so heavy with mortality
that I bend and fall,
and my bones, brittle with age,
become food for moth and worm,
be my help, O be my help!
Where my forebears went, there go I.
Yes, I know it.
Their resting-place is mine.

I know it.
Like them I am a stranger passing through this life.
Since the womb of earth is my allotted portion,
and since I've chased the wind from the beginning of my
days,
when will I come to set my house in order?
The passions You Yourself have made a part of me
have kept me rapt within the passing scene,

477

and how, enslaved to passion as I've been,
a prey to fierce and fiery hungers,
how, I ask, could I have served You as I needed to?
But now the time has come to ask:
why all this ambition, why the quest for high estate,
when tomorrow I must die?
Why this expense of spirit,
when tomorrow I mourn the passing time?
These days and nights combine to bring me to the end;
they scatter my thought to the winds,
they return my frame to the dust.
What now can I say in my defense?
What brave words remain to shield me from my truth?
My nature has pursued me, possessed me, driven and
flayed me,
a doubtful friend from childhood on.
What then do I really have besides Your presence?
Stripped of my pretensions, naked at the last, here I stand,
and only Your goodness can clothe and shelter me.
For nothing now remains but this:
Lord, I yearn only to be near You!

◆ ◆

From Psalm 63

אֱלֹהִים, אֵלִי אַתָּה; אֲשַׁחֲרֶךָּ. צָמְאָה לְךָ נַפְשִׁי, כָּמַהּ
לְךָ בְשָׂרִי, בְּאֶרֶץ־צִיָּה וְעָיֵף, בְּלִי־מָיִם. כֵּן בַּקֹּדֶשׁ
חֲזִיתִיךָ, לִרְאוֹת עֻזְךָ וּכְבוֹדֶךָ. כִּי־טוֹב חַסְדְּךָ מֵחַיִּים,
שְׂפָתַי יְשַׁבְּחוּנְךָ. כֵּן אֲבָרֶכְךָ בְחַיָּי: כִּי־הָיִיתָ עֶזְרָתָה
לִי, וּבְצֵל כְּנָפֶיךָ אֲרַנֵּן.

O God, You are my God;
at first light I seek You.

My soul thirsts for You,

my flesh longs for You,
as in a dry and weary land,
where there is no water.

So do I look for You in the sanctuary,
to behold Your power and Your glory.
Your love is better than life;
my lips will extol You.

And I will praise You with my life:
for You have been my help,
and in the shadow of Your wings
I sing for joy.

✦ ✦

Lord of all worlds, how insignificant we are in Your sight,
and how minute in Your presence! You are Creator of a
universe so vast that the effort to conceive it overwhelms
the mind. The keenest eye scans but a corner of it; the rays
of light we see today began their journey long before we
came to be. Counted from first creation, the earth we live
on was born but yesterday, and we made our appearance
on it only a moment ago.

When I consider Your heavens, the work of Your fingers;
the moon and the stars that You have established: what are
we, that You are mindful of us? What are we mortals, that
You consider us?

✦ ✦

We are feeble; we live always on the brink of death.
Scarcely ushered into life, we begin our journey to the
grave. Our best laid plans are ever at risk; our fondest
hopes are buried with us. Ambition drives us on to high
exertion; indulgence makes us waste the powers we have;
and evil seduces us to heap misery upon others. Success

and failure, love and hatred, pleasure and pain mark our
days from birth to death. We prevail, only to succumb; we
fail, only to renew the struggle.

Our days are few and full of trouble.

The eye is never satisfied with seeing; endless are the
desires of the heart. We devise new schemes on the graves
of a thousand disappointed hopes. Like Moses on Mount
Nebo, we behold the promised land from afar but may not
enter it. Our life, at its best, is an endless effort for a goal
we never attain. Death finally terminates the struggle, and
joy and grief, success and failure, all are ended. Like
children falling asleep over their toys, we relinquish our
grasp on earthly possessions only when death overtakes
us. Master and servant, rich and poor, strong and feeble,
wise and simple, all are equal in death. The grave levels all
distinctions, and makes the whole world kin.

• •

יְיָ, מָה־אָדָם וַתֵּדָעֵהוּ? בֶּן־אֱנוֹשׁ וַתְּחַשְּׁבֵהוּ? אָדָם
לַהֶבֶל דָּמָה; יָמָיו כְּצֵל עוֹבֵר. בַּבֹּקֶר יָצִיץ וְחָלָף,
לָעֶרֶב יְמוֹלֵל וְיָבֵשׁ. תָּשֵׁב אֱנוֹשׁ עַד־דַּכָּא, וַתֹּאמֶר:
"שׁוּבוּ, בְּנֵי־אָדָם!" לוּ חָכְמוּ יַשְׂכִּילוּ זֹאת, יָבִינוּ
לְאַחֲרִיתָם! כִּי לֹא בְמוֹתוֹ יִקַּח הַכֹּל; לֹא־יֵרֵד אַחֲרָיו
כְּבוֹדוֹ. שְׁמָר־תָּם וּרְאֵה יָשָׁר, כִּי אַחֲרִית לְאִישׁ
שָׁלוֹם. פָּדָה יְיָ נֶפֶשׁ עֲבָדָיו, וְלֹא יֶאְשְׁמוּ כָּל־הַחוֹסִים
בּוֹ.

Lord, what are we, that You have regard for us? What are we,
that You are mindful of us? We are like a breath; our days are as
a passing shadow; we come and go like grass which in the
morning shoots up, renewed, and in the evening fades and
withers. You cause us to revert to dust, saying: Return, O mortal
creatures! Would that we were wise, that we understood whither

we are going! For when we die we carry nothing away; our glory does not accompany us. Mark the whole-hearted and behold the upright: they shall have peace. Lord, You redeem the soul of Your servants, and none who trust in You shall be desolate.

◆ ◆

We are strangers in Your sight, O God; like all who came before us, our days on earth vanish like shadows. But the speedy flight of life, and the grave that looms on the horizon, should not dismay us; rather, let them teach us wisdom, and prompt us to put our trust in You. For only the dust returns to the dust; the spirit which You have breathed into us returns to You, its everlasting Source. Into us You have placed a portion of Your divinity; Your mighty strength is our firm support. When we become servants of Your Law, witnesses to Your truth, champions of Your kingdom, then indeed do we endow our fleeting days with abiding worth.

We are children of dust, Lord. Give us strength and understanding that we may fill our days with good. Though our days are few, help us to make them great.

◆ ◆

From Psalm 90

אֲדֹנָי, מָעוֹן אַתָּה הָיִיתָ לָּנוּ בְּדֹר וָדֹר. בְּטֶרֶם הָרִים יֻלָּדוּ, וַתְּחוֹלֵל אֶרֶץ וְתֵבֵל, וּמֵעוֹלָם עַד־עוֹלָם אַתָּה אֵל.

Lord, You have been our refuge in all generations.

Before the mountains were born, or earth and universe brought forth, from eternity to eternity You are God.

481

כִּי אֶלֶף שָׁנִים בְּעֵינֶיךָ כְּיוֹם אֶתְמוֹל כִּי יַעֲבֹר,
וְאַשְׁמוּרָה בַלָּיְלָה. זְרַמְתָּם; שֵׁנָה יִהְיוּ; בַּבְּקֶר כֶּחָצִיר
יַחֲלֹף: בַּבְּקֶר יָצִיץ וְחָלָף, לָעֶרֶב יְמוֹלֵל וְיָבֵשׁ.

For a thousand years in Your sight are but as yesterday
when it is past, or as a watch in the night.

*You sweep us away; we are like a dream at daybreak; we
come and go like grass which in the morning shoots up,
renewed, and in the evening fades and withers.*

יְמֵי־שְׁנוֹתֵינוּ בָהֶם שִׁבְעִים שָׁנָה, וְאִם בִּגְבוּרֹת,
שְׁמוֹנִים שָׁנָה; וְרָהְבָּם עָמָל וָאָוֶן, כִּי־גָז חִישׁ, וַנָּעֻפָה.
לִמְנוֹת יָמֵינוּ כֵּן הוֹדַע, וְנָבִיא לְבַב חָכְמָה. יֵרָאֶה אֶל־
עֲבָדֶיךָ פָעֳלֶךָ, וַהֲדָרְךָ עַל־בְּנֵיהֶם.

The number of our years may be many or few; yet vain toil
fills their span, for it is soon ended, and we fly away. So
teach us to number our days that we may grow wise in
heart.

*Let Your servants understand Your ways, and Your children
see Your glory.*

וִיהִי נְעַם אֲדֹנָי אֱלֹהֵינוּ עָלֵינוּ, וּמַעֲשֵׂה יָדֵינוּ כּוֹנְנָה
עָלֵינוּ. וּמַעֲשֵׂה יָדֵינוּ כּוֹנְנֵהוּ!

Let the beauty of our Eternal God be with us, and may
our work have lasting value.

O let the work of our hands be enduring!

❖ ❖

O God, Author of life and death, our wisdom is small, our
vision short. One by one our companions, passing along
the road of life, disappear from our view. We know that
each must walk the same path to the doorway of the

grave. We strain to see what lies beyond the gate, but all is darkness to our mortal sight.

Yet even the darkness is not too dark for You, O God, but the night shines as the day.

You have created us in Your image and made us share in Your enduring righteousness. You have put eternity into our hearts, have implanted within us a vision of life everlasting. This hope we cherish in humility and faith, trusting in Your endless goodness and Your wondrous love.

Into Your hands we commit the spirits of our dear ones, for You keep faith with Your children in death as in life.

Sustain us, O God, that we may meet, with calm serenity, the dark mysteries that lie ahead, knowing that when we walk through the valley of the shadow of death, You are with us, a loving Friend in whom we put our trust; You are the light of our life, our hope in eternity.

• •

Psalm 121

אֶשָּׂא עֵינַי אֶל־הֶהָרִים, מֵאַיִן יָבוֹא עֶזְרִי? עֶזְרִי מֵעִם
יְיָ, עֹשֵׂה שָׁמַיִם וָאָרֶץ. אַל־יִתֵּן לַמּוֹט רַגְלֶךָ, אַל־יָנוּם
שֹׁמְרֶךָ. הִנֵּה לֹא־יָנוּם וְלֹא יִישָׁן שׁוֹמֵר יִשְׂרָאֵל. יְיָ
שֹׁמְרֶךָ, יְיָ צִלְּךָ עַל־יַד יְמִינֶךָ. יוֹמָם הַשֶּׁמֶשׁ לֹא־
יַכֶּכָּה, וְיָרֵחַ בַּלָּיְלָה. יְיָ יִשְׁמָרְךָ מִכָּל־רָע, יִשְׁמֹר אֶת־
נַפְשֶׁךָ. יְיָ יִשְׁמָר־צֵאתְךָ וּבוֹאֶךָ, מֵעַתָּה וְעַד־עוֹלָם.

I lift up my eyes to the mountains:
what is the source of my help?
My help will come from the Lord,
Maker of heaven and earth.

483

God will not allow your foot to slip;
your Guardian will not slumber.
Behold, the Guardian of Israel neither
slumbers nor sleeps.
The Eternal is your Keeper,
the Lord is your shade at your right hand.
The sun shall not harm you by day, nor the moon by night.
The Lord will guard you from all evil,
God will protect your being.
The Lord will guard you, coming and going,
from this time forth, and for ever.

* *

If some messenger were to come to us with the offer that death should be overthrown, but with the one inseparable condition that birth should also cease; if the existing generation were given the chance to live for ever, but on the clear understanding that never again would there be a child, or a youth, or first love, never again new persons with new hopes, new ideas, new achievements; ourselves for always and never any others—could the answer be in doubt?

We shall not fear the summons of death; we shall remember those who have gone before us, and those who will come after us!

"Alas for those who cannot sing, but die with all their music in them." Let us treasure the time we have, and resolve to use it well, counting each moment precious—a chance to apprehend some truth, to experience some beauty, to conquer some evil, to relieve some suffering, to love and be loved, to achieve something of lasting worth.

Help us, Lord, to fulfill the promise that is in each of us, and so to conduct ourselves that, generations hence, it will be true to say of us: The world is better because, for a brief space, they lived in it.

• •

רַבִּי טַרְפוֹן אוֹמֵר: הַיּוֹם קָצֵר, וְהַמְּלָאכָה מְרֻבָּה,
וְהַפּוֹעֲלִים עֲצֵלִים, וְהַשָּׂכָר הַרְבֵּה, וּבַעַל הַבַּיִת
דּוֹחֵק.

Rabbi Tarfon says: The day is short, and the task is great, and the workers are sluggish, and the wages are high, and the Master of the house is pressing.

• •

All things pass away, but You are eternal. Teach us, O God, to see that when we link ourselves to You, and strive to do Your will, our lives acquire eternal meaning and value. And sustain in us the hope, for we dare not ask for more, that the human spirit, created in Your image, is, like You, eternal.

The dust returns to the earth as it was, but the spirit returns to the God who gave it.

• •

הַנְּשָׁמָה לָךְ, וְהַגּוּף פָּעֳלָךְ; חֽוּסָה עַל עֲמָלָךְ.

The soul is Yours, the body is Your work; O have pity on Your creation.

• •

In You, Lord, do I seek refuge; let me never be put to shame.

Lord, make me to ponder the end, the measure of my days; help me to realize how fleeting is my life.

485

You have made my days a mere span; my life's duration is nothing before You; those who stand firm are but a breath of wind.

They move about like shadows; they stir the air like the passing breeze; they heap up riches not knowing who will inherit them.

What hope have I then, Lord? My trust is in You.

My flesh may fail, and my heart, but God is for ever the strength of my heart and my life's destination.

I dwell in the shelter of the Most High; I abide in the shadow of the Almighty.

And I say to the Lord: You are my Refuge and my Fortress, my God in whom I trust.

◆ ◆

From Psalm 16

I have set the Eternal always before me; God is at my side, I shall not be moved. Therefore does my heart exult and my soul rejoice; my being is secure. For You will not abandon me to death nor let Your faithful ones see destruction. You show me the path of life; Your presence brings fullness of joy; enduring happiness is Your gift.

שִׁוִּיתִי יְיָ לְנֶגְדִּי תָמִיד, כִּי
מִימִינִי בַּל־אֶמּוֹט. לָכֵן שָׂמַח
לִבִּי וַיָּגֶל כְּבוֹדִי, אַף־בְּשָׂרִי
יִשְׁכֹּן לָבֶטַח. כִּי לֹא־תַעֲזֹב
נַפְשִׁי לִשְׁאוֹל, לֹא־תִתֵּן
חֲסִידְךָ לִרְאוֹת שָׁחַת.
תּוֹדִיעֵנִי אֹרַח חַיִּים, שֹׂבַע
שְׂמָחוֹת אֶת־פָּנֶיךָ,
נְעִמוֹת בִּימִינְךָ נֶצַח.

◆ ◆

486

Let us call to mind the great and good, through whom the
Lord has done wonders.

*They were leaders of the people, helping many with under-
standing and insight.*

Wise and eloquent in their teachings, they were just and
loving in their deeds.

*All these were honored in their generations; they were the
glory of their times.*

There are some who have left a name behind them, whose
remembrance is as honey in the mouth.

*People will declare their wisdom; all will tell of their
goodness.*

And there are some who have left no memorial, whose
names have vanished as though they had never been.

*But the goodness of their lives has not been lost and their
work cannot be blotted out.*

◆ ◆

I think continually of those who were truly great,
Who from the womb, remembered the soul's history
Through endless corridors of light where the hours are
        suns,
Endless and singing. Whose lovely ambition
Was that their lips, still touched with fire,
Should tell of the spirit clothed from head to foot in song,
And who hoarded from the spring branches
The desires falling across their bodies like blossoms.

What is precious is never to forget
The delight of the blood drawn from ageless springs
Breaking through rocks in worlds before our earth;

Never to deny its pleasure in the simple morning light,
Nor its grave evening demand for love;
Never to allow gradually the traffic to smother
With noise and fog the flowering of the spirit.

Near the snow, near the sun, in the highest fields,
See how these names are fêted by the waving grass,
And by the streamers of white cloud,
And whispers of wind in the listening sky;
The names of those who in their lives fought for life,
Who wore at their hearts the fire's center.
Born of the sun they travelled a short while toward the
     sun,
And left the vivid air signed with their honour.

◆ ◆

*O Lord of life, bless the memories we cherish. On this day
that, more than any other, affords us glimpses of eternity,
may the sorrows we have known be softened by our sense of
Your infinite wisdom, Your unending love, Your eternal
presence.*

May the pains of past bereavements grow more gentle; indeed, let them be transformed into gratitude to our dear
ones who have died and tenderness to those who are still
with us.

◆ ◆

Psalm 23

מִזְמוֹר לְדָוִד. יְיָ רֹעִי, לֹא אֶחְסָר. בִּנְאוֹת דֶּשֶׁא
יַרְבִּיצֵנִי, עַל־מֵי מְנֻחוֹת יְנַהֲלֵנִי. נַפְשִׁי יְשׁוֹבֵב. יַנְחֵנִי
בְמַעְגְּלֵי־צֶדֶק לְמַעַן שְׁמוֹ. גַּם כִּי־אֵלֵךְ בְּגֵיא צַלְמָוֶת
לֹא־אִירָא רָע, כִּי־אַתָּה עִמָּדִי; שִׁבְטְךָ וּמִשְׁעַנְתֶּךָ

הֵמָה יְנַחֲמֻנִי. תַּעֲרֹךְ לְפָנַי שֻׁלְחָן נֶגֶד צֹרְרָי. דִּשַּׁנְתָּ
בַשֶּׁמֶן רֹאשִׁי, כּוֹסִי רְוָיָה. אַךְ טוֹב וָחֶסֶד יִרְדְּפוּנִי
כָּל־יְמֵי חַיָּי, וְשַׁבְתִּי בְּבֵית־יְיָ לְאֹרֶךְ יָמִים.

*The Lord is my shepherd, I shall not want. He makes me lie
down in green pastures, He leads me beside still waters. He
restores my soul. He leads me in right paths for the sake of
His name. Even when I walk in the valley of the shadow of
death, I shall fear no evil, for You are with me; with rod and
staff You comfort me. You have set a table before me in the
presence of my enemies; You have anointed my head with
oil, my cup overflows. Surely goodness and mercy shall follow me all the days of my life, and I shall dwell in the house
of the Lord for ever.*

◆ ◆

O Lord of life, our times are in Your hand. One generation comes into the world to be blessed with days of peace
and safety; another goes through the valley of the shadow
enduring the cruelties of persecution and war. Heart-
breaking have been the times that have fallen to our lot, O
God. We have lived through years of tyranny and destruction; we are schooled in sorrow and acquainted with grief.
We have seen the just defeated, the innocent driven from
their homes, and the righteous suffer a martyrdom as mer-
ciless as any ages have witnessed.

At this hour of memorial we recall with grief all Your
children who have perished through the cruelty of the op-
pressor, victims of demonic hate: the aged and young, the
learned and unlettered—all driven in multitudes along the
road of pain and pitiless death. Their very presence on
earth was begrudged them, for they brought Your covenant of mercy and justice to the recollection of Your
enemies; they perished because they were a symbol of

Your eternal law; their death has brought darkness to the human soul.

They lie in nameless graves, in far-off forests and lonely fields. And the substance of many was scattered by the winds to the earth's four corners. Yet they shall not be forgotten. We take them into our hearts and give them a place beside the cherished memories of our own loved ones. They now are ours.

We pray to You, O Source of mercy, that Your Torah, to which these Your children bore witness in life and in death, may come to glow with a renewed light in the human soul; that, remembering them, we may sanctify Your name in all the world. Thus will their memory become an enduring blessing to all Your children.

We remember with sorrow those whom death has taken from our midst during the past year .... Taking these dear ones into our hearts with all our beloved, we recall them now with reverence.

In the rising of the sun and in its going down, we remember them.
In the blowing of the wind and in the chill of winter, we remember them.

In the opening buds and in the rebirth of spring, we remember them.
In the blueness of the sky and in the warmth of summer, we remember them.

In the rustling of leaves and in the beauty of autumn, we remember them.
In the beginning of the year and when it ends, we remember them.

When we are weary and in need of strength, we remember them.

When we are lost and sick at heart, we remember them.

When we have joys we yearn to share, we remember them.

So long as we live, they too shall live, for they are now a part of us, as we remember them.

✦ ✦

MEDITATION

יִזְכּוֹר אֱלֹהִים נִשְׁמוֹת יַקִּירִי....... שֶׁהָלְכוּ לְעוֹלָמָם. אָנָּא תִּהְיֶינָה נַפְשׁוֹתֵיהֶם צְרוּרוֹת בִּצְרוֹר הַחַיִּים וּתְהִי מְנוּחָתָם כָּבוֹד. שְׂבַע שְׂמָחוֹת אֶת־פָּנֶיךָ, נְעִימוֹת בִּימִינְךָ נֶצַח. אָמֵן.

May God remember for ever my dear ones . . . . who have gone to their eternal rest. May they be at one with the One who is life eternal. May the beauty of their lives shine for evermore, and may my life always bring honor to their memory.

יִזְכּוֹר אֱלֹהִים נִשְׁמוֹת כָּל־אַחֵינוּ בְּנֵי יִשְׂרָאֵל שֶׁמָּסְרוּ אֶת־נַפְשׁוֹתֵיהֶם עַל קִדּוּשׁ הַשֵּׁם. אָנָּא תִּהְיֶינָה נַפְשׁוֹתֵיהֶם צְרוּרוֹת בִּצְרוֹר הַחַיִּים וּתְהִי מְנוּחָתָם כָּבוֹד. שְׂבַע שְׂמָחוֹת אֶת־פָּנֶיךָ, נְעִימוֹת בִּימִינְךָ נֶצַח. אָמֵן.

May God remember for ever our brothers and sisters of the House of Israel who gave their lives for the Sanctification of the Divine Name. May they be at one with the One

who is life eternal. May the beauty of their lives shine for
evermore, and may my life always bring honor to their
memory.

◆ ◆

All rise

אֵל מָלֵא רַחֲמִים, שׁוֹכֵן בַּמְּרוֹמִים, הַמְצֵא מְנוּחָה
נְכוֹנָה תַּחַת כַּנְפֵי הַשְּׁכִינָה עִם קְדוֹשִׁים וּטְהוֹרִים
כְּזֹהַר הָרָקִיעַ מַזְהִירִים לְנִשְׁמוֹת יַקִּירֵינוּ שֶׁהָלְכוּ
לְעוֹלָמָם. בְּעַל הָרַחֲמִים יַסְתִּירֵם בְּסֵתֶר כְּנָפָיו
לְעוֹלָמִים, וְיִצְרוֹר בִּצְרוֹר הַחַיִּים אֶת־נִשְׁמָתָם. יְיָ
הוּא נַחֲלָתָם. וְיָנוּחוּ בְּשָׁלוֹם עַל מִשְׁכָּבָם, וְנֹאמַר:
אָמֵן.

O God full of compassion, Eternal Spirit of the universe, grant
perfect rest under the wings of Your Presence to our loved ones
who have entered eternity. Master of Mercy, let them find refuge
for ever in the shadow of Your wings, and let their souls be
bound up in the bond of eternal life. The Eternal God is their in-
heritance. May they rest in peace, and let us say: Amen.

◆ ◆

MOURNER'S KADDISH   קדיש יתום

יִתְגַּדַּל וְיִתְקַדַּשׁ שְׁמֵהּ רַבָּא בְּעָלְמָא דִּי־בְרָא
כִרְעוּתֵהּ, וְיַמְלִיךְ מַלְכוּתֵהּ בְּחַיֵּיכוֹן וּבְיוֹמֵיכוֹן וּבְחַיֵּי
דְכָל־בֵּית יִשְׂרָאֵל, בַּעֲגָלָא וּבִזְמַן קָרִיב, וְאִמְרוּ: אָמֵן.

Yit·ga·dal ve·yit·ka·dash she·mei ra·ba be·al·ma di·ve·ra
chi·re·u·tei, ve·yam·lich mal·chu·tei be·cha·yei·chon
u·ve·yo·mei·chon u·ve·cha·yei de·chol beit Yis·ra·eil, ba·a·ga·la
u·vi·ze·man ka·riv, ve·i·me·ru: a·mein.

יְהֵא שְׁמֵהּ רַבָּא מְבָרַךְ לְעָלַם וּלְעָלְמֵי עָלְמַיָּא.

Ye·hei she·mei ra·ba me·va·rach le·a·lam u·le·al·mei al·ma·ya.

יִתְבָּרַךְ וְיִשְׁתַּבַּח, וְיִתְפָּאַר וְיִתְרוֹמַם וְיִתְנַשֵּׂא,
וְיִתְהַדָּר וְיִתְעַלֶּה וְיִתְהַלָּל שְׁמֵהּ דְּקוּדְשָׁא, בְּרִיךְ
הוּא, לְעֵלָּא מִן־כָּל־בִּרְכָתָא וְשִׁירָתָא, תֻּשְׁבְּחָתָא
וְנֶחֱמָתָא דַּאֲמִירָן בְּעָלְמָא, וְאִמְרוּ: אָמֵן.

Yit·ba·rach ve·yish·ta·bach, ve·yit·pa·ar ve·yit·ro·mam
ve·yit·na·sei, ve·yit·ha·dar ve·yit·a·leh ve·yit·ha·lal she·mei
de·ku·de·sha, be·rich hu, le·ei·la min kol bi·re·cha·ta
ve·shi·ra·ta, tush·be·cha·ta ve·ne·che·ma·ta, da·a·mi·ran
be·al·ma, ve·i·me·ru: a·mein.

יְהֵא שְׁלָמָא רַבָּא מִן־שְׁמַיָּא וְחַיִּים עָלֵינוּ וְעַל־כָּל־
יִשְׂרָאֵל, וְאִמְרוּ: אָמֵן.

Ye·hei she·la·ma ra·ba min she·ma·ya ve·cha·yim a·lei·nu ve·al
kol Yis·ra·eil, ve·i·me·ru: a·mein.

עֹשֶׂה שָׁלוֹם בִּמְרוֹמָיו, הוּא יַעֲשֶׂה שָׁלוֹם עָלֵינוּ וְעַל־
כָּל־יִשְׂרָאֵל, וְאִמְרוּ: אָמֵן.

O·seh sha·lom bi·me·ro·mav, hu ya·a·seh sha·lom a·lei·nu ve·al
kol Yis·ra·eil, ve·i·me·ru: a·mein.

Let the glory of God be extolled, let His great name be hallowed
in the world whose creation He willed. May His kingdom soon
prevail, in our own day, our own lives, and the life of all Israel,
and let us say: Amen.
Let His great name be blessed for ever and ever.
Let the name of the Holy One, blessed is He, be glorified, exalted, and honored, though He is beyond all the praises, songs,
and adorations that we can utter, and let us say: Amen.
For us and for all Israel, may the blessing of peace and th'
promise of life come true, and let us say: Amen.

May the One who causes peace to reign in the high heavens, let peace descend on us, on all Israel, and all the world, and let us say: Amen.

✦ ✦

May the Source of peace send peace to all who mourn, and comfort to all who are bereaved. Amen.

תפלת נעילה ליום כפור

YOM KIPPUR CONCLUDING
SERVICE

Readings and Meditations begin on page 229

Concluding Service

נעילה

This is the house of God;
this is the gate of heaven.

Open to me the gates of righteousness;
I will enter them and thank the Lord.

Listen, O Lord, when I cry out;
be gracious and answer me!
You have said: Seek My Presence.
I seek Your Presence within my heart—
do not hide from me.

I will enter Your gates with thanksgiving,
Your courts with singing.

Give yourselves to the Lord,
and enter into God's holy space.
Go through, go through the doors.

This is the gateway to the Lord;
the righteous will enter it.

＊ ＊

Lord our God, we turn now to You once more
to cry out our longing
and the longing of all men and women
for a beginning of that wholeness
we call peace.
Ever and again, we now admit,
we have turned our backs on You,
and on our sisters and brothers:
forsaking Your Law,
denying Your truth,
ignoring Your will,
defacing Your beauty.

The intelligence You have implanted within us
we have applied to the arts of war;
with the skill we have from You
we make engines of terror and pain.

We have prayed for peace,
even as we laughed at truth;
for blessing,
but did not care to do Your will;
for mercy,
and have shown none to others.
We have prayed for impossible things:
peace without justice,
forgiveness without restitution,
love without sacrifice.

But You, our Maker, abound in grace:
so now again we turn to You,
to attach ourselves to Your purpose,
to set ourselves
on the paths that lead to Your kingdom
of peace and right, freedom and joy
for Israel and all the world.

Again, as the shadows fall, we ask forgiveness,
and again
we praise You, Lord, the Source of peace.

◆ ◆

MEDITATION

◆ ◆

Grant us peace, Your most precious gift, O Eternal Source
of peace, and give us the will to proclaim its message to all
the peoples of the earth. Bless our country, that it may

always be a stronghold of peace, and its advocate among the nations. May contentment reign within its borders, health and happiness within its homes. Strengthen the bonds of friendship among the inhabitants of all lands; and may the love of Your name hallow every home and every heart. Teach us, O God, to labor for righteousness, and seal us in the Book of life, blessing, and peace. Blessed is the Eternal God, the Source of peace.

✦ ✦

The leaves fall, fall as from afar . . . .
They fall with slow and lingering descent.
And in the nights the heavy earth, too, falls,
From out the stars into the Solitude.
Thus all must fall. This hand of mine must fall,
And lo! the other one:—it is the law.
But there is One who holds this falling
infinitely softly in His hands.

✦ ✦

The sun sinks low, the shadows fall,
The day of God is near its end.
To You, eternal Lord of all,
Let all our prayers now ascend.
O hear them, Lord, before the night;
In the evening, let there be light.

Bestow Your favor and Your grace,
And pardon us, O Lord of heaven.
The day declines—yet still a space
To us for penitence is given.
Then shall our sins be put to flight.
In the evening, let there be light.

And when the end of life draws near,
And darkness threatens to enfold us,
We shall not be dismayed by fear,

499

Our trust in You will still uphold us.
With You, eternity is bright:
In the evening there shall be light.

         ◆ ◆

Forgive your neighbors the wrongs they have done you,
and when you pray, your sins will be forgiven.
If I nurse anger against another,
can I ask pardon of the Lord?
Showing no pity for one like myself,
can I then plead for my own sins?
If I, a creature of flesh, nourish resentment,
who will forgive me my sins?

Consider that life is short, and cease to hate.
Remember mortality and death,
and live by the commandments.

Let not the fierce sun dry one tear of pain, before you
yourself have wiped it from the sufferer's eye.
But let each burning human tear drop onto your heart and
there remain; nor ever brush it off until the pain that
caused it is removed.

For transgressions against God, the Day of Atonement
atones; but for transgressions of one human being against
another, the Day of Atonement does not atone, until they
have made peace with one another.

         ◆ ◆

All rise

READER'S KADDISH   חצי קדיש

יִתְגַּדַּל וְיִתְקַדַּשׁ שְׁמֵהּ רַבָּא בְּעָלְמָא דִּי־בְרָא כִרְעוּתֵהּ, וְיַמְלִיךְ
מַלְכוּתֵהּ בְּחַיֵּיכוֹן וּבְיוֹמֵיכוֹן וּבְחַיֵּי דְכָל־בֵּית יִשְׂרָאֵל, בַּעֲגָלָא
וּבִזְמַן קָרִיב, וְאִמְרוּ: אָמֵן.
יְהֵא שְׁמֵהּ רַבָּא מְבָרַךְ לְעָלַם וּלְעָלְמֵי עָלְמַיָּא.
יִתְבָּרַךְ וְיִשְׁתַּבַּח, וְיִתְפָּאַר וְיִתְרוֹמַם וְיִתְנַשֵּׂא, וְיִתְהַדָּר
וְיִתְעַלֶּה וְיִתְהַלָּל שְׁמֵהּ דְּקוּדְשָׁא, בְּרִיךְ הוּא, לְעֵלָּא מִן כָּל־
בִּרְכָתָא וְשִׁירָתָא, תֻּשְׁבְּחָתָא וְנֶחֱמָתָא דַּאֲמִירָן בְּעָלְמָא,
וְאִמְרוּ: אָמֵן.

Let the glory of God be extolled, let His great name be hallowed
in the world whose creation He willed. May His kingdom soon
prevail, in our own day, our own lives, and the life of all Israel,
and let us say: Amen.
Let His great name be blessed for ever and ever.
Let the name of the Holy One, blessed is He, be glorified, exalted and honored, though He is beyond all the praises, songs,
and adorations that we can utter, and let us say: Amen.

∴

תפלה

אֲדֹנָי, שְׂפָתַי תִּפְתָּח, וּפִי יַגִּיד תְּהִלָּתֶךָ.
Eternal God, open my lips, that my mouth may declare Your glory.

THEIR QUEST IS OURS   אבות

בָּרוּךְ אַתָּה, יְיָ אֱלֹהֵינוּ וֵאלֹהֵי אֲבוֹתֵינוּ, אֱלֹהֵי
אַבְרָהָם, אֱלֹהֵי יִצְחָק, וֵאלֹהֵי יַעֲקֹב: הָאֵל הַגָּדוֹל,
הַגִּבּוֹר וְהַנּוֹרָא, אֵל עֶלְיוֹן. גּוֹמֵל חֲסָדִים טוֹבִים,

וְקוֹנֶה הַכֹּל, וְזוֹכֵר חַסְדֵי אָבוֹת, וּמֵבִיא גְאֻלָּה לִבְנֵי
בְנֵיהֶם, לְמַעַן שְׁמוֹ, בְּאַהֲבָה.

°Source of all being, we turn to You as did our people in
ancient days. They beheld You in the heavens; they felt
You in their hearts; they sought You in their lives.

*Now their quest is ours. Help us, O God, to see the wonder
of being. Give us the courage to search for truth. Teach us
the path to a better life. So shall we, by our lives and our
labors, bring nearer to realization the great hope inherited
from ages past, for a world transformed by liberty, justice,
and peace.*

זָכְרֵנוּ לְחַיִּים, מֶלֶךְ חָפֵץ בַּחַיִּים, וְחָתְמֵנוּ בְּסֵפֶר
הַחַיִּים, לְמַעַנְךָ אֱלֹהִים חַיִּים. מֶלֶךְ עוֹזֵר וּמוֹשִׁיעַ
וּמָגֵן. בָּרוּךְ אַתָּה, יְיָ, מָגֵן אַבְרָהָם.

Remember us unto life, O Sovereign who delights in life, and
seal us in the Book of Life, O God of life.

◆ ◆

אַתָּה גִבּוֹר לְעוֹלָם, אֲדֹנָי, מְחַיֵּה הַכֹּל אַתָּה, רַב
לְהוֹשִׁיעַ. מְכַלְכֵּל חַיִּים בְּחֶסֶד, מְחַיֵּה הַכֹּל בְּרַחֲמִים
רַבִּים. סוֹמֵךְ נוֹפְלִים, וְרוֹפֵא חוֹלִים, וּמַתִּיר
אֲסוּרִים, וּמְקַיֵּם אֱמוּנָתוֹ לִישֵׁנֵי עָפָר.
מִי כָמוֹךָ, בַּעַל גְּבוּרוֹת, וּמִי דוֹמֶה לָּךְ, מֶלֶךְ מֵמִית
וּמְחַיֵּה וּמַצְמִיחַ יְשׁוּעָה? מִי כָמוֹךָ אַב הָרַחֲמִים,
זוֹכֵר יְצוּרָיו לְחַיִּים בְּרַחֲמִים? וְנֶאֱמָן אַתָּה לְהַחֲיוֹת
הַכֹּל. בָּרוּךְ אַתָּה, יְיָ, מְחַיֵּה הַכֹּל.

°This symbol indicates that the English is a variation suggested by the theme
of the Hebrew.

502

°Eternal God, the power of Your spirit pervades all creation. When we open our hearts to You, we are filled with Your strength: the strength to bear our afflictions, the strength to refuse them victory, the strength to overcome them.

And then our will is renewed: to lift up the fallen, to set free the captive, to heal the sick, to bring light to all who dwell in darkness.

Add Your strength to ours, O God, so that when death casts its shadow, we shall yet be able to say: O Source of blessing, You are with us in death as in life!

◆ ◆

שְׁמַע נָא, סְלַח נָא הַיּוֹם, עֲבוּר כִּי פָנָה יוֹם, וּנְהַלֶּלְךָ נוֹרָא וְאָיוֹם.

Hear now! Forgive now! As the day turns to night, we praise You, the One awesome in greatness and mystery!

◆

SANCTIFICATION   קדושה

נְקַדֵּשׁ אֶת־שִׁמְךָ בָּעוֹלָם כְּשֵׁם שֶׁמַּקְדִּישִׁים אוֹתוֹ בִּשְׁמֵי מָרוֹם, כַּכָּתוּב עַל יַד נְבִיאֶךָ, וְקָרָא זֶה אֶל־זֶה וְאָמַר:

We sanctify Your name on earth, even as all things, to the ends of time and space, proclaim Your holiness; and in the words of the prophet we say:

503

קָדוֹשׁ, קָדוֹשׁ, קָדוֹשׁ יְיָ צְבָאוֹת, מְלֹא כָל־הָאָרֶץ
כְּבוֹדוֹ.

*Holy, Holy, Holy is the Lord of Hosts; the fullness of the
whole earth is His glory!*

אַדִּיר אַדִּירֵנוּ, יְיָ אֲדוֹנֵינוּ, מָה אַדִּיר שִׁמְךָ בְּכָל־
הָאָרֶץ!

Source of our strength, sovereign Lord, how majestic is
Your presence in all the earth!

בָּרוּךְ כְּבוֹד־יְיָ מִמְּקוֹמוֹ.

Blessed is the glory of God in heaven and earth.

אֶחָד הוּא אֱלֹהֵינוּ, הוּא אָבִינוּ, הוּא מַלְכֵּנוּ, הוּא
מוֹשִׁיעֵנוּ, וְהוּא יַשְׁמִיעֵנוּ בְּרַחֲמָיו לְעֵינֵי כָּל־חָי.

He alone is our God and our Creator; He is our Ruler and
our Helper; and in His mercy He reveals Himself in the
sight of all the living:

I AM ADONAI YOUR GOD! "אֲנִי יְיָ אֱלֹהֵיכֶם!"

יִמְלֹךְ יְיָ לְעוֹלָם, אֱלֹהַיִךְ צִיּוֹן, לְדֹר וָדֹר. הַלְלוּיָהּ!

*The Lord shall reign for ever; your God, O Zion, from
generation to generation. Halleluyah!*

•

קָדוֹשׁ אַתָּה וְנוֹרָא שְׁמֶךָ, וְאֵין אֱלוֹהַּ מִבַּלְעָדֶיךָ,
כַּכָּתוּב: וַיִּגְבַּהּ יְיָ צְבָאוֹת בַּמִּשְׁפָּט, וְהָאֵל הַקָּדוֹשׁ
נִקְדַּשׁ בִּצְדָקָה.
בָּרוּךְ אַתָּה, יְיָ, הַמֶּלֶךְ הַקָּדוֹשׁ.

You are holy; awesome is Your name; there is no God but
You.

504

The Lord of Hosts is exalted by justice; the holy God is sanctified by righteousness. Blessed is the Lord, who rules in holiness.

All are seated

THE HOLINESS OF THIS DAY   קדושת היום

אֱלֹהֵינוּ וֵאלֹהֵי אֲבוֹתֵינוּ, מְחַל לַעֲוֹנוֹתֵינוּ בְּיוֹם
(הַשַּׁבָּת הַזֶּה וּבְיוֹם) הַכִּפּוּרִים הַזֶּה; מְחֵה וְהַעֲבֵר
פְּשָׁעֵינוּ וְחַטֹּאתֵינוּ מִנֶּגֶד עֵינֶיךָ. בָּרוּךְ אַתָּה, יְיָ, מֶלֶךְ
מוֹחֵל וְסוֹלֵחַ לַעֲוֹנוֹתֵינוּ וְלַעֲוֹנוֹת עַמּוֹ בֵּית יִשְׂרָאֵל,
וּמַעֲבִיר אַשְׁמוֹתֵינוּ בְּכָל־שָׁנָה וְשָׁנָה, מֶלֶךְ עַל כָּל־
הָאָרֶץ, מְקַדֵּשׁ (הַשַּׁבָּת וְ) יִשְׂרָאֵל וְיוֹם הַכִּפּוּרִים.

Our God and God of all generations, pardon our sins on this (Shabbat and this) Day of Atonement; sweep away our transgressions and misdeeds, that they vanish from Your sight.

Blessed is the Lord, the King whose forgiving love annuls our trespasses year after year. King of all the world, You hallow (the Sabbath,) the House of Israel and the Day of Atonement.

♦ ♦

IN OUR DEEDS AND OUR PRAYER   עבודה

רְצֵה, יְיָ אֱלֹהֵינוּ, בְּעַמְּךָ יִשְׂרָאֵל, וּתְפִלָּתָם בְּאַהֲבָה
תְקַבֵּל, וּתְהִי לְרָצוֹן תָּמִיד עֲבוֹדַת יִשְׂרָאֵל עַמֶּךָ. אֵל
קָרוֹב לְכָל־קֹרְאָיו, פְּנֵה אֶל עֲבָדֶיךָ וְחָנֵּנוּ; שְׁפוֹךְ
רוּחֲךָ עָלֵינוּ, וְתֶחֱזֶינָה עֵינֵינוּ בְּשׁוּבְךָ לְצִיּוֹן בְּרַחֲמִים.
בָּרוּךְ אַתָּה, יְיָ, שֶׁאוֹתְךָ לְבַדְּךָ בְּיִרְאָה נַעֲבוֹד.

O Lord our God, may we, Your people Israel, be worthy in our deeds and our prayer. Wherever we live, wherever

505

we seek You—in this land, in Zion restored, in all lands—
You are our God, whom alone we serve in reverence.

· ·

FOR THE GLORY OF LIFE הודאה

מוֹדִים אֲנַחְנוּ לָךְ עַל־חַיֵּינוּ הַמְּסוּרִים בְּיָדֶךָ, וְעַל־
נִפְלְאוֹתֶיךָ וְטוֹבוֹתֶיךָ. הַטּוֹב: כִּי לֹא־כָלוּ רַחֲמֶיךָ,
וְהַמְרַחֵם: כִּי־לֹא תַמּוּ חֲסָדֶיךָ. בָּרוּךְ אַתָּה, יְיָ, הַטּוֹב
שִׁמְךָ, וּלְךָ נָאֶה לְהוֹדוֹת.

For the glory of life, O Lord, and for its wonder, we give
thanks. You are Goodness, You are Compassion. We give
thanks to You for ever.

· ·

THAT OUR CHILDREN MAY INHERIT ברכת שלום

שִׂים שָׁלוֹם, טוֹבָה וּבְרָכָה, חֵן וָחֶסֶד וְרַחֲמִים, עָלֵינוּ
וְעַל כָּל־יִשְׂרָאֵל עַמֶּךָ. בָּרְכֵנוּ אָבִינוּ, כֻּלָּנוּ כְּאֶחָד,
בְּאוֹר פָּנֶיךָ, כִּי בְאוֹר פָּנֶיךָ נָתַתָּ לָּנוּ, יְיָ אֱלֹהֵינוּ,
תּוֹרַת חַיִּים, וְאַהֲבַת חֶסֶד, וּצְדָקָה וּבְרָכָה וְרַחֲמִים,
וְחַיִּים וְשָׁלוֹם. וְטוֹב בְּעֵינֶיךָ לְבָרֵךְ אֶת־עַמְּךָ יִשְׂרָאֵל
בְּכָל־עֵת וּבְכָל־שָׁעָה בִּשְׁלוֹמֶךָ. בְּסֵפֶר חַיִּים בְּרָכָה
וְשָׁלוֹם וּפַרְנָסָה טוֹבָה נִזָּכֵר וְנִכָּתֵם לְפָנֶיךָ, אֲנַחְנוּ
וְכָל־עַמְּךָ בֵּית יִשְׂרָאֵל, לְחַיִּים טוֹבִים וּלְשָׁלוֹם. בָּרוּךְ
אַתָּה, יְיָ, עוֹשֵׂה הַשָּׁלוֹם.

°Our God, the Guide of humanity, let Your spirit rule this
nation and its citizens, that their deeds may be prompted
by a love of justice and right, and bear fruit in goodness
and peace.

Bless our people with love of righteousness.

Teach us to work for the welfare of all, to diminish the evils that beset us, and to enlarge our nation's virtues.

Bless our people with civic courage.

Bless our striving to make real the dream of Your kingdom, when we shall put an end to the suffering we now inflict upon each other.

Bless our people with a vision of Your kingdom on earth.

For You have endowed us with noble powers; help us to use them wisely, and with compassion.

Bless our people with a wise and feeling heart.

You have given us freedom to choose between good and evil, life and death. May we choose life and good, that our children may inherit from us the blessings of dignity and freedom, prosperity and peace.

◆ ◆

MEDITATION

Compassionate God, let the promise be fulfilled: "I will bring peace to the land; you shall be serene and unafraid. I will rid the land of vicious beasts, and the sword of war shall be set aside. They shall beat their swords into plowshares, and their spears into pruning-hooks; nation shall not lift up sword against nation, nor ever again shall they train for war. Justice shall roll down like waters, righteousness as a mighty stream."

◆ ◆

שָׁלוֹם, שָׁלוֹם לָרָחוֹק וְלַקָּרוֹב, אָמַר יְיָ.

Peace, peace to the far and to the near, says the Lord.

◆ ◆

507

GOD OF AWESOME DEEDS   אל נורא עלילה

אֵל נוֹרָא עֲלִילָה, אֵל נוֹרָא עֲלִילָה, הַמְצֵא לָנוּ
מְחִילָה בִּשְׁעַת הַנְּעִילָה. אֵל נוֹרָא עֲלִילָה.

מְתֵי מִסְפָּר קְרוּאִים, לְךָ עַיִן נוֹשְׂאִים, וּמְסַלְּדִים
בְּחִילָה בִּשְׁעַת הַנְּעִילָה. אֵל נוֹרָא עֲלִילָה.

שׁוֹפְכִים לְךָ נַפְשָׁם, מְחֵה פִּשְׁעָם וְכַחֲשָׁם, הַמְצִיאֵם
מְחִילָה בִּשְׁעַת הַנְּעִילָה. אֵל נוֹרָא עֲלִילָה.

הֱיֵה לָהֶם לְסִתְרָה, וְחַלְּצֵם מִמְּאֵרָה, וְחָתְמֵם לְהוֹד
וּלְגִילָה בִּשְׁעַת הַנְּעִילָה. אֵל נוֹרָא עֲלִילָה.

חֹן אוֹתָם וְרַחֵם, וְכָל־לוֹחֵץ וְלוֹחֵם, עֲשֵׂה בָהֶם
פְּלִילָה בִּשְׁעַת הַנְּעִילָה. אֵל נוֹרָא עֲלִילָה.

זְכֹר צִדְקַת אֲבִיהֶם, וְחַדֵּשׁ אֶת־יְמֵיהֶם, כְּקֶדֶם
וּתְחִלָּה בִּשְׁעַת הַנְּעִילָה. אֵל נוֹרָא עֲלִילָה.

קְרָא נָא שְׁנַת רָצוֹן, וְהָשֵׁב שְׁאֵרִית הַצֹּאן, לְתִפְאֶרֶת
וּתְהִלָּה בִּשְׁעַת הַנְּעִילָה. אֵל נוֹרָא עֲלִילָה.

אֵל נוֹרָא עֲלִילָה, אֵל נוֹרָא עֲלִילָה, הַמְצֵא לָנוּ
מְחִילָה בִּשְׁעַת הַנְּעִילָה. אֵל נוֹרָא עֲלִילָה.

God of awesome deeds, God of awesome deeds,
grant us pardon, as the gates begin to close.

God, we stand in awe before Your deeds.

We who are few in number look up to You; with trembling we praise You, as the gates begin to close.

God, we stand in awe before Your deeds.

To You we pour out our souls; blot out our sins, our dishonest ways; grant us pardon, as the gates begin to close.

God, we stand in awe before Your deeds.

Be our refuge and shield us from danger; assure us joy and honor, as the gates begin to close.

God, we stand in awe before Your deeds.

Be gracious to us, compassionate; let Your judgment fall on tyrants and those who make war, as the gates begin to close.

God, we stand in awe before Your deeds.

Remember the merits of our mothers and fathers; renew in us their spirit and faith, as the gates begin to close.

God, we stand in awe before Your deeds.

Proclaim a year of favor; return the remnant of Your flock to honor and glory, as the gates begin to close.

God of awesome deeds, O God of awesome deeds,
grant us pardon, as the gates begin to close.

✦ ✦

THE LORD WILL REIGN   בטרם שחקים

יְיָ מֶלֶךְ, יְיָ מָלָךְ, יְיָ יִמְלוֹךְ לְעוֹלָם וָעֶד!

The Lord, the everlasting King, the Lord will reign for ever!

בְּטֶרֶם שְׁחָקִים וַאֲרָקִים נִמְתָּחוּ, יְיָ מֶלֶךְ!
וְעַד־לֹא מְאוֹרוֹת זָרָחוּ, יְיָ מָלָךְ!
וְהָאָרֶץ כַּבֶּגֶד תִּבְלֶה, וְהַשָּׁמַיִם כְּעָשָׁן נִמְלָחוּ,

Before the earth and sky were formed, the Lord was King!
When heaven's lights had yet to shine, the Lord did reign!
Though like a garment earth decay, and heaven all as smoke dissolve,

the Lord will reign for ever!   יְיָ יִמְלוֹךְ לְעוֹלָם וָעֶד!

וְעַד־לֹא עָשָׂה אֶרֶץ וְחוּצוֹת, יְיָ מֶלֶךְ!
וּבַהֲכִינוֹ יְצוּרִים עֲלֵי אֲרָצוֹת, יְיָ מָלָךְ!
יַרְגִּיז אֶרֶץ מִמְּקוֹמָהּ, וַתִּכָּס עַמּוּדֶיהָ פַּלָצוּת,

Before the earth's expanse was spread, the Lord was King!
And when its creatures all were formed, the Lord did reign!
Though earth from out its orbit reel, and tremble to its lowest depths,

the Lord will reign for ever!   יְיָ יִמְלוֹךְ לְעוֹלָם וָעֶד!

· ·

All rise

The Ark is opened

510

אבינו מלכנו

אָבִינוּ מַלְכֵּנוּ, פְּתַח שַׁעֲרֵי שָׁמַיִם לִתְפִלָּתֵנוּ.

Our Father, our King, let the gates of heaven be open to our plea.

אָבִינוּ מַלְכֵּנוּ, נָא אַל תְּשִׁיבֵנוּ רֵיקָם מִלְּפָנֶיךָ.

Our Father, our King, do not turn us away empty-handed from Your presence.

אָבִינוּ מַלְכֵּנוּ, סְלַח וּמְחַל לְכָל עֲונוֹתֵינוּ.

Our Father, our King, forgive and pardon all our misdeeds.

אָבִינוּ מַלְכֵּנוּ, זְכוֹר כִּי עָפָר אֲנָחְנוּ.

Our Father, our King, remember that we are dust.

אָבִינוּ מַלְכֵּנוּ, חֲמוֹל עָלֵינוּ וְעַל עוֹלָלֵינוּ וְטַפֵּנוּ.

Our Father, our King, have compassion on us and on our children.

אָבִינוּ מַלְכֵּנוּ, חַדֵּשׁ עָלֵינוּ שָׁנָה טוֹבָה.

Our Father, our King, let the new year be a good year for us.

אָבִינוּ מַלְכֵּנוּ, חָתְמֵנוּ בְּסֵפֶר חַיִּים טוֹבִים.

Our Father, our King, seal us for blessing in the Book of Life.

אָבִינוּ מַלְכֵּנוּ, הָרֵם קֶרֶן יִשְׂרָאֵל עַמֶּךָ.

Our Father, our King, give strength to Your people Israel.

אָבִינוּ מַלְכֵּנוּ, כַּלֵּה כָּל־צַר וּמַשְׂטִין מֵעָלֵינוּ.

Our Father, our King, make an end to all oppression.

אָבִינוּ מַלְכֵּנוּ, הַצְמַח לָנוּ יְשׁוּעָה בְּקָרוֹב.

Our Father, our King, hasten the time of our redemption.

אָבִינוּ מַלְכֵּנוּ, חָנֵּנוּ וַעֲנֵנוּ, כִּי אֵין בָּנוּ מַעֲשִׂים, עֲשֵׂה
עִמָּנוּ צְדָקָה וָחֶסֶד וְהוֹשִׁיעֵנוּ.

Our Father, our King, be gracious and answer us, even when
we have little merit; treat us generously and with kindness,
and be our help.

The Ark is closed
All are seated

• •

CONFESSION OF SIN   ודוי

אֱלֹהֵינוּ וֵאלֹהֵי אֲבוֹתֵינוּ, תָּבוֹא לְפָנֶיךָ תְּפִלָּתֵנוּ וְאַל
תִּתְעַלַּם מִתְּחִנָּתֵנוּ, שֶׁאֵין אֲנַחְנוּ עַזֵּי פָנִים וּקְשֵׁי עֹרֶף
לוֹמַר לְפָנֶיךָ, יְיָ אֱלֹהֵינוּ וֵאלֹהֵי אֲבוֹתֵינוּ, צַדִּיקִים
אֲנַחְנוּ וְלֹא חָטָאנוּ, אֲבָל אֲנַחְנוּ חָטָאנוּ. חָטָאנוּ,
עָוִינוּ, פָּשַׁעְנוּ.

Our God, God of our mothers and fathers, grant that our
prayers may reach You. Do not be deaf to our pleas, for
we are not so arrogant and stiff-necked as to say before
You, Lord our God and God of all ages, we are perfect
and have not sinned; rather do we confess: we have gone
astray, we have sinned, we have transgressed.

•

אָשַׁמְנוּ, בָּגַדְנוּ, גָּזַלְנוּ, דִּבַּרְנוּ דְפִי. הֶעֱוִינוּ, וְהִרְשַׁעְנוּ,
זַדְנוּ, חָמַסְנוּ, טָפַלְנוּ שֶׁקֶר. יָעַצְנוּ רָע, כִּזַּבְנוּ, לַצְנוּ,
מָרַדְנוּ, נִאַצְנוּ. סָרַרְנוּ, עָוִינוּ, פָּשַׁעְנוּ, צָרַרְנוּ, קִשִּׁינוּ
עֹרֶף. רָשַׁעְנוּ, שִׁחַתְנוּ, תִּעַבְנוּ, תָּעִינוּ, תִּעְתָּעְנוּ.

°We all have committed offenses; together we confess these human sins:

The sins of arrogance, bigotry, and cynicism; of deceit and egotism, flattery and greed, injustice and jealousy.

Some of us have kept grudges, were lustful, malicious, or narrow-minded.

Others were obstinate or possessive, quarrelsome, rancorous, or selfish.

There was violence, weakness of will, xenophobia.

We yielded to temptation, and showed zeal for bad causes.

◆

סַֽרְנוּ מִמִּצְוֺתֶֽיךָ וּמִמִּשְׁפָּטֶֽיךָ הַטּוֹבִים וְלֹא שָֽׁוָה לָֽנוּ. וְאַתָּה צַדִּיק עַל כָּל־הַבָּא עָלֵֽינוּ, כִּי אֱמֶת עָשִֽׂיתָ וַאֲנַֽחְנוּ הִרְשָֽׁעְנוּ.

מַה־נֹּאמַר לְפָנֶֽיךָ יוֹשֵׁב מָרוֹם, וּמַה־נְּסַפֵּר לְפָנֶֽיךָ שׁוֹכֵן שְׁחָקִים? הֲלֹא כָּל־הַנִּסְתָּרוֹת וְהַנִּגְלוֹת אַתָּה יוֹדֵֽעַ?

We have turned aside from Your commandments and from Your precepts, and it has not availed us. You are just, whatever befalls us; You call us to righteousness, but we bring evil upon ourselves.

What shall we say before You, who dwell on high? What shall we plead before You, enthroned beyond the stars? Are not all things known to You?

◆

סְלַח נָא לַעֲוֹן הָעָם הַזֶּה כְּגֹדֶל חַסְדֶּךָ, וְכַאֲשֶׁר נָשָׂאתָ
לָעָם הַזֶּה מִמִּצְרַיִם וְעַד הֵנָּה.

As, in Your love, You have been patient with this people
from the time You led us out of Egypt to the present day, so,
in Your great love, may You forgive Your people now.

וַיְּאמֶר יְיָ: "סָלַחְתִּי כִּדְבָרֶךָ."

And the Lord said: I have pardoned in response to your
plea.

• •

YOU HOLD OUT YOUR HAND   אתה נותן יד

אַתָּה נוֹתֵן יָד לְפוֹשְׁעִים, וִימִינְךָ פְשׁוּטָה לְקַבֵּל
שָׁבִים. וַתְּלַמְּדֵנוּ, יְיָ אֱלֹהֵינוּ, לְהִתְוַדּוֹת לְפָנֶיךָ עַל
כָּל־עֲוֹנוֹתֵינוּ, לְמַעַן נֶחְדַּל מֵעֹשֶׁק יָדֵינוּ, וּתְקַבְּלֵנוּ
בִּתְשׁוּבָה שְׁלֵמָה לְפָנֶיךָ, לְמַעַן דְּבָרֶיךָ אֲשֶׁר אָמָרְתָּ.

You hold out Your hand to those who have rebelled
against You; Your right hand is stretched out to receive
those who turn back to You. Lord our God, You have
taught us to confess all our faults before You, so that we
may turn away from violence and oppression. In accordance with Your gracious promise, accept our repentance,
which we offer to You in all sincerity.

וְאַתָּה יוֹדֵעַ שֶׁאַחֲרִיתֵנוּ רִמָּה וְתוֹלֵעָה; לְפִיכָךְ
הִרְבֵּיתָ סְלִיחָתֵנוּ. מָה אָנוּ, מֶה חַיֵּינוּ, מֶה חַסְדֵּנוּ,
מַה־צִּדְקֵנוּ, מַה־יְשְׁעֵנוּ, מַה־כֹּחֵנוּ, מַה־גְּבוּרָתֵנוּ?
מַה־נֹּאמַר לְפָנֶיךָ, יְיָ אֱלֹהֵינוּ וֵאלֹהֵי אֲבוֹתֵינוּ? הֲלֹא
כָל־הַגִּבּוֹרִים כְּאַיִן לְפָנֶיךָ, וְאַנְשֵׁי הַשֵּׁם כְּלֹא הָיוּ,
וַחֲכָמִים כִּבְלִי מַדָּע, וּנְבוֹנִים כִּבְלִי הַשְׂכֵּל?

*We know that we end in dust, but Your compassion has no
end. For what are we? What is our life, and what our
faithfulness? What is our goodness, and what our vaunted
strength? What can we say in Your presence, O Lord our
God and God of all ages? Are not all the conquerors as
nothing before You, and those of renown as though they had
not been, the learned as if they had no knowledge, and the
wise as if without understanding?*

כִּי רֹב מַעֲשֵׂיהֶם תֹּהוּ, וִימֵי חַיֵּיהֶם הֶבֶל לְפָנֶיךָ.
וּמוֹתַר הָאָדָם מִן הַבְּהֵמָה אָיִן, כִּי הַכֹּל הָבֶל.

Many of our works are vain, and our days pass away like
a shadow. Since all our achievements are as insubstantial
as mist, how can we look upon ourselves as higher than
the beasts?

אַתָּה הִבְדַּלְתָּ אֱנוֹשׁ מֵרֹאשׁ וַתַּכִּירֵהוּ לַעֲמוֹד לְפָנֶיךָ.

Yet from the beginning You set us apart to stand erect
before You.

וַתִּתֶּן־לָנוּ, יְיָ אֱלֹהֵינוּ, בְּאַהֲבָה אֶת־יוֹם הַכִּפּוּרִים
הַזֶּה, קֵץ וּמְחִילָה וּסְלִיחָה עַל כָּל־עֲוֹנוֹתֵינוּ, לְמַעַן
נֶחְדַּל מֵעְשֶׁק יָדֵינוּ, וְנָשׁוּב אֵלֶיךָ לַעֲשׂוֹת חֻקֵּי רְצוֹנְךָ
בְּלֵבָב שָׁלֵם.

And in Your love, O Lord our God, You have given us
this Day of Atonement, that our sins may cease and be
forgiven, and that, turning away from violence and oppression, we may turn back to You and do Your will with
a perfect heart.

וְאַתָּה בְּרַחֲמֶיךָ הָרַבִּים רַחֵם עָלֵינוּ, כִּי לֹא תַחְפֹּץ
בְּהַשְׁחָתַת עוֹלָם, שֶׁנֶּאֱמַר: "דִּרְשׁוּ יְיָ בְּהִמָּצְאוֹ,
קְרָאֻהוּ בִּהְיוֹתוֹ קָרוֹב." וְנֶאֱמַר: "יַעֲזֹב רָשָׁע דַּרְכּוֹ

515

וְאִישׁ אָוֶן מַחְשְׁבֹתָיו, וְיָשֹׁב אֶל יְיָ וִירַחֲמֵהוּ, וְאֶל
אֱלֹהֵינוּ כִּי יַרְבֶּה לִסְלוֹחַ."

*In Your great mercy have compassion upon us, for You do
not desire the world's destruction. It has been said: "Seek
the Lord while there is yet time, cry out while God is near.
Let the wicked forsake their ways, those bent on evil their
thoughts. Let them return to the Lord, who will show them
mercy; to our God, who will graciously pardon."*

וְאַתָּה אֱלוֹהַּ סְלִיחוֹת, חַנּוּן וְרַחוּם, אֶרֶךְ אַפַּיִם וְרַב
חֶסֶד וֶאֱמֶת, וּמַרְבֶּה לְהֵיטִיב, וְרוֹצֶה אַתָּה בִּתְשׁוּבַת
רְשָׁעִים, וְאֵין אַתָּה חָפֵץ בְּמִיתָתָם, שֶׁנֶּאֱמַר: "אֱמֹר
אֲלֵיהֶם, חַי אָנִי, נְאֻם אֲדֹנָי אֱלֹהִים, אִם אֶחְפֹּץ בְּמוֹת
הָרָשָׁע, כִּי אִם בְּשׁוּב רָשָׁע מִדַּרְכּוֹ וְחָיָה. שׁוּבוּ, שׁוּבוּ
מִדַּרְכֵיכֶם הָרָעִים, וְלָמָּה תָמוּתוּ, בֵּית יִשְׂרָאֵל?"

You are a God of forgiveness: gracious and merciful,
endlessly patient, loving and true. You ask evildoers to
return to You, and do not seek their death; for it has been
said: "Declare to them: As I live, says the Lord God, it is
not the death of the wicked I seek, but that they turn from
their ways and live. Turn back, turn back from your evil
ways; for why should you choose to die, O House of
Israel?"

• •

דַּרְכְּךָ, אֱלֹהֵינוּ, לְהַאֲרִיךְ אַפֶּךָ, לָרָעִים וְלַטּוֹבִים,
וְהִיא תְהִלָּתֶךָ. לְמַעַנְךָ, אֱלֹהֵינוּ, עֲשֵׂה וְלֹא לָנוּ; רְאֵה
עָמְדָתֵנוּ דַלִּים וְרֵקִים.

It is Your way, our God, to be patient with all, evil and good; that
is Your greatness. Forgive us, not because of our merit, but that
Your purpose may prevail. Humbled, we stand before You,
knowing how slight is our worth.

OPEN THE GATE

Now send forth Your hidden light and open to Your servants the gates of help.

O great Lord, in Your justice and Your perfect love, open for us wisdom's gates.

◆

פִּתְחוּ־לָנוּ שַׁעֲרֵי־צֶדֶק, נָבוֹא בָם, נוֹדֶה יָהּ. דְּלָתֶיךָ
דָּפַקְנוּ, רַחוּם וְחַנּוּן; נָא אַל תְּשִׁיבֵנוּ רֵיקָם מִלְּפָנֶיךָ.
פְּתַח לָנוּ וּלְכָל־יִשְׂרָאֵל אַחֵינוּ בְּכָל־מָקוֹם: שַׁעֲרֵי
אוֹרָה, שַׁעֲרֵי בְרָכָה, שַׁעֲרֵי גִילָה, שַׁעֲרֵי דִיצָה,
שַׁעֲרֵי הוֹד וְהָדָר, שַׁעֲרֵי וַעַד טוֹב, שַׁעֲרֵי זְכִיּוֹת,
שַׁעֲרֵי חֶדְוָה, שַׁעֲרֵי טָהֳרָה, שַׁעֲרֵי יְשׁוּעָה, שַׁעֲרֵי
כַפָּרָה, שַׁעֲרֵי לֵב טוֹב, שַׁעֲרֵי מְחִילָה, שַׁעֲרֵי נֶחָמָה,
שַׁעֲרֵי סְלִיחָה, שַׁעֲרֵי עֶזְרָה, שַׁעֲרֵי פַרְנָסָה טוֹבָה,
שַׁעֲרֵי צְדָקָה, שַׁעֲרֵי קוֹמְמִיּוּת, שַׁעֲרֵי רְפוּאָה
שְׁלֵמָה, שַׁעֲרֵי שָׁלוֹם, שַׁעֲרֵי תְשׁוּבָה.

Open for us the gates of righteousness,

and we shall enter, to praise the Lord.

Open the gates; open them wide.

*We knock at Your gates, O gracious One;
do not turn us away empty-handed.*

Open the gates, Lord; open the gates
for us and for all Israel.

Open the gates of blessing for us all.

The gates of atonement, benevolence, and compassion,
the gates of dignity, excellence, and faith,

generosity and hope, insight and joy,
kindness and love, melody and nobility.

openness, purity, and quietude,
renewal, simplicity, and truth,

the gates of understanding and virtue,
the gates of wonder and zest.

Open the gates; open them wide.

Open the gates, Lord; show us the way to enter.

◆ ◆

אֱלֹהִים, הֲשִׁיבֵנוּ, וְהָאֵר פָּנֶיךָ וְנִוָּשֵׁעָה.

Restore us, O God; show us again the light of Your presence, that we may find deliverance.

◆ ◆

פְּתַח לָנוּ שַׁעַר בְּעֵת נְעִילַת שַׁעַר, כִּי פָנָה יוֹם.
הַיּוֹם יִפְנֶה, הַשֶּׁמֶשׁ יָבוֹא וְיִפְנֶה, נָבוֹאָה שְׁעָרֶיךָ!

Open the gates for us, even now, even now, when the gates are closing, and the day begins to fade. Oh, the day is fading, the sun is setting; let us enter Your gates!

◆ ◆

The day is fading; the sun is setting; the silence and peace of night descend upon the earth. Give rest now, O Author

518

of peace, to our troubled hearts; lift up the spirit oppressed by guilt. Turn, O Loved One, to Your children; turn to every broken heart and every burdened soul. Let us at this hour be sure of Your forgiveness.

From Your house, Lord, we are about to return to our homes. Enter them with us, that they may become Your sanctuaries, dwelling-places of Your spirit. Then will our home stand firm against the storms of life, to be a shelter for all that is good, and a refuge from evil.

And still another dwelling-place have You destined for us, O Source of life, an eternal home to which we shall go when our brief day on earth has passed. Open for us then the gates of everlasting peace, and keep alive in those who follow us the truths, the visions, and the hopes we have struggled to make real.

This twilight hour reminds us also of the day when, if we are faithful to our mission, Your light will arise over all the world, and Israel's spiritual descendants will be as numerous as the stars of heaven. Teach our people to recognize the meaning of our history and the challenge of our destiny, to proclaim to all Your children the truth of Israel's message: One humanity on earth even as there is One God in heaven.

You alone know when this great hope shall be fulfilled. But the day will surely come, even as none of Your words returns fruitless, without having accomplished Your purpose. Then joy will thrill all hearts, and from one end of the earth to the other will ring the exultant cry: 'Hear, O Israel, hear, all creation: The Lord is our God, the Lord is One!' Your house shall be called a house of prayer for all peoples; all nations shall flock to it and exclaim in triumphant song: 'Lift up your heads, O gates! Lift yourselves up, O ancient doors! Let the King of Glory

enter. Who is this King of Glory? The Lord of Hosts— He
is the King of Glory!'

Lift up your heads, O gates!	שְׂאוּ שְׁעָרִים רָאשֵׁיכֶם,
Lift yourselves up, O ancient doors!	וְהִנָּשְׂאוּ פִּתְחֵי עוֹלָם,
Let the King of Glory enter	וְיָבוֹא מֶלֶךְ הַכָּבוֹד!
Who is this King of Glory?	מִי הוּא זֶה מֶלֶךְ הַכָּבוֹד?
The Lord of Hosts—	יְיָ צְבָאוֹת—
He is the King of Glory!	הוּא מֶלֶךְ הַכָּבוֹד! סֶלָה.

All rise

The Ark is opened

Lord, whither can I go from Your spirit? Whither can I
flee from Your presence? If I ascend to the heavens, You
are there! If I make my home in the lowest depths, behold,
You are there! If I take up the wings of the morning, and
dwell on the ocean's farthest shore, even there Your hand
will lead me, Your right hand will hold me. And if I say:
Surely the darkness will conceal me, night will hide me
from view, even the darkness is not too dark for You; the
dark is clear as the day.

When I consider the heavens, the work of Your hands,
and when I gaze at the measureless sea of space and the
endless host of stars that sail in it; and when I set out to
understand this marvel and its tremendous Maker—then
Your greatness and power overwhelm me; Your infinite
majesty makes me tremble with awe. For the worlds
beyond count are but a breath of Your spirit, the lucent
suns only beams of Your light. O what are we, that You
have given us eyes to see something of Your truth? What
am I, that You have given me thought to fathom
something of Your purpose? Yet upon the earth with all

its abundance and beauty, forests dancing with life, mountains rising like prayers, seas roaring their creative hymn—with all the mysteries of the boundless depths and the immeasurable heights—You have chosen us to proclaim Your grandeur and to voice the longing of all being for You, O King of the universe and fountain of life! In woman and man, children of dust and offspring of heaven, You have blended two worlds: perishable earth and immortal soul; finite matter, locked into time and space, and infinite spirit, which endures through all eternity. You have given us dominion over the works of Your hands, and placed all things under our care. You have commanded us to live at peace with all living creatures, and to walk softly in their presence.

But there is that in us which darkens the soul. Called to a life of righteousness, we rebel: arrogance possesses us. The passions that rage within us drown the voice of conscience: good and evil, virtue and vice, love and hate contend for the mastery of our lives. Again and again we complain of the struggle, forgetting that the power to choose is the glory and greatness of our being. When we succumb, life loses its beauty, and within us sounds the voice of judgment: Where are you? How you have fallen, O children of the Most High!

But sure as is Your judgment, Lord, surer still is Your mercy. It is not the death of sinners You demand—only that they return to You, return to life. The gates of Your forgiveness are open wide, and all who seek to enter may be at one with You.

Aware of our weakness, Eternal God, we have come before You, longing for Your presence, Your light, Your peace. We have reflected with anguish on a life misused and filled with regrets, on opportunities neglected and promises unfulfilled. We have struggled to reach You, to turn back to You and to Your Law. Accept then our penitent spirits; be with us as our hope for the future.

Now, as evening falls, light dawns within us; hope and trust revive. The shadow that darkened our spirit is vanished; and through the passing cloud there breaks, with the last rays of the setting sun, the radiance of Your forgiving peace. We are restored, renewed by Your love.

How can we find words to thank You for Your goodness, and how can words alone be fitting thanks? And so we make this pledge: We will thank You with our lives; we will offer to You the work of our hands. Fill then our heart, our life, our work, with a constant love for You, God of the universe, Creator of all life, Lord of all being. Then shall our souls rejoice and sing: "You have turned my grief into dancing, released me from my anguish, and surrounded me with gladness: O Lord my God, I shall give thanks to You for ever!"

• •

וַאֲנַחְנוּ כּוֹרְעִים וּמִשְׁתַּחֲוִים וּמוֹדִים לִפְנֵי מֶלֶךְ מַלְכֵי
הַמְּלָכִים, הַקָּדוֹשׁ בָּרוּךְ הוּא.

We therefore bow in awe and thanksgiving before the One who is Sovereign over all, the Holy and Blessed One.

•

יִתְגַּדַּל וְיִתְקַדַּשׁ שְׁמֵהּ רַבָּא בְּעָלְמָא דִּי־בְרָא
כִרְעוּתֵהּ, וְיַמְלִיךְ מַלְכוּתֵהּ בְּחַיֵּיכוֹן וּבְיוֹמֵיכוֹן וּבְחַיֵּי
דְכָל־בֵּית יִשְׂרָאֵל, בַּעֲגָלָא וּבִזְמַן קָרִיב, וְאִמְרוּ: אָמֵן.

We sanctify Your name on earth, as we pray for the coming
of Your kingdom, in our own day, our own lives, and the life
of all Israel.

יְהֵא שְׁמֵהּ רַבָּא מְבָרַךְ לְעָלַם וּלְעָלְמֵי עָלְמַיָּא.

Let Your great name be blessed for ever and ever.

יִתְבָּרַךְ וְיִשְׁתַּבַּח, וְיִתְפָּאַר וְיִתְרוֹמַם וְיִתְנַשֵּׂא,
וְיִתְהַדָּר וְיִתְעַלֶּה וְיִתְהַלָּל שְׁמֵהּ דְּקוּדְשָׁא, בְּרִיךְ
הוּא, לְעֵלָּא מִן־כָּל־בִּרְכָתָא וְשִׁירָתָא, תֻּשְׁבְּחָתָא
וְנֶחֱמָתָא דַּאֲמִירָן בְּעָלְמָא, וְאִמְרוּ: אָמֵן.

*Let Your name be exalted and honored, though You are
beyond all the praises we can utter, all the songs we can ever
sing.*

תִּתְקַבֵּל צְלוֹתְהוֹן וּבָעוּתְהוֹן דְּכָל־יִשְׂרָאֵל קֳדָם
אֲבוּהוֹן דִּי בִשְׁמַיָּא, וְאִמְרוּ: אָמֵן.

*O Maker of heaven and earth, Divine Parent of all being,
accept the prayers and supplications of Your people Israel.*

יְהֵא שְׁלָמָא רַבָּא מִן־שְׁמַיָּא וְחַיִּים, עָלֵינוּ וְעַל כָּל־
יִשְׂרָאֵל, וְאִמְרוּ: אָמֵן.

*For us, for all Israel, for all men and women, may the bless-
ing of peace and the promise of life come true.*

עוֹשֶׂה שָׁלוֹם בִּמְרוֹמָיו, הוּא יַעֲשֶׂה שָׁלוֹם עָלֵינוּ וְעַל
כָּל־יִשְׂרָאֵל, וְאִמְרוּ: אָמֵן.

*As You make peace on high, so let peace descend on us, on
all Israel, and all the world.*

◆ ◆

(One time)

שְׁמַע יִשְׂרָאֵל: יְיָ אֱלֹהֵינוּ, יְיָ אֶחָד!

Hear, O Israel: the Lord is our God, the Lord is One!

(Three times)

בָּרוּךְ שֵׁם כְּבוֹד מַלְכוּתוֹ לְעוֹלָם וָעֶד!

Blessed is God's glorious kingdom for ever and ever!

(Seven times)

יְיָ הוּא הָאֱלֹהִים!

The Eternal Lord is God!

The Shofar is sounded
The Ark is closed
Havdalah, page 526, may be recited here
Remain standing

Benediction

And now, at the close of this day's service, we implore You, O Lord our God:

Let the year upon which we have entered be for us, for Israel, and for all the world,

A year of blessing and prosperity.

Amen.

A year of salvation and comfort.

Amen.

A year of peace and contentment, of joy and of spiritual welfare.

Amen.

A year of virtue and of reverence for God.

Amen.

A year that finds the hearts of parents united with the hearts of their children.

Amen.

A year of Your pardon and favor.

Amen.

יְיָ יִשְׁמָר־צֵאתְךָ וּבוֹאֶךָ מֵעַתָּה וְעַד־עוֹלָם.

May the Lord bless your going out and your coming in from this time forth and for ever.

Amen.

525

הבדלה

The cup is raised

בָּרוּךְ אַתָּה, יְיָ אֱלֹהֵינוּ, מֶלֶךְ הָעוֹלָם, בּוֹרֵא פְּרִי הַגָּפֶן.

Blessed is the Lord our God, Ruler of the universe, Creator of the fruit of the vine.

The spice box is raised

בָּרוּךְ אַתָּה, יְיָ אֱלֹהֵינוּ, מֶלֶךְ הָעוֹלָם, בּוֹרֵא מִינֵי בְשָׂמִים.

Blessed is the Lord our God, Ruler of the universe, Creator of all the spices.

The candle is raised

בָּרוּךְ אַתָּה, יְיָ אֱלֹהֵינוּ, מֶלֶךְ הָעוֹלָם, בּוֹרֵא מְאוֹרֵי הָאֵשׁ.

Blessed is the Lord our God, Ruler of the universe, Creator of the light of fire.

• •

בָּרוּךְ אַתָּה, יְיָ אֱלֹהֵינוּ, מֶלֶךְ הָעוֹלָם, הַמַּבְדִּיל בֵּין קֹדֶשׁ לְחוֹל, בֵּין אוֹר לְחֹשֶׁךְ, בֵּין יִשְׂרָאֵל לָעַמִּים, בֵּין יוֹם הַשְּׁבִיעִי לְשֵׁשֶׁת יְמֵי הַמַּעֲשֶׂה. בָּרוּךְ אַתָּה, יְיָ, הַמַּבְדִּיל בֵּין קֹדֶשׁ לְחוֹל.

Blessed is the Lord our God, Ruler of the universe, who

separates sacred from profane, light from darkness, the House of Israel from other peoples, and the seventh day of rest from the six days of labor.

Blessed is the Lord, who separates the sacred from the profane.

The candle is extinguished

Ha·mav·dil bein ko·desh le·chol, cha·to·tei·nu hu yim·chol, zar·ei·nu ve·chas·pei·nu yar·beh ka·chol, ve·cha·ko·cha·vim ba·lai·la.	הַמַּבְדִּיל בֵּין קֹדֶשׁ לְחוֹל, חַטֹּאתֵינוּ הוּא יִמְחֹל, זַרְעֵנוּ וְכַסְפֵּנוּ יַרְבֶּה כַּחוֹל, וְכַכּוֹכָבִים בַּלָּיְלָה.
Sha·na tova	שָׁנָה טוֹבָה...
Yom pa·na ke·tseil to·mer, Ek·ra la·eil, a·lai go·meir; a·mar sho·meir, a·ta vo·ker, ve·gam lai·la.	יוֹם פָּנָה כְּצֵל תֹּמֶר, אֶקְרָא לָאֵל, עָלַי גֹּמֵר; אָמַר שׁוֹמֵר, אָתָא בֹקֶר, וְגַם־לָיְלָה.
Sha·na tova	שָׁנָה טוֹבָה...
Tsid·ka·te·cha ke·har Ta·vor, al cha·ta·ai a·vor ta·a·vor, ke·yom et·mol ki ya·a·vor, ve·ash·mu·ra va·lai·la.	צִדְקָתְךָ כְּהַר תָּבוֹר, עַל חֲטָאַי עָבוֹר תַּעֲבוֹר, כְּיוֹם אֶתְמוֹל כִּי יַעֲבוֹר, וְאַשְׁמוּרָה בַלָּיְלָה.
Sha·na tova	שָׁנָה טוֹבָה...
Hei·a·teir, no·ra ve·a·yom, a·sha·vei·a, te·na fid·yom, be·ne·shef, be·e·rev yom, be·i·shon lai·la.	הֵעָתֵר, נוֹרָא וְאָיוֹם, אֲשַׁוֵּעַ, תְּנָה פִדְיוֹם, בְּנֶשֶׁף, בְּעֶרֶב יוֹם, בְּאִישׁוֹן לָיְלָה.
Sha·na tova	שָׁנָה טוֹבָה...

You separate sacred from profane: separate us now from our sins! Let those who love You be as many as the sands, and as the stars of heaven.

Day has declined, the shadows are gone; we call to the One whose word is Good. The sentry says: 'Morning will come, though it still be night.'

Your righteousness is a majestic mountain: forgive our sins. Let them be as yesterday when it is past, as a watch in the night.

Hear our prayer, O awesome God, and grant redemption! in the twilight, in the waning of the day, or in the blackness of the night!

שירים ותעתיקים

SONGS AND
TRANSLITERATIONS

A NOTE ON TRANSLITERATION

The system employed in this Prayerbook is, with minor deviations, the "American National Standard Romanization of Hebrew (approved 1975)."

Vowels and Consonants for Special Notice

a as in 'papa' (short) or 'father' (long)
e as in 'get' or 'the' (sheva)
eh as in 'get' (used only at the end of a word)
i as in 'bit' (short) or 'machine' (long)
o as in 'often'
u as in 'pull' (short) or 'rule' (long)
ai as in 'aisle'
oi as in 'boil'
ei as in 'veil'
g as in 'get' (hard 'g')
ch as in Scottish 'loch' or German 'ach'

Songs
שירים

I

O LORD, WHERE SHALL I FIND YOU?

O Lord, where shall I find you? Hid is Your lofty place;
And where shall I not find You, whose glory fills all space?
Who formed the world, abiding within the soul alway;
Refuge to them that seek Him, ransom for them that stray.

O, how shall mortals praise You, when angels strive in vain—
Or build for You a dwelling, whom worlds cannot contain?
I find You in the marvels of Your creative might,
In visions in Your temple, in dreams that bless the night.

Who say they have not seen You, Your heavens refute their word;
Their hosts declare Your glory, though never voice be heard.
And You, transcendent, holy, delight in Your creatures' praise,
And descend where we are gathered to glorify Your ways.

2

O GOD OUR HELP

O God, our help in ages past, our hope for years to come,
Our shelter from the stormy blast, and our eternal home.

Before the hills in order stood, or earth received her frame,
From everlasting You are God, to endless years the same.

Beneath the shadow of Your throne Your children dwell secure;
Sufficient is Your arm alone, and our defence is sure.

O God, our help in ages past, our hope for years to come,
Be now our guide while troubles last, and our eternal home.

3

AMERICA THE BEAUTIFUL

O beautiful for spacious skies,
For amber waves of grain,
For purple mountain majesties,
Above the fruited plain!
America! America!
God shed His grace on thee,
And crown thy good with brotherhood,
From sea to shining sea.

O beautiful for pilgrim feet,
Whose stern, impassioned stress,
A thoroughfare for freedom beat,
Across the wilderness!
America! America!
God mend thy every flaw,
Confirm thy soul in self-control,
Thy liberty in law!

O beautiful for heroes proved
In liberating strife,
Who more than self their country loved,
And mercy more than life!
America! America!
May God thy gold refine
Till all success be nobleness,
And ev'ry gain divine!

O beautiful for patriot dream,
That sees beyond the years,
Thine alabaster cities gleam,
Undimmed by human tears!
America! America!
God shed His grace on thee,
And crown thy good with brotherhood,
From sea to shining sea!

4

THE NATIONAL ANTHEM

O say, can you see
By the dawn's early light,
What so proudly we hailed
At the twilight's last gleaming?
Whose broad stripes and bright stars
Through the perilous fight,
O'er the ramparts we watched
Were so gallantly streaming!
And the rocket's red glare,
The bombs bursting in air,
Gave proof through the night
That our flag was still there!
O say, does that star-spangled banner yet wave
O'er the land of the free, and the home of the brave?

5

O CANADA!

O Canada! Our home and native land!
True patriot-love in all thy sons command.
With glowing hearts we see thee rise,
The true North, strong and free.
And stand on guard, O Canada,
We stand on guard for thee.
O Canada, glorious and free!
O Canada, we stand on guard for thee.
O Canada, we stand on guard for thee!

6

HATIKVAH

התקוה

Kol od ba·lei·vav pe·ni·ma,
ne·fesh Ye·hu·di ho·mi·ya.
U·le·fa·a·tei miz·rach ka·di·ma,
a·yin le·tsi·yon tso·fi·ya.

כָּל עוֹד בַּלֵּבָב פְּנִימָה,
נֶפֶשׁ יְהוּדִי הוֹמִיָּה.
וּלְפַאֲתֵי מִזְרָח קָדִימָה,
עַיִן לְצִיּוֹן צוֹפִיָּה.

Od lo a·ve·da tik·va·tei·nu,
ha·tik·va she·not al·pa·yim,
li·he·yot am chof·shi be·ar·tsei·nu,
be·e·rets tsi·yon vi·ru·sha·la·yim.

עוֹד לֹא אָבְדָה תִּקְוָתֵנוּ,
הַתִּקְוָה שְׁנוֹת אַלְפַּיִם,
לִהְיוֹת עַם חָפְשִׁי בְּאַרְצֵנוּ,
בְּאֶרֶץ צִיּוֹן וִירוּשָׁלָיִם.

So long as still within the inmost heart a Jewish spirit sings, so
long as the eye looks eastward, gazing toward Zion, our hope is
not lost-that hope of two millenia, to be a free people in our
land, the land of Zion and Jerusalem.

Transliterations

תעתיקים

ROSH HASHANAH CANDLE LIGHTING

Ba·ruch a·ta, A·do·nai E·lo·hei·nu,
me·lech ha·o·lam,
a·sher ki·de·sha·nu be·mitz·vo·tav
ve·tsi·va·nu le·had·lik neir shel
(Sha·bat ve·shel) Yom Tov.

בָּרוּךְ אַתָּה, יְיָ אֱלֹהֵינוּ,
מֶלֶךְ הָעוֹלָם,
אֲשֶׁר קִדְּשָׁנוּ בְּמִצְוֹתָיו
וְצִוָּנוּ לְהַדְלִיק נֵר שֶׁל
(שַׁבָּת וְשֶׁל) יוֹם טוֹב.

SHEHECHEYANU

Ba·ruch a·ta, A·do·nai
E·lo·hei·nu, me·lech ha·o·lam,
she·he·che·ya·nu ve·ki·ye·ma·nu
ve·hi·gi·a·nu la·ze·man ha·zeh.

בָּרוּךְ אַתָּה, יְיָ
אֱלֹהֵינוּ, מֶלֶךְ הָעוֹלָם,
שֶׁהֶחֱיָנוּ וְקִיְּמָנוּ
וְהִגִּיעָנוּ לַזְּמַן הַזֶּה.

3

READER'S KADDISH

Yit·ga·dal ve·yit·ka·dash
  she·mei ra·ba
be·al·ma di·ve·ra chi·re·u·tei,
ve·yam·lich mal·chu·tei
  be·cha·yei·chon
u·ve·yo·mei·chon u·ve·cha·yei
de·chol beit Yis·ra·eil,
be·a·ga·la u·vi·ze·man ka·riv,
ve·i·me·ru: a·mein.

יִתְגַּדַּל וְיִתְקַדַּשׁ שְׁמֵהּ רַבָּא
בְּעָלְמָא דִּי־בְרָא כִרְעוּתֵהּ,
וְיַמְלִיךְ מַלְכוּתֵהּ בְּחַיֵּיכוֹן
וּבְיוֹמֵיכוֹן וּבְחַיֵּי
דְכָל־בֵּית יִשְׂרָאֵל,
בַּעֲגָלָא וּבִזְמַן קָרִיב,
וְאִמְרוּ: אָמֵן.

Ye·hei she·mei ra·ba me·va·rach
le·a·lam u·le·al·mei al·ma·ya.

יְהֵא שְׁמֵהּ רַבָּא מְבָרַךְ
לְעָלַם וּלְעָלְמֵי עָלְמַיָּא.

Yit·ba·rach ve·yish·ta·bach,
ve·yit·pa·ar ve·yit·ro·mam
ve·yit·na·sei,
ve·yit·ha·dar ve·yit·a·leh ve·yit·ha·lal
she·mei de·ku·de·sha, be·rich hu,
le·ei·la min kol bi·re·cha·ta
ve·shi·ra·ta,
tush·be·cha·ta ve·ne·che·ma·ta
da·a·mi·ran be·al·ma, ve·i·me·ru:
a·mein.

יִתְבָּרַךְ וְיִשְׁתַּבַּח,
וְיִתְפָּאַר וְיִתְרוֹמַם וְיִתְנַשֵּׂא,
וְיִתְהַדָּר וְיִתְעַלֶּה וְיִתְהַלָּל
שְׁמֵהּ דְּקוּדְשָׁא, בְּרִיךְ הוּא,
לְעֵלָּא מִן כָּל־בִּרְכָתָא וְשִׁירָתָא,
תֻּשְׁבְּחָתָא וְנֶחֱמָתָא
דַּאֲמִירָן בְּעָלְמָא, וְאִמְרוּ: אָמֵן.

4

BARECHU

Ba·re·chu et A·do·nai ha·me·vo·rach!

Ba·ruch A·do·nai ha·me·vo·rach

le·o·lam va·ed!

בָּרְכוּ אֶת־יְיָ הַמְבֹרָךְ!
בָּרוּךְ יְיָ הַמְבֹרָךְ
לְעוֹלָם וָעֶד!

5

SHEMA

She·ma Yis·ra·eil: A·do·nai

E·lo·hei·nu, A·do·nai e·chad!

Ba·ruch sheim ke·vod

mal·chu·to le·o·lam va·ed!

שְׁמַע יִשְׂרָאֵל: יְיָ
אֱלֹהֵינוּ, יְיָ אֶחָד!
בָּרוּךְ שֵׁם כְּבוֹד
מַלְכוּתוֹ לְעוֹלָם וָעֶד!

6

VE·AHAVTA

Ve·a·hav·ta eit A·do·nai E·lo·he·cha,
be·chol
le·va·ve·cha, u·ve·chol naf·she·cha,
u·ve·chol
me·o·de·cha.
Ve·ha·yu ha·de·va·rim ha·ei·leh,

וְאָהַבְתָּ אֵת יְיָ אֱלֹהֶיךָ
בְּכָל־לְבָבְךָ וּבְכָל־נַפְשְׁךָ
וּבְכָל־מְאֹדֶךָ.
וְהָיוּ הַדְּבָרִים הָאֵלֶּה,

536

a·sher a·no·chi
me·tsa·ve·cha ha·yom, al le·va·ve·cha.
Ve·shi·nan·tam
le·va·ne·cha, ve·di·bar·ta bam
be·shiv·te·cha
be·vei·te·cha u·ve·lech·te·cha
va·de·rech,
u·ve·shoch·be·cha u·ve·ku·me·cha.
U·ke·shar·tam le·ot
al ya·de·cha, ve·ha·yu
le·to·ta·fot bein ei·ne·cha,
u·che·tav·tam al me·zu·zot bei·te·cha
u·vish·a·re·cha.
Le·ma·an tiz·ke·ru, va·a·si·tem et kol
mits·vo·tai vi·he·yi·tem ke·do·shim
lei·lo·hei·chem. A·ni A·do·nai
E·lo·hei·chem, a·sher
ho·tsei·ti e·te·chem mei·e·rets
Mits·ra·yim,
li·he·yot la·chem lei·lo·him.
A·ni A·do·nai E·lo·hei·chem.

אֲשֶׁר אָנֹכִי
מְצַוְּךָ הַיּוֹם, עַל־לְבָבֶךָ.
וְשִׁנַּנְתָּם לְבָנֶיךָ, וְדִבַּרְתָּ בָּם
בְּשִׁבְתְּךָ בְּבֵיתֶךָ, וּבְלֶכְתְּךָ בַדֶּרֶךְ,
וּבְשָׁכְבְּךָ וּבְקוּמֶךָ.
וּקְשַׁרְתָּם לְאוֹת
עַל־יָדֶךָ, וְהָיוּ לְטֹטָפֹת בֵּין עֵינֶיךָ,
וּכְתַבְתָּם עַל־מְזֻזוֹת
בֵּיתֶךָ, וּבִשְׁעָרֶיךָ.
לְמַעַן תִּזְכְּרוּ וַעֲשִׂיתֶם
אֶת־כָּל־מִצְוֹתָי, וִהְיִיתֶם
קְדֹשִׁים לֵאלֹהֵיכֶם. אֲנִי יְיָ
אֱלֹהֵיכֶם, אֲשֶׁר הוֹצֵאתִי
אֶתְכֶם מֵאֶרֶץ מִצְרַיִם
לִהְיוֹת לָכֶם לֵאלֹהִים.
אֲנִי יְיָ אֱלֹהֵיכֶם.

7

MI CHAMOCHA

Me cha·mo·cha ba·ei·lim, A·do·nai?

Mi ka·mo·cha, ne·dar ba·ko·desh,

no·ra te·hi·lot, o·sei fe·leh?

Mal·chu·te·cha ra·u va·ne·cha,

bo·kei·a yam li·fe·nei Mo·sheh;

"Zeh Ei·li!" a·nu ve·a·me·ru:

"A·do·nai yim·loch le·o·lam va·ed!"

מִי־כָמֹכָה בָּאֵלִם, יְיָ ?

מִי כָּמֹכָה, נֶאְדָּר בַּקֹּדֶשׁ,

נוֹרָא תְהִלֹּת, עֹשֵׂה פֶלֶא?

מַלְכוּתְךָ רָאוּ בָנֶיךָ,

בּוֹקֵעַ יָם לִפְנֵי מֹשֶׁה;

"זֶה אֵלִי!" עָנוּ וְאָמְרוּ:

"יְיָ יִמְלֹךְ לְעֹלָם וָעֶד!"

Ve·ne·e·mar: "Ki fa·da A·do·nai
et Ya·a·kov,
u·ge·a·lo mi·yad cha·zak mi·me·nu."
Ba·ruch a·ta, A·do·nai, ga·al
Yis·ra·eil.

וְנֶאֱמַר: "כִּי־פָּדָה יְיָ אֶת יַעֲקֹב,
וּגְאָלוֹ מִיַּד חָזָק מִמֶּנּוּ."
בָּרוּךְ אַתָּה, יְיָ, גָּאַל
יִשְׂרָאֵל.

8

TSUR YISRAEIL

Tsur Yis·ra·eil, ku·ma be·ez·rat
Yis·ra·eil, u·fe·dei chi·ne·u·me·cha
Ye·hu·dah ve·yis·ra·eil.

Go·a·lei·nu A·do·nai tse·va·ot
she·mo,
ke·dosh Yis·ra·eil.
Ba·ruch a·ta, A·do·nai,
ga·al Yis·ra·eil.

צוּר יִשְׂרָאֵל, קוּמָה בְּעֶזְרַת
יִשְׂרָאֵל, וּפְדֵה כִנְאֻמֶךָ
יְהוּדָה וְיִשְׂרָאֵל.
גְּאָלֵנוּ יְיָ צְבָאוֹת שְׁמוֹ,
קְדוֹשׁ יִשְׂרָאֵל.
בָּרוּךְ אַתָּה, יְיָ, גָּאַל יִשְׂרָאֵל.

9

AVOT

A·do·nai, se·fa·tai tif·tach, u·fi
ya·gid te·hi·la·te·cha.

Ba·ruch a·ta, A·do·nai E·lo·hei·nu
vei·lo·hei
a·vo·tei·nu, E·lo·hei Av·ra·ham,
E·lo·hei
Yits·chak, vei·lo·hei Ya·a·kov:
ha·eil ha·ga·dol,
ha·gi·bor ve·ha·no·ra, Eil el·yon.
Go·meil cha·sa·dim to·vim,
ve·ko·nei ha·kol,
ve·zo·cheir cha·se·dei

אֲדֹנָי, שְׂפָתַי תִּפְתָּח,
וּפִי יַגִּיד תְּהִלָּתֶךָ.
בָּרוּךְ אַתָּה, יְיָ אֱלֹהֵינוּ
וֵאלֹהֵי אֲבוֹתֵינוּ, אֱלֹהֵי
אַבְרָהָם, אֱלֹהֵי יִצְחָק,
וֵאלֹהֵי יַעֲקֹב: הָאֵל הַגָּדוֹל,
הַגִּבּוֹר וְהַנּוֹרָא, אֵל עֶלְיוֹן.
גּוֹמֵל חֲסָדִים טוֹבִים,
וְקוֹנֵה הַכֹּל, וְזוֹכֵר חַסְדֵי

a·vot, u·mei·vi ge·u·lah
li·ve·nei ve·nei·hem, le·ma·an
    she·mo, be·a·ha·va.
Zoch·rei·nu le·cha·yim, me·lech
    cha·feitz ba·cha·yim,
ve·cho·te·vei·nu be·sei·fer
    ha·cha·yim,
le·ma·a·ne·cha E·lo·him
    cha·yim.
Me·lech o·zeir u·mo·shi·a u·ma·gein.
Ba·ruch a·ta, A·do·nai, ma·gein
    Av·ra·ham.

אָבוֹת, וּמֵבִיא גְאֻלָּה לִבְנֵי
בְנֵיהֶם, לְמַעַן שְׁמוֹ, בְּאַהֲבָה.
זָכְרֵנוּ לְחַיִּים, מֶלֶךְ חָפֵץ
בַּחַיִּים, וְכָתְבֵנוּ בְּסֵפֶר הַחַיִּים,
לְמַעַנְךָ אֱלֹהִים חַיִּים.
מֶלֶךְ עוֹזֵר וּמוֹשִׁיעַ וּמָגֵן.
בָּרוּךְ אַתָּה, יְיָ, מָגֵן אַבְרָהָם.

10

GEVUROT

A·ta gi·bor le·o·lam, A·do·nai,
me·cha·yei ha·kol a·ta,
    rav le·ho·shi·a.
Me·chal·keil cha·yim be·che·sed,
me·cha·yei ha·kol be·ra·cha·mim
    ra·bim.
So·meich no·fe·lim, ve·ro·fei
    cho·lim,
u·ma·tir a·su·rim, u·me·ka·yeim
e·mu·na·to li·shei·nei a·far.
Mi cha·mo·cha, ba·al ge·vu·rot,
u·mi do·meh lach,
me·lech mei·mit u·me·cha·yeh
u·mats·mi·ach ye·shu·a?
Mi cha·mo·cha Av
    ha·ra·cha·mim,
zo·cheir ye·tsu·rav
    le·cha·yim be·ra·cha·mim?
Ve·ne·e·man a·ta le·ha·cha·yot
ha·kol. Ba·ruch a·ta, A·do·nai,
me·cha·yei ha·kol.

אַתָּה גִבּוֹר לְעוֹלָם, אֲדֹנָי,
מְחַיֵּה הַכֹּל אַתָּה,
רַב לְהוֹשִׁיעַ.
מְכַלְכֵּל חַיִּים בְּחֶסֶד,
מְחַיֵּה הַכֹּל בְּרַחֲמִים רַבִּים.
סוֹמֵךְ נוֹפְלִים, וְרוֹפֵא
חוֹלִים, וּמַתִּיר אֲסוּרִים,
וּמְקַיֵּם אֱמוּנָתוֹ לִישֵׁנֵי עָפָר.
מִי כָמוֹךָ, בַּעַל גְּבוּרוֹת,
וּמִי דּוֹמֶה לָּךְ, מֶלֶךְ מֵמִית
וּמְחַיֵּה וּמַצְמִיחַ יְשׁוּעָה?
מִי כָמוֹךָ אַב הָרַחֲמִים,
זוֹכֵר יְצוּרָיו לְחַיִּים בְּרַחֲמִים?
וְנֶאֱמָן אַתָּה לְהַחֲיוֹת הַכֹּל.
בָּרוּךְ אַתָּה, יְיָ, מְחַיֵּה הַכֹּל.

11

YI·HE·YU LE·RA·TSON

Yi·he·yu le·ra·tson i·me·rei fi
ve·heg·yon li·bi le·fa·ne·cha,
A·do·nai, tsu·ri ve·go·a·li.

יִהְיוּ לְרָצוֹן אִמְרֵי־פִי
וְהֶגְיוֹן לִבִּי לְפָנֶיךָ,
יְיָ, צוּרִי וְגוֹאֲלִי.

12

OSEH SHALOM

Oseh sha·lom bi·me·ro·mav,
Hu ya·a·seh sha·lom
a·lei·nu ve·al kol Yis·ra·eil,
ve·i·me·ru a·mein.

עֹשֶׂה שָׁלוֹם בִּמְרוֹמָיו,
הוּא יַעֲשֶׂה שָׁלוֹם
עָלֵינוּ וְעַל כָּל־יִשְׂרָאֵל,
וְאִמְרוּ אָמֵן.

13

AVINU MALKEINU

A·vi·nu Mal·kei·nu, she·ma
   ko·lei·nu.
A·vi·nu Mal·kei·nu, cha·ta·nu
   le·fa·ne·cha.
A·vi·nu Mal·kei·nu, cha·mol
   a·lei·nu ve·al o·la·lei·nu
   ve·ta·pei·nu.
A·vi·nu Mal·kei·nu, ka·lei de·ver
   ve·che·rev ve·ra·av mei·a·lei·nu.
A·vi·nu Mal·kei·nu, ka·lei kol tsar
   u·mas·tin mei·a·lei·nu.
A·vi·nu Mal·kei·nu, ko·te·vei·nu
   be·sei·fer cha·yim to·vim.
A·vi·nu Mal·kei·nu, cha·deish a·lei·nu
   sha·na to·va.

אָבִינוּ מַלְכֵּנוּ, שְׁמַע קוֹלֵנוּ.
אָבִינוּ מַלְכֵּנוּ, חָטָאנוּ לְפָנֶיךָ.
אָבִינוּ מַלְכֵּנוּ, חֲמוֹל עָלֵינוּ
וְעַל עוֹלָלֵינוּ וְטַפֵּנוּ.
אָבִינוּ מַלְכֵּנוּ, כַּלֵּה דֶבֶר
וְחֶרֶב וְרָעָב מֵעָלֵינוּ.
אָבִינוּ מַלְכֵּנוּ, כַּלֵּה כָּל־
צָר וּמַשְׂטִין מֵעָלֵינוּ.
אָבִינוּ מַלְכֵּנוּ, כָּתְבֵנוּ
בְּסֵפֶר חַיִּים טוֹבִים.
אָבִינוּ מַלְכֵּנוּ, חַדֵּשׁ
עָלֵינוּ שָׁנָה טוֹבָה.

A·vi·nu Mal·kei·nu, cho·nei·nu
va·a·nei·nu, ki ein ba·nu
ma·a·sim, a·sei i·ma·nu
tse·da·kah va·che·sed
ve·ho·shi·ei·nu.

אָבִינוּ מַלְכֵּנוּ, חָנֵּנוּ וַעֲנֵנוּ,
כִּי אֵין בָּנוּ מַעֲשִׂים, עֲשֵׂה
עִמָּנוּ צְדָקָה וָחֶסֶד וְהוֹשִׁיעֵנוּ.

14

MA TOVU

Ma to·vu o·ha·le·cha Ya·a·kov,
mish·ke·no·te·cha, Yis·ra·eil!
Va·a·ni, be·rov chas·de·cha a·vo
vei·te·cha,
esh·ta·cha·veh el hei·chal
kod·she·cha be·yir·a·te·cha.
A·do·nai, a·hav·ti me·on bei·te·cha,
u·me·kom mish·kan ke·vo·de·cha.
Va·a·ni esh·ta·cha·veh ve·ech·ra·a,
ev·re·cha li·fe·nei A·do·nai o·si.
Va·a·ni te·fi·la·ti le·cha,
A·do·nai, eit ra·tson.
E·lo·him, be·rov chas·de·cha,
a·nei·ni be·e·met yish·e·cha.

מַה־טֹּבוּ אֹהָלֶיךָ, יַעֲקֹב,
מִשְׁכְּנֹתֶיךָ, יִשְׂרָאֵל!
וַאֲנִי, בְּרֹב חַסְדְּךָ אָבֹא בֵיתֶךָ,
אֶשְׁתַּחֲוֶה אֶל־הֵיכַל
קָדְשְׁךָ בְּיִרְאָתֶךָ.
יְיָ, אָהַבְתִּי מְעוֹן בֵּיתֶךָ,
וּמְקוֹם מִשְׁכַּן כְּבוֹדֶךָ.
וַאֲנִי אֶשְׁתַּחֲוֶה וְאֶכְרָעָה,
אֶבְרְכָה לִפְנֵי־יְיָ עֹשִׂי.
וַאֲנִי תְפִלָּתִי לְךָ,
יְיָ, עֵת רָצוֹן.
אֱלֹהִים, בְּרָב־חַסְדֶּךָ,
עֲנֵנִי בֶּאֱמֶת יִשְׁעֶךָ.

15

RESPONSES TO THE KEDUSHAH

Ka·dosh, ka·dosh, ka·dosh
A·do·nai tse·va·ot,
me·lo chol ha·a·rets ke·vo·do.
Ba·ruch ke·vod A·do·nai
mi·me·ko·mo.
A·ni A·do·nai E·lo·hei·chem!

קָדוֹשׁ, קָדוֹשׁ, קָדוֹשׁ
יְיָ צְבָאוֹת,
מְלֹא כָל־הָאָרֶץ כְּבוֹדוֹ.
בָּרוּךְ כְּבוֹד־יְיָ מִמְּקוֹמוֹ.
"אֲנִי יְיָ אֱלֹהֵיכֶם!"

Yim·loch A·do·nai le·o·lam,
E·lo·ha·yich Tsi·yon,
le·dor va·dor. Ha·le·lu·yah!

יִמְלֹךְ יְיָ לְעוֹלָם, אֱלֹהַיִךְ
צִיּוֹן, לְדֹר וָדֹר. הַלְלוּיָהּ!

16

TORAH BLESSINGS

Before the reading

Ba·re·chu et A·do·nai ha·me·vo·rach!
Ba·ruch A·do·nai ha·me·vo·rach
    le·o·lam va·ed!
Ba·ruch a·ta, A·do·nai E·lo·hei·nu,
    me·lech
ha·o·lam, a·sher ba·char ba·nu mi·kol
ha·a·mim, ve·na·tan la·nu et To·ra·to.
Ba·ruch a·ta, A·do·nai, no·tein
    ha·to·rah.

בָּרְכוּ אֶת־יְיָ הַמְבֹרָךְ!
בָּרוּךְ יְיָ הַמְבֹרָךְ
לְעוֹלָם וָעֶד!
בָּרוּךְ אַתָּה, יְיָ אֱלֹהֵינוּ,
מֶלֶךְ הָעוֹלָם, אֲשֶׁר בָּחַר־
בָּנוּ מִכָּל־הָעַמִּים
וְנָתַן־לָנוּ אֶת־תּוֹרָתוֹ.
בָּרוּךְ אַתָּה, יְיָ, נוֹתֵן הַתּוֹרָה.

After the reading

Ba·ruch a·ta, A·do·nai E·lo·hei·nu,
    me·lech
ha·o·lam, a·sher na·tan la·nu To·rat
    e·met,
ve·cha·yei o·lam na·ta
    be·to·chei·nu.
Ba·ruch a·ta, A·do·nai, no·tein
    ha·to·rah.

בָּרוּךְ אַתָּה, יְיָ אֱלֹהֵינוּ,
מֶלֶךְ הָעוֹלָם,
אֲשֶׁר נָתַן־לָנוּ תּוֹרַת אֱמֶת
וְחַיֵּי עוֹלָם נָטַע בְּתוֹכֵנוּ.
בָּרוּךְ אַתָּה, יְיָ, נוֹתֵן הַתּוֹרָה.

17

PASSAGES RELATED TO THE TORAH RITUAL

I.

Ba·ruch she·na·tan To·rah le·a·mo
    Yis·ra·eil
bi·ke·du·sha·to.

בָּרוּךְ שֶׁנָּתַן תּוֹרָה
לְעַמּוֹ יִשְׂרָאֵל בִּקְדֻשָׁתוֹ.

II.

Ki mi·tsi·yon tei·tsei To·rah
u·de·var A·do·nai mi·ru·sha·la·yim.

כִּי מִצִּיּוֹן תֵּצֵא תוֹרָה
וּדְבַר־יְיָ מִירוּשָׁלָיִם.

III.

Le·cha, A·do·nai, ha·ge·du·la,
    ve·ha·ge·vu·ra
ve·ha·tif·e·ret, ve·ha·nei·tsach,
    ve·ha·hod, ki chol
ba·sha·ma·yim u·va·a·rets, le·cha
    A·do·nai ha·mam·la·cha
ve·ha·mit·na·sei le·chol le·rosh.

לְךָ, יְיָ, הַגְּדֻלָּה וְהַגְּבוּרָה
וְהַתִּפְאֶרֶת וְהַנֵּצַח וְהַהוֹד,
כִּי כֹל בַּשָּׁמַיִם וּבָאָרֶץ,
לְךָ יְיָ הַמַּמְלָכָה וְהַמִּתְנַשֵּׂא
לְכֹל לְרֹאשׁ.

IV.

Ho·do al e·rets ve·sha·ma·yim,
    va·ya·rem ke·ren
le·a·mo, te·hi·la le·chol cha·si·dav,
    li·ve·nei
Yis·ra·eil, am ke·ro·vo. Ha·le·lu·yah!

הוֹדוֹ עַל אֶרֶץ וְשָׁמָיִם,
וַיָּרֶם קֶרֶן לְעַמּוֹ,
תְּהִלָּה לְכָל־חֲסִידָיו,
לִבְנֵי יִשְׂרָאֵל, עַם
קְרוֹבוֹ. הַלְלוּיָהּ!

V.

Ki le·kach tov na·ta·ti la·chem,
To·ra·ti al ta·a·zo·vu.
Eits cha·yim hi la·ma·cha·zi·kim ba,
ve·to·me·che·ha me·u·shar.
De·ra·che·ha da·re·chei no·am,
ve·chol ne·ti·vo·te·ha sha·lom.

כִּי לֶקַח טוֹב נָתַתִּי
לָכֶם, תּוֹרָתִי אַל־תַּעֲזֹבוּ.
עֵץ־חַיִּים הִיא לַמַּחֲזִיקִים
בָּהּ, וְתֹמְכֶיהָ מְאֻשָּׁר.
דְּרָכֶיהָ דַרְכֵי־נֹעַם,
וְכָל־נְתִיבוֹתֶיהָ שָׁלוֹם.

VI.

Ha·shi·vei·nu A·do·nai ei·le·cha,
ve·na·shu·va.
Cha·deish ya·mei·nu ke·ke·dem.

הֲשִׁיבֵנוּ יְיָ אֵלֶיךָ, וְנָשׁוּבָה.
חַדֵּשׁ יָמֵינוּ כְּקֶדֶם.

VII.

Ye·ha·le·lu et sheim A·do·nai,
ki nis·gav she·mo le·va·do.

יְהַלְלוּ אֶת־שֵׁם יְיָ,
כִּי נִשְׂגָּב שְׁמוֹ לְבַדּוֹ.

VIII.

Ve·zot ha·to·rah a·sher sam
Mo·sheh li·fe·nei be·nei Yis·ra·eil,
al pi A·do·nai be·yad Mo·sheh.

וְזֹאת הַתּוֹרָה אֲשֶׁר־שָׂם
מֹשֶׁה לִפְנֵי בְּנֵי יִשְׂרָאֵל,
עַל־פִּי יְיָ בְּיַד־מֹשֶׁה.

544

IX.

Se·u she·a·rim ra·shei·chem,
ve·hi·na·se·u pi·te·chei o·lam,
ve·ya·vo me·lech ha·ka·vod!
Mi hu zeh me·lech ha·ka·vod?
A·do·nai tse·va·ot—
hu me·lech ha·ka·vod! Se·la.

שְׂאוּ שְׁעָרִים רָאשֵׁיכֶם,
וְהִנָּשְׂאוּ פִּתְחֵי עוֹלָם,
וְיָבוֹא מֶלֶךְ הַכָּבוֹד!
מִי הוּא זֶה מֶלֶךְ הַכָּבוֹד?
יְיָ צְבָאוֹת—
הוּא מֶלֶךְ הַכָּבוֹד! סֶלָה.

18

ARESHET SEFATEINU

A·re·shet se·fa·tein·nu
ye·e·rav le·fa·ne·cha,
Eil ram ve·ni·sa,
mei·vin u·ma·a·zin, ma·bit
u·mak·shiv le·kol te·ki·a·tei·nu,
u·te·ka·beil be·ra·cha·mim
u·ve·ra·tson
sei·der mal·chu·yo·teinu.
(zich·ro·no·tei·nu, sho·fe·ro·tei·nu.)

אֲרֶשֶׁת שְׂפָתֵינוּ יֶעֱרַב
לְפָנֶיךָ, אֵל רָם וְנִשָּׂא,
מֵבִין וּמַאֲזִין מַבִּיט
וּמַקְשִׁיב לְקוֹל תְּקִיעָתֵנוּ,
וּתְקַבֵּל בְּרַחֲמִים וּבְרָצוֹן
סֵדֶר מַלְכֻיּוֹתֵינוּ.
(זִכְרוֹנוֹתֵינוּ, שׁוֹפְרוֹתֵינוּ.)

19

HAYOM HARAT OLAM

Ha·yom ha·rat o·lam. Ha·yom
ya·a·mid ba·mish·pat kol
 ye·tsu·rei
o·la·mim im ke·va·nim im
 ka·a·va·dim.
Im ke·va·nim, ra·cha·mei·nu

הַיּוֹם הֲרַת עוֹלָם. הַיּוֹם
יַעֲמִיד בַּמִּשְׁפָּט כָּל־יְצוּרֵי
עוֹלָמִים אִם כְּבָנִים אִם
כַּעֲבָדִים. אִם כְּבָנִים, רַחֲמֵנוּ

545

ke·ra·cheim
av al ba·nim. Ve·im ka·a·va·dim,
ei·nei·nu le·cha te·lu·yot ad
she·te·cho·nei·nu ve·to·tsi cha·or
mish·pa·tei·nu,
A·yom Ka·dosh.

כְּרַחֵם אָב עַל בָּנִים.
וְאִם כַּעֲבָדִים, עֵינֵינוּ לְךָ
תְלוּיוֹת עַד שֶׁתְּחָנֵּנוּ
וְתוֹצִיא כָאוֹר מִשְׁפָּטֵנוּ,
אָיֹם קָדוֹשׁ.

20

ALEINU

A·lei·nu le·sha·bei·ach la·a·don
  ha·kol,
la·teit ge·du·lah le·yo·tseir
  be·rei·shit,
she·lo a·sa·nu ke·go·yei
  ha·a·ra·tsot,
ve·lo sa·ma·nu ke·mish·pe·chot
  ha·a·da·mah;
she·lo sam chel·kei·nu ka·hem,
ve·go·ra·lei·nu ke·chol ha·mo·nam.
Va·a·nach·nu ko·re·im
  u·mish·ta·cha·vim u·mo·dim
li·fe·nei me·lech ma·le·chei
  ha·me·la·chim,
ha·ka·dosh ba·ruch Hu.

עָלֵינוּ לְשַׁבֵּחַ לַאֲדוֹן
הַכֹּל, לָתֵת גְּדֻלָּה
לְיוֹצֵר בְּרֵאשִׁית, שֶׁלֹּא עָשָׂנוּ
כְּגוֹיֵי הָאֲרָצוֹת, וְלֹא שָׂמָנוּ
כְּמִשְׁפְּחוֹת הָאֲדָמָה; שֶׁלֹּא
שָׂם חֶלְקֵנוּ כָּהֶם, וְגֹרָלֵנוּ
כְּכָל-הֲמוֹנָם.
וַאֲנַחְנוּ כּוֹרְעִים
וּמִשְׁתַּחֲוִים וּמוֹדִים
לִפְנֵי מֶלֶךְ מַלְכֵי הַמְּלָכִים,
הַקָּדוֹשׁ בָּרוּךְ הוּא.

21

ALEINU (Conclusion)

Ve·ne·e·mar: "Ve·ha·ya A·do·nai
  le·me·lech
al kol ha·a·rets; ba·yom ha·hu
  yi·he·yeh
A·do·nai e·chad u·she·mo e·chad."

וְנֶאֱמַר: "וְהָיָה יְיָ לְמֶלֶךְ
עַל-כָּל-הָאָרֶץ;
בַּיּוֹם הַהוּא יִהְיֶה יְיָ
אֶחָד וּשְׁמוֹ אֶחָד."

22

YOM KIPPUR CANDLE LIGHTING

Ba·ruch a·ta, A·do·nai E·lo·hei·nu,
me·lech ha·o·lam,
a·sher ki·de·sha·nu be·mitz·vo·tav
ve·tsi·va·nu le·had·lik neir shel
(sha·bat ve·shel)
yom ha·ki·pu·rim.

בָּרוּךְ אַתָּה, יְיָ
אֱלֹהֵינוּ, מֶלֶךְ הָעוֹלָם,
אֲשֶׁר קִדְּשָׁנוּ בְּמִצְוֹתָיו
וְצִוָּנוּ לְהַדְלִיק נֵר
שֶׁל (שַׁבָּת וְשֶׁל)
יוֹם הַכִּפּוּרִים.

23

VE·AL KULAM

Ve·al ku·lam, E·lo·ah se·li·chot,
se·lach la·nu, me·chal la·nu,
ka·per la·nu!

וְעַל כֻּלָּם, אֱלוֹהַ
סְלִיחוֹת, סְלַח לָנוּ,
מְחַל לָנוּ, כַּפֶּר־לָנוּ!